Also by **Ashgate**

FRANCIS AMES-LEWIS
Sir Thomas Gresham and Gresham College: Studies in the Intellectual History of London in the Sixteenth and Seventeenth Centuries

DAVID LOADES
John Foxe: An Historical Perspective

OLE PETER GRELL
Calvinist Exiles in Tudor and Stuart England

KEITH LINDLEY
Popular Politics and Religion in Civil War London

DARREN OLDRIDGE
Religion and Society in Early Stuart England

and in the Collected Studies Series

JOHN GUY
Politics, Law and Counsel in Tudor and Early Stuart England

JOHN E. LAW
Venice and the Veneto in the Early Renaissance

MARION LEATHERS KUNTZ
Venice, Myth and Utopian Thought in the Sixteenth Century: Bodin, Postel and the Virgin of Venice

JOSEPH S. FREEDMAN
Philosophy and the Arts in Central Europe, 1500–1700: Teaching and Texts at Schools and Universities

BODO NISCHAN
Lutherans and Calvinists in the Age of Confessionalism

JOHN M. HEADLEY
Church, Empire and World: The Quest for Universal Order, 1520–1640

SCOTT H. HENDRIX
Tradition and Authority in the Reformation

LEWIS W. SPITZ
Luther and German Humanism

VARIORUM COLLECTED STUDIES SERIES

Cardinal Pole in
European Context

Thomas F. Mayer

Cardinal Pole in European Context

A *via media* in the Reformation

Taylor & Francis Group
LONDON AND NEW YORK

First published 2000 by Ashgate Publishing

Published 2016 by Routledge
2 Park Square, Milton Park, Abingdon, Oxon OX14 4RN
711 Third Avenue, New York, NY 10017, USA

Routledge is an imprint of the Taylor & Francis Group, an informa business

This edition copyright © 2000 by Thomas F. Mayer.

All rights reserved. No part of this book may be reprinted or reproduced or utilised in any form or by any electronic, mechanical, or other means, now known or hereafter invented, including photocopying and recording, or in any information storage or retrieval system, without permission in writing from the publishers.

Notice:
Product or corporate names may be trademarks or registered trademarks, and are used only for identification and explanation without intent to infringe.

British Library Cataloguing-in-Publication Data
Mayer, Thomas F. (Thomas Frederick), 1951–
   Cardinal Pole in European Context: A *via media* in the Reformation.
   (Variorum Collected Studies Series: CS686).
   1. Pole, Reginald, 1500–1558. 2. Catholic Church – England – Clergy.
   3. Reformation. 4. England – Church History – 16th Century.
   I. Title.
   282'.092

US Library of Congress Cataloging-in-Publication Data
The Library of Congress Control Number is preassigned as:
   00–104298

ISBN 9780860788294 (hbk)

VARIORUM COLLECTED STUDIES SERIES CS686

CONTENTS

Acknowledgements		viii
Preface		ix

TOLERATION AND RESISTANCE

I	'Heretics be not in all things heretics': Cardinal Pole, His Circle, and the Potential for Toleration *Beyond the Persecuting Society: Religious Toleration Before the Enlightenment, ed. J.C. Laursenand C.J. Nederman. Philadelphia, 1998*	107–124
II	Nursery of Resistance: Reginald Pole and his Friends *Political Thought and the Tudor Commonwealth, ed. P.A. Fideler and T.F. Mayer. London, 1992*	50–74
III	Tournai and Tyranny: Imperial Kingship and Critical Humanism *Historical Journal 334. Cambridge, 1991*	257–77

THE CONCLAVE OF JULIUS II AND THE ROLE OF DIPLOMACY

IV	The War of the Two Saints: the Conclave of Julius III and Cardinal Pole *Revised English version of 'Il fallimento di una candidatura: il partito della riforma, Reginald Pole e il conclave di Giulio III'*	1–21
V	An Unknown Diary of Julius III's Conclave by Bartolomeo Stella, a Servant of Cardinal Pole *Annuarium Historiae Conciliorum 24. Paderborn, 1992/95*	345–375
VI	If Martyrs are Exchanged for Martyrs: the Kidnappings of William Tyndale and Reginald Pole *Archiv für Reformationsgeschichte 81. Gütersloh, 1990*	286–307

VII A Diet for Henry VIII: the Failure of Reginald Pole's
1537 Legation 305–331
Journal of British Studies 26. Chicago,1987

THE ITALIAN RELIGIOUS CONTEXT

VIII Marco Mantova, a Bronze Age Conciliarist 385–408
Annuarium Historiae Conciliorum 14. Paderborn, 1984

IX Marco Mantova and the Paduan Religious Crisis
of the Early Sixteenth Century 41–61
Cristianesimo nella storia 7. Bologna, 1986

X Ariosto Anticlerical: Epic Poetry and the Clergy in
Early Cinquecento Italy 1–15
*Revised version of: Anticlericalism in Late Medieval and
Early Modern Europe, ed. P. Dykema and H. Oberman,
pp. 283-98. Leiden, 1993*

RENAISSANCE COLLECTIVE IDENTITY AND THE CREATION OF AN ICON

XI A Fate Worse than Death: Reginald Pole and the
Parisian Theologians 870–891
English Historical Review 103. Harlow,1988

XII A Sticking-Plaster Saint? Autobiography and
Hagiography in the Making of Reginald Pole 205–222
*The Rhetoric of Life-Writing, ed. T.F. Mayer and
D.R. Woolf. Ann Arbor,1995*

XIII Reginald Pole in Paolo Giovio's *Descriptio*:
a Strategy for Reconversion 431–450
Sixteenth Century Journal 16. Kirksville,1985

XIV When Maecenas was Broke: Cardinal Pole's
'Spiritual' Patronage 419–435
Sixteenth Century Journal 27. Kirksville,1996

XV	Cardinal Pole's Finances: The Property of a Reformer *First publication*	1–16
Addenda et Corrigenda		1–2
Index		1–8

This book consists of xii + 334 pages

ACKNOWLEDGMENTS

The following journals and publishers graciously allowed reprinting of the pieces that first appeared under their imprint: University of Pennsylvania Press, 1997 (I); Routledge, London (II); Cambridge University Press (III); Verlag Ferdinand Schöningh, Paderborn, (V, VIII); Verlag Gerd Mohn, Gütersloh (VI); North American Conference on British Studies, Chicago (VII); *Cristianesimo nella storia*, Bologna (IX); Oxford University Press (XI); University of Michigan Press, Ann Arbor (XII); *Sixteenth Century Journal*, Kirksville (XIII, XIV).

PREFACE

This volume assembles some of my articles on Reginald Pole (1500–1558) and his contexts published over the last fifteen of the twenty-five years I have been working on him. They prepared me to write *Reginald Pole, prince and prophet* (Cambridge University Press, in press), but aside from some of the material in chapter II this volume is an independent companion to the biography. The biggest section of my work omitted from it are studies of Pole's client Thomas Starkey.[1] The essays included here trace an evolving interpretation of a perplexing figure recently called 'hamletic'.[2] My fundamental approach is to place Pole in his contexts, English, Italian and European. These contexts are broadly defined, intellectual, political, diplomatic, and literary. They extend geographically from the university of Padua (especially the essays on the Paduan jurist and Pole's possible teacher Marco Mantova Benavides) and the nearby Val Padana (Ludovico Ariosto's religious views) to the university of Paris (the Mantova pieces as well as no. XI).[3] In terms of intellectual context, they have most to say about conciliarism and reflection on the nature of the church, including late medieval anti-clericalism, as well as discussion of the vital concept *rex imperator*, which began in the early fourteenth century.

In addition to contexts there are texts, and literary analysis supports much of my interpretation. Context and text exist in symbiosis, each dependent for its meaning on the other, neither a constant. And as was true of any well-trained humanist like Pole, his texts are rhetorical through and through, designed first and foremost to persuade (see especially no. XII). Since I began as a historian, a literary and rhetorical approach emerged slowly. I first attempted to apply it to Pole in the second essay. At the risk of immodesty, I hazard the assessment that probably the most successful piece on this score is no. XII which helped to open up the field of Renaissance life-writing. Both these pieces share in addition to close reading of texts a prosopographical approach that I adopted

---

[1] See esp. Thomas F. Mayer, *Thomas Starkey and the commonwealth: humanist politics and religion in the reign of Henry VIII* (Cambridge: Cambridge University Press, 1989).
[2] Adriano Prosperi, 'Evangelismo di Seripando', in Antonio Cestaro, ed., *Geronimo Seripando e la chiesa del suo tempo nel V centenario della nascita* (Rome: Edizioni di storia e letteratura, 1997), pp. 33–49, p. 47.
[3] For the centrality of Padua to sixteenth-century English experience of Italy, see Jonathan Woolfson, *Padua and the Tudors: English students in Italy, 1485–1603* (Toronto: University of Toronto Press, 1998).

originally when confronted by the slipperiness of Pole 'himself'. It became increasingly necessary in proportion as it became clear how much both he and those close to him invented his character and successfully handed it on. Pole's household naturally played a central role both during his life-as-lived (including by conducting espionage; see no. VII) and -as-written and then in transmitting the second to the future. No. XIII sketches some of this process, along with no. XIV nominally about Pole's patronage, but really about how ideology bound him and his coteries together, as did as well, of course, but to a much smaller degree than usual, the financial resources considered in a new piece, no. XV.

This is all relatively unfamiliar territory, since Pole is much better known as an icon than as a historical figure. I have tried in part simply to reveal his iconicity, especially in no. XI which is less about what Pole did in Paris than the interaction between what happened and what Pole said happened and how this contributed to making an icon. My earliest publication on Pole, no. XIII, is also one of my most historicist in its demonstration of how Pole's life-as-lived fed directly into his own image and then its dissemination during his lifetime, a phenomenon also considered in no. XIV.

Icon or no, Pole is mostly thought of as a religious figure, hero of resistance to Henrician ceasaropapism and to the counter-reformation. The first pair of essays, combined with a new piece, no. IV, as well as no. V inherit Pole's own image to some degree while turning it in new directions. Thus instead of loyal defender of papal monarchy against the encroachments of the Henrician state (discussed in no. III), Pole appears as one who might have broken the mold and prepared the way for a theory of toleration. No more a papalist than a statist like Thomas Cromwell, Pole resisted the new direction of monarchy in general. Instead of nascent 'absolutism', Pole defended a corporate – if oligarchical – constitution in church and state.

In the last twenty years Pole has become one of the most important figures in Italian-language scholarship on the failed reformation in Italy.[4] Identified as the leader of the *spirituali* who defended justification by faith at all costs even after they should have known that they could not do so within the Catholic church, Pole became one of the Inquisition's most celebrated victims. There are many difficulties in this argument, not least new views of the Roman Inquisition.[5] I see Pole's fate as neither inevitable nor simple and related to the problem of what to call the *spirituali*.[6] As nos IV and V demonstrate, Pole and his

---

[4] See especially Massimo Firpo, *Tra alumbrados e 'spirituali'. Studi su Juan de Valdés e il valdesianesimo nella crisi religiosa del '500 italiano* (Florence: Olschki, 1990) and *Inquisizione romana e Controriforma. Studi sul Cardinal Giovanni Morone e il suo processo d'eresia* (Bologna: Il Mulino, 1992); and Paolo Simoncelli, *Evangelismo italiano del Cinquencento. Questione religiosa e nicodemismo politico* (Rome: Edizioni di storia e letteratura, 1979).
[5] See, for example, John Tedeschi, *The prosecution of heresy: collected studies on the inquisition in early modern Italy* (Binghamton, NY: MRTS, 1991).
[6] See the introduction to *Prince and prophet*.

alignment, which I propose to call the reform tendency, were complicit in their own protracted demise. Even after their defeat in the conclave of Julius III in 1549–50, indeed even after Paul IV's election in 1555, the die had not been cast. In this argument and these essays, instead of continuing to follow the lead given by both his and others' hindsight, I have tried to treat Pole the right way around, from the beginning forward.

Perhaps the most important contribution of this collection lies in its demonstration of how widespread ideas like Pole's were. The reform tendency was not exclusively Italian. Pole, literally the original *inglese italianato, diavolo incarnato*, was neither English nor Italian, neither 'Catholic' nor 'Protestant', and belonged to neither Renaissance nor Reformation. Of late, both have split into renaissances and reformations, and although untidy, this marks a step in the right direction. Individual studies always make the big picture more complex, and this is markedly true in Pole's case. The moral of the volume is that the 'Reformation' needs renaming as much as any of the other labels assigned to Pole or his contemporaries and in order to do this successfully, historians must work on (or at least take account of) as wide a European stage as Pole trod. This will produce disappointments (the news of the recent destruction of the communal archive of Bagnoregio, a papal territory which Pole governed for five years is perhaps my saddest moment as a historian), but the comparisons therefore demanded are also certain to pay results.

THOMAS F. MAYER

Augustana College,
December, 1999

PUBLISHER'S NOTE

The articles in this volume, as in all others in the Collected Studies Series, have not been given a new, continuous pagination. In order to avoid confusion, and to facilitate their use where these same studies have been referred to elsewhere, the original pagination has been maintained wherever possible.

Each article has been given a Roman numeral in order of appearance, as listed in the Contents. This number is repeated on each page and quoted in the index entries.

I

"Heretics be not in all things heretics": Cardinal Pole, His Circle, and the Potential for Toleration

IN THE EARLY 1530S, WRITING HIS "Dialogue Between Pole and Lupset," Thomas Starkey ascribed the apparently tolerant sentiment "heretics be not in all things heretics" to his patron Reginald Pole (1500–1558). After Starkey left his service, Pole became a leading opponent of Henry VIII, cardinal, nearly successful candidate for pope, papal legate, and archbishop of Canterbury under Mary I.[1] Later, another of Pole's dependents, Andras Dudic, became known as one of the most famous sixteenth-century defenders of toleration.[2] Dudic, along with Pole's client Gianbattista Binardi and Starkey, also tried to create an image of Pole in accord with such opinions. That they did raises several problems. It might have been mere coincidence that three of Pole's satellites put forward such views, just as it will always be open to question to what degree Starkey, Dudic, and Binardi accurately represented their patron, especially in light of recent studies which demonstrate the conflicted nature of patron-client relations in the Renaissance.[3] A partial answer to the first difficulty is that Pole, to an unusual degree, was a composite construction, created through intensive interaction with his household of true believers.[4]

But Starkey's, Dudic's, and Binardi's views raise another, more serious problem. Do even they, much less those of their patron, reflect a belief in toleration? Mario Turchetti maintains that nearly all sixteenth-century advocates of leniency to those with whom they disagreed, except for Sebastian Castellio, favored reunifying Christianity without resorting to force, not permanently tolerating disparate viewpoints.[5] (I shall refer to this attitude by the terms "concordance" and "concordant.") Turchetti's special subject, François Baudouin, certainly did not see Pole as tolerant, lumping him with the notoriously vehement Albert Pighe.[6] Yet the fact that Pighe, despite valiant efforts, failed to attach himself to Pole (or any of Pole's allies) may give a first clue to Pole's position, as on the other hand do the comparatively subtle criticisms of John Calvin against certain prelates at Trent who knew the truth "but yet having nothing in order to resist manfully" did not follow it, or the stark attacks of Francesco Negri and Pierpaolo Vergerio, both converts to Protestantism and violent critics of Pole.[7]

Finding himself for much of his career uncomfortably suspended between various political and religious positions, Pole reacted by leaving his lines of communication as open as the good rhetorician he was could. Given his eminence in the mid-sixteenth century, and the strength of his "party," a large space for dialogue resulted, not only with Protestants but within the Catholic church. Unlike many of Pole's contemporaries who could sometimes talk a good line about some kind of toleration if circumstances made it impossible for them to enforce their views, Pole in practice took an unusually lenient line on heresy even when he had virtually full religious authority in England in the last four years of his life. In the light of the present state of the question, it would be strange indeed to find any kind of opening toward toleration in the Catholic church, but had Pole's tenure in England coincided with Pius IV's papacy, which followed shortly after Pole's death, the opening for dialogue, even embryonic toleration, could have been quite large.

What were Pole's views? There has been much disagreement about whether Starkey's statement reflected them, Starkey's, or some combination. Starkey was undoubtedly close enough to the notoriously taciturn Pole to have heard him discourse more than once. They had probably met at Oxford in the early 1520s, and Starkey remained in Pole's household as they moved about Europe off and on until his return to England in late 1533. Thereafter they remained in touch, right up to Starkey's death in 1538, at which point Pole was about to be declared a traitor.[8] Despite this extended period of contact between Pole and Starkey, for our purposes paternity matters less than the proper interpretation of the dictum. The real question is whether it reflects a tolerant, as opposed to a concordant, attitude to heresy.[9] If the possibility of toleration is predicated on allowing the existence of more than one truth, then it did not. Pole and Thomas Lupset, Starkey's other interlocutor, were debating whether scripture should be put into the vernacular. Pole strongly urged the utility to ordinary people of both an English liturgy and Bible (not to mention canon law).[10] Lupset objected that these were Lutheran tenets, and just look what a mess they have made. Were we to follow their lead, we would soon see as many errors in England as in "Almayn." Pole replied:

fyrst you schal be sure of thys I wyl not folow the steppys of Luther whose jugement I estyme veray lytyl, & yet he & hys dyscypullys be not so wykkyd & folysch that in al thyngys they erre, heretykys be not in al thyngys heretykys, wherefor I wyl not so abhorre theyr heresye that for the hate therof I wyl fly from the truth, I alow thys maner of saying of servyce not bycause they say & affyrme hyt to be gud & laudabul but bycause the truth ys so as hyt apperyth to me.[11]

The most important point here is that Pole believed in the unity of truth. Heretics might discover it, but it remained a single truth nonetheless. Such a notion of truth obtained throughout the "Dialogue," which, like most such blueprints of the ideal commonwealth, claimed to embrace a single vision of felicity, at least some of the time.

A crucial ambiguity undercuts many of the apparent implications of Pole's emphasis on a unitary truth: were laws or men to rule? Despite the elaborate constitutional structures Starkey designed, full of interlocking councils intended to force the rulers to virtue, the work ultimately took a Pauline twist and concluded (more or less) that the law was insufficient. This time Lupset got the big speech:

Whether yet al thes ordynance ye or al the powar of law be abul to bryng man to thys perfectyon I somewhat dowte, for as much as the perfectyon of man stondyth in reson & vertue, by the wych he both knowyth that wych ys truth & gud & also hath wyl stabyl & constant purpos to folow the same, not compelllyd by feare of any payne or punnyschement, nor yet by any plesure or profyt alluryd therto, but only of hys fre wyl & lyberty wyth prudent knolege & perfayt love movyd.

Pole agreed, adding that the law was "the pegadoge of chryst" and a means to prepare humans to achieve perfect knowledge. That, however, came only from Christ and was, as Lupset put it, "only the worke of god." Pole again agreed that to attain perfection "we must use other mean than cyvyle ordynance . . . & as nere as we may folow the exampul of our mastur chryst, the wych by no compulsyon instytute hys law, nor by any drede of fear of any thyng." Christ's original means were "exampul of lyfe, & exhortacyon" which meant ensuring good preaching and circulating translations of Erasmus. As Pole concluded, once good preachers had been provided for, and the Bible, Christ's law, and worship services put into English, "then I thynke schortly yu schold see more frute of the gospel then we have, you schold see wyhtin few yerys men wyth love dow such thyng as now they can not be brought to be no mannys law." Nevertheless, Pole reiterated that "fere of punnyschment & payne" and "desyre of honest plesure & profyt by law prescrybyd" came first, to be replaced gradually by action undertaken out of love of virtue and of Christ.[12] Thus it seems that no one could be compelled to salvation, but at the same time, the means which made salvation accessible—preaching and education—could indeed be dictated. There is slippage here, which may produce an opening toward toleration. Put into Pole's mouth, it contributed to an image of *his* tolerance.[13]

It may not be accidental that Starkey laid so much emphasis on Erasmus at the moment of this maneuver. Although his attitude changed over time and was probably always concordant rather than tolerant, it was possible to read some of Erasmus's works as leaning in the direction of toleration.[14] *Inquisitio de fide* offers perhaps the clearest instance. This dialogue between the characters Aulus and Barbatius, written as late as 1524 but before Erasmus's celebrated dispute with Luther over the will, transparently defended Luther (and by implication other "heretics") by arguing that belief in Christianity required only adherence to a very simple creed.[15] Above all, Barbatius (Luther) professed not to believe in "holy church," defining the church instead as "the body of Christ, that is, a universal assemblage of all those throughout the world who agree in the evangelic faith." Aulus pressed him on the point, and Barbatius defended himself by reference to Cyprian's explication of the creed (even though Erasmus knew the work not to be by Cyprian). Instead of any visible church, which, no matter how many good men it contained, could still be corrupted, Barbatius adhered to the "communion of the saints." That church was "no other than the belief in one God, one gospel, one faith, one hope, a joining in one spirit and the same sacraments," the last of which then disappeared from the discussion. Aulus concluded that Barbatius was as orthodox as his opponents, and let Barbatius persuade him to come to lunch to reason further. Aulus was a little concerned that he would be seen in the company of a heretic, but Barbatius convinced him, on the authority of Paul, that "nothing is more holy than to favor heretics." Aulus returned to his original pose of physician to Barbatius, but it would have been difficult to avoid the conclusion that the sick man not only did not require healing, but had done as much for Aulus as Aulus for him.

However much Starkey may have drawn on Erasmus, his example was probably more important to Dudic, who has been called the last important Hungarian Erasmian.[16] However that may be, in the late 1560s Dudic developed a position which came about as close as was possible in the sixteenth century to a demand for toleration. Already in 1568 Dudic had called on the emperor to allow "liberty of conscience" in Poland.[17] Sometime between then and 1572 he translated pseudo-Themistius, *Oratio XII, ad Valentem de religionibus* with a commentary which bluntly stated "no one may impose his opinion" about religion on any one else, and "each religion has its own rationale, as do all arts and all sciences." Yet Dudic also likened each religion to a component of an army and rooted his views in a neo-Platonic idea of charity, which probably means that he was after a new synthesis, and thus believed at bottom in concordance.[18]

One of the most important episodes in the sixteenth-century debate came in Dudic's dispute with Calvin's successor in Geneva, Theodore de Bèze, in the wake of the cases of Miguel Servetus (whom Calvin had had burned for heresy), Bernardino Ochino, and others.[19] Dudic's letter of 1 August 1570 is famous.[20] It opened with the same question Dudic had put earlier. How could one locate the true church, "about the possession of which there are now so many, so various, so sharp combats, and such a bloody dispute?" It was arrogance, Dudic several times argued, to claim sole access to truth, and worse to arm the people for religious wars. As he did frequently, Dudic pointed to the lengthy consensus behind the Catholics in wondering whether the Church could have survived for so long in what Bèze and others called darkness. Had not Christ promised to be with his church forever? If true Christians were identified by their works, what to make of all the cruelty and bloodshed practiced by Bèze and his allies? "Could you not be compared to ambushes laid for princes in a republic?" Reformed preaching, which led to such bloodshed, had helped little to uncover the truth. Surely the church had troubles with heretics, but "who might these disturbers of the Church, and destroyers of unity be?"

How to arrive at the mean? What to do when no judge could be found? Scripture, which everyone read by his own lights, could not fill that role. The fathers and church councils? Perhaps, but Dudic attacked Bèze's "inconstancy" in fleeing from those fathers who condemned his beliefs, and said Bèze knew perfectly well that the councils were against him. Dudic called the church "a fortress common to all" (a possible echo of Erasmus's emphasis on the common good), which Dudic nevertheless wished to be very careful about identifying. Not only various rulers but "whole nations" had tried to appropriate it in the name of "liberty of conscience." Returning to the question of consensus, Dudic denied Bèze's claim to superior philological ability as a guarantee of truth, again because there were so many possible leaders in it. Why follow Bèze more than another? Dudic willingly conceded the gifts Bèze immodestly claimed, but even so the Catholics might have been better still at languages, and could certainly read church history more carefully. Besides, deeds, not words, counted, and Bèze and his followers had not exactly distinguished themselves on that score, having killed so many men, disturbed so many cities, and "taught magistrates to be butchers." War was not the Christian magistrate's appropriate response to dissent. Dudic had no wish to defend Catholicism, but he admired the Roman church's "wonderful order" and readiness to do battle. Fighting it was like fighting Cadmus's constantly-renewed warriors.

Truth was still a unity for Dudic, but he could see no reason to privilege any one sect's apprehension of it over another's. All the issues between Bèze and the Catholics were and would remain "sub judice." The "Ebionites" in Transylvania and Poland were as likely to have found the truth as Bèze, or the Catholics, for that matter. Adapting the "if it walks like a duck" argument, Dudic pointed out that the reformed churches could easily be charged with usurping the prerogatives of the holy see; both obviously relied on excommunication. And a king, their preferred religious authority, could degenerate as easily as a pope. Yes, some rites needed modification, but differences among Catholics over them were small by comparison with Protestant variations, a point Dudic made at length. Although he insisted on the need for unity, which makes his "tolerant" attitude appear more "concordant," Dudic still rejected the persecution of heretics, because it disagreed with the doctrine of predestination, was more a matter of law than gospel, and violated John 18: 31, which forbade killing of any kind. It did no good to claim that magistrates actually did the killing, since anyone acting through another to commit a crime was equally guilty of it. Dudic closed by proudly admitting that he had not chosen his church, perhaps leaving the implication open that he never would.

It had taken Dudic a long time to get to this position, "concordant" if the tale were ever told, but "tolerant" *rebus sic stantibus*.[21] As a young man Dudic had spent about eighteen months in Pole's household in England, and the experience made a great impact on him. If I am right, he was very quickly promoted to a position of great responsibility, since it is likely that he was the principal author/copyist of Pole's strangest work, "De reformatione ecclesiae."[22] In 1556 Dudic extravagantly praised Pole together with their mutual friend Paolo Manuzio for their "true religion of Christ, by whom I was confirmed in the faith and by whose examples I was invited to spend life piously and holily."[23] About five years later, while at the council of Trent, Dudic repaid Pole's hospitality by engaging, along with Binardi, in a translation and adaptation of Ludovico Beccadelli's life of Pole.[24] Dudic continued to admire Pole right up to the end of his life, nearly thirty years later, long after he had definitively gone over to the Reformations, proposing a study of Pole as a model for a series of biographies of men "whom our age raises to the level of the fathers [of the church]."[25]

The question of Dudic's motives in adapting Beccadelli has long been debated, but virtually nothing has been said about Binardi, whom Dudic lauded in the preface to the *Vita Reginaldi Poli*. Dudic said he had asked Binardi for help because of his own artistic failings, and he went on to emphasize how much substance Binardi had contributed, in addition to having "polished" "totam hanc Poli effigiem."[26] Binardi had been one of the most central figures in Pole's English household because he had custody of Pole's writings and knew English. He enjoyed enough success to attract the envy of at least two competitors after his return to Italy.[27] His attitude has proven very difficult to reconstruct. For one thing, not much is known of Binardi's time in England until its very end. For another, if we can trust Ludovico Castelvetro, he busied himself turning works dictated by Pole in Italian into good Latin, including *De sacramento*, Pole's attack on Thomas Cranmer, his predecessor as archbishop of Canterbury.[28] Finally, Castelvetro called Binardi a persecutor.[29] This is more than a little ironic, since Binardi was among the very few to take Castelvetro's side in his literary dispute with Annibale Caro, well after Castelvetro had become a notorious heretic.[30]

The dearth of information about Binardi, beyond these possibly suggestive but contradictory tidbits, combined with the disagreements about Dudic's leanings and intentions, make it all the more interesting that whatever their inclinations may have been, they did not much affect the re-working of Beccadelli's original on the score of Pole's lenient attitude to heresy.[31] True, Dudic and Binardi emphasized much more than Beccadelli had the degree to which Pole combatted heresy in England, and cut out Pole's own relations with Marcantonio Flaminio, which Beccadelli had used as a major illustration of Pole's manner of dealing with heretics. Instead, they substituted the laconic "and certainly he [more than] once proved that this means of dealing with heretics is the most appropriate means." But they agreed with Beccadelli about "this means," no matter how many times employed.

He [Pole] truly, when perhaps he had fallen in with anyone, whom he understood to be in the grip of any false opinion, abhorring from the doctrine of the church, did not attack him with sharp accusations and certain inhumane reproofs, but he would admonish gently and in a friendly way, and so attempt to lead back to health. For, those who were neither public, nor contumacious, nor obstinate heretics, he thought ought to be so treated.[32]

To whatever degree reworked, the image of Pole is even more markedly concordant, with fully "tolerant" practical implications, than Starkey's had been more than thirty years earlier.

So much for the image. Before turning to test the views of Starkey, Dudic, and Binardi against Pole's practice, we may be able to get a little closer to his theory. Pole made his most explicit statement at Trent about how to treat heretics, the touchstone in discussions of toleration, unsurprisingly in the course of the debate over justification. Just before he left the council, he argued that Lutheran works on the subject should be read dispassionately. The principle "Luther said it, therefore it is false" had to be rejected. Whatever was good in such books should be kept and a *via media* sought which would lead to the truth.[33] Most of Pole's formal works, even those with promising contents, say very little. His tirade against Henry VIII, *Pro unitatis ecclesiae defensione* [*On the unity of the church*] (1536), made the obligatory point that heretics distorted the meaning of scripture, and praised John Fisher and Thomas More for having written against heresy.[34] Perhaps this is not the most likely of texts in which to seek a "soft" line. The sprawling manuscript of "De reformatione ecclesiae" appears to offer more hope, despite being well nigh unintelligible because of its at least eleven more or less independent versions, some now nearly illegible, as well as almost impossible to date.[35] Pole went on at length about the church's problems (variously blamed on the bishops and, later, on "the people") but never raised questions of heresy, except perhaps obliquely by stressing the need for discipline.[36] In a sermon prepared for delivery to the synod Pole held in London in 1555, he upbraided the clergy for giving an opening to heretics by their covetousness, and proposed as a remedy for heresy no more than instruction in good doctrine.[37] This was an exceptionally mild proposal.

But in what was probably a set of instructions to one of his subordinates in the archbishopric of Canterbury, probably the person or persons in charge of dealing with heretics, Pole spelled out a remarkably lenient approach.[38] Almost immediately Pole offered a definition of a heretic which comes close to that ascribed to him by Beccadelli, Dudic, and Binardi.

Merely holding a heretical opinion was not enough, unless one adopted it of one's own judgment and defended it obstinately, and after one had been better informed. Pole wished heretics would argue that they had been led astray by their leaders, which might well mean that they could be spared the consequences once those leaders' opinion was condemned. Heretics' confidence in their own reasoning powers was what got them into trouble, but any who blamed their beliefs on their bishop were to be spared. Instead of appealing to reason, Pole clung to the test of "paternity," or tradition. Any heretic, like Cranmer, who could not point out the father of his idea was to be condemned. Pole did not have much patience—heretics were to be admonished only once or twice before being condemned—but they had at least some chance to come around.[39]

It must be more than coincidence that Pole's position here is nearly identical to the strongest case Dudic put in favor of what has been taken to be toleration: the Catholics at least could still point to consensus over time, to tradition. Since Pole's stance cannot be safely called any more than concordant (or perhaps no more than lenient), this must raise some questions about exactly what Dudic claimed. Unlike the later Dudic, of course, Pole thought he knew what the true church was, but he had earlier had his problems with that church and would again. As his instructions about penitent heretics already indicate, Pole's practice leaned toward de facto toleration.

That was certainly the way his first life-writers put the point. Even the second set, who found the most notorious instance of his dealings with suspected heresy an embarrassment, still emphasized that he had dealt leniently with *some* heretics. Beccadelli was more forthright in presenting Pole's relations with Flaminio as an example of his *mansuetudo*. Flaminio led a contingent of Juan de Valdés's followers into Pole's household shortly after he moved to Viterbo as papal legate in 1541. Although there is room for reservations on the specifics of this point, Massimo Firpo's contention that Flaminio meant to convert Pole's household into the foremost Valdesian cell in Italy underscores the attraction it exercised.[40] As the *processi* against Pole's friends Giovanni Morone and Pietro Carnesecchi reveal, a large number of Pole's intimates held heterodox religious views, more than a few of which could be traced to Flaminio.[41]

Eventually Flaminio's close ties to Pole would help to put Pole under a cloud of quasi-official accusations of heresy emanating from Paul IV, the former Gianpietro Carafa. By at least 1550 the future pope had become deeply suspicious of Pole's "seducer" Flaminio, going so far as to visit his deathbed to be sure he died a good Christian. Both Pole and Beccadelli, however, defended Pole's relation to Flaminio by claiming that Pole had taken Flaminio under his protection in an effort to save him.[42] Be that as it may, Flaminio used Pole's patronage as an opportunity to help write the most famous product of the Italian Reformation, *Il Beneficio di Cristo*.[43] Pole and his wider circles, including Morone and Cardinal Contarini, who shortly after Flaminio joined Pole engaged in a more public effort to recuperate a group of heretics in Modena (including Castelvetro), thought very highly of the book.[44]

The *Beneficio* quickly found its way onto the Index of Prohibited Books and Pole seems to have come under Carafa's suspicion even more quickly.[45] But the opening represented by Pole's patronage of Flaminio did not close as soon as historians have thought: Pole and Carafa, although engaging in a fierce duel, left the conclave of Julius III in 1550 as members of still more or less the same group of reformers.[46] The impact of Pole's attitude to heresy during his nearly decade-long intimacy with Flaminio comes out most clearly in his attempts to prevent the council of Trent from dealing first with doctrine, in order not to offend the emperor, who was then deep in negotiations with his Lutheran subjects. Pole failed in this, as he did in the first round of discussion of doctrine over justification. This episode resulted in his infamous flight from the council, which he had earlier defined in what has been called an "ecumenical" way in line with his generally concordant views.[47]

When Pole returned to England in late 1554, he took charge of a concerted effort to return the country to Roman obedience. Although his successor as archbishop of Canterbury called him a "butcher," Pole generally stayed away from persecution.[48] John Foxe, one of the most successful of Protestant martyrologists, who thus had a special incentive to look for martyr-making enemies, offered what amounts to an encomium of Pole. Foxe could not avoid noting that Pole was a papist, but "none of the bloody and cruel sort of papists," not only because he restrained "Bloody" Edmund Bonner, the bishop of London, but also because of his "solicitous writings" to Cranmer, not to mention his own difficulties with Paul IV. All this "notwithstanding, the pomp and glory of the world carried him away to play the papist thus as he did."[49] Foxe implicitly concluded that only circumstances prevented Pole from at least practical toleration.

Pole undoubtedly prevented some of Bonner's worst excesses, at one point refusing to allow him to put on an enormous auto-da-fé.[50] In another famous instance, Pole treated the prominent Protestant John Cheke with great leniency, sufficient to persuade him to recant.[51] Cheke was deeply grateful.⁵² Whoever besides Bonner may have been responsible for the sanguinary side of the Marian Reformation, the list of suspects should not include Pole. Once again, leniency does not, any more than concordance, mean toleration, but it may perhaps be counted as a practical step toward it.

The grossest apparent exception to this pattern in Pole's practice is the treatment of Cranmer. Jasper Ridley, David Loades, and A. G. Dickens all agree that Pole badly abused Cranmer, although neither Loades nor Dickens goes to the lengths Ridley did to inculpate Pole in a plot to destroy him, for which there is no evidence.⁵³ The fact that Foxe equated Pole's behavior to that of Cheke and Cranmer suggests that bias speaks through Ridley's interpretation much more than do the sources, and versions of both pieces of direct evidence for Pole's attitude passed through Foxe's hands. They are a pair of letters to Cranmer, one a lengthy polemical treatise and the other a fragment of November 1555.⁵⁴ Not much has been said about the first, except to compare it implicitly to the second, which has been called "bitter" (Ridley) and "cold, furious and abusive" (Loades). By the standards of sixteenth-century controversial writing, however, neither the treatise, *De sacramento*, nor the letter is excessively vicious, even when they both blame the entire subversion of Henry VIII on Cranmer, and the treatise also laid to his charge murder and a long list of other crimes. In *De sacramento*, Pole distinguished his much more stringent private views from his public stance as legate, and devoted at least some sections of the treatise to trying to persuade Cranmer more or less calmly. Pole had some reservations about sending the work to Cranmer, because he had heard that it would not prove effective, but concluded that grace was always possible while life lasted.⁵⁵ A similar if even more restrained attitude came out in Pole's instructions cited above. They presented Cranmer as merely the obvious example of a heretic who could not furnish a complete tradition for his Eucharistic views, from the early church right through to the immediate past.⁵⁶

Pole was never directly involved in Cranmer's protracted trial, degradation and execution. He did, however, send Pedro de Soto, one of his most trusted agents, to reason with the imprisoned Cranmer after his trial in Oxford, and de Soto continued to be involved almost until the end.⁵⁷ Likewise, the man who finally persuaded Cranmer to produce an acceptable recantation, Juan de Villagarcia, a Spanish Dominican and then Regius professor of theology at Oxford, was a client of Pole's close spiritual ally, Bartolomé Carranza, and linked to Pole's household as well.⁵⁸ The view one takes of their actions will almost certainly depend on the attitude one takes to the whole proceeding, but there can still be no doubt that they acted much more moderately than Bonner or Henry Cole (also, it is true, a sometime dependent of Pole).

Thus it seems that even in the case of Cranmer, Pole still managed to take a more lenient, concordant stance than most of his associates or his queen. To say this is not to claim any special sanctity for Pole. Even the young Calvin could nearly adhere to concordance in the first edition of *The Institutes of Christian Religion*.[59] Rather, I mean to extend to Pole an argument about the anabaptists, and in particular their pacificism, or refusal to use force on their own or any one else's behalf.[60] Far from an entrenched principle right from the start, pacificism *became* a hallmark of most anabaptists once efforts to impose their views—the usual sixteenth-century attitude—had failed. That is, principle arose from force of circumstances. Then again, neither pacificism nor toleration could have arisen had the linguistic and conceptual resources to fill the opening created by circumstances not existed. I have suggested above that Pole's suspended position helped generate his concordant behavior, and that Pole and some of his allies, reflecting on those circumstances, made a virtue of necessity and assigned to Pole a firm belief in concordance. This was not yet toleration, but the continuing interaction between the concept of concordance and circumstances like Pole's marked a major drift toward it.

Three major consequences follow from this examination of Pole's case. First, potentially anyone finding him- or herself in circumstances like his might have come to ideas like his. Therefore, since Protestants did not monopolize such circumstances, the roots of toleration did not grow exclusively among them.[61] Second, Pole's perfectly typical case can serve as a reminder that a distinction between theory and practice is not very helpful in the Renaissance, especially in ethical matters, as Nancy Struever has recently argued.[62] Third, Pole illustrates the more general point that it is perhaps impossible to find a coherent theory of toleration then, as it sounds a salutary warning that any attempt to isolate such a theory may be doomed. But when have historians *found* a coherent anything, as opposed to inventing one? R. G. Collingwood notoriously attacked "scissors-and-paste" or "philogical" history for its incapacity to say anything interesting about the past precisely because that approach denied the active role of the historian's mind in its re-enactment. In other words, the meaning, the coherence of the past is unavoidably a product of the historian's efforts to understand.

That must be as true of the history of toleration as of any other facet of human experience.⁶³

Notes

1. *Thomas Starkey: A Dialogue Between Pole and Lupset*, ed. Thomas F. Mayer, Camden Fourth Series 37 (London: Royal Historical Society, 1989), 90. My editorial symbols have been omitted throughout. For Starkey and Pole, see Thomas F. Mayer, *Thomas Starkey and the Commonweal: Humanist Politics and Religion in the Reign of Henry VIII* (Cambridge: Cambridge University Press, 1989), passim. There is no adequate biography of Pole, but see Dermot Fenlon, *Heresy and Obedience in Tridentine Italy: Cardinal Pole and the Counter-Reformation* (Cambridge: Cambridge University Press, 1972) and Martin Haile (pseud. of Marie Hallé), *The Life of Reginald Pole* (London: Pitman, 1911). I am at work on a new life. In the meanwhile, see my summary articles in David A. Richardson, ed., *Dictionary of Literary Biography* 132 (Detroit: Gale Research, 1993) and Hans J. Hillerbrand et al., eds., *Oxford Encyclopedia of the Reformation* (New York: Oxford University Press, 1996).

2. Domenico Caccamo, *Eretici italiani in Moravia, Polonia e Transilvania (1558–1611). Studi e documenti*, Corpus Reformatorum Italicorum, ed. Luigi Firpo and Giorgio Spini (Florence and Chicago: Sansoni and the Newberry Library, 1970), 116 called the necessity of toleration Dudic's "fundamental thesis."

3. Diana Robin, *Filelfo in Milan: Writings, 1451–1477* (Princeton, N.J.: Princeton University Press, 1991), introduction.

4. For a sketch of some of Pole's relations with his clients, see Thomas F. Mayer, "Nursery of Resistance: Reginald Pole and his Friends," in Paul A. Fideler and Mayer, eds., *Political Thought and the Tudor Commonwealth: Deep Structure, Discourse and Disguise* (London: Routledge, 1992), 50–74 and "When Maecenas Was Broke: Cardinal Pole's 'Spiritual' Patronage," *Sixteenth Century Journal* 27 (1996): 419–35.

5. Mario Turchetti, *Concordia o tolleranza? François Bauduin (1520–1573) e i "moyenneurs"* (Geneva: Droz, 1984), 591–95. Turchetti argues that everyone besides Castellio who expressed tolerationist views, above all Erasmus, did so for tactical reasons. J. Wayne Baker's current work would remove the exception for Castellio.

6. Turchetti, *Concordia o Tolleranza?*, 136, drawing a contrast between Pole, Pighe and others, and Martin Bucer.

7. Mayer, *Starkey*, 264 for Pighe and Pole. I would now stress Pighe's failure to get anything worthwhile out of Pole. John Calvin, *Acta synodi Tridentinae cum antidoto*, in *Opera Omnia* (Braunschweig: C. A. Schwetske, 1863–1900, 59 vols.), vol. 7 (Corpus Reformatorum, vol. 35), col. 386. Paolo Simoncelli, *Il caso Reginald Pole: Eresia e santità nelle polemiche religiose del Cinquecento* (Rome: Edizioni di Storia e Letteratura, 1977), 54–55 and 58–59 for Negri, and passim for Vergerio.

8. Mayer, *Starkey*, chap. 8.

9. This was William K. Jordan's opinion. *The Development of Religious Tol-*

eration in England, Vol. 1, *From the Beginning of the English Reformation to the Death of Queen Elizabeth* (Cambridge, Mass.: Harvard University Press/London: Allen and Unwin, 1932; reprint Gloucester, Mass.: Peter Smith, 1965), 60–61. Jordan was typical in baldly claiming that the *Dialogue*'s implicit argument in favor of toleration was "probably" Starkey's own.

10. Starkey, *Dialogue*, 141 for the law.
11. Starkey, *Dialogue*, 89–90.
12. Starkey, *Dialogue*, 137–41.
13. See Thomas F. Mayer, "Faction and Ideology: Thomas Starkey's *Dialogue*," *Historical Journal* 28 (1985): 1–25, 19 for the argument that Starkey could not have gone too afield of Pole's views if he hoped to keep his patronage.
14. See most recently Gary Remer, "Dialogues of Toleration: Erasmus and Bodin," *Review of Politics* 56 (Spring 1994): 305–36.
15. I cite Robert Adams's translation, Desiderius Erasmus, *The Praise of Folly and Other Writings* (New York and London: W. W. Norton, 1989), 219–22. The Latin text is Desiderius Erasmus, *Opera Omnia* (Amsterdam: North-Holland, 1972), I, part 3: 371–74.
16. Agnes Rióok-Szalay, "Erasmus und die ungarischen Intellekutellen des 16. Jahrhundert," in August Buck, ed., *Erasmus und Europa* (Wiesbaden: Harassowitz, 1988; Wolfenbüttler Abhandlungen zur Renaissanceforschung, 7), 125–26. For Dudic's biography, see Caccamo, *Eretici italiani*, 110ff.
17. Caccamo, *Eretici italiani*, 117n.
18. Caccamo, *Eretici italiani*, 122, and Pierre Costil, *André Dudith, humaniste hongrois 1533-1589: Sa vie, son oeuvre et ses manuscrits grecs* (Paris: Les Belles Lettres, 1935), 348 for the likely date.
19. For discussion, see Massimo Firpo, *Il problema della tolleranza religiosa nell'età moderna dalla riforma protestante a Locke* (Turin: Loescher, 1978), 97–98, where Dudic's argument is identified with Castellio's. Partial Italian translations of the two most important letters appear on 130–33. Cf. also Costil, *Dudith*, 339–51. Cf. the next note for the bibliography of Dudic's letter.
20. *Correspondance de Théodore de Bèze*, ed. Hippolyte Aubert, Alain Dufour, Claire Chimelli, and Béatrice Nicollier (Geneva: Droz, 1983), 11: 226–48, with more accurate bibliography than in Firpo and more complete than in Mino Celsi, *In haereticis coercendis quatenus progredi liceat. Poems—Correspondence*, ed. Peter G. Bietenholz (Naples and Chicago: Prismi and the Newberry Library, 1982), 612. All references below are drawn from *Correspondance de Bèze*.
21. I argue here by analogy to Allan Megill's classification of historians' attitudes to grand narrative. "Grand Narrative and the Discipline of History," in Frank Ankersmit and Hans Kellner, eds., *A New Philosophy of History* (London and Chicago: Reaktion Books and University of Chicago Press, 1995), 151–73.
22. Alexius Horányi claimed that Dudic met Pole at Maguzzano in 1550. *Memoria Hungarorum et provincialium scriptis editis notorum* (Vienna: Anton Loew, 1775), 1: 550, apparently building on the contemporary life of Dudic by Quirinus Reuter. See Costil, *Dudith*, 64–65 and 71–73 for his time with Pole.
23. Costil, *Dudith*, 448.
24. For the date of composition of Dudic's and Binardi's adaptation, see

Gigliola Fragnito, "Gli 'spirituali' e la fuga di Bernardino Ochino," *Rivista Storica Italiana*, 84 (1972): 777–811, 803n.

25. Costil, *Dudith*, 448 citing a letter of Dudic to one Sylburg, dated Breslau, 25 February 1585.

26. Andras Dudic, *Vita Reginaldi Poli* (Venice: Domenico and Giovanni Battista Guerrei, 1563), sig. 4r.

27. Ludovico Castelvetro was one, serving up a fairly nasty life of Binardi in "Racconto delle vite d'alcuni letterati del suo tempo di M. L. C. Modenese scritte per suo piacere," printed in Giuseppe Cavazzuti, *Ludovico Castelvetro* (Modena: Società Tipografica Modenese, 1903), appendix, 7–8, and Alemanio Fino was the other, in a letter to Luca Michelonio, Crema, 29 November, probably 1565. Bergamo, Biblioteca Civica "Angelo Mai," Carte Stella in Archivio Silvestri 41/197 (hereafter Carte Stella); cf. Giuseppe Bonelli, "Un archivio privato del Cinquecento: Le Carte Stella," *Archivio Storico Lombardo* 34 (1907): 332–86, no. 346.

28. The only two manuscripts of "De sacramento" emanating from Pole's circle (London, British Library, Harl. 417, fols. 49r–68v [hereafter BL] and Città del Vaticano, Biblioteca Apostolica Vaticana [hereafter BAV], Vat. lat. 5967, fols. 141r–7v) are probably in the hand of Pole's principal secretary, Marcantonio Faita.

29. Castelvetro, "Racconto."

30. Carte Stella, 40/155 (Bonelli, no. 178).

31. See Thomas F. Mayer, "A Sticking-Plaster Saint? Autobiography and Hagiography in the Making of Reginald Pole," in Mayer and D. R. Woolf, eds., *The Rhetorics of Life-Writing in Early Modern Europe: Forms of Biography from Cassandra Fedele to Louis XIV* (Ann Arbor: University of Michigan Press, 1995), 205–22.

32. Andras Dudic, *Vita Reginaldi Poli*, in A. M. Querini, ed., *Epistolarum Reginaldi Poli*, 5 vols. (Brescia: Rizzardi, 1744–57), 1: 57.

33. Sebastian Merkle, ed., *Concilium Tridentinum Diariorum Pars Prima* (Freiburg: Herder, 1901), 82. Cf. Fenlon, *Heresy and Obedience*, 134.

34. *Reginaldi Poli ad Henricum octavum Britanniae regem, pro ecclesiasticae unitatis defensione* (Rome: Antonio Blado, [1539]), fols. VIr and XCIXr. Cf. also fol. CXIr–v, where in the midst of an exhortation to Charles V to invade England, Pole contrasted the tolerant attitude of the Turks to Christians with Henry's treatment of those who disagreed with him.

35. Some versions of the work begin with the expectation of a general council, which would seem to mean that it could have been begun as early as 1537, shortly after Pole became a cardinal, or at least in 1542 when Trent opened. The only dated manuscript (Naples, Biblioteca Nazionale, IX. A. 14) comes from 1556. It was not at all unusual for Pole to gestate a work over such a long time. The main collection of manuscripts is BAV Vat. lat. 5964, assembled in the volume backwards in terms of likely order of composition.

36. For discipline, see, e.g., fols. 105r/268r/336r. The bishops bore the brunt of Pole's displeasure at the beginning of the work, only to be replaced by the *populus*. See, e.g., fol. 146r for the bishops and fols. 50v/246v, the beginning of a lengthy treatment of the manifold faults of the *populus*.

37. BAV, Vat. lat. 5968, fols. 1ar–4v.

38. The text (BAV Vat. lat. 5968, fols. 227r–56v, headed "A fragment tow-

chinge the sacrament of the altare" and possibly related to the following section described as a sermon) was incorrectly identified by R. H. Pogson, "Cardinal Pole—Papal Legate to England in Mary Tudor's Reign" (PhD diss., University of Cambridge, 1972), 203 as being addressed to the synod. The person in question may well have been Pole's archdeacon (and part-time biographer) Nicholas Harpsfield. Bibliothèque Publique, Douai, MS 922, vol. 3, fols. 16r–17r (written in Calais, 22 May 1555) is Pole's appointment of Harpsfield and others as inquisitors in the city and diocese of Canterbury. For his contribution to Pole's myth, see "Sticking-Plaster Saint," 207–9.

39. BAV, Vat. lat. 5968, fols. 227r–29v.

40. Massimo Firpo, *Tra alumbrados e "spirituali." Studi su Juan de Valdés e il Valdesianesimo nella crisi religiosa del '500 italiano* (Florence: Leo S. Olschki, 1990), 132–38.

41. Massimo Firpo and Dario Marcatto, eds., *Il processo inquisitoriale del Cardinal Giovanni Morone*, 5 vols. (Rome: Istituto italiano per la storia dell'età moderna e contemporanea, 1981–89), passim, and Giacomo Manzoni, ed., "Il Processo Carnesecchi," *Miscellanea di Storia Italiana* 10 (1870): 189–573 passim. Cf. also Sergio Pagano, ed., *Il processo di Endimio Calandra e l'Inquisizione a Mantova nel 1567-1568*, Studi e Testi 339 (Città del Vaticano: Biblioteca apostolica vaticana, 1991) *ad indices*.

42. Pole offered that explanation of his relations with Flaminio to Carafa in 1553. G. B. Morandi, ed., *Monumenta di varia letteratura*, 2 vols. (Bologna: Istituto per le Scienze, 1797–1804), 1, part 2: 350. Ludovico Beccadelli, "Vita di Reginaldo Polo," in ibid., 326–27.

43. Benedetto da Mantova, *Il Beneficio di Cristo*, ed. Salvatore Caponetto, Corpus Reformatorum Italicorum, ed. Luigi Firpo and Giorgio Spini (Dekalb and Chicago: Northern Illinois University Press and Newberry Library, 1972), 478ff.

44. *Beneficio*, 454 for Morone's early opinion and Massimo Firpo, "Gli 'spirituali,' l'Accademia di Modena e il formulario di fede del 1542: controllo del dissenso religioso e nicodemismo," in Massimo Firpo, *Inquisizione romana e Controriforma. Studi sul cardinal Giovanni Morone e il suo processo d'eresia* (Bologna: Il Mulino, 1992), 29–118.

45. Simoncelli, *Caso*, 23–26.

46. Thomas F. Mayer, "Il fallimento di una candidatura: Reginald Pole, la 'reform tendency' e il conclave di Giulio III," *Annali dell'Istituto Storico Italo-Germanico in Trento* 21 (1995): 41–67.

47. Fenlon, *Heresy and Obedience*, 104–15.

48. Matthew Parker called Pole a *carnifex* for his treatment of Cranmer in *De antiquitate britannicae ecclesiae* (London: Bowyer, 1729), 533.

49. George Townshend and Stephen R. Catteley, eds., *The Acts and Monuments of John Foxe*, 8 vols. (London: Seeley and Burnside, 1837–41), 5: 308.

50. 26 December 1556, Bonner-Pole, in ibid., 8: 307.

51. Rawdon Brown, ed., *Calendar of State Papers and Manuscripts, Relating to English Affairs in the Archives and Collections of Venice*, 9 vols. (London: Routledge and Kegan Paul, 1873–86), vol. 6, no. 536 (hereafter *CSPV*).

52. 15 July 1556, Cheke-Pole, from the Tower of London. BL Add. MS 32091, fol. 149r–v; printed in John Strype, *Ecclesiastical Memorials Relating Chiefly to Religion, and its Reformation, under the Reigns of King Henry VIII, King Edward VI, and Queen Mary*, 7 vols. (Oxford: Clarendon Press, 1816), 3: 2, no. LIV, from a manuscript in his possession. See also the summary in John Strype, *The Life of the learned Sir John Cheke* (Oxford: Clarendon Press, 1821), 111–12. Cheke had been kidnapped and brought back to England for trial. D. M. Loades, *The Oxford Martyrs* (New York: Stein and Day, 1970), 258.

53. Jasper Ridley, *Thomas Cranmer* (Oxford: Clarendon Press, 1962), e.g., chap. 24 passim. Cf. Loades, *Martyrs*, 223 and A. G. Dickens, *The English Reformation*, 2d ed. (University Park: Pennsylvania State University Press, 1991), 294, who writes of Pole's "cold, official ferocity."

54. See note 24 for the manuscripts. The treatise was printed in Cremona by Cristofor Dracono in 1584, allegedly from a manuscript the editor's father had gotten from one of Pole's familiars in Rome. Ridley, *Cranmer*, 382 and Loades, *Martyrs*, 223 both date *De sacramento* 1554, but on unknown evidence. It probably was written before 26 October 1555, when Pole apparently referred to the work in a letter to the nuncio in Brussels (*CSPV*, vol. 6, no. 255). The second of Pole's letters, dated 6 November, is in BL Harl. 417, fols. 69r–78v; it is mutilated but still has his original signature. It is printed in John Strype, *Memorials of the Most Reverend Father in God Thomas Cranmer*, 2 vols. (Oxford: Clarendon Press, 1812), 2: 972–89.

55. 26 October 1555, BAV, Vat. lat. 6754, fols. 181r–2r; *CSPV* 6: 1, no. 255.

56. Vat. lat. 5968, fols. 227rff. A later set of sermon notes in the same volume (fols. 446r–82v) also merely blamed Cranmer in fairly mild terms for having led the English church astray.

57. Ridley, *Cranmer*, 379–80.

58. Carte Stella 40/145 (Bonelli, "Carte Stella," no. 168), Henry Pyning-Gianfrancesco Stella, London, 27 August 1559, which reported that Villagarcia had been seized in Zeeland on the orders of the Spanish Inquisition. For Villagarcia's close relations with Carranza (and hence by extension with Pole) and his time in Oxford, see J. I. Tellechea Idigoras, *Fray Bartolomé Carranza y el Cardenal Pole: Un navarro en la restauración católica (1554–1558)* (Pamplona: Institución Príncipe de Viana, 1977), 245ff. and James McConica, ed., *The History of the University of Oxford*, vol. 3, *The Collegiate University* (Oxford: Oxford University Press, 1986), 145, 325, and 353. Ridley, *Cranmer*, calls Villagarcia "Garcina" throughout.

59. John Calvin, *Selections from His Writings*, ed. John Dillenberger (Garden City, N.Y.: Doubleday, 1971), 301. Latin text in *Institutio religionis christianae (1536)*, *Opera Omnia*, vol. 2, cols. 76–77.

60. Steven M. Ozment, *The Age of Reform, 1250–1550: An Intellectual and Religious History of Late Medieval and Reformation Europe* (New Haven, Conn.: Yale University Press, 1980), 347, building on the work of James M. Stayer, *Anabaptists and the Sword* (Lawrence, Kan.: Coronado Press, 1976), esp. part 4.

61. Firpo, *Tolleranza*, 14–15 argues that toleration could only have arisen among Protestants.

62. Cf. Nancy S. Struever, *Theory as Practice: Ethical Inquiry in the Renaissance* (Chicago: University of Chicago Press, 1992).

63. R. G. Collingwood, *The Idea of History* (New York: Oxford University Press, 1956), 249–302. Megill, "Grand Narrative," 162 briefly summarizes Collingwood's argument and recasts it in terms of the imposition of coherence.

II

Nursery of resistance: Reginald Pole and his friends

During the wait for the opening of the long-delayed first session of the council of Trent in 1545, one of the papal legates to the council sought relief from studies and the heat. Two of his emissaries arranged an outing to a suburban garden. They also proposed the topic of conversation: the republic and religion. The temporary lodger in the garden agreed, and ten years later he produced what purported to be a record of the day's disputes. Marco Gerolamo Vida, Christian epic poet, theorist of chess, sometime favourite of Leo X, and bishop of Cremona, published his *Dialogues on the dignity of the republic* in 1556.[1] By then its dedicatee, Reginald Pole, had become even more famous than he had been as legate at Trent. Cousin of Henry VIII, Pole had broken with the king and been made cardinal of England in reward, had been a nearly successful candidate for the papal tiara in the conclave of 1550 and five years later became papal legate for the reconciliation of England and, finally, Archibishop of Canterbury. His friends were Alvise Priuli, a Venetian noble, and the famous humanist Marcantonio Flaminio. The audience included the other two legates, Marcello Cervini and Giulio del Monte, both later popes.

Vida, under coercion, agreed to debate Flaminio, even though he conceded that Pole knew much more about the republic. (Vida also claimed to have discussed it with him at Maguzzano the day before Pole left for England in 1553.) Vida framed his dialogues by presenting Pole as an oracle of politics and then praising him as certain to bring splendour to 'our age by literary monuments'. This image may seem thoroughly eccentric in light of the hagiographical view of Pole, but it is crucial for the understanding of Vida's work, Pole's place in it, and their century.

The dialogue opened with a fairly standard Aristotelian disquisition on the commonwealth as natural but dependent on God for its felicity. Del Monte interrupted by asking Flaminio what the poets said about life before the republic. Vida assigned Flaminio, introduced as Pole's close friend and both a poet and rhetorician, a set of speeches defending the life of nature and bitterly opposed to civilized, urban existence. Among the first problems of cities which Flaminio pointed out were the crimes and frequent exiles they produced. There is no justice in cities, but even worse, no poverty, the only source of beatitude. Men in a state of nature, by contrast, had 'no empires, no domination, no magistracies, no public council, in short there could not have been such and so profound desire of commanding' as there is now. By comparison, the first humans lived in Arcadian bliss 'in their own families and households, offended by no communities'. Of course, they all lived in peace. Flaminio continued his paean to 'pristine liberty' for some fifteen pages.

Vida's rejoinder subtly regularized Flaminio's case by rooting it in Flaminio's poetic practice, according to which real poets could not compose on command (a position Flaminio himself insisted on in his letters). Vida, by contrast, had written his *Christiad* at Leo X's behest and was therefore not a real poet, but an orator. The character Pole strenuously praised Vida's success in writing decent, Christian epic, a stance which contrasts sharply with his silence when Flaminio was introduced. Having established a hierarchy of literary practices, Vida then refuted Flaminio's views one by one. The tone is equally strident, but much more personal. Bad man, bad ideas, declaimed Vida. Worst of all, Flaminio had behaved like a rhetorician.

Instead, Vida replied 'in the mode of a logician [dialectician]' interested solely in the truth. It eventually turned out to rest in the hands of Peter, the vicar of Christ, and to be found therefore in the heavenly city. Interestingly enough, within the shelter of their garden, Vida and Flaminio agreed about tyranny, although not about the role of consent in politics or about the necessity of law. Vida clinched his case with another literary attack, offering the testimony of historians to counter Flaminio's dependence on poets. After a catalogue of the benefits of civilization and a thoroughly Augustinian discussion of the necessity of sin and hence of the coexistence of good and evil, Vida first had Del Monte joke that the company should return to the city and leave Vida, the defender of civility, all alone, and then closed by throwing everything up in the air. Vida both violated the boundaries of his garden by leaving it and accompanying his guests *up to* the city gate (but not through it) and also partially subverted his quest for verisimilitude by turning a romance episode – Del Monte's jesting – into a mobile conversation with no conclusion: Priuli told Vida later that everyone had talked about him and Flaminio on the way back, trying without success to decide whose case had been stronger.

Thus ended an apparently eccentric pastime, designed to escape the tedium of hard work and bad weather, if, of course, this conversation ever took place. That question is much less important than establishing the cultural reality of the venue Vida chose and the events which took place therein. An aristocratic group composed of three princes of the church, one bishop, two (sometime) poets, a rhetorician and an orator engaged in debate about the fundamental principles of what those 'same'

II

people were up to in the 'real' world of the council of Trent. In literary terms, within the topos of a *locus amoenus* (pleasant place), a garden, the site of romance, a battle more suited to epic was fought out between civilization and nature. By focusing on this event, its site and its principal occupant, Pole, we can unearth a wide range of resistances to new political, religious (and literary) developments in the sixteenth century. Often dismissed as frivolous, wildly unrealistic, or the product of aristocratic 'detachment', the pleasing pastimes in which Pole and his circles engaged deserve to be read more seriously.[2] Simultaneously political and literary, their play was more than escapism.

Just as Vida's garden 'resisted' the city and council of Trent by providing a protected place in which everything held dear by civilization, both civic and religious, could be called into question, so its romance episodes and open-ended dialogic structure 'resisted' the epic destruction of Flaminio which was probably high on Vida's list of motives for writing.[3] Since no one could decide who had won the debate, that left open the possibility that Flaminio not only continued to believe his Arcadian vision of reality, but might even have chosen to act on it outside Vida's garden. Likewise, Flaminio's own pastoral verse, written only in very small forms, refused the linearity and purposefulness of epic in the same way as his rhetorical speeches refused the corruption, domination and law of cities. So too did Pole's numerous dialogues – no matter how didactic some of them became – resist straightforward organization, closure and consequently interpretation. It is more than ironic that Vida chose the most ambiguous form of Renaissance literature simultaneously to exalt himself and Pole and to attempt to destroy Flaminio.

Vida's Pole, his Flaminio, and their friends offer an archetype of resistance on many fronts, especially through literature, beginning with Pole's own *De unitate* and ramifying into an enormous amount of writing. This is not a new idea, originating as it does with Pole. But the dynamics, the ramifications and the typicality of his responses have not been understood; the role of his circles in general and his household in particular as nurseries of resistance, a species of movable garden, has been largely missed in English language scholarship.[4] The list of Pole's intimates adjudged either then or later guilty of a wide range of resistances includes the Englishmen Thomas Starkey, Thomas Lupset, John Helyar, George Lily, Ellis Heywood, Nicholas Harpsfield and Nicholas Sander; Italians, beginning with Michelangelo, Giovanni Morone, Girolamo Seripando, Ludovico Beccadelli, Vittoria Colonna, Francesco Berni, Antonio Brucioli, Aonio Paleario, Donato Giannotti, Guido da Fano, Bartolomeo Spadafora, Trifone Benci, Donato Rullo, Pietro Carnesecchi and many others; Spaniards such as Bartolomé Carranza and Francisco de Navarra (both high-ranking bishops, Carranza perhaps the most celebrated victim of the Inquisition, in no small part because of his association with Pole in England); one Hungarian,

II

NURSERY OF RESISTANCE

Andras Dudic; and at least two Flemings, Christophorus Longolius and Dominic Lampsonius. The mere geographical diffusion of Pole's circles suggests a major phenomenon.

Only some of these figures can be included here, and a great deal more subtle analysis will be needed to take full account of how their circumstances intersected in Pole's nursery. Nevertheless, it should already be clear that as in the case of the literary analogue to Pole's households/gardens, the 'pleasant places' of romance, it could be hard to predict what kinds of resistance might spring up there. Pole and his coteries exhibit some ten varieties. (1) As in the case of Vida's Flaminio or perhaps Pole in the early phases of his career, they might pledge ambivalent – and therefore always unstable – allegiance to the established order. (2) Contrariwise, as Pole and the Florentine exiles Giannotti and Brucioli often did, they might engage in subversion, whether in the form of supporting armed rebellion or more devious means of undermining a regime. (3) When that failed nearly all of Pole's circle tried resistance by exile, both internal and external.[5] (4) Less seriously but equally devastatingly, they might employ humour, even if much of it now seems of a gallows variety and very little of it as subtly ironic as the paradoxical encomia of Erasmus or the simultaneous praise and blame of Francesco Filelfo.[6] A witticism could be a devastating rejoinder to tyranny. (5) Knowing when to make a joke required some of the skills of a councillor, debates over whose function became one of the principal forms of sixteenth-century resistance, not merely for Pole and followers. Similarly, discussion of prudence functions as a locus of resistance, beginning with *De unitate*.[7] (6) Pole also developed a specific form of counsel, prayer, a not-so-covert appeal to a higher power which might well judge a prince's actions in ways other than he might wish, and (7) the closely related but more threatening resistance of prophecy. (8) These two came together in the sites of martyrs, idealized figures of resistance; Pole and many of his allies proved very adept at putting hagiography to work for their purposes. (9) Hagiographical or not, rewriting events turned out to be perhaps the most successful means of resistance. (10) Finally, a favourite strategy for Pole was wars of words, resistance by definition.

A number of difficulties, not unlike the diversions in the path of a romance hero, immediately arise in trying to redraw the map of Pole's resistances. Perhaps the most serious of these is the relation between Pole's life as lived the first time through and as reconstructed after the 'fact' into a different fact by Pole and his followers; one of the most curious reconstructions was the writing out of his life of his love for gardens.[8] A related problem concerns the relation between the 'Pole' in the texts, a *persona* (almost literally meaning mask), and the Pole outside them. The outside Pole must indeed have 'authored' some of the *personae* in the limited sense that a pen in Pole's hand wrote the first texts containing

II

'his' *personae*, but 'authorization' is at least equally likely to have run in the opposite direction. To say it bluntly, the Pole in the texts differs from the Pole outside them. These two Poles of course bore a family resemblance to one another. Yet their differences make it extremely difficult to follow custom and beg the question of action and its springs by collapsing the writings, *personae* and all, into a putative self, an identity, even a fractured one. Instead, treating life and *personae* as separate but equivalent types of behaviour opens the way to taking account of the instability, indeterminacy and randomness Renaissance writers notoriously felt. These all, of course, are excellent means of resisting the 'normal politics' (or literature or religion) imposed by despots of whatever kind. The gap between *persona* and self in particular offered one of the principal sites of resistance, one of the best places to hide in plain sight.

Certainly Pole succeeded in doing that. Just four years ago still another hagiographical life of him appeared in Italy.[9] Yet however saintly Pole might have been, this cannot obscure his political purposes. A function of both his station and his education, Pole's political prowess, often in the face of difficult conditions, is beginning to emerge.[10] At a not too metaphorical stretch, the action begins with the wilful trouble-making of Pole's maternal grandfather, George, duke of Clarence, brother of Edward IV. This august ancestry meant that in the eyes of a Yorkist, Reginald's elder brother Henry, Lord Montagu, had a better claim to the throne than Henry VIII. Still, even to a Yorkist partisan the relations of 'false, fleeting, perjured Clarence' needed watching. Despite Clarence's family's uncertain loyalties and very close connection to the monarchy, Henry VII and even more his son restored Clarence's daughter Margaret. Her son Pole from early manhood set out to become a successful royal servant. Whether or not Henry VIII originally conceived the idea of supporting his cousin's education in Padua, Pole begged Cardinal Wolsey for his stipend and offered to guarantee results in practical experience and glory for the king.[11]

Longolius, one of the first inmates of Pole's household, aptly summed up the brunt of his friend's studies when he noted that Pole eagerly scrutinized the governors of his native land, in search of 'that quality you would like to see in the majority of all responsible men these days – a talent perfectly suited to the running of affairs of state'.[12] Pole would appear to have derived this concern partly from his education. His principal tutor in Padua, Niccolò Leonico, has recently been made an example of the 'profound fusion of Aristotelian philosophy and Venetian political principles' created by Venetian and Paduan humanists.[13] The ardently anti-Medicean Giannotti both recommended Leonico's political expertise at the end of *Della repubblica de' Veneziani*, designed as a blueprint to save the Florentine oligarchy from the Medici, and also further intended to use him as the main speaker in a sequel on the general principles of republicanism.[14] Giannotti, who wrote *Della repubblica* in Padua, was further connected

II

NURSERY OF RESISTANCE

to Pole through Pole's intimate Thomas Starkey, to judge from the dependence on Giannotti's work of Starkey's most important literary effort at resistance.[15]

Pole behaved for quite a time as if he meant to capitalize on his introduction to the theory of politics. In 1529–30 he dived energetically into his first big assignment from the king and persuaded the theologians of Paris to support Henry's divorce from Katharine of Aragon.[16] Nevertheless, immediately after Pole's return from Paris and despite high praise from Henry, he went into seclusion in John Colet's retirement villa at Sheen. According to Pole's later account, he honed his meterological skills then by forecasting tempests over England. Perhaps he did; perhaps this episode can be squared with the new account of Pole's behaviour in Paris by labelling it the beginning of Pole's resistance to the direction of English state-building. Some of Pole's companions in Sheen certainly did not much favour withdrawal, even if their ideas of engagement might have reflected more active resistance than Pole yet had in mind. Pole's chief secretary Starkey, for one, spent his time composing much of his 'Dialogue between Pole and Lupset' in which he simultaneously cast the character Pole as an expert on the problems of the commonwealth and urged him to put his knowledge to work as head of a revived nobility.[17] Starkey's hopes could not have outstripped Pole's by too much, lest he lose Pole's patronage.[18] Another member of Pole's household, Thomas Lupset, tried to further his career in royal service at the same time; he wrote both stoic treatises on dying well and libels against the direction of the king's policy, a combination of concerns which would prove very important to Pole a few years later.[19]

Like Giannotti, Starkey pinned his hopes on the Venetian constitution (which he discussed, as Giannotti claimed to have done, in a garden). This implicated Starkey's work in yet another web of resistances, both inside and outside Venice. Starkey's highly circumscribed image of the doge's power reflected that in Gasparo Contarini's *De magistratibus*, but ignored the real increase in his authority in the first several decades of the sixteenth century.[20] Starkey's Venice was still more republican than oligarchical. At the same time, the propagation of any image of Venice to the rest of Europe may well have made Starkey a cog in the propaganda machine responsible for the so-called 'age of Gritti', a cultural offensive launched under doge Andrea Gritti to restore Venetian prestige after the humiliation of the war of the league of Cambrai.[21] Starkey had close ties to one of the principal architects of this campaign, Pietro Bembo, to whom he may also have owed the decision to write about the serious subject of politics in the vernacular.[22]

Starkey and Pole and other members of Pole's household danced a complicated series of negotiations over the next five years, which resulted in temporary success for Starkey in royal service, an equally temporary breach with Pole, and a major swerve in Pole's itinerary, into open opposition. This came in the form of his massive broadside against Henry, *Pro ecclesiasticae unitatis defensione* (known as *De unitate*, *On the unity of the church*), written between September 1535 and March 1536. Like the rest of Pole's works, *De unitate* presents large textual problems.[23] Resistance by confusion had begun. So had resistance by prophecy, by insult, by martyrology (an especially fruitful mode for Pole), by fomenting rebellion and invasion (in two manuscripts and the first printed version of the text, not including the one Henry's advisory committee read), and by exile.

Pole claimed that *De unitate* repaid Henry for 'all the years I have spent in the labour of my studies [which] you supported'. Since these studies were overtly political and Pole treated this motive as distinct from 'the confession of Christ's name', he appears to have meant that *De unitate* was to be read as a political tract. Pole immediately claimed much skill in letters and their political use (IIIv, VIIr), and just as immediately made plain the intensity of his text's political resistance. Pole told Henry that he knew the king was not interested in the truth about 'the power of the Roman pontiff' and 'your new, and now first usurped honour, by which you have arrogated to yourself the right of the supreme headship of the English church'. Unable to agree with Henry's claim, Pole could see no option but to write and make himself guilty of treason and, worse, ingratitude. That would be the height of imprudence; the nature of true prudence becomes one of the major arguments of the work (Ir–v). Much of the strategy of *De unitate* turned on similar resistance by definition. This in turn depended on resistance by unmasking dissimulation, the highest form of political prudence.[24]

No matter how great Pole's political prudence, no matter how great the apparent contradiction between it and his strident denunciations of Henry, *De unitate* is anything but a straightforward text of resistance. For one thing, its superficial purpose – to bring the errant Henry back into the church by the shortest, epic path – frequently falls victim to romance interludes, including a meditation on the 'garden' of Henry's education and the golden age promised at the beginning of his reign, and at one of the climaxes of the work Pole's text wound up in a theatre watching a tragedy rather than in the streets of London demanding vengeance for the execution of Thomas More. Worse, while the shape of Pole's opposition to Henry may seem clear enough, the allegiance to the church he proposes as an alternative is anything but. Pole pursued resistance through various literary modes and on various fronts simultaneously. This creates a complicated web of a text.

Pole prescribed a simple remedy for Henry. The king must repent and do penance in order to re-enter the church, his mother. The meaning of this injunction is not so simple. Quite apart from the wildly spiralling family romances Pole constructed around Henry's 'mother', Pole defined the church differently from the way that his hagiographers have argued. True, he defended papal power, but as the mere title of his work must have reminded his learned readers, not necessarily at the expense of the rest of the hierarchy, particularly the bishops. The overtones were probably strong of Cyprian's most famous treatise, *De ecclesiae catholicae unitate*; although sometimes read as an unequivocally papalist statement, Cyprian actually defended a collective leadership of the church.[25] Pole, too, at several points implicitly defended episcopal authority. In his attack on Henry's argument from classical Christian precedent, Pole claimed that Constantine had intervened in the council of Nicaea only to shame the bishops into behaving themselves. That cleared the way for the council to gain the same authority as the apostles (XIXr). More importantly, when explaining Peter's primacy, Pole identified the church which never differed from Peter as the succession of the bishops 'the biggest thing the church contains' (XXXIIIv). Later Pole went so far as to define the church – along with Ockham – as 'the multitude of believers' (LXVIv).

The bishops, 'the successors of the apostles', might not individually always meet the apostolic standard, but that did not reduce the dignity of their office. Peter was important, but not singular even after he had undergone a metamorphosis produced by divine revelation of his new status. He was not even the only rock; Pole applied that label to all Christians. Peter did stand out in 'dignity and degree of excellence, nor did all get the same place of nobility in this building [of the church]' (XLVIIIv). Earlier Pole defended divine right episcopacy (XXr). Even in the heat of a protracted insistence on Peter's power, Pole both explicitly allowed that the other apostles might have had the same power, if not dignity, and he also pointed to the example of Moses and the seventy elders to illustrate that neither he nor the pope had their powers diminished by sharing them. A short and cryptic statement may tell most about Pole's attitude. Should the pope not feed Christ's sheep, he wrote, 'remedies are not lacking, by which the church can easily cure this evil' (CIr). Although Pole hurried on to talk of unity, he did so by turning to the council of Florence to refute Henry's claim that the Greeks did not recognize papal headship. Pole's mind easily turned from remedies to councils.

Pole rooted the present church in its primitive ancestor, as any humanist would. Not only did he stress its lowly social composition, but also he thought that not even the apostles collectively, much less Peter alone, had been its entire leadership – that included 'the others who [had] first fruits of the power of God's spirit' (XVr). Pole played the Augustinian card about the difference between Christ's 'doctrine' and the 'domination' of rulership to prove that Christ, and therefore, the church, did not claim coercive authority (XVIv). The clerical office, however, remained superior to the king's, since priests knew a higher form of wisdom than human prudence (XXIr). Their superiority and the entirety of their office consisted in prayer. That, like everything else the clergy did, was common to all priests (XXIIIIrff.). Likening praying priests to 'legates sent by everyone' to God was scarcely a hierocratic move, either (XXVr). (Later Pole added that priests 'stood above' kings who merely commanded, and could 'prescribe what ought to be done in the royal office'; XXVIr.) Eventually Pole came to describe the church in terms of a hierarchy of lower orders, priests, bishops, archbishops and 'he who bears the *persona* of God' (but no cardinals) (XXXVIIIr). In short, the leadership of the church was oligarchical (but not plutocratic), rather than monarchical, just as it was for Starkey and for Pole's friend and possible teacher in Padua, Marco Mantova.[26]

Ultimately Pole rested his case for the clergy on prophetic authority, which he set parallel to human prudence in secular government (XLIIv). Pole made his leanings crystal clear. He adopted a series of prophetic *personae* throughout, from David, to Moses (who also figured as a type of the secular ruler, giving rise to at least some peculiar overtones on what Pole thought of his own status), to Isaiah, probably the most frequent. Virtually the whole range of Old Testament prophets appeared. Pole frequently supported his points with one prophet or another speaking 'in the *persona* of God' (e.g. XXXVIr) and several times he made his own prophecies (e.g. XXXr). Immediately after his exhortation to Charles V to invade England, he effaced even the *persona* of prophet and claimed that the Old Testament prophets were speaking through him (CXIIIIv). The church's dependence on prophecy and revelation ran right to the very top. Peter owed his position to revelation and he alone knew precisely what it was because only he had direct, personal testimony from God (cf. XLIXr). This claim followed hard on a defence of ecclesiastical custom! Lest the point be missed, Pole quickly explained that such divine revelation had nothing to do with flesh and blood (XLVIr–v).

The principal requirement of the head of the church – elsewhere defined as nobility, although Pole never quite brought these two together – was lack of ambition. Christ had repressed 'contention over the principate [the papal office]' as 'most foreign to those who should rule the church of God, where humility, not ambition . . . should have the first place' (LIIIv). This statement posed a resistance of the first order, which Pole apparently really executed in the conclave of 1550.[27] Even stronger was Pole's claim that 'the house of God is ruled by charity' (quickly qualified as 'inflamed by the spirit of God'), which meant that no inferior should ever hesitate to correct an erring superior (LXXr). Pole maintained that the church knew God's will only thanks to 'the light of the Holy Spirit' (CIIv). Without necessarily adopting Max Weber's distinction between charismatic and routinized leadership, there is no doubt that Pole's view of the church was something less than fully hierocratic. Nor did his church require much

II NURSERY OF RESISTANCE

institutional structure – it was not, after all, a physical building, even though composed of a multitude of men.[28]

The church did, however, need nobility, and Pole made a contest over Peter's true nobility the central point of his book.[29] As Pole thereby resisted both secular and ecclesiastical absolutism, so insisting on the status of the English nobility and of himself as one noble in particular furthered the same end. At first, it might have seemed that Pole was merely establishing another claim to be heard when he reminded Henry of how the king had singled him out, 'one out of all the English nobility' (IIIv; cf. CXXr). When he turned to how Henry had thrown the succession into doubt, Pole greatly magnified his own standing in a transparently threatening way (LXXXv) by justifying on grounds of scripture the innocence of his uncle, the earl of Warwick, whom Henry VII had quietly executed (LXXXIr). Pole also warned Henry that he would never get away with repudiating Mary; among 'such a number of most noble families' any disruption of the succession was certain to lead to sedition. That is, unless Henry did away with all the nobility (LXXXIv).

Thus when Pole shortly after this reminded Henry of his educational benefits to him by suggesting an analogy for what Henry had done to the church, he did not randomly choose a republic (*civitas*) undergoing a change from rule by the privileged classes (*populus*) to rule by one. 'Consult the histories of all republics, and you will find that those republics which were constituted by the rule of the people (*populus*) suffered no greater injury then when they were reduced under the power of one' (IIIv). Only after this resoundingly aristocratic statement did Pole allow that rule by one was the 'best state' of a republic.

Even then, that 'one' could not behave as Henry had, as an 'emperor' who had conquered territory and could dispose of it as he wished. Henry might be a king and that might be the best form of rule, but a king was not absolute. Pole certainly knew Henry's more extreme claims. He reproduced the basic one that 'in a republic the cases of all citizens are referred to the king, as to the supreme head of the body politic' (XVIr). He obliquely referred to another when he applied language to Henry which echoed the famous legal maxim 'the king is an emperor in his own kingdom' (LXr). Henry had made similar noises, probably ventriloquizing his French predecessors, since early in his reign.[30] Later Pole compared Henry to the Great Turk, stressing the role of consent in England. The realm now had no more than 'a memory of its pristine liberty', despite the efforts of its best men (CIv). The king's office consisted in only two things: domestic justice and defence against foreign attack. (It will be noted that Pole allowed defensive war only.) 'Human prudence alone' could maintain civil concord (XXIr).

Pole caused himself most trouble by making it possible for 'the people' to reverse the decision by which they had constituted a single head for

59

themselves (XIIr, XXIIr).³¹ Arguing from origins Pole concluded that 'therefore on account of the people, the king, not the people on account of the king' (XXIIr). Many nations even got by entirely without kings, including the Jews. When they finally got theirs, God granted Saul 'not as a benefit, but rather for punishment' (XXIIIv, XXXVv). By talking about this transference of power in terms of the *lex regia*, Pole entered into the ongoing debate over the origins not only of royal but also of imperial power (LXr). The *lex regia* by which the Romans had allegedly transferred all their power to the emperor had been one of the proof texts medieval lawyers and political writers had used to resist various earlier moves in the direction of absolutism.³² Pole's description of how secular society was modelled on the hierarchy of the universe further carefully made room for two layers of magistrates between the 'lowest common people' and 'the command [*imperium*] of one supreme [head]' (XXXIIr). This was the same argument German Lutherans had already begun to use to justify resistance by the lesser magistrates to the direction of Charles's religious policy, as Pole almost certainly knew.³³

At the very least, a king had to listen to his councillors and friends, among whom Pole ranked himself very high (VIIr).³⁴ Bishop John Fisher and Sir Thomas More also should have been Henry's best friends; they certainly were Pole's, a point repeated often (e.g. XXXr). Henry, by contrast, was helpless, denuded of all his friends, and at the mercy of flatterers and self-servers among his advisers, Richard Sampson above all (CXVIIIv–CXIXr).

Pole engaged in one of the favourite forms of aristocratic behaviour in his confrontation with Sampson, casting most of the first two books of *De unitate* as literally a duel with Henry's champion. Sampson was like Goliath, pushing ahead of him an enormous spear and sword, the proem to his book. Then he was a gladiator, prematurely basking in the glory showered on him by the crowd. Sampson was mistaken not only in thinking he had won, but also in playing with a serious matter, or worse, deliberately deluding the English people (Xr).

Pole deserved to replace Sampson among Henry's councillors, in large part because of his pristine record of opposition to Henry's fatal politics. Here Pole offered resistance through autobiography, especially when rewriting the story of his role in Henry's consultation of the university of Paris about his divorce. As I have shown elsewhere, Pole's account may have saved his face, but it represented a much different kind of truth from that of what happened in the first place.³⁵ As in the case of his own life, Pole egregiously rewrote other kinds of history; one of the odder bits concerned the unwavering allegiance of the kings of France to the pope. Philip the Fair, to name only one of Francis's predecessors, had been erased (CVIIIv).

In both these cases, the play was the thing to Pole. He deployed a

II

NURSERY OF RESISTANCE

multitude of *personae* together with a great range of other literary devices, especially dramatic metaphors. One of Pole's best strategies was to offer a rhetorical criticism both of Sampson's book and of Henry's actions which became 'tragedies' in Pole's representation. A marginal note pithily summed up this line of attack: 'Sampson plays Goliath' (Xv). Near the beginning of book II, Pole replied at length to Sampson's rhetorical device of having Peter criticize his unworthy successors as pope. Dramatic metaphors litter this passage, above all *personae* in great plenty (XXXIIrff.). Shortly thereafter comes a long discussion of the dangers of rhetoric, but Pole objected most strongly to Sampson that he had violated verisimilitude in the characters he created, not that he had created characters at all. Sampson was a *bad* rhetorician who offended both against the 'laws of rhetors' and 'ordinary, vulgar prudence' (XXXIIIr). When explicating the equivalence of Peter and the rock on which Christ had founded his church, Pole offered a long lesson in how to read metaphors, a lesson in rhetoric (XLVIIrff.). Indeed, his entire case for Peter's superior nobility rested on what Pole explicitly termed a *similitudo*, a metaphor, that of the mystical body of the church (XLVIIIv).

At one of the climaxes of the book, Pole drew an extended theatrical analogy between the reaction of the Athenian *populus* to the death of Socrates and how Londoners had taken the execution of More. The Athenians had performed 'as if reciting words in a theatre', imitating 'some tragedy'; the Londoners, with juster cause for indignation, had not confined their rage to 'your [Henry's] theatre', but spread it wherever there were Christians. While the Athenians might have been playing, the Londoners were 'more than serious'. How could Henry have missed the implied sequel in the fate of Socrates's prosecutors, murdered by their enraged fellow citizens (XCIIIIv)?

Pole leaned very heavily on the deaths of Fisher and More in his attack on Henry.[36] Even an identification of More with Socrates was not enough; More would ultimately become a Christ-figure combating Henry's antichrist and sacrificing himself for the king (XCr, XCIIv).[37] Pole began by telling the king that 'your intelligence [*ingenio*], learning, prudence and finally experience' could never be compared to Fisher's and More's; this point later grew into several very long eulogies of More's prudence and political acumen (e.g. LXXXIXrff.).[38] Even if Henry's endowments had been superior, he still lacked the one thing needful, 'the spirit of Christ' which had made it possible for Fisher and More to understand the metaphors (*figurae*) of scripture (LXXIIv–LXXIIIr). Overtly political resistance had its place, but as in the case of the papacy, Pole found a charismatic defence much more appealing. But that did not mean that he neglected the brutally physical. Among the other uses to which Pole put Fisher and More, he dwelt at length on the ignominious manner of their deaths and the fate of their (and the other martyrs') bodies (LXXXIIIvff.). Even here, however, Pole could not resist several horrid puns on heads, including the rhetorical question 'can we doubt whose church's head [he means Satan's] cut off those heads' (LXXXIIIIr)? Pole repeatedly said he was crying while writing, but it seems that he must also have been laughing, however grimly.

Very shortly after this Pole swerved well out of the serious epic, even cosmic, path he had set himself. In order to remind Henry of how far he had already fallen, Pole recalled the high expectations for 'a golden age' early in Henry's reign. 'What did your outstanding virtues not promise, which shone in you especially in the first years of your reign?' Further, Henry's father had added to his education 'the care of letters, as streams pouring into a well-planted garden, by which, like waters, your virtues were irrigated, so that they might grow better and spread themselves more like the branches of a tree'. Making his favourite move, Pole then quoted the prophet Ezekiel to compare Henry to a tree in the Garden of Eden! This was true above all because Henry's tree had united in itself the contenders for the throne of England and thus brought the faction fights of the fifteenth century to an end. (Can Pole have been unconscious of the overlap between his garden metaphor, the genealogical one of a family tree, and the horticulturally labelled 'wars of the roses?') Henry himself had been part of a deliberately created garden, a pleasant place, but was fated to become twisted epic; quoting Isaiah this time, Pole warned that God had promised to destroy his vineyard, a proleptic move out of the idyll of Henry's early years into the current tragedy (LXXIXv).

Perhaps not by coincidence, Pole's ultimate move against Henry returned to a tragedy which began in a garden, a classic version of what Bakhtin called carnival.[39] 'The whole of this mystery is contained in Christ's passion', Pole told Henry. Only one who had 'eyes so illuminated by faith' could understand that Christ was 'the son of God, author of our felicity, and teacher of the same'.[40] Christ's bodily death set the pattern for all his 'members', who also had to suffer crucifixion of their bodies if they wished salvation. Such 'living books' revealed the will of God as no written books could, even those dictated by the Spirit. 'These books which were written in the blood of the martyrs are to be preferred to all others. These were archetypical books, in which the sole finger of God' – Pole naturally continued to think in terms of body parts – 'appears'. Pole pushed his anti-intellectual stance by continuing that any books, even divinely inspired ones, were subject to interpretation and therefore distortion, even deliberate invention, 'while those written in the blood of martyrs cannot be adulterated', a significantly physical term (XCVv–XCVIr).

Combining both martyrology and its original, Christ's passion, Pole developed the metaphor of legation which he had earlier applied to priests as emissaries to God. Before offering this (perhaps) metaphorical solution to Henry's problems, Pole assured the king that he was not 'playing

II

NURSERY OF RESISTANCE

seriously' in such a serious matter (XCVIIv). Metaphors had at least two edges. Pole tried to guard against being cut by one of them by a preemptive strike on his reader(s). Of course, the emissaries were to be Fisher, More and the monks, for all of whom Pole once more presented credentials in the form of capsule biographies. Pole quickly got back to carnival, however, via his argument against learned pretension and in favour of the ability of any 'simple Christian' to understand what he was talking about with the aid of revelation (CIIv). This Erasmian-sounding theme occurs frequently. Pole thoughtfully provided the *idiota*, the unlearned common person, with a long oration to Henry. Its point was simple: 'we do not listen to your words'. Pole's unlearned speaker concluded with Pole's own major point: 'we will not listen to words more, but now we will look at things written by the finger of God, that is, the holy martyrs' (CIIIr). As for Henry, all should pray not only that God would send him good councillors, but also that 'he might hear good councillors'. Having suggested a wide range of possible resistances, Pole left ordinary Christians only prayer (CVr).

That was not the only option. A prince and prophet like Pole could appeal to the bluntest strategy of resistance and call on Francis and Charles to attack England. Isaiah once more served to unmask 'your counsels', but Pole claimed that no one really needed a prophet to see what Henry was doing (CIXr–v). Charles above all could hardly miss it, given Henry's private injury to Charles's aunt Katharine, and the much more serious public one done to the church. Since Charles had just then scored a major victory over the church's external enemies in the battle of Tunis, he was fully prepared to deal with Henry (CXv). And if Charles somehow missed Henry's devilry, Pole told him about it. A long set oration followed, designed to shame Charles into dealing with a much more serious 'danger to the republic' (CXIr–CXIIIIr, continued on CXVIvf). Among the incentives he offered Charles, Pole included an English fifth column of 'whole legions, lurking [*latent*] in England' (CXIIv). In addition to military attack, Pole also returned to a proposal for economic warfare which he may have suggested in 1531; what would England do if its trade with the continent were cut off (CXVIIr–v)?

In the final book of *De unitate* Pole spelled out a dangerous implication he had raised earlier. He contrasted the early days 'in which the sons of the church abounded in the gifts of the holy spirit' with 'these same most corrupt times in which many judge that knowledge which is had through divine light to be almost extinct in men' (CXXVv). The same held true for secular history, whose countless examples could be understood only in the light of spiritual illumination. Since the test of successful illumination was consistency, both the church and secular power had to be in the same state as they had originally been. That was a tough standard, offering equally strong resistance on both ecclesiastical and secular fronts.

Pole then turned his back on both powers in favour of faith, sounding a note that he would strike consistently for at least the next decade. The only certain source of knowledge, faith was both the light and the fire 'through which light we believe and know [*cognovimus*] that Jesus is Christ'. 'The spirit...in that faith which is the gift of God...gives...firm and stable knowledge'. Pole then put forward a definition of faith as 'supernatural light' which gave form to unformed human belief (CXXVIIr). 'True faith', as the marginal note had it, was 'the only way to be given entry to knowledge of the divine mysteries'. That meant, 'unless you believe, you will not understand'. Everything of any value in earthly bodies came from 'the image of faith', which Pole now called Henry to contemplate. The examples of Sennacherib and Sodom and Gomorrah sufficed to show what happens to people who trust in their own powers rather than faith (CXXVIIv–CXXVIIIr).

But that was not the sort of faith Pole had in mind. He meant faith which led to felicity 'and that kingdom with God which raises us an infinite distance above our nature'. Transcendence to the maximum degree became the final resistance. Again sounding a great deal like Erasmus, Pole offered this escape, as he had before, as especially appealing because 'it easily persuades [note the rhetorical emphasis] the wise both to hold in contempt their wisdom and to be least offended to take themselves as fools' (CXXVIIIv).[41] Turning to Paul for an apostrophe of the transforming powers of divine light, Pole wound up back in the church, outside of which there could be no light of Christ (CXXIXr). Henry had no choice but to do penance and submit to ecclesiastical authority. Pole's belated introduction of the laws of the church, combined with a short argument that the scriptures owed their authority to the church may be a response to the difficulty raised by his demonstration of the power of unmediated faith (CXXXIv). In any case, Pole very shortly returned to the necessity and power of revelation, concluding his 'oration' with the words of Ezekiel 'and your iniquity will not be your ruin' (CXXXIIv–CXXXVIr).

Pole's later enemies within the church had trouble with his talk of faith. The usual story has them hounding him into withdrawal, just as Henry is supposed to have done before. Such a conclusion poses difficulties. Above all, Pole's retreat was always tactical, susceptible to reversal when the proper circumstances arose. This happened in 1537 when Pole undertook a lengthy legation designed to assist the Pilgrims of Grace to overthrow Henry. It happened in 1553 when he eagerly accepted another legation to reconcile England to the church. And it probably happened in any number of cases in between which are not well understood, for example, his pivotal role in brokering the deal by which the Farnese definitively gained the duchy of Parma.[42]

Pole would later try to squelch both dimensions of his early career, insisting that he was neither political nor a fideist. That was after he had

II

NURSERY OF RESISTANCE

lost several more rounds in his struggle with absolutism. Space precludes a complete discussion of this evolution, but suffice it to say that this was a long, drawn-out process, frequently much more responsive to short-term political demands than to those of ideology, whether Pole's (increasingly a powerful appeal for peace, at least unconsciously in part as a means of stunting the processes of state-building which depended, then as now, on aggression for their successful completion), Paul IV's (as much a Renaissance prince as Leo X, however their religious beliefs may have differed), Charles's or Mary Tudor's.[43] And Pole continued throughout to attract and nourish other resisters, on both religious and political grounds.[44]

The course of Pole's relations with Henry illustrates some of the complications in his resistance. Even after Pole entered into direct negotiations with the emperor in early 1535, sent *De unitate* in mid-1536, became a cardinal six months later, and manifested his hostility in 1537, neither Henry nor many of his supporters gave up on him, nor Pole on Henry (to read *De unitate* and its related correspondence at face – the safest – value).[45] Towards the end of Henry's reign, Pole at least gave his blessing to various efforts to regain the king, including propaganda and diplomacy, but excluding armed force.[46] Yet in the midst of the most epic moment in all these upheavals, his legation of 1537, while dodging assassins (some doubtless real) through France and the Low Countries, and retiring to another monastery – this time at Aulne – praying, reading the Bible and singing 'in the Theatine manner', Pole also scribbled a dialogue, an intellectual romance, 'On divine and human prudence'.[47]

In the context of the established view of Pole as paragon of post-tridentine Catholic faith, this work looks weird. The character Pole held the balance between the *personae* of his friends Cosmo Gheri and Priuli. Gheri, supposedly another model of the virtues of pious withdrawal, played the Aristotelian proponent of human, civil prudence. Pole cast Priuli as the obscurantist defender of an extreme form of the contemplative and religious life. The action broke off before settling the dispute. Two years later, Pole apparently reversed his position in his famous condemnation of Machiavelli's argument in favour of dissimulation – what Pole again called human prudence – in political action.[48] Or did he? Pole's first biographer maintained that 'his purity was mixed with prudence, which allowed him to foresee many things' and then continued with the story of Pole's treason![49]

It strikes me as highly important that changing scholar's bonnet for cardinal's beret, and English royal service for a career in papal diplomacy did not permanently entrench Pole's resistances. Equally significant, the same uncertainty dominated Pole's circles in Italy. The case of four famous Venetian friends is well known – Contarini, one of Pole's closest allies; Gianbattista Egnazio, who tutored some of Pole's clients; Vincenzo Querini; and Paolo Giustinian.[50] This list could easily embrace Marco Mantova, perhaps Lazzaro Bonamico, close friend and Greek tutor of Pole, and Benedetto Lampridio, another of Pole's intimates.[51] For a decade and a half between 1509 and about 1524, this group tacked back and forth between withdrawal and political action. At one point Querini and Giustinian opted for the strict monastery of Camaldoli and only just failed to induce Egnazio to follow them. Contarini wavered. The rigorous life of a solitary hermit may have attracted Mantova.

Ultimately, most of these friends wound up in active service to the church, including Contarini whom Pope Paul III plucked out of a secular career in Venice in 1535. But like Contarini, Giustinian and Querini, none of them went quietly. These three continued deep resistance to the creation of papal absolutism in texts ranging from Giustinian and Querini's *Libellus ad Leonem X* (1514) to the *Consilium de emendanda ecclesia* (1537), the product of a reforming commission chaired by Contarini (and including Pole) which would have virtually dismantled the financial props of papal monarchy by using its own instruments against it.[52] Mantova kept alive conciliarist views of the ecclesiastical constitution as late as 1541, and arranged to have them widely disseminated.[53]

Another example of permanent uncertainty about resistance and withdrawal was Pole's household manager, Bartolomeo Stella. Even Stella's admiring biographer had to admit that the strength of Stella's religious vocation fluctuated constantly – it kept giving way to a curial life and to a penchant for writing obscene verse.[54] In this Stella behaved exactly like a large circle of Roman poets and sometime courtiers with close ties to Pole. They included the notorious Francesco Berni, author of some of the most outstanding obscene poetry of the early sixteenth century, off-again, on-again familiar of Pole's reforming ally Gian Matteo Giberti, sometime 'Lutheran', constantly reforming homosexual. (He was linked most closely to Pole through Priuli.)[55] Gianfrancesco Bini, a senior papal financial official, belonged to this coterie, as did Blosio Palladio; both loved gardens, Bini writing a poem of insults delivered by the speaking garden of its title (*L'orto*) and Palladio inheriting one of the most famous Roman gardens, the Corycius (which he also immortalized in the verse collection *Coryciana*).[56] Most of these were also friends of Michelangelo, whose transcendentally personal poetry took this kind of resistance to another plane, along with his overtly political and more subtle religious resistance.[57]

Far the most well known of Pole's resisting gardeners was Flaminio. Both of his recent biographers agree that the speeches Vida assigned to him probably reflect his ideas, as both of them struggle to make sense of Flaminio's errant career.[58] By his own testimony, it was held together by the desire for freedom from the constraints of a courtier's life, which Flaminio usually had to live. His chosen mode of expression was poetry, which he wrote in Latin and only in small forms, his specialties being pastoral odes and verse epistles (his late collection of these provides a

II

NURSERY OF RESISTANCE

directory of all the usual suspects). Then again, he also wrote several highly serious paraphrases of scripture, the Psalms above all, and co-authored the most famous product of the Italian reformation, *The Benefit of Christ's Death*. However this work is interpreted – whether as rooted in the possibly heterodox beliefs of Juan de Valdés, the certainly heretical ones of John Calvin, safely traditional Benedictine piety or something else – it most assuredly ignored institutional religion, stressing an almost mystical relation between God and the chosen few.[59]

Despite the best efforts of serious-minded historians, the fact remains that Flaminio did all these things *at the same time*. To take only one example from near the end of Flaminio's life, on 4 May 1549 he described a mystical experience of rejuvenation to Caterina Cibo.[60] In another letter of nearly the same date (and certainly before 27 May) Flaminio reported that he had decided to take the advice of Vincenzo Gheri (Cosmo's brother) and finish his collection of verse epistles, which included one to Pole in which Flaminio imagined himself Pole's lap-dog.[61] The balance of Flaminio's remaining letters concern his poetry, even if the very last surviving letter offered spiritual consolation to Lelio Torelli, an important councillor of Duke Cosimo I of Florence.[62] The habit of resistance through counsel was as deeply ingrained as resistance through poetry.

Flaminio, like Pole, has proved a difficult figure to understand. Since he always successfully escaped ecclesiastical office, it has been easier to dismiss him as a playful lightweight. This will not do, in either case. All of their resistances had a political root, whatever other sources of nourishment they may also have tapped. They responded in part to a profound change in their political circumstances. In both Pole's major venues, England and Italy, very similar developments in the direction of a new kind of monarchy were under way. The difference between the two places lay only in the direction of development. In Italy Courts and princes were a relatively new thing, proto-absolutism even newer.[63] In England, established Courts (above all the royal Court) took on new meanings and functions, but ones which had already been tried without much success a century and more earlier under Richard II. Venice, together with its dependent Padua, one of Pole's most constant Italian homes, underwent oligarchical contraction and a concomitant increase in the doge's power as a result of 'the crisis of the league of Cambrai' in the first two decades of the sixteenth century; this evolution was atypical only in its relative lateness.[64] And as Paolo Prodi brilliantly argues, Rome led the way, teaching the other European monarchs how to be absolutists.[65]

A wide range of experiments in opposition began simultaneously. Seeing life as a game was one of the best cultural resources of resistance. This was the choice of Richard Lanham's 'rhetorical man'. To rhetorical man, words counted for much more than ideas, and winning the game above all. Renaissance literature, says Lanham, was 'an attempt to keep man in the rich confusion of the mixed self' through a 'fruitful collision' or a 'self-corrective oscillation' between style or play and 'pure concept'.[66] Alternation between play and seriousness in an ongoing game describes politics especially well. It was a debating contest, which the players enjoyed for its own sake. A Renaissance politician 'as poet and critic' had to be adept at 'continually moving from purpose to game, serious to rhetorical coordinates, as circumstances require'.[67] His lack of a 'central self' also made it much easier to hide from those who demanded one.

Hence Pole's usual choice of literary, even playful, modes of resistance. But resistance these undoubtedly offered. Constructing gardens, real and 'imaginary', writing pastorals, orations and dialogues, all presented a serious challenge to the nascent order. Pole's lack of success by later standards cannot obscure the importance of his resistances for a more complete understanding of late Renaissance culture. Instead, they offer eloquent testimony about the power of absolutism to quash resistance and of playing to deflect absolutism.

NOTES

1 M. G. Vida, *Dialogi de rei publicae dignitate*, Cremona, V. Conte, 1556; truncated text in an appendix to G. Toffanin, *L'Umanesimo al Concilio di Trento*, Bologna, Zanichelli, 1955. My thanks to F. W. Conrad, Robert Hariman, Dean Hammer and Paul A. Fideler for their comments on a draft of this chapter.
2 E.g. G. Fragnito, *In museo e in villa: saggi sul Rinascimento perduto*, Venice, Arsenale, 1988, p. 12, and ch. 1 passim for detachment; A. Pastore, *Marcantonio Flaminio. Fortune e sfortune di un chierico nell'Italia del Cinquecento*, Bologna, Angeli, 1981, esp. p. 139.
3 Pastore, op. cit., pp. 138–9.
4 Much more attention needs to be given to Pole's closest circle, his household. I offer some suggestions here; for the most important previous work see W. G. Zeeveld, *Foundations of Tudor Policy*, Cambridge, Mass., Harvard University Press, 1948. Newer views will depend above all on the massive studies of M. Firpo, most recently *Fra alumbrados e 'spirituali': Studi su Juan de Valdés e il valdesianesimo nella crisi religiosa del '500 italiano*, Florence, Olschki, 1990; C. Mozzarelli (ed.) *'Familia' del principe e famiglia aristocratica*, Bologna, Bulzoni, 1988; and G. Fragnito, 'Cardinals and their households', paper given at the Sixteenth Century Studies Conference, St Louis, Mo., October 1990.
5 R. Starn, *Contrary Commonwealth: The Theme of Exile in Medieval and Renaissance Italy*, Berkeley, Calif., University of California Press, 1982.
6 D. Robin, *Filelfo in Milan*, Princeton, NJ, Princeton University Press, 1991.
7 R. Hariman, 'Prudence/Performance', *Rhetoric Society Quarterly*, 1991, vol. 21, no. 2, pp. 26–35, suggests an important new construction of the problem of prudence.
8 L. Beccadelli, 'Vita di Reginaldo Polo', in G. B. Morandi (ed.) *Monumenti di varia letteratura*, Bologna, Istituto per le Scienze, 1797–1804, vol. 2, p. 325, and Andras Dudic, *Vita Reginaldi Poli*, in A. M. Quirini (ed.) *Epistolarum Reginaldi Poli*, Brescia, 1744–57 (hereafter *ERP*), vol. 1, p. 55, both had Pole snub a Roman noble who wished that Pole could enjoy the noble's new garden

II

NURSERY OF RESISTANCE

thirty years hence. For Pole's love of gardens, see his letter of condolence to Alessandro Farnese on the destruction of that prince's Roman gardens in *CSPV*, vol. 6, no. 614.

9 M. T. Dainotti, *La via media: Reginald Pole 1500–1558*, Bologna, EMI, 1987.
10 C. Höllger, 'Reginald Pole and the legations of 1537 and 1539; diplomatic and polemical responses to the break with Rome', Oxford University DPhil thesis, 1989, and my work cited below.
11 BL MS Vespasian F XIII, fos 283r–4r (not in *L&P*). The letter was dated Oxford, 6 October, and addressed to Wolsey as legate; the year must therefore be 1518 or 1519.
12 T. F. Mayer, *Thomas Starkey and the Commonweal: Humanist Politics and Religion in the Reign of Henry VIII*, Cambridge, Cambridge University Press, 1989, p. 49.
13 M. L. King, *Venetian Humanism in an Age of Patrician Dominance*, Princeton, NJ, Princeton University Press, 1986, p. 182.
14 Mayer, *Starkey*, p. 50.
15 Ibid., pp. 55–6, 67–71.
16 T. F. Mayer, 'A mission worse than death: Reginald Pole and the Parisian theologians', *EHR*, 1988, vol. 103, pp. 870–91.
17 Mayer, *Starkey*, chs 3–5, and *T. Starkey: 'A Dialogue between Pole and Lupset'*, T. F. Mayer (ed.), C4S, no. 37, pp. xiii, 1–2, 142–3.
18 Richard Lanham emphasizes that the best a courtier could hope to do was to 'become expert in drama, in stylistic manipulation, so that it will be convincing drama' which he plays before the prince, or in Starkey's case, his patron. R. A. Lanham, *The Motives of Eloquence: Literary Rhetoric in the Renaissance*, New Haven, Conn., Yale University Press, 1976, p. 153.
19 J. A. Gee, *The Life and Works of Thomas Lupset*, New Haven, Conn., Yale University Press, 1928, pp. 172–3, and Mayer, 'Mission worse than death', p. 872.
20 Mayer, *Starkey*, op. cit., pp. 59–61, and E. G. Gleason, 'Reading between the lines of Gasparo Contarini's treatise on the Venetian state', *Historical Reflections/Réflexions Historiques*, 1988, vol. 15, pp. 251–70.
21 M. Tafuri, '"Renovatio urbis Venetiarum": il problema storiografico', in M. Tafuri (ed.) *'Renovatio urbis': Venezia nell'età di Andrea Gritti (1523–1538)*, Rome, Officina, 1984, pp. 9–55.
22 Mayer, *Starkey*, p. 66.
23 T. F. Dunn, 'The development of the text of Pole's *De unitate ecclesiae*', *Papers of the Bibliographical Society of America*, 1976, vol. 70, pp. 455–68, to be used with care. The text cited is *Reginaldi Poli ad Henricum octavum Britanniae regem, pro ecclesiasticae unitatis defensione*, Rome, Antonio Blado, 1539. I have collated it roughly against the prooftext in Biblioteca apostolica vaticana [hereafter BAV], Vaticanus latinus 5970, fos 1–124r. Folio references in round brackets in the text. My translations. J. G. Dwyer (trans. and intro.) *Pole's Defense of the Unity of the Church*, Westminster, Md., Newman Press, 1965, contains many errors.
24 P. S. Donaldson, 'Machiavelli and Antichrist: prophetic typology in Reginald Pole's *De unitate* and *Apologia ad Carolum quintum*', in *Machiavelli and Mystery of State*, New York, Cambridge University Press, 1989, pp. 1–36. This piece is also very good on Pole's prophetic *personae*.
25 Pole relied heavily on Cyprian, putting him first in a list of interpreters of scripture (fo. XXXIr), for example, although he never cited his predecessor's *De unitate*. Pole did, however, use Cyprian's letter no. 59 to pope Cornelius

to defend obedience to divinely ordained priests, although the subject at issue was papal primacy alone. Pole claimed that Cyprian's whole letter made for his point, but quoted only (1) part of a sentence speaking of all the bishops as if it applied to the pope alone (LXIIv–LXIIIr; Wilhelm Hartel (ed.) *S. Thasci Caecili Cypriani Opera Omnia*, vol. 3:2, Wolfenbüttel, Herzog August Bibliothek, 1872, pp. 673–4; translated in *The Letters of St. Cyprian of Carthage*, vol. 3, trans. and notes by G. W. Clarke, New York, Newman Press, 1986, pp. 73–4); and (2) another part of a sentence calling 'the chair of Peter . . . the principal church whence arose priestly unity'. Cyprian's text continued by equating that see (if that was even certainly what Cyprian meant) with 'those Romans [not just the pope, again if that was what Cyprian meant by the 'chair of Peter'] whose faith was praised by the preaching apostle' (Hartel, p. 683; *Letters*, p. 82.) Was Pole deliberately distorting his source, or leaving it for his readers to fill in a blank? For Cyprian's text, see M. Bévenot (ed. and trans.) *De Lapsis & De Ecclesiae Catholicae Unitate*, Oxford, Clarendon Press, 1971, esp. pp. xivff. for his ecclesiology. P. O'Grady, *Henry VIII and the Conforming Catholics*, Collegeville, Minn., Liturgical Press, pp. 22 and 151 offers a start on Henrician interpretation.

26 T. F. Mayer, 'Marco Mantova, a Bronze Age conciliarist', *Annuarium historiae conciliorum*, 1984, vol. 14, pp. 385–408.

27 He spent much of his time writing another dialogue *De summo pontifice*, which argued that Christ-like humility was the principal requisite of a candidate for pope. For his acting of that role, see the detailed reports of the Venetian ambassador in *CSPV*, vol. 5, nos 595–6 and Beccadelli, 'Vita', p. 303.

28 *De unitate*, fo. XLIXv. See A. J. Slavin, Chapter 8 in this volume, for a demonstration of the utility of Weber's ideas about patrimonialism in analysing the Tudor state.

29 See Q. Skinner, *Foundations of Modern Political Thought*, vol. 1, *The Renaissance*, Cambridge, Cambridge University Press, 1978, pp. 45–6, 59–60, 81–2, 236–40 and 257–9 for an introduction to the debate on true nobility.

30 For some of these see T. F. Mayer, 'Tournai and tyranny: imperial kingship and critical humanism', *HJ*, 1991, vol. 34, pp. 257–77, and 'On the road to 1534: the occupation of Tournai and Henry VIII's theory of sovereignty', in D. Hoak (ed.) *Tudor Political Culture: Ideas, Images and Action*, Cambridge, Cambridge University Press, forthcoming.

31 At no time did Pole write about a 'pact' between king and people, as Dwyer, op. cit., p. 56, has it, translating '*quo pacto se Rex in suo munere gerat*' as 'the pact by which the king exercises his office' instead of simply 'how the king exercises his office' (XXIIIr).

32 H. Morel, 'La place de la *lex regia* dans l'histoire des idées politiques', in *Études offertes à J. Macqueron*, Aix-en-Provence, 1970, pp. 545–56.

33 See Skinner, op. cit., vol. 2, *The Reformation*, pp. 195–208, and L. D. Peterson, 'Melanchthon on resisting the emperor: the *Von der Notwehr Unterricht* of 1547', in J. Friedman (ed.) *Regnum, Religio et Ratio: Essays Presented to Robert M. Kingdon*, Kirksville, Mo., Sixteenth Century Journal Publishers, 1987, pp. 133–44, and 'Justus Mennius, Philipp Melanchthon, and the 1547 Treatise, *Von der Notwehr Unterricht*', *Archiv für Reformationsgeschichte*, 1990, vol. 81, pp. 138–57.

34 See F. W. Conrad's essay on Thomas Elyot and friendship, Chapter 3 in this volume.

35 Mayer, 'Mission worse than death'.

36 Josef Ratzinger takes Pole's major contribution to be a martyrological justifi-

cation of papal primacy. In light of Pole's attitude detailed here, Ratzinger's judgement about Pole's notion of the primacy may need modification, but there is no doubt that dead heroes meant a great deal to him: 'The papal primacy and the unity of the people of God', in J. Ratzinger, *Church, Ecumenism and Politics: New Essays in Ecclesiology*, New York, Crossroad, 1988, pp. 36–44.

37 Pole apparently also fostered this resistance by hagiographical transcendence when he returned to England twenty years later. His archdeacon of Canterbury, Nicholas Harpsfield, wrote the second life of More, and Ellis Heywood, allegedly one of Pole's secretaries, dedicated to Pole his *Il Moro*, significantly a dialogue which made More a Socratic saint. Nicholas Harpsfield, *The Life and Death of Sir Thomas More*, E. V. Hitchcock (ed.), EETS, o.s., vol. 186, 1932, pp. 4 and clxxxii–clxxxv, and R. L. Deakins (ed.) *Il Moro: Ellis Heywood's Dialogue in Memory of Thomas More*, Cambridge, Mass., Harvard University Press, 1972, p. 73. Pole's close collaborator Pedro de Soto also saved the holograph of More's *De Tristitia Christi*. T. More, *De Tristitia Christi*, C. H. Miller (ed. and trans.), New Haven, Conn., Yale University Press, 1976, vol. 2, p. 696. I am grateful to Prof. Miller for pointing this connection out to me.

38 This passage was among those cut on Contarini's advice; Dunn, op. cit., pp. 462–3.

39 M. M. Bakhtin, *Problems of Dostoevsky's Poetics*, C. Emerson (ed. and trans.) Minneapolis, Minn., University of Minnesota Press, 1984, esp. pp. 134ff.

40 This requirement excluded Henry, and may well refer to yet another mode of resistance, the belief in justification by faith to which Pole would tenaciously adhere until 1546 when Trent officially condemned it. Of another huge literature, see esp. E. G. Gleason, 'On the nature of sixteenth-century Italian evangelism: scholarship, 1953–1978', *SCJ*, 1978, vol. 9, pp. 3–25; P. Simoncelli, *Evangelismo italiano del Cinquecento. Questione religiosa e nicodemismo politico*, Rome, Istituto storico italiano per l'età moderna e contemporanea, 1979, and esp. the work of Firpo (see Note 4 above).

41 M. A. Screech, *Erasmus, Ecstasy and the Praise of Folly*, Harmondsworth, Penguin, 1988.

42 *CSPV*, vol. 5, nos 591 and 594. Pole's role was commemorated by his inclusion in the fresco of Ottavio receiving Parma from Julius III in the Farnese villa at Caprarola.

43 H. Lutz (ed.) *Friedenslegation des Reginald Pole zu Kaiser Karl V. und König Heinrich II. (1553–1556)*, Nuntiaturberichte aus Deutschland, 1. Abteilung 1533–1559, vol. 15, Tübingen, Niemeyer, 1981; for Paul IV see G. Fragnito, ' "Parenti" e "familiari" nelle corti cardinalizie del rinascimento', in Mozzarelli (ed.) op. cit., p. 572; A. Aubert, 'Alle origini della Controriforma: studi e problemi sul Paolo IV', *Rivista di storia e letteratura religiosa*, 1986, vol. 22, pp. 303–55; and R. De Maio, *Michelangelo e la Contrariforma*, Bari, Laterza, 1981; for Mary, D. Loades, *Mary Tudor*, Oxford, Basil Blackwell, 1989.

44 Guido da Fano makes one excellent example and Bartolomeo Spadafora another. A. Stella, 'Guido da Fano eretico del secolo XVI al servizio dei re d'Inghilterra', *Rivista di storia della chiesa in Italia*, 1959, vol. 13, pp. 196–238, and S. Caponetto, 'Origini e caratteri della riforma in Sicilia', *Rinascimento*, 1956, vol. 7, pp. 219–41, 281–325.

45 T. F. Mayer, 'If martyrs are exchanged with martyrs: the kidnappings of William Tyndale and Reginald Pole', *Archiv für Reformationsgeschichte*, 1990, vol. 81, pp. 305–27, and 'A diet for Henry VIII: the failure of Reginald Pole's 1537 legation', *JBS*, 1987, vol. 26, pp. 305–31. See also Höllger, op. cit. For

Pole's earlier treason, see *CSPSp*, 5:1, no. 172 (Contarini asking imperial protection for Pole); BL Add. MS 28,587, fos 7v–9v and *CSPSp*, 5:1, no. 109; Add. MS 28,590, fos 5v–6r (*CSPSp*, 5:2, no. 63); and *CSPSp*, 5:1, no. 133 (for the date, see Mayer, *Starkey*, p. 216, n. 64). Eustace Chapuys, the imperial ambassador in London, had talked up Pole's prospects already in 1532; *CSPSp*, 4:2, no. 888.

46 K. R. Bartlett, 'Papal policy and the English crown, 1563–1565: the Bertano correspondence', *SCJ*, forthcoming; J. Lestocquoy (ed.) *Correspondance des nonces en France Capodiferro, Dandino et Guidiccione 1541–1546, Acta nuntiaturae gallicae*, vol. 3, Rome, Presses de l'Université Grégorienne, 1963, nos 136ff; and T. F. Mayer, 'Reginald Pole in Paolo Giovio's *Descriptio*: a strategy for reconversion', *SCJ*, 1985, vol. 16, pp. 431–50.

47 I say scribbled because of the palaeographical problems posed by this work (BAV, Vaticanus latinus 5966, fos 3r–26r). The date is based mainly on the hand, which closely resembles that in other autograph documents stemming from this period.

48 'Apologia ad Carolum quintum caesarem', in *ERP*, vol. 1, pp. 136–8, 147–8. Pole's case against Machiavelli once more rested on martyrology, this time a defence of the power of Becket's body. Pole's identification with Becket became so complete that he had himself buried in Becket's by then empty tomb in Canterbury cathedral. He also owned a MS life of Becket by John de Grandison, now in the Bodleian (no. 2097, *Summary Catalogue of Western Manuscripts*), which bears Pole's name and the date 1539. A. Pastore, 'Due biblioteche umanistiche del Cinquecento. (I libri del cardinal Pole e di Marcantonio Flaminio)', *Rinascimento*, 1979, ser. 2, vol. 19, pp. 269–90, p. 273. S. J. Gunn helped greatly on this point.

49 Morandi (ed.) op. cit., vol. 2, p. 330, and in *ERP*, vol. 5, p. 389. I do not mean to say that Beccadelli's words accurately captured Pole's opinions, merely that the biographer thought they did. On him, see G. Fragnito, esp. *Memoria individuale e costruzione biografica*, Urbino, 1978, and *In museo e in villa*, op. cit.

50 H. Jedin, *Contarini und Camaldoli*, Rome, Edizioni di storia e letteratura, 1953; G. Alberigo, 'Vita attiva e vita contemplativa in un'esperienza cristiana del XVI secolo', *Studi veneziani*, 1974, vol. 16, pp. 177–225; G. Fragnito, 'Cultura umanistica e riforma religiosa: Il "De officio viri boni ac probi episcopi"', *Studi veneziani*, 1969, vol. 11, pp. 75–189; F. Gilbert, 'Religion and politics in the thought of Gasparo Contarini', in T. K. Rabb and J. E. Seigel (eds) *Action and Conviction in Early Modern Europe*, Princeton, NJ, Princeton University Press, 1969, pp. 90–116; J. B. Ross, 'Gasparo Contarini and his friends', *Studies in the Renaissance*, 1970, vol. 17, pp. 192–232, and 'Venetian schools and teachers fourteenth to early sixteenth century: a survey and a study of Giovanni Battista Egnazio', *Renaissance Quarterly*, 1976, vol. 29, pp. 521–66.

51 For Mantova, see T. F. Mayer, 'Marco Mantova and the Paduan religious crisis of the early sixteenth century', *Cristianesimo nella storia*, 1986, vol. 7, pp. 41–61; for Bonamico, Mayer, *Starkey*, pp. 51–3, 194, 196–7; and for Lampridio, ibid., pp. 194–6. Another of Pole's long-time friends and tutor in the ideas of Juan de Valdés, Marcantonio Flaminio, chose to use Lampridio as an example of competence in Greek in one of his religious tracts. Firpo, 'Valdesianesimo ed evangelismo: alle origini dell' "Ecclesia Viterbense" ', in *Tra alumbrados e spirituali*, op. cit., pp. 170–1.

52 W. F. Young, 'Reform ideology in the "Libellus ad Leonem X" ', paper read to the American Historical Association, New York, 1985. The text of the

II

NURSERY OF RESISTANCE

Consilium is in E. G. Gleason (ed. and trans.) *Reform Thought in Sixteenth-Century Italy*, n.p., American Academy of Religion, 1981, pp. 81–100.

53 Mayer, 'Bronze Age conciliarist', pp. 407–8.

54 A. Cistellini, *Figure della Riforma pretridentina*, Brescia, Morcelliana, 1948, pp. 71, 79, 95 and passim.

55 Still the best life is A. Virgili, *Francesco Berni*, Florence, Le Monnier, 1881. Berni's link to Priuli is mentioned on p. 253 but see also Berni's letter to his Venetian friend in A. Virgili (ed.) *Rime, poesie latine e lettere edite e inedite*, Florence, Le Monnier, 1885, pp. 319–32. Anne Reynolds offers an important fresh start on Berni's poetry in 'Francesco Berni: the theory and practice of Italian satire in the sixteenth century', *Italian Quarterly*, 1983, vol. 24, no. 94, pp. 5–15.

56 On Bini's poetry and that of this circle see S. Longhi, *Lusus. Il capitolo burlesco nel Cinquecento*, Padua, Antenore, 1983 and the life in A. M. Ghisalberti (ed.) *Dizionario Biografico degli Italiani*, Rome, Istituto dell'enciclopedia italiana, 1960– . For Palladio's garden see esp. P. P. Bober, 'The *Coryciana* and the Nymph Corycia', *Journal of the Warburg and Courtauld Institutes*, 1977, vol. 40, pp. 223–39, and for his life G. Battelli, 'Un umanista romana del Cinquecento. Blosio Palladio', *La Bibliofilia*, 1941, vol. 43, pp. 16–23, and M.-H. Laurent, *Fabio Vigili et les bibliothèques de Bologne au début du XVIe siècle*, *Studi e testi*, vol. 105, Rome, Biblioteca apostolica vaticana, 1943, p. XI.

57 Both of Michelangelo's early biographers put Pole high on the list of his intimate friends. R. Beltarini and P. Barocchi (eds) Giorgio Vasari, *Le vite de' più eccellenti pittori scultori e archittetori*, Florence, Studio per edizioni scelte, 1966, vol. 1:1, p. 109, and Ascanio Condivi, *The Life of Michelangelo*, in C. Holroyd, *Michael Angelo Buonarroti... with Translations of the Life of the Master by his Scholar, Ascanio Condivi*, London, Duckworth, 1903, p. 84. For his poetry see most conveniently J. Saslow (ed. and trans.) *The Poetry of Michelangelo*, New Haven, Conn., Yale University Press, 1990. H. Hibbard, *Michelangelo*, New York, Harper & Row, 1974, offers the best short treatment in English. For Michelangelo's political art see esp. D. J. Gordon, 'Giannotti, Michelangelo and the cult of Brutus', in D. J. Gordon (ed.) *Fritz Saxl 1890–1948: A Volume of Memorial Essays*, London, Nelson, 1957, pp. 281–96 and S. Levine, 'The location of Michelangelo's *David*: the meeting of January 25, 1504', *Art Bulletin*, 1974, vol. 56, pp. 31–49, for the politics of that statue, and for Michelangelo's general political outlook G. Spini, 'Politicita di Michelangelo', *Rivista storica italiana*, 1964, vol. 76, pp. 557–600. For Michelangelo's artistic religious resistances, which come very close to some of Pole's ideas about papal primacy, see L. Steinberg, *Michelangelo's Last Paintings: The Conversion of St. Paul and the Crucifixion of St. Peter in the Cappella Paolina, Vatican Palace*, London, Phaidon, 1975 (the most detailed treatment, with fine illustrations) and above all W. Wallace, 'Narrative and religious expression in Michelangelo's Pauline Chapel', *Artibus et Historiae*, 1989, vol. 20, pp. 107–21.

58 C. Maddison, *Marcantonio Flaminio: Poet, Humanist and Reformer*, London, Routledge, 1965, pp. 154–8, and A. Pastore, op. cit., p. 139.

59 For an excellent summary of the state of the debate, see A. Aubert, 'Valdesianesimo ed evangelismo italiano: alcuni studi recenti', *Rivista di storia della chiesa in Italia*, 1987, vol. 41, pp. 152–75.

60 Marcantonio Flaminio, *Lettere*, A. Pastore (ed.), Rome, Ateneo & Bizzarri, 1978, no. 59.

61 Ibid., no. 60.

62 Ibid., no. 66.

63 L. Martines, *Power and Imagination: City-states in Renaissance Italy*, London, Allen Lane, 1980, esp. ch. 15.
64 Gilbert, 'Religion and politics', op. cit., and 'Venice in the crisis of the League of Cambrai', in *History: Choice and Commitment*, Cambridge, Mass., Harvard University Press, 1977, pp. 247–67; W. J. Bouwsma, *Venice and the Defense of Republican Liberty: Renaissance Values in the Age of the Counter-Reformation*, Berkeley, Calif., University of California Press, 1968; and R. Finlay, *Politics in Renaissance Venice*, New Brunswick, NJ, Rutgers University Press, 1980.
65 P. Prodi, *Il sovrano pontefice: Un corpo e due anime: la monarchia papale nella prima età moderna*, Bologna, Il Mulino, 1982.
66 *Motives of Eloquence*, op. cit., p. 32 and cf. p. 219.
67 Ibid., p. 155.

III

TOURNAI AND TYRANNY: IMPERIAL KINGSHIP AND CRITICAL HUMANISM*

Almost from the first, the reign of Henry VIII witnessed high views of kingship.[1] Some instances in the first decade of his rule have attracted much attention, but one critical episode has been overlooked. In the course of the occupation of Tournai between 1513 and 1519, Henry developed and successfully tested a complete theory of imperial kingship, partly cast in a new language of sovereignty. Drawing in part on the French models liberally strewn about the English cultural landscape, Henry asserted all the prerogatives of a *rex imperator* not only against the Tournaisiens but more significantly against Leo X. This new model kingship and its implications for royal relations with the church alarmed some of Henry's agents, especially Ralph Sampson. Sampson contented himself with expostulating about the threat to his conscience to his chief, Thomas Wolsey, but others showed more alarm. One of Sampson's friends, Thomas More, a similarly junior but rising functionary, offered two meditations on the potential dangers of Henry's kingship, going much beyond the abstract admonitions against tyranny of his Latin epigrams.

As many commentators have observed, the problem of royal *Willkür* greatly

---

* My thanks to A. J. Slavin, Sir Geoffrey Elton and S. E. Lehmberg for their comments on an earlier version of some of this material; to Daniel Woolf for the invitation to present a draft of it to the Halifax Early Modern Colloquium where his comments and those of Jack Crowley were most valuable; to Brown Patterson for an invitation to present another version as a public lecture at the University of the South; and to commentators at the Folger Shakespeare Library on the present rendering, particularly Neal Wood. The American Council of Learned Societies and the Augustana Research Foundation generously provided financial assistance for a study of early Tudor political vocabulary, of which this is a part.

[1] See especially J. A. Guy, 'Henry VIII and the *praemunire* manoeuvres of 1530–1531', *English Historical Review*, XCVII (1982), 498, and 'Thomas Cromwell and the intellectual origins of the Henrician revolution', in Alistair Fox and John Guy (eds.), *Reassessing the Henrician age: humanism, politics and reform 1500–1550* (Oxford, 1986), pp. 166–7, although Guy has modified his views in *Tudor England* (Oxford, 1988), p. 110; and the woodcut at the head of Stephen Hawes's poem on the coronation reproduced in Florence W. Gluck and Alice B. Morgan (eds.), *Stephen Hawes: the minor poems* (Early English Text Society, no. 271, 1974), p. 80. (Dale Hoak is at work on the problem of imperial iconography.) Walter Ullmann, 'This realm of England is an empire', *Journal of Ecclesiastical History*, XXX (1979), 179, followed by George Bernard, 'The pardon of the clergy reconsidered', *Journal of Ecclesiastical History*, XXXVII (1986), 262, made much of the claims in the revised coronation oath, but this probably cannot date from so early in Henry's reign. Miss S. G. Lockwood discovered that Henry worked from the version of the oath in *The Statutes. Prohemium Johannis Rastell* (London, J. Rastell, 1527; STC 9518), and I have confirmed that the same oath did not appear in either the 1517 or 1519 version of this work, although it might still have circulated in some other form before that.

concerned More. As most have not noticed, he rooted his reflexions concretely in the context of Henry's grandiose assertions. In *Utopia* More offered an institutional solution in the form of a republic completely lacking sovereignty, and in *The history of Richard III* he offered a moral drama about the evils of tyranny.[2] These two works have yet more in common, for in them More saw the problem of tyranny not so much as one of perverted royal will (although princely ambition was assuredly a sin in sore need of bridles), but rather of a failure of counsel (in *Richard III*) to be remedied by a new kind of council (in *Utopia*). In *Richard III*, faction encouraged an evil-willed ruler. In *Utopia*, More designed a system to make both faction and tyranny impossible, in particular through the prohibition of what the Venetians called *broglio* (and which they, too, proscribed).[3] Specifically electioneering but more generally whispering in corners, *broglio* carried forward much of Richard's evil action. His success makes *Richard III* pessimistic. *Utopia* is not so, at least not in the same way. It does, however, reveal the magnitude of the problem in the radical extent of its engineering. Even the best of individual advisers, like John Morton, no matter how noble his 'politique driftes', would fail in his obligation to the prince. An association of equal councillors, forced to virtue by *Utopia's* institutional arrangements, might not make the same mistake.

More's treatment of tyranny and faction in tandem points to a yet broader context of reactions to Henry's schemes. More's peculiar emphasis on faction goes as much beyond other historians of Richard's reign as does his whitening of Edward IV. Albeit the one required the other in More's dramatic purpose, More's morality play did not transcend history, nor did eschatology overwhelm his concrete circumstances. It seems that *Richard III* in part addressed the political crisis surrounding the expulsion of the minions in 1519. That episode in turn was also a more direct reaction to Henry's new pretensions. Thus if we will probably never know what Henry made of *Utopia*, it and *Richard III* may tell us a good deal about what at least one of Henry's subjects made of him. The 'radical' potential in More's criticism is clearer yet in Erasmus's contemporary attacks on 'new monarchy' in general and Henry's in particular. On this point at least, More and Erasmus thought much alike, providing a powerful theoretical *locus standi* for their humanist epigoni.

Casting Henry and More as antagonists is hardly a new idea; giving their struggle an origin almost at the beginning of the reign would still operate within the established tragic view of their relationship. I shall suggest instead that Henry and More should be taken as nodal points in a complicated transformation of discourse.[4] As actors both Henry and More were caught in the toils of political language, which was then shifting away from figuring supreme power as feudal suzerainty to casting it as sovereignty. At the same

---

[2] Alistair Fox argues a close connexion between these two works, but the case is not original to him. *Thomas More. History and providence* (New Haven, 1982), esp. pp. 75–7. Cf. Richard Sylvester (ed.), *History of Richard III* (*Complete works of St. Thomas More*, II, 1963), lxv.

[3] Edward Surtz and J. H. Hexter (eds.), *Utopia* (*Complete works of St. Thomas More*, IV, 1965), 192–3 and cf. pp. 124–5.

[4] This analysis expands Guy's suggestion in 'Cromwell and the Henrician revolution', esp. p. 178.

time, political practice slowly moved toward a 'state' which monopolised violence and laid ultimate claim to allegiance. This new language and practice came to replace a culture of honour and its concomitant 'politics of violence' which had not left much space for unconditional demands on loyalty.[5]

English claims over Tournai make an almost textbook study of how an unstable blend of *auctoritas* and *potestas* cohered into something more than suzerainty.[6] Room for linguistic manoeuvre within competing traditions of discourse provided the alembic in this transformation, which the exigencies of a colonial situation converted into a new practice. The king began with the standard late medieval definition of sovereignty according to which he had final political authority over Tournai and was entitled to exercise his jurisdiction without interference from outside authorities.[7] This position strengthened as Henry turned to French models to assert that he had inherited all the authority in Tournai of his predecessors, and then used that greatly increased authority both against all his subjects, clerical and lay equally, and also to hedge in the pope's authority more narrowly than in England. Henry's actions may not always have come up to the high level of his pretensions, but they still served to frighten his own agents. A theory of imperial kingship came to maturity in Tournai.

If it does not matter much to the history of discourse who pushed this development, it still seems likely that Henry himself stood at the intersection of political thought and praxis. This point is of great importance in understanding the politics of the minions. It emerges in part by a process which eliminates one of the most likely contenders for the title of theorist of imperial kingship, Wolsey. He and his agent, Sampson, played strictly by the canonist and chivalric rules laid down by their opponents in the fight over the bishopric and got nowhere for their pains. In light of their caution, it seems proper to conclude that the strong letter to Leo which finally cut through the impasse with unequivocal statements of royal authority ought to be assigned to its signatory, Henry. As in the case of the later *Collectanea satis copiosa*, Henry would have needed help with some of the intricacies of this argument, probably from a civil lawyer, whose identity is unknown.[8] Royal officers on the

---

[5] Mervyn James, *English politics and the concept of honour 1485–1642*, Past and Present supplement, III (1978), 1, 6, 17–8, 31. For Henry's francophilia as a source of models for conduct and institutions, see David Starkey, *The reign of Henry VIII. Personalities and politics* (London, 1985), p. 77, and Guy, 'The French king's council', in R. A. Griffiths and J. Sherborne (eds.), *Kings and nobles in the later middle ages. A tribute to Charles Ross* (Gloucester, 1986), p. 278. R. J. Knecht emphasizes the importance of cultural borrowings from France in the sixteenth century, although he discusses only the impact of Huguenot political thought. *The lily and the rose: French influences on Tudor England* (Birmingham, 1987). I am grateful to Professor Knecht for sending me a copy of this, his inaugural lecture in the University of Birmingham.

[6] According to A. J. Slavin, '*Craw v. Ramsey*: new light on an old debate', in Stephen B. Baxter (ed.), *England's rise to greatness 1660–1763* (Berkeley, 1983), pp. 31, 48, such hybrid language should be expected at least as late as the restoration.

[7] Marcel David, *La souveraineté et les limites juridiques du pouvoir monarchique du IXe au XVe siècle* (Paris, 1954), pp. 67–8.

[8] Phillipe Wielant is a likely candidate, as the most serious civil lawyer among the imperial delegation in Bruges. See Edward Surtz, 'Saint Thomas More and his Utopian embassy of 1515', *Catholic Historical Review*, XXXIX (1953), 274–5, 280, and esp. 284–6. For the 'Collectanea', see

ground seem no more likely to have hit on the subtlety of Henry's case then their woolly-minded brother Chief Justice Fitzjames was to comprehend More's argument in arrest of judgment.

Claims to uniform allegiance appeared at once in the treaty of capitulation. All residents of Tournai, spiritual and temporal, were to take Henry as their 'natural et souverain Seigneur' (a phrase frequently repeated). He had 'tous et quelzconques droitz et souveraineté, dignitez, prerogatives, preheminences regalles et jurisdiction aussi amplement et en telle et semblable forme et manière' as Louis XII had. Municipal officers were thus to surrender their keys 'en signe et recongnoissance de souveraineté'. An oath of allegiance was demanded of all inhabitants; those who refused it had twenty days to vacate the *banlieue* of Tournai.[9] The oath actually administered does not survive, but a draft appears to be a fairly standard 'iuramentum fidelitatis' to Henry, the 'supremus rex'.[10]

A comparison of the treaty of surrender with its famous predecessor of Brétigny suggests that both Henry's treaty and his oath were more than feudal. Edward III's treaty did not manifest much concern with sovereignty, and the comparatively rarely used word probably stood as shorthand for the usual panoply of feudal obligations.[11] In other contemporary documents of direct relevance, for example in the title and description of Edward's new 'supreme court' for Guyenne or the opinions of the doctors of Bologna on Edward's title to the duchy, sovereignty does not appear.[12] This makes a clear contrast to Henry's treaty where sovereignty came second in his catalogue of demands and recurred frequently thereafter.

Three years later Henry expatiated at length on his inheritance of the same powers in Tournai as Louis XII exercised. Replying to a delegation from that city, Henry turned to a historical argument to rule out their claim that poverty made it impossible for Tournai to pay for its own defence. This point in turn ushered in a scheme for a thorough reform of Tournai's government, modelled on a similar review ordered by Charles VII sixty years before. Henry meant

---

Graham Nicholson, 'The nature and function of historical argument in the Henrician reformation', Cambridge University, PhD. thesis, 1977.

[9] Adolphe Hocquet, *Tournai et l'occupation anglaise* (Tournai, 1901), p. 104, treaty of capitulation, 23 Sept. 1513. It is summarized in E. G. Cruickshank, *The English occupation of Tournai 1513–1519* (Oxford, 1971), pp. 5–6, 37–9, but without this precise claim. Cf. Public Record Office (PRO), SP 31/8/144, fos. 268–9.

[10] PRO, State Papers of the reign of Henry VIII (SP) 1/230, fo. 65r-v. (J. S. Brewer, J. Gairdner and R. H. Brodie (eds.), *Letters and papers foreign and domestic of the reign of Henry VIII* [London, 1862–1932; hereafter *LP*], 1, no. 2319.) The oath is summarized in Cruickshank, *English occupation*, p. 40.

[11] David, *Souveraineté*, p. 78. The relevant articles of the treaty are in Thomas Rymer (ed.), *Foedera* (London, 1726–35), IX, 762–3, 788–90 and VI, 221. Maurice Keen reflects the standard analysis in 'Diplomacy', in G. L. Harriss (ed.), *Henry V: the practice of kingship* (Oxford, 1985), pp. 181–91.

[12] Pierre Chaplais, 'Some documents regarding the fulfilment and interpretation of the treaty of Brétigny (1361–1369)', *Camden Miscellany*, XIX, 1952 (3rd ser. vol. LXXX), pp. 53–4, 61, 70.

to hold a 'visitation of the state of the said town, as well upon the finances as upon the privileges franchises statutes and ordinances of the same'. Playing the tune of reform, the king averred that he would keep whatever worked 'as well for the conservation of the said sovereignty of the king, as for the weal and utility of the said town & of the common weal of the same' and change the rest. Drawing on the town's records, a sign that someone was taking a good deal of care over Tournai's problems (whatever modern historians may have thought of Henry's attitude), the letter recounted how King Charles had intervened in the 'person' of three members of his council to take over the government of Tournai. On the basis of their examination, Charles's commissioners had laid down 'diverse statutes and ordinances' which completely obligated the Tournaisiens to obedience.[13]

Approaching the general point, Henry paralleled the force of the confirmations he had liberally distributed almost from the first with those of his French predecessors.[14] He concluded that 'it appeareth clearly by the said reduction, that the king our said sovereign lord is abiden in the same estate and in such power & authority as those French kings were before the said reduction'. From this it followed once again that Henry, now in the place of the king of France, could 'cause due visitation upon all the estate of the said town & upon their privileges statutes ordinances franchises and liberties of the same, for to augment or diminish them, change, alter, or to revoke in all or in part'. His motive was concern 'as well for the conservation of his sovereignty, as for the weal and profit of the common weal of the said town'. Whatever reforms he instituted were subject only to the test of reason.[15] Henry here laid claim both to more extensive powers than he had over any similarly significant English town and also to more powers than his French models usually deployed.[16] Nor did Henry have any very good English precedent for his actions, or any imitators even in the *quo warranto* proceedings instituted by Charles II.[17]

---

[13] For the original visitation, see Gaston du Fresne de Beaucourt, *Histoire de Charles VII*, vol. 5, *Le roi victorieux (1449–1453)* (Paris, 1890), pp. 335–6.

[14] Although Henry has been faulted from that day to this for being too generous in these confirmations, he was only following the precedent set by French monarchs who granted large privileges (or confirmed those of their ancestors) at their accessions. Bernard Chevalier, 'The *bonnes villes* and the king's council in fifteenth century France', in J. R. L. Highfield and Robin Jeffs (eds.), *The crown and local communities in England and France in the fifteenth century* (Gloucester, 1981), pp. 113–16.   [15] SP 1/113, fos. 242r–4r.

[16] Nor did it take Henry very long to adopt the argument from the common weal to justify financial impositions. SP 1/15, fo. 36r, Henry VIII–Jerningham, 26 Mar., s.a. (*LP*, 2, no. 3055). It is of great interest, too, that when Henry's officers reported problems in Tournai which required money to remedy, they did not realize the importance of appealing to the common weal. Chevalier asserts against Henry Sée that Charles VII and Louis XI either had no coherent urban policy, or at least did not intend to keep the *bonnes villes* under their thumb. Chevalier, *Les bonnes villes de France du XIVe au XVIe siècle* (Paris, 1982), pp. 110, 118–24, and cf. pp. 101–2 for an even stronger claim that the kings were pursuing an 'operation de séduction' for the sole benefit of the towns.

[17] The closest English analogue again stems from Edward III, but a statute of 1354 gave an offending borough three chances before forfeiting its charter. *Statutes of the realm* (London, 1817),

This episode may make it appear that Henry regarded Tournai as a problem *sui generis*. The history of attempts to incorporate the city into the English legal system say otherwise. Shortly after the conquest Henry called for representatives from Tournai to the parliament of early 1514, twenty years before Calais got its voice.[18] Tournai had a similarly important place on that parliament's agenda: its first statute ordered the partial integration of the city into the English legal system.[19] Once more quickly outpacing his medieval forebears, Henry secured Chancery's jurisdiction over contracts made in Tournai as well as the Chancellor's responsibility for enforcing judgements on actions of debt handed down in English courts there.[20] The practical demands of the law attracted further attention to Tournai during this parliament. In February a new court was set up to hear appeals previously directed to the *parlement* of Paris 'en souveraineté'. Following the line of the treaty of surrender, the new court had as much authority as the *parlement* 'tout ainsi et par la manière que par avant la réduction'.[21] The purpose of the court was later amplified: since 'es matiéres d'appellacions et ressort de souveraineté [non] convenoit passer la mer', 'une court souveraine' was needed 'en laquelle on porroit avoir toutes provisions comme on feroit en sa court souveraine et de adviser premièrement gens notable pour excerser ladite souveraineté'.[22] The law of this court is not spelled out, but its substitution for Henry's court may have dictated that it be common law – or perhaps equity. In any case, this is yet another difference from Edward III's tactics in

---

I, 346–7. This legislation was in part a reaction to Edward's much more high-handed dealing with Southampton fifteen years earlier, which Susan Reynolds argues 'probably seemed less fitting as autonomous government became more established' (S. Reynolds, *An introduction to the history of English medieval towns* (Oxford, 1977), pp. 112–13). G. R. Elton, *Reform and renewal: Thomas Cromwell and the commonweal* (Cambridge, 1973), pp. 106–9 and Robert Tittler, 'The emergence of urban policy, 1536–58', in Robert Tittler and Jennifer Loach (eds.), *The mid-Tudor policy c. 1540–1560* (London, 1980), pp. 74–93 recount the much more supportive attitude of the crown towards the towns later in Henry's reign, during Thomas Cromwell's regime. Freedom to make ordinances without royal interference and handle finances was not usually spelled out in borough charters, which suggests that neither presented problems to either crown or borough, at least not on the scale of Tournai. See the table in Maurice Beresford, *New towns of the middle ages: town plantation in England, Wales, and Gascony* (New York, 1967), p. 205. Peter Clark and Paul Slack argue that before 1600 charters were taken as guaranteeing the autonomy of boroughs. *English towns in transition 1500–1700* (Oxford, 1976), p. 126. John Miller rebuts the traditional interpretation that Charles II was after quasi-absolutist power over the boroughs, arguing instead that the king merely intended to insure that loyal men ran them. At no time in his reign did the crown go any further than to claim the power to remove elected officials, and Miller found only one case where the initiative behind a new charter came from the king. 'The crown and the borough charters in the reign of Charles II', *English Historical Review*, C (1985), 25–52. My thanks to Professor Tittler for much help with the problem of the constitutional position of the towns.

[18] Hocquet, no. 27, 18 Nov. 1513; *LP*, I, no. 2450.   [19] *LP*, I, no. 2590.

[20] *Statutes of the realm*, III, 92–3. Chancery had been excluded from Edward III's Guyenne. M. G. A. Vale, *English Gascony, 1399–1453: a study of war, government and politics during the later stages of the hundred years' war* (Oxford, 1970), p. 5.

[21] Hocquet, pp. 119–20; Westminster, 26 Feb. 1514. PRO C82/401; 31/8/144, fo. 237; *LP*, I, no. 2684.107; cf. Cruickshank, *English occupation*, pp. 192–3.

[22] Hocquet, p. 130, Henry VIII–Tournai, 20 July 1515, from the now destroyed Archives communales.

Guyenne, where his *curia superioritatis* had been explicitly debarred from administering common law.[23] Perhaps Edward took somewhat better account of practicalities. Henry was still demanding in 1516 that the Tournaisiens bestir themselves and hold the court.[24]

The lieutenancy of Tournai provided another field for the play of new notions of sovereignty. As might now be expected, subtle differences show up between fifteenth-century patents and that of William, Lord Mountjoy.[25] Mountjoy got 'merum et mixtum imperium ac jurisdictionem omnimodam in cives, incolas et pro tempore inhabitantes quoscumque...ad nos regaliam et coronam nostras Franciae ratione quacumque pertinentem et spectantem seu pertinere et spectare consultam et solitam'. Even if Henry VIII had learned Henry VI's lesson and meant to keep the crowns of France and England separate, this patent still emphasized the lack of distinction between those subject to the former.[26] It combines two possibly antithetical discourses in order to produce obedience to Mountjoy 'sicuti nobis ipsis, si in persona nostra praesentes essemus'.[27] 'Merum et mixtum imperium' was the language of the civil law for legislative sovereignty, circumscribed within divine and natural laws. *Regalia*, however, the English 'regalie' or regality, had functioned in the fifteenth century as a means of *avoiding* attributing supreme authority to the crown.[28] Palsgrave, perhaps reflecting similar linguistic uncertainty, would gloss 'regality' as the sovereignty of a king.[29] The appearance of both phrases in Mountjoy's patent offered a way to broaden royal authority. Mountjoy's successor, Sir Richard Jerningham (whose patent has been lost), certainly enjoyed greater authority than his opposite numbers in Ireland specifically in the matter of appointing to offices.[30] When Jerningham baulked at dismissing certain soldiers without explicit royal warrant, he was bluntly told to get on with it; it 'should not stand with his [Henry's] honour' to fire recalcitrant soldiers by individual royal letters.[31] Henry indeed meant Jerningham to stand 'sicuti nobis ipsis'.

The struggle between Wolsey and the French bishop-elect, Louis Guillard, focused issues of sovereignty most clearly. Wolsey and Sampson went very carefully, attempting to dislodge Guillard with the established tools of injunction and appeal. Henry was more brutal, finally ending Leo's and

---

[23] Vale, *English Gascony*, p. 5.   [24] SP 1/113, fo. 238r.
[25] Vale describes the medieval patents in *English Gascony*, p. 7.
[26] Hocquet, p. 133, Mountjoy's nomination as lieutenant, 20 Jan. 1515. PRO C76/196, m. 6; Thomas Rymer (ed.), *Foedera* (London, 1741), XIII, 387; *LP*, I, no. 2617·22. Cf. Cruickshank, *English occupation*, pp. 44–5, 189.   [27] Hocquet, p. 135.
[28] David, *Souveraineté*, p. 75. For *merum et mixtum imperium* see especially the indispensable work of C. N. S. Woolf, *Bartolus of Sassoferrato: his position in the history of political thought* (Cambridge, 1913), pp. 143–60, and on the extension of Bartolo's thought about *merum et mixtum imperium* into a broader theory of sovereignty, Francesco Ercole, 'Impero universale e stati particolari: la civitas sibi princeps' e lo stato moderno', in his *Da Bartolo all'Althusio. Saggi sulla storia del pensiero pubblicistico del Rinascimento italiano* (Florence, 1932), pp. 49–156. According to Ercole, p. 81, *merum et mixtum imperium* was itself originally a hybrid term which embraced even feudal rights and jurisdiction.   [29] *Oxford English dictionary*, s.v. 'regality'.
[30] S. G. Ellis, *Reform and revival. English government in Ireland, 1490–1530* (London, 1986), p. 13.
[31] SP 1/16, fos. 110v–111r, Wolsey–Jerningham, 16 Jan., s.a. (*LP*, 2, no. 3886).

Guillard's obstructionism by blunt complaints about offence to royal sovereignty, combined with crude threats.³² One wonders whether the king knew much about the specifics of Wolsey's strategy. Following Sampson's suggestion, Wolsey first asked Francis I and Margaret of Savoy, imperial regent in the Low Countries, to intervene.³³ Francis assured the earl of Worcester that he would try to the utmost to do Wolsey 'honour & profit', but his means would not have pleased Henry. Turning to the *parlement* of Paris, which had already lost its sovereignty over Tournai to Henry's new court, Francis wrote a letter by its 'counsel and advice...for maintaining of his right of sovereignty in Flanders'.³⁴ Wolsey never evinced much interest in matters of principle – the administration of the see (and its profits) stayed in the forefront of his mind. In addition to canon law, he could muster only repeated appeals to his and Henry's injured honour.³⁵ Neither Sampson nor Wolsey ever got past the point they reached in mid-1515. Then Sampson merely recommended sticking to the course of the law, since abandoning Wolsey's claim would 'not be for the king's honour & profit', or approaching Francis again.³⁶

The affair reached its crisis in late 1516 and early 1517. Guillard won another round and moved Leo to give him the see and its temporalities. Henry responded in a highly interesting mixture of chivalric and legal language together with strictures on a pope who would offend royal sovereignty. The king's instructions to one of his agents in Rome opened by protesting that the pope's decision was 'derogatory to our dignity royal' and 'contrary to all law and justice redounding greatly to our dishonour, [and] the defeating and derogation of our right and prerogative royal within the regalie of our city of Tournai'.³⁷ After some legal toing and froing, Henry pitched his argument at a much higher level.

Truth it is that we having the supreme power as lord and king in the regalie of Tournai without recognition [cf. BL Cotton MSS, Vitellius B III, fo. 122v: recognizance] of any superior owe [cf. BL Cotton MSS Vit. B III, fo. 122v: ought] of right to have the

---

³² For the diplomatic manoeuvrings, see Cruickshank, *English occupation*, pp. 145–85.

³³ SP 1/9, fo. 121r, Sampson–Wolsey, Bruges, 23 Sept. 1514; fo. 149r, Wolsey–Worcester, draft (*LP*, 1, no. 3378); fo. 151r, Wolsey–Worcester, 22 Oct. [1514] (*LP*, 1, no. 3379).

³⁴ British Library, Cotton MSS, Caligula D VI, fo. 202r, Abbeville, 3 Oct. [1514] (*LP*, 1, no. 3331).

³⁵ See especially SP 1/10, fos. 174r ff., instructions from Wolsey to Sir William Sidney for negotiations with Francis (*LP*, 2, no. 468), and, e.g. Sampson's letter of [16] Nov. 1514, BL Caligula D VI, fo. 288r–v (*LP*, 1, no. 3445) or of 20 May 1515, ibid. fo. 294v (*LP*, 2, no. 480). Wolsey also insisted that he wished the see only because Henry had given it to him. *LP*, 2, no. 468.

³⁶ BL Cotton MSS, Galba B III, fo. 373v, Sampson–Wolsey, n.p., n.d., unsigned (*LP*, 2, no. 769).

³⁷ This letter is in SP 1/13 (a draft partly in Brian Tuke's hand) and BL Cotton MSS, Vitellius B III (*LP*, 2, no. 2871). The quotation here is SP 1/13, fo. 247r and Cotton MSS, Vitellius B III, fo. 122r. The second rendering omits 'the regalie' in the last phrase. Cf. Cruickshank, *English occupation*, pp. 179–81. The addressee was Silvestro de Gigli, who was one of three Italians working on Henry's side. The exact state of English diplomatic representation in Rome at any given moment is uncertain, but see the excellent study by William Wilkie, *The cardinal protectors of England. Rome and the Tudors before the reformation* (Cambridge, 1974).

homage fealty and oath of fidelity as well of the said pretended bishop by reason of his temporalities which he holdeth of us as of other within the precincts of the same territory.[38]

The last point had been made repeatedly since the occupation of Tournai, but it now had a stronger import for two reasons. First, although Henry was making a purely feudal demand, he had directed it against the pope; second, and much more important, the king had transcended the limits of feudal law by claiming that he made his claim as *supremus rex*. It seems that Henry had learned well his lesson from the kings of France, whose revived monarchy had relied heavily on the legal claim that *rex in regno suo est imperator*.[39]

When Henry continued, he did so in feudal discourse. As bad as was Leo's

---

[38] SP 1/13, fo. 247v; Vit. B III, fo. 122v.

[39] André Bossuat, 'La formule "le roi est empereur en son royaume". Son emploi au XVe siècle devant le parlement de Paris', *Revue historique de droit français et étranger*, 4th ser., XXXIX (1961), 371–81. The English civilian Alanus apparently invented the idea in the early thirteenth century, and it had thereafter migrated first to Sicily and the court of Frederick II and then to France and the partisans of Philip the Fair. Richard Koebner, *Empire* (Cambridge, 1961), p. 36. The great Italian jurist Bartolus of Sassoferrato extended it to argue that any *civitas* which did not recognize a superior was *sibi princeps* and therefore had all the jurisdiction of the emperor. Woolf, *Bartolus*, p. 109 and Ercole, 'Impero universale e stati particolari', pp. 81–146; cf. also Julius Kirshner, '*Civitas sibi faciat civem*: Bartolus of Sassoferrato's doctrine on the making of a citizen', *Speculum*, XLVIII (1973), 706 and Maurice Keen, 'The political thought of fourteenth century civilians', in Beryl Smalley (ed.), *Trends in medieval political thought* (Oxford, 1965), pp. 116–24. The phrase recurred frequently in pleadings before the *parlement* of Paris in the fifteenth century, but its later history is otherwise not well known. Italian civilians in the fifteenth and sixteenth centuries kept alive both the original form of this idea and also Bartolus's cognate, applying them variously to such lesser princes as the duke of Milan or non-Tuscan *civitates* like Venice; some of these legists were certainly known in England. See especially Paulus de Castro, *Consiliorum sive responsorum* (Venice, 1581), II, no. 34, fo. 17r. Other Italian jurists who made either or both cases included: Pietro Paolo Parisio, *Consiliorum* (Venice, 1593), I, no. 1, fo. 3v and no. 69, fo. 134r; Mariano Socini the elder, *Consiliorum* (Louvain, 1551), III, no. 3, fo. 6v; Carlo Ruini, *Responsorum sive consiliorum* (Venice, 1571), II, no. 200, fo. 272r; Aimone Cravetta, *Consiliorum sive responsorum* (Venice, 1568–92), I, no. 135, fo. 122v; Francesco Curzio (or di Corte) the younger, *Consiliorum* (Venice, 1571), I, no. 61, fo. 93r; Alessandro Tartagni, *Consiliorum seu responsorum* (Venice, 1597), V, 1, fo. 4r; Giason del Maino, *Consiliorum* (Lyon, 1544), IV, no. 101, fo. 10r and II, no. 227, fo. 99r. The idea appears especially prominently in the important *consilia* of Mariano Socini the younger, one of the mainstays of both the Paduan and Bolognese legal faculties in the first half of the sixteenth century, and perhaps once a partisan of Henry's divorce. See *Consiliorum sive malis responsorum* (Venice, 1580), e.g., I, no. 69, fos. 103r and 104r (a case of 1526); II, no. 100, fo. 139v; III, no. 98, fo. 158v (a general statement of the principle, relying mainly on Paulus de Castro; a case of 1547); no. 126, fo. 198r (1548); IV, no. 82, fo. 135r; 92, fo. 151r (appealing to the examples of the *doge* of Venice and the king of France; 1555), etc. Marco Mantova Benavides, who dominated the faculty of Padua almost throughout the sixteenth century, also adverted to the concept in his *Consiliorum sive responsorum*, II (Venice, 1559), fos. 66v–69v; Mantova certainly delivered an opinion favourable to Henry's divorce. For their *consilia*, see Edward Surtz, *Henry VIII's great matter in Italy: an introduction to representative Italians in the king's divorce, mainly 1527–1535* (Ann Arbor, 1978), I, 272 (Socini) and 298 ff. (Mantova). My thanks to Professor Antonio Padoa Schioppa for his hospitality at the Istituto per la storia di diritto italiano, Università di Milano, which greatly facilitated my researches on this point. However all this may be, it is much more likely that Henry learned it from a French source, perhaps directly from the *parlement* of Paris, which had continued to defend the sovereignty of the crown even when its wearer was Henry VI.

III

266

permission to Guillard to invoke the secular arm, the pope's threatened excommunication of 'all and singular the persons spiritual and temporal of our said regalie' who declined to accept Guillard as bishop was worse. To Henry it meant 'as much as to discharge our subjects there from their fidelities and allegiances towards us'. Glossed in legal and chivalric language this was 'so exorbitant and contrary to the laws of God and man, justice and reason, that it is the greatest dishonour that ever came to the pope'.[40] The point came up again later with Henry charging that 'our subjects spiritual and temporal' would be forced by the excommunication to 'maintain our rebel against us to our dishonour and unsurety'.[41]

Similar language elsewhere belied the more sweeping nature of the claims being advanced. For example, in his early legalistic complaint about how Leo had violated proper procedure, Henry argued that the pope

attempteth to take from us the superiority regalie preeminence jurisdiction and authority that we have in the region and dominion of Tournai in that he in our absence and without our knowledge hath in this great matter so much touching our honour fulminate[d] the censures and by his delegates called and adjourned us and our subjects [cf. Vit B III, 124v: delegates] out of the regalie and territory to places unsure under the obedience of other princes in derogation of our honour and contrary to justice whereas all causes be determined [cf. Vit B III, fo. 124v: determinable] within the same and no appeal or resort either to the court of Paris or elsewhere can have place there.[42]

This was the same point made in the establishment of Henry's new court in Tournai, but it had now been made to the pope and become an even more general principle than any king of England had claimed to apply within his realm. *No* case, not even an ecclesiastical one, with or without royal permission, could leave Tournai.

Henry was never one to rely on principle alone when a good threat might also help. Crudely reminding Leo of 'all the benefits we have done to him and the church of Rome', Henry complained that he would 'have good cause to think our benevolence labour costs and charges full ill employed and bestowed in that behalf'.[43] Again objecting to Leo's manner of proceeding, Henry raised the stakes by hinting that he might withdraw England's obedience from the pope.[44] Finally, all subtlety abandoned and rudely collapsing the carefully fostered distinction between the public and private persons of the pope, Henry made a threat that no Renaissance pope would take lightly (even if Alexander

---

That king's regent, the duke of Bedford, attended some sessions of the court during which the rights of the French crown were stated in no uncertain terms, and the *parlement* continued to do that throughout the English occupation. André Bossuat, 'Le parlement du Paris pendant l'occupation anglaise', *Revue historique*, CCXXIX (1963), 19–40.

[40] SP 1/13, fo. 248r; BL Cotton MSS, Vit. B III, fo. 123r.
[41] SP 1/13, fo. 248v; BL Cotton MSS, Vit. B III, fo. 124r.
[42] SP 1/13, fo. 249r; BL Cotton MSS, Vit. B III, fo. 124v.
[43] SP 1/13, fo. 248v; BL Cotton MSS, Vit. B III, fo. 123v.
[44] SP 1/13, fo. 249r; BL Cotton MSS, Vit. B III, fo. 124v.

VI really died of malaria). If Leo 'in his person would thus rigorously without ground of justice proceed against us we would not suffer it'.[45] In case the point was missed, Henry repeated it. Determined to prevent outside interference in Tournai, Henry roused himself to almost as resounding a statement – and a much blunter threat – as he had trumpeted to convocation a little more than a year before. 'The sovereignty of our regalie' would be inviolate.[46]

While Henry redefined Leo as a fit subject for assassination, he also redescribed Guillard in terms of the treaty of 1513. Originally labelled 'our disobedient and untrue vassal and subject', vassal disappeared by the dorse of the same folio and the 'subject' alone owed homage and fealty.[47] Sampson never called Guillard more than subject.[48] Henry would seem to have profited by his father's tutelage from Louis XI, who had pioneered the reduction of the duke of Brittany to mere subject, dissolving a feudal hierarchy with its fixed relationships into a pool of equal subjects, a crucial move in the direction of absolutism.[49]

All of this would be interesting enough if it had never been more than the most arid theory, but in fact Henry's tactics worked. Leo prostrated himself before the king, abjectly assuring the king that he had never meant to trench on his 'maiestate et amplitudine' nor to demean all his assistance. Attacking the weak point of Henry's letter, while tactfully avoiding its more extreme claims, Leo dismissed the invocation of the secular arm as purely formulaic. He would never have aimed such a clause 'ad tuum statum quod absit perturbandum'. Peace was a much better idea, and who had been talking about military force, anyway?[50] Although Leo took Henry's tirade seriously enough to have his brother Cardinal Giulio explain again what had happened two days later, Henry's agent Silvestro de Gigli thought the whole thing should have blown over by the next day.[51] By late March, Wolsey sounded the

[45] One wonders whether Henry might have been in touch with the Petrucci conspirators, whose leaders were arrested on 19 May 1517. Another of his agents in Rome, Cardinal Adriano Castellesi, had patched up his often rocky relationship with Wolsey at just about the time of Henry's letter, and would be accused of misprision of the conspiracy in the consistory of 8 June. Bruno Gebhardt, *Adrian von Corneto. Ein Beitrag zur Geschichte der Curie und der Renaissance* (Breslau, 1886), pp. 38–40. Castellesi, the patron of Polydore Vergil, fled to Venice saying he intended to continue on to England. Henry, however, deprived Castellesi of Bath and Wells (which went to Wolsey), as well as repossessing Castellesi's palace in Rome. Besides Wolsey's adroit seizing of an opportunity for aggrandizement, it looks very much as if he and Henry were covering their tracks by protesting too much – one of the reasons for Leo's animus against Castellesi was a harshly critical letter about him which the cardinal had sent Henry. Wolsey certainly furthered Leo's resolve to deal with Castellesi; was he too dangerous? Gigliola Fragnito, 'Adriano Castellesi', *Dizionario biografico degli italiani*, XXI, 665 ff.; and cf. Wilkie, *Cardinal protectors*, passim.

[46] SP 1/13, fo. 249v; BL Cotton MSS, Vit. B. III, fo. 124v.   [47] SP 1/13, fo. 248r-v.

[48] BL Cotton MSS, Galba B III, fo. 362r (*LP*, 2, no. 553), Sampson–Wolsey, Bruges, 3 June [1551]. *LP* gives the date as 1 June.

[49] Barthélemy-Amédée Pocquet du Haut-Jussé, 'A political concept of Louis XI: subjection instead of vassalage', in P. S. Lewis, *The recovery of France in the fifteenth century* (New York, 1971), pp. 196–215.

[50] SP 1/13, between fos. 253 and 254, Leo X–Henry VIII, 5 Feb. 1517 (*LP*, 2, no. 2873).

[51] SP 1/13, fo. 256r-v (Rome, 7 Feb. 1517; *LP*, 2, no. 2879) and fo. 258r (Rome, 8 Feb.; *LP*, 2, no. 2886).

all-clear, writing to de Gigli that he had only made such trouble out of concern for 'regiae majestatis et meum honorem'.[52] Wolsey, like Leo, ignored Henry's sovereignty. And for a good, self-interested reason: Henry's success with Leo provides a clear instance of the process of mutually advantageous exchange between the papacy and other territorial monarchs which Paolo Prodi places at the centre of early-modern state building.[53]

Thus Henry's claims, thus their effect. The king's attitude, wrapped in a complicated mixture of discourses, yet seems clear. So does that of Wolsey and Pope Leo, if more for what they do not say. Sampson was less circumspect. He was in no doubt that Henry meant to encroach dangerously on the church's prerogatives. The portrait Sampson drew of relations between laity and spirituality in Tournai so closely resembles the England of the Hunne and Standish affairs that one may be pardoned for wondering where Sampson was directing his gaze. But unlike Abbot Kidderminster or Bishop Fitzjames, Sampson stood four-square for caution. For one thing, 'sedition' among the Flemish commoners meant 'if it were the greatest lord of their own land, they would do him displeasure'.[54] Sampson also expressed reluctance even to use justifiable legal means against Guillard's officials 'because the temporalty in these parts be so minded against the spirituality so that if there should be any scisma, there should immediately many thing be taken from the spiritual jurisdiction, which was hard ever to recover', above all the bishop's financial advantages.[55] Concern for repercussions if he were to try to exercise Wolsey's spiritual authority stayed Sampson's hand throughout. This led to extremely legalistic proceedings on his part.[56]

Of course, Sampson was a lawyer so this was only to be expected. His horrified response to Wolsey's apparent suggestion that Henry's sovereignty might solve their problems was a different matter. He wrote Wolsey forthrightly that 'though [the] temporal sword divideth or taketh away temporal power or jurisdiction, yet hath it no such power nor strength canonice in spiritual jurisdiction'. Sampson, for one, would not endanger his soul by attacking spiritual jurisdiction. He assured Wolsey that 'I write thus to your grace for that mine opinion and conscience thus leadeth me. And more largely I think my conscience not informed with no saint's scrupulosity, but

---

[52] Edmund Martène and Ursin Durand (eds.), *Veterum scriptorum et monumentorum...amplissima collectio*, III (Paris, 1724), col. 1275B–C, Wolsey–de Gigli, London, 24 Mar. 1517 (*LP*, 2, no. 3045).

[53] Paolo Prodi, *Il sovrano pontefice. Un corpo e due anime: la monarchia papale nella prima età moderna* (Bologna, 1982), esp. pp. 303 ff. on the very similar negotiations between Leo and Francis I over the concordat of Bologna, from which Henry almost certainly learned a great deal.

[54] SP 1/9, fo. 107r, Sampson–Wolsey, Brussels, 6 Sept. 1514 (*LP*, 1, no. 3246).

[55] BL Cotton MSS, Galba B v, fo. 365r, Sampson–Wolsey, Tournai, 15 Dec. 1514 (*LP*, 1, no. 3545).

[56] See, e.g. Sampson's discussion of the role of the archbishop of Rheims as metropolitan in BL Cotton MSS, Caligula D vi, fo. 296r, Sampson–Wolsey, Bruges, 26 May (month endorsed) 1515 (*LP* 2, no. 512); BL Cotton MSS, Galba B III, fo. 363v, Sampson–Wolsey, Bruges, 8 June 1515 (*LP*, 2, no. 566). For Sampson's caution see, e.g. BL Cotton MSS, Calig. D vi, fo. 294r–v, Sampson–Wolsey, Tournai, 20 May 1515 (*LP*, 2, no. 480).

directed with plain truth.'⁵⁷ Such strong reservations by his agent on the ground might have been expected to produce fulminations from Wolsey; instead he acquiesced in Sampson's objections. Neither was prepared to buy the king's arguments. Better to follow standard practice and assassinate one of the principal clerical obstructionists in Tournai.⁵⁸

Henry's taste for French models is established. He imitated Charles VII's legislative sovereignty over Tournai; he borrowed his rhetoric of the common weal and history; most important, Henry cast himself as an emperor in his own realm. While still wrapped in feudal language, Henry had followed Louis XI beyond a feudal kingship.⁵⁹ He was also likely enough following the example of his own father, who probably drew heavily on his Breton experience in shaping his 'new monarchy'.⁶⁰ 'French' precedent thus provides at least one of the mechanisms through which all the baggage of Roman emperorship, which Walter Ullmann saw behind the events of 1534, entered England.⁶¹ Henry's new style directly challenged Sir John Fortescue's allegedly normative comparison of the *dominium regale* of the king of France, expressed by *rex in regno suo*, and the *dominium regale et politicum*, or limited monarchy of the kings of England. As Peter Lewis well put it, 'the practice of arbitrary rule in France... terrified' Fortescue.⁶² By whatever agency, a major rupture with tradition was underway.

In view of this demonstration, together with the work of Graham Nicholson, John Guy, Virginia Murphy, and George Bernard, it looks as if C. G. Cruickshank's musing that Henry regarded Tournai as 'the beginning of a new English empire on the continent' had things exactly right.⁶³ Nevertheless, however much Henry's views appeared fully formed in Tournai, we must resist the temptation to cut through this conjoint appeal to less 'forward-looking' traditions of discourse, and decide that the king had 'really' done whatever Thomas Cromwell accomplished in the 1530s, bar one or two details. The tangle of feudal, civil law, and specifically French language would take some unsnarling. Nor would such a major realignment of English political discourse

---

⁵⁷ BL Cotton MSS, Galba B III, fo. 363v, Sampson–Wolsey, Bruges, 8 June 1515 (*LP*, 2, no. 566). ⁵⁸ *LP*, 2, no. 2274.
⁵⁹ Bossuat, '"Le roi est empereur"', esp. pp. 380–1; P. S. Lewis, 'France in the fifteenth century: society and sovereignty', *Essays in later medieval French history*, esp. pp. 5–6, 187, and *Later medieval France: the polity* (London, 1968), pp. 84–7 outlines the fifteenth-century French idea of unlimited royal sovereignty; and for Charles VII's at least theoretically 'absolute' monarchy, see M. G. A. Vale, *Charles VII* (Berkeley, 1974), pp. 230–2. For a sketch of a similar argument, see Guy, *Tudor England*, p. 81.
⁶⁰ A. E. Goodman, 'Henry VII and Christian renewal', *Studies in Church History*, XVII (1981), 115–25. For Henry VII's experience in Brittany, B.-A. Pocquet du Haut-Jussé, *François II duc de Bretagne et l'Angleterre (1458–1488)* (Paris, 1929) is fundamental. See also R. A. Griffiths and R. S. Thomas, *The making of the Tudor dynasty* (Gloucester, 1985), ch. 7.
⁶¹ Walter Ullmann, *Medieval foundations of renaissance humanism* (London, 1977), pp. 49–50, 119.
⁶² Lewis, 'France in the fifteenth century', p. 27.
⁶³ Cruickshank, *English occupation*, p. 267. V. M. Murphy, 'The debate over Henry VIII's first divorce: an analysis of the contemporary treatises', unpublished Cambridge University PhD. thesis, 1984 shows that Henry had a coherent policy on his divorce from at least 1527.

and practice come easily. However much Sampson might eventually have his conscience adjusted, others would raise similar reservations about the new order. One of those, Thomas More, probably learned first hand from Sampson both what Henry was up to in Tournai and Sampson's construction of it. More drafted his immediate reaction in Bruges in the *streng Republikanismus* of the second book of *Utopia*. Moving from theory to practice, he expanded his meditations on tyranny and its enabling conditions in that work's first book and in *Richard III*.

On one level, Utopia's response to Henry's pretensions is perfectly clear. In the stead of monarchy, a republic. An elected prince, hedged about by the council of Syphogrants, in order to make tyranny impossible. But this is only part of the tale. European republics were often considered to possess the same ultimate sovereignty (within higher laws) as any monarch. This 'added dimension' is missing from *Utopia*, strengthening Book II's indictment of the drift of English government. The absence of the kind of sovereignty Henry claimed is not terribly surprising in this era of 'divided sovereignty'.[64] But not even that sort of shared authority is unequivocally present. One could force the text to say that ultimate control lay in the hands of the 'people', but there are yet many instances in which the prince had at least some say, including the crucial division of property. Similarly, only infrequently is a mechanism for the enforcement of the Utopians' few but good laws spelled out: responsibility rested jointly in the hands of governors, fathers, and priests. There is no provision for resolving a deadlocked conflict between them.

This is odd in light of the conclusion of Book II: 'seeing the chief causes of ambition and faction with other vices be plucked up by the roots... there can be no jeopardy of domestical dissension, which alone hath cast under foot and brought to naught the well fortified and strongly defenced wealth and riches of many cities'. The strength of Utopian domestic peace is such that no foreign powers can 'shake or move the empire'.[65] Thus although princely tyranny was much on the Utopians' minds, it was only one of many ways that pride destroyed commonwealths. Rather than collapsing Utopia into a pyschological re-education camp, however, More stressed institutional solutions. 'E poi si *non* muove'. Who settles insoluble disagreements? Rather than appeal to the man with the sword to bring to a close a long period of civil dissension as Hobbes would, More thought Utopian conciliar institutions (together with psychological means of controlling behaviour) made sovereignty unnecessary.

Thus Book II of *Utopia* solved the problem of royal tyranny in the same radical way that it dealt with private property – it abolished both. At the same time, it necessarily did away with the problem Book I spent most time on, how to counsel a prince. Hythloday had argued in the 'dialogue of counsel' that it was possible to advise successfully only in a society without private property

---

[64] Brian Tierney, '"Divided sovereignty" at Constance: a problem of medieval and early modern political theory', *Annuarium historiae conciliorum*, VII (1975), 238–56.

[65] I quote Ralph Robinson's translation, rather than the flatter version in *Utopia*, pp. 244–5, but have amended Robinson's 'sedition' to 'faction', following the Latin 'ambitionis et factionum radicibus'. *Utopia*, trans. Ralph Robinson, intro. John Warrington (London, 1951), p. 134.

and hence without ambition. That was not 'Morus's' view in his celebrated appeal to dramatistic art in counselling princes. *Utopia* thus adumbrates two positions on the councillor's role, one of which More explored further in the consciously dramatic *Richard III*.

Utopia's optimism about the effects of institutional reform makes a stark contrast to *Richard III*, which considers what happens when English conciliar institutions break down and ambition of 'sovereignty' and faction combined led to tyranny.[66] The relation between ambition, faction and tyranny was the same as in Utopia. Ambition sowed the seed of tyranny, which failure of counsel (especially in the king's council) and faction nourished. Even though More was writing about a period in which he could hardly avoid giving a great deal of attention to faction, he emphasized that aspect of Richard's reign much more than Polydore Vergil or Domenico Mancini.[67] Nearly the whole of the action of More's *Richard III* turns on council/sel and faction.[68] The first scene set the stage. It depicted King Edward on his deathbed presiding over a council meeting designed to put an end to faction. This makes a sharp contrast to Richard's first action, in which he immediately turns faction to his own evil purposes.[69] Both the first scene and More's laudatory attitude to Edward differ markedly from the way Vergil and Mancini treated that king. In order to highlight how much Edward accomplished, above all in suppressing faction, More sanctified him. The character sketch of the king noted only the tiny defect of gluttony, and reduced its significance by saying that anybody as well-fixed as Edward would be hard put to avoid that failing without a special grace.[70] Vergil's Edward, by contrast, although receiving a similar eulogy at the end of book twenty-four, was nevertheless painted in much less flattering colours in the rest of that section – made out to be faithless for turning on Warwick, a violent womanizer, and in direct contrast to More's monarch, lately fallen into avarice.[71] Mancini's King Edward came off at least as poorly. His covetousness appeared in a worse light, serving as a motive for a more blameworthy instance of faithlessness, and his 'intemperantissimus'

---

[66] Of the numerous commentaries on *Richard III*, I have found Judith Anderson's in *Biographical truth: the representation of historical persons in Tudor-Stuart writing* (New Haven, 1984) most illuminating. Her treatment parallels much of my argument. Elton has recently demanded more attention to the work, and pointed in the right direction for further interpretation. 'Humanism in England', in Anthony Goodman and Angus MacKay (eds.), *The impact of humanism on western Europe* (London, 1990), p. 263.

[67] This comparison of More's text to Vergil's *Anglica historia* is necessarily provisional, since I have not yet been able to have a look at Vergil's MS first draft, the only version even approximately contemporary with More's work. Later versions were heavily revised.

[68] This dimension was emphasized even more in the Latin text. See, e.g. *Richard III*, p. 10 (a passage where faction is the subject), p. 12 l. 7 (and commentary on 174), or p. 13 l. 17. For More's non-literal translation practice, see Sylvester's introduction, p. lvii.

[69] Ibid. pp. 11–13 and 14–19.

[70] Fox argues that More treated Edward and Richard in very similar ways to make the point that politics was a hopeless enterprise. *More*, pp. 78–81 and *Politics and literature*, pp. 120–2, especially p. 121 where Fox stresses that More 'obtrudes unflattering references' to Edward's vices 'so as to bring the idealization [of the character sketch] under control'.

[71] Henry Ellis (ed.), *Three books of Polydore Vergil's English history* (London, 1844; Camden Society, ser. 1, vol. XXIX [cited as Vergil]), p. 117 (lust and faithlessness), and p. 172 (avarice).

womanizing was described in detail.[72] While More's Edward behaved perfectly in character in his final moments as the great pacifier, putting the seal on an extraordinarily felicitous and much-lamented reign, that scene again departed from Vergil and Mancini, the first of whom merely mentioned Edward's will, while Mancini allowed that Edward may have presided over the reconciliation of Hastings and Lord Rivers.[73]

In More's description, England at Edward's death enjoyed almost as solid a domestic concord as Utopia.[74] Alas, it all depended on the weak reed of monarchy. Change Richard for Edward and ruination could not be averted. In the face of royal ambition, the council found itself helpless.[75] Once again, More's treatment differs from Vergil. Vergil had them taken in by Richard's subtlety, More by Hastings's credit and eloquence, but without describing what the councillors thought of Hastings's speech (Mancini simply made most of the councillors irresolute).[76] If the collective council failed to stop Richard, More raised the possibility that one councillor acting alone could yet accomplish his overthrow. But when More came to discuss Bishop Morton's attempt to turn Buckingham against Richard, his text abruptly ended.[77] England was not Utopia and More apparently could see no way out of the cycle within the real institutions he served. He therefore broke off writing when he discovered that even his 'hero' Morton could do no more than deploy the identical tactics that the devil incarnate, Richard, had used.[78] It was not so much that More hesitated to cast Henry VII as divine saviour, as Vergil did (at least in later versions of his *Anglica historia*), as that he appeared to believe that such a hero would be no permanent help.

Ambition, tyranny, faction, overthrow of the commonweal. Such was More's considered judgement on the reign of Richard III, and by implication perhaps on that of Henry VIII. As Richard Sylvester well noted, More changed his mind about Henry in the course of the first decade of the king's reign, substituting for the adulation of his poem on the coronation the strictures of *Utopia* and *Richard III*.[79] The change is evident in More's

---

[72] Mancini, pp. 60, 64–6.   [73] Vergil, p. 171; Mancini, p. 68.

[74] As More emphasized on the first page of his text in the thrice-repeated variation on the prime Christian virtue of *charitas*, the cement of the commonwealth (*Richard III*, p. 3). This point is here more muted in the English rendering, but comes out equally strongly in the repetition of 'love' in Edward's speech on p. 13.

[75] Fox, *More*, pp. 87–91 neatly details how the councillors *individually* failed in their responsibility to prevent tyranny, but this does not necessarily lead to the conclusion that More thought this an unalterable feature of *la condition humaine*.

[76] Mancini, p. 79; Vergil, p. 178; *Richard III*, p. 23.

[77] It should also be noted that Vergil made Buckingham the aggressor, for whom Morton acted only as one agent among many; Mancini's account ended before Buckingham's conspiracy. Vergil, p. 198.

[78] The problem of the ending of *Richard III* has attracted much inconclusive attention; Fox, the most recent student, offers two different interpretations, one linking More's decision to quit the work to the execution of the third duke of Buckingham in 1521 (*More*, pp. 104–7) and the other to his horrified realization that tyranny was ineluctable; not even Henry VII (much less Morton) could cure it (*Politics and literature*, pp. 122 and 126).

[79] Sylvester, *Richard III*, pp. c–ci; and cf. Fox, *Politics and literature*, p. 114.

superficially adulatory epigram on the conquest of Tournai. A specimen of his infamous irony, the poem played on a direct reference to Henry's new status. After noting Julius Caesar's sanguinary triumph over the town, More drew a contrast with Henry's recent success. 'Henry captured you [Tournai], captured you without bloodshed, a prince as much greater as better than Caesar', punning on *Caesar* as one of the emperor's titles and also on Henry's staking out of even larger claims.[80] We can now say a little more precisely what induced More's new attitude.[81]

If most of More's criticism of Henry's new style had perforce to be implicit, Erasmus's was explicit in all but openly calling Henry by name. *Querela pacis* and other works nearly contemporary with *Utopia* and *Richard III* level a strong attack not only on royal tyranny as a cause of war, but also as the means to the destruction of the commonwealth. Much of this broadside could have hit any European monarch, but some of it had to have been directly targeted at Henry. Above all, Erasmus openly took the part of France when lamenting princely appetites for territorial aggrandisement.[82] He argued that avarice made other princes jealous of France, the most powerful Christian country. Pretending to enlarge the *imperium Christi*, those who invade France actually

---

[80] 'De deditione Nerviae Henrico VIII Angliae regi', in Leicester Bradner and C. A. Lynch (eds.), *The Latin epigrams of Thomas More* (Chicago, 1953), 98 (no. 228); also in C. H. Miller, et al. (eds.), Thomas More; *Latin poems* (New Haven, 1984; *Complete works*, 3, 2), p. 256 (no. 244). Translation mine. More visited Tournai in the summer of 1515. Ibid. p. 404.

[81] There is one small problem. William Roper rep .ed a famous exchange between More and Henry as part of More's defence against charges of treason. Debating the power of the pope, Henry concluded by maintaining 'we will set forth that authority to the uttermost. For we received from that See our crown imperial'. More commented 'which till his grace with his own mouth told it me, I never heard of before'. William Roper, 'The life of Sir Thomas More', in R. S. Sylvester and D. P. Harding (eds.), *Two early Tudor lives* (New Haven, 1962), p. 235. The syntax is maddeningly obscure, but this could mean that More claimed not to have known about the imperial crown before 1521. More corroborated this discussion (but not the crucial point about the crown) in a letter to Cromwell, where he wrote that Henry stopped More's argument by showing him 'a secret cause whereof I never had anything heard before'. E. F. Rogers (ed.), *The correspondence of Sir Thomas More* (Princeton, 1947; reprint edn., 1970) no. 199, p. 498. I. 213. There and in her condensed edition (*St. Thomas More: selected letters* [New Haven, 1961], p. 212) Rogers speculated that this 'cause' concerned the invalidity of Henry's marriage to Katherine. More could have missed the numismatic and iconographical evidence referred to above, but his friend Cuthbert Tunstall, another of his intimates in Bruges while *Utopia* was being written, certainly knew all about the imperial crown no later than 1517 when he quoted it to the king. Guy, *Tudor England*, p. 105. Thus it must be that Roper's More meant to say that he had never heard that Henry held his crown imperial from the pope. That would strengthen the extent of his knowledge of the crown itself and perhaps therefore his reaction to it.

[82] James Tracy, comparing the *Adagia* and *Querela pacis* allowed that Erasmus 'seemed *for a time* sympathetic to France' (emphasis added), but continued by showing how Erasmus shared the gloating of his English hosts over English victories. James D. Tracy, *The politics of Erasmus: a pacifist intellectual and his political milieu* (Toronto, 1978), p. 28. For this episode, see also Jean-Claude Margolin, 'Erasme et la France', in August Buck (ed.), *Erasmus und Europa* (Wiesbaden, 1988; Wolfenbüttler Abhandlungen zur Renaissanceforschung, VII, p. 50. Later, once he had left England, Erasmus was more forthright, but still did not condemn Henry to the degree that he did his *bête noire*, Julius II (*Pacifist intellectual*, p. 33). Nevertheless, the crucial point for the consummate rhetorician Erasmus is that on severally closely-linked, particular occasions, he wrote about Henry's pretensions in a sharply critical way.

subverted the Christian commonwealth by harming its most 'beautiful and happiest part'.[83] In addition to other laments about the carving up of France, Erasmus pointed the finger squarely at Henry who, in what Erasmus thought a cruel joke, had christened his siege artillery after the twelve apostles (p. 45). Even in the almost impenetrably gnomic 'Scarabaeus aquilam quaerit' added to the 1515 edition of his *Adagia*, Erasmus got off one identifiable jab at Henry. Criticizing those rulers for whom 'the title of king is not enough', Erasmus likened them to predatory eagles (a symbol of empire) who might be called 'Britannicus' or 'Germanicus'.[84]

Henry also came in for oblique condemnation in Erasmus's extended consideration of how princely innovation provokes war. Instead of allowing constant transmigration of 'empire', a plan should be devised which would make kings put the concerns of the common people first. Erasmus hammered away at the economic motive behind princely aggression, contrasting kings' increasing demands for new taxes to support their wars with the *exemplum* of the lily in the Gospel (p. 17). Other princes, fearing that peace will make them expendable, deliberately stirred up war to distract their commons. Such tyrants were beasts who were 'noble only in their tyranny' (p. 23). Referring to the custom of putting pieces of kingdoms into dowries, Erasmus opined that 'free cities are those which a king rules, slaves those which a tyrant squeezes' (p. 34). Once the boundaries of a particular jurisdiction had been established, they should be preserved and the ruler should turn his efforts to improving the condition of the country he hands on to his successors (p. 35).

Here, as elsewhere, Erasmus emphasized the importance of consent in any decision to make war. Likewise free cities were those with a say in what the king did. Thus consent and the common good went hand in glove, as did 'rule' (in various forms of *imperare*) and free (*liber*, etc.). The ruler must above all have the welfare of the commonwealth at heart, and the commons must act to curb princely ambition. 'The princes know that they ought to act for the people, not themselves, in order that their majesty, happiness, riches, and their splendour should be measured by these things, which truly make them great and excellent.' Borrowing More's metaphor from *Utopia*, Erasmus exhorted kings to regard the commonwealth as fathers did their families. Rulers should 'exercise their rule (*imperium*)', 'remembering always that they were men ruling men (*hominem imperare hominibus*), citizens citizens, above all Christians Christians'. The *populus* had reciprocally always to act out of 'public utility'. Only 'the consent of the citizens' could restrain the prince's 'evil desires' (pp. 33–4). They stood to lose most by war (cf. the extended treatment of the suffering inflicted on the common people on pp. 25–6). Adverting once more to familial imagery, Erasmus contended that 'if the happiness of the prince is

---

[83] Desiderius Erasmus, *Querela pacis* (Basel, Froben, 1517), p. 24. All translations are mine.

[84] Margaret Mann Phillips, *The 'adages' of Erasmus. A study with translations* (Cambridge, 1964), pp. 234 and 240. Erasmus did not neutralize his twin epithets until the 1533 edition. Mann argued that Erasmus's main target was Julius II, but this argument cannot apply to the passages quoted (ibid. p. 105). Then again, Erasmus excluded Henry from his catalogue of notorious aggressors in 'Spartam nactus es, hanc orna', also of 1515.

to rule daughters (*imperare filiabus*), then he ought much rather to embrace peace' (p. 42).[85] Even though Erasmus knew it could jeopardize his patronage in England, he sketched most of these points in a letter of early 1514, written in an effort to stop the war between France, England and the Empire.[86] Erasmus's more general attitude to monarchy at this time was nearly identical to More's: both made the institution of kingship, not the failings of individual rulers responsible for incessant warfare in Europe.[87] Undoubtedly More and Erasmus differed in the fixity of their gallophobia. That may have made Erasmus more even-handed in his criticism of European rulers, while More's chauvinism, manifested *ad nauseam* in his controversy with Germaine Brie, would only have reinforced his objections to specifically French-style monarchy.[88]

More and Erasmus were not the only ones to see the dangers of apeing French monarchy. The close agreement between More, Erasmus and the senior councillors who engineered the removal of Henry's riotous young companions puts both humanists and practical politics in a different light, some current harsh strictures on English 'Erasmianism' to the contrary notwithstanding.[89] Recently reinterpreted as a fit of moral francophobia rather than a factional crisis orchestrated by Wolsey, both views of the expulsion may yet have an element of truth, rooted once more in opposition to Henry's new French ways.[90] Until late 1518 the king's exalted claims to sovereignty threatened to mean the replacement not of the thoroughly Frenchified minions in the privy chamber, but of the *consiliarii nati* in the council chamber. The councillors who forced Henry to rid himself of his evil companions saw them as pandering to the king's every whim, and thereby fostering tyranny. The minions riding through the streets of Paris with Francis I, throwing eggs at sober *bourgeoises*, became an icon of French monarchy to the councillors, not simply of the excesses of French manners.[91] Wolsey, for his

[85] This passage is paralleled by another in 'Aut fatuum aut regem nasci oportere', in the *Adagia* of 1515, pp. 221–2.

[86] To Anton van Bergen, 14 Mar. 1514. P. S. Allen (ed.), *Opus epistolarum Desiderii Erasmi Roterodamensis*, I (Oxford, 1906), no. 288. An English translation in *The correspondence of Erasmus*, trans. R. A. B. Mynors and D. F. S. Thomson, notes W. K. Ferguson (Toronto, 1975; *Collected works of Erasmus*, II), but it needs to be used with caution whenever political terms are in question. In this case, for example, 'altercatio cuius sit ditio' is rendered as 'a question about sovereignty', when that is the *last* thing *ditio* meant.

[87] Tracy, *Pacifist intellectual*, p. 36, although he is more cautious in his conclusion about the parallels between their work. The traditional portrait of More and Erasmus as alter egos is becoming a little frayed. See especially Richard Marius, *Thomas More* (New York, 1985), passim; it is probably significant that Marius and Elton endorsing his conclusion ('Humanism', p. 275) put More and Erasmus closest in the mid-1510s. Hubertus Schulte Herbrüggen offers the latest restatement of the usual view in 'Erasmus und England: Erasmus und More', in Buck, *Erasmus und Europa*, pp. 91–110.   [88] Marius, *More*, pp. 243–9.

[89] Fox, in Fox and Guy, *Reassessing the Henrician age*, chs. 2, 3.

[90] Greg Walker, 'The "expulsion of the minions" of 1519 reconsidered', *Historical Journal*, XXXII (1989), 1–16 and Starkey, *Reign*, pp. 74–81.

[91] Walker, '"Expulsion"', pp. 13–15 labels English indignation over the minions' 'dissoluteness' a social rather than a political reaction, but it would be difficult so easily to separate politics and culture in the early sixteenth century.

part, was every bit as gallophobic as either More or the king's council; the Venetian ambassador's original report linking Wolsey and the council as agents of the expulsion may yet have captured their joint action and its motive.[92]

In More's eyes, the continued dominance of Henry's dissolute young companions would have been an instance of precisely the failure of both counsel and council that he dreaded. Thus the suggestion offered above about why More stopped writing *Richard III* may be too pessimistic. Perhaps the solution to the conundrum is that the council which he had just joined had disappointed his dismal historical expectations and actually thrown the rascals out at the same time as it and Wolsey, acting together, had satisfied some of More's Utopian vision by an institutional reform of the privy chamber. Henry got the sop of French-model titles, but the sober new councillors behind them were anything but followers of French models.[93] As a result, a lesson in the dangers of faction and tyranny was no longer as urgently needed.[94]

This interpretation suggests that despite the deep concern about Henry's new kingship expressed in both *Utopia* and *Richard III*, More had made an accommodation shortly after he got his place among the king's councillors. This is not so hard to understand, especially in a world in which the court was increasingly the only game in town. Others of More's contemporaries who would come to seem equally saintly did exactly the same thing.[95] Nor did More's attitude prevent Henry from making an offer to him. At least in the first decade of his reign, both Henry and More played by the same rules. Yet the language within which they manoeuvred was in flux, opening the possibility of a rupture which would break more than words. A very clear example of this is how the two used the 'same' highly significant word, sovereignty.[96] Unlike Henry, More once gave 'desire of vainglory and sovereignty' a thoroughly traditional meaning as synonymous with *praecellendi cupiditas* and 'immoderate appetite of worship' (*ardor gloriae*).[97] Both were something which happened among the nobility ('estates' or *illustri viri*) and within the realm (*regnum*).[98] In another instance, More translated 'execrable desire of sovereignty' as *execrabilis imperandi sitis*, thereby perhaps inadvertently revealing how the 'same' imperial claims Henry was putting forward were inextricably rooted in the 'same' language More used to criticize them (p. 5). One doubts that Cromwell or Henry saw the consequences of pursuing sovereignty as the destruction of the commonweal when they consistently

[92] Walker, '"Expulsion"', pp. 3–4.
[93] Starkey, *Reign*, pp. 80–1, and Walker, '"Expulsion"', p. 9.
[94] This suggestion about More's attitude and its coalescence with that of Henry's conservative councillors must remain speculative. For the little known of More's politics so early in his career, see J. A. Guy, *The public career of Sir Thomas More* (New Haven, 1980), ch. 1.
[95] See T. F. Mayer, 'A mission worse than death: Reginald Pole and the Parisian theologians', *English Historical Review*, CIII (1988), 870–91.
[96] Michel Foucault, *The archaeology of knowledge*, trans. A. M. Sheridan Smith (New York, 1972), p. 110 on polysemia.
[97] This is probably also the meaning Vergil's anonymous mid-century translator gave the word. Mancini attributed no similar motive to Richard. [98] *Richard III*, pp. 13–4.

appealed to that 'same' key term. There may not have been a 'Tudor despotism' but the resources of language available to Henry made a discourse of despotism possible. Contrariwise, More's political humanism offered a 'critical theory' which could enable resistance to it.[99] In both cases, mutual incomprehension would levy a high price on both language and those who used it.

---

[99] I owe the description of humanism as 'critical theory' to Paul A. Fideler's unpublished 'Christian humanism and poverty: reflections on common weal, commonwealth, and policy', which he kindly let me read.

IV

THE WAR OF THE TWO SAINTS: THE CONCLAVE OF JULIUS III AND CARDINAL POLE

Almost as soon as Paul III died on 10 November 1549, many observers thought Reginald Pole, a cardinal since 1536, the leading candidate to succeed him.[1] Pole failed to be elected in intricate fashion. The conclave of Julius III in which this happened has not received much attention since the turn of the century, but it should count as one of the pivotal moments not only in the history of the Italian reformation, but also of the reformation generally.[2] It is not too much to say that most previous discussion needs to be revised in light of new evidence. Mountains of diplomatic reports and other documents force me to argue against the prevailing interpretations according to which the outcome was decided within the first week. Perhaps more important, cardinals

---

[1] The title comes from Matteo Dandolo's dispatch of 18 December 1549 (ASVe:APR, 7, fo. 147r). The following abbreviations are used: *Algunas cartas* Alberto Vazquez and R. Selden Rose, eds, *Algunas cartas de Don Diego Hurtado Mendoza, 1538-1552* (New Haven: Yale University Press, 1935); ASF:AMP Archivio di stato, Florence, Archivio mediceo del principato; ASM:AG Archivio di stato, Mantua, Archivio Gonzaga; ASVe:APR Archivio di stato, Venice, Archivio Proprio Roma; BAV Biblioteca apostolica vaticana; BPP Biblioteca palatina, Parma; *CRP The correspondence of Reginald Pole*, ed. Thomas F. Mayer (forthcoming); *CSPSp* Gustav A. Bergenroth, et al., eds., *Calendar of letters, despatches and state papers, relating to the negotiations between England and Spain* (London: Longman, et al., 1862-1954); *CSPV* Rawdon Brown, ed., *Calendar of state papers and manuscripts...in the archives and collections of Venice* (London: Longman, et al., 1864-98; nine volumes); *CT Concilium Tridentinum*, ed. Sebastian Merkle, Stephan Ehses, Gottfried Buschbell, et al. (Freiburg: Herder, 1901-1966; 12 vols); Druffel A. von Druffel, *Beiträge zur Reichsgeschichte 1546-1551* (Munich: Rieger, 1873-82; 3 vols), 1; *ERP* Angelo Maria Querini, ed., *Epistolarum Reginaldi Poli [libri]* (Brescia: Rizzardi, 1744-57; 5 volumes); *MMB* G. B. Morandi, ed., *Monumenti di varia letteratura* (Bologna: Istituto per le scienze, 1797-1804; 2 volumes); *PM* Massimo Firpo and Dario Marcatto, eds., *Il processo inquisitoriale del Cardinal Giovanni Morone* (Rome, 1981-1996; 6 volumes). An earlier version of this piece appeared as 'Il fallimento di una candidatura: Il partito della riforma, Reginald Pole e il conclave di Giulio III' in *Annali dell'Istituto storico italo-germanico in Trento*, 21 (1995), pp. 41-67.

[2] See especially Giuseppe De Leva, *Storia documentata di Carlo V in correlazione all'Italia*, 5 (Bologna: Zanichelli, 1894, reprint of 1864 ed.), pp. 64-92.

connected to the Inquisition formed only one group among many, and they did not play a determining role.³ Instead, Pole and the reform tendency caused their own downfall. This last point emerges most clearly from the sharp division between Pole and his leading opponent, Gianpietro Carafa.

One of Pole's appeals and simultaneously largest drawbacks arose from his identification with those cardinals who wished an overhaul of the papal bureaucracy, and consequently, a change in the direction in which the papal monarchy had developed since at least Innocent III.⁴ Pole had been tied to such aspirations from the time of the *Consilium de emendanda ecclesia* and had come to be singled out as wishing to do away with both the Datary and the Penitentiary, the most sensitive organs of that bureaucracy. He was also said to have wished to send the bishops to their dioceses and to prevent cardinals from holding bishoprics, both points in the *Consilium*.⁵ But Pole's attractiveness on the score of doctrine ought not to be underestimated, coupled with expectations that he was just what was needed to revive the council of Trent.⁶ Neither Pole's allies nor his enemies missed these possibilities, and it is likely that the potential for his manipulation provided one more appeal to some of his most potent supporters. Pole encouraged hopes that he might act as a sort of figurehead by scarcely involving himself in the negotiations, unlike the other leading contenders. About the only evidence of his participation comes from the ambassador of Urbino who noted that despite dealing with Pole and Marcello Cervini at length, neither had expressed any interest in the papacy.⁷ The Venetian ambassador, Matteo Dandolo, an old friend, immediately after the end of the conclave reported Pole as having told his backers that he refused to do anything to secure his election, surrendering himself as always to God's will.⁸ This remained his public position throughout the conclave. Some of his competitors seized on the chance to make Pole dance to their tune. Just before the conclave Ippolito d'Este, cardinal of Ferrara, blatantly advised Henry II to cover an attack on England by having Pole made legate for a crusade.⁹ Ercole

---

[3] Against the interpretation in Paolo Simoncelli, *Il caso Reginald Pole: eresia e santità nelle polemiche religiose del Cinquecento* (Rome: Edizioni di storia e letteratura, 1977), pp. 60–76, and above all Massimo Firpo, *Inquisizione romana e Controriforma. Studi sul Cardinal Giovanni Morone e il suo processo d'eresia* (Bologna: Il Mulino, 1992), *passim*, especially p. 377.

[4] Amadio Ronchini, *Lettere di Girolamo Muzio giustinopolitano conservate nell'Archivio governativo di Parma* (Parma: F. Carmignani, 1864), p. 109 vs. Archivio di stato, Siena, Archivio del Balìa (hereafter ASS:AB), b. 720, no. 57.

[5] See, *e.g.*, Muzio, p. 109, and ASVe:APR, 7, fo. 133r (*CSPV*, 5, no. 596).

[6] *E.g.*, ASS:AB, b. 720, no. 67 or ASM:AG, b. 888, fos 430-35.

[7] ASF, Archivio di Urbino (hereafter ASF:AU), Cl. I G f. CXXIV, fos 368r–71r.

[8] ASVe:APR, 7, fo. 129r (*CSPV*, 5, no. 595).

[9] Guillaume Ribier, *Lettres et Memoires D'Estat, Des Roys, Princes, Ambassadeurs, et autres Ministres, sous les Regnes de François premier, Henry II et François II* (Paris: F. Clouzier, 1666; 2 vols), 2, p. 250.

Gonzaga, one of the leaders of the Imperial party who did his best to undermine Pole's candidacy, might well have acquiesced in the emperor's orders to vote for Pole in the hopes that their agreement about dismantling the papal bureaucracy would benefit his nephew the duke of Mantua.[10] And more than a few observers, including Pole's first biographers, thought that Alessandro Farnese saw little beyond a wide-open opportunity to aggrandize his family under Papa Polo (an idea which may not have been completely foreign to Paul, either).

Remarkably little firm planning about a successor took place in the months before Paul's death. The Imperial camp and the group around Farnese took a very long time to coalesce behind Pole. The two leaders of the Imperial party in Italy, Gonzaga and Cristoforo Madruzzo, were deeply divided both politically and personally from Farnese, as was the imperial ambassador in Rome, Diego Hurtado de Mendoza.[11] Gonzaga, Madruzzo and Mendoza agreed very well among themselves and backed Giovanni Salviati, a leader of the Florentine exiles, explicitly as an anti-Farnese candidate. Mendoza cooperated fully, even well after Cosimo I, duke of Florence and alleged director of the Imperial party from the outside, discovered and thereby essentially ruined the scheme.[12] The emperor steadfastly refused to hear any talk of Salviati. Cosimo backed Juan Alvarez de Toledo, cardinal of Burgos, in large part because he was a relative – an uncle of Cosimo's wife and brother of the viceroy of Naples – and the emperor's first choice among his vassals.[13] All the same, his candidacy too appeared to have failed before the conclave opened.[14] The general impression is one of frantic scrambling.

---

[10] *PM*, 2:1, p. 280; ASVe:APR, 7, fo. 133r (*CSPV*, 5, no. 596). Cf. ASM:AG, 1918, fos 455r-9v, 465, and 477r and ASF:AMP, 611, fo. 135. See also ASM:AG, 888, *passim* and ASVe:APR, 7, fo. 149r (*CSPV*, 5, no. 602) and fo. 203r (*CSPV*, 5, no. 640).

[11] Erika Spivakovsky, *Son of the Alhambra. Diego Hurtado Mendoza, 1504-75* (Austin: University of Texas Press, 1970), chapter 10.

[12] *E.g.*, ASM:AG, 1918, fos 455r-9v. Cf. Thomas F. Mayer and Peter E. Starenko, 'An unknown diary of Julius III's conclave by Bartolomeo Stella, a servant of Cardinal Pole', *Annuarium historiae conciliorum*, 24 (1992), pp. 345-75, pp. 363n and 367n [this volume no. V]. The plot was disclosed to Cosimo by Salviati. ASF:AMP, 621, fos 99v and 113v and *e.g.*, ASF:AMP, 3463a, fos 78v-81r and 83r-4v. Firpo (*PM*, 2, p. 557n) attributed the diary to Stella, and when I published this text, I followed his lead. I have since decided this proposition lacks solid support. The text bears no indication of its author, and I have found no autograph documents by Stella to which to compare it. It may well be, as I suggested ('Unknown diary', p. 353), that the diary was written after the conclave. For the sake of convenience, I shall continue to refer to the text as Stella's.

[13] *E.g.*, ASF:AMP, 13, fos 167r-8v and 174r-v; 611, fos 188r-94v; 323, fos 54v-5r; and many other documents. For Charles's wishes, *CT*, II, no. 400B.

[14] See, *e.g.*, ASF:AMP, 3463a, fos 84v-5v, and fos 88v-92v (Luigi Serristori, ed., *Legazioni di Averardo Serristori Ambasciatore di Cosimo I a Carlo Quinto e in Corte di Roma (1537-1568)* [Florence: Le Monnier, 1853], pp. 211-6).

The Conclave of Julius III and Cardinal Pole

Despite both Paul's well-known recommendation to Cardinal Alessandro that Pole should succeed him and an anonymous piece of advice from one of Farnese's intimates, Pole did not emerge until almost the last minute, according to the oddsmakers between the pope's death and 13 November.[15] Farnese's adviser suggested the best tactic to get him elected, which Farnese would indeed try: a surprise adoration.[16] Pole led an exemplary life and his only major drawback was that his likely severity would discomfit many, among them Paul's (and Alessandro's) relatives and many of the clergy. This charge circulated widely, probably even more widely than reservations about his theology.[17] Others objected as well, especially Gonzaga. At one point he sent an agent to Benedetto Buonanni, the Florentine ambassador's secretary, with a lengthy catalogue of Pole's weaknesses, stretching from defective views of justification to plans to force beneficed clergy to reside.[18] At another, he easily overcame Madruzzo's weak support by the argument that Pole was too holy to be elected.[19] This marks not only another fracture in the Imperial front, but within the reform tendency, of which Gonzaga was a principal (if not necessarily principled) member.[20]

Despite the apparent solidity of the Gonzaga-Madruzzo-Mendoza cabal, Farnese somehow usurped the leadership of a heterogeneous group composed on the one hand of the Farnesiani, his natural affinity (four cardinals were his close relatives) together with those who, in Paolo Giovio's words, were still

---

[15] BAV, Barb. lat. 5366, fo. 134v (cited by Simoncelli, *Caso*, p. 63n). At the pope's death he stood fourth in the wagers and the Florentine ambassador also rated him one of four possibilities. ASVe:APR, 7, fo. 107r (*CSPV*, 5, no. 587); *Legazioni*, pp. 207-11; ASS:AB, b. 720, no. 23; and ASVe:APR, 7, fo. 111r (*CSPV*, 5, no. 588).

[16] Public Record Office, London, PRO 31/9/66, pp. 351-60, from Biblioteca Minerva, Rome, cod. XX. IX. 8, 'Avvertimenti dati al Card. Farnese per il conclave nella morte di Pavolo Terzo'. It may be that this text is actually evidence of an organized campaign against Pole. Most of its content and even one exact phrase appear in a report of a speech Cardinal Gonzaga's agent made against Pole to Buonanni (ASF:AMP, 395, fo. 22r).

[17] See, *e.g.*, ASF:AU, Cl. I G f. CXXIV, fos 368r-71r, and *Lettere di Muzio*, p. 109 and ASF:AMP, 395, fo. 22r.

[18] ASF:AMP, 395, fo. 22r. Buonanni, one of the most copious informants about the conclave, served for most of it as an attendant to Alvarez (*CT*, 2, p. 123). He had more than a little sympathy for Pole, at one point praying God to pardon those who tried to prevent his election. ASF:AMP, 613, fo. 140r. Unfortunately, Buonanni's dispatches for this moment do not survive, although a large number of them have been found in the Archivio di stato in Florence. My thanks to my former student John Frymire for much help in transcribing them.

[19] ASM:AG, b. 1918, fo. 455v.

[20] *CRP*, no. 464. Gonzaga told Pole that his oration to the fathers at Trent made such a strong impression on him, that he completely repented his past sins. See also Gigliola Fragnito, 'Ercole Gonzaga, Reginald Pole e il monastero di S. Benedetto Polirone', *Benedictina*, 37 (1987), pp. 253-71 and Sergio Pagano, ed., *Il processo di Endimio Calandra e l'Inquisizione a Mantova nel 1567-1568* (Vatican City: Biblioteca Apostolica Vaticana, 1991). ASM:AG, 1918, fo. 455v for the agreement with Madruzzo.

hungry (that is, they had profited under Paul but were worried about keeping their gains), and on the other of the Imperial confederation.[21] But if Farnese meant to construct and maintain a party, he had a hand in some stupid moves before the conclave opened, quickly lost some of his most important followers, and could barely maintain cohesion even in his family nucleus. I shall offer only two examples. On the day of Paul's death, the leading imperialist cardinal Francesco Sfondrati resigned the bishopric of Capaccio to one of the leading Farnesiani, Girolamo Verallo, but Sfondrati reserved to Farnese a pension on the see of 1,500 *scudi*, apparently the price of the bishopric of Cremona to which Sfondrati transferred.[22] Similarly, in 1547 Farnese had induced the exiled Portuguese cardinal Miguel de Silva to resign the wealthy see of Viseu to him, apparently promising to see him well compensated. In fact, de Silva had to wait more than two years before he got the financially nearly worthless see of Massa Marittima, and only after Farnese had first given it to his secretary.[23] Both would desert Farnese, Verallo with disastrous consequences.

Thus before Farnese ever made his choice, there were reasons to wonder about the success of any candidate he supported. And despite the advice and the odds, Farnese took his time making a selection. On 16 November it was reported that he had rejected Pole as non-Italian and for other, unspecified, reasons.[24] On the 20th, Charles V sent contingency instructions, naming Pole as one of his four choices, and the Imperial party among the cardinals seems already to have hit on him.[25] Not all its members agreed, it seems, since the duke of Urbino's ambassador, escorting the duke's brother cardinal Giulio della Rovere, still deeply discounted Pole's chances on 25 November.[26] Farnese, for his part, lobbied that long for Cervini, whom he several times tried to substitute for Pole later, despite the emperor's determined opposition.[27] Farnese's eventual selection of Pole probably compounded both their difficulties, especially since Farnese had first courted Carafa, who fell out of Farnese's graces by refusing to support the arrangement by which Parma would go to Ottavio Farnese.[28] It may, however, be that Pole was forced on Farnese by Farnese's own backers. When he tried to transfer Pole's votes on several occasions, he failed, and Mendoza insisted

---

[21] G. G. Ferrero, ed., Paolo Giovio, *Lettere*, 2 (Rome: Tipografo dello Stato, 1958), no. 324.
[22] ASF:AMP, 3268, fo. 408r, and Conrad Eubel and J. Van Gulik, *Hierarchia catholica medii et recentioris aevii* (Münster: Bibliothek Regensberger, 1913), 3, pp. 152 and 181.
[23] *Ibid.*, pp. 26 and 237.
[24] ASF:AMP, 611, fos 179r–86v.
[25] ASF:AMP, 395, fos 15r–16r and *CT*, 2, no. 400A.
[26] ASF:AU, Cl. I G f. CXXIV, fos 372r–6v.
[27] ASF:AMP, 611, fos 188r–94v and fos 69r–70r. Cf. also *Algunas cartas*, pp. 146–8.
[28] ASVe:APR, 7, fo. 118r–v (*CSPV*, 5, no. 594). ASF:AMP, 395, fo. 43v said Farnese was backing Pole in part because Pole intended to forward Farnese's plans about Parma.

that Farnese had been very loath to back Pole.²⁹ According to Gonzaga, Farnese chose Pole because he was 'so good and of such holiness of life' that no one would dare to oppose him.³⁰ Angelo Massarelli on 21 November recorded a deal by which Madruzzo reneged on his promise to Gonzaga to support Salviati and brought about a reconciliation between Gonzaga's brother Ferrante and Farnese such that they all decided to support Pole.³¹ If so, they managed to give a good impression to many other observers of doing anything but until at least the end of the month when the conclave finally opened.

All these political and family rivalries fed into one more division which may finally have had the greatest impact on Pole's candidacy. As Mendoza and many others noted, there were the old and the rich cardinals, and the young and the poor.³² Many observers thought the old and the rich opposed Pole to a man. I have not done a complete study of the college and thus cannot say with authority exactly which cardinals belonged to which group. From a crude analysis of all its Italian members, together with the three or four foreigners for whom I have found data, the division according to age stands up: the Imperial-Farnese alignment averaged 40.5 years old, while their opponents were almost a decade older. A study of economic status is much more difficult, but it should eventually prove possible to label cardinals as rich or poor depending upon whether they received the standard papal pension to 'poor' cardinals, which is probably close to what contemporaries meant. At the moment, it appears that more of Pole's opponents were rich than poor, and an economic motive could well have undergirded the defections from Farnese of others besides Verallo, especially Girolamo Capodiferro, who had been datary for almost a decade.

Before passing to a narrative of events, two words about the mechanics of the conclave. Each cardinal was assigned a cell by lot. Pole's had an important location, at the bottom of the Sala regia, putting him both at the cross of the 'T' between the Sistine chapel and the consistorial hall, and also just outside the new Capella paolina. A more central location would not have been possible. Cardinal Georges d'Armagnac had the cell directly opposite Pole, and Madruzzo on the diagonal from Pole.³³ Each cardinal was allowed three conclavists, although some managed to have more, at least before the reform of the conclave in late January. It is not entirely clear who attended Pole. Alvise Priuli is certain (see below), the other two less so. According to Massarelli's diary, they were Gianbattista della Ripa, and Tommaso Madius or

---

²⁹ *Algunas cartas*, pp. 146-8 and 164-73. Cf. ASF:AMP, 395, fo. 369v and 3268, fo. 596.
³⁰ ASM:AG, b. 1918, fo. 479r.
³¹ *CT*, 2, p. 19.
³² Druffel, no. 352 (pp. 306-12); cf. *CSPSp*, 10, pp. 483-6 and, *e.g.*, *Algunas cartas*, p. 150; ASF:AMP, 611, fos 73r-4r; and *CT*, 2, p. 50.
³³ *CT*, 2, pp. 27-8.

Maggio, who had been with Pole since at least Trent.³⁴ It has also been claimed that Bartolomeo Stella and Thomas Goldwell were Pole's conclavists, but despite the existence of diaries of the conclave attributed to both, there is no evidence that they were present in any capacity, nor can Madius and Goldwell have been the same person, despite their common Christian name, since Madius came from the diocese of Como.³⁵

Various machinations of Cardinal d'Este prevented the conclave from opening until 29 November, more than a week late.³⁶ Next, Giandomenico de Cupis, dean of the college of cardinals, tried his hand, and he managed to delay the first voting until 3 December.³⁷ At that point, the Holy Spirit took over.

At least that was Cervini's explanation (and less modestly, Pole's), and for lack of any more rational one, it will have to do. It is not impossible that God and Alessandro Farnese may for once have been on the same side.³⁸ The leading candidate in the first *scrutinium* turned out to be Pole, by a wide margin. He had twenty-one votes, with Alvarez second at thirteen, Sfondrati and de Cupis tied at twelve, and Carafa at ten.³⁹ (The cardinals could vote for as many candidates as they wished on each ballot, although the usual number seems to have been about three.) Much later as part of one of his long excuses for Alvarez's failure, Mendoza claimed that Pole's support had arisen spontaneously.⁴⁰ This might be true, but it would probably be necessary to identify more precisely the 'reformers' in the conclave in order to demonstrate the proposition, an even more difficult job than classifying the cardinals according to economic status. Pole's supporters included all the cardinals known as reformers, except for three painful exceptions: Carafa, Nicolò Ridolfi (like Salviati a Florentine exile) and de Cupis. Carafa can be explained away easily enough, and many would say that the other two can as well. Ridolfi's commitment to reform has been doubted, but it seems to me that the evidence of a 'conversion' to a brand of religious piety not far removed from

---

³⁴ *CT*, 2, p. 125.
³⁵ *PM*, 2, p. 557n; Giuseppe Silos, *Historiarum clericorum regularium [liber]* (Rome: Mascardi, 1650; 2 vols), 1, p. 305 and Bibliothèque municipale, Douai, MS 922, vol. 3, fo. 58v. The 'diary' attributed to Goldwell is little more than a record of votes. English College, Rome, MS 303, fos C–D among several loose sheets pasted in at the front of the volume. It was printed in translation by Vincent Cronin in *Rome* and then reprinted in *The tablet*, 114 (1909), 28 August, pp. 340–42, 'How cardinal Pole nearly became the second English pope'. George B. Parks, 'The Reformation and the hospice 1514–1559' in *The English hospice in Rome, The venerabile*, 21 (1962), pp. 193–217, p. 213n offers a more correct description of the MS.
³⁶ Druffel, pp. 296–7; Ribier, 2, pp. 252–4; and Ludwig von Pastor, *Geschichte der Päpste im Zeitalter der katholischen Reformation und Restauration*, 5 (Freiburg: Herder, 1919), p. 8.
³⁷ Druffel, pp. 296–7.
³⁸ Pastor, p. 14 and *CT*, 2, pp. 44–6.
³⁹ *CT*, 2, p. 38.
⁴⁰ *Algunas cartas*, p. 169.

Pole's is convincing.⁴¹ De Cupis was said to be almost as rigid a moralizer as Carafa, and he had been a leading member of most of Paul III's reform commissions.⁴² But all three harbored papal ambitions, and all were strongly French.

Even without these three possible allies, on 4 December Pole reached twenty-four of the twenty-eight votes necessary.⁴³ Farnese, capable of recognizing a good thing when it was presented to him on a plate, then put in train the scheme of having Pole adored, that is, elected by acclamation rather than a formal *scrutinium*.⁴⁴ According to Cardinal Bernardino Maffei, the manager of the Farnese party and better disposed to Pole than most other observers inside the conclave, constant toing and froing consumed most of the night until Pole refused to agree to the plot, which had already inspired a French threat of a schism.⁴⁵ According to Agostino Oldoino's scrupulously researched biography of Pole, Pole had communicated his refusal through Priuli.⁴⁶ Pole's own account of this dramatic moment in a letter to Francisco de Navarra shortly after the conclave confirms the contemporary record, and added that Pole had been persuaded to accept Farnese's overtures, but had then changed his mind.⁴⁷ Maffei's diary recorded Pole's unmoving reaction, which would become the key to Beccadelli's story of the conclave.⁴⁸ It seems likely that part of Pole's objection stemmed from politics. He might very well have known that Farnese had been slow to come around to him, and also have wished to avoid being too beholden for his election. In any case, Farnese's precipitate action probably did Pole more harm than good, especially annoying the 'old' cardinals.⁴⁹

Never the less, things looked very promising. Maffei reported that three French partisans, Giovanni Maria Ciocchi del Monte, Federico Cesi (by my calculations Cesi was a floating vote) and Nicolò Gaddi had been induced to

---

⁴¹ Cf. Randolph Starn, *Donato Giannotti and his Epistolae* (Geneva: Droz, 1968), pp. 48–50 (with some reservations) and Achille Olivieri, *Riforma ed eresia a Vicenza nel Cinquecento* (Rome: Herder, 1992), p. 239. Marcantonio Flaminio planted Jacopo Bonfadio on Ridolfi at nearly the same moment at which Valdés's followers fanned out from Naples. Firpo, *Alumbrados*, p. 178.
⁴² Pastor, pp. 79, 131-3, 138 and A. M. Ghisalberti, ed, *Dizionario biografico degli italiani* (Rome: Istituto dell'Enciclopedia Italiana, 1960–), 33, p. 603.
⁴³ *CT*, 2, p. 41.
⁴⁴ *CT*, 2, p. 42.
⁴⁵ *CT*, 2, pp. 43ff. Cf. 'Unknown diary' pp. 356-7 and ASVe:APR, 7, fo. 133r (*CSPV*, 5, no. 596), picked up in Beccadelli's and Dudic's lives.
⁴⁶ Alfonso Chacón, *Vitae et res gestae pontificum romanorum et S. R. E. cardinalium*, 3, ed. Agostino Oldoino, SJ (Rome: Filippo and Antonio De Rubeis, 1678), col. 630. Oldoino greatly expanded the entries in the first and second editions of Chacón.
⁴⁷ *CRP*, no. 573.
⁴⁸ *CT*, 2, p. 47; *MMB*, 1:2, p. 303.
⁴⁹ Druffel, no. 352 (cf. *CSPSp*, 10, pp. 483-6) and ASF:AMP, 613, fo. 209r.

vote for Pole, so annoying Salviati that they had to promise to vote for Pole only after he had reached twenty-six.[50] Given the stiffening for the Imperial party provided by the arrival of Cardinal Pedro Pacheco, Pole's election seemed a mere formality.[51] The three native French cardinals desperately sent a message to Claude d'Urfé, Henry's ambassador, that unless he resorted to 'some stratagem' they were lost. D'Urfé did the best he could and blustered first and lied second. He passed a message into the conclave that Henry would refuse to acknowledge an election in which the French cardinals did not participate, and added that they were already at Corsica. Even he did not expect this ruse to work. Pole had picked up three more votes while the ambassador was writing his report and d'Urfé considered his election certain.[52] So did the bankers, who put Pole's odds up to 90 or 95%, and his conclavists who disassembled (or looted) his cell. Pontifical vestments were made, and one later commentator even thought he had written an acceptance speech.[53] Soldiers were sent to guard the English hospice, in anticipation of uproars when Pole was elected.[54]

Things did not go as predicted the next day. For a start, it proved difficult to get the two grand factions together.[55] Probably to ensure that an election would be held, Pole and Alvarez approached de Cupis, but their discussion may have had even more significance. Once the meeting began, Carafa sprang to his feet and accused Pole of heresy, waving 'a *processo* or articles (*un processo o capitulos*)' with a list of Pole's errors.[56] Pole replied as if Carafa were mad, 'sometimes laughing and sometimes citing authorities from Holy Scripture'. Carafa certainly did not intimidate Pole. Mendoza even had Pole admit that he had expressed Lutheran positions at Trent, if only as devil's advocate. Pole appealed to powerful witnesses to corroborate his testimony, del Monte and Cervini, the other two legates to Trent. They supported his story to such effect that some of the cardinals proposed a vote of censure against Carafa.[57] Instead, the college proceeded to an election, in which Pole once again garnered twenty-four votes. When the secret balloting had ended, Rodolfo Pio da Carpi rose and said he wished to change his vote to

---

[50] *CT*, 2, p. 43. Cf. ASF:AMP, 613, fo. 143v.
[51] ASS:ADB, 720, no. 67 and ASF:AMP, 395, fo. 23v; and ASVe:APR, 7, fo. 132r (*CSPV*, 5, no. 596).
[52] Ribier, 2, pp. 254–6.
[53] ASVe:APR, 7, fo. 133r (*CSPV*, 5, no. 596), and ASF:AMP, 3463a, fos 94v–8r (*Legazioni*, pp. 218–21, incorrectly dated 5 December). Antonio Maria Graziani, *De casibus virorum illustrium* (Paris: Antoine Cellier, 1680), p. 219 for the oration. The work was written before Graziani died in 1611.
[54] Parks, 'Reformation and the hospice', p. 214.
[55] *CT*, 2, pp. 44 and 48; 'Unknown diary', p. 357.
[56] Druffel, no. 52 and *CT*, 2, pp. 46 (Massarelli) and 45 (Maffei).
[57] Druffel, no. 352.

Pole. Farnese did the same. And then deep silence descended on the Capella paolina. Finally, de Cupis asked whether anyone else wished to change his vote to Pole and, when no one rose to speak, he declared the election over. All contemporaries assigned the principal reason for Pole's failure to Carafa's attack, but it must be emphasized first, that Carafa had a great deal of help, and second, that he and his allies alone probably did not undo Pole. Their moment had been prepared well in advance.[58] Florentine agents reported Pole's ill repute *della fede* at the end of November, drawing in part on Carafa's steady aspersions, as did Ferrante Gonzaga's informant Girolamo Muzio; Carafa was heard to say that Pole should clear himself of the charge of claiming that alms given by a mortal sinner did no good without grace; and one of Cervini's nephews noted on 2 December that a *processo* against Pole was being brandished in the conclave.[59] This celebrated *processo* might seem to have been Carafa's major contribution, but in fact it was de Cupis who had dredged it up and brought it into the conclave, at least according to Mendoza who would not have missed an opportunity to pin what he called 'an unheard of, illegal thing' on Carafa.[60] Undoubtedly Carafa and his allies had some kind of impact on Pole's candidacy, but there is another more complicated, more political, and more inclusive explanation of what happened on 5 December. Had Pole received one more vote, any one of several schemes would have guaranteed his election, not including an Imperialist (or more likely Farnese) trick by which it was claimed that a candidate who came within one vote could have a free one![61]

The roster of possible suspects for the missing vote is long, but worth attention as a demonstration of the relatively small role Carafa played.[62] It also underlines the importance of the recent deaths of *spirituali* among the cardinals. The simplest plot, recorded by Ludovico Beccadelli and corroborated by other sources, probably had nothing to do with Carafa. It would have had del Monte publicly switch to Pole, and he was one of the cardinals least likely to be affected by Carafa's attack.[63] The blame in this case might attach to an unsuspected villain, Priuli. According to one source, Farnese had gotten a promise from del Monte and Cervini to accede to Pole,

---

[58] Simoncelli (*Caso*, pp. 70-1) discovered that Carafa had prepared his ground carefully, but missed many of the steps in his campaign, including the use of *processi*, which Simoncelli thought to be new in 1555.

[59] ASF:AMP, 395, fo. 22r and 3463a, fos 88v-92v (cf. *Legazion*i, p. 215); Muzio, p. 109; and *CT*, 2, pp. 47n and 530.

[60] Druffel, no. 362, p. 329. Muzio (p. 114) noted that some cardinals had been said to have brought in writings damaging to Pole, but did not name Carafa, as Firpo (*Inquisizione romana*, p. 196) appears to make him say.

[61] *CT*, 2, p. 50 (Maffei). For another scenario, see, *e.g.*, ASF:AMP, 613, fo. 143v.

[62] For the most comprehensive list, see ASF:AMP, 3463a, fos 98r-100v.

[63] *MMB*, 1:2, p. 306 and Druffel, no. 352, p. 311n.

but Cervini would do so only after del Monte had already risen. Priuli failed to visit del Monte during the night, and he was so put off by this *salvaticheza* that he changed his mind about voting for Pole.[64] Priuli might of course have been following Pole's resolve not to do anything to forward his candidacy, and he may also have thought so little of these 'external ceremonies' that it did not matter whether Pole was actually elected pope, but even this politically-inclined anonymous analyst thought a mere visit would have sufficed to hold del Monte's vote.[65]

'Stella's diary' inculpated Verallo for breaking a promise to vote for Pole.[66] Another contemporary source precisely supports this claim, which also appeared in Bernardo Segni's *Istorie fiorentine*, written shortly afterwards.[67] From the first Verallo probably tried to sell his vote.[68] Another leading suspect for the missing vote is Innocenzo Cibo, who had any number of reasons for opposing Pole, including his wealth, ambitions, role as defender of the *libertà d'Italia*, plain orneriness, and, perhaps, stupidity.[69] In a letter to Cosimo, Cibo explained that he had stopped voting for Pole after he had once gained twenty-four votes and an accession, but had failed to gain either Gaddi or del Monte 'in the morning', which seems to be a reference to 5 December.[70]

One person accused of having failed to vote for Pole, Alvarez, probably is not guilty, and may even have largely been responsible for Pole having as much success as he did.[71] Before the vote he approached Pole privately and asked him to defend himself against the charge of heresy. Pole refused to do so in public, at least not before the accuser made himself known. Once he did, Pole hoped that God would punish him for his lies. Pole convinced Alvarez of his innocence.[72] Even more, according to 'Stella' Alvarez refused de Cupis's

---

[64] BAV, Urb. lat. 845, fos 172v–4v (Druffel, no. 352, p. 311n).

[65] Cf. Maffei in *CT*, 2, p. 51. For Priuli's alleged views, see the possibly entirely unreliable testimony of Lorenzo Davidico in Dario Marcatto, *Il processo inquisitoriale di Lorenzo Davidico (1555–1560). Edizione critica* (Florence: Olschki, 1992), pp. 117–18.

[66] 'Unknown diary', p. 357.

[67] ASF:AMP, 395, fo. 99r and Bernardo Segni, *Istorie fiorentine dall'anno MDXXVII al MDLV*, ed. G. L. Gargani (Florence: Barbera, Bianchi, 1857), p. 483.

[68] ASF:AMP, 613, fo. 140r and Druffel, nos 359 and 361.

[69] Druffel, no. 352; *CT*, 2, p. 48; and ASF:AMP, 3463a, fos 94v–8r and 3969, no. 36.

[70] ASF:AMP, 611, fos 2r–3r.

[71] ASF:AMP, 613, fo. 143r; ASF:AMP, 3463a, fos 102r–5r (*Legazioni*, pp. 221–2); *CT*, 2, pp. 972–3; Archivio di stato, Parma, Archivio Gonzaga di Guastalla, 42/6 (1548-50), fos 7r–8r; ASF:AMP, 611, fos 73r–4r. 'Unknown diary', p. 357 also exculpated Alvarez. Buonanni sent Cosimo both an affidavit signed by three cardinals attesting that Alvarez had voted for Pole on 5 December and his own certificate listing all of Alvarez's votes up to that point. ASF:AMP, 613, fos 172r and 173r. Paolo Simoncelli, 'Diplomazia e politica religiosa nella chiesa della Controriforma', *Rivista di storia e letteratura religiosa*, 18 (1982), pp. 415–60, p. 432 missed Pole's exoneration of Alvarez, although citing a passage of the 'Apologia' very nearby.

[72] *CT*, 2, p. 47.

blandishments designed to induce him to stand himself, instead, and best of all, as we have seen, he cooperated with Pole to bring de Cupis to hold an election. Thus when Pole himself later cleared Alvarez, we can believe him.[73] So much for the conspiracy of inquisitors.

Yet more significance may attach to Alvarez's action. Even if de Cupis remained opposed to Pole, the symbolic value of the dean of the college of cardinals appearing together with Pole and Alvarez could have been enormous. Some commentators thought that the French might have gone over to Pole if del Monte had voted for him, thereby averting a schism, and it could be that a few French votes came loose anyway after Alvarez manipulated de Cupis, only to be offset by the defection of Farnese rebels.[74] The French votes very likely included d'Armagnac's, which he reportedly had promised to Paul when Pole, said to be d'Armagnac's great friend, reached twenty-seven.[75] If there is anything to this supposition about the French, it dents the leading alternative interpretation of 5 December as a victory for the Francophile party. Instead, the scene of De Cupis, Alvarez and Pole together highlights the contradictions internal to the reform tendency, and the degree to which it harmed itself. De Cupis, Alvarez, Pole (and, of course, Carafa), all with equally strong reforming credentials, fought one another to the brink of fiasco. But I must stress 'to the brink'. The die might have been cast on 5 December, but if so it landed on a corner.

Alvarez may not bear responsibility for Pole's failure on 5 December, but he caused a major crack in the imperial front just after that, even if it is a little difficult to be certain when and why. The discovery that Pole had once voted for Morone, d'Armagnac and Maffei so scandalized Alvarez that he drew up two ballots of his own, one naming Pole and the other Morone, and left it to chance which he submitted. Morone came up on top.[76] Pole had cast the offending ballot on 7 December.[77] Another Florentine reporter in the conclave, Pedro de Toledo, claimed that Alvarez had not voted for Pole in the fifth and sixth scrutinies, that is on 7 and 8 December, which squares with Buonanni's certificate of 7 January.[78] On 15 December it was reported that Alvarez had voted for Pole through the first five scrutinies, to the best of Buonanni's recollection.[79] Both Alvarez and later Juan de Ayala confronted

---

[73] Ignacio Tellechea Idigoras, 'Pole y Paolo IV. Una celebre apología inedita del cardenal Inglés (1557)', *Archivum historiae pontificiae*, 4 (1966), pp. 105-54, p. 140.
[74] See above all ASF:AMP, 3969 no. 33 and 3268, fo. 637r.
[75] ASF:AMP, 3463a, fos 98r–100v, but cf. 395, fo. 155v and Muzio, p. 116.
[76] ASF:AMP, 613, fo. 143r. According to Antonio Caracciolo, Carafa exposed Pole's ballot. BPP, MS pal. 638, fo. 153r.
[77] *CT*, 2, p. 50.
[78] ASF:AMP, 3969, no. 26 and 613, fo. 173r.
[79] ASF:AMP, 613, fo. 143r.

The Conclave of Julius III and Cardinal Pole 13

Pole about his votes, and he satisfied both, Alvarez by promising never again to vote for d'Armagnac or Maffei, or at least convincing Alvarez that his motives were pure.[80] The Florentine ambassador, Averardo Serristori, told a different tale of Alvarez's motives, reporting that he had decided that Pole had no chance and that Farnese should therefore switch to him.[81] It may also be that Alvarez got his back up about this time because of his enemy Pacheco's arrival.[82]

Alvarez had help, in a manner which might at first seem to restore some credence to the theory that blames Pole's 'bust' on the Inquisition. Cervini, who although declaring himself neutral before the voting of 5 December had none the less gladly gone as an ambassador to the French in order to get them to come to an election, like Alvarez announced that Pole's ballot of the 7th had scandalized him, and it apparently helped to trigger other attacks on Pole as unskilled in governing, too young, a foreigner, and a heretic.[83] Basing himself on a retroactive interpretation of the failure of 5 December as God's will, Cervini said that he thought Pole unelectable and could not vote for him sincerely. This may sound like a convenient excuse to cover complicated machinations, but that possibility turns out to be irrelevant. Despite his long rationalization, Cervini never the less cast his ballot for Pole.[84] Over the course of the next few days, as Pole failed several more times, Massarelli, Cervini's conclavist, noted that Cervini slowly changed his mind, but this turns out to have been wishful thinking on Massarelli's part, or perhaps a reconstruction after the fact. Otto Truchsess's conclavist dated the beginning of Cervini's tergiversations to the aftermath of 5 December.[85]

During the rest of the first half of the month the campaign against Pole directed by de Cupis and Carafa recycled the familiar charges, and Pole bore them stolidly.[86] On 11 December he tried to make a concession speech, thanking the cardinals for the honor done him, confessing himself not up to the task, and asking them to vote for someone else. The longer the delay, the more certain it was that the Holy Spirit had not chosen him. Some replied that he was not at liberty to stand down, and two days later Cervini not only acceded to Pole, but gave an oration praising him (only to turn around a few days later and rejoin the opposition).[87] Just as Pole gained the important support of one of

---

[80] *CT*, 2, p. 50. For Alvarez, see, *e.g.*, ASF:AMP, 3969, no. 26, and 613, fo. 173r.
[81] ASF:AMP, 3463a, fos 102r–5r.
[82] ASF:AMP, 3463a, fos 98r–100v. For Alvarez's and Pacheco's enmity, *e.g. Algunas cartas*, pp. 156-60.
[83] *CT*, 2, p. 51.
[84] *CT*, 2, pp. 44, 50 and 51.
[85] *CT*, 2, p. 973.
[86] Druffel, no. 357, pp. 318-9.
[87] ASVe:APR, 7, fos 137r–8v (*CSPV*, 5, no. 599); Druffel, no. 360, pp. 325-6.

the other consciences of the college, he lost the votes of Verallo, Tiberio Crispi, and probably most important, Capodiferro.[88] The biggest change, however, was the deadlock produced by the arrival of more French cardinals. Pole might yet have been able to count on one of them, his old friend Jean du Bellay, although another imperial observer judged that du Bellay, while personally well-inclined to Pole, threw him his support only as a means of undermining the imperial party.[89] Bellay had earlier had a very high opinion of Pole, according to Pole's brother Sir Geoffrey, intervening on his behalf with Henry VIII, perhaps in 1538, and praising Pole in the strongest terms, writing to the effect that 'all men were but shades in comparison of him' and claiming that Pole was always ready to excuse Henry.[90] Mendoza, faced with this new sit-uation, assured the emperor that if Pole were elected and a schism resulted, that at least the imperialists had taken the spiritual high ground.[91] One thing is clear: the French had confused everything. Two observers on the imperial side disagreed wildly about what they wanted. Toledo thought the French so feared Pole that they had offered their votes to Alvarez in order to block him. This fantastic scheme is not much stranger than Mendoza's report that the French had no instructions to reject Pole, whom they liked because he lived like them 'in the Holy Spirit'.[92] In any case, obstinacy was the order of the day, as in the amusing duet between Cardinals de Cupis and Truchsess, each blaming the other camp and threatening to elect their own candidate, whatever the other side wished.[93]

In mid-December Carafa's run began, the French resolving 'let us oppose a saint to a saint (*opponamus sanctum sancto*)', as Dandolo put it.[94] Despite the continuing resolve of the imperialists not to veer from Pole, Farnese acceded to Cardinal Guise about the time Carafa began to stand, which threatened to throw all into even greater confusion and angered many of the imperialists.[95] Guise and Farnese, who together dominated the conclave, were up to something, perhaps a plot to abandon Pole.[96] Their scheme included the long visit Guise paid to Pole on 16 or 17 December, which happened to be

---

[88] ASF:AMP, 3268, fo. 508 and 395, fo. 155r.
[89] Druffel, no. 360.
[90] PRO, SP 1/139, fo. 7r–v (J. S. Brewer, *et al.*, eds, *Letters and papers, foreign and domestic of the reign of Henry VIII* [London: HMSO, 1862–1932; 32 vols], 13:2, no. 822).
[91] Druffel, pp. 319–24, but the citation to Ribier which Druffel gave in support of Mendoza's claim says nothing about an alleged permission from Henry II to du Bellay.
[92] ASF:AMP, 3969, no. 36.
[93] *CT*, 2, p. 69.
[94] ASVe:APR, 7, fo. 147r (not in *CSPV*). Cf. 'Unknown diary', p. 358.
[95] Druffel, no. 361; cf. 'Unknown diary', p. 359, and *CT*, 2, pp. 62–4.
[96] *CT*, 2, p. 62 but cf. ASF:AMP, 3969, nos 29–30.

the time Carafa's vote total shot up.⁹⁷ Guise, probably responding to an overture from the imperial camp on Pole's behalf, found Pole in the Capella paolina, and broached four topics with him.⁹⁸ First, he apologized for not having talked to him before, explaining that he had not wished to annoy the cardinals opposed to Pole's election. Second, he congratulated Pole on his success. Third, he expressed sorrow that Pole's opponents doubted his orthodoxy, citing as evidence his withdrawal from Trent in order to avoid the conclusion of the decree on justification, which meant either that he disagreed with the majority of the council, or wished to avoid displeasing the emperor. Finally, Guise went beyond this veiled attack and got to the point. Since Pole was not fit to govern the temporalities of the church, he should withdraw from the running. Pole replied with compliments to Guise's first two points, and answered the second two together. His first response to doubts about his actions at Trent was to liken himself to Christ who had similarly suffered from untrue allegations, and then added later that he had left only for reasons of health, which still bothered him, as was 'notorious'. In between, he said that only God could decide whether he could govern the church. However close Pole and Carafa may have come to speaking the same language, Pole and Guise seemed to have no points of contact beyond the forms of courtesy. Despite attempts to keep this meeting secret, Guise's main accusation had already been made public, as he acknowledged, perhaps referring to Carafa's speech. On 16 December Ayala related Pole's difficulties directly to several developments in the French camp, and to Pole's reactions. Pole, he wrote, had been brought down by charges of heresy, failing to vote for himself, and, implicitly, by cardinal du Bellay's refusal to follow through on his convictions and back Pole.⁹⁹

A week after his French-supported candidacy began, Carafa tried a fairly naked ploy. On 22 December he gave a speech in which he thanked the cardinals for their votes, and suggested that they turn to someone else who

---

⁹⁷ *CT*, 2, pp. 62–4 and ASF:AMP, 613, fos 155r-6r. Dermot Fenlon, *Heresy and obedience in Tridentine Italy: cardinal Pole and the counter reformation* (Cambridge: Cambridge University Press, 1972), p. 135 says that Guise accused Pole of having abandoned Trent for doctrinal reasons, drawing the charge from Morandi's notes to Beccadelli. Morandi (*MMB*, 1:2, p.303n) cited Maffei's diary as published by Gregorio Leti in *Conclave nel quale fu Creato Papa il Cardinale de Monti detto poi Giulio Terzo* in *Conclave dei pontefici romani* (Geneva: De Tournes, 1667; cf. Franco Barcia, *Bibliografia delle opere di Gregorio Leti* [Milan: Franco Angeli, 1981], p. 127) but this gave Tournon as Pole's attacker and said nothing about Guise. Tournon is a result of textual corruption. Maffei had written 'Theatinus', that is, Carafa. BAV, Vat. lat. 12526, fo. 172r and cf. *CT*, 2, p. XXVIII. Gualteri (*CT*, 2, p. 64), however, had blamed Guise. Pastor (p. 22) made this meeting an open attack on Pole's orthodoxy and called it similar to the stormy scene of 22 December. Frederick Baumgartner, 'Henry II and the papal conclave of 1549', *Sixteenth century journal*, 16 (1985), pp. 301–14, p. 307 does not notice this episode.
⁹⁸ *CT*, 2, pp. 60 and 62.
⁹⁹ Druffel, no. 360.

could be elected.¹⁰⁰ Although Carafa did not mention Pole by name, he immediately rose to reply. His words survive in multiple versions.¹⁰¹ Of these, 'Stella's' seems a virtual transcription, which perhaps deserves pride of place.¹⁰² Carafa had charged that some candidates enjoyed running even though they had no chance, and Pole took that as a reference to him, 'finding myself in the same boat, one might say'. Pole praised Carafa's stress on the scandal arising from delay, and assured him that he had tried to persuade Farnese to adopt another candidate. De Cupis's charge that he had engaged in electioneering stung Pole, and Pole had then warned Farnese that he refused to have anything to do with such *pratiche*. It seems as if Pole had the attempted adoration in mind, because he insisted that he would come to the papacy only through 'the door'. If it seemed God's will, he would immediately withdraw his candidacy. Pole might have laughed at Carafa's surprise attack on him earlier in December, but his tone this time was personal and in 'Stella's' rendering narrowly political. Pole chose to respond almost exclusively to charges that his party had engaged in electioneering. 'Stella's' version highlights how Pole took Carafa's criticisms of his orthodoxy as direct attacks on himself, not a matter of mere theological debate. 'Stella's' text also reveals a degree of impatience on Pole's part, as if he resented the fact that he had to deal again with a problem he thought solved. To judge from 'Stella's' version, Carafa must have stung Pole quite badly. And he continued to try to make trouble, brandishing another *processo* accusing Pole of keeping heretics in his house, doubtless a reference to Marcantonio Flaminio.¹⁰³

After the excitement of the 22nd, very little happened for several weeks. The equality between the two camps led to continued efforts to strike a compromise, including at the very highest level. Mendoza several times asked the emperor to approach Henry II about Pole, but Charles refused.¹⁰⁴ Things had come to such a pass that even the bettors began to make ridiculous wagers, including on Adriano Castellesi, a cardinal who had died in 1521 (although his body had never been found).¹⁰⁵ As one conclavist put the situation by late December, 'every day in order to pass the time they canvas [*scrotiniano*] England [Pole] and the Theatine [Carafa]'.¹⁰⁶ Informants on the scene were

---

¹⁰⁰ 'Unknown diary', pp. 347 and 359-60.
¹⁰¹ ASF:AMP, 613, fo. 161r-v; *CT*, 2, p. 71; ASM:AG, 888, fos 425r-29v; BPP, MS pal. 638, fo. 152v; ASVe:APR, 7, fos 150r and 152v (*CSPV*, 5, nos. 603-4); *CSPSp*, 10, pp. 14-16.
¹⁰² 'Unknown diary', pp. 359-60. This summary supports–if it is not the origin of–Beccadelli's claim that neither Pole nor his backers ever made any effort to have him elected. *MMB*, 1:2, p. 303 and *ERP*, 1, p. 21 for Dudic.
¹⁰³ 'Unknown diary', p. 361.
¹⁰⁴ *E.g.*, *Algunas cartas*, pp. 152-4; *CT*, 11, no. 401B and p. 532n; and Druffel, no. 371.
¹⁰⁵ ASF:AMP, 395, fo. 269r-v.
¹⁰⁶ ASVe:APR, 7, fo. 165r.

reduced to writing 'bible'-sized letters for lack of anything better to do.[107] Conclavists not only engaged in dress-up, but played a practical joke on the cardinals by locking them in a loggia, whence they had to be rescued with the master of ceremony's spare key.[108]

By mid-January, many observers had given up on Pole, despite an uproar in the Borgo on the 13th generated by rumors of his election.[109] De Cupis then tried a similar maneuver to Carafa's veiled suggestion that Pole cease to stand, offering his vote and all those he controlled for a quick election. Pole urged the cardinals to the same end, but he could dispose only of his own vote, since those he had been given were not his to release.[110] One of the votes he looked most likely to lose was della Rovere's.[111] Pole, allegedly so far above the fray, responded with an impressive piece of timing. He dedicated his dialogue 'De summo pontifice', which cast della Rovere as the questioner, to him on 20 January 1550. This happens to have been the moment of heaviest pressure on della Rovere to desert the Imperial party and switch to Carafa, an effort in which Carafa took direct part. 'Stella' wrote that de Cupis had expected della Rovere's vote already on 17 January, and according to two reports to Mantua, Carafa shortly thereafter went to work on della Rovere, until he agreed to vote for Carafa only when he was missing one vote, at which point Carafa gave up.[112] That was because Carafa needed della Rovere, not to put himself over the top, but to break the Imperial front in the first place. By keeping della Rovere's vote safe, Pole once more bested Carafa. The dedication was a thinly veiled piece of both flattery and strict admonition to the fourteen- (or maybe sixteen-) year-old della Rovere. It cannot be an accident that Pole several times noted that he had showed the work to della Rovere's uncle Cardinal Gonzaga, both reminding della Rovere that he was supposed to follow his uncle's lead and also perhaps giving Gonzaga a subtle hint to keep della Rovere in line. Pole had known della Rovere before the conclave, and they spent time during it discussing topics including the best pope.[113]

A Mantuan agent, Gianfrancesco Arrivabene, had della Rovere give a generally very good account of himself, apparently on the basis of a report from Endimio Calandra, whom Arrivabene called della Rovere's *commensale*

---

[107] ASF:AMP, 3268, fo. 539r–v.
[108] ASVe:APR, 7, fo. 168v (*CSPV*, 5, no. 618).
[109] ASF:AMP, 3268, fos 579r–80r and ASS:AB, b. 721, no. 15.
[110] ASS:AB, b. 721, no. 14.
[111] ASF:AMP, 3969, no. 22.
[112] 'Unknown diary', p. 365; ASM:AG, 888, fos 460r–61v and 485r–7v; and ASF:AMP, 3969, fos 11r–12r.
[113] *CRP*, nos 554, 576 and 559. Another version of 'De summo pontifice', described as *extra conclavi scripta*, begins with effusive thanks from della Rovere to Pole for his *paternam ac singularem tuam erga me benevolenciam dum in conclavi essemus* (BAV, Vat. lat. 5965.1, fo. 1br).

and who was also one of Gonzaga's conclavists.[114] On 12 November 1549 Cardinal Gonzaga had reported to his brother Ferrante that he had asked the duke of Urbino, della Rovere's brother, to order della Rovere to follow his (Gonzaga's) orders.[115] Some observers, for example Serristori and Toledo, expected him to follow Gonzaga's lead implicitly, while worrying that he would not without a little encouragement from time to time.[116] That Gonzaga thought it necessary to engage della Rovere's brother the duke's mediation suggests that their fears were justified.

Perhaps drawing on the confidence engendered by this victory over Carafa, shortly thereafter on 30 January, Pole confronted him in his cell, and according to both Pole and 'Stella', they emerged, in 'Stella's' words, 'reconciled and satisfied (*reconciliati et satisfatti*)'. (It is possible that 'Stella' meant a different meeting than Pole did, since he reported another agenda than Pole: Flaminio.)[117] We should by now suspect that there were important political implications to this conference, whatever the topics discussed. Its timing underscores an apparent French opening to Pole, orchestrated by du Bellay as a reply to Guise's insistence that the French cardinals swear never to vote for Pole.[118] Guise and du Bellay were on opposite sides of the French factional wars, and each move by one provoked a reaction from the other. Du Bellay had a bloc of at least five cardinals including himself.[119] According to Buonanni on 3 January he had it from a highly-placed source that some thought that the French had not excluded Pole and it might prove easy to elect him.[120] On the 8th he amplified that to read that du Bellay was spreading this news.[121] Toledo said a week later that du Bellay had written a letter to Mendoza to that effect, and Ayala had shown it to some cardinals (although apparently Toledo himself had not seen it).[122] Du Bellay, adopting Mendoza's line of trying for a high-level agreement between Henry and Charles, was cooperating with Montmorency, who was said to wish for any pope who could bring peace.[123] Guise responded by asserting that Farnese could control his votes only as long as he backed Pole (a report directly confirmed by another observer on 17 January), an attempt to bring the Farnese-Imperial faction to abandon Pole.[124]

---

[114] ASM:AG, 888, fo. 483r.
[115] ASM:AG, 1918, fos 455r-9v.
[116] ASF:AMP, 395, fo. 22r and ASF:AMP, 3463a, fos 94v-8r.
[117] 'Unknown diary', p. 366.
[118] ASVe:APR, 7, fo. 170v (*CSPV*, 5, no. 621).
[119] ASF:AMP, 613, fo. 185r and cf. fo. 175v. ASF:AMP, 3969, fos 11r-12v; Druffel, no. 383, p. 349.
[120] ASF:AMP, 644, fo. 411r-v.
[121] ASF:AMP, 613, fo. 175v.
[122] ASF:AMP, 3969, fos 15r?-16*v.
[123] *Ibid.* and ASF:AMP, 395, fo. 369v together with Druffel, no. 381.
[124] ASF:AMP, 395, fo. 369v and 3268, fo. 596.

At the end of the month, the possibility of a French rapprochement arose again, according to the Florentine bishop Gianbattista Ricasoli, one of the guardians of the conclave.¹²⁵ For three days, he said, the French had 'not fled' from Pole because Pietro Carnesecchi had written from the French court that he was 'not abhorred' (*non abhorrito*) and even venerated there. More important, Ricasoli also thought Montmorency had written in Pole's favor, news apparently confirmed by Cosimo's secretariate.¹²⁶ Then again, Simon Renard later said that Montmorency had told him that Pole was unconditionally rejected.¹²⁷ The French cardinals were none the less worried enough about Carnesecchi's actions on Pole's behalf to have Carnesecchi's four-year-old *processo* exhumed and sent to France in order to undermine him at the court.¹²⁸ Guise steadfastly refused to consider Pole. Despite this, his name continued to be proposed in negotiations between the two factions until almost the end.

The conclusion of the conclave depended in part on Pole's actions. On 26 January it was decided to elect deputies for its reform, including Pole.¹²⁹ Their proposals, originally sketched by de Cupis, included expelling officials (especially secretaries) of secular princes serving as conclavists and reducing their number substantially, as well as reducing the cardinal's rations (which took almost a week to implement).¹³⁰ The cardinals were to return to their original cells, unless they were ill, in which case they could have one of the usual infirmary cells. No more than three persons were allowed in a cell at once, nor could cardinals eat with another cardinal, nor send anything from the serving dishes to anyone except their own conclavists. They could not leave their cells between five at night and dawn. None were to have secret talks. No one was to leave or enter the conclave except for canonical reasons. Arrangements for bringing in food were tightened up, and no one was to open windows unless two deputies were present. Writings could be sent only through the hands of the master of ceremonies or his clerics. No one was to

---

[125] Ricasoli had earlier been said to be deep in the counsels of Salviati's backers, so he might have had better contacts in the French camp than most other imperial observers. ASF:AMP, 395, fo. 22r and 3268, fos 566r–8v.

[126] ASF:AMP, 3268, fo. 637r. Cf. ASF:AMP, 13, fos 324r–9v and 395, fos 521r and 547r. Oddone Ortolani, *Per la storia della vita religiosa italiana nel Cinquecento. Pietro Carnesecchi* (Florence: Le Monnier, 1963), p. 73 claimed Giacomo Manzoni, ed., 'Il processo Carnesecchi', *Miscellanea di storia italiana*, 10 (1870), pp. 189–573, pp. 359–60 corroborated Carnesecchi's role, but Carnesecchi merely said that he had talked to the Grand Chancellor (whose name he remembered as Oliviero) at some point during a *sede vacante*, and that the Chancellor thought well of Pole. François Olivier was Grand Chancellor in 1549. Ribier, 2, pp. 236–40.

[127] *CSPSp*, 10, pp. 21–3.

[128] ASF:AMP, 3268, fos 593r–4v.

[129] *CT*, 2, pp. 107–9 and 'Unknown diary', p. 366. Cf. ASF:AMP, 644, fo. 425r; 3268, fos 631r–3v and 638; ASS:AB, b. 721, no. 31; *CSPV*, 5, no. 635; and ASF:AMP, 395, fo. 701r–v.

[130] *CT*, 2, pp. 113–14 and cf. 115–21.

have anything to do with those outside the doors except the prelates appointed to guard the conclave. In short, the conclave's constant communication with the outside was to be severely reduced if not cut off, and political intrigues were to be made impossible within it.

On 2 February 'Stella' noted two odd events. First, he wrote that Pole had come away from a ballot in the morning 'when he should have been created pope' relieved that there would be no pope that day. Second, a gentleman had come into the conclave claiming that Pole was a heretic who pretended to be a good man.[131] There is very little evidence to clarify this mysterious entry, save perhaps Arrivabene's note that Pole was recovering in the wagers on 4 February.[132] Two days later Arrivabene sent in a most interesting report on Pole's behavior, his difficulties, and the other cardinals' attitude to him. He was 'revered most of all', and the master of ceremonies identified only him and a few others as *reverendissimo* when reading the ballots. Pole rose at midnight in order to study and write, and 'lives angelically and with the appearance of infinite peace of mind'. He had three problems: heresy, incompetence in governing, and the likelihood that he would give the states of the church to the emperor. Pole had defended himself against the first two charges by referring to his works (perhaps not the most convincing rejoinder to the second), and as for alienating church property, no one could think him so impious as to try to give the emperor anything he had never given the church. Finally, it sounds as if Pole had rehearsed the central argument of 'De summo pontifice' in discussing the requisites of the 'complete prince'. No one in the conclave, said Pole, was fit to govern, all were 'weak and imperfect'. He concluded, according to Arrivabene, by affirming that he had never done anything except God's will.[133] Judging from this dispatch, Pole's chances might have appeared still to be very good.

In fact, they were dead. Almost as soon as Arrivabene sent his letter, del Monte was elected pope.[134] 'Stella' first recounted the horse-trading on 6 February between Guise and Farnese, and then Cardinal Durante's visit to Pole to ask his approval of their plan. Farnese himself came to accompany Pole to the Paolina where a rump, missing the imperialist leaders, agreed to the election.[135] Afterwards, as the cardinals made reverence to the new pope, Julius III, he singled Pole out for a special, tearful embrace.[136] The next

---

[131] 'Unknown diary', p. 368.
[132] ASM:AG, b. 888, fo. 481.
[133] *Ibid.*, fos 485r–7v.
[134] Ribier, 2, p. 264; ASF:AMP, 621, fo. 206v; ASVe:APR, 7, fos 205r–6r; ASM:AG, b. 888, fo. 493r; *Algunas cartas*, pp. 194–7.
[135] 'Unknown diary', pp. 368–70.
[136] Massarelli said Julius cried through the whole ceremony and did not note any distinctive treatment of Pole. *CT*, 2, p. 142.

morning the election was carried out in somewhat peculiar fashion, a sort of cross between a ballot and an adoration. The cardinals then once more made their obedience, filing past Julius and kissing his foot. 'Stella' said nothing of any special treatment for Pole at this moment, which makes it appear that Beccadelli and Andras Dudic confused it with that of the previous night in their dramatic account of the new pope raising Pole up and embracing him.[137] In any case, this treatment was pretty generally meted out, including to Dandolo and Mendoza.[138]

A conflicted conclave, dominated by political contingencies. It turns on the self-destruction of the reform tendency. The fault lines within it still need full mapping, but one clear fracture runs throughout, between Pole and Carafa. Pole's disdain for Carafa is as clear as Carafa's certainty that Pole was a dangerous heretic. And here lay the rub. It has been argued that while Pole could only with difficulty cover his dislike of Carafa with an ideological and political blanket, Carafa could not only do that with ease, but also rally a party to his banner of orthodoxy.[139] Since he also had the institutional machinery of the Inquisition on his side, Carafa could put Pole and his 'party', largely founded on personal and therefore unstable relationships, at a marked disadvantage. Although much of this is getting ahead of the story, it holds true to some degree already in 1549–50. Had Carafa been elected, the Inquisition would have been unleashed. Had Pole won, it might have been brought almost to a full stop. Inquisition or no inquisition, Pole's defeat marked the last moment at which a rapprochement with the Protestants might have occurred, the real loss the reform tendency brought on itself and Europe.

---

[137] *MMB*, 1:2, p. 306 and *ERP*, 1, p. 25.
[138] ASVe:APR, 7, fos 207v and 210v.
[139] Firpo, *Inquisizione romana*, pp. 252 and 305–6.

V

An Unknown Diary of Julius III's Conclave by Bartolomeo Stella, a Servant of Cardinal Pole

THOMAS F. MAYER

PETER E. STARENKO

The conclave of Julius III, one of the longest in history, was also one of the leakiest.[1] Despite constant protests from within and without, a steady deluge of information poured out from both conclavists and cardinals, when outside agents did not themselves obtain entry to the conclave.[2] In addition, at least

---

[1] C. DE LEVA, Storia documentata di Carlo V in correlazione all'Italia, 5 vols. Venice, 1869-95, 5, 63-93 (another version in: RSI 1 [1884] 632-53); L. VON PASTOR, Geschichte der Päpste im Zeitalter der katholischen Reformation und Restauration 6, Freiburg, 1923, 5-44 (done almost completely from Angelo Massarelli's diary); G. CONSTANT, Une rivalité Franco-Allemande en conclave d'election de Jules III, in: Revue hebdomadaire (18 February 1922) 333ff.; G. MÜLLER, Die Kandidatur Giovanni Salviatis im Konklave 1549/50. Zwei Briefe Pietro Bertanos vom Hof Karl V, in: QFIAB 42 (1963) 435-52; D. FENLON, Heresy and Obedience in Tridentine Italy. Cardinal Pole and the Counter Reformation, Cambridge, 1972, 226-34; E. SPIVAKOVSKY, Son of the Alhambra. Diego Hurtado Mendoza, 1504-75, Austin, Texas, 1970, chapt. 10; F. BAUMGARTNER, Henry II and the Papal Conclave of 1549, in: SCJ 16 (1985) 301-14. An NEH Fellowship at Villa I Tatti: The Harvard University Center for Italian Renaissance Studies made possible some of the research for this article.

[2] I have used the following ambassadors' reports: Matteo Dandolo (Venice, calendared in part in CSPV); Gianfrancesco Arrivabene and Alessandro Palombo (Mantova); Diego Hurtado de Mendoza, Charles V's agent (partly calendared in Calendar of Letters, Despatches, and State Papers relating to the Negotiations between England and Spain, vol. 9, hg. v. M. HUME – R. TYLER, London, 1912 and mainly printed in A. VÁZQUEZ – R. ROSE (Hg.), Algunas Cartas de Don Diego Hurtado Mendoza, 1538-1552, New Haven, 1935); Claude d'Urfé, Henry II's agent (printed in G. RIBIER, Lettres et Memoires D'Estat, Des Roys, Princes, Ambassadeurs, Et autres Ministres, sous les Regnes de François premier, Henry II et François II, Paris, 1666, vol. 2); Scipione Gabbrielle (Siena); Averardo Serristori, Gianbattista Ricasoli, Nofri Camaiano, Agostino d'Angulo, Antonio Guiducci, Pedro de Toledo (probably the son of Cosimo I's brother-in-law the viceroy of Naples, also named Pedro, for whom a very full dossier of reports survives) et al. (Florence). The Florentine reports include the invaluable and nearly complete series of bulletins from Benedetto Buonanni, secretary of the legation in Rome, who was in the conclave and whose

five conclavists kept diaries, mainly printed in CT: Antonio Massarelli, conclavist of Marcello Cardinal Cervini, the longest and most widely cited diary; Bernardino Cardinal Maffei; Luigi Firmani, the master of ceremonies; Sebastiano Gualteri, bishop of Viterbo and Alessandro Farnese's conclavist; and Pierpaolo Gualteri, who seems to have been no close relation of Sebastiano and was in the conclave as Maffei's conclavist (I cite his diary and not Sebastiano's below).[3] Three of these five diaries present a somewhat unflattering view of the candidacy of the early front-runner, Reginald Pole. It is therefore of great interest that a diary kept by Bartolomeo Stella, one of Pole's conclavists and a longtime intimate, has come to light. Catalogued at the end of the nineteenth century by Giuseppe Bonelli, the manuscript – Carte Stella in Archivio Silvestri 40/76 of the Biblioteca Civica, Bergamo – seems never to have been studied.[4]

Stella's is the only diary to emanate from the circle of a contender. Cervini, Massarelli's patron (and also Gualteri's at some point), was at center stage for much of the conclave and frequently mentioned as a suitable candidate, but he never had a serious chance because of Charles V's hostility. Maffei, apparently the only cardinal to keep a diary, was never a candidate. Apart from its *prima facie* importance arising from the circumstances under which it was written, Stella's text contains a good deal of information not to be had from other sources. For example, it offers a detailed account of Julius III's election and coronation, neither of which surviving diplomatic documents report well.[5] Perhaps most important, through both what it says and does not say Stella's journal provides a new perspective on Pole's relations with Gianpietro Caraffa, so often portrayed as an unequal duel between the saintly Pole and the personification of evil.[6]

---

letters Serristori usually merely forwarded. Pastor could not find them, to judge from his appendices. (My former student John Frymire and I are at work on an edition of this wonderful source.) The series of avvisi from Rome which begins immediately after Julius III's election is almost nonexistent during the conclave – I have found only one.

[3] See the discussion of sources in the introduction to CT 2. Sebastiano Gualteri was born in Orvieto and Pierpaolo in Arezzo. That would certainly not preclude close family ties, but none have come to light.

[4] G. BONELLI, Un archivio privato del Cinquecento: Le Carte Stella, in: ASL 34 (1907) 332-86.

[5] ASF:AMP 3463a, Serristori's register of letters from Rome, skips from 21 January to 24 (?) February, and all the other Florentine agents' correspondence has similar gaps. Dandolo's letter of 8 February is very summary (ASV:APR 7, fos. 205r-6r), as are Gabbrielle's of 8 and 9 February (ASS:ADB, nos. 43 and 45). There is no report at all in ASM:AG. For the diarists, cf. CT 2, 139-43.

[6] For a similar suggestion of the need for a re-reading of their relations on the basis of the celebrated "agape" at S. Paolo fuori le mura in 1553, see M. FIRPO, Inquisizione romana

In this more like Pole's second biographer Andras Dudic than his first Ludovico Beccadelli, Stella downplayed Caraffa's attacks on Pole's orthodoxy. He recorded nothing about Caraffa's opening salvo on 2 December, or an earlier whispering campaign, perhaps emanating from Caraffa. Gualteri noted that Caraffa was overheard casting aspersions on Pole's beliefs, and one of Cervini's nephews wrote on 2 December that a "processo" against Pole was being brandished in the conclave.[7] Diego Hurtado de Mendoza, the emperor's agent, reported on 5 December that Caraffa had openly attacked Pole on the 2d, but had been routed by Pole and his allies. Pole had replied partly by laughter and partly by treating Caraffa as a "loco."[8] Benedetto Buonanni (on 27 November, see below) and Averardo Serristori (respectively ambassador's secretary and ambassador of Cosimo) had already reported Pole's ill repute "della fede" on 30 November.[9] Again, Stella ignored the "bellissima oratione," a concession speech, which Matteo Dandolo, the Venetian ambassador, said Pole gave on 9 December.[10] Yet Stella virtually transcribed Pole's speech of 22 December in which he refused Caraffa's invitation to decline to stand in future *scrutinii*. Pole might have laughed at Caraffa's surprise attack on him earlier in December, but his tone this time was personal and in Stella's rendering, anyway, narrowly political. Pole responded almost entirely to charges that he had engaged in what the Venetians called *broglio*, electioneering. Stella's version highlights how Pole took Caraffa's criticisms of his orthodoxy as direct attacks on himself, not part of a mere theological debate. Stella's text also reveals a degree of impatience on Pole's part, as if he resented the fact that he had to deal with Caraffa again, a problem he thought already solved. Rebuked publicly earlier in the month and now again, Caraffa turned to disseminating reports of Pole's heresies through other means, according to Stella's entry of 26 December.

The need for a more careful assessment of the relations between Pole and Caraffa and their bearing on the conclave also arises from Stella's unique report of 30 January that Pole and Caraffa had closeted themselves for two hours, discussing Marcantonio Flaminio. Flaminio, one of Pole's closest allies (if that

---

e Controriforma. Studi sul Cardinal Giovanni Morone e il suo processo d'eresia, Bologna, 1992, 238-43, who yet tends to conform to the usual view of Caraffa.

[7] CT 2, 47n and 11, 530n. Memories of that processo were still fresh in the conclave of Paul IV. G. COGGIOLA, I Farnesi ed il Conclave di Paolo IV, in: Studi storici 9 (1900) 61-91, 203-27, 449-79 here 72. For Caraffa's attack see Antonio Caracciolo's life of Caraffa (partially quoted in M. FIRPO – D. MARCATTO (Hg.), Il processo inquisitoriale del Cardinal Giovanni Morone, 1, Rom 1981, 132-4).

[8] A. DRUFFEL, Beiträge zur Reichsgeschichte 1546-1551, München, 1873, no. 352; cf. HUME – TYLER, Calendar, 483.

[9] ASF:AMP 3463a, fo. 88v-92v (cf. Legazioni di Serristori, 215).

[10] Dispatch of 11 December (ASV:APR 7, fos. 136v-8r; CSPV 5, no. 599).

should not be put the other way around), would die just after the conclave with both Pole and Caraffa in attendance, Caraffa because he regarded Flaminio as the most heretical member of Pole's entourage.[11] Yet according to Stella anyway, Pole and Caraffa left their discussion "reconciliati et satisfatti." Especially in light of Stella's political reading of Pole's duel with Caraffa in December, there may well have been important political implications to this reconciliation. This story also closely parallels views about Flaminio and Pole which Caraffa expressed in 1553, which have usually been held to be insincere.[12] Caraffa had long received much – if soft – French support, which could mean that the timing of this reconciliation corroborates an apparent French opening to Pole, even though Stella said nothing of it. (His mysterious entry for 2 February about a messenger arriving to tell an unnamed cardinal that Pole was a heretic may have some connection to these events.)

Whatever Stella said or did not say about the French, he offered an otherwise not much noticed villain in place of Caraffa. Stella's story of the disappointment of 5 December assigned the blame for Pole's missing final vote to Girolamo Cardinal Verallo, whom Stella wrote had broken a promise to support Pole. Stella may have had this information from one of Verallo's conclavists, Latino Giovenale.[13] Various reporters put forward other culprits. Massarelli obliquely assigned the missing vote to Giulio del Monte, as did Beccadelli. Neither mentioned Verallo.[14] Mendoza thought the defector was Innocenzo Cibo.[15] Gualteri agreed with Mendoza, while apportioning a share of responsibility to cardinal Verulanus (Ennio Filonardi). It is thus remotely possible that Stella or Gualteri confused Filonardi's title with Verallo's surname.[16] Since Massarelli had earlier called Filonardi one of Pole's principal supporters and he

---

[11] M. FIRPO, Tra allumbrados e "spirituali". Studi su Juan de Valdés e il valdesianesimo nella crisi religiosa del '500 italiano, Florenz, 1990, passim.

[12] FIRPO, Inquisizione romana 240. The text is in MORANDI, I:2, 348-52.

[13] Latino Giovenale (or Juvenale) de' Manetti is only known to have been in the conclave as one of Cardinal Crispo's attendants, who did not survive the expulsion of superfluous *conclavisti* (ASF:AMP 3969, letters of Pedro de Toledo, Pedro de Toledo?-Cosimo, 22 December 1549 and CT 2, 125 and 128). Did Stella mean to say that Giovenale had earlier been one of Verallo's aides, referring to his defection in the phrase "dicono che latina [sic] iuvenale deserto verallo?" It certainly seems to have been possible for *conclavisti* to transfer their allegiance. Stella may have been privy to Giovenale's confidences because of an earlier association in Rome. For him see L. DOREZ, La cour du pape Paul III, 1, La cour pontificale, Paris, 1932, chapt. 3, which stops short of the conclave.

[14] CT 2, 46-7 and BPP MS 973/3, fo. 21v.

[15] DRUFFEL, Beiträge, no. 352.

[16] CT 2, 48.

was undoubtedly a leading member of the Imperial party (as was Cibo, in theory), the likelihood increases that Gualteri made a mistake.[17]

That Gualteri probably erred combined with other reports of Verallo's behavior tends to confirm Stella's account. One letter in particular, an anonymous account of 6 December sent to Florence, precisely supports Stella's claim.[18] For what it is worth, Bernardo Segni encapsulated Verallo's guilt in his brief account of the conclave.[19] Gualteri's judgment that Verallo's accession to Juan Alvarez, cardinal of Burgos on 8 December was a ploy to stop Pole suggests that Verallo at first played some kind of complicated game.[20] Many observers had considered him a distant possibility, and the ambassador of the duke of Urbino even called him one of Farnese's two horses.[21] Mendoza's agent Juan de Ayala later placed Verallo on a par with Caraffa in making trouble for Pole.[22] Whatever Verallo was up to, Massarelli assigned him to the anti-Pole camp on 11 December.[23] The next day Ricasoli named Verallo along with Capodiferro and Crispo as "rebellati da Farnese," and yet another Florentine, Nofri Camaiano, wrote that Farnese was very upset by Verallo's behavior.[24] Buonanni judged Crispo and Verallo lost by 13 December, Verallo having succumbed to a large bribe.[25] Pedro de Toledo, Cosimo's principal agent in the conclave, thought on December 14 that neither Verallo, Crispo, nor Cervini would vote for Pole under any circumstances.[26] By the 15th Verallo had come

---

[17] CT 2, 44. If Filonardi were the cardinal in question, his opposition to Pole may have had a similar root to de Cupis's: he had engaged in a protracted financial dispute with Stella which Pole had needed all his authority to resolve. ERP 2, nos 76 and 77. Carnesecchi certainly thought financial disputes made dangerous enemies (G. MANZONI, [Hg.], Il Processo Carnesecchi [= Miscellanea di storia italiana 10], Turin 1870, 189-573, here 462 and 472). For the general problem see B.M. HALLMAN, Italian Cardinals, Reform and the Church as Property, 1492-1563, Berkeley, 1985.

[18] ASF:AMP 395, fo. 99r, 6 December 1549.

[19] Bernardo Segni, Istorie Fiorentine dall'anno MDXXVII al MDLV, hg. v. G. GARGANI, Florence, 1857, 483.

[20] CT 2, 55 and ASF:AMP 3967, fo. [6v].

[21] ASF, Archivio di Urbino Cl. I G f. CXXIV, fos. 372r-6v, Paolo Mario to the duke of Urbino, 25 November 1549. Paolo Giovio's judgment of Verallo as "worthy of all good" but hedged in by dangers was not atypical. Giovio, Lettere, II, hg. v. G. FERRERO, Rom, 1958, no. 324.

[22] DRUFFEL, I, no. 357, pp. 318-9, Ayala-de Mendoza, before 13.12.49.

[23] CT 2, 55.

[24] ASF:AMP 3268, fo. 507 and ASF:AMP 395, fo. 155r.

[25] ASF:AMP 613, fos. 139r and 140v.

[26] ASF:AMP 3969, no. 36.

out in open opposition by acceding fulsomely to Caraffa.²⁷ Yet his position remained equivocal. Mendoza told Charles on 20 December that he had made a mistake in excluding Capodiferro, Verallo and Coria, all of whom were not his enemies (Mendoza explicitly contrasted them to del Monte and Caraffa who were), although the next day Buonanni aligned Verallo with Pole's hard-core opponents.²⁸ Massarelli judged on 26 December that Verallo was French, but had been bribed to join the Imperial ranks.²⁹ Ayala gave the size of his first bribe as 12,000 dineros.³⁰ And even Charles could hope to regain his support, instructing Mendoza to clarify what Farnese had written, since it might mean that the French would lose his vote.³¹ But Massarelli's label was inexact and Charles's hopes probably vain: other observers continued to call Verallo a Farnese rebel.³²

Perhaps Verallo's difficult experience as nuncio to the Emperor immediately before the conclave had something to do with his actions and attitude to an Imperial candidate like Pole.³³ Charles certainly excluded him from consideration from the outset.³⁴ Or he may be yet another cardinal with an economic grievance – Charles was holding up his very recent appointment to the bishopric of Capaccio –, as well as a position in the papal bureaucracy which he may have thought Pole threatened.³⁵ Verallo was a referendary of both *Segnature*, and Pole was alleged to have wished to dismantle both the papal chancellery and the penitentiary, and immediately after the conclave he was appointed to a commission for reform of the datary, the most sensitive organ of the papal financial bureaucracy.³⁶ The other scanty evidence about Verallo's allegiances

---

²⁷ CT 2, 60.

²⁸ Vásquez – Rose, Algunas Cartas 153; ASF:AMP 613, fo. 159r.

²⁹ CT 2, 74 and 94. Massarelli's judgment probably led Pastor (Geschichte, 6) greatly to simplify things by calling Verallo French from the outset.

³⁰ Druffel, I, no. 359, pp. 324-5, Ayala-de Mendoza, 16 December and no. 361, pp. 326-9 Ayala-de Mendoza, 17 December.

³¹ CT 11. 532 (24 December): Farnese's letter has not been found.

³² See the anonymous map of party lines included in Stella's diary and Pandolfo Pucer's letter to Cosimo (ASF:AMP 395, fo. 401r, 10 January 1550).

³³ H. Jedin, Storia del concilio di Trento, 2, trans. G. Basso and I. Rogger, Brescia, 1962-1974, passim.

³⁴ Geschichte, 6 and CT 11, 525.

³⁵ CT 11, 531. HCE, 3, 152.

³⁶ Firpo – Marcatto, Processo Morone, II:2, 847-8 (cf. F. Tamburini, La Riforma della Penitenzieria nella prima metà del sec. XVI e i cardinali Pucci in recenti saggi, in: RSCI 44 (1990) 110-40, here 121) and A. Ronchini, Lettere di Girolamo Muzio giustinopolitano conservate nell'Archivio governativo di Parma, Parma, 1864, 109 Muzio to Ferrante Gonzaga, 26 November 1549, claiming that none of the candidates was more feared

would appear to give him similar views to Pole's. He shared Pole's strong support of the Jesuits and of Nicholas Bobadilla – perhaps the most eccentric of the early Jesuits – in particular.[37]

Many observers joined Stella in putting the fiasco of 5 December down to division between the Imperialists and the Farnesiani. Gabbrielle was one.[38] Serristori was another. He heard reports that Cardinals Cibo, Girolamo Doria, Gianangelo de' Medici, and Giulio della Rovere had failed to vote for Pole.[39] The Ferrarese ambassador also told Serristori that della Rovere had not voted for Pole, although Ercole Gonzaga, della Rovere's uncle, had. Serristori thought it very unlikely that della Rovere had not followed Gonzaga's lead, an opinion which Toledo shared.[40] Serristori reported three days later that the same quadrumvirate had failed to back Pole.[41] Two weeks later Farnese wrote a letter (reported by Camaiano) complaining of della Rovere, Cibo, and de' Medici, but the next day the Florentine Agostino d'Angulo still thought Cibo and della Rovere would stay with the Imperial party for the time being.[42] Worse, Serristori also thought that Alvarez had failed to vote for Pole, and that he and Cibo both harbored hopes of somehow winning French support.[43] Although his account lacks enough circumstantial detail to allow one to date the moment he had in mind, Farnese wrote Cosimo later that Alvarez had cost Pole the papacy by refusing to vote for him on one occasion.[44] An undated summary of the

---

than Pole because he would "in somma dispopolorebbe Roma et ruinerebbe gli officii." CT 2, 158.

[37] A. CHIACON, Vitae et res gestae pontificum romanorum et S. R. E. cardinalium III, ed. A. OLDOINO, SJ, Rome, 1678, col. 735 and NICOLAI ALPHONSI DE BOBADILLA, Gesta et Scripta, Madrid, 1913, 40, in which Bobadilla reported from Vienna, probably in December 1542, that he was reading Paul with the nuncio Verallo.

[38] ASS:ADB, 720, no. 71 (6 December 1549).

[39] Gualteri agreed about Cibo. CT 2, 48.

[40] ASF:AMP 3463a, fos. 94v-8r, 6 December (cf. Legazioni di Serristori, 220, which however misread French for Ferrarese) and ASF:AMP 3969, no. 36 (14 December).

[41] ASF:AMP 3463a, fo. 98r-100v.

[42] ASF:AMP 395, fo. 256v, 20 December and ibid., fo. 269r.

[43] ASF:AMP 3463a, fos. 102r-5r, 12 December. In late January, just before he left the conclave ill, Cibo gave a long speech opposing Pole on the grounds that Charles already had too much power in Italy, and that at least the papacy should remain in Italian hands. ASV:APR 7, fo. 202r, 21 January 1550 (CSPV 5, no. 637, redated 31 January, but this must be a mistake. Cibo did not return to the conclave until 2 February according to Stella, and Ricasoli reported that he was absent on 30 January and expecting to return within two or three days, which fits perfectly with Stella's entry [ASF:AMP 3268, fo. 639]). Cibo may thus have earlier joined those who objected to Pole's nationality, as Maffei recorded in explaining his defeat on 5 December. CT 2, 51.

[44] ASF:AMP 611, fos. 73r-4r, 11 January 1550.

conclave by one of Otto Truchsess's conclavists likewise assigned the blame for Pole's failure to Alvarez and Cibo.[45] Mendoza was right to be very worried about dissension in the Imperial ranks long before the conclave began. On 6 May 1549 he lamented "que son tan pocos y tan divididos los unos con los ostros" and saw no hope of unifying the feuding Imperialists.[46]

Thus Stella's fixing of blame to Verallo has fairly solid support. This is not the case with another big point noted only by Stella, the consultation between Farnese and Caraffa on 24 January "si disse per conslari [sic] lo vol far papa." But without other corroboration and despite the deep suspicions entertained by nearly everyone of Farnese's motives, perhaps this putative unholy alliance ought not to be assigned to his ledger, even as a mere talking point.[47] It is, however, another moment at which Stella differs from Massarelli. As we have already begun to see, Stella's diary, together with many other sources, raises serious questions about the coverage of Massarelli's widely admired record. Perhaps most suspicious, Stella said nothing about the clamor for Pole throughout the night of 7 December, the disassembling of his cell by his conclavists in anticipation of his election (something it would have been surprising for Stella to miss), or yet another complicated scheme to make him pope through Cervini's assistance (but Massarelli might have known such negotiations better than Stella). And no one, including Stella and the exceedingly well-informed Toledo, said anything about the Imperial plot to abandon Pole, which Massarelli recorded on 16 December.[48] Massarelli was undoubtedly less than scrupulous about observing the Imperialists, as emerges from his complete failure to note the arrival of Charles's instructions of 19 December (see below). He would also appear to have had an animus against Pole in particular, which could be interesting in light of Massarelli's dependence on Cervini. Then again, Massarelli may have meant a similar plan to abandon Pole emanating from the Farnese camp. On 16 December Farnese wrote Cosimo defending Pole, but asking the duke to tell Charles that Cervini's election would be best for Italy, a line he continued to pursue.[49] Massarelli would likely have known of any approach to his patron, and in this case, anyway, loyalty to Cervini might have given him

---

[45] CT 11, 972-4.

[46] VÁZQUEZ – ROSE, Algunas cartas, 134.

[47] Mendoza had a particularly dim view of Farnese's intentions, at one point offering Cardinals Gonzaga and Madruzzo (whom he intensely disliked; Mendoza must have harbored overwhelming antipathy for Farnese!) as witnesses to "quan de mala gana vino Fernes en Polo," together with his own testimony that Farnese wanted Cervini to become pope. VÁZQUEZ – ROSE, Algunas Cartas, 148 (17 December).

[48] CT 2, 61-2. ASF:AMP 3969, nos. 29-30. Cf. Dandolo's dispatch of 18 December 1549 (ASV:APR 7, fo. 147r).

[49] ASF:AMP 611, fos. 69r-70r.

an extra motive to wish ill to Pole. This could also be an instance in which Stella chose to portray Pole above the fray, or – almost the same thing – in which his backers did not consider it necessary to keep him informed of their plans.

In addition to sometimes contradicting majority views on questions of fact, Stella's diary raises possibly irresolvable problems of chronology. A few of these may stem from the possibility that Stella wrote up (or rewrote) his diary after the fact. The strongest evidence for this theory is the double entry for 31 December, combined with a confusion about whether there was a vote on Epiphany, 6 January (there was not, according to everyone but Stella), and the reversed entries for 1 and 2 February. Then again, the double entry may have been caused by a lapse of memory between fos. 2v and 3r, and it is possible in the second case that Stella was simply confused about the dates, since there was a *scrutinium* on only one of these two days, as he correctly reported, but under the wrong date. Stella's chronology nevertheless differs in important ways from that recorded by many other observers. For example, in his entry for 5 December, he may have meant to refer to the French protest recorded by the other diarists under the previous night's events (and reported by ambassador d'Urfé himself as having happened on the 4th). Stella may also have been a day off in recording the high-point of Giovanni Morone's candidacy, which Stella assigned to 16 January, but in this case there was considerable disagreement about the date. All of this suggests that precision about chronology was difficult to obtain, even for participants, however soon after the events Stella may have written his journal.

Otherwise, most of Stella's portrait of Pole fits well into the process by which the original Pole became the plaster saint which has dominated historiography almost down to the present day.[50] (The biggest exception, Pole's speech of 22 December, therefore takes on all that much higher relief.) If Stella had to suppress evidence, so be it, including important information found in Pole's biographers, for example, Caraffa's original attack on Pole and the strong criticism of him which other observers picked up during the early going.[51] Was the circumstantial detail Stella substituted intended as a smokescreen? Then again, Stella's diary reveals the degree to which it was easy for Pole to be made to stand above the fray. By Stella's account, Pole was almost completely left out of consideration by his supporters after the first week of December, perhaps including during the French initiative of late January. In the early going, however, Stella assigned Pole a much more important role than any of the other diarists, especially in his negotiations in company with Cardinal Alvarez, the

---

[50] "A Sticking-plaster Saint? The Making of Reginald Pole" in T. MAYER – D. WOOLF, eds. The Rhetoric of Life-Writing in the Later Renaissance, forthcoming, University of Michigan Press.

[51] See the summary of charges in Beccadelli, BPP MS 973/3, fo. 19r.

other principal Imperial candidate, with the cardinal dean Giandomenico de Cupis on 5 December, an episode to which Pole later refered in his celebrated "Apologia" to Paul IV.[52] But after that point Pole's only return to prominence came as a member of the commission for the reform of the conclave, appointed on 26 January. Pole was not even consulted until after the deal for del Monte was completely set, Stella frankly admitting "non sapeamo cosa alcuna" until Durante Cardinal de' Duranti came to ask Pole's blessing. Gualteri, one of the diarists most favorable to Pole, gave him a much greater role at the conclusion.

Stella had the right credentials to play a major role in shaping the dominant image of Pole. By the time of the conclave, Stella (1488-1554) had been in Pole's service off and on probably since 1537 when he may have joined his first papal legation to Flanders.[53] He was certainly both important enough and close enough to Pole by 1539 for Pole to deploy all his resources to defend him in the financial dispute with Cardinal Filonardi discussed above. A native Brescian and laureate in both law and theology, Stella had been a member of the Oratory of Divine Love in Rome and also close to Caraffa, with whom he seems to have fallen out by the mid-1530s. He may have been introduced to Pole by the bishop of Verona, Gianmatteo Giberti, who went with Pole in 1537 and whom Stella must have known in Rome in the 1520s. Stella was at Viterbo with Pole in the 1540s and then at Trent, officially as his secretary.[54] For the next decade until his death Stella was probably almost continuously in Pole's household. Stella, along with his nephew Gianfrancesco and Vincenzo Parpaglia, was one of the key members of Pole's establishment. To judge from Stella's surviving writings, he shared religious beliefs with Pole, and with Michelangelo, whom Cistellini calls Stella's life-long friend.[55] Pole is said to have

---

[52] J. TELLECHEA IDIGORAS, Pole y Paulo IV. Una célebre apología inédita del cardenal Inglés (1557), in: AHP 4 (1966) 140.

[53] The best study of Stella is A. CISTELLINI, Figure della Riforma pretridentina, Brescia 1948, 56-103, including an appendix of correspondence between Stella and Laura Mignani, 213-95, together with P. GUERRINI, in: Brixia Sacra, 9 (1918) 81-93. For Pole's legation see, T. MAYER, If Martyrs are Exchanged with Martyrs: The Kidnappings of William Tyndale and Reginald Pole, in: ARG 81 (1990) 305-27 and id.: A Diet for Henry VIII: The Failure of Reginald Pole's 1537 Legation in: Journal of British Studies 26 (1987) 305-31.

[54] His presence in Viterbo in 1542 is attested in Archivio di Stato, Viterbo, Archivio notarile distrettuale di Viterbo, 1622, fo. 16v, and in 1544 in Archivio storico (Biblioteca comunale degli Ardenti), Viterbo, Riforme del Comune, 42, fos. 222rff. and 257r (where he is called maggiordomo). According to Carnesecchi, he was among "omnes familiares" of Pole in Viterbo. "Processo," 254.

[55] Cf. his poem on the death of Christ in BCM:CSAS 42/29 (BONELLI, no. 364), printed by CISTELLINI, 238-40 and what Bonelli considered a sonnet to Pole, BCM:CSAS 42/45 (BONELLI, no. 385).

written three epitaphs for Stella (only one of which I have been able to find), and the career papal bureaucrat Gianfrancesco Bini eulogized him in a series of sonnets, including one to Michelangelo.[56] He was buried outside Brussels, where he had gone as part of Pole's entourage on his final legation.

A note on the text: Stella wrote his journal in a very small, quick hand, which results in frequent difficulties of transcription. The virtual lack of punctuation, combined with uncertainty about how to expand certain abbreviations, makes getting its sense that much more difficult. With four exceptions, all dates are supplied in [].

Descrizione del conclave di Julio III

(1r) veneri
La vigilia de sant Andrea [29 November] s'intro in conclavi,[57] cantata la messa del spirito sancto in capella s'ando in conclavi in processione tutti li cardinali dapoi andorno a disnar, a casa loro poi a 21 hore si congregorno in conclavo fecero congregatione chiamorno li prelati et baroni et conservatori li dettoro il giuramento secondo il solito delle custodie steti aperto il conclavi sino a 6 hor' di notti che usci don diego[58]

Il di [30 November] fu detto alquante messe de cardinali preti cardinali chi non disse missa si communicorno da chi disse messa, et alcuni con tutti li diaconi si communicorno disse lultima messa il Revrendissimo decano, et communico, non fu fatto altro la detta mattina doppo disnare furon scritti tutti li familiari de cardinali con li officiali del conclavi, si mandorno dapoi nella capela de Papa Paulo, et furon chiamati fuor a uno a uno secondo il scritto per il maestro de cerimonium presente li Revrendissimi deputati camerlengo Carpi de Cupis[59]

---

[56] Both Pole's epitaphs and Bini's sonnet are printed in CISTELLINI, Figure, 100-01. For Michelangelo, see G. POGGI – P. BAROCCHI – R. RISTORI, eds. Il Carteggio di Michelangelo, Florenz 1979, 4, nos. MCLXXIII and MCLXXV.

[57] CT 2, 26. Giovanni Salviati sang the mass. The list of cardinals who entered at the beginning is on 27.

[58] CT 2, 29-30. Massarelli had Mendoza present at the first congregation after the closure and everyone not a conclavist excluded at 4 of the night. But he noted that some people hid and left secretly before dawn; Mendoza would appear to have been one of those.

[59] Cf. CT 2, 30. Stella did not mention – as both Massarelli and Firmani do – that some Imperialist cardinals tried to force the first vote on this evening.

V

Domenica [1 December] doppo la messa che fu detta dal sacrista presente tutti li cardinali excepto theatino fecero portan ogni cardinali il suo dal maestro de cerimonium si lesse la scabillo [sic] bolla de Julio, dapoi fu letto dal detto maestro di cerimonie la forma del Iuramento, et finito de uno in uno ando facendoli giurato sopra il crucifisso del messali commenzando dal decano, el qual posite due mani insieme sopra detta figura disse in voce alta che ognun potea intendersi de cardinali come conclavisti queste parole ita me deus adiuvet in dei evangelium cosi de man in man per ordine fecieno tutte il medesimo dapoi mandorno tutti li conclavisti fuor ce non stetero molto a uscire in quel menzo li conclavisti fecero la lor congregatione ancora per far signar li lor privilegii dopo disnare li Reverendissimi deputati Theatini Croce Santa [sic] Trani vescovi crescentio veralo preti camerlengo et gaddi cardinali diaconi fecero congregatione per dar ordine del modo de la elettione nella stessa capella paulina/[60]

Lunedi [2 December] dapoi la solita messa detta dal sacrista coram Revrendissimis a hore 16 nel solito habito di rocheto, et mozeta fecero portar li scrite che dali suoi conclavisti familiari et mandati fuora fecero li capitali duro fino a 19 hore detta mattina fu letta la lettera del Imperator ad patres di 20 novembre 1549 detto de li conclavisti fecero obligar li familiari di li Revrendissimi che sel suo cardinale sia papa li debon pagar 1000 ducati[61]

Martedi [3 December] andorno ala solita messa con le crocie finita seli portorno li scabelli grandi col carticello con carta pene inchiostro et li fogli dimonstrato scritti li nomi de tutti cardinali per il scrutinio nel quale riuscito monsignore Revrendissimo con voti 21 doppo disnar a 22 hore e fatta congregatione per distribuir li castelli et tetti della ghiesa alli Reverendissimi che non hano in commenda[62]

(1v) Mercori [4 December] a circa 16 hore intro in conclavi el cardinale d'ghien spagnolo intrato[63] che fa si spoglio del abito da cavalcar et intro con li

---

[60] CT 2, 33-4. Stella omitted a dispute over the manner of voting, whether public or private.

[61] CT 2, 35 puts the figure at 6000 scudi; cf. Appendix I for the complete list of privileges granted to conclavists, not given by Massarelli, and Appendix III, a copy of an agreement for a conclavist's remuneration.

[62] CT 2, 36-9. Massarelli described a croccia as being like a Benedictine habit or that of the Canons lateran. In the distribution of offices Pole received Ascoli for one year and Bagnoregio (of which he had been governor since 1547) for life.

[63] Massarelli (CT 2, 41-2) overlooked the arrival of the important Imperialist Pedro Pacheco, perhaps forgotten in the chaos of this dramatic evening. Dandolo, writing to Venice on 5 December, by contrast, thought that Pole's failure to be elected might have hinged on Pacheco's arrival, which delayed the proceedings. ASV:APR 7, fo. 132r (CSPV 5, no. 596). Gabbrielle reported that Pacheco immediately went into a clandestine meeting, to-

altri nela capella paulina se disse la messa dal solito sacrista dapoi il maestro delle cerimonie li lesse la bolla de Julio come fece a tutti nel primo congresso et lesse listessa forma del iuramento poi giuro nel modo delli altri ita me deus adivet [sic] et sancta dei evangelia fatto questo se portorno li scabelli del scrutinio alli Reverendissimi cardinali et fecero uscir li familiari stetero serati per spacio de 2 hore resto il Revrendissimo Cardinale polo con 24 voti et se voleva la sera lo volevano adorar non volse dicendo che a se difero la matina seguente perche se era volunta di dio tanto seria la matina come la sera[64]

Giobbia [5 December] a circa hore 17 introrno nella solita capella fu gran mutinamento dalli francesi et per le loro con li altri stetero assai a risolversi del venir a messa finalmente venero a poco a poco Trani fu da monsignore revrendissimo nostro con Burgos contessero insieme un pezo et Trani resto confuso di certe cose che opponeva fu detta la messa et fatto il scrutinio monsignore revrendissimo nostro con 24 voci et farnese et carpi fecero accesi *si verallo non mancava la parola, monsignore reverendissimo restava papa dicono che latina [sic] iuvenale deserto verallo [ab.] chieti ne hebbe 16 Trani con li soi complici per voler romper la compagnia che favorisce monsignore revrendissimo nostro tento Burgos con promessa de volerlo far papa esso recuso fu tentanto [sic] Cueva et rebuffo che nele parlo fu tentato san Agnolo con minaccie che perse via la penitentiaria niente fecero fu gran parole tra il camerlengo et crispo che sia pertinace con vilenie insieme[65]

Veneri [6 December] doppo la messa fu fatto il scrutinio resto monsignore revrendissimo con 22 voti chieti 16 si scopersi un hora avanti la messa un trattato della parte aversa che pensavano far veruli[66] il di sbalso hebbe voce. ... finito il scrutinio si domanda fuoco per brusar li voti [fino chel papa riesce. del.] che cosi si usa far sino che riescera il papa

---

gether with the expectation that Pole would be proclaimed the next morning. ASS:ADB, 720, no. 67.

[64] Massarelli noted this scheme briefly (CT 2, 42-3). Maffei's diary (CT 2, 43n) gave it much more attention, corroborating Stella's account of Pole's refusal to be adored and describing in detail the maneuvering which almost produced Pole's election. Stella's text in turn provides some confirmation of BECCADELLI'S version of this crucial episode ("Vita di Reginaldo Polo," BPP, MS 973/3, fos. 20v-1r; ERP 5, 372; MORANDI 303-4; cf. A. DUDIC, Vita Reginaldi Poli, in: ERP 1, 23). For Salviati's candidacy, see also below, 367-368. Dandolo's report of 5 December (ASV:APR 7, fo. 132v-3r [CSPV 5, no. 596]) largely agrees with Maffei's and Stella's on Pole's actions, but makes de Cupis the villain who insisted on having an election. Since de Cupis had just quarrelled with Pole over the abbey of Canalnuovo, his motives do not appear very noble. ASV:APR 7, fo. 107r; CSPV 5, no. 587.

[65] Cf. CT 2, 46-7 and D'Urfé's account of his *stratageme* in RIBIER 254-6, 6 December (but reporting actions from the 4th).

[66] CT 2, 48, for Cardinal Filonardi's temporary prominence. The following ellipsis in the text was probably left for Filonardi's vote tally.

V

Sabato matina [7 December] fu in gran predicamento Burgos d'esser papa per esser stato praticato la notte avanti dalli aversarii per divertir li nostri dal proposito ma non stetero molto su tale opinione andorno alla messa a 18 hore dapoi si fece il scrutinio che si domanda secreto che cosi usano far in questo conclavi ma si suole alle volte far aperto che volo, monsignore Reverendissimo hebbe voti 24 Burgos ... [i.o.][67]

Domenica [8 December] non fu scrutinio et si suol far ma la parte che non vorebbe il papa se non a suo modo trovo [sic] occasione col far dir messe dalli suoi adherenti ad un altare solo lun doppo laltro che fu si longo che fece passar [ab.] il tempo del scrutinio[68]

Lunedi [9 December] fu scrutinio al modo solito monsignore Reverendissimo hebbe voti 22 *senza accesso [ab.] et intromo a 17 hore[69]

Martedi [10 December] fu scrutinio al modo solito a hore 17 si comenzo la messa monsignore Reverendissimo hebe voti 22 senza accesso[70]

Mercori [11 December] fu scrutinio al solito monsignore Reverendissimo hebbe voti 22 intromo a hore 17[71]

Giobbia [12 December] fu scrutinio more solito venne la mattina a 15 hore li cardinali guisa vandomi parisi et chatiglion si lesse la bolla et giuroron la sera vene il cardinali di Tornon monsignore Reverendissimo hebbe 23 voti[72]

(2r) Veneri [13 December] fu scrutinio more solito monsignore Reverendissimo hebbe voti 23[73]

Sabato [14 December] fu scrutinio more solito monsignore Reverendissimo hebbe voti 23 [monsignore di chieti 22 del.][74]

Domenica [15 December] fu scrutio [sic] dalli francesi a concorrentia del nostro *hebbe chieti 22 voci [ab.] et hebbe accesso dal cardinale de monte qual disse che sapea la mente del papa che volea che che [sic] chieti fusse papa ma pochi li crederono[75]

---

[67] CT 2, 49. Alvarez had fourteen votes.
[68] CT 2, 50.
[69] CT 2, 52.
[70] CT 2, 53.
[71] CT 2, 54-5.
[72] Cf. D'Urfé, RIBIER 257-8. Massarelli (CT 2, 53-7) had the five French cardinals arrive over the course of two days, the first four on 11 December and Tournon on the 12th.
[73] CT 2, 57.
[74] Stella must have deleted this information because it was wildly wrong; Carafa had only nine votes. CT 2, 58.
[75] CT 2, 59-60.

Lunedi [16 December] fu scruti [sic] et chieti hebbe voti 24 per la concorrentia di nostro 23 soliti non hebbe accesso chieti perche tutti detteno il voto per superar il nostro[76]

Martedi [17 December] fu scrutinio monsignore Reverendissimo hebbe li voti 23 soliti chieti 18 guisa 18 et due accessi farnese et cornaro[77]

Mercori [18 December] fu scrutinio monsignore Reverendissimo hebbe voti 23 chieti 19[78]

Giobia [19 December] fu scrutinio monsignore Reverendissimo hebbe voti 23 chieti 20[79]

Veneri [20 December] fu scrutinio monsignore Reverendissimo hebbe voti 23[80]

Sabbato [21 December] non fu scrutinio[81]

Domenica [22 December] fu scrutinio monsignore Reverendissimo hebbe voti 23 chieti 20 el qual fece un oratione persuadendo che non lo voglino nominar piu vedendo non poter suceder et dicendo che sono altri che se compiacciono nel sentirsi nominar che facendo opera [two words lost in holes] pisani[82] deveriano far il medesimo vedendo non poter ottener pregar che non fusse piu nominato et si fecci experienza daltri monsignore sentendo questo toccar a se rispose perche sento toccar a me me bisogna risponder ritrovandomi si puo dir in eadem navi, io dico che monsignore Reverendissimo Theatino ha parlato santamente in questa parte maxime havendo risguardo al ben publico che tanta dilatione non po senon portar male et scandolo dando a pensar alla christianita delle nostre discordie cosi exorto che se nomini qualche altro, et gia piu presto che hora ho fatto simil officio con chi piu mi pareva necessario che e stato con monsignore Reverendissimo farnese il qual mi rispose che *per lui non lo facevano et [ab.] faron l'officio con tutti *persuadendolelo che per amor suo non faccevano cosa altra [ab.] dapoi mi parso il Reverendissimo decano con dirmi de non so che pratica che si faceva contra le ordinationi et contra la bolla io hebbe gran dolore sentendo dir tal parole sentendome inocente, et ri-

---

[76] CT 2, 61-2.

[77] CT 2, 62-4. Massarelli gives Guise's second *accesso* as Miguel de Silva. Stella did not note the apparently cordial visit Guise paid Pole, described by Gualteri at length.

[78] CT 2, 65-6.

[79] CT 2, 66-7.

[80] CT 2, 68-9. Massarelli recorded a highly dramatic confrontation between Truchsess, perhaps one of Pole's most determined supporters, and de Cupis, over who deserved blame for the deadlock. Truchsess haughtily told de Cupis "nos creabimus Polum pontificem, velitis nolitis," and the other cardinals prevented de Cupis from replying.

[81] CT 2, 70.

[82] As the French Venetian cardinal, it makes sense that Francesco Pisani should have seconded Caraffa. Cf. CT 2, 31 and 55 and bel. 00.

V

tornai a passar a monsignore Reverendissimo farnese dicendoli che havea inteso del Reverendissimo decano tal parole che avertir si bene chio non intendeva che per me si facesse pratica alcuna et se intendero di pratica che se lor non me volevano lassar me io lassaria loro che non intendeva ne intendo voler penetrar al [? hole] pontificato nisi per ostium mi rispose che non solo non praticava ma che anche havea fatto officio con li Reverendissimi che unitamente si communicassero et che dapoi la communione li voleva relassar in conscientia quel viacolo [? hole] che a loro parese tener alla voluta di esso, et cosi fece *et li risposero [ab. del. et trovo] che non lo fano per causa sua ma ogniun per lor conscientia lo fano, et vedendo cosi io pensando che le cose sia da dio non posso resistere alla voluta di dio, ma se voi iudicati che sia *piu honor de dio et che sia per riportato [ab.] maggior beneficio di dio che io renuntia *et mi separaro per [ab., but placement unclear] a questa speranza di papato non solo lo faro in questo ma ancor al cardinalato pregar [aft. illegible del.] dio per voi et per la chiesa universale santa croce doppo il scrutinio usci fuor del conclavio[83]

---

[83] CT 2, 70-1. Massarelli summarized Pole's speech as follows: se numquam quesivisse pontificatum neque aliquem rogasse, ut ei vota daret; nescireque an aliqui essent, qui amicitiae vel benevolentiae causa in cum suffragia conferrent. If there were any such, they should stop it. Si autem nullo moti affectu humano, sed tantum ut eorum conscientiis satisfacerent ei vota sua dabant, cum non posse neque debere eorum conscientias astringere, sed eos liberos relinquebat. But if Pole knew that votes for him were impeding the election of someone else, he would not only renounce his votes, but give up both cardinalate and life if that could help the church. Gualteri reported Pole's oration more briefly: Cogor ... aut sequi [Caraffa's example], aut causam adducere cur non sequar, ut me invidiae et ambitionis onere liberem [agreeing with Stella's report of Pole's having taken offense]. Egi pluries cum his omnibus, qui in me suffragia contulerunt, especially Farnese, whom I would stop if they were only supporting me out of good will. Eos igitur omnes per viscera Iesu Christi etiam atque etiam rogo, ne tantum benivolentiae tribuant, ut diutius in comitio perseverandum esse cogitent ac christianum gregem pastor carentem in graviora pericula adduci permittant. Arrivabene's retrospective dispatch of 12 January 1550 had Pole say that he "conobbe che egli lo provocava tacitamente a dover ragio[ne ?hole] disse, che anch'egli rendeva infinite gratie al Signore Dio, di haverlo sempre fatto conoscente del poco valore suo, et come egli non meritasse di essere coronato di cosi grande successione, ma che non volea tuttavia rendere alcuna gratia a quei R.mi Card.i et Ill.mi Sig.i di conclavi che l'haveano voluto far Pontifici, poi che non esso havea mai praticato cosa alcuna per questo, ne domandatone alcuno di loro, et più anche perche le parea che a certo modo volessero gareggiare con lo spirito santo, che si credeva che non l'eleggeva a cosi grandi dignità." ASM:AG 888, fos. 425r-29v. Dandolo's dispatch of 23 December noted only Caraffa's speech in a brief two line summary, but a newsletter from a conclavist which he enclosed gave a short version of Pole's speech, "che fu molto commendato." Pole said that "benche non volesse liberare i suoi voti, come colui che non gli havere procurati, tuttavia offerendosi cedere al capello, non pur alla speranza o timore che dir si possa." ASV:APR 7, fos. 150r, 152v; CSPV 5, nos. 603-4, 23-4 December. Stella's summary supports – if it is not

(2v) lunedi [23 December] scrutinio monsignore Reverendissimo hebbe voti 21 chieti 20 non intromo al scrutinio cornaro ne doria [? hole] per haver la gota medici usci finita la messa per sentirsi indisposo [sic]⁸⁴

Martedi [24 December] fu scrutinio monsignore Reverendissimo hebbe 23 chieti 20⁸⁵

il di di natale [25 December] non fu scrutinio si communicorno li diaconi cardinali dal decano li altri la piu parte dissero tre messe guisa fu il primo che disse la messa di mezanotte non si disse in capella all matutino in generale ne manco nulla [? hole] ordinamento come si suol far la notte di natale se communicorno con le crochie

Mercori di di natale

Giobbia [26 December] fu scrutinio monsignore Reverendissimo hebbe voti 23 chieti 20 il quale non cessa tuttavia dandando seminar male quanto po di monsignore Reverendissimo et gia ha fatto un processo con dir che favorisce et nutrisse heretici in casa sua con molte altri malignita et inventioni false la sera nacque un rumore de voler far papa il cardinale Burgos li cardinali francesi andorno cercando [? hole] fin un gran pezo di notte per obviar stando in timore⁸⁶

Veneri [27 December] fu scrutinio monsignore Reverendissimo hebbe voti 23 Burgos 20 Trani 21 chieti 20 furon accessi coria a augusta et chieti a Trani avanti il scrutinio nel metter le crochie uno conclavista in campio della crochia prese la coperta da letto et la puose al suo patrone movendo luno da un canto da laltro per trovar li al capo un altro suo compagno che si era acorto del Trani prese la crochia *preso di se [ab.] ma primo lasso far li suoi atti al primo suo compagno con la coperta col patrone⁸⁷

Sabato [28 December] fu scrutinio monsignore hebbe li soliti voti chieti 20 Trani 12 [? hole] la sera a due hore di notte intro in conclavi il cardinale dampoisa et bologna in habito con li pilori senza rocheta⁸⁸

Domenica [29 December] fu scrutinio monsignore hebbe li 23 voti chieti 22 per la venita [sic] delli 2 francesi dopo disnar fu congregatione si dissi che'l

---

the origin of – the passage in which BECCADELLI claimed that neither Pole nor his supporters ever made any effort to have him elected. BPP, MS 973/3, fo. 18r (ERP 5, 370; MORANDI, 303; DUDIC, ERP 1, 21).

⁸⁴ CT 2, 72. Massarelli noted the illnesses of del Medici and Doria on 24 December, but not Corner's absence.

⁸⁵ CT 2, 72-3.

⁸⁶ CT 2, 74, which made no mention of further machinations on Caraffa's part and makes the Imperialists the party terrified by word of the imminent arrival of three more French cardinals.

⁸⁷ CT 2, 75. Massarelli, who had an eye for a joke, did not notice the episode of the bedsheet, of which Stella, also a humorist in his youth, clearly did not approve.

⁸⁸ CT 2, 76.

populus romanorum noleva se guardia delli prelati come suo de more ecc. [? hole]/⁸⁹

Lunedi [30 December] fu scrutinio monsignore hebbe voti 23 chieti 20 la sera ritorno tutti in cappela paulina ma non fu congregatione venero lettere del imperatore si disse che excludeva salviati ridolphi santa croce et monte che non vol siano elleti [? hole] in papa⁹⁰

ultimo dicembre [31 December] Martedi fu scrutinio monsignore hebbe voti 23 la sera 23 hore intro lorena in habito di cardinal in rocheto con la mozetta, bologna deve andar fuora per li continui dolori⁹¹

(3r) Martedi [31 December] fu scrutinio monsignore Reverendissimo voti 23 chieti 20 li cardinali primo vescovo primo diacono primo prete andorno per li voti dali amalati more solito⁹²

Mercori primo genaio [1 January] non fu scrutinio ando fuor a 21 hore il cardinale di bologna per il mal dela pietra presente li deputati alla porta Trani camerlengo et carpi⁹³

Mercori [1 January] non fu scrutinio per la circuncisione⁹⁴

Gioibbia [2 January] fu scrutinio monsignore hebbe li 23 voti chieti 21⁹⁵

Veneri [3 January] fu scrutinio monsignore hebbe voti 23 chieti 22 la sera fu congregatione come son soliti fate li nostri in camera di Trento⁹⁶

---

⁸⁹ CT 2, 77-8.

⁹⁰ CT 2, 79. Charles's letter of 19 December (CT 11, 529-31) was noted by Mendoza in his reply of the 31st. VÁZQUEZ – ROSE, Algunas Cartas 156. From Stella's entry and Dandolo's claim that the letter arrived on Sunday, which would have been the 29th (ASV:APR 7, fo. 162v; CSPV 5, no. 613), it appears that Mendoza did not answer the Emperor immediately upon receipt of his letter.

⁹¹ CT 2, 81.

⁹² Stella might have erred in giving Caraffa's tally; Massarelli gave him twenty-one votes.

⁹³ CT 2, 81 had Boulogne leave the same day Lorraine arrived, 31 December, but this does not accord with d'Urfé's report probably of 2 January (although dated 20 January in RIBIER) that Boulogne and d'Amboise had entered the conclave (he did not say when) but that Lorraine was still expected. RIBIER 258-9. He probably arrived shortly thereafter, since he stood at 10% in the banks on 1 January according to Dandolo, and Massarelli had him cooperating with Guise on the 2d. ASV:APR 7, fo. 162r (CSPV 5, no. 613) and CT 2, 82. Stella's wording under 31 December ("deve andar fuora") could corroborate d'Urfé's report, making it possible that Massarelli somehow anticipated events. From Henry's letter of 6 February, it appears that Boulogne may never have returned. RIBIER 263-4.

⁹⁴ CT 2, 81. Stella here did the same thing as he did with Christmas, making two separate entries for the day of the week and for its holiday.

⁹⁵ CT 2, 82. Stella again gave Caraffa one vote fewer than Massarelli did.

⁹⁶ CT 2, 83 for the vote. Cf. Juan de Ayala's report to Mendoza of 19 December (VÁZQUEZ – ROSE, Algunas Cartas 195n) for the cardinal of Trent's cell as the usual locus

Sabato [4 January] fu scrutinio li voti al modo solito[97]

Domenica [5 January] fu scrutinio monsignore Reverendissimo hebbe li soliti voti chieti 22[98]

Trani fu in predicamento di papa et 4 di avanti secretamente andando per li cardinali diceva io son insicuro se me dato il voto vostro sara in avantagio pur lo reconoscero questo faceva astutamente per inganar li per haver il lor voto farnese hier sera dapoi la congregatione stete un gran pezo con lui che fece crescer lopinione et suspitione altri che soleno darli il voto per honorarlo volsero contarlo contra dicendo che lanimo loro non è che sia[99]

Lunedi [6 January] fu scrutinio li voce secondo il solito monsignore voti 23[100]

Martedi [7 January] non fu scrutinio per lepiphania doppo disnar andorno quasi tutti li cardinali nell coridor li conclavisti li seroron dentro exortandoli a far il papa non fu fatto cosa alcuna[101]

Mercori [8 January] fu scrutinio li voti al solito doppo disnar fu si gran pioza che non si po tolerar apena[102]

Giobbia [9 January] fu scrutinio monsignore hebbe voti 23 soliti[103]

Veneri [10 January] fu scrutinio hebbe voti 21 manco il voto de viseo, et cibo, li quali non lo volsero piu dar fu congregatione da trento la sera[104]

---

for meetings of the Imperial party. He was Cristoforo Madruzzo, who at least later was an admirer of Pole. BECCADELLI reports his pride in having known the man Madruzzo called "santo Polo" (BPP MS. 973/3, fo. 37v; MORANDI, 333; ERP 5, 391). But in the conclave Madruzzo backed Salviati at least as strongly as Gonzaga did, and like Gonzaga he was among the last four cardinals who refused to agree to Julius III (cf. bel. 7 February). For Madruzzo's support of Salviati, see, e.g., ASF:AMP 3463a, fos. 85v-8v, 25 November 1549, or Cardinal Cibo's letter to Cosimo I of 17 December (ASF:AMP 611, fos. 2r-3r).

[97] CT 2, 83.
[98] CT 2, 84.
[99] Cf. Toledo's letter of 4/5 January in ASF:AMP 3969, no. 24 and Ricasoli's dispatch of 7 January in ASF:AMP 3268, fo. 570r. Camaiano reported the next day that de Cupis's run had broken down because of powerful opposition from Crescenzi and Santa Fiore. ASF:AMP 395, fo. 386r.
[100] CT 2, 85. Cf. the introduction for Stella's confusion about this entry.
[101] CT 2, 85.
[102] CT 2, 87.
[103] CT 2, 88.
[104] Cf. CT 2, 89 and two newsletters enclosed in Dandolo's dispatch of 11 January (ASV:APR 7, fos. 171v-2r and 173r; CSPV 5, no. 620 and 619 [order reversed from original codex]); Dandolo himself thought Cibo might still vote for Pole if he were thought to have a chance (fo. 169v; CSPV 5, no. 621). Cibo defended his defection – for which he had been taken to task in a letter from Cosimo of 14 January – in a reply to the duke of the 18th, but managed to avoid giving his reasons. ASF:AMP 611, 4r-6r. Ricasoli had a very low

Sabato [11 January] fu scrutinio monsignore hebbe voti 21[105]
Domenica [12 January] fu scrutinio al solito[106]
Lunedi [13 January] non fu scrutinio per lottava dela epiphania[107]
Martedi [14 January] fu scrutinio al solito con li voti 21, si disse che farnese vol mutar in un altro li voti la sera avanti fu gran pratica per Burgos, li francesi hebbero nova dela morte dela regina di navara[108]
(3v) Mercori [15 January] fu scrutinio li voti al solito si disse che guisa disse a farnese che se li voleva servir di 3 voti laltro di lo serviria lui di 9 per polo fu scoperto che era una insidia per far riuscir papa lorena[109]
Giobbia [16 January] fu scrutinio morone fu in gran predicamento desser papa hebbe voti 26[110]

---

opinion of Cibo, whom he thought had been buried alive for many years (ASF:AMP 3268, fo. 557r-8r, dated 4 January, but actually 4 February), a judgment shared by Toledo who thought no cardinal had less credit than Cibo, who had seriously impeded an election (ASF:AMP 3969, fos. 11r-12r, 22 January; cf. also his letter of 27 January, ibid., fos. 8r-10v). Cibo's vote had been thought unsafe for some time. A Florentine news summary dated 8 January assigned him to a group of cardinals who had always voted for Alvarez, but "per niente voglio Pollo" (ASF:AMP 395, fo. 369r). Ricasoli and Arrivabene both reported Viseo's defection on 12 January, and both attributed it to a French trick by which Farnese was persuaded to let Viseo run, but then failed to support him. ASF:AMP 3268, fo. 588; ASM:AG 888, fos. 425r-29v, a report corroborated in part by Palombo on 15 January, who, however, assigned the initiative to Viseo. Palombo also thought it likely that Doria would join Cibo and Viseo in defecting (ASM:AG 888, fos. 439r-40v). Ricasoli called this a rumor, while adding Durante's name to the list of possible defectors [ASF:AMP 3268, fo. 588]. According to Toledo, Doria had already deserted Pole by mid-December (ASF:AMP 3969, nos. 29-30). Cardinal Gonzaga wrote Antoine Perrenot de Granvelle on the 10th that Cibo and Viseo had deserted Pole, the second for reasons of conscience. JEDIN, Storia 3, 308n. As it turned out, all four cardinals informed Farnese on 14 January that they would vote for Pole no longer. Camaiano to Cosimo, ASF:AMP 395, fo. 434r. D'Urfé put all four in the French column in his summary dispatch of 2 January. RIBIER 258-9.

[105] CT 2, 90.
[106] CT 2, 91.
[107] CT 2, 92 does not omit a *scrutinium* on this date, but Stella was correct that it was the octave of Epiphany. This helps to reinforce the supposition that Stella reversed the entries for 6 and 7 January.
[108] CT 2, 93-4, which, however, said nothing about a campaign for Alvarez; contrariwise, Stella failed to note the beginning of Morone's run, for which see below, 16 January.
[109] CT 2, 94-5, which does not mention any plot on Lorraine's behalf. For his candidacy, see BAUMGARTNER, "Henry II" 309.
[110] It would appear that Stella's chronology is off. The apogee of Morone's candidacy came on 15 January according to Massarelli, who gave him only thirteen votes on the 16th and fourteen on the 17th (CT 2, 95-7). Dandolo, who thought Morone's candidacy was taken as something of a joke (ASV:APR 7, fo. 175v; CSPV 5, no. 627) agreed with Massa-

Veneri [17 January] Trani penso esser papa per una pratica coperta fatta che havea praticato tanti voti che supplivano al numero, ma per una congregatione che fu fatta nella stantia di oria [i.e., Doria] dali farnesiani et imperiali fu ordinato che nessun desse voto a parte francesa urbino che gia havea promesso il voto suo a Trani che piu volte lo havea praticato prima ma promessa generale cioe che lo serviria una volta, rispose nella congregatione che si trovava haver promesso a una persona a che non potea mancar ogni volta che saria stato rechiesto ma heri li faria avisati del di quando saria rechiesto la sera avanti, Trani havendo havuto la sua promessa ha compito che hebbe il numero non parlo a urbino se non la matina per coglierlo a l'improviso accio non lo potesse dir et discoprir la cosa urbino che si trovava haver fatto la promessa davisar la sera avanti li rispose che'l voto non lo poteva dar quella matina per alcuni rispetti et questo fece andati in vano il pensier suo et desentimo alcuni che aveano promesso resto con voti 17 monsignore 21 chieti 21 una ne per se[111]

Sabato [18 January] fu scrutinio solito[112]

Domenica [19 January] similmente[113]

Lunedi [20 January] fu il medesimo li voti al solito si comenzo a dar le robba *in vano [ab.] alla finestra del conclavi dalla famiglia di cardinali ali medesimi dentro senza passar per man de officiali parti [aft. del. la sera] la detta matina ridolphi con dolori principiati il di avanti usci nel hora del scrutinio[114]

Martedi [21 January] fu scrutinio al solito li voti a 22 hore fu congregatione per le cose di parma se se [sic] li deve mandaro lettera o non/ la cena si levo il modo di servir chacunno [? hole] principiato fu veduto al solito la sera fu congregatione da Trento duro piu di 2 hore dali nostri[115]

Mercori [22 January] fu scrutinio li voti al solito la sera fu congregatione[116]

---

relli's tally of the rest of Morone's votes. Then again, Palombo assigned Morone's trial run to 14 January (ASM:AG 888, fos. 439r-40v), and Ricasoli reported his 26 votes on the 17th (ASF:AMP 3268, fo. 596). The news of Morone's spurt did not make it to poor Gabbrielle until 18 January. ASS:ADB, 721, no. 21. Cf. BECCADELLI, BPP, MS 973/3, fo. 21r (ERP 5, 372-3; MORANDI, 305) and DUDIC, ERP 1, 24.

[111] CT 2, 97. There is another hiccup in Stella's chronology, since Massarelli assigned de Cupis seventeen votes the day before.

[112] CT 2, 98.

[113] CT 2, 99.

[114] CT 2, 101 and ASV:APR 7, fo. 187v (CSPV 5, no. 630). D'Angulo wrote Cosimo on 19 January that Ridolfi was so sick that he was expected to leave the conclave the next morning. ASF:AMP 395, fo. 521r.

[115] CT 2, 102-3.

[116] CT 2, 104.

V

Giobbia [23 January] fu scrutinio li voti soliti ma viseo fece acesso a chieti la sera ando fuor Cibo[117]

genaio 24/ Veneri scrutinio voti al solito la sera farnese stete piu di due hore con chieti si disse per conslari [sic] lo vol far papa[118]

(4r) 25 genaio sabbato fu scrutinio li voti soliti[119]

domenica [26 January] non fu scrutinio a 22 hore fu congregatione intorno il maestro di cerimonie [dopo? hole] disnar chiso [sic] fino a 24 hore trattorno de reformar il conclavi, et gionsero alli 4 [sic] deputati soliti theatino polo pazecho viseo borbon et augusta che non si mandi fuor lettere ne avisi et non si fatti bancheti et [aft. del. ne] si manda fuor li conclavisti che non hare che far[120]

lunedi [27 January] fu scrutinio [aft.del. congregatione] con li soliti voti Trani 23 doppo disnar fu congregatione delli deputati della reforma in casa del sacrista nelle stantie del cardinale oria[121]

martedi [28 January] fu scrutinio dopo disnar congregatione ut supra[122]

mercori [29 January] il medesimo con li stessi voti doppo disnar congregatione delli deputati per la reforma fu aperto li luoghi di santa croce per lorena et borbone[123]

Giobbia [30 January] fu scrutinio li voti medesimi doppo disnar congregatione di deputati per la reforma la sera andorno fuor molti conclavisti non restando se non tre per ciascuno ma la natione spagnola con francesa volsero un confessor ciascuna che se intendesse pubblica persona la sera monsignore ando da theatino stete con lui circa a 2 hore et ha molte cose che li disse nego haver detto della cusa [sic] fatta di Messer marcantonio ancorache non la fussa negar restar reconciliati et satisfatti[124]

---

[117] CT 2, 105. Dandolo reported Cibo's illness on 22 January (ASV:APR 7, fo. 188r; CSPV 5, no. 630), and his expected return to the conclave on 25 January (ASV:APR 7, fo. 188r; CSPV 5, no. 633). Cf. ASF:AMP 3268, fo. 627r-8r, 24 January, a report that Cibo had left the conclave the evening before. According to Stella Cibo did not reenter until 2 February, which accords with Ricasoli's report of 30 January that he was expecting to reenter within two or three days. ASF:AMP 3268, fo. 639.

[118] CT 2, 106. No other commentators mention this episode.

[119] CT 2, 107.

[120] CT 2, 107-9.

[121] CT 2, 109, giving de Cupis twenty-two votes, the same total Guiducci reported (ASF:AMP 395, fo. 614r).

[122] CT 2, 110.

[123] CT 2, 111. Firmani (CT 2, 110n) noted the rearrangement of cells under 28 January. As the master of ceremonies, he should have known best.

[124] CT 2, 112-21, including the *capitula* for the reform of the conclave. There is a rough draft of some of them in BCM:CSAS 42/3-4 (BONELLI, no. 96). Cf. ASF:AMP 3268, fo. 639.

Veneri [31 January] fu scrutinio al modo solito doppo disnar al sono di campanella usciron molti conclavisti alli ordinati dandar fuora dapoi li deputati cardinali della reforma andorno visitando li cele de cardinali si ci sono busi [sic =? abusi] la sera andorno fuor altri conclavisti et in tre di sono usciti circa a 70 la sera a circa un hora di notte vene nove chel cardinale ridolphi era morto di morte subitanea, et *la matina [ab.] prima era nova che dovea intrar in conclavi[125]

Domenica [2 February] *al matina [ab.] quando monsignore si dovea crear papa finito il scrutinio fu il primo a uscir del scrutinio con la faza allegra et disse per questa matina non haveremo papa et il di avanti che a intrar gentilhomo che andasse aparlar a un certo cardinale con dirlo che li dicesse da parte sua che'l cardinale d'Inghilterra era heretico che avertisse bene, et la sera intro cibo in conclavio[126]

(4v) sabato [1 February] fu scrutinio li voti al solito la sera furno gran bolbimento de altri cardinali tre francesi armignac schiatiglion e tornon stetero da trenta per bon pezo, il simile fece farnese con santa Fiore in cella di sant'Angelo poi altri con moron trento medici mantua, et altri insieme, finalmente fu detto che si praticava di far papa salviati fu congregatione di deputati, duro 2 hore[127]

---

[125] CT 2, 112. Cf. ASV:APR 7, fos. 197v-8r (CSPV 5, no. 638) and ASS:ADB, 721, no. 34 for both Ridolfi's death and the expulsions, which Gabbrielle made a matter of comfort, not strictness. Oddly, the Florentine agents said very little about Ridolfi's death. Did Cosimo not need the news, having had a hand in poisoning one of his chief rivals?

[126] By referring to a *scrutinium* on 2 February, Stella contradicted both his own entry below and Massarelli, who recorded that especially fierce in-fighting prevented one being held (CT 2, 132). Stella once more reversed this entry with the next for Sabato, 1 February.

[127] CT 2, 129-30, which reported another boost to Salviati's hopes, including accessions from Gonzaga, della Rovere, Ranuzio Farnese and Cervini. Cf. ASF:AMP 3268, fos. 539 and 557r-8r. Salviati had been Gonzaga's candidate from the beginning. Cf. ASM:AG 1918, fos. 455r-59v, Gonzaga's summary to his brother Ferrante of his negotiations with Madruzzo, dated 12 November; ASM:AG 1918, fo. 465, a letter two days later attributing the initiative for Salviati to Ferrante; and especially ASM:AG 1918, fo. 477r, Gonzaga's summary dated 19 November of what he had told an unidentified nuncio in Siena. Gonzaga had even gone so far as to approach Cosimo directly on 17 November (ASF:AMP 611, fo. 135). See also the detailed correspondence in ASM:AG 888 from envoys in Rome during the conclave, all supported by Dandolo (e.g., 21 December; ASV:APR 7, fo. 149r [CSPV 5, no. 602] or 5 February 1550; fo. 203r [CSPV 5, no. 640]). Gonzaga also tried to wreck Pole's chances before the conclave opened, at one point sending his agent Capilupo (probably Camillo) to Buonanni with a huge catalogue of Pole's failings, extending from unsound views on justification (a point on which Capilupo adduced Caraffa's support) to plans to force all beneficed clergy with cure of souls to reside. ASF:AMP 395, fo. 22r, 27 November 1549; unfortunately, Buonanni's dispatches do not survive for this date. Gabbri-

V

368

Domenica [2 February] non fu scrutinio fu fatto la beneditione delle candelle con le crochie et distributione dal decano *si comunicoron molti cardinali alcuni da augusta altri dal decano altri dissero messa [ab.] si comenzo a servir secondo la reforma un ferculo solo, che fu di due galli ne lesse con menestra et sapore che dio voglia seguita cosi, vene il compagno de messer bino doppo disnar a intimar la congregatione generale a 21 hore duro fino a notte[128]

Lunedi [3 February] fu scrutinio li voti al solito si parla assai che salviati era in una pratica di farsi papa si disse ancor che ridolphi e morto di veneno si parla ancor che Trani stava in bona pratica di papizar Suoi (?) 23 voti salviati 19[129]

Martedi [4 February] fu scrutinio li voti al solito fu posto su la rota ne avanti per il buso intromo dopo [? hole][130]

Mercori [5 February] fu scrutinio li voti ut supra la sera fu congregatione di deputati in la camera doria[131]

Giobbia [6 February] fu scrutinio li voti ut supra si incontro farnese e guisa la sera insieme et si tentorno lun laltro di far un papa guisa disse a farnese che proponesse che li piacceva fuor di polo, e la nation spagnola che accetaria alcun delli altri, et lui li respose che dalla sua parte proponesse alcun de altri fuor de salviati e Trani che resolveriano farnese propose santa croce non fu accetato propose dalaltra parte monte et si contentorno tutti dui et cosi ognun dala sua parte pratico li soi et conclusero insieme la sera ando farnese da trento con dir li che haveano concluso in monte lui bravo et contrasto molto et vene mantua dapoi parti et fu rechiamato et poi partiron farnese se ne ando con la sua resolution li spagnoli con trento et gli altri spagnoli si consultorno assai insieme

---

elle kept close watch on Salviati's candidacy for Siena and corroborated Stella's entry in his dispatch of 3 February (ASS:ADB, 721, no. 36). Marin Cavallo reported to Venice on 25 January that Charles was resigned to Salviati, but the news could not have reached Rome so soon. In any case, it turned out to be false, as Cavallo admitted later. CSPV 5, nos. 632 and 639.

[128] CT 2, 132. "Messer Bino" was Gianfrancesco Bini, an old friend of Stella's and fellow poet, prominent papal bureaucrat, and (just possibly) author of a history of the conclave. See DBI and the discussion in CT 2, XXI-II, which is not entirely convincing in denying that Bini wrote a history; nor did the editor examine all the MSS with Bini's name attached to them, as he admitted.

[129] CT 2, 133. For Ridolfi's poisoning, see Dandolo's highly circumstantial report on his autopsy (ASV:APR 7, fo. 203v; CSPV 5, no. 640); Pirro Olivo's dispatch to Mantova of 22 January (ASM:AG 888, fos. 462r-3v); and Arrivabene's of 4 February (ASM:AG 888, fo. 481r).

[130] CT 2, 134.

[131] ibid.

ma non poterno interrompare che gli altri gia haverano praticato la conclusione et fermata, delle a un pezo si comenzorno a congregar per andarlo adorar[132]
(5r) Veneri [7 February] non sapeamo cosa alcuna se non del veder praticar durante ando avanti et ritorno [? hole] a dir che ogniun si preparava per adorar monte[133] cosi si vidde venir tutti i francesi andar in capella, et dapoi chieti dala creboro (?) dapoi salviati e Trani poi vene durante adir a monsignore che farnese veniva et che tutti eran daccordo monsignore si misse el rocheto in quel tanto vene farnese et unaltra compagnia et chiamo monsignore polo andiamo in capella et vene fuor di cella et andorno in capella di compagnia vene dapoi Burgos con coria dapoi monte con alquanti altri *et fu posto [ab.] a sede su la sedia papale nel laltare [ab.] in tanto che passava il numero si sero la porta della capella e stando in aspettation del resto dei cardinali Burgos con coria et certi altri andorno verso la porta per *andar fuora dicendo [? hole] che volea andar a chiamar trento farnese saccorse che volerno partir et disse al baronino maestro de marangoni che non lassasse uscir nissuno si fusse Christo, in quel tanto si vide venir Agusta [sic] et si apirlo [sic] la porta che erano fose 36 o 40 carpi mando uno per lui che stava in letto amalato a prometter si messero accader ogniun secondo lordine loro primo escono preti e diaconi dapoi fu chiamato al maestro de cerimonie et lesse il nome di tutti li cardinali dapoi farnese disse che ogniun che confirmava la elettione del papa alzasse la mano tutti alzorno il brazo un noti (?) fu rogato dapoi disse che bisognava ancora andar abrazarlo et che si comenzasse disse Trani da che si ha da far faciamolo speditamente levo su et andolo a biazar dapoi salviati dapoi chieti et per ordine tutti gli altri quando ando il nostro lo abbrazo molto et baso et li vene le lacrime agliochi[134] et finito labbrazamento ogniun se ne ando comenzando primo lui trento cueva

---

[132] CT 2, 135n for Maffei's report of this crucial maneuver, the origins of which can be dated more precisely from this entry. Dandolo moved the original meeting between the two leaders back another evening, but his report was delayed until 8 February, so he could have missed a day. ASV:APR 7, fo. 205r; CSPV 5, no. 642. Cf. BECCADELLI, BPP, MS 973/3, fo. 21v (ERP 5, 373; MORANDI, 305) and DUDIC, ERP 1, 25.

[133] CT 2, 140-2 describes some of these *pratiche*, but Gualteri's diary gave Pole a more prominent role and made Maffei (not Durante) Farnese's emissary to Pole. If Durante really were the go-between, this might help to explain Pole's liking for a man whom many others regarded as beneath contempt, including Massarelli (CT 1, 197). Most important, shortly after the conclave Pole intervened energetically and successfully with Ignatius Loyola to get Bobadilla as Durante's confessor when Durante went to reside in his see of Brescia, despite the high demand for and short supply of Jesuits. Pole had not even been able to keep Bobadilla for himself a decade before. Cf. Monumenta Ignatiana, series 1, St. IGNATIUS DE LOYOLA, Epistolae et Instructiones, 3, Madrid, 1905, MHSJ, 3, 611 and 614 and BOBADILLA, Gesta, 167.

[134] BECCADELLI and DUDIC gave this moment an even more dramatic treatment. BPP, MS 973/3, fo. 21v (ERP 5, 373; MORANDI, 306) and ERP 1, 25.

pazego et mantua non si ritrovorono andorno dapoi in camera sua a far lobidienza tutta la notte si stete in piedi il nostro ando a letto a 8 hore il cardinale de guisa ando a visitar il papa, et dapoi lui molti altri a 13 hore si sono la campanella dal maestro de cerimonie li cardinali si misseno a ordine con il rocheto et mozeta per andar in capella et ogniun de essi fece il suo voto aperto nominando solo il papa dicendo eligo in summum pontificem Reverendissimum dominum cardinalem de monte et congregati in capella vestirono le croccie dapoi al

(5v) udirono la messa del sacrista finita la messa mandorno fuor li conclavisti dettero li voti per ordine nel modo solito del scrutinio mettendo le sue nel calice della messa li soliti tre cardinali primo vescovo primo prete et primo diacono li lesseno dapo [sic] fatto andorno a mostrar la croce con nominar il papa al modo solito finito fecero signar alquante supliche stando a sede per [? hole] mezo laltar sopra la sede pontificale dapoi lo messero a sedir in mezo del altare et aprirno la capella li conclavisti intorno con le cape pavonanze il papa fu spogliato de suoi pani et vestito pontificalmente con la mittra et a sedri sul mezo di laltare li cardinali in quel tempo deposero le crocie et vestire le cappe et per ordine [---zo ? hole] il decano abasarli al piede le mani et al volir la faza de lana e laltra guancia in quel tempo si muoeva la porta che va a san pietro che gia haven commenzata avanti che li conclavisti fussero intrati finita la obedienza andorno in san pietro portato il papa delli palafreneri anche del papa morto giunti in san pietro singinochio avanti laltare di san pietro dapoi fu posto aseder in mezo laltare et li cardinali fecero la medesima obedienza per ordine come la prima dapoi le baso le piedi molti altri finito si levo et disse alta voce si nomen domini benedictum et finito dete la benedicione li cantori respondendo finito ando alle stantie papale con molti cardinali di compagnia portato ut supra il camerlengo gli diede il possesso de le stantie et poi col resto de cardinali se ne ritornonno alle lor stantie/

Francesi[135]	Imperiali.	Farnesiani
1 Guisa 1.	22 Burgos. 1.	32 Farnese 1.
2. Parisi 2.	23 Trento. 2.	33 S. Fiore 2.
3. Vandomo 3.	24 Augusta. 3.	34 S. Angelo 3.
4 Satigliene. 4.	25 Mendozza. 4.	35 S. Croce. 4.

---

[135] A loose sheet in a different hand. The document can probably be dated by the anticipated arrival of Lorraine and Boulogne, that is, before 31 December or shortly thereafter (see the entry for 1 January above). Then again, if the crosses next to Ridolfi's and Filonardi's names indicate that they had died during the conclave, the list could have been reworked almost at the end of the conclave, after Ridolfi's death. There are many such lists of party alignments, all of which need to be precisely localized in time. Cf. the most accessible version (of 17 January) printed in CT 2, 97.

5 Turnone. 5.	26 Cueva. 5.	36 Maffei. 5.
6 Scialone. 6.	27 Pazeceo. 6.	37 Morone. 6.
7 Medone. 7.	28 Mantoa. 7.	38 Crescentio. 7.
8 Armignac. 8.	29 Carpi. 8.	39 Sfondrato. 8.
9 Lorena. 9.	30 Doria. 9.	40 Durante. 9.
10 Bologna. 10.	31 Cibo. 10. [2]	41 Inghilterra. 10.
11 Ferrara. 11.		42 Savello. 11.
12 Trani. 12.		43 Cornaro. 12.
13 Salviati. 13.		44 Ragusa. 13.
+14. Ridolfi. 14.+		45 Viseo. 14.
15 Pisani. 15.		46 Urbino. 15.
16. Gaddi. 16. [1]		

[1] Questi sono della parte Francese: ma Lorena et Bologna non sono ancora giunti: si aspettano. Tra questi Italiani tre attendono al papato, che sono Trani, Salviati, Ridolfi.

[2] Questi imperiali hanno seguito in Inghilterra il Cardinale Farnese salvo che alcuna volta Burgos et Cibo hanno vacillato. Ma essendo hora chiari, che non possono esser essi, sono risoluti di seguire in Inghilterra per quanto s'intende.

17 Crispo. 1.	47 Monti. 1.
18 S. Giorgio. 2.	+ 48 Veruli. 2. +
19 Verallo. 3.	49. Cesis. 3.[4]
20 Sermoneta. 4.	
21. Chieti. 5. [3]	

[3] Questi sono quelli, che hanno lasciato il Cardinale Farnese. Ma Chieti nol vuole seguire senon nel Cardinale Burgos.

[4] Monti attende al papato anch'esso: pure si dice che non potendo essere, verrà in Inghilterra. Il simile di Veruli, et ancho piu fermamente. Cesis, il quale ha vacillato alcuna volta, dicono che anch'esso verrà in Inghilterra.

A fare il papa vi bisognano i Duo terzi.

Appendix I

Summarium facultatum concessarum conclavistis in electione felicis recordationis paulus papa III (BCM, Archivio Stella 40/33 [Bonelli, no. 23])

Recipit ipsos conclauistas in suos familiares, et ut tales nominentur
Facit ipsa prothonotarios, et quod gaudeant priuilegiis et si non deferant habitum prothonotarii
Item comites palatinos
Item facit ipsos nobiles etiam quo ad assecutione benefficiorum
Item dat licentiam quoscumque doctorandi extra curiam
Item creandi Notarios
Item legittimandi bastardos
Item concedit priuilegium archiui quoad creationem notariorum, et legitimationem illegitimorum
Item dat exemptionem ab ordinario
Item dat exemptionem a gabellis et decimis
Item absoluit ipsos a quibuscumque excessibus et symonie et heresis etiam si insorduerint per annum
Item remittit fructus male perceptos
Item dat gratias expectativas ad tres collocationes et ad presentes valorum C. ducatorum
Item quod possit herede expectatiuam extra rationem
Item concedit prerogativas ad instar vere descriptorum
Item describit ipsos post primum et ante secundum
Item dispensat cum nobilibus ad quattuor incompatibilia cum aliis ad tria et ad unum regulare
Item ad quecumque pro illegitimo etiam ad ordines, et ad successionem, et ad honores et officia
Item dat licentiam de non promovendo ad septenium
Item concedit quod illegitimi non teneantur facere mentionem de defectu in quibusuis concessionibus
Item di promovendo ad ordines a quocumque et extra tempora etiam in curia
Item de fructibus percipiendis etiam in absentia
Item dicendi officium cum sotto clerico seu presbytero per cum eligendo
Item stationes urbis
Item dat licentiam absoluendi pariochianos etiam in casibus ordinis reservatis
Item comutandi uota
Item audiendi leges
Item attendandi ad bienium
Item testandi
Item dat conseruatoriam ad vitam etiam pro familiaribus: vicariis, et capellanis

Item concedit facultatem resignandi et permuttandi extra curiam tam conclauistis quam illis qui in eorum [ad. del. omnibus] fauorem, etiam sempliciter resignaverint cum derogati relictorum de infirmis et supensione gratiarum
Item mandat expeditum literas gratis super omnibus per missis
Item quod detur fides transumpti
Sub datum Romae apud sancto petro tertio nones nouembris anno primo [one line missing]

Appendix II
Descrizione delle esequie di Paolo III
(BCM, Archivio Stella, 40/79 [Bonelli, no. 94])

in la morte del papa morsi alo 10 novembre a hore 13 et circa un 4o in monte cavallo nelle stantie: napoli fu portato in letica a palazo con [ill.] senza la croce avanti acompagnato con la guardia di sguilari et cavalli leggieri, hebbe drieto il maestro di casa con poca famiglia
Di .10. fu portato nella salla del concistorio et exatterato lavato etc poi vestito pontificalmente, li cardinali si congregorno nella salla de pontifici passando per la sala del concistorio con le cappe pavonanze, et gionti avanti il morto si fermorno ciascun a dir un de profundis sub silentio poi fatti poco dinclinatione di capo andarano al loco della congregatione mentre si faceva detta congregatione li penitentieri fecero portar il papa nella capella di Julio processionalmente finita la congregatione li cardinali creati da detto papa andorno a detta capella et gionti fa levato il corpo et portato in Santo Pietro nella capella di Sisto, poi fatto se ne andorno a casa loro, lassando sempre li penitentieri presso al morto/
di 11 laltri di detti cardinali a 19 hore si congregorno nella sala del concistorio andorno sino in detta sala con mantelletti pavonanzi, mazze, et valise, come si suole far gionti si spogliorno il mantelletto et restorno in rocheto con la mozeta, finita la congregatione et usciti delle sale si vestirno detti mantelletti/
3° di fu fatta la congregatione nel modo sopradetto nel sopradetto habito, et la sera tardi fu sepulto il papa
4° di medesima congregatione nel solito habito commenzo a 21 [corr. from 20] hora
5° di medesima congregatione nel medesimo habito
6. di medesima congregatione nel medesimo habito
[NB: The remaining text was almost certainly written at a different time.]
10. di il p° di de lexequie li cardinali *creati del papa del papa morto [sic; ab.] andorno con le cappe di pavon violaceo li altri con le cape de zambeloro andorno a seder nella capella di papa sisto canto la messa il decano fece loratione ms Romulo, dapoi finita la messa si vestirno con par.te? et puiali? [cf. pluiali

bel.] li 4 primi cardinali *col decano [ab. del. dui (?) cioe decano verali et Theatini, ostiense, albanense, et sabinense, et carpi], andorno con le mitre ad castrum doloris et si fece le solite cerimonie che si usa *cantante libera me domine [ab.] doppo lexequie, dapoi ritornati si spogliorno, et remessero le cappe pavonanze, et andorno in congregatione. duro tutto sino a 21 hore, erono [sic] 32. cardinali et limbassatori di Franza, et Venetia

11. di messa ut supra la canto carpi con listesse cerimonie doppo la messa del vestirsi cinque cardinali con mitre et pluiali erono [sic] carpi che canto la messa, morone, Trento, medon et santa croce, dapoi andorno in congregatione duro sino a 22 hore/

12. nel solito habito messa con le solite cerimonie et li cinque cardinali ne lultimo della messa con li puiali andorno ad castrum doloris, dapoi fu congregatione con le solite cape fini a 19 hore

Adi 13. messa ut supra la congregatione fini a 19 hore/

Adi 14. messa ut supra la congregatione fini a 18 hore

Adi 15. fu domenica non fu messa ne congregatione/

Lunedi messa solita congregatione duro sino a 19 hore

Appendix III
Agreement for remuneration of conclavist
BCM, Archivio Stella 40/80 (Bonelli, no. 96)

In conclaui per obitum foelicis recordationis Pauli iii

Nos episcopi, Presbyteri, et diaconi, S.R.E. Cardinales, uniuersalem ecclesiam representantes, Pro electione futuri Romani Pontificis facienda in Unitate sancti spiritus in conclaui nostro simul congregati, Prospicientes quod dilecti nostri familiares, et alii, qui in dicto conclaui nobis seruiendo de presenti remanserunt, de relictis eorum rebus et negociis, in dicto presente conclaui se includere non formidarunt, et in illo vigilias et alios labores non paruos, non sine eorum graui iactura sustinere non cessant, ac similes et maiores etiam cum vitae discrimine sustinere proponant, Hac igitur consideratione moti promittimus, et nostrum quibus, qui in Rom. Pont. fuerit electus promittit quod omnia et singula Beneficia quomodo qualificata, vbique etiam in romana curia vacante et existentia, cuius cunque annui valoris dummodo consistorialia non sint, nec ad S. R. E. Cardinalium Collationem spectan., eisdem Conclavistis, pro rata dividenda iusta ordinationem Deputatorum eorundem Conclavistarum, conferre et de illis etiam providere. Nec non summam sex milium scutorum anni in auro Pro Cam.ra R.mi D. Car.lis in Pont. eligendi solvendam, infra mensem a Die electionis: Necnon quatuor cannas Panni rosati de meliori sorte, pro eorum quorum, Necnon mandata de providendo cum Prerogativis et aliis gratiis, privilegiis et indultis concedi solitis, pro ut latius in Mandato et supp.bus de spure conficiendis et segnandis explicabitur. Ac ex nunc volumus promittimus et decernimus, ac nostrum quibus, qui in Rom. Pontificem electus fuerit, vult promittit et decernit promissa omnia et singula eisdem Conclavistis, ut profertur, concessa, ac si inter capitula in presente conclavi per nos facta, eum similibus notis electis et decretis concessa, data, facta, et posita eiusdemque obligationis roboris et momenti fuisse et esse, ac pro talibus effectuatur haberi, atque irritum et inanae quicquid secus a quoquam quavis auctoritate scienter vel ignoranter attemptari contigerit etiam decernet:

Abbrevations

ASF:AMP	Archivio di Stato, Florence, Archivio Mediceo del principato
ASM:AG	Archivio di Stato, Mantova, Archivio Gonzaga
ASS:ADB	Archivio di Stato, Siena, Archivio del Balia
ASV:APR	Archivio di Stato, Venice, Archivio Proprio Roma
BAV	Biblioteca Apostolica Vaticana, Rome
BCM:CSAS	Biblioteca Civica "Angelo Mai," Bergamo, Carte Stella in Archivio Silvestri
BPP	Biblioteca Palatina, Parma
ERP	Epistolarum Reginaldi Poli, ed. A. Querini, 5 vols., Brescia, 1744-57
CT	Concilium Tridentinum Diariorum Pars Prima, ed. S. Merkle, Freiburg, 1901 [= vol. 1]; Concilium Tridentinum Diariorum Pars Secunda, ed. S. Merkle, Freiburg, 1911 [= vol. 2]; and Epistolarum Pars Secunda [= vol. 11], 2d ed., ed. G. Buschbell, Freiburg, Herder, 1966
Morandi	Monumenti di varia letteratura, ed. G. Morandi, Bologna, 1797-1804, I:2
CSPV	Calendar of State Papers and Manuscripts, Relating to English Affairs in the Archives and Collections of Venice, vol. 5, ed. R. Brown, London, 1873
Legazioni di Serristori	Legazioni di Averardo Serristori Ambasciatore di Cosimo I a Carlo Quinto e in Corte di Roma (1537-1568), ed. G. Canestrini, Florence, 1853.

VI

If Martyrs are to be Exchanged with Martyrs: The Kidnappings of William Tyndale and Reginald Pole*

The history of the English Reformation has often been written in the light of hindsight, particularly when dealing with the major figures whose well-known views of themselves and their contemporaries have appeared to coincide with more modern historiographical prejudices. The Olympian conflict between Reginald Pole and Thomas Cromwell provides a perfect illustration of how a political contest with strong ideological overtones became a cosmic drama. In order fully to understand this process, Pole's self-fashioning or the creation through literary means of a *persona* for himself deliberately at odds with his demonic opponents, chief among them Cromwell, needs much more attention.[1] The following materials contribute a little toward that goal, but they will concentrate on bringing Cromwell further out of the shadow of Pole's diatribes against him. The inaccuracy of some of these has been exposed, although mainly in terms of Cromwell's domestic accomplishments.[2] The story can also

---

* The title of this article is paraphrased from John Foxe. An earlier version was read to the Tudor and Stuart Seminar, University of London. I would like to thank Professor Conrad Russell for the invitation to speak. Some of the following material is extensively reworked from my "A Diet for Henry VIII: The Failure of Reginald Pole's 1537 Legation," *Journal of British Studies* 26 (1987): 305-31. – ABBREVIATIONS: Unless otherwise noted, documents are cited according to their numbers. – B.L.: British Library (documents cited by folio). – CSPSp: P. de Gazangos, *et al.*, eds.: *Calendar of State Papers, Spanish* (London, 1862-1954). – ERP: A. M. Quirini, ed.: *Epistolarum Reginaldi Poli* (Brescia, 1744-57). – Lestocquoy: J. Lestocquoy, ed.: *Correspondance des nonces en France Carpi et Ferrerio, 1535-1540* (Rome, 1961). – LP: J. S. Brewer, J. Gairdner and R. H. Brodie, eds.: *Letters and Papers Foreign and Domestic of the Reign of Henry VIII*, (London, 1862-1932). – Mozley: J. F. Mozley: *William Tyndale* (New York, 1937). – SP: Public Record Office, London, State Papers of the Reign of Henry VIII (documents cited by folio).

1. S. J. Greenblatt: *Renaissance Self-Fashioning, from More to Shakespeare* (Chicago, 1980), develops this approach, which is applied to another episode in Pole's career in T. F. Mayer: "A Mission Worse than Death: Reginald Pole and the Parisian Theologians," *English Historical Review* 103 (1988): 870-91.

2. P. Van Dyke: "Reginald Pole and Thomas Cromwell: An Examination of the *Apologia ad Carolum Quintum*," *American Historical Review* 9 (1904): 696-724; see also G. R. Elton: *The Tudor Revolution in Government: Administrative Changes in the Reign of Henry VIII* (Cambridge, 1953), 7, 73-4, and his "The Political Creed of Thomas Cromwell," in

be pursued in the theatre of Europe and analyzed within the context of a factional and ideological crisis beginning with the kidnapping of William Tyndale in 1535 and running through late 1538.

Cromwell and Pole had neatly symmetrical strengths and weaknesses, but Cromwell faced the more difficult task. (I shall defer consideration of the relative importance of Cromwell and Henry VIII until the end of this paper and write for the moment as if Cromwell were mainly responsible for the actions against Pole). At the most fundamental, there was a large disproportion in the difficulty of accomplishing the worst that either side could do. Cromwell had somehow to engineer the physical destruction of a cardinal, while Pole had merely to accede to his friends' wish that he publish his attack on Henry, *De unitate* (1536). Pole's mission took place in the context of the serious threat posed in late 1536 by the Pilgrimage of Grace, a widespread rebellion in the north of England, stimulated by a complex mixture of political and religious grievances (for example, opposition to the dissolution of the smaller monasteries and other religious innovations or, perhaps, resentment on the part of peers excluded from politics at the center).[3] As J. P. Moreau argues, Pole and his ideas could have provided much of the coherent program and leadership the Pilgrims lacked.[4] In theory, Pole could draw on much greater resources than Cromwell, and in practice he had at least two inestimable advantages, the full support of the papal diplomatic apparatus, the best in Europe, and the attitude of the

---

Studies in Tudor and Stuart Politics and Government, 2, *Parliament/Political Thought* (Cambridge, 1974), 217-20.

3. The classic narrative is M. H. and R. Dodds: *The Pilgrimage of Grace 1536-7, and the Exeter Conspiracy, 1538* (Cambridge, 1915). Since then an enormous literature on the causes of the Pilgrimage has grown up, including A. G. Dickens: "Religious and Secular Motivation in the Pilgrimage of Grace," in: G. J. Cuming, ed.: *Studies in Church History* 4, (Leiden, 1968), 39-54; C. S. L. Davies: "The Pilgrimage of Grace Reconsidered," *Past and Present* 41 (1968): 54-76; M. E. James: "Obedience and Dissent in Henrician England: The Lincolnshire Rebellion, 1536," in his *Society, Politics and Culture: Studies in Early Modern England* (Cambridge, 1986), 188-269; S. J. Gunn: "Peers, Commons and Gentry in the Lincolnshire Revolt of 1536," *Past and Present* 123 (1989), forthcoming; G. R. Elton: "Politics and the Pilgrimage of Grace," in: B. C. Malament, ed.: *After the Reformation: Essays in Honor of J. H. Hexter* (Philadelphia, 1980), 25-56; C. Haigh: *The Last Days of the Lancashire Monasteries and the Pilgrimage of Grace* (Chetham Society, 3rd ser. 17 [1969]) and his *Reformation and Resistance in Tudor Lancashire* (Cambridge, 1975), 118-38; R. B. Smith: *Land and Politics in the England of Henry VIII: The West Riding of Yorkshire, 1530-46* (Oxford, 1970), 165-212; S. M. Harrison: *The Pilgrimage of Grace in the Lake Counties* (London, 1981); and J. A. Guy: *Tudor England* (Oxford, 1988), 149-53.

4. J. P. Moreau: *Rome ou l'Angleterre? Les réactions politiques des catholiques anglais au moment du schisme (1529-1553)* (Paris, 1984), 248, 251.

VI

imperial authorities in the Netherlands, beginning with the regent Mary of Hungary. This compounded a structural difficulty facing Cromwell, which would continue to bedevil English intelligence operations into the twentieth century: finding agents able to move about in the Netherlands, or at least persuading Englishmen to keep quiet about their aims. Pole had no problem with the former, thanks to the resources of the English exile community. Further, England was either without high-level diplomatic representation in the Netherlands or forced to employ inexperienced men (a problem which Cromwell brought on himself). Finally, the basic weakness of Cromwell's position at home underlay all three of his problems in the field, and translated once again into an embryonic strength for Pole.

Contrary to the views of some modern historians, assassination and kidnapping as instruments of policy were anything but innovations introduced to England in the reign of Elizabeth.[5] Rather, they had a respectable pedigree and had been revived early in Henry's reign in various attempts either to kill or suborn Richard de la Pole.[6] Nor were these tools regarded the least bit squeamishly. At roughly the same time Richard Sampson, Thomas Wolsey's agent in Tournai, almost offhandedly suggested to his master that one particularly annoying Tournaisien clergyman could be caught and disposed of for a small fee.[7] In 1527 Wolsey himself while on a diplomatic mission to France, was supposed to see that an envoy from Queen Katherine was "by some secret means ... stopped and molested." Wolsey agreed to intercept the messenger without letting him know that Henry and he were after him.[8] Near the end of Wolsey's long run as chief minister, several attempts to kidnap Tyndale were made on his orders.[9] A little later Stephen Vaughan, perhaps acting for Cromwell, tried to engineer the kidnapping of Friar Peto.[10] Thus when various agents went after Tyndale and Pole, they were acting in a vibrant tradition.

John Foxe recounted Tyndale's end in great detail, drawing on a memoir written by one of those who tried to save him, Thomas Poyntz.[11] Foxe blamed Harry Phillips for the execution of the whole plot. Phillips began by ingratiat-

---

5. R. L. Pollitt: "The Abduction of Dr. John Story and the Evolution of Elizabethan Intelligence Operations," *Sixteenth Century Journal* 14 (1983): 131-56.
6. C. G. Cruickshank: *The English Occupation of Tournai 1513-1519* (Oxford, 1971), 208-13.
7. *LP* 2: 2274.
8. SP 1/42: 211r (*LP* 4: 3278) and 215r (*LP* 4: 3283).
9. *LP* 4. III: 5402 and 5462.
10. *LP* 6: 1324.
11. Quoted *in extenso* by Mozley, 295-301.

VI

ing himself with Tyndale, who was living in the house of the Merchant Adventurers in Antwerp. Once he had Tyndale's confidence, Phillips went to Brussels where he lined up support, especially from the procurator-general, Pierre du Fief, and then returned to Antwerp while Poyntz was away and lured Tyndale out of his sanctuary into a trap. Tyndale was arrested about May 21, 1535, whisked into the hands of the procurator-general and imprisoned in the castle of Vilvoorde. Belatedly, Poyntz stirred Cromwell to act, but no letters from England had much effect. Poyntz continued to try to save Tyndale à l'outrance, chasing back and forth to England and after various imperial officials. For his pains he found himwelf accused of heresy and imprisoned, once more at the instance of Phillips and du Fief. These two even managed to neutralize orders in Tyndale's favor from more senior imperial officials, and insured his condemnation and execution.[12]

We know a great deal about Phillips, a forerunner of the type of "criminal adventurer" which proliferated in modern espionage.[13] He was the son of Richard Phillips, sometime member of Henry VII's household, customer of Poole, five times MP, and, curiously enough, perhaps a client of Cromwell.[14] Harry turned on his family, most of whom he apparently robbed in an effort to satisfy gambling debts run up in London.[15] Despite this, he pursued a successful career as a student, taking a B.C.L. in Oxford in 1533 and later perhaps actually studying in Louvain.[16] He claimed to have powerful patronage in the diocese of Exeter from Thomas Brerewood and John Underhill, both prebendaries of the cathedral.[17] Brerewood was chancellor of the bishop of Exeter and his vicar-general in spirituals, as well as a doctor of both laws, canon of St. Paul's, royal chaplain, and once promised the deanery of Exeter by Cromwell.

Like Phillips, Foxe's other villian, du Fief, was a man of parts. He has had an excruciatingly bad press, largely because of the understandably negative attitude to him which Francisco de Enzinas (Dryander) developed after du Fief

---

12. Mozley, 309 ff. See further D. D. Smeeton: *Lollard Themes in the Reformation Theology of William Tyndale* (Kirksville, Missouri, 1986), 73-4.

13. C. G. Andrew: *Secret Service: The Making of the British Intelligence Community* (London, 1985), 108 ff. For a sketch of Phillips's career, see Mozley, 297-9.

14. See S. T. Bindoff, ed.: *The House of Commons 1509-1558* (London, 1982), s.n. "Phillips, Harry."

15. SP 1/100: 95 r-102 v.

16. See A. B. Emden: *A Biographical Register of the University of Oxford A.D. 1501 to 1540* (Oxford, 1974), s.n. "Phillips, Harry."

17. See Mozley, 298; Emden, *Biographical Register*; and the entries in J. Le Neve: *Fasti ecclesiae anglicanae*, compiled J. M. Horn, 3, *Salisbury* (London, 1962) and 9, *Exeter* (London, 1964).

VI

imprisoned him, combined with the notoriety deriving from the present case.[18] He held the post of procurator-general of the council of Brabant from at least 1523, apparently for the next thirty years.[19] The theory of his office is clear, even if the near total destruction of the records of the council of Brabant to which he was responsible and of his office make it extremely difficult to learn much about how he exercised it.[20] Although he could indeed torture prisoners, and although the form of most cases of prosecutions in his name automatically highlighted his involvement, and although his wide powers were much abused and became a license to extort, in fact the procurator could almost never proceed without authorization from the council of Brabant, and was liable to punishment if he engaged in an unjustified prosecution. Of greatest importance here – he stood in the place of the emperor (or the duke before him). This almost certainly means that the operation had Charles V's full support.

Phillips and du Fief, however vile their character, could never have brought their scheme off alone, especially where not only Wolsey's but also Henry's own auspices had proved insufficient to secure success.[21] But it is difficult both to establish the degree of du Fief's responsibility, which hinges on the origin of a "commission" which Phillips may have had, and also to trace its origin. Thomas Theobald, who had been set to spy on Phillips after Tyndale's arrest, reported to Archbishop Cranmer that Philipps claimed to have "had a commission out also for to have taken Dr. Barnes & George Joye with other."[22] The earliest apparent reference to it came through an English merchant in Antwerp, George Collins, who on May 1, 1535, passed on a tip from Robert Flegge, who

---

18. C. A. Campan, ed.: *Mémoires de Francisco de Enzinas*, 1 (Societé de l'Histoire de Belgique. Collection des Mémoires relatifs à l'Histoire de Belgique, 13, 1862).

19. Du Fief was nominated on February 17, 1523 and died in 1553; see A. Gaillard: *Le conseil de Brabant* (Brussels, 1898-1902), 379. He began participating in heresy trials almost immediately after his appointment; see P. Kalkoff: *Die Anfänge der Gegenreformation in den Niederlanden*, 2 (Schriften des Vereins für Reformationsgeschichte, 81, 1904), 79, 107. P. Fredricq found him identified as procurator-general in a document of 1536 ("La fin de William Tindale," in *Mélanges d'histoire offerts à M. Charles Bémont* [Paris, 1913], 476) and Campan cited a case of 1543 involving du Fief as procurator-general (*Enzinas*, 355, 369, 491, 18).

20. See Gaillard, *Conseil de Brabant*, 348-65. See also P. Alexandre: *Histoire des origines, des développements et du rôle des officiers fiscaux dans les anciens Pays-Bas* (Brussels, 1891), 16 f., 20, 31, 126 f.

21. *LP* 5: 265, 354, and especially 1554. Cf. also Mozley, 130-3, 240; S. E. Lehmberg: *Sir Thomas Elyot, Tudor Humanist* (Austin, 1960), 106-7, 111; and F. W. Conrad: "A Preservative against Tyranny: The Political Theology of Sir Thomas Elyot" (Ph. D. diss., Johns Hopkins University, 1988; Ann Arbor, University Microfilms), 109-11.

22. See Mozley, 304.

had in turn been warned by the stadhouder of Bergen, Cornelis Bogaert, that "a commission came from the procurator-general of Brabant [du Fief] to take three Englishmen whereof one is Dr. Barnes."[23] This report has been taken to mean that du Fief invented the entire plot.[24] But if Poyntz was right to allege that Tyndale was captured "by procurement out of England," du Fief was only a high-powered agent.[25]

Phillips could well have had powerful backing at home, as he insisted. The cost of the operation led Theobald to observe that "either this Phillips hath great friends in England ... or ... he is well beneficed in the bishopric of Exeter."[26] Edward Hall chronicled the rumor that Tyndale had been captured "not without the help and procurement of some bishops of this realm."[27] Du Fief's importance suggests one heretofore overlooked clue to these clergymen's identity: good diplomatic contacts in the Low Countries. This further implicates J. F. Mozley's *bête noire*, John Stokesley, but it may mean that others like Cuthbert Tunstall also took a hand.

Like Stokesley, Tunstall had a long record of trying to root out heresy both at home and in the English merchant community in the Low Countries. Tunstall interrogated at least one person accused of knowing Tyndale's works.[28] In August 1529, Cromwell's agent Vaughan fell foul of a commission sent out by Tunstall and Thomas More.[29] Less than a year later the bishop attended Henry's condemnation of the heresy in Tyndale's New Testament.[30] By 1535, however, Tunstall had long been replaced in London by Stokesley and would have been relatively out of touch with the continent. Nevertheless, he had been on numerous missions to the Low Countries in the 1510s and '20s and had returned to Cambrai in mid-1529. Vaughan, bearing no grudge, wanted him back three years later to negotiate a new commercial treaty.[31] Tunstall must still have been at least *persona grata* with the imperial authorities in 1535.

23. For Collins's warning, see Mozley, 300. See also C. J. F. Slootmans: "Engelsche Lutheranen op de Jaarmarkten te Bergen-op-Zoom," *Taxandria* 49 (1942): 56, and his *Jan metten Lippen, zijn familie en zijn stad* (Rotterdam-Anvers, 1945), 323.

24. O. de Smedt: *De Engelse Natie te Antwerpen in de 16e Eeuw (1496-1582)*, 2 (Antwerp, 1954), 637.

25. Mozley, 309. Cf. ibid., 299-300, and R. Demaus: *William Tyndale. A Biography*, ed. R. Lovett (Amsterdam, 1971; reprint of the 1886 edition), 386-91.

26. Mozley, 305.

27. E. Hall: *The Union of the Two Noble and Illustre Famelies of Lancastre and Yorke* (London, 1809), 818.

28. *LP* 5: 589.

29. *LP* 4. III: 5823.

30. *LP* 4. III: 6402.

31. *LP* 4. III: 5744 and 5: 804.

VI

Stokesley, coming to London at the beginning of More's chancellorship fresh from a diplomatic tour of Europe which may have included a meeting with the emperor's party in Bologna, inevitably took an even more active role against Tyndale than Tunstall had. In December 1531 he examined James Bainham, who owned four of Tyndale's works.[32] Stokesley's celebrated feud with Hugh Latimer began about the same time.[33] But of greatest importance in the present context is the fact that Stokesley's attack on heresy led him into conflict with Cromwell. From almost the moment Cromwell first achieved a position of importance in mid-1532, he was known as an opponent of Stokesley, and he received a steady stream of requests for protection against Stokesley's heresy-hunting throughout the bishop's life.[34] Their dispute intensified during 1534 and 1535, with Cromwell trying to trap Stokesley in a liasion with a nun who had borne a child and, more seriously, to condemn him as at least lukewarm on the Supremacy. Stokesley defended himself by claiming that he could not remember exactly what he had preached and agreeing with an ill grace and veiled threats to let George Browne preach in London.[35] At precisely the time of the attack on Tyndale, Stokesley was sitting in judgment on twenty-three Flemish heretics.[36] The most damning evidence against Stokesley is that several of his servants were seen in the Low Countries. Sometime late in 1532 or early in 1533 Tyndale reported the appearance in Antwerp of John Tisen "with a red beard and a black-reddish head," but he stayed away from the English.[37] At nearly the same time, Vaughan suggested that Cromwell find out what another of Stokesley's servants, a notary named Docwraye, had been doing in Antwerp.[38] Thus Stokesley had motive, means and probably opportunity.

It still remains to explain how Cromwell suffered such a humiliating defeat. While it is true that he officially distanced himself from Tyndale already in 1531, he was ready enough to accede to Vaughan's urgings in 1536.[39] Richard Demaus suggested that domestic events, notably the proceedings against More

---

32. *LP* 5: 583.
33. E.g., *LP* 5: 607, 704, 860.
34. *LP* 5: 926, 1083, 1176, 1203, 1432; *LP* 6: 99; and so on, including *LP* 9: 1115, 1150.
35. *LP* 6: 907; *LP*, 8: 1019, 1043, and especially 1054.
36. *LP* 8: 771.
37. *LP* 6: 403.
38. *LP* 6: 934; cf. Mozley, 300.
39. For the events of 1531, when Vaughan's ardor for Tyndale nearly got him into serious trouble with Henry, see W. C. Richardson: *Stephen Vaughan, Financial Agent of Henry VIII. A Study on Financial Relations with the Low Countries* (Baton Rouge, La., 1953), 31-4; and G. R. Elton: *Reform and Renewal. Thomas Cromwell and the Common Weal* (Cambridge, 1973).

and John Fisher, absorbed too much of his attention.[40] Cromwell's hand would also have been weakened by the king's apparent refusal to let Cromwell write in his name.[41] It could be that Henry (and perhaps Cromwell) still resented Tyndale's attack on the divorce as well as his lack of cooperation when he was offered a second chance. But Cromwell tried hard enough when he finally intervened in September 1535, even if his level of involvement must have tailed off by March 1536 when Vaughan was still urging him to act. By then the plot against Anne was in motion, and Cromwell was watching his every movement.[42]

Vaughan probably put his finger on the major reason for Cromwell's failure, the lack of anyone in Flanders in a position of authority on whom he could rely, a problem compounded by ideological differences.[43] The post of ambassador in Brussels was left vacant after John Hackett's death in 1534 until the emergency appointment of John Hutton in 1537, while Cromwell concerned himself much more with protecting his interest in Hackett's estate than in guarding his diplomatic flank.[44] Or it may be that the best candidates to represent England there could not pass the test of ideological purity which Cromwell increasingly applied, while the men he might have preferred, perhaps including Vaughan or William Lok, were unacceptable to Henry. The appointment of Thomas Wriothesley as Hutton's successor in 1538 simultaneously indicates that Cromwell had both belatedly realized the importance of the post and that he had extreme difficulty in finding a man on whom he could rely. Wriothes-

---

40. Demaus, *Tyndale*, 395.

41. Cromwell at least made a note to ask Henry whether he should write (*LP* 9: 498). Vaughan thanked Cromwell for his two letters for Tyndale on September 9 (*LP* 9: 275), and Hall (*Union*, 818) referred only to letters from Cromwell, but Foxe made all letters from England anonymous. *Acts and monuments*, ed. S. R. Cattley (London, 1838), 5: 123-4.

42. The final word on the coup and counter-coup of 1536 has yet to be said: G. R. Elton sketched their main lines in *Reform and Reformation England 1509-1558* (Cambridge, Mass., 1977), 250-3; but see more recently D. R. Starkey: *The Reign of Henry VIII: Personalities and Politics* (London, 1985), 108-18; J. A. Guy: "Privy Council: Revolution or Evolution?," in: C. Coleman and D. R. Starkey, eds.: *Revolution Reassessed: Revisions in the History of Tudor Government and Administration* (Oxford, 1986), 77-80 (the fuller account can be found in R. M. Warnicke: "The Fall of Anne Boleyn: A Reassessment," *History* 70 (1985): 1-15; "Sexual Heresy at the Court of Henry VIII," *Historical Journal* 30 (1987): 247-68; and G. W. Bernard: "Politics and Government in Tudor England," *Historical Journal* 31 (1988): 160-62. The main point at issue concerns the degree of Cromwell's responsibility; of late the balance of opinion is shifting against assigning the major portion of blame for Anne's demise to him.

43. See Mozley, 312.

44. *LP* 8: 752, and 9: 562, 1296.

VI

ley's handling of the renegade Phillips, whom he probably deliberately let slip through his fingers together with a large sum of money, was an almost certain sign that he would not support Cromwell's ideological politics.[45]

In 1535 the nearest substitute for an English ambassador, the governor of the Merchant Adventurers in Antwerp, failed to intercede for Tyndale.[46] Nor did Cromwell have any kind of effective local agent. Blinded by faulty or insufficient information, Cromwell directed one of his letters to a man disinclined to help because of his hostility to the Reformation, Antonius van Glymes, marquess of Bergen.[47] On the other hand, Cromwell had good reason to turn to the authorities of Bergen, knowing of their strong desire to preserve commerce with England. A delegation had just been to London, and had even promised to defy the emperor, if he ordered them to cease trading with the English.[48] And the stadhouder of Bergen may have leaked word of Phillips's mission to Flegge out of a desire to protect good commercial relations with England.[49] Thus Cromwell may only have been mistaken to rely on the authorities of Bergen too much. Then again, better intelligence might have shown his allies' limits. Cromwell's own domestic ideological and factional ties produced little better results. He could mobilize only Theobald, a client of the earl of Wiltshire "with some assistance from Cranmer," and then Robert Farrington to track Phillips, but they were much too unimportant to help much.[50]

Thus round one went unequivocally to Stokesley and his friends. Although Cromwell robbed them of the full fruits of their triumph over Anne Boleyn in mid-1536, the conservatives almost certainly hoped both then and later that Pole would retrieve their victory by returning home and regaining Henry's favor. This was probably particularly true of the vast majority of them who had refused the violent option of the Pilgrimage of Grace. Although faced with a more difficult problem given the much higher level of concern over Pole, the conservatives successfully helped to scupper at least three attempts to capture

---

45. *CSPSp* 5.I: 122. For differing opinions on Wriothesley's religion see G.R.Elton: "Thomas Cromwell's Decline and Fall," *Cambridge Historical Journal* 10 (1951): 152; D. Hoak: *The King's Council in the Reign of Edward VI* (Cambridge, 1976), 347; A.J.Slavin: "The Fall of Lord Chancellor Wriothesley: A Study in the Politics of Conspiracy," *Albion* 7 (1975): 272-4, 275; Bindoff, *House of Commons*, 3: 663-6, and J.Murphy: "The Illusion of Decline: the Privy Chamber, 1547-1558," in: D.R.Starkey, ed.: *The English Court from the Wars of the Roses to the Civil War* (London, 1987), 123, 133.

46. Mozley, 311.

47. Mozley, 312-14; Slootmans, *Jan metten Lippens*, 323, 325.

48. *CSPSp* 5.II: 215.

49. Slootmans, "Engelsche Lutheranen," 56.

50. See Mozley, 304, 320-1; E.W.Ives: *Anne Boleyn* (Oxford, 1986), 306-7.

or assassinate him. Their opposition may have so taxed even Cromwell's formidable political skills that he had little left for diplomatic maneuvering. Pole's own aims, especially once they were fully incorporated into papal policy, combined with imperial interest, meant that Pole's legation posed a serious threat. And as R. B. Merriman long ago noted, Pole's diplomacy worked over the long term to defeat Cromwell.[51] The lord privy seal was right to be worried.

In the course of a key document in his self-creation Pole gave the king's council a thoroughly innocuous version of his plans the day after his appointment in February 1537. The pope had given him the legation, Pole wrote, because of Pole's zeal for the church. His assignment covered "three great matters": "peace with the princes beyond the mountains," "abolishing of heresies and resisting against the Turk." Pole continued in a now badly mutilated passage that he had special charge to see "if God might open any gate [where]by I might enter to do you that good" which he had always hoped to do. The Latin version of this letter is more blunt. Pole was looking for a gate which would allow him "dissentientes vos in opinionibus ecclesie componerem." It is of great significance that Pole concluded by alluding to his new prophetic *persona*, declaring that he hoped to give a twist to the old saying about prophets and honor.[52] Pole remained studiedly vague throughout his legation about his aims, often promising that he would give his correspondent more information at another time or asking him to wait for further particulars from one of Pole's companions.[53] The one exception is a letter to his ally Gasparo Contarini, which breaks off at precisely the point where he began to set down his plans.[54] It was normal practice to avoid committing anything dangerous to writing, but the inference must not be drawn that because no such plans survive, Pole was incapable of translating his strong sense of strategy into tactics.[55]

---

51. R. B. Merriman: *Life and Letters of Thomas Cromwell* (Oxford, 1902), 1: 211.

52. SP 1/119: 60 r–v (English), 69 r (Latin), Rome February 16, 1537 (*LP* 12: 444). Cf. P. S. Donaldson: "Machiavelli, Antichrist, and the Reformation: Prophetic Typology in Reginald Pole's *De unitate* and *Apologia ad Carolum quintum*," in: R. L. DeMolen, ed.: *Leaders of the Reformation* (Selinsgrove, 1984), 211–46.

53. For example, *ERP* 2: 24, 14.

54. *Ibid.*: 15. This letter can be dated by the report of the vice-legate of Piacenza that Pole reached his city on March 3, and intended to leave on the 5th. Archivio di Stato, Parma, Carteggio Farnesiane Interno, busta 3, January–June 1537 (unfoliated).

55. R. H. Pogson: "Cardinal Pole – Papal Legate to England in Mary Tudor's Reign" (Ph. D. thesis, Cambridge University, 1972; Cambridge: Cambridge University Library), 27 and 31. Pogson relied on Pole's biographer Ludovico Beccadelli, who was drawing on Pole's own later recollections of his actions in Paris in 1529-30, but see my "A Mission

VI

Despite Pole's careful self-presentation, he could not fully conceal his aims. They appear at greatest length in a position paper for Paul III about any mission to England. Pole stated bluntly that its major object, the reestablishment of "the accustomed authority," would require the pope to send "someone confirmed to them [the Pilgrims] in the name of your holiness, to help not only with words, but again with deeds, who would need to have a certain quantity of money" to give the "so well deserving" rebels. This support was a hedge against a trick by Henry, who might promise to attend to the insurgents' demands only to destroy their leaders once he had them in his hands.[56] The pope incorporated Pole's hypothetical advice into the secret part of the bull appointing him legate *a latere*. Paul equably accepted the prospect of returning Henry to the faith by force. If this could not be, better it were that he and all his supporters should die rather than endanger the salvation of others. The pope very much hoped the Pilgrims would rebel again, and ordered Pole to encourage them when they did so by a crusading indulgence.[57] A letter was drawn up at the same time as Pole's appointment instructing Erard de la Marck, cardinal of Liège, to provide Pole with money for the rebels, but it is not yet known whether it took effect.[58] Pole certainly had the enthusiastic support of the nuncio in Paris, Rodolfo Pio, who probably planned much of his legation.[59] In light of the short time between Pole's memorandum to the pope (probably January 1537), his bull of appointment (February 15) and his letter to the king's council (February 16), self-fashioning here comes to look uncommonly like prevarication.

Near the middle of his legation, Pole reiterated most of his memorandum in a letter to the pope. Refusing a nearly direct order to abandon his mission, he insisted that the people of England needed him to put the fear of God into their leaders, as was already happening. If he left Flanders, the people would despair and their enemies would be left securely in control. This would also violate Pole's new principle – elaborated in *De unitate* – that the people should always be consulted, and better, could be relied on to rebel once more since the

---

Worse than Death" (as in n.1) for both Pole's great practical success and how he reworked that episode.

56. See also *ERP* 2: cclxxvii-viii.

57. *LP* 12.I: 779. Cf. G. B. Parks: "The Parma Letters and the Dangers to Cardinal Pole," *Catholic Historical Review* 46 (1960): 310-11, one of the few pieces to get Pole's aims right.

58. C. Baroni: *Annales ecclesiastici*, 32 (Paris, 1878): 454, a partial letter dated February 15, 1537.

59. See my "A Diet for Henry VIII," 307-9.

cause of the recent disturbance had not been removed. Thus, repeating himself almost literally, Pole argued that the faithful English Catholics deserved a permanent envoy in Flanders, "who should be ready not only in word but in deed."[60] Pole disagreed with Contarini that it would be an affront to his dignity to stay in Flanders indefinitely, and reiterated that his departure would give victory to his opponents.[61]

Pole owed his safe refuge in Flanders to imperial protection. True, Charles tried first to suppress Pole's legation; when that failed he instructed an envoy bound for England that open support had to be withheld until Pole clearly had tangible backing and had either toppled Henry or had at least brought the English people to the point where they would certainly rid themselves of the king. Nevertheless, the emperor instructed his sister to use her judgment about how much to help Pole.[62] Mary cast a diplomatic blanket over Pole and must have ordered de la Marck, the chief of her council, to shelter him. When Hutton tried to bring her to prevent Pole from entering Flanders, she lied to him and told him Pole was already within her domain.[63] Once Pole reached Liège and de la Marck's hospitality he felt himself perfectly safe. According to one of Pole's reports to the pope, de la Marck had saved him from repeated ambushes, and the citizens of Liège would do anything for his welfare.[64] As the English may have known, the emperor took a reasonably active interest in Pole's possible uses from 1535 onward and some imperial agents were most impressed by his value to an attack on England, including the ambassador in London, Eustace Chapuys.[65] The imperial ambassador in Rome also knew Pole's attitude and the full details of his mission.[66]

Thus the odds appear to have been against the English before ever they began to entrap Pole. Some of them could have been in little doubt about Pole's hostility to Henry and the urgency of the situation. At least the committee which read *De unitate* must have known his attitude well; it almost certainly

---

60. *ERP* 2: 19 (pp. 51–4).
61. *ERP* 2: 28.
62. *LP* 12.I: 123; B. L. Add. MS 28,589: 248 r (*LP* 12.I: 696).
63. SP 1/120: 209 r, 235 r–v (*LP* 12.I: 1293, 1306).
64. *ERP* 2: 21 (p. 59), 24 (p. 66).
65. See my "The Life and Thought of Thomas Starkey," (Ph.D. diss., University of Minnesota, 1983; Ann Arbor: University Microfilms), 114–17.
66. *LP* 12.I: 123; B. L. Add. MS 28,589: 217 v (*LP* 12.I: 1141). Pole unfairly regarded the ambassador as a major obstacle; Archivio di stato Parma, Epistolario scelto, busta 13: 2 r.

VI

reached Cromwell through his man Richard Morison.[67] Even though Pole accepted Contarini's advice and cut his invitation to Charles to invade England, Contarini was not around to prevent Pole from putting the identical threat into the covering letter.[68] Michael Throckmorton was to warn Henry about the dangers which might arise "of outward power of those princes to whose honor it is judged to appertain to defend the laws of the church against all other princes or nations that will impugn them."[69] The French also passed some of their full information to the English.[70] Despite this knowledge, none of the English operations came even close to success. First, diplomatic efforts with Francis failed ignominiously. Stephen Gardiner began by dawdling on the way to an audience with Francis at which he was to ask the French king to honor his treaty with Henry and hand Pole over as a traitor. As a result, Pole entered Paris without difficulty.[71] Next, Gardiner failed to let Hutton, the new ambassador in Brussels, know of his difficulties.[72] Then he flagrantly breached his orders and struck a deal with Francis by which Pole would merely be expelled from France. Finally, Gardiner and Sir Francis Bryan allowed Pole not only to escape but to leave them in the dark about his intentions.[73]

The second phase turned rougher. In it, Peter Mewtas appeared in Paris with orders to kill Pole with a "hand goon."[74] He was also to prod Gardiner and Bryan to fulfill their separate instructions both to "research and try out the mystery of Pole's so sudden departure from Paris and likewise to have good espiall continually upon him," and to try to "have the said Pole by some means trussed up and conveyed to Calais." Bryan was specially charged to find "such fellows for the enterprise ... as [are] by secret wise and for their courage meet for that purpose."[75] Bryan's men may have fulfilled the second requirement, but they bungled the first. He enlisted Sir Thomas Palmer, knight porter of Calais,

---

67. See my *Thomas Starkey and the Commonweal: Humanist Politics and Religion in the Reign of Henry VIII* (Cambridge, 1989), 232.
68. See T. F. Dunn: "The Development of the Text of Pole's *De Unitate Ecclesiae*," *Papers of the Bibliographical Society of America* 70 (1976): 463.
69. B. L. Cleopatra E VI: 347 v–348 r.
70. *LP* 12. I: 625.
71. SP 49/5: 21 r (*LP* 12. I: 760); *LP* 12. I: 865; Lestocquoy, 215, 252.
72. *LP* 12. I: 817.
73. B. L. Add. MS 25,114: 257.
74. SP 1/138: 192v (*LP* 13. II: 797). There is a brief and incomplete discussion of Mewtas's mission in M. L. Robertson: "Thomas Cromwell's Servants: The Ministerial Household in Early Tudor Government and Society," (Ph. D. diss., University of California–Los Angeles, 1975; Ann Arbor, University Microfilms), 242.
75. B. L. Add. MS 25,114: 262 r (*LP* 12. I: 1032), 258 r, 263 r.

and he in turn found three or four other soldiers, the "Wingfield connection," and received the large sum of £100 for them.⁷⁶ They chased Pole into Hainault, but the cardinal learned of their plans and the gaff was blown. Henry called off any further pursuit on May 18, unless Bryan and Gardiner could persuade their agents to work in hopes of a future reward.⁷⁷

Thus the last chance fell to Hutton. At least he took his job seriously. His dispatches always bore at least the endorsement "haste post haste/haste post haste" and he strove diligently to fulfill his charge from Henry "to have continual espialls to the intent I might the better advertise your grace of the estate and conversation of your grace's traitor Pole."⁷⁸ Hutton's most serious handicap was a lack of agents. He was forced either to borrow men from the Calais garrison or to take his chances amongst the English exiles in order to effect his designs. Hutton's success in the latter is well indicated by Pole's "turning" of his most promising recruit.⁷⁹ Nor did Hutton always expend his energies in the most obviously productive ways, unless he and Cromwell were working to a secret agenda. He spent a good deal of time trying to catch Phillips by persuading him to smuggle letters into England baked in loaves of bread, but the plot miscarried.⁸⁰ Although Hutton would almost certainly have had to take part in another alleged scheme to deal with Pole – the offer of large numbers of troops in exchange for him – there is no independent confirmation of this story told by Pole's first two biographers.⁸¹

The dramatis personae of these attempts against Pole point to the last and most intractable problem facing Cromwell overseas. The English diplomatic establishment was anything but his tool. Experienced men like Gardiner and Bryan at best passively obstructed the lord privy seal's designs, while his own men either, like Mewtas, lacked much understanding of how to approach assassination subtly or, like Hutton, were out of their depth. The embassy in Paris was especially troublesome. Bryan allegedly told all to one of his opposite numbers in the French Privy Chamber, who may even have been the gentleman

---

76. SP 1/120: 276 r (*LP* 12.I: app. 4).

77. B. L. Add. MS 25,114: 265 r (*LP* 12.I: 1235).

78. SP 1/121: 136 r (*LP* 12.II: 107).

79. SP 1/120: 136 v, and *ERP* 2: 24 (pp. 66-7). Phillips explained to Hutton that the prospect, one William Vaughan, had refused to cooperate further for conscientious reasons (SP 1/121: 152 r).

80. *LP* 12.I: 1293.

81. L. Beccadelli: "Vita del cardinale Reginaldo Polo," ed. G. B. Morandi: *Monumenti di varia letteratura* (Bologna, 1797–1804), 1. II: 295; A. Dudic: *Vita Reginaldi Poli*, in *ERP* 1: 16.

VI

whom Francis sent to warn Pole as soon as the legate reached Paris.[82] Nor did Bryan and Gardiner prevent their machinations from coming to Pio's notice.[83] Just when Pole was made legate, Gardiner had to be strenuously called to account for advising Henry that the Pilgrims deserved a hearing. Whoever reprimanded Gardiner complained that the bishop must "have had some advertisement from some person of that faction that would put you in fear of things, [in order] to win you again to their naughty opinion."[84] Sir John Wallop, the English resident in Paris, may have been the culprit. Wallop kept both himself and Pio informed about the Pilgrimage of Grace, and, more important, he publicly expressed sympathy for Pole.[85] Almost as bad from Cromwell's point of view, Wallop complained to the nuncio in July 1536 about Cromwell's interference in Stokesley's efforts to suppress unauthorized preaching.[86] If Chapuys can be trusted, Wallop was an even older enemy of Cromwell than Stokesley. Five years after the event, Chapuys claimed that Wallop attacked Cromwell immediately after Wolsey's fall and Cromwell had sought Henry's protection as a result.[87] Gardiner and Cromwell were permanently at odds, as the dispatch of Mewtas to keep an eye on Gardiner indicates.[88] Other key components of the English diplomatic apparatus may also have been doubtful in Cromwell's eyes, including Richard Pate, ambassador to the emperor, who had supported Mary in 1536, and closer to home Peter Vannes, Henry's Latin secretary who handled much incoming diplomatic correspondence.[89] The newly arrived Pio had assured Vannes of his good will in April 1535, at the same time as the nuncio asked to be recommended to Stokesley, Gardiner and Bryan.[90] Although like Cromwell a minion of Wolsey, Vannes was never Cromwell's man, becoming dean of Salisbury after his fall.[91] It may well be that Cromwell recruited Thomas Starkey in 1535 as an alternative to Vannes.[92]

If so, another of Cromwell's weapons turned in his hand. Every member of Pole's family, Elizabeth Darrell (and probably therefore her lover, Sir Thomas

---

82. SP 1/138: 217v–218r (*LP* 13.II: 804); Lestocquoy, 215 (*LP* 12.I: 931).
83. Lestocquoy, 215, 217.
84. B. L. Add. MS 25,114: 247v.
85. Lestocquoy, 194 (pp. 232-3); *LP* 12.I: 165.
86. *LP* 11: 52.
87. *CSPSp* 5.I: 228.
88. B. L. Caligula E 2: 233r.
89. See Ives, *Anne Boleyn* (as in n. 50), 347 (Pate is made ambassador in Rome).
90. LP 8: 622.
91. See L. Stephen and S. Lee, eds.: *The Dictionary of National Biography*, 20 (Oxford, 1917): 134-136.
92. See my *Starkey* (as in n. 67), 203-5.

Wyatt), Sir Edward Neville and an enormous number of servants knew all about the moves against Pole, probably courtesy originally of Starkey.[93] And Palmer's expedition was no more help. One of his servants eventually tipped his master's hand to Pole, but Palmer's sortie was doomed before it ever left Calais.[94] He chose dependents of Sir Robert Wingfield, whose ferocious quarrel with the deputy of Calais, Lord Lisle, virtually guaranteed problems.[95] Cromwell's protégé John Bale's attack on the bishops in the privy council could be generalized to include the large number of Pole's friends in places of power. "When so ever any godly enterprise is therein doing, be it never so privily handled, yet shall the pope, the prelates of Italy, Spain, France, Flanders and Scotland have sure knowledge thereof by your secret messengers, and you again their crafty compassings to deface it if it may be."[96]

If we continue to work outward from Pole and backward to England we quickly uncover a large number of potentially disaffected people in key positions, many of whose seats were clustered in one vital area of southern England, eastern Hampshire and western Sussex. Calais, whence Cromwell both tried to conduct diplomatic relations with the Low Countries before Hutton's appointment and to recruit most of the personnel who chased Pole, was probably especially infertile ground for him. Palmer owed his principal allegiance to Lisle, who would be brought down in 1540 in part by charges of having a private talk with Pole with whom he probably sympathized.[97] Palmer's men, or at least the Wingfields, were probably clients of the Duke of Suffolk, an indefatigable opponent of Anne Boleyn.[98] Perhaps the Calais Act of 1536, which

---

93. See my "Diet for Henry VIII," 323.

94. SP 1/121: 137r (*LP* 12.II: 107). The Welsh chronicle of Calais supports this story, making Palmer responsible for both the kidnapping and assassination plots against Pole; M. St. Claire Byrne, ed.: *The Lisle Letters* (Chicago, 1981), 4: 223.

95. *LP* 12.I: 440, 555, 625.

96. *The Epistle exhortatory of an English Christian unto his dearly beloved Country of England* (Basel?, 1544), sig. xxvv.

97. For Palmer's tangled career, see *Lisle Letters*, indices. A. J. Slavin treats Lisle's religious views and his political position in Calais in "Cromwell, Cranmer and Lord Lisle: A Study in the Politics of Reform," *Albion* 9 (1977): 316-36.

98. For the Wingfields, see the genealogical chart in S. J. Gunn: *Charles Brandon, Duke of Suffolk 1484-1545* (Oxford, 1988), 48-9 and 119, 137, for the duke's relations with Anne. I am indebted to Dr. Gunn for help with the numerous Wingfields and Suffolk's politics. Ives, *Anne Boleyn* (as in n. 50), 379, also discusses Suffolk's attitude to the Queen. It may also be significant that Sir Richard Wingfield's widow was the source of some of the most damning evidence against Anne, which may have found its way to Suffolk through the Wingfields. *Ibid.*, 377-80.

VI

required the officers of Guisnes to be resident, accounts for the arrival of William Lord Sandys in April 1537, but he was as disaffected as he was experienced. This arose in part from Cromwell's handling of Sandys's long-running dispute with Lisle and a more recent controversy with Sir Robert Wingfield. Sandys frequently stayed away from Court after 1534, often pleading illness, and usually staying at The Vyne in Hampshire. He assured Chapuys in early 1535 that the emperor "had the hearts of all this kingdom."[99] Sandys wrote Cromwell from Guisnes of his pleasure at the capture of his old ally, Lord Darcy, but in wholly conventional terms and at the end of a letter defending himself for failing to report apparently seditious rumors.[100] Cromwell once again undermined Sandys's position by issuing a commission to Lisle to investigate his activities and, according to Sandys, failing to protect Sandys's interests in some other unspecified way.[101]

In England itself, the majority of the short list of councillors Henry gave the Pilgrims in December 1536 as well as many of their neighbors should also be added to the column of Pole's admirers. These include Sir William Paulet, the Marquess of Exeter, leader of what has been called the only proper faction in England in the 1530s, Sir William Fitzwilliam, bishops Sampson and Tunstall, the Duke of Norfolk, the Earl of Shrewsbury, and Sir John Russell.[102] I do not argue that disaffection or religious conservatism necessarily meant support for Pole, but if there were even a rough equivalence between these two the odds were strongly in Pole's favor. Yet someone wanted Pole destroyed. Who? The traditional answer from all but one wavering dissenter has been Henry. Nevertheless, the question might be reopened in light of the factional and ideological alignments sketched here.

The strongest evidence for Henry's guilt comes from the French ambassador, reporting at the height of the scare triggered by the discovery of the Exeter conspiracy in late 1538. Louis de Perreau, sieur de Castillon, wrote Montmorency in November that Henry had long ago expressed his resolve to exterminate the White Rose "house of Montagu," along with the remainder of the Poles.[103] This report has frequently, and again recently, been taken as overwhelming proof of Henry's primacy, the more so when Castillon's "long ago" has been interpreted to refer to a time shortly after his arrival in England in

---

99. *LP* 8: 48.
100. *LP* 12.I: 961.
101. *LP* 12.I: 151, 171, 172, 589.
102. See my "Diet for Henry VIII," 324–27.
103. *LP* 13.II: 753.

1537, when Henry's anger over Pole's cardinalate was still fresh.[104] Castillon's reports deserve more careful handling. Mere chronology should raise eyebrows, since we are asked to believe that Castillon waited more than a year before passing on his information.[105] Further, many of the details in his report are wrong, including a false but possibly revealing title for Pole's grandfather. While pretending detailed knowledge of the "White Rose," Castillon made him the duke of Lancaster and therefore assigned him to exactly the wrong side. This may cast doubt on the value of his sources, while his further comment that "I believe that few of the lords have an assured position in this country" may reveal his party allegiance.

Castillon offered another lead to his motives when he put this dispatch into context in a companion letter of the same date which lacks all the excited trappings of this one. Writing to Jean Cardinal du Bellay, Castillon admitted first that "we are in the worst possible favor with these gentlemen here" and second that "I know not what will come" of the arrests of Exeter and Montagu (whom the ambassador also identified merely as being of "the most noble of this kingdom").[106] It would therefore appear that Castillon engaged in a little editorializing in his first report. If we consider to whom that letter was addressed, together with Castillon's antipathy to Henry and especially what the ambassador took to be the king's religious policies, then the pronounced coalescence between Castillon's analysis of English affairs and that offered by both Pio and Pole increases the likelihood that Castillon hewed much more closely to a party line than to any imagined duty to report reliably. His letter went to Francis's chief minister, Anne de Montmorency, who strongly favored peace with the Empire and therefore opposed an alliance with Henry.[107] Castillon's violent denigration of Henry gave Montmorency exactly what he needed to support his case.[108] At the same time, Castillon constantly pressed Montmorency to move the pope to slap an interdict on anyone, especially Flemings, who traded

---

104. C. Höllger: "The Destruction of the Pole Family," unpublished paper. I am grateful to Mr. Höllger for letting me see a copy of his work.

105. He arrived in London sometime between June 6 and September 9, 1537 (*LP* 12.II: 46, 670).

106. *LP* 13.II: 752.

107. D. L. Potter: "Diplomacy in the Mid-sixteenth Century: England and France, 1536–1550," (Ph. D. diss., Cambridge University, 1973; Cambridge University Library), xiii. Jean Kaulek erred in thinking that Castillon was very concerned to preserve an English alliance. *Correspondance politique de MM. Castillon et de Marillac* (Paris, 1885), xvi.

108. *LP* 12.II: 1285; 13.I: 56, 274 (calling Henry "a little sick in the head" because he was prepared to believe that a peace between Francis and the emperor was possible); 13.II: 78.

VI

with England. Once that was done, the people of England would take care of Henry.[109] This had been Pole's scheme in theory (and then as policy) since 1531.[110] Finally in December 1538 Castillon fired off one more outburst which could have been lifted verbatim from one of Pio's dispatches of some years earlier or, for that matter, from the unexpurgated version of *De unitate*, with their assurance of intense popular dissatisfaction and suggestion of the same remedy for Henry's misbehavior.[111] Perhaps Castillon's reference to the White Rose also becomes more explicable in light of Pio's obsession with that non-existent party, and Pole's intense interest in his origins and exalted standing.[112] Finally, Castillon's sententious commentary on the arrests fits this theory of his party allegiance. Alas, we know next to nothing about Castillon's life in 1535 and 1536. Nevertheless, the circumstantial case presented here reinforces the suspicions of a partially closed loop feeding the image of Henry the ogre.

Thus Castillon's testimony requires discounting. This does not exonerate Henry, any more than the fact that most of what transpired in 1537 was done in his name incriminates him. Without reviving the "king or minister" debate, some evidence should be laid against Cromwell at least as strong as Castillon's against Henry. As Sir Geoffrey Pole confessed, Starkey told him "that the lord pr[ivy] seal if the king was not of a good nature for one Pole's sake would destroy all Poles." Cromwell singled out this statement as part of the evidence which he at one point thought to use to attaint Starkey posthumously along with the Exeter conspirators.[113] It will be noted that this statement contained nothing treasonous, at least not against Henry. Depending upon Sir Geoffrey's

---

109. *LP* 13.I: 205, 274, 844.

110. It appeared originally in Cranmer's report on Pole's divorce opinion as the most serious way in which the emperor could threaten England. B.L. Lansdowne 115: 2r (also printed in N. Pocock: *Records of the Reformation. The Divorce, 1527–1533* [Oxford, 1870], 2: 130-1).

111. "The time could not be more favorable, both on account of his [Henry's] inhuman cruelties to religion [the honor of the church runs constantly through Castillon's dispatches], which ought to make him the enemy of all Christians ... as they [Montmorency and Francis] are in hand to forbid all commerce with the English, they should agree to get rid of them altogether, and deliver the kingdom as a prey." This would be easy once again because "the people are inconceivably discontented ... [therefore] chase them out of their den of cruelty and heresy." Castillon continued at great length about how to divide the conquered country and repeated his plan for a papal interdict. Quoted from the text in *LP* 13.II: 1162.

112. See my *Starkey* (as in n.67), 155-6.

113. SP 1/138; 215v; *LP* 13.II: 804.2. Starkey's name was marked in the margin of a later copy of this evidence, in the same way as those actually attainted were. See also SP 1/139: 39r.

memory and when Starkey spoke to him, this evidence is at least as reliable as Castillon's, for although Starkey fell under a cloud in 1536 and never again regained Cromwell's trust, he remained in Henry's favor until his death in 1538.[114] For what it is worth, Pole echoed Starkey's remark almost exactly in conversation with Sir Geoffrey's servant, Hugh Holland. "Would the lord privy seal so fain kill me? Well, I trust it shall not lie in his power, the king is not contented to bear me malice."[115] Pole also wrote Henry after *De unitate* that Cromwell had been "most fervent of all touching the suasion of my return."[116] Latimer's testimony from the other side of the fence supports Starkey's and Pole's evidence. As he wrote Cromwell in December 1538, "I heard you say once, after you had seen that furious invective of cardinal Pole [*De unitate*] that you would make him to eat [his] own heart."[117]

Of course, all these sentiments, save Latimer's, may have both been carefully crafted to avoid the treason laws, and also sprung from the common reflex to blame the minister rather than the king. Nevertheless, the extent of Cromwell's plans for Pole as well as the men he chose to execute many of them give substance to Pole's claims. It is easy to see what Cromwell intended in approving Holland's role as financial conduit for Pole's partisan John Helyar or in proclaiming himself "good lord" to Geoffrey Pole when his dealings with Holland became known.[118] He went yet further, and registered greatest success with his own two men in the field. Mewtas almost certainly shared religious sympathies with Cromwell, judging from his "eyes only" report that Gardiner had written against Latimer and shown the draft to Wallop.[119] Mewtas alone received orders to kill Pole. Even if Bryan really said he would assassinate the legate, that exceeded his instructions which never told him to do worse than tie Pole up and spirit him to Calais. Hutton's diligence almost certainly arose from his allegiance to Cranmer, perhaps also for religious reasons. The archbishop steadily sought favor for him, at one point telling Cromwell that Hutton was "most bound unto you of all men."[120] A conventional sentiment no doubt, but sympathy for reform could well explain Hutton's more tangible interest in Phillips.

All of this – deep plots, careful choice of the right agents, ideological motiva-

---

114. See my *Starkey*, 231–6, 243–6.
115. SP 1/138: 192 v.
116. B. L. Cleopatra E VI: 341 r.
117. B. L. Cleopatra E IV: 323 r (*LP* 13. II: 1030).
118. SP 1/139: 154 r (*LP* 13. II: 875).
119. B. L. Caligula E 2: 233 r.
120. *LP* 13. II: 25. See also B. L. Harleian MS 6148: 43 r (*LP* 7: 568).

VI

tion – squares much better with the character of Cromwell we have been taught over the last thirty years than it does with that of his vacillating, if allegedly bloodthirsty, master. Judging from the denoument of Pole's legation, it looks as if Merriman – the exception to the universal condemnation of Henry mentioned earlier – got the story nearly right.[121] The protracted and probably sincere efforts to get Pole back to England by peaceful means which continued into August 1537 smack much more of the temporizing Henry, and Stokesley, his old comrade-in-ideological-arms and Cromwell's enemy, had a major share in this campaign.

Thus Pole's self-creation turns out to contain a germ of information which accords well with an independent analysis. Cromwell does seem to have been his chief antagonist. There is a paradox here. The force of the conflict between these two provided much of the energy which Pole converted into his own guiltless *persona*, which comes much less near the truth than his caricature of Cromwell. With benefit of hindsight, Pole later wrote what he had to write in order to explain what he had become. But the process by which he (and therefore unavoidably Cromwell) reached that point proves much more interesting than the plaster saint which emerged at its end. One of its most important episodes began with Tyndale's kidnapping when ideology and factional conflict began to work themselves out in espionage. Assisted by this development, a breach opened between Pole and Henry no earlier than 1537 and a critical turning-point in the English Reformation had passed. The divide between the cousins owed much to ideological politics but happened almost in spite of faction.

Pole's version of events came to dominate historiography through the continuation of the process which he began in three sixteenth century works: Paolo Giovio's *Descriptio Britanniae, Scotiae, Hyberniae et Orchadum* (Venice, 1548); Ludovico Beccadelli's life of Pole (written 1561); and Andras Dudic's adaptation and translation of Beccadelli done a few years later.[122] All three agreed that Pole was the injured party, who had come, as Giovio put it, "in order to remind Britain by familiar and pious words, what was necessary to heal the king's

---

121. Merriman, *Cromwell* (as in n. 51), 1: 205–7.
122. Giovio's intentions and motives are discussed in my "Reginald Pole in Paolo Giovio's *Descriptio*: A Strategy for Reconversion," *Sixteenth Century Journal*, 16 (1985): 431–50. For the dates of the last two works, see Morandi, *Monumenta letteraria*, 1. II: 272, and G. Fragnito: "Gli 'spirituali' e la fuga di Bernardino Ochino," *Rivista storica italiana* 84 (1972): 803 n. For Dudic at Trent, see most recently L. Szczucki: "Miedzy ortodoksja a nikodemizmem (Andrzej Dudycz na soborze trydenckim)," *Odrodzenie i Reformacja w Polsce* 29 (1984): 49–90. I have been unable to read this article, but I am grateful to Dr. Szczucki for sending me a copy.

mind."¹²³ Beccadelli was a little more forthright and gave Pole a more credible if inaccurate motive, noting that he had been sent "to give encouragement to the Catholics in England" "with much more zeal to return the king to the Catholic religion, than to make war," which Beccadelli at least admitted may have entered Pole's mind.¹²⁴ For the rest, however, it was all a matter of Pole dodging scurvy English assassins inspired no doubt by the enormous prices Henry was alleged to have put on his head. Dudic was, as often, more circumspect. Instead of encouraging the English Catholics, which did after all leave the means open, Dudic wrote only that Pole had been sent "to preserve them in the faith of the church." He continued as Beccadelli had that Pole would try to get Henry back into the church, but the mere implication that Pole might use violent means had disappeared.¹²⁵ Both Beccadelli and Dudic ended with Pole welcoming assassins the way a person who wants to go to sleep greets someone who helps him undress. They saw no contradiction between the attitude here ascribed to Pole and his careful quest for a secure "corner" (as he called it) in which to hole up and from which to conduct further operations. These latter entirely escaped their notice. The editing of these early biographers may not have been as subtle as Pole's own self-creation, but their efforts did as much violence to what Pole did. Instead of the strong feelings and inclinations on both sides we are left with only the plots against Pole. Cromwell lost all these skirmishes, while yet managing to win a battle, but thanks to the power of Pole's pen, never had a chance in the war. Pole's spoils were three new *personae* – his, Cromwell's, and Henry's – and much of the history of the Reformation.

VII

A Diet for Henry VIII: The Failure of Reginald Pole's 1537 Legation

The triennium 1536–38 marks the crisis of Henry VIII's reign. The palace coup that toppled Anne Boleyn in May and June 1536 and apparently left Thomas Cromwell more firmly in control instead ushered in a series of further threats to both Cromwell and Henry. The upheaval of the Pilgrimage of Grace convulsed the north in late 1536 and early 1537 and looked for a time as if it would shake Henry's throne. The Pilgrims' calls for the upstart Cromwell's removal forced the chief minister to withdraw behind the scenes for a time, always a tricky maneuver. The battle of wits and wills between the king and his cousin and sometime protégé Reginald Pole runs as counterpoint throughout these dislocations. Pole's intemperate attack on Henry's divorce from Catherine of Aragon, *De unitate,* arrived at the extremely sensitive moment of June 1536 and announced the beginning of an eighteen-month struggle that finally led to an irreparable breach between Henry and Pole. *De unitate* has often been taken to signal Pole's crossing of the Rubicon. It should certainly have discomfited Pole's potential allies just as many of his partisans thought they had jockeyed themselves into power by engineering Anne's downfall. In fact, the work had a minimal effect, mainly because the committee entrusted with reading it was heavily stacked with Pole's friends. Henry probably never saw *De unitate*. Despite its violent language, neither Pole nor his supporters were then quite ready to give up on Henry. Early the next year the situation changed. Paul III created the new cardinal Pole a legate and dispatched him to Flanders, traditional locus of plots against England. Pole's legation has usually been dismissed as the comic-opera machinations of a slightly befuddled, if saintly, scholar wholly unequipped to deal with the rigors of European diplomacy.

Instead, this essay will argue that Pole's mission represented a real challenge to England; and English policymakers so took it, Cromwell chief among them.

Pole's bull of appointment publicly charged him to arrange matters between Christian princes in preparation for a general council that in turn would lead to common efforts against the Turks. Any other matters concerning the church also came within his purview. In keeping with standard diplomatic practice, these open instructions told only half the story. The pope secretly ordered Pole to aid the Pilgrims, although Paul failed to give Pole any specific pointers about how to do that.[1] Pole's public mandate failed to fool the English, who mounted three separate operations designed to get Pole into their clutches or to eliminate him. Neither of the two sides enjoyed much success in trying to undo the other, but not for lack of effort. The potential of Pole's legation failed to materialize because he never convinced Charles V to give him material support, but imperial agents, including the emperor's sister, gave much aid and comfort. Pole's cardinalate, which he claimed provided the only protection he needed, probably did comparatively little to help him. Rather, English plots to snare or assassinate him blundered from one fiasco to another as Pole's friends sabotaged them. Cromwell may have been at the tiller, but much of the rest of the English government refused to answer the helm. The struggle for dominance triggered by Anne's fall created what should have been a perfect opening for Pole. Had the Pilgrimage lasted a little longer, had Paul III thrown in a few *scudi,* and had Charles abandoned caution, Pole's legation would have been the most serious episode in the triad of coup, Pilgrimage, and Pole because it would have served as a catalyst to revive and unite the parties who made both coup and rebellion. A deeper understanding of Pole's place in the crisis of 1536–38 requires not only attention to English faction politics but also a descent into the murky world of espionage. A fair amount is known about Renaissance diplomacy, but next to nothing is known about its counterpart in intelligence operations.[2] The skulduggery of Pole and his opponents offers a glimpse of the underside of English statecraft.

---

[1] J. S. Brewer, J. Gairdner, and R. H. Brodie, eds., *Letters and Papers, Foreign and Domestic, of the Reign of Henry VIII,* 21 vols. (London, 1862–1932), vol. 12, pt. 1, no. 779, March 31, 1537.

[2] Garrett Mattingly's *Renaissance Diplomacy* (Boston, 1955) is a classic. R. L. Pollitt has recently begun serious study of Elizabethan intelligence operations; see, e.g., his "The Abduction of Doctor John Story and the Evolution of Elizabethan Intelligence Operations," *Sixteenth Century Journal* 14, no. 2 (1983): 131–56, and "From Ambassador to Prison Spy," *Studies in Intelligence* 29, no. 2 (1985): 69–78.

The papacy's diplomatic organization, the most highly developed in Europe, undergirded Pole's legation. A deep darkness shrouds the ins and outs of maneuvering in the Curia, but Pole had the full support of some key members of the diplomatic establishment, in particular, of the men in the best positions to help.[3] The nuncio in Paris, Rodolfo Pio, realized Pole's value early. No sooner had John Fisher been executed in mid-1535 than Pio wrote Cardinal Palmieri that Pole should have the dead bishop's red hat. A letter of recommendation addressed to the second most powerful man in the Curia went outside normal channels. Usually Pio reported to Ambrogio Ricalcato, who handled correspondence with all nuncios.[4] Pio had met Pole when both studied at Padua and still knew enough about him to refer Palmieri to two of Pole's closest friends, Gianmatteo Giberti and Gasparo Contarini.[5] The nuncio also pointed out the effect the appointment of a member of the White Rose faction like Pole would have on English politics.[6] By August 1535 Pio had given up on Henry, writing that "one could not and should not hope for any good outcome" of the king's policy.[7] Pio knew about *De unitate* just a month after the dispatch of the presentation copy and had some idea of its content: he thought Pole had written entirely in favor of papal power.[8] The outbreak of the Pilgrimage in October 1536 immediately raised Pio's ambitions for Pole. In late November, apparently in response to a query about the Englishman, he reported that Pole "could do service to God by going to England whenever any insurrection should arise." In the meantime Pio advised that Pole should publish some of his writings and have them distributed, especially in England. The English feared most that Pole would do exactly that.[9]

---

[3] Ludwig von Pastor's standard *History of the Popes from the Close of the Middle Ages* (ed. R. F. Kerr [St. Louis, 1914], vol. 11) contains nothing; and Carlo Capasso's *Paolo III (1534–1549)* ([Messina and Rome, 1924], 1:387 ff.) has little more.

[4] J. Lestocquoy, ed., *Correspondance des nonces en France Carpi et Ferrerio, 1535–1540* (Rome, 1961), p. xxiv.

[5] Ibid., no. 39, July 4, 1535.

[6] Brewer et al., eds., vol. 8, no. 986, July 4, 1535. This probably summarizes the letter cited in n. 5 above, but Brewer et al. usually present much fuller versions of Pio's letters than the often brief resumes in Lestocquoy, ed.

[7] Biblioteca Apostolica Vaticana, MS Vaticanus Latinus (Vat. Lat.) 12909, fol. 16r, August 21, 1535 (a register of Pio's correspondence). I am grateful to the Vatican Film Library of St. Louis University for a Mellon Fellowship, which allowed me to consult this document.

[8] Lestocquoy, ed., no. 158, Lyon, June 26, 1536 (Brewer et al., eds., vol. 10, no. 1212).

[9] Brewer et al., eds., vol. 11, no. 1173; and Lestocquoy, ed., no. 181 (an innocuous summary).

VII

308

Pole's strategy may well have rested on Pio's plotting. At any rate, early on the nuncio sketched out the means Pole would later adopt to bring Henry to submit. In fact, Pio had little choice but to resort to scare tactics like suspending papal censures against Henry over the king's head since he knew well enough the lack of adequate means to do more.[10] Three weeks before the pope appointed Pole, Pio suggested that Paul send him at least as far as the frontier of France because Pole could "again inflame these good people better than any other, and use the censures, like arms of your Holiness, in their behalf." The analogy can hardly have been flippant.[11] The advance planning for the legation involved Pio intimately. Pole informed Pio very early of his dispatch, telling the nuncio as well that he had delayed leaving Rome in order to reply to letters sent from the king's council.[12] In January 1537 Pio sat on pins and needles over the fate of one of Pole's men whom the French had caught in Picardy. He probably meant Michael Throckmorton, one of Pole's most trusted associates and a highly effective double agent.[13] Throckmorton showed himself not only capable of much greater speed than Pole but also eager to keep Pio in the picture. He returned to Paris by January 26 on at least his second trip since mid-December and had a long audience with Pio as soon as he arrived. It is highly interesting that Pole's personal servant Throckmorton acted as principal messenger on official papal business.[14]

Pio maintained close ties to other possibly and actually disaffected Englishmen than Throckmorton. At the same time as the nuncio learned of *De unitate,* he reported that the English ambassadors in Paris had indiscretely told him they hoped Mary would be legitimized and that England would return to the church.[15] This gave Pio quite an opening, and he exploited it. He repeatedly noted the favorable inclination of Sir John Wallop, one of the ambassadors, to Pole and to good religion.[16] Pole used Pio to keep Wallop informed of his actions, at one point sending the nuncio a copy of his January 1537 letter to the council with explicit instructions to give it to the English ambassadors.[17] How

---

[10] Brewer et al., eds., vol. 12, pt. 1, no. 34.

[11] Lestocquoy, ed., no. 194, Paris, January 18–19, 1537; Brewer et al., eds., vol. 12, pt. 1, no. 165.

[12] Biblioteca Apostolica Vaticana, MS Vat. Lat. 12909, fols. 141r–141v, February 28, 1537.

[13] Brewer et al., eds., vol. 12, pt. 1, no. 34. Throckmorton's identity confirmed by Lestocquoy, ed., no. 192, p. 228.

[14] Lestocquoy, ed., no. 197, Paris, February 2, [1537].

[15] Ibid., no. 158, Lyon, June 26, 1536.

[16] Ibid., nos. 200, 210; Brewer et al., eds., vol. 12, pt. 1, no. 705.

[17] Brewer et al., eds., vol. 12, pt. 1, no. 705.

much Pio had to work on Wallop to neutralize him is hard to say, but he effectively deprived the English of one important piece in any moves projected against Pole, especially since Wallop stood high in Francis I's favor. Pio also did his best to encourage French hostility by, for instance, passing on Francis's chief minister's suggestion that an Englishman in Rome (Pole?) should see to the publication of the censures. The French played a duplicitous game throughout but on balance leaned in the direction Pio wished.[18] Whatever Pio's sources, they gave him less than perfect intelligence about the circumstances requiring Pole in England. Pio viewed the course of the Pilgrimage much too optimistically, but in this he once more behaved exactly as Pole would. The nuncio knew already in early January 1537 that the disturbances had largely died away. Yet in mid-February and again in mid-March he noted, first, that the insurgents might well overpower the king and create an ideal opportunity for Pole and, second, that "the people . . . are more enraged than ever" by Henry's trickery.[19] Even in mid-April Pio remained stolidly convinced that the English lied when they reported that they had quashed the trouble and that Henry's treachery upset the people more than before. When next they rose, as they certainly would, that would spell the end for the king.[20] Just to remove any doubt about his attitude, Pio reiterated that no opportunity to hurt Henry should be lost.

Pio thus eagerly awaited Pole's arrival in Paris, projected for the first day of Easter. As always, Pole missed that date. He finally entered the French capital on April 10, but the next day Giberti, accompanying Pole partly because of the bishop's ties to England, sent Pio a full report on Pole's comparative lack of success with Francis.[21] The nuncio had gone with the court to Amiens but made plans to confer with Pole as the latter withdrew to safety at Cambrai.[22] Two days later Pio reported that Pole had left too quickly and thereby aborted the meeting.[23] Once Pole reached Cambrai he dispatched a long letter to Pio explaining why he had failed to meet him. Even though he had been forced out of Paris, Pole would not lay the blame at Francis's feet, faulting the king only for his friendship with Henry, which dictated that Francis hand Pole over.

[18] Ibid., vol. 11, no. 1250; Lestocquoy, ed., no. 184, December 4, 1536.
[19] Brewer et al., eds., vol. 12, pt. 1, nos. 463, 665.
[20] Ibid., no. 923.
[21] Ibid., no. 908.
[21] Lestocquoy, ed., no. 215; Brewer et al., eds., vol. 12, pt. 1, no. 931, Amiens, April 13, [1537].
[23] Brewer et al., eds., vol. 12, pt. 1, no. 949.

More important, Pole gave Pio a detailed briefing on the aims of his legation, especially its third point covering the restoration of stability in England. (For the rest, he stuck to his public instructions about peace and a council.) At first glance, the proposals sound tame. Pole insisted that he had eschewed force. There were two ways to cure a disease: surgery, or a resort to arms; and diet, the method he preferred.[24] Pole left the latter unexplained, but similar plans elsewhere in Pole's writings may elucidate it. Pole's idea of diet meant causing violence indirectly. When this notion first arose in his divorce opinion written sometime in early 1531, he suggested that, if the emperor simply broke trade relations between the Low Countries and England, the latter's enraged merchants would do the rest.[25] The scheme reappeared in Thomas Theobald's report to Archbishop Cranmer of a talk with Throckmorton in Padua in 1538. Theobald also noted Throckmorton's comment about Pole's disappointment in the pope's failure to proceed vigorously against England.[26] Pole must therefore have feigned caution with Pio. It is extremely unlikely that Pole did not know exactly where Pio stood and much more probable that Pole feared or (more deviously) hoped that the English would intercept his letter. Pio probably remained one of Pole's admirers long after this legation. He may well have passed a detailed account of it to Paolo Giovio, who incorporated it in his *Descriptio Britanniae, Scotiae, Hyberniae et Orchadum*.[27]

Pole and his companions officially kept other people besides Pio in the dark about Pole's mission. Throckmorton and Giberti regularly insisted on the strict nonviolence of his plans. Pole joined Throckmorton in assuring Cromwell of his benign motives, and Pole later told Erard de la Marck, cardinal of Liège, merely the cover story about his legation.[28] Giberti, Throckmorton, and Pole tried hard to persuade almost everyone, even if they met with small success. Pole's image as the shy, retiring, unworldly type might not seem to square with the requirements of diplomatic deviousness, but it might be argued that

---

[24] A. M. Quirini, ed., *Epistolarum Reginaldi Poli* (Brescia, 1744–57), 2:35–37; place and date corrected from Biblioteca Apostolica Vaticana, MS Vat. Lat. 12909, fol. 139r, as Cambrai, February 19, [1537].

[25] Thomas Cranmer to the earl of Wiltshire, British Library (BL), Lansdowne MS 115, fol. 2v, June 13, [1531].

[26] BL, Nero MS B. VI, fols. 125r, 138r. Theobald may have been an agent of the Boleyn faction. He signed another nearly contemporary letter to Wiltshire "godson" (Brewer et al., eds., vol. 13, pt. 2, no. 337). Cranmer received a full intelligence report from him in August 1538, together with a request for funds (ibid., no. 117).

[27] T. F. Mayer, "Reginald Pole and Paolo Giovio's *Descriptio*: A Strategy for Reconversion," *Sixteenth Century Journal* 16, no. 4 (1985): 431–50, 435–36.

[28] Quirini, ed., vol. 2, no. 18, Cambrai, April 27, [1537].

CARDINAL POLE'S LEGATION 311

Pole fit the job nearly perfectly. A taciturn man, not the least bit above dissembling, Pole displayed extraordinary caution throughout his legation.[29] He refused to commit much of his thinking to paper, frequently noting that he would write his mind in another letter or referring to a missive from one of his companions for further particulars.[30] The creation of this record may have involved more than caution. When Pole found himself with unexpected time in Piacenza, he sat down to spell out fully what he intended in a letter to Contarini, but the only surviving copy of this letter breaks off at the point at which he actually began to describe his plans.[31] One must begin to suspect that someone tampered with Pole's correspondence. If this is a case of bowdlerization, it failed to conceal Pole's aims.

When it counted, Pole carefully laid out precisely what he had in mind. Before he was appointed legate, he prepared a position paper for Paul III about the goals of any hypothetical mission to England. Its main object, of course, had to be the restoration of the "accustomed authority," but Pole feared that this required that the pope dispatch "someone confirmed to them [the Pilgrims] in the name of your holiness, to help not only with words, but again with deeds, who would need to have a certain quantity of money" to pay the "so well deserving" rebels. They needed such support because Henry might prevaricate, pretending that he would give the insurgents justice. Once the king had them in his clutches, however, he would execute the leaders.[32] Judging from the bull appointing Pole a legate *a latere*, the pope adopted most of Pole's suggestions, but with even less circumspection. The king might have to be returned to the faith by force, but if even that failed, it were better that he and his supporters should die rather than take others to hell. Paul did not practice conservative medicine; diet would not have a trial. The pope firmly hoped that the rebels would rise again and felt that Pole should encourage them, in part by a crusading indulgence.[33]

About the middle of his legation, when his Roman backers began to urge him to abandon it, Pole wrote a remarkable letter to the pope,

[29] Christopher Longolius, a friend from Pole's first visit to Padua, called the Englishman "prodigiously taciturn" (F. A. Gasquet, *Cardinal Pole and His Early Friends* [London, 1927], pp. 29–30).

[30] For example, Quirini, ed., vol. 2, nos. 24, 14.

[31] Ibid., no. 15. This letter preserves the place of writing. The vice-legate of Piacenza reported to the pope on March 4 that Pole had arrived there the day before, intending to leave the next morning. He reached Asti by March 8 (Archivio di Stato, Parma, Carteggio Farnesiane Interno, busta 3, January–June 1537 [unfoliated]).

[32] Quirini, ed., 2:cclxxvii–viii.

[33] Brewer et al., eds., vol. 12, pt. 1, no. 779.

repeating the substance of his earlier memorandum. Pole refused a practically direct order to return, arguing that he must stay to help the people. They needed one of their own to put terror into their misguided leaders, and Pole presented evidence—the actions of English agents against him—of how much some people feared him. His departure would lead to the greatest desperation of the people, who ought always to be consulted, and leave their opponents secure. Opportunities could often arise from the people, especially since the cause of the disturbance had not disappeared. Therefore the faithful English deserved a nearby leader, someone stationed permanently in Flanders, "who should be ready, not only in word, but in deed."[34] Unlike his Roman supporters, Pole thought it no affront to his dignity to hole up in a "corner" in Liège, and he offered to stay indefinitely.[35] In fact, his departure would give his enemies a victory.[36] Giberti echoed Pole's decision, despite his lack of enthusiasm for Pole's mission.[37]

Pole's overt hostility to England had cropped up comparatively recently, but it arose fully fledged. In the correspondence over *De unitate* in mid- and late 1536, Pole repeatedly adopted the same medical analogy he employed in the letter to Pio from Cambrai, but this time he plumped for surgery. He was a physician faced with such a serious wound in Henry that he had to probe it to the very bottom.[38] *De unitate* itself contained a long passage addressed to Charles V, asking him to intervene in England. Pole took Contarini's advice to prune it from the presentation copy but then restored the threat to the instructions he gave Throckmorton for oral delivery to Henry. Pole's messenger should warn the king what dangers hung "off outward power off those pryncis to whose honour ytt ys iudgyd to apperteyne to defend the lawes off the churche ageinst all other pryncis or nations thatt wyll impugne them."[39] At about the same time, trying on his new prophetic personality developed in *De unitate,* Pole composed a long letter to James V of Scotland and invited him to imitate the faithful Israelites by

---

[34] Quirini, ed., 2, no. 19:51-54.

[35] Gasparo Contarini to Alvise Priuli (Pole's right-hand man), May 22, 1537, warning him that Pole could make his own decision about how long to stay, but not at the expense of his dignity (Franz Dittrich, ed., *Regesten und Briefen des Cardinals Gasparo Contarini [1483-1542]* [Braunsberg, 1881], Inedita, no. 17, p. 267).

[36] Reginald Pole to Contarini, Liège, July 21, 1537, Quirini, ed., vol. 2, no. 28.

[37] Brewer et al., eds., vol. 12, pt. 1, no. 1053.

[38] Pole to Cuthbert Tunstall, August 1, 1536, BL, Cleopatra (Cleop.) MS E. VI, fol. 351r.

[39] Thomas F. Dunn, "The Development of the Text of Pole's *De Unitate Ecclesiae*," *Papers of the Bibliographical Society of America* 70 (1976): 458-68, 463. BL, Cleop. MS E. VI, fols. 347v-348r.

taking action against England.⁴⁰ The legate adopted exactly the same line in a June 1537 letter to Contarini. Pole refused to despair, for just as the Israelites prevailed over the sons of Benjamin, so the aroused people of England would triumph through divine providence.⁴¹ Who better than he to interpret heavenly intentions or even help them along a little? Pole's celebrated attack on Cromwell the Machiavellian cannot obscure his own interest in similar tactics.

In addition to the will, the personality, and powerful support, Pole possessed some of the means to implement his designs. If in the end Francis and Charles refused troops, Pole had a small body of agents of his own. Nothing much is yet known about the composition of Pole's traveling household except that, according to one English report, it numbered twenty-one, all Frenchmen or Italians.⁴² Superficially, it might appear that Pole would therefore have suffered the critical handicap of a dearth of agents able to slip in and out of England. In fact, his case was not so bleak.

Throckmorton played a pivotal role. He apparently shuttled back and forth between England and the Continent almost at will, partly because he convinced Cromwell that he kept a careful eye on Pole. Throckmorton fed the lord privy seal just enough true information to keep him hooked. For example, he reported in February 1537 that Pole had delayed his departure from Rome in order to answer the council's letter but also added fatuously that Pole would burn all the copies of *De unitate* if only Henry would renounce his usurped titles. Right from the first, Throckmorton proved himself a master of duplicity. He would not, he wrote Cromwell, come directly back with Pole's answer to the minister's letters but would rather accompany Pole in an effort to persuade him to change his mind, "for as your lordschype know full well grete men arr not lyghtly perswadyd & he specialle." Throckmorton also claimed that he had not yet sent any letters because he had no intelligence worth the cost of the post. This was true enough if he could do no better than the neutral report of Pole's intentions the letter contains. In much the same offhand manner Bishop Gardiner would later display, Throckmorton closed by assuring Cromwell that the news of Pole's departure would still reach England before the legate

⁴⁰ Quirini, ed., 1:173. For Pole's new persona, see Peter S. Donaldson, "Machiavelli, Antichrist, and the Reformation: Prophetic Typology in Reginald Pole's *De Unitate* and *Apologia ad Carolum Quintum*," in *Leaders of the Reformation*, ed. Richard L. DeMolen (London, 1985), pp. 211–47.

⁴¹ Quirini, ed., vol. 2, no. 24.

⁴² John Hutton to Thomas Cromwell, April 1537, Public Record Office (PRO), State Papers (SP) 1/119/46v–47r (Brewer et al., eds., vol. 12, pt. 1, no. 1061).

arrived in France.[43] In August, just a few days before Pole finally fled Liège for Rome, Throckmorton again wrote Cromwell. He observed ingenuously that the lord privy seal had apparently expected him back long before, but Throckmorton pleaded in his defense that he had assumed that the minister had consented to his remaining with Pole since no letter had come from Cromwell. Throckmorton had meant to leave Pole at Paris, but when no word came from England, Pole convinced him to stay. Nothing all that remarkable in such a turn, but when Throckmorton continued that after they had arrived in Cambrai he could not abandon Pole to the dangers presented by the king's agents "as I suppose youre lordschype selffe wyll sey the same," one can begin to understand the violence of Cromwell's eventual response. Throckmorton coolly rehearsed once more what Pole had meant to accomplish, emphasizing that he had proposed nothing against the king's honor. Prayers remained the means of choice, especially because of the late rebels' uproar. Pole's stubbornness again led Throckmorton to decide to stay with him in order to work on his conversion some more. Besides, Throckmorton wrote his putative master, he still did not have anything worthwhile to report. Better for Cromwell to leave him in place than to waste time and effort on however many spies he might have.[44] Up to this point, at least, Throckmorton apparently took Cromwell in completely.[45] He later gloated about how he had deceived Cromwell and Richard Morison.[46]

While Throckmorton pulled the wool over Cromwell's eyes, other agents chipped in. One of the Italians in Pole's household, Bernardino Sandro, seems likely to have run a fairly low level espionage effort, judging from evidence collected in the wake of the so-called Exeter conspiracy. He was a close friend of Pole's protégé Thomas Starkey, who had left Pole's household for the king's, but Starkey and Sandro continued to correspond. Pole may therefore have assigned the mission to Sandro because of his superior knowledge of English conditions, which he derived from Starkey. In any case, Sandro entrusted two knives to one Hugh Holland for delivery as a token to John Walker, Pole's business agent in London. According to Sir Geoffrey Pole, Walker would be asked to join Pole in the Low Countries after he received them.[47] Why? Pole hardly made it a practice to encourage a

---

[43] PRO, SP 1/114/34v–36r (Brewer et al., eds., vol. 12, pt. 1, no. 429).
[44] PRO, SP 1/124/76r–77v.
[45] PRO, SP 1/124/144 (Brewer et al., eds., vol. 12, pt. 2, no. 619).
[46] BL, Nero MS B. VI, fol. 138v.
[47] Jerome Ragland's examination, October [28?], 1538, PRO, SP 1/138/40v (Brewer et al., eds., vol. 13, pt. 2, no. 702.3); confirmed by John Collins's interrogation, November 14, PRO, SP 1/139/31v (Brewer et al., eds., vol. 13, pt. 2, no. 829.2).

mass exodus, flatly telling his brother Geoffrey not to leave England.[48] Perhaps the obvious symbolism of the knives holds significance. It looks as if Pole had a use for a practical man of affairs. Walker was probably one of Pole's most faithful servants and may have associated with him since Pole's days at Magdalen College, Oxford, when Walker served as the university messenger.[49] Unfortunately, Walker seems not to have received the knives and never to have been caught up in any plot.

Pole could count on active support from others like Walker, though. An unbalanced and, worse, unreliable mind probably produced Geoffrey Pole's braggadocio and threats that he would thrust his dagger into anyone who would kill his brother, but similar mutterings from Morgan Wells might demand more serious consideration. Wells apparently freely confessed that he would kill Peter Mewtas with a handgun if the latter succeeded in doing the same to Pole and that he would not wait for Mewtas to return to England but would go after him on the Continent.[50] Jerome Ragland, right-hand man of Pole's older brother, Henry, Lord Montagu, knew of the widespread grumblings in the various Pole households.[51]

One last Pole dependent had even better credentials for mischief. A seaman and unsuccessful pirate, Hugh Holland plied back and forth between Sir Geoffrey and Pole on several occasions during the legation.[52] At one time, Holland found his way to Pole's refuge at Awne Abbey and had an audience with Pole in which he told the cardinal of some of the plots afoot, but only after a thorough vetting by Throckmorton.[53] This particular visit gave rise to one of the counts in Holland's indictment. Whatever Holland's own talents, his role as lifeline for John Helyar, parish priest of Pole's mother the countess of Salisbury, made him appear even more dangerous and takes up much more space in the articles against him. When Helyar fled England for reli-

---

[48] Two examinations of Jerome Ragland, PRO, SP 1/138/35r, 40v (Brewer et al., eds., vol. 13, pt. 2, nos. 702.1, 702.3).

[49] At least a John Walker was appointed messenger in 1509 (W. T. Mitchell, ed., *Epistolae Academicae*, Oxford Historical Society, n.s., vol. 26 [Oxford, 1980], p. 8. Sandro called Walker "nostro" (BL, Nero MS B. VII, fol. 118r) and reported a gift of money from him, "un servitio d'amico" (BL, Nero MS B. VII, fol. IIIv). In early 1538 Walker still held the keys to John Colet's house at Sheen, which contained some of Pole's "stuff" (Brewer et al., eds., vol. 13, pt. 1, no. 422).

[50] PRO, SP 1/139/23r (Brewer et al., eds., vol. 13, pt. 2, no. 828.2).

[51] Ibid.; and Jerome Ragland's examination, PRO, SP 1/138/33r–34r (Brewer et al., eds., vol. 13, pt. 2, no. 702.1).

[52] The charge of piracy is recorded in Brewer et al., eds., vol. 7, no. 316. The attempt failed when Holland fell asleep and his victims captured him.

[53] PRO, SP 1/138/192v (Brewer et al., eds., vol. 13, pt. 2, no. 797).

VII

316

gious reasons in mid-1535, Holland conveyed him and a servant to Paris at Geoffrey Pole's request. Holland continued to carry messages between the latter and Helyar and also took Helyar's brother-in-law John Fowle back and forth to the Continent.[54]

None of this may sound dangerous, and it has usually been taken as part of the manufactured plot concocted by the government to strike at disaffected aristocrats in 1538. Consideration of Helyar's full significance must wait for a moment, but now we may note that the government did anything but overreact to the threat he posed. At a time when the possibility that Pole might publish *De unitate* seriously concerned the makers of policy, the last thing they needed to worry about was another accomplished propagandist. Such Helyar could have been. Like Starkey and Pole an Oxford man, Helyar matriculated at Corpus Christi College in 1522 and took his B.A. the following year. He honed his literary talents under the Catalan humanist Juan Luis Vives while holding a fellowship of his college.[55] Helyar had the proper instincts to become a propagandist as well since he was almost certainly the English student at Louvain who suggested to Pole that English attacks on papal supremacy badly needed confutation.[56] Helyar had more than his Louvain education in common with later seminary priests, for either in Paris or in Venice he met Ignatius Loyola and was sufficiently impressed to copy the Spaniard's *Spiritual Exercises* into his notebook, thereby producing the oldest extant manuscript.[57] Under Pole's patronage he became the manager of the English hospice in Rome, where he died before December 1541.[58]

Pole attracted other clerics and literary men into his orbit. Lord Montagu's chaplain, John Collins, once possessed a copy of a treatise by Pole's close friend Thomas Lupset that argued that the proper venue to discuss spiritual matters was not the royal palace "in the midst of drinking." Collins thought the work sufficiently incriminating to burn it.[59] He also told Wells, the volunteer assassin-slayer, to "be of good mynde and make a crosse in his forhedd" after he disclosed his plans.[60] Another clergyman from the same region, George Crofts,

[54] PRO, SP 1/138/191r.
[55] Henry de Vocht, *History of the Foundation and the Rise of the Collegium Trilingue Lovaniense, 1517-1550* (Louvain, 1951-55), 3:423.
[56] Marie Hallé [Martin Haile], *Life of Reginald Pole* (London, 1911), p. 224.
[57] Paul Dudon, *St. Ignatius of Loyola* (Milwaukee, 1949), p. 213n; de Vocht, p. 424.
[58] de Vocht, p. 425.
[59] John Archer Gee, *The Life and Works of Thomas Lupset* (New Haven, Conn., 1928), p. 172.
[60] PRO, SP 1/139/23r; confirmed by John Collins's examination, PRO, SP 1/139/30v.

chancellor of Chichester Cathedral, found himself caught up in the investigation of the Exeter conspiracy too. He had the patronage of Sir Thomas West, Lord Delawarr, who will require further attention.[61] Aside from his appearance in the Exeter inquiry, which suggests some contact with Pole's allies, Pole's South Harting parish lay in Chichester diocese and may have tied him to Crofts. Both men were also at Oxford together, although in different colleges.[62] Pole had foot soldiers and clergy in some numbers to call on. Whether or not he did, the mere existence of such people gives further substance to Pole's capacity for subversion.

One large strike against the English magnified Pole's threat before they turned to more violent means to try to stop him. English agents had very little room for diplomatic maneuver in the places where it counted—Paris and Brussels. Francis simply ignored his treaty with Henry, but some people in Brussels went further, offering physical protection and some degree of moral support. Both the French and the imperialists must have known the consequences of their actions and have chosen more or less deliberately to fuel English fears. Pole's true purpose was among the most poorly kept secrets in Europe. When his creation as cardinal was under discussion, one of the imperial ambassadors in Rome reported to his master that the pope intended to send Pole with money to aid the insurgents.[63] Six months later Count Cifuentes again wrote that Pole's public charge did not exhaust his instructions. He would go secretly to the rebels.[64] In the meantime, the French had the full story and sent some details to England with the bailly of Troyes in early March.[65] By then the news was old hat; the English had an anonymous report shortly after Pole became a cardinal in December 1536.[66] Whether or not they knew his legation's true intent, even its cover story endangered England. A truce between Francis and the emperor would make her position precarious. With the benefit of hindsight and the reading of imperial correspondence, historians know that Charles refused almost from the outset to think much of Pole's mission, instructing his Roman representatives to discourage

---

[61] Brewer et al., eds., vol. 12, pt. 1, no. 2. See n. 131 below.

[62] For Crofts's Oxford career between 1513 and 1519, see Bishop Sherburne's register, vol. 2, West Sussex Record Office, Chichester, Ep MS 1/1/4/51v; and *Dictionary of National Biography* (*DNB*).

[63] Brewer et al., eds., vol. 12, pt. 1, no. 123.

[64] BL, Additional (Add.) MS 28,589, fol. 217v (Brewer et al., eds., vol. 12, pt. 1, no. 1141).

[65] Brewer et al., eds., vol. 12, pt. 1, no. 625.

[66] PRO, SP 1/113/3r (Brewer et al., eds., vol. 11, no. 1353.2).

Pole's appointment or at least his dispatch to the rebels.[67] But Charles *was* interested in Pole's uses, as the English might well have known and certainly suspected.[68] The emperor's further orders in March 1537 to an envoy destined for England still expressed extreme caution. Pole could not receive open support until he clearly had men and money and had either actually overthrown Henry or at least screwed the people's resolve to do so to the sticking point.[69]

This is vintage Charles, but his designs for Mary of Hungary, his sister and regent in Brussels, appeared more threatening. She was to test the wind and either support Pole or make her excuses.[70] As it turned out, she tried more eagerly to assure Pole's safety than Francis had done—not much help, perhaps, but just exactly what Pole hoped for and just exactly what he needed in the circumstances. The blundering of English agents accounts for part of Francis's success guarding Pole, but Mary's achievement was largely her own and that of the chief of her council, the cardinal of Liège. Pole had not felt safe in Cambrai, as Giberti reported, and Pole likened his stay there to forty days in prison.[71] Concerns about security evaporated once Pole reached Liège, where de la Marck's "divine goodness" saved him from repeated ambushes, as Pole wrote the pope.[72] Pole claimed the citizens of Liège would do anything for his safety.[73] Mary's own diplomacy worked remarkably well. She lied to John Hutton, the English agent in Brussels, telling him that Pole was already in Flanders. She therefore could not prevent his entry, and she insisted that she could not interfere with a legate anyway. By then, the crisis had passed, and Pole had nestled safely under de la Marck's wing.[74]

By the time Pole made it to Liège, three of the four major operations against him had run their course. The first involved a primarily diplomatic initiative assigned to one of the English ambassadors to Francis, Stephen Gardiner. He received explicit instructions by March 28 to repair immediately to the French court and prevail on Francis to

---

[67] Brewer et al., eds., vol. 12, pt. 1, no. 123.

[68] For a brief sketch of some of Pole's intrigues with the emperor dating back at least to August 1534, see T. F. Mayer, "The Life and Thought of Thomas Starkey" (Ph.D. diss., University of Minnesota, 1983), pp. 114–17.

[69] BL, Add. MS 28,589, fol. 248r, March 21, 1537 (Brewer et al., eds., vol. 12, pt. 1, no. 696).

[70] Ibid.

[71] Brewer et al., eds., vol. 12, pt. 1, no. 1053; Quirini, ed. (n. 24 above), 2, no. 24:64.

[72] Quirini, ed., 2, no. 21:59, Liège, June 10, 1537.

[73] Ibid., no. 24, p. 66.

[74] PRO, SP 1/120/209r, 235 (Brewer et al., eds., vol. 12, pt. 1, nos. 1293 [May 26], 1306 [May 30]).

surrender Pole since a treaty with Henry obligated the French king to hand over any English traitors.[75] Gardiner hit a snag at once when he could not gain an audience until shortly before April 8. He nonchalantly informed Henry that there was no hurry, despite the fact that Pole entered Paris on April 10.[76] Less than adequate intelligence hampered the English throughout, but this is a particularly glaring example. Gardiner also seems not to have followed orders to let Hutton know if Francis refused to cooperate.[77] This limping effort quickly collapsed. Gardiner again contravened his orders and struck a deal with Francis whereby the king would insist merely that Pole leave France. The bishop never explained his blatant dereliction. Both he and Sir Francis Bryan, troubleshooter for France, had delayed a second time in approaching the French king, with the result that they not only failed to stir him to hand Pole over but also botched simply locating Pole and learning his intentions. Henry was not pleased.[78]

The arrival of Peter Mewtas began a new phase, one of active espionage. Mewtas apparently had orders to kill Pole with a "hand goon" as well as to check on Bryan and Gardiner.[79] Those two had already been asked to "reserche and trye out the mystery of Poles so sodayne departure from Paris and likewise to have good espiall contynually upon hym."[80] Now they should see if they could "have the said pole by some means trussed up and conveyed to Calais." Bryan, presumably as the military man of the two, had particular charge of recruiting "suche felowes for the enterprise . . . as [are] by secret wise and for their corage mete for that purpose."[81] By this time Pole had reached the relative safety of Cambrai, thus increasing Bryan's difficulties.[82] He turned to Sir Thomas Palmer, knight porter of Calais, to run the operation. He in turn recruited three of four soldiers, the "Wingfield connection," and was paid £100 for them.[83] Palmer chased

[75] Ralph Sadler's report to Cromwell, PRO, SP 49/5/12r (Brewer et al., eds., vol. 12, pt. 1, no. 760).

[76] Henry VIII to Stephen Gardiner and Sir Francis Bryan, April 4, [1537] (Brewer et al., eds., vol. 12, pt. 1, no. 865). Pio reported Pole's entrance on April 13 (Lestocquoy, ed. [n. 4 above], no. 215, p. 252).

[77] Brewer et al., eds., vol. 12, pt. 1, no. 817, April 3, 1537.

[78] BL, Add. MS 25,114, fol. 257, April 15, [1537].

[79] This plan crops up on numerous occasions in the records of the Exeter conspiracy investigation—e.g., in Holland's interrogation, PRO, SP 1/138/192v (Brewer et al., eds., vol. 13, pt. 2, no. 797). Mewtas reported on Bryan and Gardiner sometime before April 25, [1537] (BL, Add. MS 25,114, fol. 262r [Brewer et al., eds., vol. 12, pt. 1, no. 1032]).

[80] BL, Add. MS 25,114, fol. 258r, April 15, [1537].

[81] BL, Add. MS 25,114, fol. 263r, April 25, [1537].

[82] Quirini, ed., vol. 2, no. 18, April 26, [1537].

[83] Sir Thomas Palmer to Cromwell, [May 6?, 1537], PRO, SP 1/120/276r (Brewer et al., eds., vol. 12, pt. 1, app. 4).

VII

Pole in person as far as Hainault.[84] And nothing further happened. Pole learned of Palmer's movements, and the elaborate plan, complete with a mythical horse-buying expedition as cover, miscarried. Henry called off the affair on May 18, unless Bryan and Gardiner could persuade those involved to continue on a contingency basis.[85]

Two operations, two abject failures. To move on to Hutton, he was new in his post in Brussels, having arrived at 9 A.M. the day before Pole reached Paris. As had Gardiner, Hutton initially took his assignment a bit casually and delayed his first official audience. After a stern rebuke for failing to follow his instructions to see the regent Mary immediately, Hutton treated the business with all due seriousness.[86] He marked his dispatches about Pole at least "hast post hast/hast post hast," and he seems to have taken to heart his commission "to have contenuall esspialles to thyntent I myght the better advertis your grace of thestat & conversacion off youre gracis traitor pole."[87] He went so far as to employ multiple agents in order to check their evidence, a degree of care displayed by none of the other "spy masters" involved, save Cromwell himself.[88] Alas, all Hutton's efforts came to nothing. His rather harebrained schemes to have letters smuggled into England baked in loaves of bread have often led to a comic-opera attitude to his labors, but Hutton deserves better.[89] The almost total lack of suitable agents, a perennial plague for the English in Brussels, posed the most serious difficulty.[90] The shortage forced Hutton either to import men from Calais or, even worse, to draw from the English exile community, hardly the best material to use against one of its prominent members. Pole apparently "turned" William Vaughan, Hutton's most promising recruit.[91] Hutton's elaborate dealings with the truly vile Harry Phillips

---

[84] Hutton to Cromwell, Brussels, May 9, [1537], Brewer et al., eds., vol. 12, pt. 1, no. 1168.

[85] BL, Add. MS 25,114, fol. 265r (Brewer et al., eds., vol. 12, pt. 1, no. 1235).

[86] PRO, SP 1/118/177r (Brewer et al., eds., vol. 12, pt. 1, no. 940), a minute of a letter to Hutton, perhaps sent April 15, [1537].

[87] PRO, SP 1/121/136r, June 17, 1537 (Brewer et al., eds., vol. 12, pt. 2, no. 107).

[88] Hutton to Cromwell, May 26, [1537], PRO, SP 1/120/210v–211r (Brewer et al., eds., vol. 12, pt. 1, no. 1293). It may be significant that Hutton was concerned to corroborate the testimony of one of Palmer's servants; see below.

[89] PRO, SP 1/120/210.

[90] Thomas Wriothesley later had the same problem in his attempts to capture Harry Phillips and two other traitors, but this incident would bear investigation (see Brewer et al., eds., vol. 14, pt. 1, nos. 233, 246–48, 264, 438, etc.).

[91] Hutton to Cromwell, June 17, [1537], PRO, SP 1/120/136v; and Pole to Contarini, June 10, [1537], Quirini, ed., 2, no. 24:66–67. Harry Phillips wrote Hutton that Vaughan, after originally cooperating, had found Hutton's later instructions "ayenst ys conscyence" (Louvain, June 22, 1537, PRO, SP 1/121/152r).

promised more success (despite the loaves of bread chicanery), but the most charitable explanation of them must be that Hutton was up to something not quite directly to the point of his assignment: he seemed much more intent on capturing Phillips.[92] The near impossibility of undetected movement through the border territory, and sometimes of any movement, exacerbated the severe handicap of agents who could pass for Flemings.[93] Combined with Pole's thick local cover, these two drawbacks stacked the deck against Hutton and his masters, perhaps insurmountably.

All told, a dismal record of incompetence. The wooly minded English (as Henry complained at one point) were played for fools by the wily French or Liègois or Welsh or whomever. But were they? A common thread runs through most of these instances of misfeasance in addition to the problems about which the English could do little, and it leads to an explanation of the blundering of at least Gardiner, Bryan, and Palmer. How much Pole knew and how he found out gives us one end of that thread. All the English plans were betrayed to Pole, without exception. As Hutton learned, one of Palmer's servants whom Palmer had set to spy on Pole revealed all his master's plotting.[94] Before Palmer and his men set out, they had aroused suspicions in Calais.[95] The men he chose—the Wingfield crew—were almost exactly the wrong men for the job. Sir Robert, the patriarch of the family, was at loggerheads with Lord Lisle, the deputy of Calais, which virtually assured some sort of bungling.[96] Bryan was later alleged to have tipped his hand to a friend in the French Privy Chamber who had alerted Pole.[97] This may have been the same gentleman Francis sent to Pole to warn him of plots against him as soon as the legate arrived in Paris.[98]

---

[92] Phillips betrayed virtually everyone with whom he came in contact, beginning with his mother. See the sheaf of pleading letters in PRO, SP 1/100/95r–102v.

[93] Throckmorton was, of course, captured once; and Pole had to wait for some time for a safe-conduct to move from Cambrai into imperial territory. While he was holed up in Cambrai, any stranger was subject to arrest; and when Vaughan took a stab at killing Pole, he was betrayed by the leaky mail (Quirini, ed., 2, no. 24:67).

[94] Hutton to Cromwell, June 17, [1537], PRO, SP 1/121/137r (Brewer et al., eds., vol. 12, pt. 2, no. 107). The Welsh chronicle of Calais corroborates this story; it makes Palmer responsible both for the attempt to trap Pole by stealth and for the assassination plot (Muriel St. Clair Byrne, ed., *The Lisle Letters*, 6 vols. [Chicago, 1981], 4:223).

[95] PRO, SP 1/120/276r (Brewer et al., eds., vol. 12, pt. 1, app. 4).

[96] For Wingfield's relations, see Brewer et al., eds., vol. 12, pt. 1, no. 440. John Hussey frequently referred to the hostility between Lisle and Wingfield (e.g., ibid., nos. 555 [August 21, 1537], 625 [September 1, 1537]).

[97] By Elizabeth Darrell, among others, according to Geoffrey Pole in 1538 (PRO, SP 1/138/217v–218r [Brewer et al., eds., vol. 13, pt. 2, no. 804]).

[98] Lestocquoy, ed. (n. 4 above), no. 215 (Brewer et al., eds., vol. 12, pt. 1, no. 931).

VII

Bryan's and Gardiner's schemes, appropriately dressed up with blood-curdling threats, came to the papal nuncio's ears almost as soon as their orders arrived. "This ribald of Winchester [Gardiner] has performed those offices against the legate with the French king that one could expect from devils and not from men," wrote Pio.[99] As for Bryan, Pio made it appear that he had actually overheard him boasting that, "if he found him [Pole] in the middle of France, he would kill him with his own hand." Pio's accurate information about Bryan's official intention to "make the ultimate attempt to have the legate into his hands and take him to England to put him in the catalogue of martyrs" pales by comparison.[100] Pole and Pio, of course, kept closely in touch, even if their planned meeting fell through. The French capital seems to have provided an almost hopeless environment for secrecy.

England was little better. Not that much security should be expected of government by council under the best of circumstances, but the problem involved more than inadvertent leaks. Factionalism in the highest reaches of the English government offered Pole his biggest opportunity, much as he might have hoped for from various underlings. The list of Pole's assistants among the lower orders compiled above reads a good deal like the inventory of Exeter's servants taken after his death, which minutely detailed who was tall and who strong, with an obvious eye to their military effectiveness. The drawing of this parallel is not entirely accidental. The question of the reality of the Exeter conspiracy cannot be reopened here, but it undoubtedly turned up serious disaffection in its wake. The Carewe-Exeter faction stood at center stage then, as it had done for several years. E. W. Ives dignified it as the only properly political faction until the late years of Henry's reign.[101] It was in full working order when it successfully helped to plot Anne's fall, and it probably continued to function during the legation crisis. They were the group to which Pole would naturally have attached himself. The English court still felt the aftershocks of the palace coup of May–July 1536, and they revealed fault lines that could have doomed Cromwell, already forced to withdraw from the limelight by the Pilgrimage of Grace. Simply put, Pole's friends outnumbered his enemies in places of power.

Because the study of Henrician faction is still in its infancy, full proof of this case would require a separate essay. Nevertheless, some

---

[99] Ibid.
[100] Lestocquoy, ed., no. 217.
[101] E. W. Ives, "Faction at the Court of Henry VIII: The Fall of Anne Boleyn," *History* 57 (1972): 169–88, 180.

of the story can be sketched here. In the first place, numerous people deliberately tried to warn Pole of his danger, whatever Bryan and Gardiner may have been up to. The monitions probably came ultimately from Starkey, Pole's longtime companion. Starkey told Montagu about Mewtas, and Montagu passed the information to Elizabeth Darrell, although she professed not to remember where she had heard the story.[102] She was probably by then already Sir Thomas Wyatt's mistress and thus perhaps receiving confidences from him too, including some about his contacts with Pole. Wyatt could have told her about Bryan's misstep in Paris.[103] From Darrell the news spread to Sir Geoffrey Pole, who relayed it back to Montagu, and both told the countess of Salisbury.[104] Possibly Sir Edward Neville's version came from an independent source. He informed the marchioness of Exeter, partly in song, thereby proving himself the complete courtier.[105] Sir Geoffrey also gave a report to Holland, who delivered the by-then nugatory particulars to Pole.[106]

In Paris, almost certainly more than a faux pas lurked behind Gardiner's deal with Francis. Earlier, in February 1537, Gardiner had received a severe rebuke for daring to advise Henry that he ought to yield to the Pilgrims on some points. Whoever added the reprimand suggested that Gardiner must "have had some advertisement from some personne of that factyon that wolde put you in feare of things to wynne youe agayne to their naughty opynyon."[107] Wallop might likely have swayed Gardiner. This supposition rests in part on Wallop's public sympathy for Pole and also on his report to Pio on the progress of the Pilgrimage, which the ambassador claimed to have from a French source.[108] Mewtas's dispatch on Gardiner contained some highly classified information (Cromwell was to keep it to himself) that

---

[102] PRO, SP 1/138/174r. For Darrell and Wyatt, see Kenneth Muir, *Life and Letters of Sir Thomas Wyatt* (Liverpool, 1963), pp. 82–83.

[103] Wyatt passed through Paris in early April on his way to Valladolid. He is known to have talked to Gardiner but may well have seen Bryan as well. Patricia Thomson interprets the difficult evidence to indicate friendly relations between Wyatt and Bryan (E. A. Rebholz, ed., *Sir Thomas Wyatt: The Complete Poems* [Harmondsworth, 1978], p. 25; and Patricia Thomson, *Sir Thomas Wyatt and His Background* [Stanford, Calif., 1964], pp. 62, 64, and app. C).

[104] PRO, SP 1/138/160r (confirmed by 138/215r), and 139/221r (Brewer et al., eds., vol. 13, pt. 2, no. 955).

[105] PRO, SP 1/138/158v, November 12, 1538 (Brewer et al., eds., vol. 13, pt. 2, no. 765).

[106] PRO, SP 1/138/192v.

[107] BL, Add. MS 25,114, fol. 247v, February 17, [1537].

[108] Lestocquoy ed., no. 194, pp. 232–33, January 18–19, 1537 (Brewer et al., eds., vol. 12, pt. 1, no. 165).

VII

Gardiner had written against Hugh Latimer and shown in draft to Bryan.[109] At this time, Gardiner had some measure of support among the lower clergy too, if not quite on the scale Pole had. Gardiner figured among Helyar's patrons, and in 1537 one Stephen Caston, clerk, delivered himself incautiously of the opinion that Gardiner was being kept overseas for a purpose since if he returned to England many things would change.[110]

True, Gardiner did report Helyar's flight, but not until well after the priest had gone.[111] The extent of Helyar's patronage beyond Gardiner lays open one of the most serious centers of opposition to the direction of policy. Sir William Paulet and Sir Antony Windsor, two landowners in the vicinity of Helyar's second benefice at East Meon, Hampshire, were almost as unreliable as Gardiner, and Paulet nearly equaled the bishop in importance. According to Holland's testimony, Paulet had gone out of his way to protect Helyar, much farther than his duty as a principal lord in Hampshire would have required. He once sent Helyar's brother-in-law to Louvain for a certificate that the priest was studying there in order to have the sequestration of his benefice released, and Paulet had earlier received at least one letter from Helyar.[112] Such would later be accounted treasonable behavior. Paulet served on the commission against Anne, and G. R. Elton has recently pointed to Paulet's aloof stand at just this time as a sign of his dissatisfaction with Cromwell.[113] Norfolk would execute quite a few of Paulet's tenants in the clearing operation after the Pilgrimage.[114] Windsor, brother of Andrew Lord Windsor, keeper of the Great Wardrobe for forty years and once governor of the princess Mary's household, ran Helyar's parish in his absence.[115] Windsor's estate lay close by East Meon, as did the principal estate of Lord Lisle, for whom Wind-

---

[109] BL, Caligula MS E. 2, fol. 233r.

[110] Brewer et al., eds., vol. 12, pt. 1, no. 960, Southampton, April 17, 1537.

[111] J. A. Muller, ed., *The Letters of Stephen Gardiner* (Cambridge, 1937), no. 50, July 26, 1535. In 1538 Holland recalled taking Helyar to Paris about "the beginning of somer was iij or iiij yeres" ago (PRO, SP 1/138/191r).

[112] PRO, SP 1/138/191v–192r (Brewer et al., eds., vol. 13, pt. 2, no. 797).

[113] Ives (n. 101 above), p. 177; and G. R. Elton, "Politics and the Pilgrimage of Grace," in *After the Reformation: Essays in Honor of J. H. Hexter*, ed. Barbara C. Malament (Philadelphia, 1980), pp. 215–46, pp. 213–14.

[114] Duke of Norfolk to the Council, February 19, 1537, Brewer et al., eds., vol. 12, pt. 1, no. 468.

[115] John Helyar wrote Sir Antony Windsor on June 10, (probably) 1537, thanking him for handling his parochial affairs (PRO, SP 1/121/91r). Sir Antony had a long-standing interest in the parish. William Edwards, vicar from 1502 to 1522, left his white horse to Windsor in gratitude. My thanks to Frederick Standfield, East Meon's village historian, for this information.

sor acted as receiver general. The brothers held conservative religious views. Sir Antony's will committed his soul to God "and to the blessed Virgin and all the holy company of heaven," and it went on to order masses of the five wounds. Whether or not this emblem had any distinctively conservative meaning, it did, of course, appear on the Pilgrims' badge.[116] It may not be a coincidence that Palmer owed chief allegiance to Lisle, and charges of having secret conference with Pole helped to bring down the deputy in 1540.[117]

One can extend the list of the high and mighty with more than passing sympathy for Pole, and many of them had their principal seats in exactly the same part of the country as Paulet, Windsor, and Lisle. To look no further than the sadly insecure Privy Council, suspicion falls on six of the men on the short list Henry presented to the Pilgrims in later 1536. The marquess of Exeter, based at Halnecker, West Sussex, heads both the roster of councillors and that of suspects. In 1532 he had expressed high regard for Pole, who disappointed Exeter gravely by leaving England at a time when "we nobles" should have provided a remedy, as Exeter put it.[118] The Carewe-Exeter faction probably hoped for great things from Pole both at the time of *De unitate* and later. Sir William Fitzwilliam had been linked to Exeter when both were excluded from the council in 1536.[119] Later, as the earl of Southampton with his seat at Cowdray, also in West Sussex, Fitzwilliam tried to cover up the first signs of Geoffrey Pole's misdeeds in 1538 as well as those alleged against his mother. The only evidence, he wrote Cromwell, came from an old woman, a midwife, and a young woman with a small baby.[120] The speed with which he turned on Cromwell at the latter's fall hardly lends much support to the view that would make him one of the lord privy seal's allies. Despite Pole's attack on him in *De unitate,* Richard Sampson should probably be counted, both as a conservative and because of the attainder of Crofts, the chancellor of his cathedral in 1538. Even if Cuthbert Tunstall were being kept away from council meetings in later 1536, Pole had asked for him as a reader of *De unitate* and had his wish granted. This speaks volumes about the conservatives' strength, as does the composition of the rest of the committee charged to examine Pole's work, the

---

[116] Byrne, ed. (n. 94 above), 1:277–79; and Joyce Youings, *Sixteenth Century England* (Harmondsworth, 1984), p. 213.

[117] Byrne worked out more of Palmer's tangled career, which may be traced through her indices (see Byrne, ed.). Much of his life remains shrouded in deepest obscurity.

[118] Cited in Hallé (n. 56 above), p. 88.

[119] Ives, p. 176.

[120] The earl of Southampton to Cromwell, September 20, 1538, PRO, SP 1/136/205r.

members of which included Starkey.[121] Tunstall would flee ignominiously before the Pilgrims, perhaps out of mixed sympathy and caution. Religious conservatism marked Norfolk and George Talbot, earl of Shrewsbury, even if both helped to suppress the rebellion.[122] It may not be entirely fanciful to suggest that the duke of Suffolk, erstwhile enemy of Anne, might at least have sat on the fence over the Pole issue. If, as shall be suggested, Henry did not pursue Pole with violence, then Suffolk might have followed his fundamental political principle of loyalty to Henry and waited to see which way the king would jump. Then again, the duke had promoted anticlerical views in 1529, and he too helped to put down the Pilgrimage.[123]

Of those on G. R. Elton's slightly longer list of councillors active during the Pilgrimage, Sir John Russell stands out. Pole claimed that Russell had gladly delivered his divorce opinion to Henry in 1531, whatever the consequences, so highly did he think of Pole.[124] In June 1535 Edmund Harvel, a prominent member of Pole's Venetian circle and principal conduit of information about the writing of *De unitate*, wrote Starkey asking him to thank Russell for his favor.[125] In 1536 Russell's chaplain got into trouble for knowing the content of *De unitate*, and Russell involved himself with the opposition to Anne.[126] Perhaps because of his attitude toward her, Russell joined the court conservatives and supported Mary as heir apparent in 1536. He helped Norfolk, Suffolk, and Bryan to turn back the Pilgrimage, but he twice fell foul of Henry. Early on the king accused Russell of "slackness," and Russell's decision to ignore Henry's oral instructions and issue a general pardon to the rebels without delay angered the king. Russell

---

[121] Pole made this request in his instructions to Throckmorton when he sent his servant to deliver *De unitate* (BL, Cleop. MS E. VI, fol. 348v). The committee's makeup is reconstructed from Geoffrey Pole's recollection of a conversation with Starkey about Sampson's and Tunstall's opinions of the book and from Starkey's own letter to Pole (BL, Cleop. MS E. VI, fol. 379v).

[122] J. J. Scarisbrick has recently documented Shrewsbury's religious views in *The Reformation and the English People* (Oxford, 1984), p. 8; and G. W. Bernard amplifies Scarisbrick's evidence and explains why Shrewsbury remained loyal, despite numerous grievances (*The Power of the Early Tudor Nobility: A Study of the Fourth and Fifth Earls of Shrewsbury* [Brighton, 1985], pp. 50–52).

[123] J. A. Guy, *The Public Career of Sir Thomas More* (New Haven, Conn., 1980), pp. 106–7. Many thanks to S. J. Gunn for advice on Suffolk's politics.

[124] Biblioteca Marciana, Venice, MS Marciana Ital. X. 24 (6527), fol. 7v, a draft letter to Protector Somerset, probably from 1549 (*Calendar of State Papers, Venetian*, vol. 5, no. 575). Diane Willen makes Russell a close ally of Cromwell's (*John Russell, First Earl of Bedford: One of the King's Men* [London, 1981]).

[125] BL, Nero MS B. VI, fol. 107r, June 15, 1535.

[126] Richard Manchester, undated, PRO, SP 1/113/194v (Brewer et al., eds., vol. 11, no. 1470); Ives, p. 176; and Willen, p. 23.

CARDINAL POLE'S LEGATION 327

was also a good friend of both Lisle, whom he supported as best he could in the latter's "exile" at Calais, and Paulet.[127] Further, Starkey alleged that the council's principal secretary, Thomas Wriothesley, said that Cromwell's vengeance against the Poles went much too far.[128] Wriothesley held a manor at Micheldever, Hampshire, and would eventually establish his family in that county.[129] Wriothesley, Southhampton, Russell, and Bryan suffered a collective attack of a mysterious ailment that kept them away from court at the time of the Exeter business, and Bryan was quite literally thrown out of court in December 1538.[130] Gardiner, of course, was bishop of Winchester, which was not far west of the hotbed on the Hampshire-Sussex border, and a religious conservative. A cast of the net just a bit outside the council, but in the same part of the country, hauls in the West family. Its head, Lord Delawarr, presented Crofts to a benefice at Shepton Mallet, Somerset.[131] Cromwell treated Delawarr shabbily, forcing him out of his ancestral seat at Boxgrave Priory, Chichester. If family ties could have overridden local antagonisms, then one of Delawarr's opponents, Thomas Fiennes, might have come down on the Pole side of the fence. He was Montagu's brother-in-law through his marriage to another daughter of George Nevill, Lord Abergavenny.[132] Another cast within the Poles' marriage relations lands the Hastings—or at least one of the servants of Francis, Baron Hastings, son of the first earl of Huntingdon. George Legg originally told Morgan Wells of Mewtas's mission.[133] To paraphrase Morison, members of the king's council (and others) had indeed uttered the king's secrets (and more).[134]

Some of this treatment of Pole's likely supporters has been unavoidably impressionistic, but when one enters the waters in search of his principal enemies, navigational aids become few and far between. On the face of it, only two candidates appear, Henry and Cromwell, but the question has never been thrown open before, so the terms of

[127] Willen, pp. 22, 24, 25, 26–28.
[128] The transcript reads, "Mr. wryothesley said thatt this examinatt [Geoffrey Pole] and other of his famylie must nott be made Cok[ney]es and after the sayd sterkey sayd further, that the lord pr[ivy] seal if the king was nott of a good nature for one poles sake wold destroy all poles" (PRO, SP 1/138/215). The syntax is obscure; it could be that Starkey was echoing Wriothesley.
[129] Brewer et al., eds., vol. 13, pt. 2, no. 318.
[130] Ibid., no. 1120.
[131] Cranmer to Cromwell, November 14, 1538, ibid., no. 832.
[132] For the Fiennes pedigree, see ibid., vol. 14, pt. 2, nos. 481, 436 (72); *Sussex Archaeological Collections*, vol. 58 (London, 1915), pp. 64–65. I am grateful to A. J. Slavin for help on this point and on Sussex politics in general.
[133] For Francis Hastings, see PRO, SP 1/139/23r; and *DNB*.
[134] Richard Morison, *An invective . . . ayenst treason* (London, 1539), fol. Eiv.

VII

reference may demand expansion. Evidence exists to support both traditional answers, although the balance of opinion places the onus on Henry. But as the Dodds sisters long ago recognized, even if the sort of hatred for Pole that most recently Muriel St. Claire Byrne posited consumed Henry, that would not constitute "a really satisfactory explanation of any human being's actions."[135] Aside from deeds done in the king's name that someone else could well have instigated, the strongest evidence for Henry's primacy comes from the French ambassador. Writing at the height of the Exeter scare, Castillon informed the constable Montmorency that Henry had long ago told him of his resolve to exterminate the "house of Montagu," a part of the White Rose, together with the rest of the Pole family.[136] Castillon may well have heard whatever Henry said through the common Continental filter of the "White Rose" and thereby distorted the king's remark. It will also be noted that the ambassador did not connect Henry's determination to Pole's legation or indeed directly to Pole for any reason.

On the other hand, we have seen Wriothesley's opinion that Cromwell pulled the strings behind the plots, and Pole provides some measure of confirmation. In a letter to Henry, which was part of the *De unitate* correspondence, he wrote that Cromwell had been "most fervent off all touchyng the swasion off my retorne," even more vehement than the king.[137] It appears that the hoary old tale of the schemes to do in Pole after the arrival of his blockbuster may contain some truth and that Cromwell may well have enlisted others besides the unwitting Starkey in a campaign to ensnare the latter's former master. During the approach to *De unitate*, Starkey wrote Pole that Sir Edward Baynton, Pole's "old lovar & frend [to] whome the kyngys plesure ys not unknowen . . . apon hys behalfe wyllyd me thys to wryte to you."[138] Baynton probably acted on Henry's orders, but he gave his allegiance to Cromwell. His precise affiliation is no easier to work out than that of most other Henrician courtiers. He was once Anne's vice-chancellor but nevertheless has been made an adherent of the Carewe-Exeter faction in 1536.[139] This seems improbable unless Baynton joined the conservatives for other than ideological reasons. Baynton probably held advanced religious opinions, the sort of thing Cromwell increas-

---

[135] Byrne, ed. (n. 94 above), 4:224–25, 6:221–23. Madeleine H. Dodds and Ruth Dodds, *The Pilgrimage of Grace and the Exeter Conspiracy* (Cambridge, 1915), 2:277–78.
[136] Brewer et al., eds., vol. 13, pt. 2, no. 753.
[137] BL, Cleop. MS E. VI, fol. 341r.
[138] BL, Cleop. MS E. VI, fol. 374r.
[139] Ives (n. 101 above), p. 176.

ingly valued.[140] Perhaps, therefore, he rather acted in concert with Cromwell in 1536. Baynton may have allied himself with the conservatives in soliciting Pole's opinion as ammunition against Anne once Cromwell had decided to abandon her.

Cromwell certainly took an interest in Pole and his family. He planted Throckmorton on Pole, or so he thought. Holland alleged that Cromwell knew of his role as Helyar's financial agent and had approved the arrangement. Cromwell also declared himself "good lord" to Geoffrey Pole and one Ayer when they were delated for knowing about Holland's trips abroad.[141] Was Cromwell stringing them along to see if he could snare someone bigger? We know that Henry and Cromwell disagreed over Gardiner's orders in April 1537, but not why.[142] Was this dispute a symptom of a more basic rift over Pole? This may be inadmissible evidence, but Pole always protested his loyalty to and love for Henry while singling Cromwell out as the villain of the piece.[143]

The relatively greater success of the two men in the field on whom Cromwell could unreservedly rely further suggests that he may have been the primum mobile. Probably only Hutton and Mewtas solidly supported the government's designs and shared Cromwell's religious views. Hutton was Thomas Cranmer's man, so much so that he appears in the State Papers almost coevally with Cranmer. In 1533 or so Cranmer asked John Tregonwell to favor his friend Hutton with the lord chancellorship.[144] About a year later, the archbishop again asked for help for Hutton, "to whom, for many considerations, I owe as special favour as to any man else of his like state and degree."[145] After Hutton's efforts in the Low Countries, Cranmer tried hard to procure him some suitable reward from Cromwell that would allow him to retire to England. "If you could make him an abbot or a prior . . . he were bound unto you, as he is nevertheless most bound unto you of all men."[146] As a city man, Hutton would have doubly likely adhered to the Boleyn faction, Cranmer's staunch allies, whom Pole's supporters had just helped to overthrow.[147] Revenge against them by doing in Pole

---

[140] Maria Dowling, "Anne Boleyn and Reform," *Journal of Ecclesiastical History* 35 (1984): 32, 38. My thanks to Dowling for much assistance with Baynton's religion.

[141] PRO, SP 1/139/154r (Brewer et al., eds., vol. 13, pt. 2, no. 875).

[142] Brewer et al., eds., vol. 12, pt. 1, no. 1109.

[143] For just one example, even if secondhand, see PRO, SP 1/138/192v. Holland reported that Pole had told him "wold the lord pryvey seall so fayn kyll me, well I trust it shall nott lye in his powur, the king is not contentyd to bear me malice."

[144] Brewer et al., eds., vol. 6, no. 1093.

[145] BL, Harleian MS 6148, fol. 43r (Brewer et al., eds., vol. 7, no. 568).

[146] Brewer et al., eds., vol. 13, pt. 2, no. 25.

[147] Ives, passim.

would have been the order of the day for Hutton. Ties to religious reformers might also explain his interest in Phillips, Tyndale's betrayer. Cromwell probably dispatched Mewtas, the handgun specialist, as his personal agent. He shared religious sympathies with Cromwell, concluding one of his reports with the pious hope that the "holy goste send youe your desire," hardly the ordinary closing between servant and senior minister.[148] Cromwell also used his leading servant, Ralph Sadler, to carry orders to Gardiner, and Sadler apparently held a brief to report on Gardiner's behavior. He carefully noted that the bishop seemed pleased with his instructions.[149]

The extraordinary lengths to which someone willingly went to continue negotiations with Pole smack much more of Henry's temporizing than of Cromwell's usual aggressiveness. It cannot be said that Henry had dealt with Pole impatiently or refused to give him numerous chances to do the king's bidding, as Pole had once done and as Henry hoped he would again.[150] The protracted efforts to get Pole back to England after *De unitate* have always been written off as mere deviousness. All the same, Pole's longtime friend Starkey, who risked his neck to warn Pole in 1537, handled some of the correspondence, without betraying any uneasiness over the honorability of Henry's intentions. Henry may well have dealt treacherously with a Robert Aske, but to do the same to his own cousin, and a graft of his own setting (to paraphrase Morison once again), would have been a different kettle of fish. Similarly, the council kept open until the last the option of a conference on neutral territory if only Pole would come as a private citizen. He could pick those the English would send as negotiators, as he did in the reading of *De unitate*.[151] This was, perhaps, deceit. But given the strength of Pole's friends on the council and Henry's tokens of esteem, this offer might rather be presumed sincere.

---

[148] BL, Caligula MS E. 2, fol. 233r, April 16, 1537.

[149] PRO, SP 49/5/12r (Brewer et al., eds., vol. 12, pt. 1, no. 760).

[150] There is very little evidence of an open breach between Pole and Henry before the conclusion of this legation. Pole later tried to date their rupture back to 1529-30, claiming his mission to the Paris theologians in search of a favorable opinion on Henry's divorce had been thrust on him. This can no longer be maintained. Pole tried to serve Henry with every appearance of real enthusiasm.

[151] Hutton reported that Throckmorton thought Nicholas Wilson the best man for the conference, and he was duly commissioned (PRO, SP 1/124/167r, September 2, [1537], [Brewer et al., eds., vol. 12, pt. 2, no. 635]; see also instructions for Wilson and Nicholas Heath, PRO, SP 1/124/145r–152v [Brewer et al., eds., vol. 12, pt. 2, no. 620]). In this memorandum Cromwell claimed to have consulted Tunstall and John Stokesley, bishop of London, about how best to approach Pole (PRO, SP 1/124/147v–148r).

VII

CARDINAL POLE'S LEGATION

As is often the case, it has proved difficult to determine who in the highest reaches of English and papal government directed Pole's legation and the measures taken against it. Nevertheless, both sides fielded agents capable of various and sundry missions, whether as propagandists or as assassins. Neither met with much success, but without benefit of hindsight, trying to see the crisis as contemporaries did, we must admit that Pole's legation endangered England. He collected valuable support from both Francis and Charles (through his sister), not to mention the papacy and papal diplomats. If none furnished quite as much assistance as Pole might have hoped, their aid more than furnished the English a prima facie case for strong measures against Pole. Factional struggles largely frustrated those plots, and disagreements between Henry and Cromwell may have entered in too. These internal divisions offered Pole his best opening. He possessed the will to harm England, behaving in anything but the saintly manner he and his partisans have foisted on later historiography. Both sides were fully prepared to adopt whatever means seemed necessary to obtain their increasingly ideologically determined goals. Some of the best tactics involved espionage, always a live option when diplomacy failed.

VIII

Marco Mantova: A Bronze Age Conciliarist

The sixteenth was the "secolo d'oro" of the legal faculty at Padua, when it was the most celebrated school in Europe. Even humanists recommended it highly, despite its resolute commitment to Bartolist jurisprudence.[1] For more than half that time one of its most famous professors was Marco Mantova Benavides, but since then his life and thought have attracted little attention.[2] It is of great interest, though, that Mantova was a latter-day conciliarist, at a time and place of critical importance. Even Hubert Jedin and Remigius Bäumer did not uncover him in their thorough surveys of conciliar thought in the early sixteenth century, despite recognizing the importance of Padua, and turning up two much more obscure figures, however great their influence.[3] Only Ludwig Pastor mentioned Mantova's *Dialogus de concilio* in passing.[4] Lately, his legal thought has been accorded some importance as a transitional form between Bartolist and humanist jurisprudence, but its content still has not been touched.[5]

---

[1] B. BRUGI, L'università dei giuristi in Padova nel cinquecento: Saggio di storia della giurisprudenza e della università italiane, in: AVT 1 (1922) 1—92, here 2. Brugi presents ample evidence of humanist regard for the faculty, which could be easily multiplied.

Of the many people who have generously read this article, I would like to single out Dennis Gilkey, Wayne C. Bartee, James Tracy, Elizabeth G. Gleason, Gregorio Piaia and S. E. Lehmberg for particular thanks. The Newberry Library provided a fellowship which supported part of my research, as did the Graduate School of the University of Minnesota. My thanks and more to Prof. Antonio Padoa Schioppa of the Istituto di storia del diritto italiano, Milan, whose magnificent library made possible this study's completion.

[2] His career can be reconstructed from J. FACCIOLATI, Fasti gymnasii patavini, Padua 1757. In the period of interest he had just moved into the first ordinary chair of civil law. The best study remains a short one in G. VEDOVA, Biografia degli scrittori padovani, Padua 1832, 564—580. See also the brief sketch in R. TERPENNING, Pietro Bembo and the cardinalate: Unpublished letters to Marco Mantova, in: Lettere italiane 32 (1980) 75—86, here 79 f.

[3] H. JEDIN, Geschichte des Konzils von Trient I, Freiburg 1951, 29. R. BÄUMER, Nachwirkungen des konziliaren Gedankens in der Theologie und Kanonistik des frühen 16. Jh. (= RST 100), Münster/W. 1971, 8 ff.

[4] L. PASTOR, The history of the popes from the close of the MA 11, ed. R. F. Kerr, St. Louis 1950, 161. Prof. Gleason may include Mantova in her study of arguments for papal *plenitudo potestatis* in the early sixteenth century.

[5] E. HOLTHOEFER, Die Literatur zum gemeinen und partikularen Recht in Italien, Frankreich, Spanien und Portugal, in: Handbuch der Quellen und Literaturen der neueren europäischen Privatrechtsgeschichte II: Neuere Zeit (1100—1500) I: Wissenschaft, ed. H. COING, Munich 1977, 103—500, 110 f. and 139 f.

This paper attempts two things. The first is to treat one set of conciliar ideas in a rigorously historical fashion, and the second serves that end by considering them in their entirety. That is, it does more than merely set Mantova in context, it tries to treat his thought in an integral, text-based, fashion. That, in turn, requires an effort to escape from prevailing historiographical categories, many of them originally imposed by sixteenth century strife of parties.[6] Hence the somewhat detailed attention to method. In short, rather than forcing Mantova's text to answer a set of questions, this study tries to discover what problems he considered important, which makes a rather close analysis of how his text was assembled necessary. Such an approach will also highlight Mantova's contribution, in the traditional sense, especially on the score of the people's participation in the government of the church.

In part Mantova's neglect grows out of an older fashion in the study of conciliarist thought, which, considering it a unified phenomenon (usually a heresy), studied only the Olympian figures in whom that doctrine's essence could be most easily isolated. This largely idealist approach is still the dominant style; even in most of the newer studies of lesser figures, what is sought are contributions of lasting value. But Giuseppe Alberigo has argued forcefully that understanding conciliarism will only be possible when its study has been historicized, when each of its varieties has been firmly located in context and the lines of affiliation between individual thinkers carefully worked out.[7] If this is to be done, though, one of the principal yardsticks of importance must be a particular theorist's contemporary standing, not the value of his ideas to the sorting out of modern problems of ecclesiastical government. By this measure there could have been few more significant conciliarists in the sixteenth century than Mantova. His case also suggests the importance of Alberigo's observation that one of the more important current generalizations — the opposition of papalism and conciliarism — is much too simple. Mantova, in common with most of those who thought about the problem of pope and council, combined elements of both these "ideal types". And, given the widespread currency of the belief in the importance of the cardinals in the fourteenth and fifteenth centuries, it would be surprising if one party had been able to coopt them as thoroughly as Francis Oakley maintains.[8] Again, while Mantova shows the

---

[6] This effort bears some similarity to that of P. SIMONCELLI, Il caso Reginald Pole: Eresia e santità nelle polemiche religiose del cinquecento, Roma 1977, which attempts to trace how the "myth of Pole's holiness," originally created to defend his party from heresy proceedings immediately after his death, came to dominate historiography.

[7] G. ALBERIGO, Chiesa conciliare. Identità e significato del conciliarismo, Brescia 1981, 344 f., 14 f.

[8] J. Thomson has singled out Antonio Roselli in the midfifteenth century as one of the last figures in whom some compromise between papalism and conciliarism was still possible, and F. Oakley has argued that the "curialist oligarchic" tendency, in which the cardinals were assured a prominent place in the ecclesiastical structure, fed only into the former. In the early sixteenth century these two streams diverged. J. THOMSON, Papalism and conciliarism in Antonio Roselli's *Monarchia*, in: MS 37 (1975) 445—458, here 458; F. OAKLEY, Almain and Major: Conciliar theory on the eve of the reformation,

clear impact of Panormitanus, as would be expected from Jedin's observation that the survival of conciliarism into the sixteenth century was largely due to him, Mantova owed an even greater debt to an earlier conciliarist, Francesco Zabarella.[9] If Gregorio Piaia is correct that Zabarella did, after all, make heavy use of Marsilio of Padua, then his disguised role in later conciliar thought may need yet another assessment. Although Mantova did not make anything of Zabarella's stress on the *pars potior*, which Piaia thinks was borrowed in part from Marsilio, the two points of Zabarella's thought which Brian Tierney identified as distinctive both crop up in Mantova: corporation theory to define the powers of the pope (Zabarella's "fundamental premise"); and the limited and derivative nature of papal *plenitudo potestatis*.[10]

No doubt there is some sense in which the later practitioners of scholastic jurisprudence were *epigoni*.[11] There is also some truth in the charge that they became so wrapped up in their texts and commentaries that their constitutional theory became divorced from the world of practical politics. The most celebrated instance was their continued emphasis on the role of the emperor in areas where he no longer had the slightest importance. These criticisms could be applied to Mantova, who is guilty of an egregious (but conscious) digression on the symbolism of the imperial crown, was sometimes inclined to pile up citations, and did make the emperor the principal safeguard of the church's welfare, if the pope failed.[12] Levelling such charges, though, is an essentially ahistorical operation which demands that these texts have something of direct relevance to say to us and that they say it in an immediately accessible way.

---

in: AHR 76 (1965) 637—690, here 688. For Alberigo's criticism of the papal-conciliar opposition, see his Il movimento conciliare (XIV—XV sec.) nella ricerca storica recente, in: Stud. medievali ser. 3,19 (1978) 913—950, here 918, and Chiesa, here 15n. He points to the misleading classification of arguments about the cardinals at 34. He also suggests that the labels moderate, balanced and extreme conciliarism too clearly reveal their polemical roots and lead to confusion rather than comprehension, 345. In this article the terms conciliarism and conciliar thought will be used interchangeably. The latter makes the phenomenon seem a bit less monolithic, and hence might be preferred. "Moderate," "conservative," and the like are used generically, not to refer to any party.

[9] JEDIN, Trient 15.

[10] G. PIAIA, La fondazione della teoria conciliare in Francesco Zabarella, in: Scienza e filosofia all'università di Padova nel quattrocento, ed. A. POPPI, Trieste/Padua 1983, 431—461, especially 442 ff.; Prof. Piaia here modifies somewhat the earlier views of W. Ullmann, B. Tierney and T. Morrissey. B. TIERNEY, Foundations of the conciliar theory: The contribution of the medieval canonists from Gratian to the great schism, Cambridge 1955, 221, 225. I am grateful to Prof. Piaia for sending me a copy of his article in draft.

[11] W. ENGELMANN passed one of the severest judgments on the late fifteenth and early sixteenth century Bartolists, condemning them in particular for their excessive reliance on authorities: Die Wiedergeburt der Rechtskultur in Italien durch die wissenschaftliche Lehre, Leipzig 1938, 239—242.

[12] This last point proved popular in some strange places, cropping up, for instance, in Thomas Starkey's treatise on the English commonwealth, written during the first years of the Henrician reformation. See his Dialogue between Reginald Pole and Thomas Lupset, London 1948, 120. The date is established in T. MAYER, Faction and ideology: Thomas Starkey's Dialogue, in: Historical Journal, forthcoming.

This too often degenerates into an historical beauty pageant (and an opportunity for historians to show off their superior knowledge): one thinker is cleverer than another, one age more "creative". This is not to say that Mantova's *De concilio* is a very penetrating work, even by the standard of his near contemporaries at Paris of that of the grand master of early sixteenth century Bartolist jurisprudence and defender of the council of Pisa, Filippo Decio.[13] These were all willing to attack highly controversial questions and make some new applications of old ideas, however closely Jacques Almain and John Major may have followed Jean Gerson. Mantova was largely content to remain within the bounds of the debate on the constitution of the church as they had been drawn by the middle of the fifteenth century, and on many major issues went no further than Zabarella had in its early years.

We can apply other standards of historical relevance to subvert inherited categories. Two of the best are popularity of work and of author. There can be no doubt of either in Mantova's case. After his *Dialogus* appeared in 1541 from the press of an unknown Paduan printer, it went through at least three editions in the century, including one at Louvain just eight years later, in addition to an appearance in the *Tractatus universis iuris*, intended as a summary of the state of legal knowledge. The tract was reprinted as late as 1671, closing a publishing history equal to that of Erasmus's *Ciceronianus*.[14] The author's standing as a legist was unassailable. A student of both the most important late fifteenth century jurists, Giason del Mayno and Carlo Ruino, he spent all of his long career at Padua, from 1523 to 1582. He was an enormously prolific writer. Besides numerous legal treatises, many of them designed to simplify the hard places of the civil and canon law for beginning students, he produced works on moral philosophy and vernacular poetry commentary, as well as three fairly well known *Novelle*.[15] These latter indicate something about contemporary assessments of Mantova, since they probably mean that he was a member of the distinguished Paduan literary circle, the Infiammati, whose members included Lazzaro Bonamico and Sperone Speroni.[16] Even if Mantova may have fallen a

---

[13] For the Parisians see F. OAKLEY, Almain and Major, and Conciliarism in the sixteenth century: Jacques Almain again, in: ARG 68 (1977) 111—132. Decio is treated by BÄUMER, Nachwirkungen 36 f., 52 ff., 90 ff., and *passim*.

[14] The record of editions is taken from the British Library Catalogue of Printed Books. A. GAMBARA details the editions of Erasmus's work in his translation, Il ciceroniano o dello stile migliore, Brescia 1965, xiv.

[15] They have been reprinted several times, e. g. in: Novelle di Marco Mantova scrittore del sec. XVI, Bologna 1862.

[16] The Infiammati lack a comprehensive study, but see G. TOFFANIN, Il cinquecento, Milan ⁵1954, 111; H. HARTH's introduction to Sperone Speroni, Dialogo delle lingue, Munich 1975, 7; B. NARDI, Saggi sull'aristotelismo padovano dal secolo XIV al XVI, Florence 1958, 341; E. GARIN, L'umanesimo italiano. Filosofia e vita civile nel rinascimento, Bari 1965, 205; and J. TEDESCHI, Notes toward a genealogy of the Sozzini family, in: Italian reformation studies in honor of Laelius Socinus, Florence 1965, 275—318, here 296.

bit short by the chief standard of professional competence — his surviving *consilia* fill a mere two volumes — he was consulted on some critical cases, including Henry VIII's divorce wherein he delivered an opinion favorable to the King and got himself into deep trouble with the Signory as a result. Twenty years later it could still be singled out for attack in a Catholic defense of Queen Catherine.[17]

Mantova's popularity is attested not only by two historians of the university, one of them a humanist, but also by another "hostile witness," Viglius Zwichem van Aytta, protégé of Erasmus and of one of the first of the humanist jurists, Andrea Alciato.[18] Despite his contempt for the barbarism of the Paduan jurists, who were *"plane rudes"* when it came to *"literatura humanioris"*, Viglius praised Mantova for his "deligence", and noted that he could "by his sharp native intelligence, faithful memory and pronunciation, hold the attention of his hearers."[19] Antonio Ricoboni, humanist scholar of the *gymnasium patavinum*, recorded that when Mantova lectured, all the other halls were empty, while the legal historian Guido Panziroli still preserved the memory of Mantova's "ability of speaking in extemporaneous Latin."[20] His teaching abilities, reflected in his success as a lecturer, emerge from his introductory texts as well. Unfortunately, much of the precise content of Mantova's instruction is irrecoverable, since he would ordinarily have exposed only his more advanced students to conciliar ideas, and then only in private tuition. At least we can say a great deal about how Mantova taught his select students.

Besides the general difficulties in the study of scholastic jurisprudence referred to above, there are some peculiar to Mantova, especially his attempt to write a realistic dialogue. The exchange between him and his friend Roberto Maggio, sometime papal legate to Venice and then apostolic protonotary, is one of give and take, not merely a framework within which one character delivers *ex cathedra* pronouncements while the other sits obediently at his feet.[21] An attempt at realism may also have lain behind the characters' tendency to

---

[17] E. SURTZ, Henry VIII's great matter in Italy: An introduction to representative Italians in the king's divorce, mainly 1527—1535, Ann Arbor 1978, 297—301 considers Mantova's opinion. Nicholas Harpsfield refuted it at length in his A treatise on the pretended divorce between Henry VIII and Catharine of Aragon, ed. N. POCOCK, London 1878.

[18] C. HOYNCK VAN PAPENDRECHT, Vita Viglii ab Aytta Zuichemi ab ipso Viglio scripta, in: Annalecta ad historiam scissi Belgii potissimum attirentia I, The Hague 1743, 9. For a modern treatment, see R. STINTZING, Geschichte der deutschen Rechtswissenschaft I, Munich 1880, 221.

[19] Viglius to Erasmus, in: Opus epistolarum Desiderii Erasmi, ed. P. S. ALLEN 9, Oxford 1934, 2994; PAPENDRECHT, Analecta II, 56.

[20] A. RICOBONI, De gymnasio patavino commentariorum libri sex, in: Thesaurus antiquatum et historiarum Italiae, Louvain 1721, 74; G. PANZIROLI, De claris legum interpretibus libri quattuor, ed. O. PANZIROLI, Venice 1637, 346.

[21] According to MARIO COSENZA, Maggio received the dedication of Francesco Asulano's edition of the Decameron in 1522. Biographical and bibliographical dictionary of the Italian humanists III, Boston 1962, 2072. F. C. CHURCH called him nuncio; P. P. Vergerio was then his secretary. The Italian reformers, 1534—1564, New York 1932, 72. He is called protonotary in Mantova's preface.

pursue several ideas which both agreed were not strictly relevant.[22] Perhaps the work was designed to simulate the famous "contentions" between faculty members at Padua which Viglius found so stimulating.[23] Mantova's use of the favorite humanist form of the dialogue is one sign of his transitional position in the history of legal scholarship, since except in literary form he was dealing with a scholastic problem in an essentially scholastic fashion. Mantova did not find such an approach entirely congenial. In one place, speaking in his own persona, he rebuked Roberto for his prolixity in assembling support for papal primacy, telling him bluntly that two or three citations would have done nicely, instead of the half-page Roberto adduced.[24] Nevertheless, Mantova provides a clear instance of the difficulties produced by multiplication of authorities, at least in the early going, as well as of real canonist inconsistency, emphasized by Tierney.[25] Bad as these problems were in the case of Decretists and Decretalists, they had become worse by the early sixteenth century. As Walter Ullmann several times observed of Cardinal Zabarella, this means it is sometimes almost impossible to determine what a particular citation had to do with the point it was intended to support.[26] Whether or not these jurists seemed incoherent to contemporaries — perhaps their minds worked in ways different from ours, according to other memory systems for example — they can be hard for twentieth century historians to follow.

This situation may well have been exacerbated by the speed with which Mantova apparently wrote, or dictated, the work. He had no qualms about admitting that his own preparation had taken only three days, though this could be merely a conventional disabling statement, or a concealed boast.[27] Perhaps if the haste was real, it sprang from a desire for topicality, in response to the calling of a council for Vicenza in 1537 (that originally called to Mantua two years earlier). Nor did he hesitate to reveal, after being reproached for a particularly scathing attack on the cardinals, that he had not read the works of any of the counterexamples of Caraffa, Contarini, Bembo and Sadoleto, Roberto brought up. This particular instance, too, is typical of the debate's nature.

---

[22] The work may thus reflect its author's rhetorical training. If so, WALTER ONG's observation that such writers were certain to create characters who "generate dramatic fiction," would apply as well to Mantova. Tudor writings on rhetoric, poetic and literary theory, in: Rhetoric, romance and technology, Ithaca, N.Y. 1971, 48—103, here 66. See also D. MARSH, The quattrocento dialogue: Classical tradition and humanist innovation, Cambridge, Mass. 1980, 3.

[23] Viglius to Erasmus, above.

[24] M. MANTOVA, Dialogus de concilio, Venice 1541, f. Dv. I have not distinguished Mantova as author from Mantova as character. Context should make clear which is meant.

[25] TIERNEY, Foundations 163, 218.

[26] W. ULLMANN, Origins of the great schism: A study in fourteenth century ecclesiastical history, London 1948, 221 f.

[27] Roberto complimented Mantova that he had been *brevi quidem temporis intervallo, immo triduo, homo vehementer occupatus*. MANTOVA, f. Ciiar—v. This could be a conventional phrase to indicate that Mantova could have done much better, if he wanted to.

Mantova, despite his violent language, declared himself persuaded by Roberto's defense, but the two crossed swords again in the conclusion of the passage. Mantova begged Roberto to lend him some of these cardinals' books. "I wish and I passionately desire and I ask you to produce them, so that I may read them." Roberto retorted "[t]hey are for sale, you may buy them for yourself, and you will free me this bother, since, besides," he added a bit sheepishly, "I gave mine to Lombardus Amulius."[28]

These difficulties are not insuperable. The dialogue form is relatively easy to decode, at least on the surface. Mantova posed Roberto as the expert, claiming at the very beginning that he had set out to write on the council only in order to stimulate Maggio to do something better. Who played what role is not always certain, though, as when the two debated the requisites for a bishop's education when Mantova did not quite succeed in keeping straight who was defending the necessity of a humanist training.[29] Most of the debates which reach resolution do so through serious discussion; Roberto was not invariably the winner. Often the two agreed in some of the more violent criticisms Mantova levelled at the state of the church, but the most intemperate attacks he placed in his own mouth and then left it up to Roberto to persuade him to tone them down. One of the clearest instances is Mantova's blast against the order of cardinals.

> Would that today likewise they were such as you have said [i. e., paragons], and such they ought to be, and not giants, who groaned under the waters, who cannot be useful, nor take care, but glory to be first. They hold their necks stiff, they speak grand things, meditate on the sublime, and finally they do nothing because they are ignorant. Add the fact that neither in their work is their truth, nor honesty in their ways, nor finally faith in their counsels, greedy for money and things and riches, not following Christ, nor virtue, or an abundance of spiritual gifts.[30]

He also maintained that there were many priests in name, but few in deed, complained vigorously of the obesity of abbotts, making it a valid reason for excluding them from a council, and warned of the dangers of *otium* and the abuse of hunting by clerics.[31] All these seem to indicate that Mantova had more than a trace of evangelism in his make-up, as one of his arguments against papal primacy in matters of the faith seems to confirm. Since faith alone justified, its control could not possibly be left to a single, conceivably heretical,

---

[28] F. Fiiv.
[29] Ff. Gr—Hiir.
[30] F. Eiiav. *Utinam hodie tales essent, quales dixisti, qualesque esse debent, & non gigantes, qui gemuerunt sub aquis ... qui non prodesse possunt, nec curant, sed praeesse gloriantur, cervicem erigunt, grandia loquuntur, sublimia meditantur, & nihil denique quia nesciunt, perantur. Adde quod nec in verbo eorum est veritas, non honestas in moribus, nec denique in consiliis fides, quaesitum pecuniae, & rerum, ac divitiarum, non Christum sequentes, neque virtutum, aut donorum spiritualium affluentiam.*
[31] F. Cr—v. Roberto launched the original attack on the wealth and idleness of the clergy, contrasting them with the saints, even if he later rebuked Mantova for his strictures on them, f. Biibv. For the abbotts, f. Iiivff.

individual.³² Like many other evangelicals, though, Mantova had nothing but praise for pope Paul III, except for one veiled criticism.

The lack of finality in some debates combined with the nature of Mantova's sources presents the major problem in understanding his thought. Probably the former is a function of the latter, at least in part. Mantova depended heavily on Decretist and Decretalist writings which had left unresolved many difficulties which would become burning issues. His favorite later canonists, Zabarella and Nicola de Tudeschis (Panormitanus) were content respectively either to propose emergency measures to remedy a temporary situation, a schism, or to adhere fairly closely to earlier thinking. Hence Mantova's usual method. He began with a strongly hierocratic statement and then qualified it until, in those cases where he reached a resolution, he adopted a more moderate one. In many instances, Mantova seems to have worked from current pro-papal arguments and then whittled them down on the strength of his sources. Even so, it seems as if he were deliberately ignoring all the heated arguments of the fifteenth century.

Not that he was ignorant of the history of its great councils. He was familiar with all of them, and approved their most important actions. Constance and Florence fell under the head of useful councils, the latter for promoting union with the Greeks, the former for its role in ending the Great Schism and remedying heresy. Combined with his borrowings from Zabarella, one of the major forces behind the decrees of Constance, this seems almost a wholesale endorsement of its constitutional theory; he gave no sign of disapproval of any of its accomplishments.³³ Despite his apparently somewhat conservative leanings,

---

³² As Roberto argued, *dum sumus in hoc corpore, ut inquit Paul. ij. ad corinth. v. ambulare debemus, scientes quod non iustificatur homo ex operibus legis, nisi per fidem ... quomodo igitur his, idem esse cum deo pontificis consistorium, posseque eum a nemine iudicari, vel ulli omnino subesse velis, non video, si hereticus accusetur,* f. Diiar. The survival of two volumes of Mantova's letters in Museo Correr and the Marciana in Venice, and a third in the Law Library of the University of California, Berkeley, may well be further evidence of his evangelical leanings, especially since the latter was marked up for the printer. TERPENNING, Bembo 80 f. They could all thus be another example of that favorite evangelical print medium, the *lettere volgari*. See A. J. SCHUTTE, The *lettere volgari* and the crisis of evangelism in Italy, in: Renaissance Quarterly 28 (1975) 639—688. I hope to pursue research in these letters in the near future. Mantova's search for patronage may also indicate something about his religious leanings. At one point in his Observationes legalium libri X, Louvain 1546, 198 he called Cristoforo Madruzzo and Pietro Bembo *illustrissimis mihique dominis & patronis semper observandissimis* (in a passage dated 1540). At about the same time, he wrote to Gianmatteo Giberti's vicar Filippo Stridonio proposing to dedicate one of his works to the bishop. A. PROSPERI, Tra evangelismo e controriforma: G. M. Giberti (1495—1543), Rome 1969, 233. All these, including Bembo, were members of the party of Evangelicals. See P. SIMONCELLI, Pietro Bembo e l'evangelismo italiano, in: Critica storica 15 (1978) 1—63, and D. FENLON, Heresy and obedience in Tridentine Italy: Cardinal Pole and the counter reformation, Cambridge 1972. Among Mantova's students was Contarini's sometime secretary, Girolamo Negri. G. MARANGONI, Lazzaro Bonamico e lo studio padovano nella prima metà del cinquecento, in: Nuovo arch. veneto 1 (1901) 118—151, here 127. If Fenlon is correct about the Evangelicals' hopes for reunion with the Protestants through a general council, then Mantova shared that central belief. FENLON, Heresy 18, and see below, n. 75.

³³ MANTOVA presented a long resumé of Constance's history and accomplishments, f. Liiav, followed by a shorter one for Florence, f. Liiir.

Mantova innocently asked why general councils were rare, given the canons of Basel. He accepted Roberto's explanation that too frequent councils would be a detriment, since they should handle only issues of great weight, but he was still not completely convinced, citing the number of councils celebrated under Constantine, and emphasizing how valuable they were.[34] When he came to support his case that the council was to decide between rival claimants to the papacy, he backed it up by the Constance decree *Frequens*.[35] On the other hand, he did not ignore all the troubled history of the fifteenth century. He noted Eugenius IV's translation and dissolution of Basel in support of a general right for the pope to do both.[36] He also tacitly rejected one of Basel's major procedural innovations by arguing that, in order to avoid maximum confusion, only one important figure should reply (vote) for the others in meetings of the council, rather than counting heads.[37] The rewriting of the history of the councils, begun by Juan de Torquemada and other of Eugenius's partisans and carried to an extreme by Mantova's contemporary Albert Pighius, had yet to make an impression on him.[38]

The Paduan legist did not set out to write a systematic treatise on the constitution of the church. Rather, he applied legal method, in which persons were to be treated before the matter of the case, and Ciceronian-Aristotelian according to which, as Mantova and Roberto agreed, the essence and the *quidditas* of a phenomenon could only be derived from its definition, to give him his two basic questions: who had a right to attend a council; and how might one be called in case the pope were unable or unwilling.[39] Consequently, his constitu-

---

[34] *M. Sed aliud dicas quaeso, quare est quod concilia generalia ... raro fiunt ... quemadmodum in concilio basilen. fuit alias determinatum ...? R. Quia magno esse videntur detrimento Christianis, et plus dico tibi, quod generale solum hoc ratione raro celebratur.* To Mantova's objection about Constantinian councils, Roberto replied *multa quidem esse possunt, et raro quoque facta, et non ita generaliter ut nunc, adeo ut nec tantum detrimenti etiam pateretur tunc Christianitas,* f. Lv—Liiv.

[35] *M. ... si duo de papatu contenderent, an concilium inter eos iudiceret. R. Certe negligentia fuerat praetermissum, nunc diligenti responsione compensanda, et dicendum breviter quod sic ... et in cano. concilij constantien. incip. frequens, continetur apertius,* f. Niiar.

[36] *M. ... si papa scilicet concilium dissolvere possit. R. ... et ita etiam fecit Eugenius IV qui basilen. concilium dissolvit, seu transtulit ... Hoc idem iam decisum est supra taliter et firmiter tenere debeamus, subsistente iusta et legitima causa dissolui ab eo posse,* f. Niiv—Niiar.

[37] *M. ... debet ne unus ... in concilio pro omnibus respondere? R. Debet utique ... alias confusio esset maxima in ipsarum rerum decisione, et finiretur nunquam,* f. Nv—Niir. For Basel's procedures, see A. J. BLACK, Monarchy and community: Political ideas in the later conciliar controversy 1430—1450, Cambridge 1970, 16.

[38] For Torquemada, BLACK, Monarchy, *passim*. The whole of the sixth book of Pighius's Hierarchiae ecclesiasticae assertio is a blistering attack on conciliar ideas, focusing on Constance and Basel and singling out Jean Gerson as the father of that aberration. His ideas are treated briefly in H. JEDIN, Stud. über die Schriftstellertätigkeit Albert Pigges, Münster 1931, and by ALBERIGO, Movimento 919 ff. G. PIAIA, Marsilio da Padova nella riforma e nella controriforma: Fortuna ed interpretazione, Padua 1977, cap. V/2 provides the fullest account of Pighius's related blast against Marsilio.

[39] F. Car and Kiiv. "*M. Crederem ego prius* [speaking of a council] *a definitione esse sumendum exordium, ut quid sit is (Ci. teste) de quo disputatur, intelligamus. R. Nec secus sciam, tum vel maxime quia definitio ipsiusmet rei, quae definitur, quiditatem ac essentiam ostendit, et verus est docendi modus. Immo Aristo. dicebat,*

tional considerations were largely in the nature of emergency measures to be adopted when the normal situation had gone awry. The implications of many of his proposals were left undrawn, perhaps because that seemed unnecessary. Whether out of innate conservatism, lack of knowledge, or adherence to what Tierney has called "divided sovereignty", Mantova apparently saw no need to spell out many of the precise relations between parts of a council, council and pope, or pope, council and emperor, the issues of constitutional moment he did touch on.[40] Unanimity was expected, as emerges from his definition of a council. As Roberto put it, "a council therefore is called from a common intent, from which the faithful ... assembling in one, direct all contrariness [*obtuitum*] of mind, so far that who dissents from themselves, do not have a council, because they cannot consent in one."[41] In his general approach Mantova may have been following Zabarella, as in his primary concern about how to handle a papal schism, hardly a matter of great contemporary relevance, but Zabarella's reason for writing.

Given this emphasis on unity, it is not surprising that Mantova's discussion was dominated by the corporate metaphor.[42] The pope, the first conciliar person, was the head of the church and the council, since power was given to him alone, even if the church received its share at the same time.[43] If the council were not headed by the pope, it would not be directed by Christ, especially since all Christ's gifts were diffused into the body from the head.[44] Roberto continued with the standard texts supporting the pope's position as vicar of Christ, and concluded that without him the council would be headless. There could be no question but that the pope had all of Christ's plenitude of power.[45]

nos essentialia cognoscere non posse alicuius rei, nisi nominis definitionem accipiamus, quae nihil aliud est, quam brevis et circumscripta rei adhuc explicatio. Mantova's explicit agenda included only the first of these questions. The other question on it, what matters ought to be dealt with in a council, received very little attention, f. Aiiv.

[40] B. TIERNEY, "Divided sovereignty" at Constance: A problem of medieval and early modern political theory, in: AHC 7 (1975) 238—256, here 244.

[41] F. Kiibv. R. *Concilium igitur dictum est ab intentione communi ex quo fideles ... convenientes in unum, omnem mentis obtuitum dirigunt ... adeo ut qui sibimet dissentiunt, concilium non agant, quia non consentiunt in unum.*

[42] This metaphor has attracted much study, but we are not much closer to understanding it than was GIERKE, Das deutsche Genossenschaftsrecht III, Berlin 1883, 112, 547—555. Fundamental is E. KANTOROWICZ, The king's two bodies: A stud. in medieval political theology, Princeton 1957. One of the better recent studies is P. ARCHAMBAULT, The analogy of the "body" in renaissance political literature, in: Bib. d'humanisme et renaissance 29 (1967) 21—52.

[43] *R. ... ut sibi* [the pope] *soli potestas tributa sit, quamvis Pape et ipsi ecclesie simul data fuerit,* f. Ciibr. When Mantova did get to the rest of the conciliar persons, he did very little more than discuss the etymology of their titles and some of their qualifications, ff. Fiibr (patriarchs), Hr (bishops and metropolitans), Iiiv—Iiibv (abbotts).

[44] *R. ... et qui non habet ipsum* [the pope] *pro capite, non habet Christum ... et presertim ibi, ut ab ipso quasi a quodam capite dona sua, velut in corpus omne diffunderet,* f. Ciibr.

[45] *Sine eo quoque concilium corpus acephalum dicatur ... idest sine capite, ergo (ut iam diximus), iuxta illud Paul ad ephe. i et ipsum dedit caput super omnem ecclesiam, quae est corpus ipsius, et plenitudo eius, qui omnia in omnibus adimpletur,* ff. Ciibr—v.

Thus as head of the church, the pope held the primacy in everything, including the council, which represented the universal church.[46] Therefore he alone called a council. Any Christians who dared to assemble one without him were to be punished, since they had put themselves outside communion with the apostolic see, a clear indication of Mantova's attitude to the council of Pisa.[47]

Thus did Roberto deliver an unabashedly hierocratic disquisition on the pope's power and position. Things began to unravel when he went on to mention the two classic cases — contention over the papacy, or a pope accused of heresy — when someone else had the right to convene a council, and then added that one might be otherwise assembled if the pope neglected to call one when that was to the church's prejudice.[48] Mantova refused to accept either of the original exceptions, since the pope was elected by the cardinals and could not be judged by the council he assembled.[49] Pushing even further, Mantova argued that the pope had *imperium* (left undefined) and formed a consistory with God, leaving even the cardinals out of consideration. His power came direct from God, not by delegation, and he had no superior but God.[50] Then Roberto presented what proved to be the stumblingblock, by agreeing that all that Mantova had said was true, except in cases in which the faith was threatened. Then much could be undertaken against an absolute ruler, and, in particular, the council might judge a pope.[51] It is at this point that he delivered the long homily on justification by faith. Mantova rejoined that the pope was untouchable since he was chosen by the Holy Spirit, but Roberto again objected that a council was necessary to make it possible for the Holy Spirit to inspire a new election in the event of a schism. The council was then to depose both contenders and elect a third candidate. To this Mantova assented, since it would mean avoiding scandal in the church, than which nothing could be worse.[52]

---

[46] *R. ... ipsum esse caput corporis ecclesiae ... in omnibus primatum tenens, ut igitur concilium, in quo universalis ecclesia representatur,* f. Dr.

[47] *R. ... qui* [the pope] *solus, seu ad quem ipsius concilij congregatio spectat ... et ne conventiculum, seu conciliabulum dicatur, initumque sit, et inane quicquid in eo agatur, puniunturque graviter, sine eius auctoritate ad ipsum congregantes, ut sedis apostolicae maxime communione careant,* f. Dr.

[48] F. Diir.

[49] *Quod non congreget, si de pontificatu contendat, cum a cardinalibus eligatur ... et pari modo si negligens sit, sed quod ipse concilium minime congreget, ut a concilio iudicetur, mirum mihi visum est,* f. Diiv.

[50] *[I]dem imperium habens, ex ipsius dei commissione, et non delegatione, quia tunc secus, adeo ut tenuerint alibi doctores nostri ... quod superiorem non habeat, quod nulli omnino subsit, et quod unum denique eius sit consistorium cum deo,* f. Diiar.

[51] *R. Ne tibi mirum videatur Mantua, quia vera haec omnia sunt, si non agatur fidei quaestio, quae adeo magna et gravis est, ut multa contra iuris regulas recepta sint, et maxime ut Papa a concilio iudicetur, superiorem habet tunc, subsit alt.ri, nec idem cum deo sit consistorium eius,* f. Diiar.

[52] Mantova's objections are on f. Diiav. *R. [S]ed esse posse etiam ut de electione contendatur, quamobrem et eo tunc concilium congregandum esse dicimus, propter scisma, et universalis ecclesiae statui consulatur, quoniam eo tunc is, quem concilium probaverit, spiritus sanctus instinctu electus dicetur, eritque pontifex. ... Immo dico tibi amplius, utrumque a concilio repelli, scandali ratione, tertiumque eligi posse. ... M. Et recte quidem, immo ea ratione, nunquam deberet nisi tertius eligi, quoniam si scandalum timendum est, in ecclesia magis ac magis timeri debet,* f. Diibv.

This was not Mantova's final word. Near the end of the *Dialogus* he had Roberto retract, though unconsciously, his earlier statement about the pope and the church's power by putting a strong pronouncement into his mouth that Christ gave all power to the disciples equally.[53] Mantova still affected to be his old unreconstructed hierocratic self, objecting yet again that the pope's was the highest power, and could not be subjected to conciliar judgment. The pope alone could interpret, limit, or even remove conciliar *statuta*.[54] The pope was above the council and dominated it by right. He had no superior and could do as he pleased as lord of all, drawing his power from God.[55] Roberto brought this whole edifice crashing to the ground by the same argument which had worked originally. This was all very true, he said, but only in matters of positive law, not the faith and the *status ecclesiae*. In both these, quoting an old legal maxim, the world was greater than the city, the pope had to submit to the council's judgment. Mantova meekly assented.[56] This was not quite the end of the matter, since among the unanswered questions at the end of the treatise was one whether a council could dispense from or even abolish a papal constitution, or interfere in reserved matters.[57] It appears that Mantova was at least willing to consider extending the council's authority yet further.

It may be suggested that Mantova was only following his sources reaching this conclusion, in modifying and finally almost abandoning an original strongly pro-papal statement. When he had argued that the council should be dominated by the pope, most of the citations he adduced referred merely to a judicial supremacy, but he had thrown in the canon *Haec est fides* which made the pope alone the judge of the faith.[58] Roberto's fatal objection, that the Petrine commission had been granted to all the apostles, he drew from two canons which he had used in the first place to shore up the pope's absolute supremacy, *Ita dominus* and *In novo*. Both had earlier received emphasis for their conciliar slant, particularly the latter, which spoke of the disciples wishing to have Peter as head of their *consortium*.[59] Since Mantova, like Zabarella, though with a bit less vehemence, stressed the cardinals' role in the church, and both thought the apostolic model should be normative, this canon could well have been a major

---

[53] *Et plus quia Christus soli Petro, quamvis ipsi per prius potestatem non dedit, sed omnibus apostolis communiter, quando dicit accipite spiritum sanctum*, f. Mv.

[54] *Tamen Papae potestas maxima est, et adeo maxima, ut eius facta concilij iudicio non subiaceant, ... unde etiam ipse, et solus quidem ipsius concilij statuta interpretatur, immo limitat, et tollit*, f. Miir.

[55] *Et supra concilium est, quoniam quicquid facit, facit absque dubio ut deus, ita ut eius voluntas pre caeteris, et iure merito dominari debeat ... nec superiorem habet in hoc mundo ... et tanquam dominus (habet enim potestatem a deo, alij autem praelati ab ipso ...) trahens ad se omnia*, f. Miiv.

[56] *Haec sine dubio vera sunt Mantua, et intelliguntur ... respectu eorum, quae sunt iuri positivi, non in concernentibus fidem, et universalem statum ecclesiae, quia tunc maior est orbis urbe*, f. Miiar.

[57] *Si possit concilium tollere papae constitutionem item dispensare, absolvere, et alia facere, quae ad solum papam spectat, vel ipsi soli reservata sunt*, f. Piiiv.

[58] C. 24 q. 1. c. 14 (FRIEDBERG I 968).

[59] D. 19 c. 7 (FRIEDBERG I 62). D. 2 c. 2 (FRIEDBERG I 69 f.).

source of Mantova's conciliarism. Roberto had almost given the game away at the start, when, in the course of criticizing the state of the clergy, he noted, nearly in passing, that the presbyters not only bore the type of the apostles, but held their former place in the church; in other words, he probably meant to emphasize the apostolic succession and perhaps apply it especially to the cardinals.[60]

Mantova assigned an important role to them in the council and in ordinary government of the church. A council could not be held without the pope's *fratres*, members of one body with him.[61] Outside of it, the cardinals control the pope, the "door of God", by their advice: "just as a door is governed by a hinge *[cardine]*, so the church is moderated by the reasonable counsels of the cardinals."[62] In this he was of one mind with Zabarella, who argued that the pope was, like the emperor, *legibus solutus*, but both nonetheless should live according to their laws.[63] To enable him to do that better, difficult business was to be transacted only with the cardinals' advice, and the pope dared not make general laws for the church without it.[64] Again like Zabarella, Mantova used corporation theory to explicate the cardinals' position, but this was made explicit only in the case of their right, based on their election of the pope, to call a council, if both pope and emperor refused: "call consequences of an election pertain deservedly to them."[65] As for Mantova, for Zabarella the pope and cardinals were parts of the same body, which meant the church was in the pope as its head, and the cardinals as members.[66]

Nevertheless, Zabarella's application of corporation theory is more thoroughgoing than Mantova's with the result that some of his ideas on the ecclesiastical constitution are much clearer. Perhaps the greater immediacy of the schism came through in his more careful working out of the relations between a *universitas* and its constituent parts, which led him to posit that if the *maior* &

---

[60] R. ... *praesbiteros, qui discipulorum typum gerunt, quicque in eorum loco in ecclesia Dei constituti sunt*, f. Biiar.

[61] R. *Cardinales igitur pontificem sequuntur, ... et sine quibus concilium esse, aut congregari, minime potest, quos fratres appellat. ... Immo ipsorum in specie caput est, ipsique membra eius, et corpus adeo unitum*, f. Eiiv.

[62] R. *[Q]uemadmodum ostium cardine regitur, ita sanis ecclesia consiliis Cardinalium moderatur, a cardine, et a romana ecclesia, quae est cardo, et aliarum caput, a domino constituta, habens pontificem, ostium dei, et cardines*, f. Eiiar.

[63] *Et licet princeps sit solutus legibus, tamen secundum eas vivere decet*. F. ZABARELLA, Tractatus de schismate, in: De iurisdictione, autoritate, et praeeminentia imperiali, ac potestate ecclesiastica, ed. S. SCHARD, Basel 1566, 688—711, 701.

[64] *Ex his infertur quod praedixi, scilicet quod id quod papam dicitur omnia posse, intelligitur quando facit consilio habito cum fratribus. ... Papa sine Cardinalibus non potest concedere legem generalem de universale statu Ecclesiae*, 702.

[65] M. *[S]i neuter* [pope or emperor] *congregare nolit ... ad quem spectabit congregatio?* R. *Ad collegium Cardinalium, ex quo sunt in possessione eligendi papam ... ita ut ad ipsos spectet etiam, et de iure merito, omnia, quae sunt ad electionem consequentia*, f. Oiiav.

[66] *Et in eo quod dixi, aliud papam, aliud sedem Apostolicam, videtur intelligenda sedes Apostolica, pro ecclesia Romana, quae non censetur esse solus papa, sed ipse papa cum Cardinalibus, qui sunt partes corporis papae, seu Ecclesia quae constituitur ex papa tanquam capite, et ex Cardinalibus tanquam membris*, 701.

potior pars of the church, the cardinals, withdrew from obedience to a pope, then the whole church was said to.[67] Furthermore, when considering how the *plenitudo potestatis* is distributed in the church, Zabarella again placed it in the pope as head, in the cardinals as members, of the church, drawing on Johannes Monachus.[68] This is also the basis of his famous dictum that the *plenitudo* was in the pope as the church's principal minister, but fundamentally in the church itself.[69]

About the council's final say in matters of the faith, Mantova was unambiguous. Although it would be an extraordinary thing for council and pope to contradict one another, Mantova had Roberto say that if they did, "the opinion of the council ought to be preferred, since it is assembled with the aid of the Holy Spirit, ... [and because it is] dangerous to the cause of the faith to rely on the judgment of one man, especially when he may sin."[70] Zabarella said much the same, both stating flatly that the council was above the pope in matters of the faith, and arguing that conciliar legislation could not be tampered with by the pope, since it had been suggested by the Holy Spirit.[71] Both also appealed to the apostolic model, in which, as Zabarella put it, Peter "coruled" with the council.[72] Towards the end of the tract, Mantova reinforced this point, turning to his other major source, Panormitanus, for the opinion that the pope could not decide questions of the faith alone, since the promise of indefectibility was made to the whole church. It was heresy to hold against a council, in particular the first four ecumenical ones. Though a council could err, it would never do so persistently in the faith.[73]

The answer to the second question which most worried Mantova, who would call a council in the event of a papal schism?, revolved around his idea of

---

[67] *Cum ergo maior et potior pars Catholicorum ab obedientia recessit, sic recessit dicitur tota Ecclesia, quia quicquid maior pars universitatis facit, tota universitas fecisse dicitur*, 700.

[68] *Ubi considerandum quod licet dicatur papa habere plenitudinem potestatis, non debet tamen sic intelligi quod solus possit omnia. Sed intelligitur quod papa, id est, ecclesia Romana quae representatur in papa, tanquam in capite, et Cardinalibus, tanquam in membris*, 701.

[69] [*Q*]*uod papa habet plenitudinem potestatis, debet intelligi non solus, sed tanquam apud universitatem, ita quod ipsa potestas est in ipsa universitate tanquam in fundamento, et in papa tanquam principali ministro*, 703.

[70] *R. Crederem ego concilii sententiam esse praeferendam, quando quidem . . . id ipsum spiritu sancto cooperante congregetur. . . . Considerando quoque . . . periculosum fore fidei causam unius hominis iudicio relinquere, cum maxime peccare possit*, f. Mr—v.

[71] *Cum autem agitur de fide, synodus est maior quam papa*, 701. *Et si dicatur quod hoc est imponere legem principi, qui est solutus legibus, non Dei, quales sunt leges concilij, quae spiritu sancto suggerente promulgantur*, 704.

[72] *Et in hoc etiam apparet quod licet Petrus fuerit princeps Apostolorum tamen plenitudo potestatis non fuit in eo solo . . . Petrus in concilio tanquam unus in congregatione corregnavit. . . . Et hinc mos antiquus habuit, quod omnia difficilia terminabantur per Concilium et crebro fiebant*, 705. Mantiova phrased the idea similarly. *Apostoli simili modo . . . cum Petro statuebant, quamquam ipsum ut caput et summum pontificem haberent*, when they celebrated the first council at Antioch, f. Mr.

[73] *M. Nunquid . . . agere, seu pertinaciter tenere contra concilium, heresis sit? R. Absque dubio, maxime contra 4 paulo supra enumerata. . . . M. Ergo concilium errare non potest. R. Immo potest. . . . [N]ec errare simpliciter potest seu perseveranter, in spectantibus ad fidem, et mores, sicuti nec ecclesia, pro qua Christus indefinenter oravit, ne deficeret*, f. Liibv.

representation, the concept Alberigo has argued was central to all conciliar thinking.[74] Here Zabarella's importance to Mantova is most pronounced, since not only did he share the cardinal's vision of the nature of the council's representation of the church, but he took over almost word for word most of Zabarella's derivation of the emperor's right from his position as representative of the Christian people.[75]

Near the end of *De concilio* Roberto gave four reasons a council could be assembled without the pope's authorization:

[i]f it is contended about the papacy, as has been said widely above, and so by reason of schism, which is the greatest evil in the church of God ... [or] if the pope himself is found diverging from the faith, or if the good of the whole church is plundered, or the pope himself again is a notorious sinner, and indeed such or in such sin, that the whole church of God is equally scandalized.[76]

These are all standard justifications for calling a council *papa nolente*. Mantova's suggested means to do so were equally well established. As a good civilian, Mantova objected to Roberto's first suggestion that the cardinals issue the call, and plumped for the emperor instead. Roberto, though, objected in turn that the emperor had only taken a hand in the early church when its power had failed; after Constantine diminished the *imperium* he handed on to his successors (by the Donation), emperors could no longer be directly involved.[77] Mantova retorted by pointing out a few more cases in which emperors had both elected and deposed popes, arguing that this gave them the right to call a council, and challenged Roberto to disagree. "I will deny [your cases] more boldly," he replied, and pointed out that not only did Mantova's instances not indicate what he thought they did, but that the emperor's right to intervene, once conceded by the papacy, had since been revoked.[78] Roberto then went further and

---

[74] ALBERIGO, Movimento 933—936 (for the importance of the concept), 935 (for its meaning). See also Chiesa, 348. PIAIA, Zabarella 458 f., agrees with his emphasis.

[75] Whether this put Mantova into the camp of those impatient with Paul III's hesitations over the calling of a council must remain an open question for the moment. It seems distinctly possible, though, since he noted that a general council would have put an end to the Lutherans, f. Miibv. Zabarella's opinion became very nearly the majority view by the early sixteenth century. Almost everyone adopted Huguccio's claims for the cardinals, and even "papalists" like Jacobazzi followed the order of devolution Zabarella proposed. Filippo Decio, Piero del Monte (also educated at Padua) and Matthia Ugoni drew explicitly on his views. BÄUMER, Nachwirkungen 48—58.

[76] R. *Si de papatu contendatur, et sic schismatis ratione quod in ecclesia dei maximum est malum ... si a fide adhuc papa ipse devius inveniatur. Vel si bonum agatur universalis ecclesiae aut ipse papa rursum notorius peccator sit, et taliter quidem, sive peccato tali, ut tota ecclesia dei pariter scandalizetur*, f. Piir.

[77] M. *... postquam his casibus Papa caput non est concilij, neque concilium congregat, quis illud congregabit?* R. *Cardinales.* M. *Ego secus crederem.* R. *Quid?* M. *Quod Imperatoris esset onus, nec ab re, quoniam in quoque Honorium Imperatorem alias fecisse comperi. ...* R. *Verum est, nec ego secus sentio, sed patrocinando, quando ecclesiae potestas deficiebat ... et cum primum Con[stantinus] ipsi ecclesiae donando Imperium, id ipsum successoribus minuit*, f. Er.

[78] M. *Dubito ergo valde, quia Imperator etiam eligit pontificem, seque ipsius electioni immiscet. ... Immo et deponit, ut Otto primus Theutonicorum Rex Ioannem duodecimum. ... [E]rgo et concilium congregat, et non negabis.* R. *Negabo audacius, ex quo id ad tempus, et ex causa concessum est, posteaque revocatum, nec antedicti Ioannis depositio iure facta fuit, vel si iure facta est, eam Leonis auctoritas prius comprobavit*, f. Er—v.

tried to exclude the emperor from the council altogether, except when the faith was being discussed.⁷⁹ To this Mantova scoffed that there had never been a council which did not deal with the faith, at which point Roberto tried to claim that the question was entirely out of bounds, since it did not concern the members of a council. Mantova came back with a flat assertion that it did, which left Roberto no alternative but to appeal to authority. "It must not be doubted sanely, where we have clear authorities, and most obvious examples," said he.⁸⁰ At the conclusion of this episode Roberto reversed the usual case and asked Mantova why he had not brought up the Donation of Constantine, to which he replied that he would not, since it was still *sub judice*. Nevertheless, he believed it to be valid, since *imperium* proceeded from God, so that by giving some of his authority to the church, Constantine had merely returned it to its efficient cause. Roberto accepted that argument, but warned Mantova that others might not.⁸¹ Near the end of the dialogue Mantova persuaded Roberto to agree that the emperor should be present in order to strengthen the faith, adopting a common argument, which Zabarella also shared, that the emperor should be present by right, not by the sufferance of the council. On the first try, Roberto had refused to accept this.⁸²

Mantova's defense of the emperor's role in summoning a council, of a piece with his general emphasis on the emperor, is taken over *in toto* from Zabarella's *De schismate*, including most of the same sources. Zabarella began with the same historical evidence we have just seen Mantova cite. Both then based the emperor's role on his status as *advocatus et defensor ecclesiae*, though Mantova added a bit of classical finery to their parallel insistence on the emperor's concern with world peace and that of the city of Rome. While both cited the passage in Luke about a city divided against itself, Mantova fleshed that out with a tag from Sallust and a long excursus on the benefits of unity. Mantova severely condensed Zabarella's third question, but adopted its conclusion that the cardinals should call a council if pope and emperor refuse. He then returned to an almost literal following of Zabarella's account, when he continued that the emperor should step in, if the cardinals were paralyzed by internal dissent.

---

⁷⁹ *Immo dico tibi, quod nec est ipse Imperator, scilicet nec alius laycus, de his, qui concilio adesse debent, nisi invitentur specialiter, vel causa fidei tractanda sit,* f. Er—v.

⁸⁰ *M. Dic quaeso, quod nanque concilium unquam factum fuit, in quo non sit fidei questio tractata. R. Quid sum, satis mihi est, quod de personis conciliaribus non sit, praeterquam eo casu, ut diximus. M. Ita est, et vere non possum omnia haec probare, adeo ut nec dubitem amplius. R. Nec sane dubitandum est, ubi auctoritates claras habemus, exemplaque apertissima,* f. Eiir.

⁸¹ *R. De Constantini donatione nihil locutus es, quod unum a te maxime expectabam. M. Nec loqui intendo, cum adhuc lis (ut aiunt) sit sub iudice, cumque semper tenuerim ego, dicant alij quid velint, absque dubio valuisse, quoniam a deo processit imperium, illiusque deus causa efficiens fuit . . . et ecclesiae donando, donat deo. R. Nec ego secus tenendum censui, quamvis multa sint etiam, quibus contrarium facile suaderi posset,* ibid.

⁸² *M. Ego quoque hoc idem semper sum arbitratus, adeo ut Imperator iure merito . . . concilio adesse possit, non ad potentiam ostendendam, sed ad fidem confirmandam. . . . R. Non licet dubitando. . . .,* f. Pr. *Sed cum agitur de fide, Imperator potest interesse concilio, non ad potentiam ostendendam sed ad fidem confirmandam . . . et interest suo iure et non ex gratia concilij,* p. 691.

Zabarella, *De schismate*, pp. 689, 691	Mantova, *De concilio*, ff. Oiiav—Oiibr
Quis habebit congregare Concilium? Respondeo, quod olim Imperator congregabat Concilium. [The historical examples follow.] Postea constitutum est quod ad solum Romanum pontificem spectet talis congregatio. . . . Et hoc quando est unicus papa, sic loquuntur illa iura. Quando autem sunt plures qui contendunt de papatu, . . . debet congregari Concilium ad sollicitudinem Imperatoris. . . . Interest enim ipsius Imperatoris, ut sit pax in Romana civitate . . . & sic fortius inter est, quod sit pax in toto orbe, in quo esse non potest stante in contentione papatu, quia ut in Evangelio dicitur: Omne regnum in se divisum desolabitur. Et quod ad Imperatorem spectet, talis sollicitudo, ratio est, quia est advocatus et defensor Ecclesiae. . . . [Zabarella next discussed the cardinals' right.] [Q]uaero si eveniat, quod collegium Cardinalium sit divisum, & non concordat in convocando Concilium . . . ad quem spectabit talis convocatio? Respondeo, quod ad Imperatorem. casus videtur 65. dist. c. fin. ubi negligente illo, ad quem devolvitur congregatio vicinorum episcoporum, pro ordinandis episcopis locorum, proprij populi convocant convicinos episcopos. Proprie autem Imperator repraesentat totum populum Christianum, cum in eum translata sit iuris dictio & potestas universi orbis. ff. de orig. iur. 1. 2. . novissime C. de veteri iure enucliando. 1. . cum enim. loco ipsorum ergo populorum habet congregare Concilium, & sic ω revolabit ad α, quia extremitas retrahitur ad principium. 35. dist. c. ab exordio, ut enim dixi in secunda questione, convocatio conciliorum ab initio fiebat per Imperatorem, sed postea reservata est papae. Deficiente igitur ipso papa, seu non convocante, deficientibus ijs qui succedunt loco papae, scilicet Cardinalibus, seu non convocantibus revertimur ad ius pristinum. Sic dicimus in simili, quod cum quis non potest consequi iusticiam, a superiore licitum est sibi sua authoritate sua recuperare, ut eleganter notatur prima dist. c. Ius gentium. in gloss. & per Innocent. de restitut. spol. c. olim 1.	Immo ut prius videretur dicendum Imperatorem ipsum ad hoc tenere, ex quo olim etiam ad ipsum congregarunt Constantinus [etc. The same historical examples.] R: Verum est, sed hodie pontificis onus videretur, ad sollicitudinem tamen (ut dictum fuit) ipsius Imperatoris, cuius maxime interest pacem esse in romana civitate, & multo magis in toto orbe, quod esse non potest, si de papatu contendatur, dicente Luc. XI. omne regnum in se divisum desolari [erit. . . . If neither pope nor emperor will call, the right then passed to the cardinals.] M: nisi & ipsi dissentiunt in convocando, vel alia quacunque de causa, quia tunc necessario esset onus hoc alij devolvendum. . . . Quis ergo convocabit ipsum [concilium]? R: Imperator hoc casu solus & non alius ad ipsius sollicitudinem, ut supra, quia cum in eo translata sit iurisditio & potestas universi orbis. 1. I. novissime ff. de orig. iur. 1. 1. cum enim C. de veti iu. enu. repraesentat totum populum Christianum, & sic omega revolabit ad alpha retraheturque extremitas ad principium ut in cano. ab exordio 35. dist. & in 1. si unus, in pactus, in ver. quod in specie ff. de pactis ex quo convocatio, ut diximus, olim fiebat per imperatorem, postea per papam, deficiente ergo papa, & his eius loco subrogantur, seu non convocantibus, ad ius pristinum reverti debemus & est simile in eo, qui iustitiam consequi non potest a superiore, ut auctoritate propria sibi ipsi ius dicat secundum Inno. in ca. olim 1. de resti. spo. & not. in cano. ius gentium. 2. dist. & ar. in cano. nos ad fidem 16 di. in cano. fi. 95 dist. ubi negligente illo ad quem devolvitur congregatio vicinorum episcoporum pro ordinandis episcopis locorum, ipsi populi convocant convicinos episcopos.

Mantova's version differs from Zabarella's only in some minor rearrangement.

It seems that Mantova here regarded the emperor's as a delegated jurisdiction, as appears from his second last argument that this situation paralleled one in which a subordinate could not get justice from his superior. This appears even more clearly in his concluding argument that the emperor's right, founded on the *lex regia*, is also parallel to the people's right to call together other bishops to ordain their's if the bishop whose right that was refused.[83] Since Roberto also argued that the disciples made elections to replace lost members in order to avoid a schism, it would seem that reversion of papal election from cardinals to council was a temporary return to the original state of things by a suspension of the ecclesiastical *lex regia*. Certainly this was the way Zabarella argued.[84]

Mantova took over the definition of the council as one "in which the whole church is represented," which Zabarella had also used.[85] He cited his Paduan predecessor further to specify that the pope and all the bishops made up a general council, "representing the whole church," and standing in for "a general collection of the assembling faithful."[86] When discussing the council's representation of the church, one of the principal questions in Mantova's mind, as in Zabarella's, was that of obedience, but while Zabarella was most interested in whether or not it could be withdrawn through representatives, Mantova made enforcement the central question. In one place, he brought in Panormitanus to the effect that no one was exempt from the canons, but then modified this opinion, apparently following Pietro de Ancharano, to exclude non-Christians from obedience.[87] In an even clearer instance, immediately after writing of a council representing the whole church, he cited the canon *Maiores*

---

[83] Thus does the picture of what HANNAH PITKIN called descriptive representation become muddied: The Concept of Representation, Berkeley / Los Angeles 1967, 100—106. Pitkin unaccountably obscures her own distinction between this sort and representation as "acting for" when she considers parliamentary representation to be the latter, but overlooks (at that point) the proctorial status of its members. It is possible that Mantova's long digression on the requirements for the emperor's election and the symbolism of his crown (ff. Niibv—Oiiv) is not entirely beside the point, since he inserted it in the midst of his discussion of the emperor's right to call a council. Perhaps he meant it to elucidate the emperor's representative nature, since the tripartite crown symbolized the three parts of the world. If so, this is left an implication.

[84] *Ex quo colligitur, quod maior est potestas populi, quam magistratus ipsius. Ex hoc dicit Guill. de Cun. ... non ambiguitur: populum Romanum posse revocare potestatem datam principi,* ZABARELLA 709. Zabarella drew this implication much more sharply than Mantova. See TIERNEY, Foundations 226 f. for discussion and H. MOREL, La place de la *lex regia* dans l'histoire des idées politiques, in: Études offértes à J. Macqueron, Aix-en-Provence 1970, 545—556 for more on this important controversy.

[85] [C]*oncilium in quo universalis ecclesia representatur*, f. Dr.

[86] *Concilium breviter nihil aliud est, nisi generalis quaedam fidelium venientium collectio, auctoritate summi pontificis regulariter convocatum*, f. Kiiar. *Generale autem ... papae et omnium episcoporum, universalem ecclesiam repraesentans*, f. Lv. Defining the *ecclesia*, Zabarella called it *totam congregationem Catholicorum, et principales ministros fidei, scilicet praelatos, qui totam congregationem repraesentant*, 702. Mantova's emphasis here may be a sign that he had only the first of the three tracts which Schard put together to make De schismate. Hence his borrowing mainly of Zabarella's ideas tending in the direction of an episcopal council. ALBERIGO, Chiesa 86. But cf. ULLMANN, Schism 195 f. for the difficulty of distinguishing the three and the need for a critical edition.

[87] R. ... [I]*nfideles concilio adesse nec possint, nec debeant. ... M. Falleris, quia plerunque ipsi quoque vocati et impetiti admittuntur, puta si contra praecepta legis aliquid faciant. R. Verissimum is est utique, ut puniantur, non ut prosint concilio, ex quo omnes sumus oves Christi. ... M. Sed quomodo hoc ipsum esse potest, cum dicat Apostolus ... de his qui foris sunt nihil ad nos sensusque sit eos canonibus non ligari. ... Immo quod nec aliter esse potest, cum praedicta intelligantur respectu excommunicationis*, f. Kiiav. His citation of Ancharano appears to be an error, at least *consilium* 242 in the edition I consulted contained nothing relevant.

which decreed that whatever "the assembled synod should promulgate against a certain heretic may not be suffered to be mutilated by any retractions afterwards."[88]

Mantova never spelled out the mechanics of how the council represented the church, but his concern with obedience would indicate that he probably followed Pierre d'Ailly and most other earlier conciliarists in assuming that the members of the council appeared as the proctors of their constituents, as representatives to an essentially judicial proceeding, while at the same time the whole council including the pope and cardinals represented the essence of the church, or stood in its place symbolically.[89] It has been argued that neither of these is a "democratic" view, at least in practice, and normally this must have been the case.[90] When, however, an emergency situation arose, then, as we have seen, Mantova and Zabarella were willing to follow many other conciliarists and argue for a progressive devolution of power, even, if necessary, back to the people who could make a new dispensation.

However important the people's residual power in an emergency, and however vociferously its representatives meeting in council might demand the right to judge the pope, neither led to any permanent jurisdictional authority of people or council over pope. As Alberigo has shown, it was a fatal simplification by some opponents of conciliarism which made it appear that by demanding obedience from schismatic popes the council was also claiming judicial superiority. These opponents thereby broke with earlier thinking which had never maintained that obedience necessarily implied jurisdictional inferiority.[91] In fact, the situation was much more complicated, since both pope and council were thought to share authority between themselves. How confusing this model could seem to participants may be seen from one of the unanswered questions at the end of *De concilio*, which asked if the council had jurisdiction if the pope were present. This *may* mean that Mantova thought of the council's authority as delegated by the pope. Such a query would only make sense in the case of a vicar general's jurisdiction, for instance, which lapsed in the presence of his principal.[92] Thus Mantova made a clear, if largely implicit, distinction

---

[88] C. 24 q. 1 c. 2 (FRIEDBERG I 966).

[89] F. OAKLEY, The political thought of Pierre d'Ailly: The voluntarist tradition, New Haven 1964, 148, 154. For their functions as proctors, see G. POST, *Plena potestas* and consent in medieval assemblies, in: Stud.. in medieval legal thought: Public law and the state, 1100—1322, Princeton 1964, 96—162, especially 115ff. and 154—162. There are some reasons for hesitation in accepting Post's argument, since his rebuttal of S. CHRIMES's deemphasis of *plena potestas* is not entirely convincing: English constitutional ideas in the fifteenth century, Cambridge 1936, 80 and cap. 2, *passim*; POST's critique, f57 f. For clear statements from Henry of Langenstein and Conrad Gelnhausen, see ALBERIGO, Chiesa 38, 49. These are the two standard sorts of medieval representation, according to H. HOFMANN, Repraesentation. Stud. zur Begriffsgeschichte von der Antike bis ins 19. Jh., Berlin 1974, cap. 13 and 14.

[90] ALBERIGO, Chiesa 348 f.

[91] Ibid. 35 f.

[92] P. HINSCHIUS, System des katholischen Kirchenrechts mit besonderer Rücksicht auf Deutschland I, Berlin 1888, 182, and II, Berlin 1888, 207—213.

between jurisdictional superiority, conceded only to the pope, and authority over doctrine, ultimately left in the hands of the council. He did not draw the conclusion Giovanni Gozzadini did slightly earlier that the council held its authority because it represented the church; consequently God judged in its midst.[93] This seems to be a position almost peculiar to Gozzadini, but it was probably an extrapolation from the same tradition Mantova represented, in which an overriding concern with the sovereignty of Christ could lead to a universalist ecclesiology which could also mean the exaltation of the pope because he personalized the church, provided he looked after its welfare.[94]

Given these two sorts of authority, it was perfectly possible for the council to do two types of representing at once: on the one hand, it might represent the pope by exercising his jurisdiction, provided he had delegated it to the assembly, and, on the other, it could represent the universal church by passing final judgment on questions of the faith. Or, Mantova may have been thinking, much as did Almain, of both pope and council representing the church, but in turns, as it were. Because the church was a regal polity, the pope was its most immediate representative; it had no other, since there was no permanent representative body. But when one met in the form of a council, then the pope's authority lapsed in its favor.[95]

Although equally obscure on the surface, Mantova's great interest in which persons were entitled to attend a council, similar again to Zabarella's and d'Ailly's, may have arisen from an only partially articulated notion of representation. Zabarella had emphasized the role of *personae praecipuae* (the pope and the bishops), and d'Ailly thought a council more representative than the pope or the *ecclesia romana*, because it better approximated the composition of the whole church. The wise and influential had a special right to represent the community because they were largely responsible for it.[96] In short, although full clarity cannot be squeezed from Mantova's ideas on representation, they fit him squarely into one major tradition of conciliar thought.

One cannot resist the impression that Mantova went back primarily to that tradition, to the beginning of the fifteenth century, and that he ignored much of the heated debate about pope-council relations after that. Not only were his prescriptions about what to do in a crisis mainly concerned to avert a papal schism, but he also adamantly refused to draw out any constitutional implications from his emergency measures, as if numerous attempts to do just that, with large consequences, had not already been made. Was he being deliberately obtuse, extremely cautious, or was he, perhaps, simply badly prepared to write a short book on conciliar theory? If, as modern scholarship would have it, he

---

[93] BÄUMER, Nachwirkungen 24. *Quia propter hoc concilia habent suam auctoritatem, quia repraesentant ecclesiam universalem.*
[94] ALBERIGO, Chiesa 348.
[95] OAKLEY, Almain Again 123.
[96] OAKLEY, d'Ailly 149, 154.

were either much affected by the papal reaction, or contrariwise, by the dying glow of Paduan conciliarism, why go back to the fifteenth century for his chief inspiration? It may be that he was as deliberately ambiguous as the framers of *Haec sancta*, and for the same reason. The same solutions appealed to both, because they lived in the same constitutional epoch.[97] This may be claiming too much. Tierney adopts a sort of Kuhnian view that new answers could only arise when the questions had changed, which has much to recommend it. Nevertheless, there are still different sets of responses to any given agenda of questions, so it still matters which batch a later thinker adopts. Even if we are no longer to think of influence, the icons Mantova chose to father his ideas on give a different cast to his thought, at the very least, from that it would have had, had he chosen to absorb much of Nicholas of Cusa, for example. From the standpoint of the study of broad movements of ideas, this may not seem a very important point, but to a biographical approach and to the tracing of actual lines of affiliation, it is of the essence.

Mayhap the reason for Mantova's choice is no more obscure than a large measure of Paduan aristocratic pride, as well as the impact of the traditions of its law school, where Zabarella and Panormitanus had been master and pupil. The Venetian Signory may also have tried to dictate a "moderate" position for Paduan faculty. It could be interested in the political implications of what its professors said, as in the case of Henry's divorce, and Vicenza, the site of the proposed council, was in Venetian territory. It further seems possible to argue the reverse of some scholars' belief that conciliarism influenced later theories of secular government. In the case of Padua, the fifteenth century heyday of conciliarism may well have been a product of the limiting of secular political opportunities for its native aristocracy after the Venetian conquest in 1405. This would apply well to the cultured aristocrat, Mantova. Thus he may have been merely conforming both to the traditions of his order and of his notoriously conservative profession in leaning so heavily on Zabarella. Indeed, it could be argued that Mantova sometimes depended so slavishly on Zabarella that, whether or not the concept of influence can still be made to work as an explanatory device, in Mantova's case we must speak of simple plagiarism.[98] Quite apart from Mantova's independent judgments within the general framework laid down by Zabarella, such a judgment is only relevant to a philosophical or history of ideas approach, not to a more fully historicized one of the type adopted here. What counts is that Mantova circulated Zabarella's ideas, in whatever form.[99]

---

[97] B. Tierney, Hermeneutics and history: The problem of *Haec sancta*, in: Essays in med. hist. to B. Wilkinson, ed. T. Sandquist and M. Powicke, Toronto 1969, 354—370, 367, and: Divided sovereignty 254.

[98] Quentin Skinner has done much to demolish the old model of influence, especially in: The limits of historical explanation, in: Philosophy 41 (1966) 199—215.

[99] Those ideas could be summed up under Kantorowicz's rubric of non-absolutist organicism: Two Bodies 220, 230 f., and *passim*.

This suggests that the most important measure of Mantova's stature and meaning in context is his roster of students, since only through them can we study the diffusion of his teaching, a major part of any effort to historicize the investigation of conciliarism. This will require a separate study, but some of his more important pupils may be noted here. As important as this approach is in Oakley's golden and silver ages of conciliarism, the fifteenth and early sixteenth century, it is even more so in the "bronze" age when conciliarist ideas spread to places which had previously shown themselves proof against them, especially, if only for a brief time, England. Thus if Mantova's stature alone and his *De concilio* are insufficient reason for studying him, then his role as mentor to a whole cadre of English law students who later played key roles in justifying the Henrician Reformation should be. Among them were almost certainly Thomas Starkey, Richard Morison and Henry Cole, the first and last of whose thought was heavily influenced by some sort of conciliarism.[100] Mantova may also have been important to a later wave of English students. In 1555 he acted as one of John Orphinstrange's promoters when he received his civil law degree. At roughly the same time Francis Walsingham, later Queen Elizabeth's principal secretary, also studied at Padua, but it is not known with whom.[101] The tally of Mantova's Italian students is even more impressive, from his patron Cristoforo Madruzzo, bishop of Trent during the council and one of King Ferdinand's chief councillors (surely this connection is worth study?), through Giovangelo de' Medici later Pope Pius IV, to Pier Paolo Vergerio. It may be no accident that Simon Schard, the imperialist propagandist who published the first integral edition of Zabarella's *De schismate*, was also a student of Mantova.[102] During his fifty years at Padua Mantova seems to have been active in disseminating a view of the church as a cooperating community to large numbers of enthusiastic students.[103]

In addition to Mantova's long-term impact, there is evidence for the more immediate reception of *De concilio*. As soon as the work reached one of its two

---

[100] Morison and Cole are attested in the register of the English nation at Padua in the mid-1530s. G. A. ANDRICH, De natione anglica et scota iuristarum universitatis patavinae ab anno 1222 usque ad annum 1738, Padua 1892, 130. Starkey's presence is less directly documented, but see T. MAYER, The Life and Thought of Thomas Starkey, PhD. Diss. Minnesota 1983, 54 f., and cap. 4, *passim* for his conciliarism. P. SAWADA makes a case for Cole's by attributing an anonymous tract to him: Two anonymous Tudor treatises on the general council, in: JEH 12 (1961) 197—214.

[101] K. BARTLETT, English students at Padua, 1521—1558, in: Proceedings of the PMR conference IV (1979) 89—106, here 99 and appendix 106, which prints some documents related to Orphinstrange's *laurea* exam. I am indebted to Prof. Bartlett for sending me a copy of this paper.

[102] VEDOVA, Scrittori 566.

[103] Even in 1568 Mantova was still a firm believer in Zabarella's view of the church. It consisted "essentially in the assembly of the faithful, representatively in the cardinals and virtually in the pope," but the word was "taken besides in different ways, for the *congregatio fidelium* and for the general council." Gymnasium scholasticum, in Analysis variarum quaestionum, Venice 1568, f. 194r—v. Even the idea of the pope's virtual representation of the church could be an awkward translation of Zabarella's ministerial theory.

interlocutors in Bologna, Roberto Maggio wrote Mantova that "I have read and reread it all, and if when I saw it in Padua it appeared beautiful, learned and elegant, now it has seemed much more. I have not given a copy of it to the *frate*, as you wrote to me, but to the Reverend Governor of this city, who knows your holiness because he studied in Padua some years ago and he has commended it much, and perhaps at some time he will thank you personally."[104] While Maggio might be expected to have a high opinion of a work which made him appear such a learned lawyer, the judgment of the "governatore" of Bologna is of more interest. In February 1542 he was Fabio Mignanelli, then vice-legate. Mignanelli was a career papal diplomat and client of the Farnese whose religious attitudes and in particular his concern for reform through a council have not received a very good press.[105] But at just this moment, Mignanelli was going through something of a spiritual crisis regarding his vocation, writing Cardinal Cervini to tell him that he had asked license to return to his diocese "to learn to live as a bishop and die as a Christian."[106] Although Mignanelli was barely present at Trent, despite direct orders to stay to the bitter end, he certainly wrote a good line about his concern for its success. In 1540, during one of his legations to Vienna, he wrote Paul III that "in my weak opinion, your holiness has no other than a single remedy in hand" to assemble a council to reform the church.[107] Mignanelli, according to his own testimony, studied in Padua, but with Pier Paolo Parisio, not Mantova.[108]

Five years later, Maggio again wrote Mantova that he was reading the dialogue, "since the pope would wish that it were supplied here (Bologna), and

---

[104] *Io l'ho letto et riletto tutto, et se allhora che lo vidi in Padova mi parue bello, dotto, et elegante | hora molto piu mi è paruto. Ne ho dato uno non a frati, come essa mi scriveva ma al Reverendissimo Governatore di questa Città, il quale conosce V. S. perche studiò in Padova gia alcuni anni et molto l'ha commendato, et forse à qualche tempola ringratiarà ancora personalmente.* MS 63, Law Library, Robbins Collection, University of California - Berkeley, 47, February 18, 1542. This letter was also printed in A. VALSECCHI, Elogio di Marco Mantova Benavides, Padua 1839, 41—42. Mantova's letters and those to him exist in abundance, though many are merely formal recommendations, but little has been done to pursue Lionello Puppi's assurance that they would repay study. S. BETTINI and L. PUPPI, La chiesa degli Eremitani di Padova II, Vicenza 1970, 99—100. Prof. Ronnie H. Terpenning and I hope shortly to publish at least a summary of a large volume of vernacular letters to Mantova. Its existence in at least three manuscripts is another sign of Mantova's 16th century stature.

[105] For his career up to 1538 see especially: Nuntiaturberichte aus Deutschland I/3 : 1, Gotha 1893, 41, and for his activity in and attitude to Trent, G. ALBERIGO, I vescovi italiani al Concilio di Trento, Florence 1959, 137, 259—260, 354 and: Concilium Tridentinum X, 629n. 6. Alberigo thinks Mignanelli's career above all marked by "l'ambizione personale congiunta con la diffidenza e lo scetticismo che gli erano stati inculcati a Roma verso il Concilio." Most of the evidence for his early career comes from the preface to his will, written in 1546 when he was about to set out for Trent in order to follow the precept *dispone domui tuae, quia morieris tu, et non vives.* Giornale de' Letterati per l'Anno 1751, Rome 1753, 73. There is at least one family archive in Siena, heretofore not much explored, and another may still exist in Rome. Mignanelli's presence in Bologna is documented in A. CASADEI, Lettere del cardinale Gasparo Contarini durante la sua legazione di Bologna (1542), in: Arch. stor. ital. 118 (1960) 77—30, 220—285, 85.

[106] ALBERIGO, Vescovi 137.
[107] JEDIN, Geschichte I 330.
[108] Giornale de'Letterati 69. He also put in a year in literary studies there.

the imperial majesty in Trent. I have had it read to many of these lord prelates on your behalf and that of justice."[109] Thus during the time of Trent's temporary translation Maggio was still an eager exponent of Mantova's work. At the moment, the "lord prelates" mentioned are unidentified, but one of his circle whom he spoke of as joining the reading was a servant of Cervini's. Not only does this letter testify to the high opinion both pope and emperor were alleged to hold of the work, but it documents its presence in one important milieu at a sensitive time. Paul III may well have known the work. Mantova wrote him in 1540 that he had dared to write on the council and argued strongly that it was the pope's duty to see one assembled, another testimony of Mantova's sincerity.[110]

This paper has attempted to treat Marco Mantova's conciliar thought as a unit and to sketch some historical reasons for its importance. It has taken a more biographical and text-based than strictly intellectual approach, and has tried to make sense of the literary workings of his *Dialogus* which dealt with a scholastic problem in the quintessentially humanist form of a dialogue. This more comprehensive method has demonstrated that Mantova does not fit some prevailing generalizations about conciliarism, for instance the opposition between papalism and conciliarism, especially since he, while definitely not at the former pole, continued to place stress on the cardinals, sometimes taken to be a mark of the former alone in the early sixteenth century. His thought has been shown to be worth attention, however strange or even incoherent it may seem to modern tastes, by two more historical standards: popularity of work and author, and roster of students. It has been suggested that Mantova was an Evangelical, which may help to explain some of his ideas about the ecclesiastical constitution. Those ideas moved within a largely early fifteenth century domain. Partly under the impact of these models, partly under that of his sources, but mainly probably as a result of his method, Mantova was usually cautious in drawing any clear constitutional implications from his suggestions about how to remedy a schism. On any point he began with an extreme pro-papal statement and then gradually whittled it down. It seems very likely that this was also how he taught, given his emphasis on Socratic putting of questions. He taught large numbers of students in the most important law school in Europe, and his work circulated in the highest circles. In short, this popular legist provided one important channel through which the stream of Paduan conciliarism could flow. If we abandon a mechanical model of influence, but still try to pay attention to the concrete realities of the transmission of ideas through people and books at particular times and places, then this is all we need to know. Whether his ideas still seem useful is of considerably less importance.

---

[109] *Siamo venuti al termine del suo Dialogo de Concilio, poi che N. S. vorrebbe che si fornisce qui, et la Mta. Cesarea in Trento. Io l'ho fatto leggere a molti di questi signori prelati in favor vostro et della giusticia.* Berkeley MS. 63, 191, October 5, 1547.

[110] Biblioteca Nazionale "Marciana", Venice, MSS. Italiani 6606, f. 68v.

IX

Marco Mantova and the Paduan Religious crisis of the early sixteenth century

The War of the League of Cambrai put an end to Venetian aspirations to great power status and administered a tremendous shock to her elite. A great crisis gripped Venice as members of her most distinguished families turned their backs on civic and family duty and entered a life of religion.[1] If anything, though, the war traumatized the aristocracy of Padua even more severely. Not only did Venice respond to the crisis by closing ranks and moving more rapidly towards a narrow oligarchy, but it also added insult to injury by suppressing a revolt in Padua inspired by her defeat at Agnadello in 1509. Both definitively brought home the limits to opportunity for the *terraferma* aristocracy. Marco Mantova Benavides, a scion of one of the leading Paduan aristocratic families, responded to those restraints much as his Venetian peers did. Born in 1489, Mantova belonged to the generation most vulnerable to disappointment. An argument *post hoc, ergo propter hoc* does not support a causal link, but the temporal sequence remains. Even a single cause as potent as a major war, though, is unlikely to have plunged a whole generation in Venice and Padua into a profound psychological and existential crisis. The same thing happened for what must have been different reasons in England at roughly the same time. Nevertheless, even if

F. Gilbert, Venice in the Crisis of the League of Cambrai and Religion and Politics in the Thought of Gasparo Contarini, in History: Choice and Commitment, Cambridge Mass. 1977, 247-267 and 269-291.

we may debate causes, it is certain that Mantova and his Venetian contemporaries were torn between the *vita activa* and the *vita contemplativa*. This hoary old topos makes a much too simple contrast, but nonetheless it marks out the ends of a spectrum that ran gradually through many shades of compromise. Those who chose with drawal usually did not propose to spend their time in meditation, and Mantova elected to remain in the world and at the same time nurture a more personal religion. His beliefs resonated strongly with the frequently republican or civic humanist ideals of the *vita activa*, and made Mantova deeply dissatisfied with the institutional church. Humanism in the narrower sense of literary method may somehow have lain at the root of his religious quest. In short, Mantova wove his complex personality from three strands: humanism; intense religiosity; and loyalty to republicanism, albeit often in a disguised form.

For most of the sixteenth century Mantova taught in the University of Padua's legal faculty, the nobility's sole remaining institution of cultural defense. Authorities differ over the nature of his legal training, but one claimed that some of it came from Giason del Mayno, the great fifteenth century jurist and student of the pure text of Bartolus.[2] Mantova's vast roster of students demonstrates his contemporary stature. They came from all over Europe, especially the Holy Roman Empire, and many of them were later prominent, including one pope. Mantova wrote prolifically, pouring out a steady stream of works, numbering at least thirty-nine titles.[3] Legal historians now credit Mantova with creating a method intermediate between the *mos italicus*, Bartolist method, and the new humanist currents of *mos gallicus* or historical jurisprudence. Once upon a time labeling a member of the sixteenth century law school at Padua a humanist would have raised eyebrows. Humanists sent their sons

---

[2] G. Panziroli, De claris legum interpretibus, Venice 1637, 351. Girolamo Negri's Oratio... in funere viventis Mantuae, in Epistolarum orationumque liber, Padua 1579, f. 60v singled out only Hieronimo Butigella at Pavia. Peter Denley pointed to the university's role in a paper at the Warburg Institute, May 1981 and see also François Dupuigrenet-Desrousilles, L'università di Padova dal 1405 al Concilio di Trento, in G. Arnaldi, Storia della cultura veneta, II Vicenza 1976, 607-647, 623.

[3] T.F. Mayer, Marco Mantova: Bronze Age Conciliarist, in Annuarium Historiae Conciliorum 14 (1984) 385-408, 406 lists more important students and A. Valsecchi, Elogio di Marco Mantova Benavides, Padua 1838, 38-40 and G. Vedova, Biografia degli scrittori padovani, Padua 1832, 573 give his most complete bibliography.

there, but continued to regard it as Bartolus' citadel.[4] Viglius Zwichem van Aytta's testimony illustrates how Padua simultaneously attracted and repelled humanists. Viglius, who studied under Mantova in the early 1530s, reported to his master Erasmus that «the professors of civil law satisfy me abundantly», and he urged a friend to come to Padua because the teaching was far superior to that in France, where Viglius had been trained by Andrea Alciato, one of the principal inventors of the new jurisprudence. Mantova was among those singled out for his success holding Viglius' attention. Despite recognizing Mantova's eloquence, though, Viglius concluded that all the lawyers were «unacquainted with more humane literature».[5]

If Viglius were right, things had changed since the circle of Paduan lawyers around Lovato Lovati and Albertino Mussato had given birth to their own variety of humanism at the turn of the fourteenth century. The loss of civic liberty in Padua had quickly aborted this tradition, but important points of contact between law and humanism remained, and Lovati's and Mussato's heirs were likely to be found among Paduan jurists, even if changed circumstances muted the civic component of their humanism.[6] Viglius might have judged the Paduans fairly as lawyers because he hoped to pursue a career in imperial service and therefore needed to learn the civil law as a current legal system. Partisanship, though, burst through when he assessed his Italian hosts as hopeless litterateurs.

---

[4] E. Holthoefer, Die Literatur zum gemeinen und partikularen Recht in Italien, Frankreich, Spanien und Portugal, in Handbuch der Quellen und Literaturen der neueren europaeischen Privatrechtsgeschichte, ed. Coing, II, 103-500, 139-140. B. Brugi's fundamental L'università dei giuristi in Padova nel Cinquecento, in Archivio veneto-tridentino (1922) 1-92 detailed the humanists' attitude.

[5] Viglius' first and last judgments in Opus Epistolarum Desiderii Erasmi Roterodami, ed. P.S. Allen, IX Oxford 1902-1956, 2994; letter to Hector Hoxvinius in Analecta ad historiam scissi Belgii potissimum attirentia, ed. C.P. Hoynck van Papendrecht, II The Hague 1743, 146; opinion of Mantova, ibid., I, 56; and Viglius' legal training from his autobiography, ibid., I, 9.

[6] D. Hay, The Italian Renaissance in its Historical Background, Cambridge 1961, 73 (building on Roberto Weiss' work). G. Piaia, La fondazione filosofica della teoria conciliare in Francesco Zabarella, in Scienza e filosofia all'università di Padova nel Quattrocento, Trieste-Padova 1983, 431-461, 434; M. Cortesi, Una pagina di umanesimo in Eichstätt, in Quellen und Forschungen aus italienischen Archiven und Bibliotheken, 64 (1984) 227-260, 229, 254ff.; and P. Nardi, Mariano Sozzini, Giureconsulto senese del Quattrocento, Milano 1974, all provide evidence of humanism in the Paduan law school.

This may or may not do justice to most of the faculty. It is simply wrong in Mantova's case.

Mantova's strong interest in Italian as a literary language immediately gives the lie to Viglius' canard, as does the number of his students who referred to their training in *buone lettere* under Mantova.[7] He engaged so heavily in literary matters that he had to defend himself against the charge of neglecting his professional career. As he reassured a young friend in one of his Italian works, merely because he took himself off to his villa to read works in *nostra materna lingua* he had not abandoned all his legal training.[8] In his youth Mantova threw himself into Italian, writing three short *novelle* and one longer one in it by 1525. Mantova emphasized the necessity of eloquence in these works, and devoted one of them to this primary humanist virtue. The hero of *Della eloquenza* not only won the woman, but also praised the political use of polished speech «for reasoning amongst the multitude of men», a nice republican (or civic humanist) touch.[9]

The *Discorsi sopra i dialoghi di M. Speron Sperone* reveal a deep humanist culture and close ties to humanist luminaries. Mantova accorded his fellow Paduan the ultimate tribute by comparing him favorably to Petrarch and Boccaccio, on top of calling him a demigod. Unreserved praise poured down on Speroni, the dominant force among Paduan humanists at mid-century and long a faithful servant of his native city. With the possible exceptions of Lucian and Plato, Mantova thought no one had written better dialogues, both in terms of content and rhetorical form. Not even Quintillian, many humanists' favorite Roman rhetorician, could handle metaphors and other rhetorical devices as well as Speroni. His literary academy probably reinforced Mantova's leanings, even if he was never formally a member, perhaps because law was off-limits in its discussions. Mantova compared Speroni's Italian style to Lazzaro Bonamico's Latin and Bonamico had long been prominent among Paduan humanists, and made a natural member of Speroni's circle. Mantova habitually associated with such men. Earlier he had been a

---

[7] For one famous example, Marino Cavalli. University of California, Berkeley, Robbins Law Library MS. 63, Lettere di Marco Mantova, § 213, (Venice, December 6, 1531).
[8] Discorsi sopra i dialoghi di M. Speron Sperone, Venice 1561, f. A4r.
[9] Della eloquenza, in Novelle, ed. Luigi Pescasio, Mantova 1973, 109, 110.

friend of Bonamico's colleague Benedetto Lampridio, as well as of better-known figures such as Pietro Bembo, Trifone Gabriele and the Venetian pedagogue Giovambattista Egnazio, among numerous others.[10]

Dialogue, the quintessential humanist form, shaped a good deal of Mantova's work, including the *discorsi* just considered and most of his *novelle*. Much of Mantova's dialogue-writing sprang from a typically humanist emphasis on education. Quite apart from his Italian literary work, Mantova cast many of his legal commentaries in master-student form or as questions and answers drawn straight from the lecture-hall intended to help beginning students through the rougher patches in civil and canon law. Whatever Viglius may have thought, Mantova thus adopted the same approach as Erasmus had in his favorite teaching device, the colloquy.[11] Dialogue underpinned some of Mantova's more high-powered legal work, too, particularly *De concilio*.[12] Here Mantova made a serious effort to create a realistic interchange, perhaps trying to simulate the contention between faculty for which Viglius recommended Padua. At one point the character Mantova rebuked Roberto for prolixly piling up citations, one of the favorite humanist charges against the Bartolists. Mantova could also be hard on himself. He sheepishly admitted that his violent attack on the order of cardinals missed the mark because he had failed to take account of any examples which did not support his jaundiced view. He could not, since he had read none of the good cardinals' works. Roberto won that round, but the two crossed swords again at the end of this passage. Mantova

---

[10] Discorsi..., ff. 5r-6v; G.A. Kennedy, Classical Rhetoric and its Christian and Secular Tradition from Ancient to Modern Times, Chapel Hill N.C. 1980, 198 for Quintillian's popularity; Discorsi..., f. 6v for praise of Bonamico. Mantova does not appear in S. Maylender, Storia delle Accademie d'Italia, III Bologna 1929, 267-270, but there is no thorough study of Speroni's gl'Infiammati. Egidio Cathani's letter confirms Mantova's friendship with both Lampridio and Egnazio (Lettere di Mantova, § 249, Mantova, April 27, 1540). Three letters from Gabriele (§ 29-30 and 242) appear in the same collection. For Bembo, see below, 33.

[11] Mantova shared more than the form of his pedagogy with the great Dutch humanist. As had Erasmus, Mantova insisted on the value of humane literature even in the training of bishops. Marco Mantova, Dialogus de concilio, Venezia 1541, ff. Hiiv-Hiiar.

[12] The calling of a council to Vicenza in 1536 inspired De concilio, and Mantova completed the work by August 12, 1540 when he referred to it in his Observationes legalium, Louvain 1546, 196 as libellum editum.

begged Roberto to lend him some of the cardinals' writings, but he retorted «they are for sale, you may buy them for yourself, and you will free me from this bother. Besides, I gave mine to someone else».[13] Labored perhaps, but the last touch of humor enlivened the dialogue.

Mantova's deep-seated passion for literature burst out at the height of a profound religious crisis in his early thirties. It is surely significant that he chose to recount the upheaval in Italian. *L'heremita*, published in 1521, detailed Mantova's struggle to escape from the corrupt world. The subtitle promised a tract on the knotty problem of predestination. Most of the work is once more a dialogue, shot through with humanism. Its hero delivered himself of all manner of deep spiritual insights, but «Mantova» often paused to reflect upon and praise his graceful presentation. They discussed poetry several times and «Mantova» declared it «certainly superior to law!» At the climax of the argument over justification Mantova took time out for a defense of Petrarch's poetry, which he later expanded into a separate work.[14]

L'heremita cost Mantova much effort. Unlike many of his other works, it abounds with thick description, from the excitement of a wild boar hunt, or the tranquillity of a mountain spring, to the serenity of the hermit's aerie, which Mantova painted in loving detail. He took pains over the hermit's portrait, identifying him as Girolamo di Lancilao degli Anselmini. In addition to a wealth of circumstantial evidence about his life and character, the book's strange ending leads one to suspect that Mantova did not invent the hermit and rooted the whole encounter in fact. Despite «Mantova's» firm resolve to imitate his spiritual father and become a hermit himself, when degli Anselmini died «Mantova» gave up his intention and disconsolately returned to teaching. So strange a twist could have been modelled on experience.[15] Mantova regularly used his friends as characters. His godson Roberto Maggio was his interlocutor in one work and asked to be included in others. At least one of the other figures in *L'heremita*, Francesco Niconitio, existed outside the *novella*. Given the propensity of many of Mantova's fellow

---

[13] De concilio, f. Fiiv.
[14] Venezia, printed by Zorzi Ruscone. Ff. Biiiibr, Cv for poetry and the praise of Petrarch. Annotazioni brevissime sopra le rime di M. Francesco Petrarca appeared in Padua in 1566; Valsecchi, Elogio..., 40.
[15] Ibid., f. Fiiiv.

humanists to reshape their identities through their writings, and their small concern for the boundary we now draw between truth and fiction, establishing the hermit's reality is probably a hopeless conundrum and a problem which would have made no sense to Mantova.[16]

«Real» or not, Mantova's Anselmini is vividly limned and should have been an ideal spiritual guide. He remained a Pisan patriot and recommended his noble father's services to the republic, even though both family and city had objected to his religious vocation. He had been a law student at Padua, but had come under the sway of an itinerant preacher from Florence and chosen to imitate him. Women he shunned (a point Anselmini emphasized) and in all things followed the example of the apostles. The friar, though, had been learned in three languages and Anselmini's new vocation left him time to cultivate humanist interests. He chose the *Colli Euganei* for his hermitage because he had visited Petrarch's grave there as a youth. Anselmini defended poets against Mantova as *amici d'ogni vivere honesto*, who wrote out of divine inspiration. The hermit even showed Mantova some of his own verses written shortly after his conversion. The two had much in common.[17]

Ardor flashed through Mantova's prose. Mother-son imagery, for instance, dominates the effusive greetings between «Mantova» and his mentor.[18] The hermit inflamed «Mantova» with divine love, fostering a deep discontent with his mundane life. (Mantova was about to assume his first permanent teaching post, and the prospect must not have agreed with him). «Mantova» suffered through a horrendous dream of wandering in a terrible desert full of wild beasts, which ended as evil men assaulted him. After he awoke, he hurried up the mountain in the full heat of the morning to unburden himself of *tale horribile e spaventevolle visione*. «Mantova» begged the hermit to interpret the dream, which he did, though reluctantly. Anselmini first ruled out a number of physical causes and afterwards

---

[16] Maggio appeared in De concilio and asked to be made a part of other writings in a letter of December 8, 1542 (Lettere di Mantova, 186). Niconitio's 1540 letter is § 246 in the same volume. S. Greenblatt, Renaissance Self-Fashioning, from More to Shakespeare, Chicago 1980, speaks to both the question of self-creation and the unimportance of our division between truth and fiction. See also the vast literature on Paolo Giovio, as just one example.
[17] Defense of poets on ff. Ciiir, Ciir and Biiiibv-Cr.
[18] E.g., f. Biiir.

finally considered the dream's content. The desert is the world unworked by men, *con l'aratro della penitenza... non d'orationi seminato*. It therefore cannot collect the fruit of grace. The animals are vices and the chase, unsurprisingly, symbolized Mantova's desire to escape the world.[19]

The hermit framed his case in the manner of a Paduan natural philosopher. Anselmini began his crucial explanation of predestination in good Aristotelian fashion by pointing out that everything has its proper place, a rock, for example, should fall. A more Averroist side to the saint came out when he discussed the powers of natural science and of natural reason and wound up with a nearly classic statement of double truth. In one place, natural science was queen of the others and could penetrate God's secrets. Later, though, the hermit claimed that natural reason was insufficient to lead men to knowledge of divine mysteries. Following nature's order led only to a moral life.[20] At the same time, neo-platonism heavily marked the hermit's message and «Mantova's» reflections upon it. Worldly hopes, thought «Mantova», could never be maintained because of life's inherent instability. Circumstances changed constantly. «Et a cosi fatta instabilità soggiacente che niente un giorno niente un'hora niente un sol momento di tempo, in quell'esser medesimo, in quel stato istesso può rimanere». Life finally ended in death without ever gaining any stability. Despair of the world drove Mantova to accept the neo-platonic solution: one could achieve permanence only through contemplation of divine truth.[21]

The balance tilted toward withdrawal for most of the dialogue, but Mantova finally presented a compromise compounded of equal parts of it and a more active outlook. Initially, the hermit insisted on escape. Fly the world and never look back. Those who thought the present age the worst were probably correct — the only way out was to imitate himself and other hermits.[22] The hermit, though, sketched a remarkably active contemplative regimen for his would-be disciple. As he told Mantova, every day I say the divine offices at night and in the morning. I eat only what I grow in my garden and do not drink wine. Thrice weekly I discipline myself *a dio ignudo*.

---

[19] Ff. Biiv-Biiiiar.
[20] Ff. Ciiiv and Eiiiicr.
[21] The quotation on f. Fiiiir, a tail-piece to the discussion on ff. Diiiibr-Eiiiicv.
[22] Ibid.

I sleep on the ground. I read only books leading to knowledge of the truth. «Mantova», weeping, judged the hermit to have become a perfect man. He had gained mystical release, but only through the hard work that made one worthy of grace. Life was labor.[23]

This formula solved Mantova's problem, but in order to secure his full assent the hermit had to lead him through a long discourse on justification. «Mantova» at first argued that baptism guaranteed salvation. Anselmini would have none of that, insisting that only «the smallest number» of the elect would gain eternal life. God wished to show mercy, but most people's own neglect doomed them. Only the good were predestined; God created the rest in order to demonstrate his justice as well as his mercy. The bad fell into trouble because of original sin, which lays the pure soul open to the blandishments of bodily passions. The body cannot help but be attracted by all the beauty surrounding it. If one perseveres in the hard work of goodness, though, assurance of salvation will follow.[24]

The tension inherent in this compromise between personal religion and the demands of the world led Mantova to set high standards not only for himself, but also for everyone else. The clergy regularly failed to measure up. In *L'heremita*, they came first among bad men who succumbed to carnal temptation, because they had lost *la disciplina di Cristo*, as Mantova explained in a nearly contemporary work.[25] The hermit launched into a long tirade against clerical vice. Priests were guilty of visiting women at the hour when they should have been celebrating mass, of crimes against nature, and they and the friars committed just about any other imaginable sin, including usury and whoring.[26] A similarly extended and sharp criticism appears in another *novella*. The clergy imitated the *semplici colombe* and instead of remaining beside the pure water of the Gospel defending Christians from the *pessime et cative ombra de gli eretici*, they observed the seven deadly sins, ignoring the seven laws.

---

[23] Ff. Aiiiidr-v and Diiiiv.
[24] Ff. Eiiv-Fiiv.
[25] Della avaritia de' principi moderni, in Novelle..., 105.
[26] L'heremita, ff. Eiiiicv-Fiir.

They provided examples of the worst customs, falling

nelle guerre, ne gli odi, nelle dissensioni, nelle discordie, ne gli homicidi, ne gli adulteri, ne e stupri, nelle sodomie, nelle ruine de miseri et infelici soggetti, nelle destrution de castella subversioni di Città, arsure di contadi, rubbamenti, saccheggiamenti, tirannie et altri mancamenti imperversati, che e temporali et laichi non sono, perduta la pace, abbandonato l'amore, infreddata la charità, il zelo lassato da canto et ultimamente relati, poco pensando chi si siano, la persona di cui rappresentino.[27]

One passage in *De concilio*, although written much later, helps to explain the violence of Mantova's attitude. He included abuse of hunting in a catalogue of superficially much more serious clerical failings. Once again, though, Mantova saw this lapse as a serious breach of discipline, the clergy indulging in a pastime he denied himself. Smack in the middle of his spiritual odyssey in *L'heremita* «Mantova» took several days off to go hunting with his wordling friends. Shortly afterwards the hermit treated him to the attack on clerical sins mentioned above and spelled out his disappointment in his pupil's backsliding. Mantova learned his lesson. If he could bridle his delight in hunting, then so could the clergy.[28]

Assurance of salvation through constant effort sums up the essence of Mantova's crisis and how he resolved it. Penetrating this abstract formula to the existential and psychological reality behind it causes much more difficulty. Giuseppe Marangoni long ago put his finger on the prime difficulty of doing any literary study of Padua — lack of sources.[29] He might not have been so pessimistic had he known of Mantova's massive correspondence, but this rich collection is nearly useless for the early part of Mantova's career. Letters to and from him are sparse before the late 1530s. Mantova's own collection of his letters contains nothing earlier than 1539. Spotty coverage, though, ties the smallest knot in interpreting Mantova's *epistolario*. All his Italian in-letters survive in a collection prepared for the printer by Mantova's nephew Giovanni.[30] The motives

---

[27] Avaritia, 105.
[28] De concilio, f. Cr-v, and L'heremita, ff. Ciiiiv-Diiir for the trip.
[29] G. Marangoni, Lazzaro Bonamico e lo studio Padovano nella prima metà del cinquecento, in Nuovo archivio veneto n.s. 1 (1901) 118-151, 119.
[30] Mantova's own collection is in the Biblioteca Marciana, Venice, MSS. Marc. ital. X 91 (6606). The Latin letters from this volume were printed as Epistolae familiares... M. Mantova Benavidii, Padua 1578. The companion Italian letters

behind this obscure figure's epistolary portrait of his uncle remain buried. Whithout them and the literary purpose of the whole large volume, the use of individual letters is a very risky business. A volume of correspondence was every bit as much a literary work as *L'heremita*, but the absence of non-literary documents forces us to extract such clues as we can from literary works, and then proceed by inference.[31]

Two strong hypotheses emerge from *L'heremita*. First, it reflects the acute phase of Mantova's crisis, and second it bears the strong impress of his university environment. No evidence exists to corroborate the first suggestion, and the badly damaged University archives for this period hamper the investigation of the second. Nevertheless, Averroist Aristotelianism and neo-platonism marked both *L'heremita* and the university, so one may conjecturely connect them.[32] Better yet, at least one Paduan philosopher blended them in a manner highly reminiscent of Mantova. Nicolò Leonico, long professor of Greek, reinterpreted Aristotle in terms of Plato, particularly on the burning topic of the nature and immortality of the soul. In his *Dialogi*, he often sounded like Mantova's hermit. Prayer and contemplation were the quickest means to gain felicity and escape from contamination and impurity. Since the body gets in the way of the true and beautiful, we must be glad to be freed from it by death. Leonico, though, pursued his neo-platonism more ruthlessly than degli Anselmini, perhaps because he was an old man

---

appeared the same year as Lettere famigliari diverse, also from the press of Lorenzo Pasquati in Padua. Giovanni Mantova's volume is now in the Robbins Law Library at the University of California, Berkeley, where it was discovered by Ronnie H. Terpening. I am most grateful to Prof. Terpening for many assistances with this collection. Another, but very imperfect version, of these letters is in the Biblioteca del Seminario, Padua, cod. DCXIX, v. 5, assembled by G. Gennari in 1748.

[31] Terpening points out some of the pitfalls in handling a letter-collection prepared for the printer in Pietro Bembo and the Cardinalate: Unpublished Letters to Marco Mantova, in Lettere Italiane 32 (1980) 75-86 and G. Fragnito digs into more of them in her Per lo studio dell'epistografia volgare del cinquecento: Le lettere di Ludovico Beccadelli, Bibliothèque d'humanisme et renaissance, 43/1 (1981) 61-87.

[32] B. Nardi's Saggi sull'aristotelismo padovano dal secolo XIV al XVI, Florence 1958 is fundamental. Neo-platonism is less studied, but see A. Stella, Tradizione razionalistica patavina e radicalismo spiritualistico nel XVI secolo, in Annali della Scuola Normale Superiore di Pisa. Lettere, Storia e Filosofia, ser. 2, 37 (1968) 275-302, 288.

when he wrote his dialogues. A vital spirit linked all parts of the world and all animate natures and gave them life. Everything proceeds from God and flows back to him. The impress of divine unity produces natural order. All beings bear two essences: to remain in God and to return to him.[33] Distaste for the active life was an obvious corollary of Leonico's yearning for the divine. Nevertheless, he may not have differed as much from Mantova as may appear from these late writings. Donato Giannotti thought it made perfect sense to have his character Trifone Gabriele recommend Leonico's political wisdom, and Giannotti was anything but in favor of the *vita contemplativa*. Whatever Leonico's political opinions, his neoplatonism cannot be doubted, nor the strength of the syncretic impulse which led him through his long commentaries on Aristotle's natural sicence. Mantova could well have known Leonico, judging from the latter's interest in the law school.[34] Whether or not Leonico «influenced» Mantova, his case confirms that ideas like Mantova's flourished in Padua and could fit together into a similar synthesis.

So much for the second hypothesis. If the first remains untested, at least some scraps of evidence delimit the length of Mantova's struggle. When it began is the tougher nut to crack. Two letters from Alessandro Tyberino dated 1517 prove that Mantova's interest in religion and saintly men antedated *L'heremita*. Tyberino wrote from the village of Pitigliano just west of Lago di Bolsena to recommend Fr. Giovambattista, a native of the place, both as a theologian and as a man. His general was sending the clergyman to take over as the priest of the convent of S. Maria dei Servi in Venice, and Tyberino did not want him to go without letters to Mantova. Tyberino's florid praise worked. In his second letter, he thanked Mantova for «your most loving demonstrations» to Fr. Giovambattista. Tyberino must have spent time in Padua, since he could not have known Mantova by reputation so early, yet rightly expected that he would take an interest in a religious man. Alas, Fr. Giovambattista has thus far

---

[33] N. Leonico, Dialogi, Venice 1524 and an improved edition printed at Louvain by Gryphius in 1542, ff. LXVr-LXVIr (Venice ed.) and all the rest from Sadoletus, sive de precibus from the Gryphius version, passim.

[34] M. P. Gilmore, Myth and Reality in Venetian Political Theory, in Renaissance Venice, ed. J.R. Hale, Totowa N.J. 1973, 431-443, 436 for Giannotti on Leonico. He judged law to be well taught at a time when philosophy was not. Letter to Reginald Pole, Biblioteca apostolica vaticana, MS. Rossiana 997, f. 55v, February 8, 1531. I am grateful for an Andrew W. Mellon fellowship from the Vatican Film Library, St. Louis University which allowed me to consult this volume of Leonico's miscellanea.

eluded capture. Might his arrival have triggered or reinforced Mantova's spiritual turmoil? [35]

Pietro Barignano's 1524 letter may indicate that Mantova struggled long and hard. Barignano shared *L'heremita's* pessimism about the times and sympathized with «Mantova's» desire to escape, but embraced a much different remedy: bread, wine and poetry. He promised to send Mantova some madrigals and immortalize his name, but Mantova's response to either proposal is not recorded.[36] Nor can we be certain that the hermit's insistence on chastity reflected one of Mantova's central concerns. If so, *Della eloquenza*, which turns on a contest over a woman, must signal that the danger had passed. Unfortunately, its precise date is unknown, although its modern editor suggests 1528.[37]

Pascale Marino's letter of 1529 establishes a solid *terminus ad quem* for this phase of Mantova's life, nearly consistent with the date indicated by *Della eloquenza*. Marino wrote *de profundis*, but he proposed to resolve his trauma in the opposite way from Mantova by entering a monastery. He wrote bluntly. He had decided that he must speedily do something about *questa misera vita ambitiosa & gonfiata* and that meant giving up the law. No one who professed to be a good Christian could possibly consider such a career. If Mantova thought about Marino's resolve, perhaps he would also turn *ad altro che ad ambitione*. I am not joking, Marino insisted. «Se volete degli honori & diventar glorioso, procurate la gloria di dio che l'acquisitarete immortale non la cercando havendola acquistata per questa via, i propheti santi, i martiri, gli apostoli, et finalmente christo, la qual cosa farete, se vi sforzarete di imitarlo quanto in voi sia possibile». Marino exhortò Mantova in a way remarkably like degli Anselmini's. He claimed to know Mantova well and in a later letter Mantova spoke of their *amicizia anticha*. Marino's letter must therefore mean that Mantova had wholeheartedly embraced the *vita activa*.[38]

Marino, though, mistook the depth of Mantova's religious conviction. His teacher was anything but a man of the world. Literature and religion remained vital. *L'heremita's* struggles were

---

[35] Lettere di Mantova, §s 74 and 75 July 13 and October 4, 1517.
[36] Ibid., § 176, Pesaro, December 12, 1524.
[37] Novelle..., 41.
[38] Lettere di Mantova, § 251 (Venice, December 28, 1529) and Marc. Ital. X 91 (6606), § 52 (January 5, 1556).

fresh twenty years later when Niconitio wrote Mantova and asked for a copy of his tract on predestination.[39] At roughly the same time, Mantova grappled with many of the same issues — salvation and the state of the church — in a Ciceronian dialogue, *De concilio*. The clergy still fell short of Mantova's expectations. Disgust with clerical hunting was only one sign of his insistence on a strenuous life for churchmen. In another choice instance «Mantova» blasted the order of cardinals.

Utinam hodie tales essent, quales dixisti, qualesque esse debent, & non gigantes, qui gemuerunt sub aquis... qui non prodesse possunt, nec curant, sed praeesse gloriantur, cervicem erigunt, grandia loquuntur, sublimia meditantur, & nihil denique quia nesciunt, perantur. Adde quod nec in verbo eorum est veritas, non honestas in moribus, nec denique in consiliis fides, quaesitum pecuniae, & rerum, ac divitiarum, non Christum sequentes, neque virtutum, aut donorum spiritualium affluentiam.[40]

The cardinal's uselessness stands out from this string of grievances. Mantova harped on the dangers of clerical idleness and hounded lazy clergy throughout the work. He and his interlocutor Roberto early agreed that the clergy were called to the active life. Many were priests in name only, and Mantova complained vigorously of abbots' obesity, making it sufficient reason to exclude them from a council.[41]

Otium was the strongest blasphemy in Mantova's vocabulary, even though he had changed his mind about how one achieved salvation. Now he believed in justification by faith, and rested *De concilio's* major argument against unrestrained papal authority on it. Since faith alone could save, the church could not possibly leave its control to a single, conceivably heretical, individual.[42] The possibility of sanctification disappeared, but reliance on faith did not undercut the necessity of the *vita activa*. In fact, Mantova argued against papal authority in the course of sketching out a republican constitution for the church, which would foster the active life of at least some believers. He may have drawn on the fundamental justification for the secular republic when formulating his case for an ecclesiastical one. As Mantova put the theory many years later, the

---

[39] Lettere di Mantova, § 246 (Cracow, December 10, 1540).
[40] De concilio, f. Eiiav.
[41] Ibid., ff. Cr-v and Iiivff. for the abbots.
[42] Ibid., f. Diiar.

respublica existed to generate virtue. Mantova did not spell out the mechanism, but he probably meant to adopt the common theory that a republic offered an arena in which citizens could exercise themselves in order to become virtuous.[43] In *De concilio*, despite his harsh strictures on them, Mantova left the cardinals in a position almost identical to that of the leaders of any oligarchical republic, say Venice, except that the pope kept just a bit more of their «divided sovereignty».[44] Mantova defended the cardinals' role in the council and in the day-to-day government of the church. The ultimate authority over matters of belief and the *status ecclesiae* had to be a general council. It contained the cardinals and other *personae praecipuae* who represented the rest of the church, just as the wise and influential exercised authority over any community.[45]

Mantova's conciliarism and the circumstances which may have helped to generate it suggest a complex interplay between thinking about the constitution of the church and that of the secular state.[46] That is, the venerable road between conciliarism and republicanism went two ways. As either the secular or ecclesiastical political sphere shrank, republican ideas moved into the other. The history of Paduan conciliar thought through Mantova fits this model closely. Some care must be exercised, since filiopietism played a large part in Mantova's thinking and his models placed severe constraints on what he could say. His conciliarist streak fit a long tradition stretching back to Francesco Zabarella and Nicola de Tudeschis (Panormitanus) and Mantova drew heavily on both.[47] Members of the same legal faculty often subscribed to similar doctrines, but

---

[43] Mantova, Gymnasium scholasticum in Analysis variarum quaestionum, Venice 1568, ff. 260v-261r. J.G.A. Pocock lucidly analyzes republican theory in The Machiavellian Moment: Florentine Political Thought and the Atlantic Republican Tradition, Princeton 1975, especially I, cap. 3.

[44] Brian Tierney coined this useful term and has done a great deal to elucidate its meaning. See, in particular, «Divided Sovereignty» at Constance: A Problem of Medieval and Early Modern Political Theory, in Annuarium Historiae Conciliorum, 7 (1975) 238-256.

[45] Mayer, Bronze Age Conciliarist... 404.

[46] «Conciliarism» is a term of convenience only. It does not designate a uniform phenomenon and means exactly the same as «conciliar thought». G. Alberigo argues powerfully for the necessity of a fully historical approach to conciliarism, especially in Chiesa conciliare. Identità e significato del conciliarismo, Brescia 1981, 344, 14. The term «conciliar thought» may perhaps be preferred because it smacks more of this historical diversity.

[47] Mayer, Bronze Age Conciliarist..., 392, 396-402, especially p. 401. See also Piaia, Zabarella..., for more on the earlier tradition.

more than ideological affinity united Mantova and his predecessors. That Padua, once a birthplace of Italian humanism, should also foster conciliarism is probably not an accident. When Zabarella borrowed from Marsilio of Padua, motives very close to his «radical» compatriot's may have inspired him. Marsilio wrote to defend a secular republic *in extremis*, and Zabarella transferred Marsilio's ideas to the *respublica christiana* after any hope for their earthly *patria* had disappeared.[48] Much later, as the realm of ecclesiastical politics in turn contracted, some of those ideas percolated back into thinking about the secular state. In between, the Paduan public sphere shrank further than it already had when the Carrara gained power or Venice first conquered the republic in 1405 and that constriction helped to push Mantova to revive the almost moribund tradition of Paduan conciliarism. This fairly simple schema cannot tell the whole story, but it does provide a concrete historical framework in which Paduan conciliar thought may have developed.[49]

Concern about a limited future was probably no longer uppermost in Mantova's mind when he composed *De concilio*. After 1541 when he succeeded to Pietro Bembo's position, Mantova did not have to fear for his personal standing, but he wanted more.[50] Mantova intended his dialogue to have practical effect and gain wide-spread recognition for him, perhaps as compensation for lost

---

[48] Piaia, Zabarella..., 457-461 argues that Zabarella modelled his conciliar case on Marsilio's theory of the role of the *congregatio civium* in the *respublica*. Nicolai Rubinstein places Marsilio's ideas in the context of the decline of civic liberty in Padua. Marsilio da Padova e il pensiero politico italiano del trecento, in Medioevo 5 (1979) 143-164.

[49] Francis Oakley has been in the forefront of those modifying Figgis's claim that conciliarist ideas trickled into «democratic» secular ideas. See in particular On the Road from Constance to 1688: The Political Thought of John Major and George Buchanan, in Journal of British Studies 2 (1962) 1-31 and G. Piaia has done much to trace the currency of Marsilio's ideas in his Marsilio da Padova nella Riforma e nella Controriforma: Fortuna ed Interpretazione, Padova 1977, and C. Condren, George Lawson and the *Defensor Pacis*: On the Use of Marsilius in Seventeenth Century England, in Medioevo 6 (1980) 595-617. Hubert Jedin and Remigius Baeumer present the most complete surveys of Paduan conciliar thought, though both missed Mantova. Jedin, Geschichte des Konzils von Trient, I Freiburg 1951, 29 and Baeumer, Nachwirkungen des konziliaren Gedankens in der Theologie und Kanonistik des fruehen 16. Jahrhunderts, Münster 1971, 8ff. This tenative framework may begin to answer Alberigo's call for a historical approach to conciliar thought (above note 46).

[50] L. Puppi-M. Universo, Padova, Bari 1982, 155, summarizing Puppi's La chiesa degli Eremitani di Padova, Vicenza 1970, 99-100.

opportunities at home. He dedicated the work to Pope Paul III and freely advised him about the necessity of a council. A number of other high-ranking churchmen read the book (or had it read to them), including some Tridentine fathers during the council's translation to Bologna and the papal legate governing that city. Mantova kept his correspondents hard at work presenting copies of *De concilio* or inquiring which bookseller had it in stock.[51]

De concilio disappointed Mantova's hopes, probably because it contributed little new, apart from the justification by faith argument. It was no systematic work, either: Mantova's humanist form created problems in handling a subject always previously treated in scholastic fashion. His primary concern — how to prevent the pope from triggering a schism — had been much more pressing in the early fifteenth century than in Mantova's day. Mantova, though, trained professional ecclesiastical bureaucrats, unlike many northern contemporary conciliarists, some of whom thought in more creative ways. When he minced no words about where final spiritual authority lay, he did so before people who could apply his ideas practically. When he insisted on the cardinals' crucial role and lectured on their responsiblities, students like Cristoforo Madruzzo would have taken his words to heart.[52] Mantova's success as an educator may not have satisfied him, but his opportunity to spread conciliar ideas in the classroom singles him out for historians' attention.

Some have argued that a desire like Mantova's for a general council was a major article of faith among the religious group variously labeled *spirituali* or evangelicals. Again, if belief in justification by faith is indeed this coterie's central belief, then Mantova must be included.[53] He certainly had many contacts with

---

[51] Mayer, Bronze Age Conciliarist..., 406-408 and Lettere di Mantova, e.g., § 234 (Pisa, December 21, 1542), § 106 (Rome, April 1, 1552) and perhaps § 252 (Venice, August 20, 1541).

[52] The passage De cardinali in Mantova's Observationes legalium ended with a commendation to Madruzzo, p. 198. Vedova, Scrittori..., 566 listed Madruzzo as Mantova's student. Madruzzo's letters never failed to underline his indebtedness to Mantova, e.g. Lettere di Mantova, § 2 (Trent, December 13, 1539).

[53] D. Cantimori, Submission and Conformity: «Nicodemism» and the Expectations of a Conciliar Solution to the Religious Question, trans. E. Cochrane, in E. Cochrane ed, The Late Italian Renaissance 1525-1630, London 1970, 244-265, 257-258. Cantimori's net spread over more than what are now called spirituali, but they fall somewhere in Cantimori's spectrum. D. Fenlon, Heresy and Obedience in Tridentine Italy: Cardinal Pole and the Counter Reformation, Cambridge 1972, 18 states the case for sola fide most strongly.

people identified as its members, from Reginald Pole and Gasparo Contarini to Gianmatteo Giberti, Pietro Bembo and Madruzzo. Mantova knew Pole when the Englishman studied in Padua in the 1520s and later approached him for patronage for his nephew Giovanni. Mantova asked Luigi Quirini to gain audience with Contarini almost as soon as he was made a cardinal, but for unknown reasons. Contarini's secretary, Girolamo Negri, was a student and friend of Mantova, and by a strange quirk of fate they wrote one another's funeral orations. Giberti knew of Mantova in 1532 when his vicar Phillipo Stridonio asked Mantova for a legal opinion and the lawyer later proposed to dedicate a work to the bishop. Bembo felt close enough to Mantova to address a series of letters to him at the turning point of his life while he waited for his cardinalate. Madruzzo remained Mantova's friend and supporter long after leaving Padua.[54]

Quite apart from the difficulty of putting more flesh on these bare bones of personal contacts, another more fundamental problem lies in the way of accepting Mantova's candidacy as a *spirituale*. This time the sticking point lies not so much in evidence as in historiography. Massimo Firpo argues forcefully that historians must apply the label evangelism a good deal more carefully than they have if they would avoid emptying it of content. The cases of Marcantonio Flaminio and Ludovico Beccadelli are particularly instructive. Many times, too, the *spirituali* come out heretics, which raises yet another knotty point. Before the lines hardened at Trent, would beliefs like Mantova's have been heretical or *almeno eterodosso*, whether or not they were evangelical?[55]

---

[54] Pole: Mantova to Pole, Padua, March 6, 1555 (Marc. ital. X 91 [6606], § 43 [Iitalian series], ff. 34r-v); Contarini: Lettere di Mantova, § 157 (Quirini to Mantova, May 29, 1535), and Negri's funeral oration for Mantova, f. 61v; Giberti: Lettere di Mantova, § 206 (from Stridonio, Verona, March 17, 1532) and A. Prosperi, Tra evangelismo e controriforma: G.M. Giberti (1495-1543), Rome 1969, 233 for Mantova's suggestion; Bembo: Terpening, Bembo, and P. Simoncelli, Pietro Bembo e l'evangelismo italiano, in Critica storica 15 (1978) 1-63 identifies Bembo as an evangelical; Madruzzo: Lettere di Mantova, §s 2 and 6-10 and Mantova's to him, Marc. ital. X 91 (6606), §s 9, 21, 40, 56, 63 and 69; for both Bembo and Madruzzo, Mantova's reference to them as his patroni in Observationes legalium, 198.

[55] M. Firpo, review of Marcantonio Flaminio, Lettere, ed. A. Pastore, Rivista storica italiana 41 (1979) 653-662, 656-659 for Flaminio and Beccadelli. For the latter see also G. Fragnito, Per lo studio dell'epistografia..., 63-4; ibidem, Memoria individuale e costruzione biografica, Urbino 1978, 158-164. Paolo Simoncelli

Not in Venice, and if Mantova is any yardstick, not in the Veneto, either. Padua sometimes harbored real heretics, often in the law school, but much of Mantova's anti-clericalism sprang from contempt for the clergy's abject failure to deal with heresy. Undoubtedly, too, Paduan orthodoxy, nourished in its scholastic environment, often diverged from that of Venice, but Mantova's crisis and its resolution fit neatly into Giuseppe Alberigo's analysis of the Venetian pattern.[56] Mantova suffered from the symptomatic inner inquietude of Paolo Giustiniani and his friends, reflected in a burning need for a secure personal destiny.[57] As a result, Mantova's thinking converges on numerous points with Giustiniani's, especially in *L'heremita*. The solitary life attracted both and Giustiniani and Mantova insisted on chastity far more than usual. They may well have sought a pure and authentic religious observance out of humanist motives.[58] Mantova agreed that lack of virtue not doctrinal error threatened the «ruin and dissolution» of the church, as Giustiniani phrased it. Or as Contarini put the same idea, the governors had to lead by example, another Venetian commonplace.[59] Most important, Mantova eventually shared this circle's belief in justification by faith.

Unlike Contarini, Mantova had been severely tempted to follow Giustiniani's lead, which he perhaps knew directly through Giusti-

---

originally labeled Mantova «almeno eterodosso» in Il caso Reginald Pole: Eresia e santità nelle polemiche religiose del Cinquecento, Roma 1977, thinking of L'heremita, as prof. Simoncelli tells me.

[56] Stella, Tradizione razionalistica..., especially for Matteo Gribaldi Moffa, pp. 282-284; P.J. van Kessel, The Denominational Pluriformity of the German Nation at Padua and the Problem of Intolerance in the 16th Century, Archiv für Reformationsgeschichte 75 (1984) 256-275; K.R. Bartlett, The English Exile Community in Italy under Queem Mary I 1553-1558, University of Toronto PhD. thesis 1978; all describe the prevalence of «heretics» in the university and its law school. Stella, Tradizione razionalistica..., 287 underlines the religious difference between Padua and Venice.

[57] G. Alberigo, Vita attiva e vita contemplativa in un'esperienza cristiana del XVI secolo, Studi veneziani 16 (1974), 177-225. Alberigo's is only one of many analyses of this crisis, but his has the great merit of putting its impact on Venetian religiosity immediately on the level of lived experience.

[58] Ibid., 178, 222, 184.

[59] G. Fragnito, Cultura umanistica e riforma religiosa: Il «De officio viri boni ac probi episcopi, Studi veneziani 11 (1969) 75-189, p. 89 for Giustiniani's 1509 formulation, and pp. 115 and 117 for Contarini's version.

niani's widely-circulated letters.[60] Nevertheless, Mantova chose to take a path much more like Contarini's administrative reform, turning his back on ascetic withdrawal. One of the Venetian cardinal's models may also have inspired Mantova. Savonarola apparently showed Contarini the possibility of church reform, and a Florentine preacher converted Mantova's hermit. The two cases parallel each other inexactly, but Mantova could have intended his audience to associate any friar from Florence with the most notorious of them all. Little importance attaches to this point, but the course of Mantova's life after his early thirties hinged on his chioce of a broadly Contarinian reform.[61]

Mantova could be much more interesting than a mere epigone of Contarini, or an example of how Venetian religiosity penetrated its hinterland. His experience suggests a complicated symbiosis between the university and its clientele. The *studio* of Padua trained the Venetian elite, often in religion and philosophy as well as in statecraft and one could posit a weak causal link between university education and religious questioning. Mantova's trials allow us to extend the model. The next step saw the Venetian tremor ripple back to Padua and probably help to trigger Mantova' crisis. The interplay extends yet further. Mantova's teaching and example could well have reinforced the Venetian upheaval and helped to bring it to an end.

Thus Mantova's career deserves study because of his success as a teacher, both of Venetians and of churchmen, as well as, of course, of Venetian churchmen. More than that, Mantova completed the transition from humanist Christianity through Catholic Reform to Counter Reformation, unlike Contarini or Pole. This combined with his ordinary mind — precisely its value — make him well worth further study, even if he cannot interest students of the Reformation quite as much as a towering figure like Contarini. Much as *De concilio* was expurgated in later editions, Mantova slowly edited his own life. By the time of his death and burial in an elaborate tomb in the Chiesa degli Eremitani just across the street from his palace, the would-be hermit had become a pillar of the Paduan and Venetian

---

[60] Alberigo, Esperienza cristiana..., 202. Mantova could have found somewhat the same thing closer to home in the ascetic Ludovico Barbo. Stella, Tradizione razionalistica..., 287.
[61] Alberigo, Esperienza cristiana..., 222 and note 77.

religious establishment. Along the way Mantova expanded sympathy for Giustiniani's and Contarini's beliefs into friendship with Rodolfo Pio and Carlo Borromeo, as well as with Cornelio Musso, the famous preacher and one of the theologians behind Trent's decree on justification. Mantova's attraction to Musso and other Conventual Franciscans or even better to Borromeo symbolizes neatly his compromise between *vita activa* and *vita contemplativa*.[62] His successful public career, lifelong interest in the church and tremendous literary output demonstrate how fruitful that decision could be.

---

[62] For Pio, see his letters to Mantova in Lettere di Mantova, § 3 and 5, and 115-6 for Mantova's recommendation of Paolo Abondio to Pio in 1552-3 and Pio's acceptance of him, and Marc. ital. X 91 (6606), §s 34, 44, and 81. For Musso, Lettere di Mantova, § 39 (Rome, December 16, 1553), recalling a meeting between the two and a promise of help from Mantova. Musso studied in Padua and spent a good deal of time there in later years. In 1567 Mantova apparently had a personal interview with Borromeo (Lettere di Mantova, f. 343) and dedicated his Dialogismos (Venice, 1572) to the bishop. It may be significant that this work was one of those intended for beginning law students. The single largest block of «Lettere di Mantova» concerns Mantova's efforts to help Fr. Antonio Maria Thito, a Conventual Franciscan from Bologna, secure a preaching post in the Duomo of Padua; §s 118-128 (1553-1555, from Thito) and §s 36-7, 59 and 64 and Marc. ital. X 91 (6606), § 7, all bearing on the case.

X

ARIOSTO ANTICLERICAL EPIC POETRY AND THE CLERGY IN EARLY CINQUECENTO ITALY*

Ludovico Ariosto's *Orlando Furioso* (final version 1532) is one of the longest poems in Italian.[1] This together with its constant rough and tumble, and pelting here and pelting there, puts a great deal of pressure on its characters' identities. Its eponymous 'hero' loses himself in a fit of feral love madness; Ruggiero, the focus of the sub-plot about the founding of the house of Este, Ariosto's patrons, makes one blunder after another; and Astolfo, a clownish figure to be sure, first appears as an enchanted tree, takes an eccentric voyage to the moon, and another, concentric one around the earth.[2]

Some of this is satire, but virtually all of the poem trades in Ariosto's notorious irony, leaving the text and its readers suspended between established pieties.[3] Yet, for all this, two kinds of characters and one crucial attitude remain fairly constant, perhaps because they do not last long enough to suffer from the consistent inconsistency that plagues the larger characters. However this may be, the *Furioso* knows only two types of hermits and two of monks, evil and good (although the lines between them can be blurred and monks are mainly evil). Of secular clergy there is almost no word, except for several hearty whacks at the papacy and courtier prelates. Nor are they missed. Ariosto *anticlericale* chose his targets carefully.[4] Ariosto's anticlericalism has

---

* This article is a slightly revised version of the one published under the same title in Peter J. Dykema and H.A. Oberman, ed., *Anticlericalism in Late Medieval and Early Modern Europe* (Leiden, 1993), pp. 283-98.
[1] My thanks to Heiko A. Oberman for the invitation to write this article and to the Interlibrary Loan staff of Augustana College. I owe my introduction to Ariosto to an NEH Institute 'From Ariosto to Tasso', directed by Albert R. Ascoli and David Quint. Ascoli read this piece carefully (and quickly); I hope it is less heavy-handed than it would have been without his advice.
[2] For the best treatment of Astolfo, who is also important to my interpretation, see Peter V. Marinelli, *Ariosto and Boiardo: The Origins of 'Orlando Furioso'* (Columbia, Mo., 1987), passim.
[3] For the degree to which the poem accomplishes its suspensions, see Albert R. Ascoli, *Ariosto's Bitter Harmony: Crisis and Evasion in the Italian Renaissance* (Princeton, 1987), e.g., p. 342.
[4] I am aware of the vexed problem of the relation of author and text and have tried not to skip too blithely over the gap. Cf. above all Michel Foucault, 'What is an Author?' in Paul Rabinow, ed.,

not been the subject of much comment, aside from a seminal essay of Carlo Dionisotti, and both he and Emilio Zanette drew exclusively on the *Satire*.[5] Dionisotti used these autobiographical verse epistles as some of his strongest evidence for a 'situazione ambigua fra laicato e stato ecclesiastico' which characterized the literary generation of the first half of the sixteenth century. This ambiguity arose in part from uncertainty about the benefits of marriage, at least in Ariosto's case. Dionisotti fairly reductively traced the 'disenchanted' compromise which ended this moment to Ariosto's disappointed hopes for a curial career. Earlier, the *Furioso* had reflected 'una situazione più aperta e ambiziosa'. Certainly the anticlerical passages of the *Satire,* especially the extended attack on courtier clerics which occupies about half of the second satire, put things more bluntly than the *Furioso* usually does, but the overall treatment of the problem in the final edition makes much the same points as the *Satire*. Since Dionisotti wrote, scholarship, much of it following his lead, has transformed the religious landscape of early sixteenth-century Italy, making it possible at least to raise the issue of the relation between Ariosto's anticlericalism and reform.

The *Furioso's* anticlericalism, and its place in a long tradition going back at least as far as Dante and Boccaccio, shows most obviously in its dim view of the vast majority of monks.[6] Ariosto embedded a vicious attack on monasteries in one of the poem's most strongly parodic passages, Archangel Michael's descent from heaven (14.76-97).[7] In response to Charlemagne's

---

The Foucault Reader (New York, 1984), p.118; Ascoli, *Bitter Harmonies,* passim; and Jonathan Crewe, *The Trials of Authorship: Anterior Forms and Poetic Reconstruction from Wyatt to Shakespeare* (Berkeley, 1990), p.14, who calls Foucault's stance 'an irrevocable critical advance'.

[5] Carlo Dionisotti, 'Chierci e laici', in *Geografia e storia della letteratura italiana* (Turin, 1967), pp. 47-73, esp. pp. 59-61. Emilio Zanette offers a similarly biographical reading of the anticlericalism of *Satira* 2 as a product of family romance in *Personaggi e momenti nella vita di Ludovico Ariosto* (Naples, 1970), pp. 502-13. I borrow my title from Zanette.

[6] Sorting out the relative weight of poetic tradition and Ariosto's immediate historical moment would go well beyond the scope of this paper, which mainly makes a case for the importance of his poem as an interpretation of some of his circumstances, without denigrating a more 'intertextual' reading. On this score, it may be significant that the *Orlando Innamorato* of Ariosto's immediate predecessor in Ferrara, Matteo Mario Boiardo, contains virtually no anticlericalism. About the only passage concerns an inept friar who rather than trying to rescue Orlando according to his directions, instead tries to prepare him for death (1.6.16-38). Ariosto claimed to be continuing Boiardo's work. Matteo Maria Boiardo, *Orlando Innamorato,* trans. with intro. and notes by Charles Stanley Ross (Berkeley, 1989). Emilio Bigi compares the first of Ariosto's hermits to a Mohammedan *incantatore* in 1.20.1-8 and 22.1-6, but Boiardo never called him a hermit or a friar. Ludovico Ariosto, *Orlando Furioso,* ed. Emilio Bigi (Bologna, 1982), 1, p. 139. I cite Bigi's text throughout.

[7] Echoing Benedetto Croce, Thomas M. Greene argues on the basis of this passage that 'the Christianity of the *Furioso* is not so much disbelieved as made insubstantial', and that Michael's mission represented an 'Olympian toying with a beloved thing'. Founded in part on an intertextual reading of the poem, this judgment seems to me to go too far, once the poem is placed in

apparently heart-felt prayer for help for his forces besieged in Paris, God dispatches Michael both to order Silence to aid the Christian relief force coming from England and also to set Discord to work in the pagan camp. Michael naturally searches for Silence in monasteries of both friars and cloistered monks, 'dove sono i parlari in modo esclusi,/ che 'l Silenzio, ove cantano i salteri,/ ove dormeno, ove hanno la piatanza, e finalmente é scritto in ogni stanza' (14.79; references are to canto and stanza). He also expects to find Peace, Quiet and Charity, but none is any longer in residence, and Piety, Humility, and Love have decamped, too. Astounded, the archangel discovers that Gluttony, Avarice, Wrath, Pride, Envy, Sloth and Cruelty have replaced them.

At least Michael can accomplish one of his missions, since he does meet Discord there, acting as patron saint of lawyers. Thus Michael is spared the trip to her native habitat in Hell among the damned, instead finding her 'in questo nuovo inferno/ (chi 'l crederia?) tra santi ufficii e messe'. Michael, who does not make much of an archangel, thinks this odd *(strano)*, but no more, perhaps thereby strengthening Ariosto's sarcasm at the expense of the monks. When Discord, taking Pride with her, prepares to leave the monastery, she leaves a substitute, Fraud, 'a guerreggiare il loco, fin che tornasse, e a mantenervi il fuoco', while Pride appoints Hypocrisy her *vicaria* and *locum tenens* (18.26–7). But Discord cannot be relied upon; in canto twenty-seven Michael has to go back to the monastery where he finds her enjoying herself during elections as the monks pelt one another with their breviaries. Michael must give her a thorough beating, some of it with a crucifix, before she promises to execute his orders (37–8).[8]

In the course of looking for Silence, Michael takes Discord's advice to question Fraud, who sometimes keeps company with him. When asked how to find Silence, Fraud replies,

> ... Già costui solia
> fra virtudi abitare, e non altrove,
> con Benedetto e con quelli d'Elia
> [i.e., with Benedictines and Carmelites]
> ne le badie, quando erano ancor nuove: ...
> Mancati... quei santi
> che lo solean tener pel camin ritto,

---

immediate context, and, indeed, to resemble the way an inquisitor might have read it. *The Descent from Heaven: a Study in Epic Continuity* (New Haven, 1963), pp. 119–24.

[8] Is this beating an echo of Machiavelli's notorious advice on how to deal with Fortune in *The Prince*, chap. 25? Bigi (2, p. 1150) notes a distinction between Michael's two scenes with Discord. He calls the first a satire on ecclesiastical corruption, and this one a much broader parody of popular preachers who made 'supernatural religion' too concrete.

> dagli onesti costumi ch'avea inanti,
> fece alle sceleraggini tragitto (14.88-9).

Thus Silence moves only in the circles of Treachery, Murder, and forgers, although if Michael is quick enough, he might catch her in the cave of Slumber. The monks have not only failed themselves, but their mission to the world has also broken down.

The point is reinforced a few pages later when Astolfo and his companions temporarily detour into the Holy Land. There

> Purgati de lor colpe a un monasterio
> che dava di sé *odor di buoni esempii,*
> de la passion di Cristo ogni misterio
> contemplando n'andar per tutti i tempii
> ch'or con eterno obbrobrio e vituperio
> agli cristiani usurpano i Mori empii.
> L'Europa é in arme, e di far guerra agogna
> in ogni parte, fuor che ch'ove bisogna (15.99; emphasis added).

The call for a new crusade runs throughout the *Furioso,* and apparently was seriously meant (see below). Its linkage here to observant monasticism in the east, which sets an example to laymen, drives home the failings of western monks.

Yet the *Furioso* does not present monasticism in an unrelievedly evil light. One male monastery apparently serves as an example to the others, and there are two ambiguous references to female convents. The house held up for imitation, Vallombrosa, almost provides the setting for both key actions in the dynastic plot.[9] Ruggiero meant to be baptized and to marry Bradamante there, and thereby found the Este. Vallombrosa is described as 'una badia ricca e bella, né men religiosa, e cortese a chiunque vi venia' (22.36), that is, as both a religious and a chivalric institution. Unfortunately, another romance turning in the plot disrupts Ruggiero's intention. Later, when he does finally come to the point of baptism again, he regrets having been so cavalier the first time around, even if his decision is still heavily utilitarian (41.47; cf. Bigi, 2, 1681 and 1684).

When Orlando attempts to persuade the disconsolate Fiordiligi to leave Brandimarte's tomb, he offers to build her a convent if she wishes to serve God (43.184); under the circumstances, unrelieved by the possibly comic

---

[9] Bigi (1, p. 934n) theorizes that the name Vallombrosa is invented, despite the fame of the monastery; he suggests that it replaced Valspinosa – the house's name in the first two versions of the poem – for reasons of alliteration.

strokes surrounding the death of another woman deprived of her lover, Issabella, this seems to reflect a relatively positive attitude. It may, however, be significant both that Orlando proposes the idea and also that he deems it necessary to create a new house. Earlier, a convent also figures in Issabella's story, when her hermit protector set out to take her to an unnamed nunnery outside Marseilles, which is described in terms similar to those applied to Vallombrosa as full of 'sante donne ... ricchissimo ..., e di edificio bello' (24.92). This well-intended scheme misses fire, but the attitude to the monastery itself again seems positive. It is unfortunate (although perhaps not accidental) that Ariosto did not identify it. It might reinforce the clue provided by Vallombrosa.

Issabella's story offers one instance of the vital roles played by hermits in the *Furioso*. As in the case of the regular clergy, so a superficially ambiguous attitude to hermits, the most irregular kind, runs through the poem. The first two of them, both necromancers, behave very differently toward Angelica, the object of nearly everyone's desires. When she makes her first escape from pursuit, a hermit, 'devoto e venerabile d'aspetto' and 'di conscienza scrupulosa e schiva', assists her by conjuring a demon out of a book to lay a false trail for her pursuers (2.12-15).[10] His double in canto eight also 'aids' Angelica's flight, but via an attempted rape and into the hands of captors who will eventually offer her as a sacrifice to the Orc (and after which Ruggiero will again attempt to rape her). The hermit is explicitly identified as demonic, but 'a lei fingendo divozione quanta avesse mai Paulo o Ilarione', two famous anchorites. He succeeded in consoling Angelica 'con alquante ragion belle e divote' before drugging her to sleep and failing in his assault on her only because of his aged debility (8.44-50, 61). The first of these encounters marks a straight and indispensable romance moment in the plot, the second a 'comic' episode.

A third hermit exercises both plot functions at once, and while apparently good, he is probably meant to appear a ridiculous figure upon reflection. Astolfo, the 'anti-hero', encounters him in Egypt. The hermit's location in one of the homes of anchoritism perhaps reinforces his significance. He warns Astolfo of a terrible giant in his path, and urges him to cross to the other bank of the Nile. Astolfo, who is also a holy fool, refuses, thinking only of the safety of subsequent travelers. Thus fails another romance diversion, within one of the grandest romance diversions in the poem. The valence of the episode comes into question when the hermit, in blessing Astolfo, prays that God send the Archangel Michael to protect him (15.42-8). Michael is an intensely conflicted figure at best, who has so far appeared only by making a

---

[10] Cf. Bigi's note (1, p. 139) on the symbolic value of this hermit and a sketch of similar figures in chivalric literature.

complete mess of God's command to set Discord at work in the pagan camp outside Paris. His protection might not be worth much. Perhaps Astolfo does not need it. The final hermit in this group might again seem to be the first 'good' one. Coming upon a distraught Issabella just after the death of her lover Zerbino, he combines functions much as the last hermit did. He consoles Issabella, albeit disinterestedly, as he talks her out of suicide, and then fosters her escape. Nevertheless, his actions have sufficiently ambiguous results for both Issabella and himself to cast a cloud over his portrayal as a good hermit. His much lengthier introductory description immediately puts distance between him and his brother hermits thus far.

> Il venerabile uom, ch'alta bontade
> avea congiunta a natural prudenzia,
> et era tutto pien di caritade,
> [as the first necromancer had been also]
> di buoni esempi ornato e d'eloquenzia,
> alla giovan dolente persuade
> con ragioni efficaci pazienzia;
> et inanzi le puon, come uno specchio,
> donne del Testamento e nuovo e vecchio.

Unsurprisingly, this paragon proves his worth to be more than verbal by further persuading Issabella 'come non fusse/ alcun, se non in Dio, vero contento' and that she should enter a nunnery. Again distancing himself from the rapist hermit, this one is physically strong enough, despite his age, to help Issabella lug Zerbino's corpse around for days and morally strong enough not to trust himself alone with her. Instead he sets off to take her to a convent outside Marseilles (24.87–93).

So far, so good. Alas, they encounter the archpagan Rodomonte several cantos later. Once more deploying his eloquence to best effect, the hermit provides 'scudo e falda' for Issabella's chastity. Rodomonte for some reason suffers 'con lunga noia quel monaco audace', before seizing him by the hair, spinning him twice around his head, and flinging him into the sea. The narrator professes not to know what became of the hermit, although he notes the possibility that he drowned 'per non saper notare'. The hermit's end is 'comic', but Issabella's is less so. Having failed in her original attempt at suicide, she tricks Rodomonte into chopping her head off, with nearly immediate effect (it manages to call Zerbino's name three times as it rolls downhill: 29.4–27). Thus it seems the hermit's virtue served no higher end than to postpone Issabella's death and ensure his own.

The moral of the story of Ariosto's final hermit is much different. At the climax of the dynastic plot the holiest hermit of all converts Ruggiero,

Ariosto Anticlerical

preparing the way for marrige to Bradamante, which depends on his embracing Christianity. Nevertheless, it is probably not an accident that Ruggiero finds himself subject to the hermit's good offices only *after* a shipwreck led his *conscienza* to fear that Christ was pursuing a vendetta against him. Promising to convert, Ruggiero is miraculously rescued and led, according to God's plan, to meet his hermit on top of a cliff. Ruggiero thus comes to the point of no return without human intervention. His hermit, unlike the others, is 'di molta riverenzia e *d'onor* [the principal chivalric value] degno' (41.47–52; emphasis added). As Ruggiero approaches, the hermit calls out 'Saulo, Saulo ... perché persegui la mia fede?' which the narrator glosses as the Lord's saving intervention with Paul.

Drawing on a complete revelation of Ruggiero which he had received the night before, the hermit faults him for thinking he can escape God (Ruggiero thus becomes Jonah, bizarrely enough) and then consoles him with the parable of the laborers in the vineyard. Once he had instructed Ruggiero in the faith, the hermit told him most of what God had shown him of Ruggiero's future, omitting only the fact that once he had married Bradamante Ruggiero had only seven years to live before dying by treachery (41.52–67). Rather than a duplicitous way to convert Ruggiero, this is probably meant to figure the value of the hermit's prudence. But nothing in the dynastic plot is simple.[11]

Ruggiero's hermit returns two cantos later to heal Oliviero, one of the Christian champions in the three-cornered duel which marks Orlando's reappearance as defender of the church. Once again, the hermit had been forewarned, this time by the saints. Disdaining medicaments, he went into his chapel and prayed for Oliviero's recovery. Once blessed by the hermit, Oliviero's nearly severed foot was, naturally, better than ever. The narrator intrudes to expostulate 'Oh virtù che dà Cristo a chi gli crede!' (43.192) leaving unclear whether this applies to the hermit, Oliviero or both. If to Oliviero, it removes the necessity of even the holy hermit's mediation. Then again, this language closely resembles that applied to Astolfo a few cantos earlier, when his prayer led to the transformation of rocks rolling downhill into enough fully equipped horses to mount 80,102 foot soldiers for his campaign against Biserta (38.33). This is undoubtedly more comic than Oliviero's healing, but humorous or no, Astolfo also needs no human mediation to get his herd. The restoration of Oliviero's foot is not the end of the episode. The wisest of the pagan kings, Sobrino, witnessed the 'miracolo grande et evidente', and asks *'con cor di fede attrito,* d'iniciarsi al nostro sacro rito'

---

[11] Greene, *Descent from Heaven*, p. 123 calls Ruggiero's conversion 'unconvincing', without demonstrating the point. Andrew Fichter, by contrast, hinges his interpretation of the *Furioso* as Christian epic in part on Ruggiero's transformation. Christian epic may also be a little strong – Ariosto was no Marco Girolamo Vida – but Fichter's analysis deserves consideration. *Poets Historical: Dynastic Epic in the Renaissance* (New Haven, 1982), chap. 3, esp. pp. 99–102.

(emphasis added; see below). Once baptized, Sobrino also recovered his health through the hermit's prayer. During the subsequent *agape,* the hermit keeps up his sorely needed catechesis, although he does bow to persuasion and drinks wine and eats meat (43.188-96).

There can be no question about the importance of this explicitly figured love feast, nor of the hermit's domination of it. The proem to the next canto, in which the story continues, hammers home the point.

> Spesso in poveri alberghi e in picciol tetti,
> . . . meglio s'aggiungon d'amicizia i petti,
> che fra ricchezze invidiose et agi
> de le piene d'insidie e di sospetti
> corti regali e splendidi palagi,
> ove la caritade é in tutto estinta,
> né si vede amicizia, se non finta.

Playing a consistent anti-courtier theme, Ariosto highlights the behavior of the 'santo vecchiarel' in tying a permanent 'nodo' of 'amor vero' between Orlando and his companions, most of whom had fought one another at one time or another, 'ch'altri non avria fatto [the *nodo]* in real corte.' This unfeigned male bonding continues through stanza eighteen, and the hermit is called 'prudente', 'santo', 'devoto', 'monaco saggio', and finally Ruggiero's 'mastro santo' in the true faith (44.1-18). Thus this hermit, anyway, transcends the limits and the failings of both religious and political institutions, acting directly under divine guidance.[12]

By comparison with the attention given to monks and hermits, the secular clergy hardly appear in the *Furioso*. Again by comparison to the superficial ambiguity in Ariosto's attitude to regulars and irregulars, the seculars never appear in a flattering pose, with one possible exception. This may not be entirely fair, since in fact most of the secular clergy never come on stage at all, save for one scene. In the funeral of Brandimarte, all the clergy process, both regulars and secular, but it would be difficult to make much of this very bit part (43.175). Instead, only prelates represent the secular clergy, and even that elite group comes down to almost the pope alone, usually Leo X. Very early on there is one harsh attack on courtier prelates when the evil giant Erfilla wears vestments 'di quella sorte ch'i vescovi e i prelati usano in corte', except for their color (7.4). In the first two versions of the *Furioso* the target

---

[12] There is one more holy hermit, with a very minor role. He helps to heal one of Bradamante's wounds by cutting her hair (25.24). That, however, earns him the sobriquet 'servo di Iesù'. Bigi, 1, p. 298n.

of this barb had been even clearer: the *romana corte*.[13] Later, Charlemagne assigns archbishop Turpin of Rheims, wearing full pontificals, to undertake the catechesis of the newly converted Marfisa (38.23). Turpin also joins in the fighting, and the poem quietly mocks his authority as historian throughout, but neither kind of portrait has anticlerical overtones.[14]

The popes, mainly Julius II and Leo X, do not escape so lightly. Julius II comes in for criticism in 40.42 in the midst of an apostrophe to Alfonso d'Este, who, under attack by a 'pontifice irato', refused to surrender his territory as Ludovico il Moro had turned his over to Louis XII, to his cost. Leo X attracts more attention. In canto seventeen a proem on tyranny as God's reward for sin introduces an extended call for a crusade to free Christians from the Turks and Moors. Drawing a contrast with the time when the Franks ruled 'la sacra stanza/ dove in carne abitò Dio onnipotente', the narrator bemoans the fact that now 'i superbi e miseri cristiani,/ con biasmi lor, lasciano [the holy places] in man de' cani.'

> Dove abbassar dovrebbono la lancia
> in augumento de la santa fede,
> tra lor si dan nel petto e ne la pancia
> a destruzion del poco che si crede.
> Voi, gente ispana, e voi, gente di Francia,
> volgete altrove, e voi, Svizzeri, il piede,
> e voi, Tedeschi, a far più degno acquisto;
> che quanto qui cercate é già di Cristo.

Next the kings of France and Spain are upbraided for killing Christians instead of recovering Jerusalem and Constantinople, and so it goes for three more stanzas. Then comes Leo's turn.

> Tu, gran Leone, a cui premon le terga
> de le chiavi del ciel le gravi some,
> non lasciar che nel sonno si sommerga
> Italia, se la man l'hai ne le chiome.
> Tu sei Pastore; e Dio t'ha quella verga
> data a portare, e scelto il fiero nome,

---

[13] Bigi, 1, p. 298n.

[14] In 26.23 he is called 'il buon Turpin, che sa che dice il vero,/ e lascia creder poi quel ch'a l'uom piace', and in 30.49 the narrator comments that 'scrive Turpin, verace in questo loco.' Sexism may be responsible for Marfisa drawing the prelate Turpin, rather than a hermit like the one Ruggiero – who turns out to be her brother – got.

perché tu ruggi, e che le braccia stenda,
si che dai lupi il grege tuo difenda (17.73-9).

The attack on Leo is heightened by the portrait earlier in the same canto of another 'pastor', the monstrous Orco who ravaged Norandino's bridal party (17.32).[15] Machiavelli offered the same advice about Leo's behavior, but more temperately!

Similarly Machiavellian echoes hang over part of the explication of Merlin's allegorical carvings. One depicted a beast with ears of an ass, the head and teeth of a wolf, the claws of a lion and the rest pure fox. He was shown wreaking havoc all over Europe, but he had saved his worst for the court of Rome 'che v'avea uccisi cardinali e papi:/ contaminate avea la bella sede/ di Pietro, e messo scandol ne la fede.' This beast, which turns out to be avarice, is eventually slain by a coalition made up of Francis I, Maximilian, Charles V, Henry VIII, and a 'Leon' with the numeral 'X' on his back (26.31-6). This whole passage, and hence the transparent reference to Leo, is at least ironic, if not more broadly drawn.

This self-subversion of Leo's portrait characterizes most of the *Furioso's* anticlericalism, making it as hard to decipher as the rest of the text. How can Leo be both the lion who helps to kill avarice, and one of its victims? How can he be both shepherd, and the one who yanks Italy by the hair? Ariosto's anticlericalism is undoubtedly complicated, but perhaps not indecipherable. His text offers two clues to his attitude to the clergy, which can then be put into a larger context of a possible set of religious beliefs.

The variegated functions of the hermits suggest one line of analysis. The necromantic hermits were distinguished from one another neither by their place in the plot nor, obviously, by their addiction to necromancy. Predicting the future was not itself objectionable; indeed prophecy is one of the devices which holds the *Furioso's* plot together, and the best of the hermits, Ruggiero's, engages in it at length. Perhaps Ariosto meant to draw a distinction between the black arts and divinely inspired prophecy, even if Ruggiero's hermit says much the same thing as Merlin, one of the two chief prophets and the son of a demon. Instead, their actions lead to the assignment of different values to the two hermits: the first helps Angelica, while the second causes her great harm. The same point clarifies the ambiguity surrounding Issabella's hermit. He may have suggested either the wrong kind of 'holy' action, withdrawal, or perhaps within the wrong kind of monastery, by comparison again to Ruggiero's hermit who pushes him finally into permanent, holy action in the world. There may also be a parallel between Issabella's hermit and Ruggiero's, and Ruggiero's own, gradual education, in

---

[15] I am grateful to Ascoli for pointing out this parallel.

which he fails both the first test after his instruction from Logistilla, and also to carry out his original intention to convert.[16]

It is probably not an accident that Ruggiero's hermit acts outside all the institutions in the poem, whether of chivalry, monasticism, formal religion, or the court. The Christian love he foments can come to fruition, thinks Ariosto, only from a place apart from all of them, through the mediation of a holy hermit in direct contact with God, whose own designs he merely forwards.[17] If this hermit is meant to be taken at face value, then great importance attaches to Ariosto's praise of the monastery of Vallombrosa and of the eastern house in which Astolfo and his companions undergo penance. Vallombrosa, the only monastery named in the poem, was, like most eastern monasteries, as nearly eremitic as a communal institution could be, and like its near neighbor Camaldoli, a place of strict observance. Thus it seems Ariosto put forward an exemplary clerical life, which should hold both for the clergy and the laity.[18] But even this paragon may not be entirely necessary. It must be stressed that God worked Ruggiero's conversion without human assistance, once Ruggiero had repented. Similarly, in at least three places laymen pray, and more or less rapidly have their wishes granted, again without clerical intervention. Two of these prayers may be in part parodic, or at least they occur in the midst of

---

[16] Ascoli treats Ruggiero's education by Logistilla in depth in *Bitter Harmony,* chap. 3, esp. section iii.

[17] Nevertheless, one measure of the distance between Ariosto and Tasso is the much greater importance accorded to Peter the Hermit as a leader of the first crusade in *Gerusalemme liberata*.

[18] It may prove important that Vallombrosa was a historical place and the rest of Ariosto's monasteries probably fictitious, but too little work has yet been done on how Ariosto 'processed' history (at the same time as he may sometimes have attempted to write it) in order to pursue the implications of this distinction. Little is likewise known about Vallombrosa and its congregation in the early sixteenth century. At the close of the previous century it underwent a schism triggered by a new group of 'observant' houses modelling themselves on the reform stemming from the Benedictines of Santa Giustina in Padua. This suggests some measure of laxity in the rest of the order. The abbot elected in that crisis, Biagio Milanesi, was a great patron of culture, which may partly explain Ariosto's interest in the monastery. (Then again, if the observants held some of the same theological views as their Benedictine brothers, that could have been a more important lure for Ariosto, given my suppositions about his religious beliefs. On the traditional but still Pauline theology of Santa Giustina, see Barry Collett, *Italian Benedictine Scholars and the Reformation* [Oxford, 1985].) At the same time, Milanesi in particular and the order as a whole were subjected to an unrelenting Medici vendetta which led finally to Milanesi's deposition and replacement by a Medici outsider who held the generalcy for twenty-five years. Perhaps in an effort to dilute any further interference, the order changed its constitution in 1540 to make the abbot general's term one year only. Caught between the pressures of rigorists within and state-building without, all may not have been quite as the intensely eremitic image of Vallombrosa would seem to say. For a brief sketch of the later history of the order see R. N. Vasaturo, et al., eds. *Vallombrosa nel IX centenario della morte del fondatore Giovanni Gualberto* (Florence, 1973) and D. F. Tarani, *L'ordine vallombrosano* (Florence, 1921), which includes useful lists of abbots general and of houses (for which see also the map in H. Jedin, et al., eds., *Atlas zur Kirchengeschichte* [Freiburg, 1987]). There was none in Ferrara, and not many in the whole of the Val padana.

parodies. When Charlemagne prays for divine assistance in 14.69ff., God responds by sending the bumbling Michael, whose assistance only takes effect fifteen cantos later. We have already noted Astolfo's petition which produced an avalanche of horse-rocks and the language in which it was described. But if the narrator's comment on Astolfo's prayer may parody it and undercut some of the force of Ariosto's later praise in very similar terms for Ruggiero's hermit's prayer for Oliviero's foot, the apparent sincerity of *those* terms might also be turned back onto Astolfo's prayer.

Irony, then. Still, one of these prayers is offered by a layman, one by an irregular cleric. The point that no one other than the individual offering the prayer need have anything to do with it seems to be underlined at the beginning of the siege of Biserta. For the only time in the poem, aside from Charlemagne's prayer

> Come veri cristiani Astolfo e Orlando,
> che senza Dio non vanno a rischio alcuno,
> ne l'esercito fan publico bando,
> che sieno orazion fatte e digiuno; ...
> E così, poi che le astinenzie e i voti
> devotamente celebrati foro,
> parenti, amici, e gli altri insieme noti
> si cominciaro a convitar tra loro,

thus echoing the scene at Ruggiero's hermit's love-feast a little earlier. All this simple, Christian behavior is undertaken at the orders of two laymen. Meanwhile, inside Biserta,

> ... i *sacerdoti santi*
> supplicando col populo dolente,
> battonsi il petto, e con dirotti pianti
> chiamano il lor Macon che nulla sente.
> Quante vigilie, quante offerte, quanti
> doni promessi son privatamente!
> quanto in publico templi, statue, altari,
> memoria eterna de' lor casi amari!
>
> E poi che dal Cadi fu benedetto,
> prese il populo l'arme, e tornò al muro (40.11-14; emphasis added).

Despite (because of?) this massive clerical intervention, Biserta is doomed. The explicit parallel is striking between infidel preparations, dependent on the clergy (including the Imam [Cadi]), and Christian, which make no mention even of their presence.

The clergy, then, aside from the monks of Vallombrosa and the Near East, and a few hermits, have virtually no role in *Orlando Furioso,* and especially not at critical moments.[19] Laymen manage their own religious affairs perfectly capably, with the aid of the odd prophet, even possibly un-Christian ones.[20] These twin emphases on lay control and on prophecy appear to fit Ariosto's poem neatly into the context of the *religione cittadina* of Ferrara. It appears that Ariosto's beliefs especially overlapped with the dukes' commitment to secular control of religious observance.[21] This they maintained in part through patronage of the strictest religious orders, above all Observant Dominicans, the order of Savonarola. Some of his followers, including the native Ferrarese Francesco Silvestri, were active in Ferrara and the ducal court about the time the first edition of the *Furioso* appeared, but I have not yet found any direct links to Ariosto.[22] Unsurprisingly, the dukes and their subjects, together with their near neighbors in Mantua, assigned great importance to prophecy as an alternative, but acceptable, source of religious authority.[23]

These coincidences in turn open the almost unasked question of Ariosto's relation to reform. Although it is much too early for more than preliminary observations, Ariosto's attitudes may have been rooted in a loosely evangelical religion, like that of some of his Venetian contemporaries, the so-called *spirituali,* which would also come to prominence in the Academy of

---

[19] The absence of anticlericalism in the lunar episode (34.68-35.30) poses a large unresolved problem. Ariosto's poem ironizes virtually every other dimension of human and divine existence in this extended tale. See David Quint, *Origin and Originality in Renaissance Literature: Versions of the Source* (New Haven, 1983), pp. 81-92 and Ascoli, *Bitter Harmony,* pp. 285-304.

[20] Ariosto's ideas about secular supremacy probably have something to do with his complicated attitude to the Empire, on which see most recently Alberto Casadei, *La strategia delle varianti. Le correzioni storiche del terzo 'Furioso'* (Lucca, 1988).

[21] Adriano Prosperi, 'Le istituzioni ecclesiastiche e ie idee religiose', in *Il Rinascimento nelle corti padane* (Bari, 1977), pp.125-163, esp. p.128 where Prosperi cites one of Ariosto's letters as evidence that he was a 'fedele interprete' of the duke's ideology of temporal superiority. Cf. the conclusion of the essay (p. 162) where Prosperi provides evidence against Dionisotti's claim for Ariosto's biographically rooted 'suspension' - his descendants deployed exactly the same strategy on the score of benefices in the 1590s as Ariosto did in the 1510s and 1520s.

[22] After having been prior at Mantua in 1513 and at Ferrara in 1516, Silvestri rose to become general of the Dominicans a decade later. Gabriella Zarri, 'Pieta e profezia alle corti padane: le pie consigliere dei principi', in *Corti padane,* pp. 201-37, 223ff. and note 69 for other Savonarolans active in the area. For Savonarola's own prophecies and their survival after his death see Donald Weinstein, *Savonarola and Florence: Prophecy and Patriotism in the Renaissance* (Princeton, 1970), especially chap. 10.

[23] Zarri, passim; for the situation at the eastern end of the Val padana in Venice at roughly the same time, see most recently Bernard McGinn, 'Circoli gioachimiti veneziani (1450-1530)', trans. R. Rusconi, *Cristianesimo nella storia* 7 (1986): pp. 19-39.

Modena in the decade after Ariosto's death.[24] Perhaps Ariosto found in Pietro Bembo, now thought to have been a key *spirituale* from early on, more than a neo-platonic target, a linguistic model, and a close friend.[25] Marcantonio Flaminio, one of the authors of *Il Beneficio di Cristo* and a major force in Valdesian spirituality later, joined Bembo among those welcoming Ariosto's ship to shore near the end of the *Furioso* (46.13-15).[26] It may then not be irrelevant that one of Bembo's Paduan friends, Marco Mantova, combined anticlericalism and resistance to hierocratic pretensions with fideism.[27] Finally, there may be an analogue to the appeal of Camaldoli to Venetians in Ariosto's praise for Vallombrosa, but its links to Ferrara remain to be uncovered.[28]

In addition to these contextual hints, Ariosto's text could support this theory, especially in its constant references to *fede* (as in Sobrino's conversion), *benefizio,* and grace, sometimes explicitly contrasted with merit, as in Drusilla's defiant death in 37.73-4, as well as the poem's denigrating of clerical mediation in salvation. Perhaps most suggestive, Ariosto paralleled Ruggiero's conversion to that of Paul, a primary inspiration behind the highly amorphous *spirituali*. It also seems likely that the *Furioso* contains a good dose of Erasmus, who likewise made Paul one of his principal champions.[29]

Generalizations from one case have little value, but the popularity of the *Furioso* in the sixteenth century make it worth comparing its attitudes to one of the most important recent analyses of anticlericalism. The *Furioso* fits only some of R. W. Scribner's six categories of anticlericalism.[30] Its political

---

[24] There is now a large literature on the Academy of Modena, much of it the work of Massimo Firpo. See esp. 'Gli 'spirituali', l'Accademia di Modena e il formulario di fede del 1542: controllo del dissenso religioso e nicodemismo', *Rivista di storia e letteratura religiosa* 20 (1984): pp. 40-111. Cf. Albano Biondi, 'Streghe ed eretici nei domini estensi all'epoca dell'Ariosto', *Corti padane,* pp. 165-99, esp. pp. 183ff., which also contains a good deal of material on popular anticlericalism.

[25] Ascoli, *Bitter Harmony,* pp. 89, 99, 111-13, 116, 222-3, and Paolo Simoncelli, 'Pietro Bembo e l'evangelismo italiano', *Critica storica* 15 (1978): pp. 1-63.

[26] Massimo Firpo, 'Valdesianesimo ed evangelismo: alle origini dell' "Ecclesia Viterbense"', in *Libri, idee e sentimenti religiosi nel Cinquecento italiano* (Modena, 1987), pp. 53-71, and in Massimo Firpo, *Tra alumbrados e 'spirituali:' studi su Juan de Valdís e il valdesianesimo nella crisi religiosa del '500 italiano* (Florence, 1990), pp. 155-84, and passim for Flaminio.

[27] Thomas F. Mayer, 'Marco Mantova and the Paduan Religious Crisis of the Early Sixteenth Century', *Cristianesimo nella storia* 7 (1986): pp. 41-61 [this volume, no. IX].

[28] See esp. James Bruce Ross, 'Gasparo Contarini and his Friends', *Studies in the Renaissance* 17 (1970): pp. 192-232; Felix Gilbert, 'Religion and Politics in the Thought of Gasparo Contarini', in T. K. Rabb and J. E. Seigel, eds., *Action and Conviction in Early Modern Europe* (Princeton, 1969), pp. 90-116 (also in *History: Choice and Commitment* [Cambridge, Mass., 1977], pp. 247-67); and Giuseppe Alberigo, 'Vita attiva e vita contemplativa in un'esperienza cristiana del XVI secolo', *Studi veneziani* 16 (1974): pp. 177-225.

[29] Ascoli, *Bitter Harmony,* passim, esp. pp. 335-6.

[30] R.W. Scribner,'Anticlericalism and the Reformation in Germany', in *Popular Culture and Popular Movements in Reformation Germany* (London, 1987), p. 243.

dimension shows clearly, especially in attacks on Leo X and on courtier prelates, as it does in the poem's nearly direct support for lay control of religious observance. The stronger form of personal responsibility for salvation brings the *Furioso*'s attitudes under the head of sacred anticlericalism, although without reference to the economic dimension of clerical monopoly of sacred power. Similarly, anticlericalism's sexual aspect recurs, as in the attempted rape of Angelica set against the self-control of Issabella's hermit. Making Discord both chief denizen of monasteries and also patron of lawyers takes aim at the monks' legal authority. Yet the social side of anticlericalism and most of its economic overtones are almost entirely absent. That may well be traced both to Ariosto's own ambiguous position 'fra laicato e stato ecclesiastico', and to his dependence on income from his benefices until very late in his life. Thus the *Furioso*'s irony may have served to protect Ariosto from its own unmasking which could have threatened his hard-won position. Nevertheless, the *Satire* depicts Ariosto as a 'chierico anticlericale'; his greatest poem, perhaps not by chance, displays a narrator and characters who hold very similar opinions.

XI

A Fate Worse than Death: Reginald Pole and the Parisian Theologians

IN his recent *Il caso Reginald Pole*, Paolo Simoncelli expressed scepticism about historians' ability to penetrate the 'myth of sanctity' which shrouds his subject.[1] Simoncelli had good reason for concern, especially because Pole himself contributed heavily to the shaping of subsequent accounts. Confessionally motivated historians compounded the problem by taking Pole's stories at face value and treating his life as a *tabula rasa* for the free play of their passions. By following the well-worn channels of earlier scholarship, more modern studies have largely failed to alleviate these difficulties. The balance is beginning to swing against the naive acceptance of Pole's stories, but no one has examined the discrepancies in them in detail nor tried to explain what Pole was up to when he constructed these narratives.[2] Consequently, few new sources have come into play and little historical criticism has been applied to better-known material. Only Paul Van Dyke, W. Gordon Zeeveld and G. R. Elton have adopted rigorous standards in their treatment of a few episodes in Pole's career.[3]

The difficulty of decoding Pole's narratives shows up clearly in the case of his 1529–30 mission to the theologians of the University of Paris. Nearly forty years ago Zeeveld pointed to the difference between Pole's contemporary accounts and what Zeeveld called his later 'ration-

---

1. Paolo Simoncelli, *Il caso Reginald Pole. Eresia e santità nelle polemiche religiose del Cinquecento* (Rome, 1977), p. 241. My thanks to G. R. Elton, A. J. Slavin (in particular) and Lynn Zastoupil for their helpful comments, and to Brendan Bradshaw for an enthusiastic dissent. Unless otherwise noted, all translations are my own.

2. Ludwig von Pastor first read Pole's mission carefully, but in passing, in *The History of the Popes from the Close of the Middle Ages* (3rd edn., trans. R. F. Kerr, St. Louis, 1950), xi. 163. Until recently only a few historians followed Pastor's lead, especially J. K. McConica, *English Humanists and Reformation Politics under Henry VIII and Edward VI* (Oxford, 1965), p. 106. The momentum has built of late, including Peter S. Donaldson, 'Machiavelli, Antichrist, and the Reformation: Prophetic Typology in Reginald Pole's *De Unitate* and *Apologia ad Carolum Quintum*', in Richard L. DeMolen (ed.), *Leaders of the Reformation* (Selinsgrove, 1984), p. 213; J.-P. Moreau, *Rome ou l'Angleterre? Les réactions politiques des catholiques anglais au moment du schisme (1529–1553)* (Paris, 1984), p. 251; Jasper Ridley, *Henry VIII* (New York, 1985), p. 282; and Maria Dowling, *Humanism in the Age of Henry VIII* (London, 1986), pp. 51–2 (with doubtful chronology). J. A. Guy, by contrast, took Pole at his word, at least on the score of reluctance: *The Public Career of Sir Thomas More* (New Haven, 1980), p. 178.

3. Paul Van Dyke, 'Reginald Pole and Thomas Cromwell: An Examination of the *Apologia ad Carolum Quintum*', *American Historical Review*, ix (1904), 696–724; G. R. Elton, *The Tudor Revolution in Government: Administrative Changes in the Reign of Henry VIII* (Cambridge, 1953), pp. 7, 73–4, and 'The Political Creed of Thomas Cromwell', in *Studies in Tudor and Stuart Politics and Government*, ii. *Parliament/Political Thought* (Cambridge, 1974), pp. 217–220; and W. Gordon Zeeveld, *Foundations of Tudor Policy* (Cambridge, Mass., 1948), pp. 66–71. J. A. Froude in *History of England from the Fall of Wolsey to the Defeat of the Spanish Armada* (London, 1872–75), iii. 29 hinted at worse than inaccuracy, and T. F. Dunn, 'Cardinal Pole and Codex Vaticanus Latinus 5970', *Manuscripta*, xxii (1978), 82, warned that Pole's memory could not be trusted.

alization'.[1] Zeeveld was right. Ordinary historical criticism reveals manifest inconsistencies in Pole's versions of his behaviour and motives, which some fresh evidence reinforces. Zeeveld erred only in stopping short in an inquiry which was a bit beside his main point. Thus the historical object 'what Pole did in Paris' needs reconstitution, and that is this paper's principal goal. But the no less historical *datum* 'what Pole said he did, to whom, when, and for what reasons' must be held in tension with it. Attention to 'what Pole did' would serve only to convict him of mendacity, while the traditional focus on 'what Pole said he did' distorts the history of events around him over which he tried to exercise retrospective control. The problem is how to understand Pole's perspective without allowing it to determine everything else we see. Historians cannot implicitly continue to follow Marie Hallé's critical rule of thumb, that if Pole had not told the literal truth from *Pro ecclesiasticae unitatis defensione* (*De unitate*; 1536) forward, 'Pole would have to be given up as a reliable authority on any subject, at any time'.[2]

Alas, the study of sixteenth-century psychology – especially of individuals – has not advanced much since Lucien Febvre's numerous broadsides recommending it as a legitimate field to explore.[3] The tendency instead has been to import modern psychological theories which may or may not apply. For example, current work on cognitive biases (the nearly inescapable shackles on 'rational' thinking) seems to offer powerful insight into how and why Pole created a self at variance with his earlier actions, but the very notion of a self may well prove problematic in the case of a Renaissance man like Pole.[4] However deadly in earnest Pole may have been, his training prepared him much better for that humanist play with language which negated the seriousness of a central self.[5] No self, no ego; no ego biases, no field for cross-temporal and cross-cultural psychology. On the other hand, if we look not for selves, but for *personae* in nearly the original Greek sense of masks we may come closer to understanding Pole's actions. Peter S. Donaldson has demonstrated the utility of such an approach by delineating how Pole took on a prophetic role when uttering *De unitate*'s grim threats against Henry.[6] Elements of this rhetorical pose and no doubt others crop up in Pole's recounting of his Parisian mission. Yet a third line of

1. Zeeveld, *Foundations*, p. 66.
2. Marie Hallé [Martin Haile], *Life of Reginald Pole* (London, 1911), p. 72. Athanasius Zimmermann, *Kardinal Pole, sein Leben und seine Schriften. Ein Beitrag zur Kirchengeschichte des 16. Jahrhunderts* (Regensburg, 1893), p. 36, and Philip Hughes, *The Reformation in England*, i. 'The King's Proceedings' (London, 1950), p. 158 adopted similarly sweeping approaches.
3. See, for example, the first two essays in Peter Burke (ed.), *A New Kind of History: From the Writings of Lucien Febvre*, trans. K. Folca (New York, 1973).
4. Anthony G. Greenwald, 'The Totalitarian Ego: Fabrication and Revision of Personal History', *American Psychologist*, xxxv (1980), 603–18.
5. Richard A. Lanham, *The Motives of Eloquence: Literary Rhetoric in the Renaissance* (New Haven, 1976).
6. Donaldson, 'Prophetic Typology', *passim*.

analysis may contribute to explaining his stories. Humanists felt a profound ambivalence about entering public service, as they should have done to fulfil the dictates of the *vita activa*. Henry VIII seems to have inspired more than his share of hesitation in his servants, as the well-known case of Thomas More illustrates. The same phenomenon ran through many of the king's other subjects, including Pole and most members of his circle, among them Thomas Lupset and George Lily. While playing a big part in Paris, Lupset also wrote a lost treatise arguing that a drinking bout in the royal palace was an improper venue for discussing religion.[1] While Lily at one time hoped to see England become a second Rome under Henry's leadership, he followed Pole into exile.[2] Much as his clients did, Pole could at one point bring himself to serve Henry, only to discover later that his attitude had hardened and ambivalence become opposition. Thereafter literal truth to life fell a casualty to the conversion of Pole's early guarded acceptance into open denigration of his erstwhile patron. It is not difficult to understand how Pole might have edited his life in order to remove most of the ambivalence, leaving him instead with no more than the reservations, albeit much more strongly phrased as a result. One end of an original spectrum wound up attracting all the events stretched between it and its opposite. Doubleness of the sort Sir Thomas Wyatt felt dissolved into hostility.

Pole thus ultimately broke down the dialectical tension between engagement and detachment which Stephen Greenblatt posits as a major element in what he calls Renaissance self-fashioning.[3] Some of Greenblatt's theory also relies on modern psychological categories, but his results provide some validation for their adoption. Of greater importance here and of greater reliability, Greenblatt attempts to explain the complex relations between literature and life which led some men to an 'increased self-consciousness about the fashioning of human identity as a manipulable, artful process'.[4] Greenblatt identifies the sixteenth century as a period of 'resolutely dialectical' change in the 'structures that govern the generation of identities', leading to a profound sense of displacement 'from a stable, inherited social world'.[5] Greenblatt's ultimate aim at a 'poetics of culture' goes far beyond the scope of this paper, but his more particular goal of mapping the interrelations between the 'symbolic structures' of texts and those in the careers of their authors describes my object exactly. In other words, Greenblatt's

---

1. J. A. Gee, *The Life and Works of Thomas Lupset* (New Haven, 1928), pp. 172–3.
2. Lily to Thomas Starkey, B[ritish] L[ibrary] Nero B vi, fo. 165r, 22 Apr. 1535 (*L[etters and] P[apers Foreign and Domestic of the Reign of Henry VIII]*, ed. J. S. Brewer, J. Gairdner and R. H. Brodie (London, 1862–1932), viii. no. 581). For Lily's career, see Edward L. Hirsh, 'The Life and Works of George Lily', (Yale University PhD. thesis, 1935).
3. Stephen Greenblatt, *Renaissance Self-Fashioning, from More to Shakespeare* (Chicago, 1980), pp. 22, 46.
4. *Ibid.*, p. 2.
5. *Ibid.*, p. 8.

interest in the impact of power on the '"I" in meaning, characteristic modes of expression, [and] recurrent narrative patterns' agrees exactly with my approach to Pole.[1]

Greenblatt develops a set of criteria which both explain how self-fashioning arose and help to delineate its modes. Most of Greenblatt's points shed light on the intentions embedded in Pole's texts, if not yet on the motives beneath them. So far as possible, I will follow Greenblatt as a guide to Pole's overt, literary behaviour, leaving the inner workings of his psyche on one side, in common with Quentin Skinner's insistence that intellectual historians leave motive out of consideration.[2] Nevertheless, Greenblatt's basic point about the source of self-fashioning is sufficiently compelling (and sufficiently safe) to adduce here. Above all, he argues, the phenomenon was a function of mobility.[3] None of his subjects inherited a status which would allow him to root his identity in a 'caste'.[4] At first glance, Pole does not fit this stipulation, but, in fact, he may have felt the problem of rootlessness with particular acuity, since his superficially rightful position depended entirely on Henry's favour. The grandson of the Duke of Clarence did not take warmly to such an irregular status.[5] Greenblatt's second factor describes Pole's circumstances perfectly. Pole most certainly fashioned his *persona* under the pressure of a double relation of 'submission to an absolute power or authority' and opposition 'to something perceived as alien, strange, or hostile'. The pope was the first and Henry the second, the one a distorted image of the other. Any self-fashioning necessarily operated in connection with a 'threatening other' which had to be discovered and destroyed. Likewise, Pole fits Greenblatt's requirement that there be more than one alien and more than one authority at a time. In addition to the pope, Pole repeatedly appealed to the emperor for help against Henry, or to any other secular prince he thought might render aid. Similarly, as *De unitate* makes plain, Pole assigned Henry a whole cast of more or less demonic assistants. Greenblatt's final two points fit Pole perhaps best of all and most help to explain his behaviour. Not only did he fashion his self almost entirely through language, but he also went to such excessive lengths in attacking the alien Henry that he assuredly threatened the authority of the pope and (by encouraging popular rebellion) of the emperor in the eyes of many of his potential supporters, and therefore

1. *Ibid.*, p. 4.
2. Quentin Skinner, '"Social meaning" and the explanation of social action', in P. Laslett, W. G. Runciman and Q. Skinner (eds.), *Philosophy, politics and society*, ser. iv (Oxford, 1972), 144–47.
3. Greenblatt, *Self-fashioning*, p. 1.
4. *Ibid.*, p. 9.
5. Pole's aristocratic pride is clear from at least *De unitate*, in which he stressed his Plantagenet descent and accused Henry of plotting to dispose of the nobility, which the king held in contempt. T. F. Dunn, 'The Development of the Text of Pole's *De Unitate Ecclesiae*', *Papers of the Bibliographical Society of America*, lxx (1976), 463; and Reginald Pole, *Ad Henricum octavum Britanniae regem, pro ecclesiasticae unitatis defensione* (Rome, 1539), fos. lxxxir, lxxxiiir.

put his own *persona* at risk as well. In short, Pole's self was a dearly won creation, its standing always precarious. Hence his eagerness to affirm it over and over again in writing, in an attempt to convince himself of its reality.

Pole set down his Parisian activities in five different forms, before he settled on the version he gave his two contemporary biographers, Ludovico Beccadelli and Andras Dudith. We can chart the accelerating pace of Pole's loss of innocence in these texts. Pride of place belongs to the famous tale in *De unitate*, not so much because it came first as because most students follow this version. Writing in late 1535 and early 1536, Pole recounted how he could

> remember nothing ever in my life more bitter to have befallen me than that famous legation entrusted to me (then being in Paris) by your order, especially since I had gone there advisedly in order that I should not for any reason be a partaker of their counsels, which were then being stirred up in your house against you yourself.... At which time I certainly remember, having been grieved by that unexpected message, as soon as I could (for at that time grief robbed me not only of my voice, but almost even of thought) I replied to you to excuse my inexperience, and to ask you to send someone more exercised in that sort of thing. That you immediately did, and if you had not, assuredly any sort of death would have been easier for me than that office. That office, plainly, I never accepted, although I suffered the part to be played by me for that occasion, provided that another was present to whom you had committed that whole business in which I had said I was inexpert. And I was plainly most inexpert. Not indeed that I did not know the equity of the case, but the more I did know it, the less apt I knew myself to the doing of the thing according to your will.[1]

Pole partly reversed himself in his next version, a letter to the king's Council dated 16 February 1537. He did not refer directly to Paris, but instead he introduced the story of his interview with Henry later in 1530 in order to illustrate the depth of his love for the king. In so doing Pole admitted that 'I shall somwhat declare myn owne vyleness off mynde wythall', but he also cast some oblique light on his earlier attitudes.

> [W]hen I sawe/and my frendes sawe the same/ thatt there was butt one gate open to entre in to the kyngis favor/ att thatt tyme which was by favoreng the mattier off dyvorse/ albeit my conscyence could never perfettlye agree to the same/yett nott wythstondyng so called apon [by] my frendes wythe so meny persuasions showeng whatt occasyon thys was to avaunce my selffe yn all honour/to the greate furtheraunce off all my frendes/ thatt suerlye I could nott butt enclyne thereto.

Pole's friends, too, expressed reservations about the divorce, but assured him that he could best serve God and country by joining in Henry's suit. Pole gave in. 'I suffred my selffe so to be per[suad]yd

---
1. *De unitate*, fos. lxxviiiv-lxxixr.

thatt I remember I sayd then to doctour [fo]x/ whiche had bene wythe me for the kyngis mattier/ thatt I truste I had founde awaye to satysfye hys grace'.¹

A few years later, Pole elaborated on his motive for going to Paris. As he explained to Charles V, fear of the Machiavellian Thomas Cromwell had driven him. Cromwell approached Pole soon after Pole's return from Italy (perhaps in 1528) and asked for his opinion about the issues dividing the Council. A short time after their conversation, the problem of divided counsels became more acute; Henry abandoned the advisers who would not support the divorce and those who had originally proposed it began to waver. Cromwell seized the opening this situation offered, and thereafter Henry came to rely on his 'insane prudence, which feared neither God nor man'. At that point Pole remembered Cromwell's recommendation of *The Prince* and took it as 'an admoniser that I flee the cruel land, which the goodness of God has fled (as I later interpreted it)'.²

The whole event became yet more dramatic perhaps eight or nine years later. In a letter to King Edward, Pole pointed to the divorce as 'fons et origo' of all the 'tempests' threatening the realm. Instead of simply 'fleeing from the face of the bow' as he had put it in 1539, now Pole described himself as behaving shortly after his return from Italy as 'beasts wandering in an open field are wont to do when they are faced with an approaching storm – they take themselves into a wood or some cave'. He therefore had begged Henry to allow him to go to Paris to study theology. This was partly a ruse 'by which he should more easily dismiss me'. Pole stuck to his meteorological metaphor, continuing 'and so immediately I left, hoping to find myself a place where no part of the approaching storm should touch me'. This letter also established the final version of what Pole did in Paris after receiving Henry's mandate to treat with the theologians, that is, as little as possible.

> Here I do not say how I avoided the tempest overwhelming me. Much would be said beside the present point. What I have just said will be enough for you to understand that as much care as human advice could provide was not lacking in order that I not be called to the side of his cause. I was thrown into greater danger, whence I would never have come out sound, had I not been rescued by a certain goodness of God.³

Beccadelli and Dudith preserve many of the elements of Pole's own tales, which they probably had directly from him. Although Pole cannot therefore be held accountable for their works, they nevertheless

---

1. P[ublic] R[ecord] O[ffice], State Papers of the Reign of Henry VIII (SP) 1/116, fo. 57r-v.
2. Reginald Pole, 'Apologia ad Carolum Quintum', in A. M. Quirini (ed.), *Epistolarum Reginaldi Poli* (Brescia, 1744–57), i. 136.
3. 'Epistola ad Edouardum regem', in *Epistolarum*, iv. 313 and 'Apologia', p. 136 for the bow analogy.

XI

form part of the same corpus of evidence.[1] Both credited Pole with sufficient foresight to apprehend the coming tempests or calamities in England, and therefore plan an escape under pretext of studying in Paris. Both had Pole ask Henry and his mother for permission to go, but Beccadelli added that Pole went 'con bona gratia sua [Henry's]'. After Pole reached Paris, Henry wrote to him to include him in the general design of securing university opinions on the divorce. This shook Pole, who had thought to find a safe harbour in Paris, but he merely disabled himself as inexperienced and asked for someone more practised to handle the negotiations. Henry acceded to Pole's request and sent a member of his Council whom Pole graciously lodged and to whom he left the care of the whole business. Thus with Beccadelli and Dudith we come full circle. Their stories coalesce almost exactly with *De unitate*. By 1547 or so Pole had settled on the version he wished to pass on to posterity.

Later biographers have treated these accounts as a seamless web corresponding point to point with what happened, and have further bolstered the stories' reliability by claiming that the recipients of all but the last two knew the facts of the case and could easily have caught Pole in any lie.[2] The latter assertion is easier to dispose of. No one in a position to judge ever read any of Pole's stories about Paris. The passage in *De unitate* never arrived in England, because Pole took Cardinal Contarini's advice and cut it from the manuscript he sent the king. Neither Henry nor the various committees which actually read the work could have assessed that tale. This is particularly important. Thomas Starkey had been with Pole in Paris and figured prominently in two of these *ad hoc* bodies.[3] The printed editions of *De unitate*, which all scholars have cited, preserve the complete text. There is no reason to think that Pole dispatched the letter to Edward, nor did it appear in any edition of *De unitate* for which it may have been meant as a preface. The only extant copy came from the archive of Pole's friend Stanislaus Cardinal Hosius.[4]

Pole's last two versions may well have reached their intended destinations, but in one case the arrival imports little, and in the other casts

---

1. Ludovico Beccadelli, *Vita del cardinale Reginaldo Polo*, and Andras Dudith, *Vita Reginaldi Poli S. R. E. cardinalis*, in *Epistolarum*, v. 360-1 and i. 7-8. A cricital edition of these texts is badly needed. Beccadelli wrote his life in 1561, and Dudith translated and adapted it the following year at the Council of Trent. Ludovico Beccadelli, *Monumenti di varia letteratura*, ed. G. B. Morandi (Bologna, 1797-1804), i (ii). 272 and Gigliola Fragnito, 'Gli "spirituali" e la fuga di Bernardino Ochino', *Rivista storica italiana*, lxxxiv (1972), 803n.

2. Hallé, *Pole*, p. 72 and Wilhelm Schenk, *Reginald Pole, Cardinal of England* (London, 1950), pp. 25, 31.

3. Dunn, '*De Unitate*', 463 for Contarini's intervention. Dunn, 'Pole and Vat. lat. 5970', 80 says flatly that Henry never read the work. For Starkey and the rest of these committees, see T. F. Mayer, *Thomas Starkey and the Commonweal: Humanist Politics and Religion in the Reign of Henry VIII* (forthcoming, Cambridge University Press), ch. vii.

4. *Epistolarum*, i. 257. Even Hallé admitted that it was 'doubtful' that the letter reached the king: *Life*, p. 344.

a revealing light on Pole's purposes. Charles V could have had little detailed knowledge of the events in Paris. Nor would the emperor have had any motive for testing Pole's accuracy. Finally, there is the letter to the Council. This rates as one of the most popular documents involved. Three copies exist, one in English and one in Latin in the Public Record Office and yet another in Latin in the Biblioteca Apostolica Vaticana.[1] Neither of the PRO versions is autograph, although the English is more likely the original. It bears Pole's signature, while the Latin trails off with 'Valete'. The Latin very nearly translates the English and differs only in some small particulars from both the Vatican copy and Angelo Quirini's printed edition. Pole's standard practice explains the multiple copies. He always sent duplicates of all letters to England which passed through France, lest he lose touch because of war or the actions of English spies.[2] This particular letter went via the hands of a papal secretary to the nuncio in Paris, who was to send it to England either by the English ambassadors in France or the French envoys in England.[3] But Pole may have aimed the letter at a wider public than the Council. Perhaps he referred to it when he instructed the nuncio to pass a copy of his letter to the Council to the English ambassadors in Paris for their own information.[4] This letter's wide circulation may help to explain the workings of Pole's memory. When writing to the Council, which then included Edward Foxe and the Duke of Norfolk, either of whom could have vetted his testimony, Pole admitted his ambition and desire to satisfy Henry. But Pole told the much more restricted audience of Henry and the emperor a considerably less literal story, expecting that neither could test his assertions. He insisted repeatedly that he had written *De unitate* for Henry's eyes alone.[5] This is not to convict Pole of lying, but to suggest how he may have both edited his memory and taken on a suitable *persona* depending upon his rhetorical purposes.

Other contemporary evidence and a connected narrative of events in Paris show that not even the letter to the Council accords strictly with Pole's certain or probable actions. Four letters – two from Pole, one to him and another to the Earl of Wiltshire – constitute the standard corpus of evidence since Hallé originally assembled it in 1911. All four tear holes in Pole's account, despite difficulties in interpreting them. An undated letter ostensibly written at Norfolk's direction told Pole that he was to be 'heartily congratulated' for his effort in the

---

1. The eighteenth-century copy in the Vatican was perhaps Quirini's text. Most of the differences between printed edition and MS. (e.g. *pejus* for *prius*) could have been compositors' errors. *Epistolarum*, i. 179–87 and Biblioteca Apostolica Vaticana, Vaticanus latinus 12909, fos. 143r–57r.
2. *LP*, xii (i). no. 1243.
3. Vat. lat. 12909, fo. 141v, Pole to Rodolfo Pio, Rome, 2 Feb. 1537.
4. *LP*, xii (i). no. 705, Pio-Ambrogio Ricalcati, 23 Mar. 1537.
5. Beginning with Edmund Harvel's assurance to Starkey in 1535 that Pole 'keepith it [*De unitate*] secret to himselff for after him he wold the king scholdbe first reader of his worke'. BL Nero B vi, fo. 139r (*LP*, ix. no. 1029).

king's cause, the more so 'because it [his "duty"] was done unasked by the king's command'. The anonymous amanuensis reported having heard Henry exult that Pole had become 'a patron of his cause'.[1] If we knew who wrote this letter and whether he sent it, it would give the lie to Pole's repeated claim that the legation had been thrust on him. Since we do not, Hallé may well be right that it was a 'figment' designed to convince a third party of the addressee's good intentions.[2] Lack of date again hampers the use of the letter to Wiltshire. Its purport is clear. Henry ordered Wiltshire to deliver his letters to the theological faculty if it appeared to him and 'D. consanguinei nostri [Pole]' that they already had a majority and the letters would therefore seal the case.[3] Hallé assigned this document to the denouement of the affair after Wiltshire returned to Paris in 1530 but before Foxe arrived. Consequently Henry had no choice but to bring Pole into action. This is plausible, but the prominent role Pole played earlier makes it unlikely.

One defect or another reduces the value of these first two letters. Pole's own missives of 13 May and 7 July suffer from no such handicaps. Both magnified Pole's own role. His first progress report emphasized that 'monser de langey' had assured Pole that King Francis's letters to the faculty were 'as effectually wryten as could be desyred for your grace [sic] purpose'. Pole also underlined his concern about the course of events. The English ambassador reported to him and kept him steadily informed. He had promised Pole that other letters would arrive shortly, and when they did not Pole carefully repeated how that worried him. He pointed out 'what dowht both monser de langes & I wer [in] bycause the letters dyd not appere', as he had already written Henry in a now lost letter.[4] To put it bluntly, this letter recorded Pole's intimate involvement. His second runs even more strongly against his later interpretations. Hallé struggled to explain it away, but the letter has received too little attention since. It provides incontrovertible proof of Pole's activity and (as has been previously overlooked) his desire to gain credit for the whole business. Pole reported to Henry that a successful end to the negotiations was at hand, but the sealing of the theologians' opinion had been delayed, despite all 'solycytyng of our parte that were your agentes here/ which never ceasyd to labour all that laye yn us for the expedytion of yt bothe wythe the primeyr

---

[1]. BL Vitellius V xiv, fo. 279r. Nicholas Pocock worked over all the phrases quoted, but his suggestions seem plausible: *Records of the Reformation. The Divorce, 1527–1533* (Oxford, 1870), ii. appendix no. 21 (*LP*, iv (iii). no. 6252).

[2]. Hallé, *Life*, p. 20. The author must have known Pole. He called the invitation to write 'gratissima', and the next, mutilated, passage begins 'tuam amicitiam'.

[3]. Vit. B xiv, fo. 278r (Pocock, *Records*, ii. appendix no. 22 [*LP*, iv (iii). no. 6253]). Pocock did a good deal of reconstruction of this burned document, some of it highly doubtful, as the editors of *LP* pointed out. In particular, Pocock read the magiscule 'D' in a phrase near its end as an 'F', and took it to begin Francis Bryan, but the 'D' was more likely the initial letter of *Dominus*, which therefore referred to the person already given that title, Pole.

[4]. SP 1/57, fo. 99r (*LP*, iv [iii]. no. 6383).

president and wyth all suche as we thougth [sic] myght in ony parte furdre or ayde us thereyn'. Quite aside from emphasizing his own efforts, Pole used language in praising Foxe which sounds nothing like an attempt to blame everything on him. Instead, Pole tried to extract benefit for himself from Foxe's work. As he wrote the king,

> Mr fox who wythe his prudence, dylygence, and greate exercyse in the cause hathe most holpe to resyst all these craftes and inventions of the adversaryes and to bryng it to that poynt as your most desyred purpose hathe bene to have ytt, and most acordyng to the hope that I had of hym at the begynnyng and furst brekyng of the mattier amongst the facultye here, when I somewhat fearyng and forseyng suche contentions altercations and empechmentes as bye most lykelode myght ensue dyd gyve your Grace advertysement how necessarye I thought yt was of mr fox [sic] presence.[1]

While this report parallels that in *De unitate*, all the subtle differences run contrary to the latter's thrust. Here Pole extolled Foxe in more than conventional terms, pointed out the 'hope' he had of the new envoy's success from the start, and emphasized again that it had been his idea to have Foxe sent in the first place. Rather than disqualify himself, Pole intensified the difficulties he and Foxe faced in order to derive maximum benefit from their success.[2]

Pole probably did not exaggerate his role here any more than his joint action with Wiltshire probably sprang from necessity, as Hallé thought. The rather thin and difficult documentary corpus presented thus far needs the more complete context provided by a reconstruction of the complex diplomatic manoeuvrings between England and France over Henry's divorce and the ransom of Francis's sons. Although some of this story cannot avoid speculation and such circumstantial evidence cannot say much about Pole's attitude, it nevertheless underscores his active role. English representation both to the University of Paris and to Francis changed constantly. Pole alone remained at his station throughout. Some English agents performed ineffectively, leaving Pole to soldier on as best he could. Almost all of them held subordinate posts under Pole, and between mid-February and late April, or, better, late May, Pole ran things by himself. The English could have expected opposition from the Spanish party in the faculty, but some of their supposed allies among the French proved almost as obstructive, and forced the English to fend for themselves. Once again, much of the extra burden fell on Pole. The evidence suggests that beginning in the late winter of 1529–30 Henry saw Pole as his principal agent in Paris.

The sort of mission Pole would undertake was in the air long before

---

1. SP 1/57, fo. 248r (Pocock, *Records*, i. no. 194, p. 563; *LP*, iv [iii]. no. 6505). Pole inserted 'presence' but apparently forgot 'his'.

2. Pole was always generous with recommendations, so that his kind words for Foxe should not be overstressed. See e.g., his legatine correspondence in 1537 in which he proposed to keep the papal secretary informed of 'ogni loco dove trovo commodita'. Archivio di stato, Parma, Carteggio Farnesiane 293, Piemonte, 1532–1546, Pole-Ricalcati, 8 Mar. 1537 (unfoliated).

he left for France. The suggestion to consult the universities surfaced in early August 1529 and Henry and his advisers seized on it with enthusiasm. From the first, they expected the French to contribute substantially. Jean du Bellay, Francis's ambassador in London wrote to the king's chief adviser, Anne de Montmorency, at the end of the month that Henry and Wolsey were pressing him hard to go to Paris 'in order secretly to show the most learned men of the kingdom the matter of the divorce ... and debate it with them, and show them the arguments of the adverse party in order to draw some good advice and argument from them, and when I should find these, send them surely here'.[1] The bishop stalled them on Francis's orders. Probably the other strand of Anglo-French diplomacy was woven into French hesitation. Francis had to worry about offending the emperor, who was holding his sons hostage under the terms of the treaty of Madrid. When du Bellay's brother Guillaume, sieur de Langey, came to England about the same time to treat for the ransom, he too was importuned for assistance with the divorce in return for large financial concessions.[2] In mid-September du Bellay agreed to return home secretly in order to solicit opinions under the pretext of seeing his dying father.[3]

Pole set out for Paris in mid-October, according to one of du Bellay's dispatches. The bishop gave no hint that Pole meant to do anything other than 'see the country in continuing his education'.[4] He received a year's exhibition in advance on the 16th.[5] At almost precisely the same time the French ambassador informed Montmorency that John Stokesley would leave shortly in company with George Boleyn 'for the reasons mentioned in my other letters', which, of course, included the divorce.[6] Stokesley had been a major cog in the divorce enterprise since 1527.[7] Stokesley and Boleyn's mission changed regular English diplomatic representation right at the outset. They replaced the resident ambassador, Sir Francis Bryan.[8] On 25 October Eustace Chapuys, imperial ambassador in London, reported that Stokesley had left for Paris 'for the sole and express purpose of consulting the Parisian doctors' on the divorce.[9] Chapuys may or may not have had the full

---

1. Joachim Le Grand, *Histoire du divorce de Henri VIII, roi d'Angleterre et de Catherine d'Aragon*, iii. *Preuves* (Paris, 1688), p. 339 (*LP*, iv [iii]. no. 5862).
2. V.-L. Bourrilly, *Guillaume du Bellay, sieur de Langey* (Paris, 1905), pp. 77–81.
3. Le Grand, *Divorce*, p. 355 (*LP*, iv [iii]. no. 5945).
4. Remy Scheurer (ed.), C[orrespondance du cardinal] J[ean du] B[ellay], i (Paris, 1969), no. 41, 12 Oct. (*LP*, iv [iii]. no. 6003).
5. *LP*, v. no. 315.
6. *LP*, iv (iii). no. 5983, 4 Oct. 1529.
7. Virginia M. Murphy, 'The Debate over Henry VIII's First Divorce: An Analysis of the Contemporary Treatises' (Cambridge University PhD. thesis, 1984), pp. 19–20, 88, 93.
8. SP 1/56, fo. 104r; Le Grand, *Divorce*, p. 376, Henry VIII-Montmorency, 8 Oct. 1529.
9. C[alendar of] S[tate] P[apers,] Sp[anish], ed. Pascual de Gazangos, iv (i) (London, 1884), no. 194. De Gazangos's transcriptions and translations have been checked against Chapuys's originals in the Haus-, Hof-, und Staatsarchiv, Vienna, Staatenabteilung England.

story, since he insisted that Stokesley's departure was a 'matter of certainty' but could not confirm that he had been 'lately sent' until 6 December.[1] Norfolk, temporarily in control, no doubt kept Chapuys in the dark in an effort to forestall interference. This forced him to rely on unofficial contacts, or perhaps garbled reports reaching him indirectly from official sources.[2] Whenever Stokesley finally left, it strains credibility to believe that even Henry's most obtuse adviser could have failed to link Stokesley's departure with Pole's and to realize the latter's value as an emissary. It is difficult to say whether Pole could have realized that he was heading into a hornet's nest. Du Bellay shuttled back and forth in secret, but the project of consulting the universities was fairly widely known. The best channel of information for what would become the Aragonese party did not yet exist, since More became Lord Chancellor only about the time that Stokesley left for France.[3] More had known Pole since at least 1523, but there is no trace of contact between them in 1529, even if More had known what was afoot.[4] The academician Pole must have known the stature of the University of Paris and hence have at least guessed its likely role in any consultations about the divorce. It may be significant that he apparently saw no difficulty in going there.

In early November the affair began to intensify. Pedro de Garay warned the emperor about it for the first time on the 11th.[5] This Spanish theologian would anchor Catherine's party in the faculty. By the end of December Henry had already received some disappointing results, despite the dispatch of Boleyn, by then Lord Rochford.[6] Slightly better news came on 12 January 1530 – sixteen doctors had pronounced in the king's favour. All the same, two others acting in concert with the imperial ambassador were doing their best to thwart Henry's agent. Chapuys's failure to identify the troublemakers causes little difficulty. They were probably Garay and Noël Beda, the faculty syndic. It is more unfortunate that Chapuys could not put a name to the Englishman.[7] Perhaps he meant Stokesley, who certainly knew all about the two theologians' antics in early January. On the 16th

---

1. *CSPSp*, iv (i). no. 124.
2. Guy, *More*, p. 99 for Norfolk.
3. *Ibid.*, p. 138. For Pole's ties to this group, see S. E. Lehmberg, *The Reformation Parliament 1529–1536* (Cambridge, 1970), p. 30.
4. E. F. Rogers (ed.), *St. Thomas More: Selected Letters* (New Haven, 1961), no. 35.
5. He referred to this letter in another of 9 Apr. 1530. *CSPSp*, iv (i). no. 285. For him see the entries in James K. Farge, *A Biographical Register of Paris Doctors of Theology* (Toronto, 1980). Farge argues that a letter from one Ambrosio de la Serna to Catherine's physician (*CSPSp*, iii (ii). no. 578), which Gazangos dated November 1528 and Bourrilly 1529 (*Langey*, p. 94) actually belongs in 1531. Farge's most telling point is that the other of the two doctors mentioned, Alvaro de Moscoso, did not receive his degree until May 1530 and therefore could not have taken full, indeed decisive, part in any faculty meetings before that. James K. Farge, *Orthodoxy and Reform in Early Reformation France: The Faculty of Theology of Paris, 1500–1536* (Leiden, 1986), p. 143.
6. *CSPSp*, iv (i). no. 241, 31 Dec.
7. *Ibid.*, no. 249.

he reported that Rochford was off trying to convince Francis to adopt measures which

> we with our counsell here have divised and thought expedient for the staying and repressing of the Autoritie of doctour Beda and of the furye of the unlernyd Spanyard doctour petre garray, whiche by his Importune sute, and beryng abowte to certaine simple doctours ... a byll whiche the said Beda, not withstonding the greate maistres [Montmorency's] monition, hath with his adherentes sith Christmas signed and delyvered to the saide Spanyard against our opinion.[1]

Stokesley joined Wiltshire's embassy to the pope and left Paris shortly after filing this report. Once the English learned of skullduggery in the faculty, a replacement for him should have been a priority.[2] The French had thought little of Stokesley, a mere doctor of theology and as yet not even a bishop. In the report to Wiltshire just cited Stokesley wrote that du Bellay had sent letters to Pole, but none either to Stokesley's party or to the Frenchman's own relatives.[3] This might have further significance. Perhaps Pole already had an important position, at least as far as du Bellay knew, and he certainly outranked Stokesley and Rochford.[4] At the minimum, Stokesley's warning of troublemaking should have raised storm signals in London, even if they had not been flying when Pole left.

Wiltshire moved sluggishly throughout his embassy. Chapuys heard on 20 January that the earl and Edward Lee were to leave the next day and pick up Stokesley. Wiltshire did indeed receive his commission to treat with the pope and other European rulers about action against the Turk on the 21st, but did not depart from London for four more days.[5] He spent about three weeks in Paris, although he could claim no credit for Henry's success in inducing thirty-five doctors to take his side.[6] All the same, Henry's letter to Wiltshire and Pole could have fallen into this period, the more so since it concerned letters to the faculty like those which Henry had just dispatched.[7]

Rochford stayed in Paris only about as long as Stokesley did. Either Boleyn proved an inept agent, or his position depended solely on the immediate influence his father could exert in the court. Already in mid-January a replacement was being prepared, and Chapuys even wrote that he had been sent.[8] The imperial ambassador probably mis-

---

1. SP 1/56, fo. 211r, Stokesley to Wiltshire (?), 16 Jan. 1530. Text also in *State Papers Published under the Authority of Her Majesty's Commission*, vii. *Henry VIII*, v (London, 1849), no. 267, but with very odd orthography.
2. *CSPSp*, iv (i). no. 250.
3. SP 1/56, fo. 211v (*LP*, iv [iii]. no. 6147).
4. Zeeveld, *Foundations*, p. 68, where both his emphasis and chronology are suspect.
5. *CSPSp*, iv (i). nos. 252, 255.
6. *Ibid.*, no. 255, p. 443.
7. Wiltshire was at Moulins (*CJB*, no. 51) and Stokesley reached Lyons by 24 Feb. (*LP*, iv [iii]. no. 6242). For events between January and May, see Farge, *Orthodoxy*, ch. iii.
8. *CSPSp*, iv (i). no. 250, 13 Jan.

read events once again, but a difficult incident confronted him. According to French records, John Wellisbourne replaced Rochford. His appointment poses two problems. First, unlike both Bryan and Rochford he was not a member of the Privy Chamber until May 1530.[1] This weakened his standing in the French court considerably, since it signalled disrespect to Francis and a lack of English interest in Wellisbourne's mission.[2] The second difficulty with Wellisbourne's embassy would seem to reflect the same attitude. A gap of more than a month intervened between Rochford's retirement to London on 12 or 14 February and Wellisbourne's appointment on 15 March.[3] The English either left themselves without a resident, despite Stokesley's cautions, or Wellisbourne's hosts dawdled in taking official notice of his arrival, which may amount to the same thing. If the former, this may indicate that Pole discharged his role satisfactorily by himself. Even after Wellisbourne's installation, he probably did not help much. He spent most of his time touring provincial universities and reporting that he had little idea what was going on.[4]

Henry confirmed Pole's official involvement on 1 May when he formally asked the theologians to consider the case. The king's letter listed his arguments briefly and then adduced sources to support them. In addition to various English writings, Henry asked the learned doctors to listen to 'the noble and faithful man, our friend the sieur du Bellay de Langey and lord Reginald Pole our dearest relative, the exhibitors of these letters.... We ask you to treat with them as in undoubted faith in these matters which they relate (?) to you in our name'. This almost unnoticed document cannot have certified de Langey's original appointment, since he was active from at least early February and probably long before.[5] He had a hand in encouraging the English to approach the faculty and Stokesley's instructions singled him out as the person whose 'counsail & avice' the envoy should particularly heed.[6] Therefore his linking with Pole may indicate that this consultation was far from Pole's first appearance, too. The language reads

---

1. *LP*, iv (iii), Grants in May.
2. R. J. Knecht, *Francis I* (Cambridge, 1982), p. 209. For the mechanics of members of the Privy Chamber as royal stand-ins and for their rarity in that role, see David Starkey, 'Representation through Intimacy: A Study in the Symbolism of Monarchy and Court Office in Early Modern England', in Ioan M. Lewis (ed.), *Symbols and Sentiments: Cross-cultural Studies in Symbolism* (London/New York, 1977), pp. 200–2, 222.
3. *CSPSp*, iv (i). no. 265, p. 467 and *Catalogue des actes du François Ier* (Paris, 1887–1910), ix. 99.
4. BL Add. MS 25, 114, fo. 32r.
5. Bibliothèque Nationale, Paris, MS latin 16,576, fo. 273r-v. The seventeenth-century faculty beadle, Philippe Bouvot, probably made this transcription, perhaps not from the original. It is merely signed 'Henry', but a scribe who was writing quickly and who was unfamiliar with the king's signature could have missed its 'R' suffix. I owe identification of the hand to J. K. Farge. Hallé, *Pole*, p. 70, and Zeeveld, *Foundations*, p. 68, misdated this letter.
6. SP 1/56, fo. 106r and *State Papers*, vii. no. 264, p. 223. *CSPSp*, iv (i). no. 257 reported de Langey's deep involvement. When he returned to London by the middle of the month, the French resident's report on his activities put the divorce last, after an affair of piracy. Le Grand, *Divorce*, p. 443.

as if Henry meant to give the two an enhanced, more formal standing. Nor was this, obviously, the initial approach to the faculty. It seems unlikely that all the smoke and fire from August onwards meant nothing.

Pole threw himself into his new role. At about the same time as Pole's letter to Henry of 13 May, the king wrote to Nicholas Dorigny, president of the *chambre des enquêtes*, that he 'understands by his beloved cousin Raynald Pole's letter that the French king hath enjoined the said Dorigny to promote his cause there'. He urged Dorigny to be 'diligent and receive the direction of Raynald Pole'.[1] Pole thus bore direct responsibility for Dorigny's success in engineering the Parisian canonists' decision of 23 May against the pope's power to dispense from divine law.[2] Like his master, Lupset became deeply enmeshed in the Parisian negotiations. He was almost certainly the English student whom Chapuys reported on 23 April had come from Paris to deliver a briefing on de Langey and the quality of the opinions he had solicited.[3] On the 29th Lupset received a payment of one hundred crowns. The chronology cannot be a coincidence.[4] Lupset earned a further £10 'by way of rewarde' on 30 May, and Cardinal Wolsey gave him several more benefices in the last few months of their lives.[5] J. A. Gee's conjecture that Lupset initiated Pole's engagement may be correct.[6] Lupset acted as a messenger between Paris and London in the later stages of the affair; Pole first heard of his recall from him.[7] Earlier, Pole instructed Lupset to 'demand off mosr. langy ij bokes for mr fox', one of them a 'librum conciliorum'.[8] Lupset's actions render important the way Lily interpreted the time Lupset spent with Pole in Paris. In his *elogium* of Lupset, Pole's long-time intimate Lily noted that Lupset had rejoined Pole's household at a time when Pole had 'very opportunely gone to France, enjoying the king's high favor'.[9] No bent bows here. Despite their shared ambivalence to Henry, Lupset may well have tried to promote himself on his patron's coat-tails, much as Starkey did at the same time.[10]

Pole later tried to blame the whole business on the 'mr fox' of his instructions, but Edward Foxe came late. He indeed immersed himself

---

1. *LP*, iv (iii). no. 6394.
2. *Ibid.*, no. 6400. Dorigny wrote to Henry directly two days later. *Ibid.*, no. 6404. Bourrilly also credited this opinion to Pole. *Langey*, p. 100.
3. *CSPSp*, iv (i). no. 290.
4. Gee, *Lupset*, p. 138.
5. A. J. Slavin, 'Profitable Studies: Humanists and Government in Early Tudor England', *Viator*, i (1970), p. 322n.
6. Gee, *Lupset*, p. 138.
7. SP 1/57, fo. 248v.
8. SP 1/55, fo. 193r.
9. Gee, *Lupset*, p. 136. Beccadelli's language echoed Lily's (see above) and may have been borrowed from the 1548 edition of Lily's *opuscula*.
10. T. F. Mayer, 'Faction and Ideology: Thomas Starkey's *Dialogue*', *Historical Journal*, xxviii (1985), 18–20.

in the divorce in the first five months of 1530, but at home. Foxe tried to persuade both English universities to pronounce for Henry, and handled the life-line for the king's special agent in Italy, Richard Croke.¹ As late as mid-May he remained in England, although he may have crossed the Channel toward the end of the month.² Foxe unquestionably appeared in Paris only at the end of June, when an agent to the provincial universities wrote to him in the rue de la Madeleine.³ Pole's letter of 7 July confirmed Foxe's recent arrival. Pole concluded that he had heard from Foxe how much the king wished him to return, and that was not the sort of information one kept under one's hat.⁴ If Foxe had come to France in May, he must have gone home at least once more. This would mean that he served to second Pole, shuttling back and forth while Pole stayed on the ground. The short time Pole and Foxe spent together combined with Foxe's likely absences suggests that the case for cooperation between them has been overstated.⁵

By the time Foxe appeared on the stage, the play had entered its final scene. The recalcitrant theologians began their deliberation on 12 June, finally under full pressure from de Langey.⁶ He had been dragging his feet by royal command in order to avoid offending the emperor, but an English threat to complain to Henry induced him to act.⁷ The English representatives had witnessed a tumultuous faculty meeting in which threats had been shouted back and forth and one doctor had torn up the beadle's roll of opinions. The ambassadors left 'forte mutinés & interpretans cette affaire en très-mauvaise part', as de Langey reported to Francis. This led him to worry that

> I have dissembled too much; because if on the one hand we should fear to irritate the emperor ... on the other, perhaps, it is no less to be feared that the king of England, annoyed by too long dissimulations, will make Monsieur de Briant retire without doing anything, or find means to achieve his ends with the consent of the emperor.⁸

Bryan most concerned de Langey, but probably because of the ransom, not his role in the divorce, if any.⁹

Just at the climax it becomes very hard to track the principal English

---

1. *LP*, iv (iii). no. 6218, *CSPSp*, iv (i). no. 265 and *LP*, iv (iii). nos. 6303, 6308. For Croke, see *LP*, iv (iii). no. 6409.
2. *LP*, iv (iii). no. 6377, a letter from London of 12 May. A warrant for payment to the customer of Dover and Foxe's own note to that officer record his passage to Calais, but the warrant bears the date 21 Henry VIII. PRO E 101 324/24. nos. 2 and 3.
3. SP 1/57, fo. 198v and address (*LP*, iv [iii]. no. 6481).
4. SP 1/57, fo. 248v (*LP*, iv [iii]. no. 6505).
5. Zeeveld, *Foundations*, p. 69.
6. *CSPSp*, iv (i). no. 353.
7. Le Grand, *Divorce*, pp. 458–59 (*LP*, iv [iii]. no. 6449).
8. *Ibid.*, p. 466.
9. Knecht, *Francis I*, p. 223.

players. A letter from Norfolk to Montmorency a few days after de Langey's last report confirms the impression that Bryan stood on the periphery. Norfolk thanked Francis's chief minister for entertaining Bryan, but then continued immediately that Norfolk had learned that the divorce negotiations had gone awry. If Bryan had been in the midst of things, surely Norfolk would have noted that he had heard of the latest catastrophe from him.[1] Pole may have had to share centre stage with Wiltshire after the latter's return from Italy, but Wiltshire never appeared in any of Pole's reports or later accounts. Given Pole's vehement hostility to the earl's daughter, one might have thought Wiltshire would have been especially likely to figure prominently in Pole's stories, had he done much in the first place. Wiltshire's movements, however, are uncertain. He returned from Bologna in May and spent the latter part of the month with the court at Angoulême.[2] On 12 June when the English threatened to write to him about the disturbances amongst the theologians he could not have been in Paris, but on the 15th when they double-crossed de Langey and complained anyway, Wiltshire wrote to Norfolk (?) from Paris that Francis had better write more strongly to the faculty.[3] But the royal displeasure might have hampered Wiltshire's effectiveness. Even before he got back to England in late July, Norfolk told Chapuys that Wiltshire had made an utter mess of things by his abject failure to make headway with either pope or emperor. The duke had never seen Henry so displeased with an ambassador.[4] Personal rivalry may well have blown Norfolk's report out of proportion, but Pole's failure to mention Wiltshire may also reflect his disgrace. In any case, as the earl's standing went down, Pole's would have improved in proportion.

The matter came to a head in the first days of July. On the 5th a nearly hysterical Garay sent the emperor a detailed report, insisting that a papal bull should condemn all the principal actors. Charles finally endorsed Garay's plan, but they were too late.[5] The opinion had been formally sealed on the 2nd and a notarial transumpt made by the 6th. By 11 July Chapuys knew that the French ambassador in London had the news.[6] Stokesley carried the signed and sealed opinion home with him, although he could have had little to do with procuring

---

1. Le Grand, *Divorce*, p. 471. The summary in *LP*, iv (iii). no. 6461 made Norfolk's involved syntax worse by having his agents inform him about the course of the negotiations.
2. SP 1/57, fos. 106–9 (*LP*, iv [iii]. no. 6393). One James Clyffe wrote Edmund Bonner on 29 May that Wiltshire was still at Angoulême (*ibid.*, fo. 137r; no. 6411), but this could be a second-hand report of the news just cited.
3. *LP*, iv (iii). no. 6455. Bourrilly badly distorted this moment by ascribing this document to the English ambassadors in Paris, writing to Wiltshire: *Langey*, p. 99.
4. *CSPSp*, iv (i). no. 373, 11 July 1530. Wiltshire was at Ortonay on the way home by the 19th. *State Papers*, v. 248n.
5. *CSPSp*, iv (i). no. 354 and *LP*, iv (iii). no. 5452.
6. *LP*, iv (iii). no. 6497 and *CSPSp*, iv (i). no. 373.

it. Pole journeyed back to England at the end of July.¹ The business had not quite run its course. Poor de Langey had to make a Parisian's ultimate sacrifice and stay in the capital through the first half of August to make certain the decision would stick.²

Thus far the story of the difficult business from the English perspective. Filling in the French side enhances the precariousness of the English position. Most of Henry's chief French allies were broken reeds, and at least shared de Langey's reluctance to press Henry's case. Garay accurately singled out de Langey, Guillaume Petit and the *premier président* of the *parlement* of Paris, Pierre Lizet, as the principals.³ The ransom always interested de Langey more than the divorce. His brother Martin, who was himself deputed to escort Bryan, passed over de Langey's assistance to Henry in a few lines of his memoirs and moved on to a detailed discussion of the ransom of the princes. He confined himself to his brother's early intervention in 1529 and skipped over his allegedly decisive actions in 1530 altogether. Martin du Bellay made it crystal clear that Francis and de Langey helped Henry out of financial necessity, but also explained that de Langey was chosen as envoy to the theologians because of his reputation among European universities.⁴ A similar motive may account for Lizet's enlistment. He succeeded Jean de Selve on 20 December 1529 at the instance of Admiral Brion. He also took orders from Montmorency, but probably only as from the grand master, not from a patron.⁵ Lizet acted reluctantly for Henry, as Stokesley quickly discerned. Much pressure had to be brought to bear even to get him to execute Francis's orders. The opposition leader Beda was a close friend, and Lizet continued to obstruct the French king's wishes even after the affair had ended. Nevertheless, Lizet probably acted as royal agent rather than *premier président*. But again, as Stokesley recognized, Lizet could make the faculty come around immediately. Many of its members owed him,

---

1. *LP*, iv (iii). no. 6450, p. 2898, Stokesley to Henry, 13 July. Zeeveld cited a ledger of Pole's expenses (SP 1/55, fo. 193v [?]) as further evidence of his return, but this could almost as easily have come from another trip in 1528. Both Beccadelli and Dudith left Pole in Paris for a year (*Epistolarum*, v. p. 361 and i. p. 8), which would mean he returned in October or November 1530. This would fit better with their stories about Henry's eagerness to have Pole's opinion at the end of the year. Then again, Stokesley's letter and Zeeveld's conjecture support Pole's own letter of 7 July.

2. Bourrilly, *Langey*, p. 105.

3. *CSPSp*, iv (i). no. 370. For Petit see Farge, *Register*, p. 369 and R. Garcia Villoslada, *La universidad de Paris durante los estudios de Francesco de Vitoria, O. P.* (Rome, 1938), pp. 334–35.

4. Martin du Bellay, *Les mémoires de messire Martin du Bellay*, in Claude Petitot (ed.), *Collection complète des mémoires relatifs à l'histoire de France*, ser. i, xvii–xix (Paris, 1821), pp. 89–90. The younger du Bellay seems otherwise to have played no role. An error in *LP* misled Zeeveld into calling him *conseiller* of the *parlement* of Paris, and therefore into concluding that an entry in Pole's expense ledger 'for wyne of the consalar' referred to him, especially since one 'Martyn' was also on the list. *Foundations*, p. 66, citing *LP*, iv (iii). no. 5541 (Le Grand, *Divorce*, p. 313), a letter from du Bellay to 'Monsieur du Bellay conseiller en la Court de Parlement de Paris'. The du Bellay addressed was René, later Bishop of Le Mans. Eduard Maugis, *Histoire du parlement de Paris de l'avènement des rois Valois à la mort d'Henri IV*, iii (Paris, 1913), 169.

5. Bourrilly, *Langey*, p. 96 and Maugis, *Histoire*, i. 148–49.

'for this monsr. lysot maynteyned the facultie moche late in a certayne debate that they had and hath many of them at his devotion'. Stokesley went on to put his finger on a basic problem. '[H]e is thought moche papale and yet a mervellose greate dissembler/ and therfor we doubte how to use hym'.[1]

Hallé took Garay's list of protagonists as exhaustive, and on that assumption absolved Pole of any major role. This overlooks Garay's remarkable failure to mention *any* Englishmen, as well as evidence which suggests that some of Garay's colleagues knew of Pole's actions. It is likely that in 1536 Pedro Ortiz rested his somewhat restrained testimonial to Pole's worthiness for an enterprise against England in part on information derived from friends on the theological faculty of Paris six years before. Ortiz wrote to the emperor that Pole was now a good Catholic, but had once tried to secure Parisian opinion in favour of the divorce.[2] Ortiz had been friendly with Charles Pinelle in Rome in 1530 and Pinelle was then in contact with Alphonso de Herera, one of Catherine's staunch partisans in the faculty.[3] Then again, Ortiz's objectivity may not be above reproach. In 1537 Pole regarded him as one of the major stumbling-blocks to his legation against England.[4]

Pole began his passage to good Catholicism within a year of his stay in Paris. By the middle of 1531 he had definitely although probably not publicly come out against the divorce. This change of mind could reflect on Pole's doings (or at least his attitude) in Paris. Unfortunately, next to nothing is known about what happened to him in the period after he returned home, and even the evidence for his new stand comes at second hand. Pole later took this *Zeitwende* to mark his breach with Henry, the beginning of overt opposition. By Pole's own account, for which there is no supporting evidence, Henry tendered him the see of either Winchester or York late in 1530, if Pole would come out for the divorce. Pole edited this event in exactly the fashion he did the happenings in Paris, slowly reworking it into a scene of divine election.[5] This dramatic story may be unreliable, but it seems tolerably certain that Pole's contemporary biographers accurately reported that he retired into John Colet's house at Sheen when he came back from

---

1. SP 1/56, fo. 211v (*State Papers*, v. no. 267, p. 228). My thanks to Nancy Lyman Roelker and Linda L. Taber for help with Lizet's role.
2. BL Add. MS 28, 589, fos. 152v–53r (*LP*, xi. no. 1160).
3. Farge, *Orthodoxy*, p. 142, citing *LP*, v. no. 265. Farge identifies Herera with de la Serna.
4. Archivio di Stato, Parma, Epistolario Scelto, busta 13, Polo, fo. 2r, to Ricalcati from Cambrai, 7 May 1537.
5. The first account appeared in the letter to the Council cited above, but the next two not until 1547 or thereabouts in the letter to Edward and another to Protector Somerset, Biblioteca Marciana, Venice, MSS. Italiani x. 24. (6527), fo. 7v (summarized in C[alendar of] S[tate] P[apers,] V[enetian], ed. Rawdon Brown, v (London, 1873), no. 575, p. 242). The final version appeared in both Beccadelli and Dudith, but also in Nicholas Harpsfield, *A Treatise of the Pretended Divorce between Henry VIII and Catharine of Aragon*, ed. Nicholas Pocock (Camden Society, new ser. no. xxi, 1878), pp. 13–4, written in 1557 before either of the two biographies.

Paris, apparently having changed his mind about rewards.[1] Perhaps Pole already had second thoughts about the service he had just done for his cousin. In any case, if we can trust Thomas Cranmer's report to Wiltshire, by June of 1531 Pole had written to Henry that 'he had *never* pleasure to intromytte hymselfe in this cause'. As Cranmer continued, Pole conceded that Henry could be right about the divorce, but 'that he sholde be a doar therin, & a setter forwarde therof, he cowde *never* fynde in hys harte'.[2]

These two 'nevers' are ambiguous in the extreme. If they both bear a temporal meaning, then Pole already claimed that he had stood aloof throughout the Parisian broils. On the other hand, the first might mean 'no', which would say that Pole had contributed without enthusiasm. It would then fit Pole's letter to the Council which seven years later also explained that 'my conscyence could never perfettlye agree' to assist Henry. The second could have been intended to emphasize that Pole thought he could no longer under any circumstances support the divorce. Then again, Cranmer's words may well not bear close analysis as a representation of what Pole wrote. Cranmer was, after all, chaplain to Anne Boleyn, and if Pole had even begun to waver on the divorce Wiltshire might well have wished to rush to discredit him in Henry's eyes. To stoop to the truly sordid, Cranmer may even have seen Pole as a competitor and have had reasons of his own for wishing to eliminate him. Too much should not be made of all this, especially because Pole's opinion made an impact, even if we know next to nothing about its content. According to Pole, Sir John Russell presented his writing to Henry, who read it.[3] If Henry saw the opinion (and if we accept Cranmer's version of it), the apparent lack of recriminations against Pole would suggest that the king took Pole to mean that he had grappled with the theologians reluctantly and had since concluded that the long list of political considerations his opinion outlined – dynastic problems uppermost – ended the possibility of even limited support for the king's policy. Thus Henry may have treated Pole in the same way he did Lord Chancellor More, allowing him to oppose the divorce in private, provided that he did nothing to hamper the king's pursuit of it. Nevertheless, ambivalence may have begun to turn toward irreconcilable conflict. The balance of evidence about Pole's actions in Paris indicates that open disagreement took much longer to develop than Pole averred in *De unitate*.

A more complete scenario of the Parisian drama makes Pole's importance hard to miss. One may even suspect that an ulterior motive lay

---

1. Beccadelli, p. 361. Harvel's letter to Starkey of 18 June 1531 corroborates this report. BL Nero B vi, fo. 169r (*LP*, v. no. 307).
2. BL Lansdowne 115, fo. 2r. Emphasis added. Also printed in Pocock, *Records*, ii. 130–31.
3. Marciana Ital. x. 24. (6527), fo. 7v, undated (*CSPV*, V. no. 575).

behind Henry's decision to allow Pole to leave England in 1529. However that may be, the circumstances surrounding Pole's departure and du Bellay's letters to him in January 1530 suggest Pole's participation almost from the beginning. The lack of any English representative of a similar social position from the middle of February until at least late May would have forced Pole into a more visible role, if only by default. Henry had good grounds for distrusting most of the Frenchmen involved, and he seems not to have thought much of most of the agents acting in his name. The king would have wanted his own man on the ground, someone he felt owed him a large debt of loyalty. Such was Pole, who responded to his responsibility by hoping for full credit from his exertions. Read in the light of independent evidence, Pole's version of his time in Paris in *De unitate* comes to seem a remarkably adroit piece of equivocation.

A work which T. F. Dunn discovered in the Biblioteca Vaticana sheds further light on what Pole may have been up to in *De unitate*. His 'Oratio ab Henrico rege ad deum exercenda' was probably a model of the abject repentance Pole expected from Henry after the king had read that work.[1] The prayer drags on and on and is almost without intrinsic interest. This little work must none the less raise eyebrows, particularly when combined with Pole's claim that Henry had once agreed with him about the divorce.[2] The subject of Henry VIII could trigger an approach to the fantastic in Pole. The pressures arising from his powerfully conflicting feelings about the king no doubt motivated Pole's attempts to wash his hands of any participation in the divorce.

We can now better appreciate why many historians have found Pole's narratives seductive. His coherent account of both action and motivation offered a prize no biographer could afford to inspect too closely. Even Wilhelm Schenk's moderate conclusion that Pole took 'some part in the business', 'however odious it may have seemed to him', adhered as closely as possible to Pole's line.[3] But the point of this investigation is that Pole did not write history. Pole and his contemporaries knew the distinction between truth and fiction in historical writing perfectly well, some recent analyses notwithstanding. As one of the Renaissance historians it used to be fashionable to excoriate for his disregard of the truth put it

> History and encomium are very different. History has the light of truth, and for this it is the mistress of the life of man [quoting Cicero]. Encomium adopts rhetorical places [*luoghi*], and praises the man with the unfurled banner without any fear of falling into the teeth of lies; and is quiet about

---

1. Dunn, 'Pole and Vat. lat. 5970', p. 80.
2. Marciana Ital. x. 24. (6527), fo. 7v, where Pole alleged that his brother, Lord Montague, had reported that Henry had said of Pole's opinion 'che io [Pole] aveva detto il vero'.
3. Schenk, *Pole*, p. 28.

all the vices which often accompany the most distinguished virtues .... In encomium they seek the fame of eloquence and favor among the lords.[1]

Pole may not have had Paolo Giovio's quest for fame in mind when writing about his relations with Henry, but he certainly relied heavily on epideictic rhetoric. Accusation and denigration, blame and barb helped to control Pole's stories.[2] He may also have written under the influence of the genre of realistic *novelle*, like those of his Paduan acquaintance Marco Mantova Benavides.[3] No matter how rhetorically crafted, Pole's self-portrait has as much historical reality as the unadorned activity behind it. Thus far historians have taken the former for the latter, but we need a much more subtle analysis of the interplay between them. A more historical approach can provide both an internal critique of the interpretation descended from Pole and an explanation of how and why he came to launch that tradition.[4]

---

1. Paolo Giovio to Girolamo Scannapeco, 1534, in Paolo Giovio, *Lettere*, ed. G. G. Ferrero, i (Rome, 1956), no. 60, p. 174. For Rudolf Agricola's famous *loci* on which Giovo drew here, see Walter J. Ong, *Ramus, Method and the Decay of Dialogue* (Cambridge, Mass., 1958), ch. v, and Cesare Vasoli, *La dialettica e la retorica dell'Umanesimo: 'invenzione' e 'metodo' nella cultura del XV e XVI secolo* (Milan, 1968), pp. 147–82.
2. John W. O'Malley, *Praise and Blame in Renaissance Rome: Rhetoric, Doctrine and Reform in the Sacred Orators of the Papal Court, c. 1450–1521* (Durham, N. C., 1979), ch. ii.
3. Mantova wrote at least four *novelle*. For them see T. F. Mayer, 'Marco Mantova and the Paduan Religious Crisis of the Early Sixteenth Century', *Cristianesimo nella storia*, vii (1986), 41–61 and p. 58 for his tie to Pole.
4. See T. F. Mayer, 'Reginald Pole in Paolo Giovio's *Descriptio*: A Strategy for Reconversion', *Sixteenth Century Journal*, xvi (1985), 431–50, for a study of another episode in the creation of Pole's modern image.

XII

A Sticking-Plaster Saint?
Autobiography and Hagiography in
the Making of Reginald Pole

"An image...adorned with all the virtues and excellencies which today might come together in a Christian gentleman."[1] Such was the portrait Ludovico Beccadelli, Reginald Pole's first biographer, promised his readers, and such became the dominant image of Pole.[2] If it will ever prove possible to get behind that portrait, attention must be directed not only to the dissemination of what Paolo Simoncelli calls Pole's "myth of sanctity," but also to the means Pole employed to launch his own hagiography.[3] This article studies the creation and diffusion of one particular episode in Pole's own presentation, his refusal in late 1530 to take Henry VIII's offer of the archbishopric of York in exchange for support of the king's divorce from Catherine of Aragon. Instead, as Pole came to claim, he had prophesied against the king, acting under divine inspiration. In creating his persona of prophet (together with its mirror image of martyr), Pole slid from humanist into Counter-Reformation historiography. Although in the process he played with language in the way his humanist education had taught him to do, Pole's serious approach and that of his successors led them to negate the playful intentions in much humanist historiography.[4] Thus, an originally heavily rhetorical story became a transparent account of what had happened, and the realist axiom that the saintly Pole always told the truth (or at least serious stories) came to dominate historiography.[5]

Pole first unveiled his prophetic persona in 1536 in *De unitate,* his savage attack on Henry, and only gradually worked it into the story of his climactic interview with the king.[6] How this retroactive control developed emerges from an analysis of the intricate relationship between

XII

Pole's own writings and those of his biographers. The accounts Beccadelli, Andras Dudic, and Nicholas Harpsfield gave depended directly on the point Pole had reached in his reconstruction when they knew him. Pole first adverted to the event in the immediate aftermath of *De unitate,* in the form of Latin and English renderings of a reply to the king's council. Two years later, in 1539, when he and Beccadelli spent six months together in Spain, Pole still told much the same story, which Beccadelli faithfully reproduced as "what Sig. Reginaldo told me," the only one of these authors to make that claim. (Beccadelli had also been at Padua in 1533–36 at the tail end of Pole's extended stay and then became secretary to Pole's close ally Gasparo Contarini, who loaned him to Pole in 1539.)[7] A decade further on, Pole returned to the episode in a 1549 draft letter to Protector Somerset, before producing his final reckoning in two prefaces to *De unitate,* both addressed to Edward VI and written between mid-1553 and mid-1555 (despite the king's death two years earlier); Angelo Maria Querini printed one of these in the eighteenth century, but the other has not been previously noticed.[8] Within the next few years, Pole probably gave copies of this preface to Dudic, whom he met about 1550, and to Harpsfield, archdeacon of Canterbury during Pole's tenure as archbishop.[9] Alexius Horányi claimed that Dudic met Pole at Maguzzano in 1550, and Dudic may have been Pole's secretary after Pole's return to England in the 1550s; he certainly was profoundly impressed by Pole.[10] Judging from the number of preferments Harpsfield received from Pole, they, too, must have been close.[11]

In the Latin of the letter to the council, Pole rhetorically asked the Duke of Norfolk, "If I had wished to assent to the king's opinion, would anyone have been preferred to me in the archbishopric"?[12] Although Pole made a great deal of his opposition, he admitted that he would have liked the benefice. Seeing that the sole road to advancement ran through support for the divorce, Pole gave in to various blandishments "and directly I decided to satisfy the king." Once Henry was notified of Pole's resolve, "he met me in the door of a secret ambulatory in the house of York at Westminster (I can never forget that place).... When I saw him...I could no longer say what I had previously thought out," despite the "human chain" between them, reflected in the king's face, "which I loved above the rest."[13] It is perhaps significant that this is the only version of the interview that reached the eyes of anyone who could pass on its relation to what had passed between the two royal cousins.[14]

This simple story of a change of mind became much more complicated by the mid-1550s; fortunately, although the second version of the preface to Edward is longer than the first, they do not vary significantly in content (I quote the more readily available printed version). When telling Henry's son about his original resolution to cooperate with his father, Pole added the editorial comment "and so I really judged, blinded in my effort following men more than obeying God." Once the interview began, strange things happened. Pole saw himself singled out by divine favor in such a way that

> when ... I tried to enter the case, here I do not say I hesitated to have explained insufficiently what I wanted to say, but, oh divine goodness! so my tongue was plainly hampered, and my mouth obstructed, that I could not utter a word about what I had considered. When I yet began to speak, I said everything which attacked his opinion, as whose defender I had been expected to come.

Pole explained that his love for God and king—no longer king alone—was responsible for his change of heart.[15] Much the same account appears in the letter to Somerset. In addition to confirming that Pole's new story of his prophetic inspiration had supplanted the straightforward report of 1537, this second account offers a large clue about how Pole used autobiography to suit his rhetorical purposes. In the letter to Somerset, the story functioned as an exemplum designed to shame the protector by illustrating how Henry, "having an opportunity of knowing my sincerity in a matter very contrary to his feelings, would not, however, be angry with me nor ridicule me as you do."[16]

Harpsfield, Beccadelli, and Dudic, in that order, produced their renditions of the tale between about 1557 and 1562, almost reversing the sequence in which they came into contact with Pole.[17] The last two texts have frequently been taken as mirror images, a perception the two authors encouraged.[18] In fact, their accounts here differ most. Harpsfield veered between them. While all began by having Pole resort to prayer, Beccadelli kept it simple ("but in this deliberation, [Pole] turn[ed] to prayer, as he was wont to do"), Dudic dramatized ("while Pole was engaged in this so difficult and so dangerous deliberation, he eagerly fled to God, and prayed that in such a time he might not fail"), and Harpsfield went Dudic one better and spelled out for what exactly Pole prayed, making him ask "God to direct and govern his doings in this matter, that they might be conformable to truth, right and justice, and to His blessed will and pleasure." Despite the general similarity of Dudic's text to Harpsfield's, this could be one of several spots at which Dudic carefully criticized Pole, having him pray for inerrancy and then immediately waver. Pole himself said nothing about any kind of prayer in his letter to Edward.[19]

After this request for divine advice, Beccadelli adhered closely to Pole's original story in the letter to the council, while the other two reproduced Pole's later versions. According to Beccadelli, Pole discovered that

> he could never enter . . . into the spirit to conform himself to the king's will . . . , but he resolved to speak freely as he thought, and not as a flatterer, but truly as a relative and servant, since, the truth known, one must abstain from offending against it. The which he did with much eloquence and modesty, nor did he wish that anyone aside from the king should know his opinion.[20]

Pole's becoming modesty and faith in the power of the "truth" to convert Henry disappeared in the other two accounts. Instead of a direct refusal to support the king, Harpsfield and Dudic had Pole painfully work out a compromise, which God then prevented him from offering the king. Once their Pole recovered from the dumb fit featured in Pole's later reworkings, these two portrayed Pole telling Henry the opposite of what he had intended to say.

Strong verbal resemblances clinch the case for Harpsfield's and Dudic's dependence on Pole's finished versions. For example, where Pole wrote to Edward that "ne verbum quidem effari potuerim," Dudic merely cast that into the third person as "nullum verbum effari posset," and Harpsfield, departing from his usual practice, embroidered that into "he could not, if his life had stood on it, a great while utter one word." Pole continued "cum autem loqui tandem coepissem, omnia dixerim" [When, however, I began to talk, I said everything] against Henry, and Dudic once more followed with "[t]andem vero cum loqui coepisset, ejusmodi fuit ejus oratio, ut alia omnia diceret" [Yet truly, when he began to speak, this was his speech, that he said all the other things (against the king)], while Harpsfield wrote more expansively "[a]fterward, when he came to himself and recovered his speech, he spake quite contrary to that thing which he was determined to have spoken, and showed the king very plainly and openly that he wonderfully disliked the divorce."[21]

All these texts were plainly intended as hagiography. Dudic made his aim as explicit as Beccadelli's opening sentence: he had set out not only to translate Beccadelli's original, but also to modify it in order to demonstrate that Pole was on a par for sanctity with the martyred Thomas More and John Fisher. Dudic also adopted Beccadelli's conclusion that Pole belonged in the company of martyrs.[22] Pole looks a little out of place in Harpsfield's legal treatise on the validity of Henry's marriage to Catherine, but his figure was intended to function in much the same way as it had for Dudic, as an example of "the most notable captains" who fought against the divorce, again along with More and Fisher. By promoting Pole to equality with them, Dudic and Harpsfield completed the absorption of Pole's persona of martyr, which Pole had fashioned in *De unitate* by implicitly comparing himself to Fisher and More.[23]

The motives behind these authors' reactions to Pole's self-presentation need more work.[24] The problem is especially acute in the case of Dudic's adaptation. On the one hand, Dudic had a collaborator, Giovanni Battista Binardi, about whom little is known. Thus far we have scarcely more than Dudic's own account of his relations with Binardi, who had been one of Pole's secretaries, and to whom Dudic apparently deferred. He had asked Binardi for help because of his own artistic failings, and he went on to emphasize how much substance Binardi had contributed, in addition to having "polished...this whole image of Pole" [totam hanc Poli effigiem].[25]

Ludovico Castelvetro's polemical attack on Binardi offers the only biography I have unearthed.[26] According to Castelvetro, Binardi came from very humble origins (one of the points Castelvetro considered most damaging) and had worked his way up as a tutor until he had gained an assignment as secretary to Cardinal Bernardino Maffei. On Maffei's death in 1553, Binardi had immediately passed to Pole's service. Perhaps the most scandalous suggestion Castelvetro made—one that students of Pole have ignored—is that Binardi, hoping for preferment, hired his pen to Pole, writing many works in Italian—especially letters and a treatise on the sacraments—which were then translated into Latin and published as Pole's own.[27] Or perhaps Castelvetro's assertion is a garbled version of Beccadelli's claim—which might be more reliable—that Binardi had served as Pole's *Latin* translator.[28] If both these stories are true, the corpus of "Pole's" work will need serious reduction! According to the spy Francisco Delgado, Binardi had custody of Pole's manuscripts when they were in England.[29] On Pole's death, Binardi accompanied his lifelong companion Alvise Priuli to Paris and then set off for Italy alone.[30] Shortly thereafter, he played a major role in the planned edition of Pole's works.[31] Binardi eventually entered the service of Cardinal Bernardo Navagero, by whom Castelvetro supposed he was richly rewarded.

Castelvetro offered the summary judgment (although it may apply only to Binardi's tenure as visitor of Roman prisons) that "he was in all his actions vain and simple [*semplice*], if not a persecutor." This last suggests that the root of Castelvetro's animus to Binardi was religious. If so, it may have sprouted from Castelvetro's difficulties in Modena in the early 1540s when he had been a member of a "heretical" conventicle whose beliefs Pole and his allies had been called upon to investigate and correct.[32] The notoriously irascible Castelvetro's account of Binardi and his involvement in Pole's works may have been meant to repay Pole. One of Castelvetro's accusers was another ally of Pole, Pietro Bertano.[33] Then again, Castelvetro had earlier been friendly with Binardi, and Binardi (and Gianfrancesco Stella) had a very high opinion of Castelvetro's literary theories as late as 1559; this put them in a distinct minority in a major literary dispute.[34] Thus, Binardi would appear to have had the perfect qualifications of a "ghost writer," if Castelvetro can be trusted. To this moment, alas, no manuscript of Dudic's work has surfaced.[35]

On the other hand, Dudic's own later conversion to Calvinism has cast a shadow over his work. G. B. Morandi argued that Dudic was actually attacking Pole from a crypto-Protestant position.[36] Domenico Caccamo, Gigliola Fragnito, and Lech Szczucki all reject Morandi's thesis.[37] Nevertheless, one of the coauthors of Dudic's life may have meant to make a number of subtle criticisms of Pole. In addition to the possibly negative comparison to other heroes who had died for the faith, for example, it was similarly noted that two of the four men created cardinal with Pole had gone on to become pope. "Dudic" noted this again when discussing the same two serving together with Pole as legates to the first session of Trent.[38] But in 1556, Dudic had extravagantly praised Pole, together with their mutual friend Paolo Manuzio, for their "true religion of Christ, by whom I was confirmed in the faith and by whose examples I was invited to spend life piously and holily."[39] Near the end of his life, Dudic expressed a similar opinion in offering his study of Pole as a model for a series of biographies of men "whom our age raises to the level of the fathers [of the church]."[40] Thus the theory of Dudic the crypto-critic may not work, but if these apparently negative comments actually were Binardi's, the situation becomes even more complicated. Likewise, the meaning of Beccadelli's ties to Pole's allies the *spirituali*, in whose defense Beccadelli is generally agreed to have written, requires further attention.[41] Furthermore, Harpsfield's legendary zeal for the Counter-Reformation may not explain his handling of the image of Pole as well as further attention to his numerous historical works.[42]

The accident of print denied much immediate impact to Beccadelli's and Harpsfield's intentions and motives, for Dudic alone achieved the honor of type in the sixteenth century. This may be explained by the fact that Dudic had a compelling motive to seek patronage from Emperor Ferdinand, to whom he dedicated the *Vita*. Beccadelli, by contrast, had lost hope of further preferment after the death of his patron Marcello Cervini (the short-lived pope Marcellus II), even if he had not yet broken irrevocably with Cardinal Morone when he wrote his "Vita."[43] Or perhaps Beccadelli really was sufficiently pleased with Dudic's text to abandon his own original.

The mere availability of Dudic's text no doubt accounts in part for the appearance of his dramatic adaptation of Pole's own reworked image in the second edition of Nicholas Sander's *De origine ac progressu schismatis anglicani*. Given the wide circulation of this work, it is worth trying to determine who modified Sander's account of Henry's first divorce in order to emphasize Pole's role. Sander himself could not have selected this particular "remarkably truthful" vignette, to adapt T. G. Law's characterization of the whole work.[44] The first edition of 1585 (Cologne, but actually Rheims) contains only a compressed reference to Pole's contretemps with Henry. As Sander put it, since "nothing" in England could compare to Pole, "therefore first the king offered him an archiepiscopal prerogative, if yet he should first promise, by eloquent words, that he would support the king's divorce by all effort. When Pole heard such a foul added condition, he rightly refused to sit in the chair of pestilence."[45] Before a new edition of *De origine* appeared in Rome the following year, Dudic's version of the interview had replaced this passage. While the second edition usually follows Dudic almost literally, it also contains details from Pole's own late versions that do not appear in Dudic, for example, the fact that Henry met Pole in a small, internal chamber. These could have come from Pole's own letters, provided once again by Hosius, but it is curious that Sander, who had been Hosius's theologian at Trent and then followed him to Poland, did not include them.[46] Alternatively, whoever prepared the second edition might somehow have had access to a copy of Beccadelli's text, which also contains these details.

In any case, how these changes were made between editions is still uncertain. Until twenty years ago, it was accepted that Sander's fellow Jesuit Robert Persons bore responsibility both for the original edition and for its Roman successor. Much of the former case is conjectural and rests in the main on Joseph Gillow's etymological identification of Persons with the "Iodocus Skarnhert" who had persuaded Rishton to publish Sander's work. Despite his skepticism about "Skarnhert's" identity, J. H. Pollen did think that Persons was responsible for the second edition, arguing that because his annotations stopped early in Sander's manuscript, he must have made the rest of his additions on a copy of the 1585 edition. Eusebio Rey put forward an especially freewheeling and almost entirely unsupported argument for Persons's primacy.[47]

As flimsy as the case for Persons's original involvement was, that for his role in the second Roman edition has even weaker support and has been largely destroyed by Joseph Simons. On the basis of a comparison of the first two editions with Persons's annotations on Sander's manuscript, Simons argued that the recusant leader William Allen already had a hand in the first edition, and definitely prepared the second, into which he incorporated Persons's notes.[48] This could well be true; Persons's marginalia on Sander's manuscript did not incorporate Dudic's story.

Whoever intruded the tale, the complete supplantation of the first edition of *De origine* by the second guaranteed the survival of Pole's self-creation.[49] This critical phase began quickly. In 1587, the Rome edition was reprinted in Ingolstadt (and twice more the following year) as well as translated into French; in 1589, it was adapted into Spanish by another Jesuit, Pedro de Ribadeneira, and both it and Sander's original were recast into Italian by the Dominican Girolamo Pollini in 1594. Ribadeneira adopted the main outline of Dudic's story, but toned down the climax a little, writing merely that when Pole tried to tell Henry the compromise formula he had worked out, "se turbó, (cosa maravillosa) y de repente se cortó de tal manera, que por un buen trato no pudo hablar palabra. Despues volviendo en sí comenzó á hablar y á decir todo lo contrario de lo que habia pensado" [he became disturbed (a marvelous thing) and suddenly turned in such a manner that for a good space of time he could not speak. Afterward coming to himself, he began to speak and to say all the contrary to what he had thought out]. Pollini dedicated *L'Historia ecclesiastica della Rivoluzion d'Inghilterra* (Rome: Guglielmo Facciotti, 1594) to Allen, and it bore a privilege of Clement VIII, together with a *nihil obstat* from the famous Spanish Jesuit and moral theologian, Juan Azor. Although the first edition was apparently suppressed, Pollini brought out another three years later.[50] If Sander's history and Pole's story appeared to be standard Counter-Reformation fare at that point, in the seventeenth century they became usual features of other sorts of historiography. The catalog of the British Library lists fifteen editions of *De origine* before 1700, and that is certainly not the total. Law's judgment (in his *DNB* article on Sander) that Sander's work "formed the basis of every Roman Catholic history of the English Reformation" is no exaggeration. In one instance, the Florentine patrician Bernardo Davanzati compressed and rearranged Dudic's treatment of Pole's interview in his *Lo schisma d'Inghilterra,* except that he did not attribute Pole's dumbness to divine intervention.[51] Although Davanzati frequently followed Johannes Sleidan's *De statu religionis et reipublicae Carolo V Caesare commentarii,* he could not have in this case; Sleidan did not mention Pole before his legation of 1537.[52] Davanzati's sympathetic attitude to Pole could well have arisen from his experience in the as yet little-explored circles around Cosimo I, which had earlier displayed a good deal of interest in defending Contarini's reputation and contained a number of figures of more-or-less heterodox religion.[53] One of Cosimo's partisans, Benedetto Varchi, had a very high opinion of Pole and some of his friends.[54] The Accademia fiorentina also included Dominicans, one of whom was interested in revising heretical literature, which may suggest a tie between Pollini and Davanzati.[55] Or, the link between Davanzati and Pole could be as direct as Beccadelli, who entered the service of the Medici in 1563 at the conclusion of Trent.

Undoubtedly the most important of the later adaptations and translations of *De origine* was that of François Maucroix (1676, with at least three more editions by 1715, including one of The Hague). From it descends modern historiography of the English Reformation. Maucroix's work served as "the proximate cause" (Law) of Gilbert Burnet's *History of the Reformation,* the first volume of which, published in 1679, in turn led to Joachim Le Grand's reply in his *Histoire du divorce de Henri VIII* (Paris, 1688) and thence directly to the great burst of interest in church history in the first half of the eighteenth century.[56] Even though Maucroix had apologized for Sander's partisanship in his

XII

preface, when he chose to translate the equally partisan Dudic in 1677 as a sequel, he manifested intentions as blatantly hagiographical as most of his predecessors.[57] Maucroix gave few clues about his motives. He wrote only in his brief preface that everything Dudic had written was "la verité" [the truth] and that although he did not wish to give a eulogy of Pole, "je diray seulement, qu'il seroit difficile de trouver dans un même homme, tant de Noblesse, de Pieté & de Doctrine, que dans le celebre Cardinal POLUS" [I would only say, that it would be difficult to find in a single man so much nobility, piety, and learning as in the famous Cardinal Pole].[58] Why either work should have interested a protector of the Jansenists and a "convinced Gallican" is puzzling.[59] Perhaps this is evidence both of the reception of Pole's tolerant attitude to Protestantism and also that he was read as much less of a staunch papalist than he has been made out to be in later scholarship. Such an interpretation would fit the views expressed in *De unitate*.[60]

By the mid-eighteenth century, the time of Thomas Phillips, another sometime Jesuit and author of the first modern biography of Pole, the corner had been turned and Pole's tale come to be read fully seriously.[61] Both Phillips and his critics so took it, as the replacement of salvation history by scientific history merely substituted one objectivist epistemology for another. Gloucester Ridley, for example, insisted that he would "never rely on Pole's testimony when not supported by others," but he yet blithely assessed the York interview as an instance of "the common weakness of irresolute men, [who] fluctuating between the choice of a present and future advantage, and, loath to quit either, lose both."[62] Benjamin Pye offers an even more egregious instance. The translator and annotator of Beccadelli argued at length in his preface that "a biographer seems to be by profession a writer of panegyric" who therefore "often makes a sacrifice of truth without scruple," before concluding that "it would be absurd...to make such effusion of the fancy...the basis and ground-work of real history." Despite a few doubts about the documentary record, Pye nevertheless accorded Beccadelli's story enough credence to judge that it showed Pole in a very bad light: "he prevaricated with his prince; he deceived his friends; he acted disingenuously with himself."[63]

This outcome is the more surprising in that it ignored the conclusion reached by the dean of Anglican historians of the Reformation and the man probably most responsible for renewed interest in Pole, Bishop Burnet. But Burnet, Ridley, and Pye all held Pole to the same serious standard. Burnet flatly rejected Pole's tale as a fabrication only because, as he thought, it had no external support.⁶⁴ A key episode, invented by Pole as part of his prophetic persona, could not be expunged from historiography, even by hostile critics like Pye who displayed sensitivity to the rhetorical demands of biography. Pole's well-fashioned autobiography proved too seductive.

NOTES

A preliminary version of this article was read at the meeting of the Renaissance Society of America at Harvard in 1989. My thanks to the Gladys Krieble Delmas Foundation, Villa I Tatti: The Harvard University Center for Italian Renaissance Studies, and the National Endowment for the Humanities for their support of further work.

1. Ludovico Beccadelli, "Vita del cardinale Reginaldo Polo," in G. B. Morandi, ed., *Monumenti di varia letteratura* (Bologna: Istituto per le scienze, 1797–1804), 1:2, 277 reads *ponno*, as do most of the manuscripts; *possino* supplied from Newberry Library Case MS fE5.P7536, fol. 1ʳ. I am at work on a critical edition and translation of Beccadelli's and Andras Dudic's lives of Pole.

2. Paolo Simoncelli, *Il caso Reginald Pole: eresia e santità nelle polemiche religiose del Cinquecento* (Rome: Edizioni di storia e letteratura, 1977), 17 and 241; and Gigliola Fragnito, "Aspetti della censura ecclesiastica nell'Europa della controriforma: l'edizione parigina delle opere di Gasparo Contarini," *Rivista di storia e letteratura religiosa,* 21 (1985): 3–48, 24. For Pole's place in English recusant historiograpy and subsequent Catholic writing, see B. H. G. Wormald, "The Historiography of the English Reformation," in T. Desmond Williams, ed., *Historical Studies,* 2 (1958): 50–58, esp. 58.

3. Simoncelli, *Caso Pole,* 17.

4. Sergio Bertelli, *Ribelli, libertini e ortodossi nella storiografia barocca* (Florence: La nuova Italia, 1973), esp. chap. 1. Richard A. Lanham, *The Motives of Eloquence: Literary Rhetoric in the Renaissance* (New Haven, CT: Yale University Press, 1976), esp. chap. 1, develops the fundamental humanist dialectic between serious and playful behavior.

5. Athanasius Zimmermann, *Kardinal Pole, sein Leben und seine Schriften. Ein Beitrag zur Kirchengeschichte des 16. Jahrhunderts* (Regensburg: F. Pustet, 1893), 36. Cf. Martin Haile [pseud. of Marie Hallé], *Life of Reginald Pole* (London: Isaac Pitman and Sons, 1911), 72.

6. Peter S. Donaldson discovered Pole's prophetic persona in *De unitate,* Pole's savage attack on Henry, but did not bring out the dialectic between it and Pole's martyr-self: "Machiavelli, Antichrist, and the Reformation: Prophetic Typology in Reginald Pole's *De unitate* and Apologia ad Carolum quintum," in

Richard L. DeMolen, ed., *Leaders of the Reformation* (Selinsgrove: Susquehanna University Press, 1984), 211–46.

7. Beccadelli, "Vita," 287. For Beccadelli's stint with Pole, see Antonio Giganti da Fossombrone, "Vita di Monsignor Lodovico Beccadelli," in G. B. Morandi, ed., *Monumenti di varia letteratura* (Bologna: Istituto per le scienze, 1797–1804), 1:1, 17. Cf. also Gigliola Fragnito, "Beccadelli, Ludovico," *Dizionario biografico degli Italiani* (Rome: Istituto della Enciclopedia italiana, 1960–).

8. The letter to Somerset bears various dates in the manuscripts, but the best is probably 12 October 1549 from Biblioteca Apostolica Vaticana [hereafter BAV] Vat. lat. 5968, fols. 258^r– 74^v. Querini's text of the preface to Edward is in *Epistolarum Reginaldi Poli* (Brescia: Rizzardi, 1744–57) [hereafter *ERP*], 4, 306–53; his dating by implication is on XXII–XXVII (endorsed indirectly by Thomas F. Dunn, "Cardinal Reginald Pole and Codex Vaticanus Latinus 5970," *Manuscripta,* 21 [1978]: 75–82, at 81). This text came from Johann Georg Schellhorn, *Amoenitates historiae ecclesiasticae et litterariae* (Frankfurt and Leipzig: Daniel Bartholomäus, 1737), 192–276; Querini later acquired the manuscript from Schellhorn. It is now part of Brescia, Biblioteca Civica Queriniana [hereafter BCQ] MS F III 7, m. 1. The presence in the Queriniana of two other pieces of the codex as it existed before Schellhorn sold it to Querini clinches its provenance. This manuscript came from Pole's friend Stanislaus Hosius via Charles XIII of Sweden, who stole it from Hosius's bishopric. From him it passed to various German bibliophiles before its sale to Querini. It might be in Seth Holland's hand. The other manuscript of the preface is Bergamo, Biblioteca Civica "Angelo Mai" [hereafter BCM], Archivio Stella, 40/76, a version in the hand of Pole's secretary, Marcantonio Faita, which must have passed into the possession of Pole's longtime business agent, Gianfrancesco Stella. (The archivist who cataloged the Archivio Stella, probably Giuseppe Bonelli himself, guessed it was dated 1548. See Giuseppe Bonelli, "Un archivio privato del Cinquecento: le Carte Stella," *Archivio storico lombardo,* 24 [1907]: 332–86, no. 93.) The presence of a marginal note in the same unknown but contemporary hand on each manuscript proves their close relationship in time. The initial impulse to the preface to Edward probably came from Gianpietro Caraffa's suggestion that Pole republish *De unitate,* as mentioned in Pole's letter to Girolamo Muzzarelli of 9 August 1553 (misdated 6 August in *ERP*, 4, no. 37, 92; original in BAV Vat. lat. 5967, fols. 358^r–65^v, with wrapper and seal; as Heinrich Lutz argues, this probably means the letter was never sent: *Nuntiaturberichte aus Deutschland,* Erste Abteilung, vol. 15, *Friedenslegation des Reginald Pole zu Kaiser Karl V. und König Heinrich II. (1553–1556)* [Tübingen, 1981], XIXn). Caraffa could have hatched his scheme, possibly intended to incriminate Pole further, at any time after their famous "reconciliation" in April 1553 (reported by Filippo Gherio to Beccadelli on 29 April in Morandi, ed., *Monumenti di varia letteratura,* 1:2, 347–53). Muzzarelli endorsed Caraffa's proposal both then and again

on 1 September (*ERP,* 5, no. 64, esp. 124; no original of his letter has been found, but there is a contemporary copy in Naples, Biblioteca Nazionale "Vittorio Emanuele III," IX. A. 14, fols. 45ʳ–47ᵛ, and the copy in BCQ, MS F III 7, m. 2, fols. 7–8, may be not much later). Cf. the discussion of these two important letters in Massimo Firpo, *Inquisizione romana e Controriforma: Studi sul Cardinal Giovanni Morone e il suo processo d'eresia* (Bologna: Il Mulino, 1992), 238–50. Caraffa's urgings and the news of Edward VI's death (which reached Rome about 6 August and Maguzzano, Pole's residence, about a week later; cf. *Friedenslegation des Reginald Pole,* nos. 2 and 4) came very close together, which suggests that despite his protests to the contrary, Pole went to work immediately on the preface. The appearance of Pier Paolo Vergerio's edition of *De unitate* in Strasbourg in 1555 provides a *terminus ad quem* for the first of these prefaces, and *a quo* for the second. In the first, Pole wrote as if the anonymous edition that had spurred him to write had not yet appeared, and in the second as if it had. The balance point between these two *termini* can be dated from Pole's letter to Otto Truchsess of 19 June 1554 (*ERP,* 4, no. 53, to be used cautiously in light of its variations from the minute in BAV Vat. lat. 5967, fols. 367ʳ–71ᵛ) in which Pole asked Truchsess's help in learning whether Vergerio's edition had yet appeared. Cf. Simoncelli, *Caso Pole,* 120–31, which, however, offers no further help in dating this key episode. That Edward was dead by that time poses no difficulty in dating—Pole was, after all, proposing to reprint *De unitate,* a work that addressed Henry VIII in the first person throughout. There are yet two more autograph but fragmentary versions of the preface in BAV Vat. lat. 5971, fols. 1ʳ–57ᵛ and 117ʳ–149ᵛ, neither covering this episode.

9. Dudic could also have gotten his copy after Pole's death from Cardinal Hosius, who encouraged Dudic to translate Beccadelli, and who was well known for his aid to English Catholic exiles, among them Nicholas Sander. A. Horányi, *Memoria Hungarorum et provincialium scriptis editis notorum,* 1 (Vienna: Anton Loew, 1775), 550, apparently building on the contemporary life of Dudic by Quirinus Reuter; Pierre Costil, *André Dudith, humaniste hongrois 1533–1589: Sa vie, son ouevre et ses manuscrits grecs* (Paris: "Les Belles Lettres," 1935), 61–73, and Domenico Caccamo, *Eretici italiani in Moravia, Polonia e Transilvania (1558–1611). Studi e documenti* (Florence: Sansoni; Chicago: The Newberry Library, 1970), 110, for Dudic's high opinion of Pole.

10. See *ERP,* 1, 257 for the MS, and H. D. Wojtyska, *Cardinal Hosius, Legate to the Council of Trent* (Rome: Gregorian University Press, 1967), 211–16 for his relations with English Catholics. See Costil, *Dudith,* 104, for Hosius's encouragement.

11. Nicholas Harpsfield, *The Life and Death of Sir Thomas Moore,* ed. E. V. Hitchcock, intro. and notes by R. W. Chambers (London, Early English Text Society, o.s., no. 186 [1932]), xxi.

12. Public Record Office, London, SP 1/116, fol. 65ʳ and *ERP,* 1, 182. The

English version, which was probably Pole's original (it is autographed and signed), is phrased considerably differently and much less rhetorically. The purpose of the Latin rendering, its connection to the copy in the BAV printed by Querini, and the precise relation between all three letters remains to be worked out.

13. Ibid., fol. 66^{r-v}.

14. Wilhelm Schenk argued to the contrary in *Reginald Pole, Cardinal of England* (London: Longmans, 1950), 31n, but see T. F. Mayer, "A Mission Worse than Death: Reginald Pole and the Parisian Theologians," *English Historical Review,* 103 (1988): 870–91, esp. 876–77.

15. *ERP,* 4, 330–31; BCQ, MS F III 7, m. 1, fols. 107^v–108^r; BCM, Archivio Stella, 40/76, fols. 14^v–15^r, which has the following text: "Itaque plane cupiditate hominis plusquam Dei obtemperandi obcaecatus iudicabam.... ingressum in causam quaererem si hic non dicam me in ipsa principia haesitasse me non satis expressisse quod dicere volui. Sed o bonitatem divinam ita mihi et lingua plane impedita est, et os obstructum ac ne verbum quidem ullum effari potuerim de iis quae mecum meditatus fueram, cum autem loqui inciperem, omnia dixerim quae cum sententiam oppugnarent, cuius defensor optatus veneram."

16. BAV Vat. lat. 6754, fols. 3^r–27^v; fol. 5^r has the most legible extant text. That in Vat. lat. 5968, fols. 258^r–74^v, stems more directly from Pole, but nearly all of this version can no longer be read. There are other copies in BL Add. MS 41577, fols. 3^r–27^v, dated in a different hand 8 April 1548; BL Add. MS 25425, 3–27; and Venice, Biblioteca Marciana, MSS italiani X. 24 (6527), fols. 6^r–22^v, summarized in *Calendar of State Papers and Manuscripts, Relating to English Affairs in the Archives and Collections of Venice,* ed. Rawdon Brown, 5 (London, 1873), no. 575, p. 242, where it is dated 7 September.

17. For the dates of composition, see Nicholas Harpsfield, *A Treatise on the Pretended Divorce between Henry VIII and Catharine of Aragon,* ed. Nicholas Pocock (London, Camden Series, n.s. 21 [1878]), 13–14); Morandi, *Monumenti di varia letteratura,* 1:2, 272; and Gigliola Fragnito, "Gli 'spirituali' e la fuga di Bernardino Ochino," *Rivista storica italiana,* 84 (1972): 777–811, 803n. For Dudic at Trent, see most recently Lech Szczucki, "Miedzy ortodoksja a nikodemizmem (Andrzej Dudycz na soborze trydenckim)," *Odrodzenie i Reformacja w Polsce,* 29 (1984): 49–90. I have been unable to read this article, but I am grateful to Dr. Szczucki for sending me a copy.

18. Gigliola Fragnito, *Memoria individuale e costruzione biografica* (Pubblicazioni dell'università di Urbino, serie di lettere e filosofia, Urbino, 1978), 64n, 161.

19. *ERP,* 4, 330; BCQ, F III 7, m. 1, fol. 107^v; BCM, Archivio Stella, 40/76, fol. 14^v.

20. Beccadelli, "Vita," 286–87.

21. *ERP,* 4, 330 (BCQ, F III 7, m. 1, fol. 107ᵛ–108ʳ); BCM, Archivio Stella 40/76, fol. 14ᵛ, adds a few words; Dudic, *Vita Reginaldi Poli,* in *ERP,* 1, 9; Harpsfield, *Divorce,* 206. Harpsfield's somewhat stultifying, if fully rhetorical, treatment of Pole resembles the way he rewrote William Roper's life of Thomas More. See Judith H. Anderson, *Biographical Truth: The Representation of Historical Persons in Tudor-Stuart Writing* (New Haven, CT: Yale University Press, 1984), 15, 49–51.

22. Andras Dudic, *Vita Reginaldi Poli* (Venice: Domenico and Giovanni Battista Guerrei, 1563), sig. 3ᵛ; *Vita,* in *ERP,* 1, 65, repeating Beccadelli, "Vita," 333. Querini did not reprint Dudic's preface in *ERP,* but his text is otherwise almost identical to the Venetian edition.

23. *Reginaldi Poli ad Henricum octavum Britanniae regem, pro ecclesiasticae unitatis defensione* (Rome: Antonio Blado, 1539), esp. fols. LXXXIII–XCV.

24. Quentin Skinner sketches the useful distinction between motives and intentions in "'Social Meaning' and the Explanation of Social Action," in P. Laslett, W. G. Runciman, and Q. Skinner, eds., *Philosophy, Politics and Society,* series 4 (Oxford: Blackwell, 1972): 136–57, esp. 144–47. I differ from him in suggesting that both should be taken into account, with intentions and their textual warrant controlling motives that must be established by inference from texts. This method thus comes fairly close to that espoused by Eric Cochrane in *Historians and Historiography in the Italian Renaissance* (Chicago: University of Chicago Press, 1981), xvii.

25. Dudic, *Vita,* sig. 4ʳ.

26. Castelvetro's broadside was printed in part by Girolamo Tiraboschi in *Biblioteca modenese,* 1 (Modena: Società tipografica, 1781), 274–76. The original is in the Biblioteca Estense, Modena, Alpha H 1, 11. The short biographical notice of Binardi in *Nuovi documenti su Vittoria Colonna e Reginald Pole,* ed. Sergio Pagano and Concetta Ranieri (Città del Vaticano: Archivio segreto vaticano, 1989), 47n, must be used with caution. Most previous notices have no value.

27. Given the evidence of multiple pens in all of Pole's works written during Binardi's service, there is probably more than a grain of truth in this allegation. Cf. especially the numerous versions of Pole's "De Reformatione Ecclesiae" in BAV Vat. lat. 5964. The partial manuscript in the British Library of Pole's "De sacramento," which Castelvetro singled out as Binardi's work, is in Faita's hand, and the copy in the Marciana is later, possibly made from the printed edition.

28. Fragnito, "Censura ecclesiastica," 23n.

29. J. I. Tellechea Idigoras, "Pole, Carranza y Fresneda: cara y cruz de una amistad y de una enemistad," in *Fray Bartolomé Carranza y el cardenal Pole: Un navarro en la restauracion católica de Inglaterra (1554–1558)* (Pamplona: C. S. I. C., 1977), 137 and 139 (noting his intimate involvement in the discussion of Bartolomé Carranza's *Catechismo,* later judged heretical).

30. See the letters between Binardi and Priuli in BCM, Archivio Stella, 40/160–61.

31. Fragnito, "Censura ecclesiastica," 24 and 35, together with Binardi's important letter to Giovanni Morone in BAV Vat. lat. 6414, fols. 191^r–2^v.

32. Massimo Firpo, "Gli 'spirituali,' l'Accademia di Modena e il formulario di fede del 1542: controllo del dissenso religioso e nicodemismo," *Rivista di storia e letteratura religiosa,* 20 (1984): 40–111, now in *Inquisizione romana,* 29–118.

33. T. Sandonnini, *Ludovico Castelvetro e la sua famiglia* (Bologna: Nicola Zanichelli, 1882), 42–43, 81.

34. See Binardi's letter to Stella, BCM, Archivio Stella, 40/155.

35. The manuscript in the Queriniana, MS G. V. 1, is a copy of the text printed in Venice, written by Querini's sometime amanuensis, Abbot Schannat.

36. G. B. Morandi, ed., *Monumenti di varia letteratura* (Bologna: Istituto per le scienze, 1797–1804), 1:2, 274 and his notes.

37. Caccamo, *Eretici italiani,* 112–13, argues that although Dudic's true beliefs were much more radical, he had not openly broken with the Catholic church before the end of Trent; Fragnito, "Censura ecclesiastica," 39; and Szczucki, "Andrzej Dudycz," according to the English summary.

38. *Vita,* in *ERP,* 1, 14, and 19.

39. Caccamo, *Eretici italiani,* 112–13. For Manuzio's religion, see Fragnito, "Censura ecclesiastica," 26–28, Simoncelli, *Caso Pole,* 40–42, and A. J. Schutte, "The *Lettere Volgari* and the Crisis of Evangelism in Italy," *Renaissance Quarterly,* 28 (1975): 639–88.

40. Costil, *Dudith,* 448.

41. Hubert Jedin, *Il tipo ideale del vescovo secondo la riforma cattolica* (Brescia: Morcelliana, 1950), 49, 54–55; Simoncelli, *Caso Pole,* 191–92, argues for this thesis most strenuously; but see Fragnito, *Memoria,* 157–59; and idem, "Per lo studio dell'epistographia volgare del Cinquecento: le lettere di Ludovico Beccadelli," *Bibliothèque d'humanisme et renaissance,* 43 (1981): 61–87, 64, and 87, in which she disputes current views of Beccadelli's religion. Fragnito considers Beccadelli a lifelong adherent of Contarini, but not a *spirituale* (a term she would now restrict to Pole's immediate circle). See Fragnito, "Censura ecclesiastica," esp. 36 where Beccadelli not only becomes a key instrument in the campaign to rehabilitate Pole, but also a promoter of the "banca di vescovi Contarini."

42. See his entry in Sidney Lee and Leslie Stephen, eds., *The Dictionary of National Biography* [hereafter *DNB*] (Oxford: Oxford University Press, 1917).

43. Fragnito, *Memoria individuale,* 145–55; and "Censura ecclesiastica," 32–41. Fragnito obliquely makes "Dudic's" text part of the campaign engineered by Morone, even though she theorizes that the cardinal would not have approved its anti-Carafa polemic ("Censura ecclesiastica," 39–40). The latter, like Mo-

rone's putative, but undocumented, attitude, is difficult to detect; in all the cases where Carafa is mentioned by name, "Dudic" referred to him more respectfully (and at greater length) than Beccadelli. "Dudic" also seemed much more concerned with the prerogatives of the *Sancta romana ecclesia* than Beccadelli, which also reverses Fragnito's analysis.

44. T. G. Law, "Nicholas Sanders," in *DNB*.

45. Nicholas Sander, *De origine ac progressu schismatis anglicani*, ed. Edward Rishton (Cologne [Rheims], 1585), 57. The manuscript of Sander's work confirms that these are his words and not Rishton's: English College, Rome, Liber 1388, fol. 43^r. I am greatly indebted to the Rector of the English College and to T. M. McCoog, S. J., for procuring me a photocopy of this section of Sander's MS.

46. Wojtyska, *Cardinal Hosius*, 211–12 and 216.

47. J. Gillow, *A Literary and Biographical History or Biographical Dictionary of the English Catholics*, 12 vols. (London: Burns and Oates, 1885–1905), 5:279; J. H. Pollen, "Dr. Nicholas Sanders," *English Historical Review*, 6 (1891): 18–35, esp. 24 (cf. Thomas McNevin Veech, *Dr. Nicholas Sanders and the English Reformation* [Louvain: Bibliothèque de l'Université, 1935], 234); Pedro de Ribadeneira, *Historias de la contrareforma*, ed. Eusebio Rey (Madrid: Editorial Católica, 1945), 856–60; and T. H. Clancy, *Papist Pamphleteers. The Allen-Persons Party and the Political Thought of the Counter-reformation in England, 1572–1615* (Chicago: Loyola University Press, 1964), 16.

48. Robert Persons, *Certamen ecclesiae anglicanae*, ed. Joseph S. F. Simons (Assen: Van Gorcum, 1965), 301–4.

49. Something similar happened to the tales Sander told about Sir Thomas More. See Beatrice Corrigan, "Sir Thomas More: Personage and Symbol on the Italian Stage," in D. B. J. Randall and G. W. Williams, eds., *Studies in the Continental Background of Renaissance English Literature: Essays Presented to John L. Lievsay* (Durham, N. C.: Duke University Press, 1977), 91–108.

50. For the first German editions, see *The National Union Catalogue: Pre-1956 Imprints* (London: Mansell, 1968–81); Pedro de Ribadeneira, *Historia del cisma de Inglaterra* (Cadiz: Revista Medica, 1863), chap. 16, 86. For Pollini, Piero Rebora, "Una controversia anglo-toscano nel secolo decimosesto," in *Civiltà italiana e civiltà inglese: studi e ricerche* (Florence: Le Monnier, 1936), 101–5. Cf. also Giulio Negri, S. J., *Istoria degli scrittori fiorentini* (Ferrara: Bernadino Pomatelli, 1722), 304, and for Pollini's treatment of More, Piero Rebora, "San Tommaso Moro e l'Italia," in *Civiltà italiana*, 75–79.

51. *Lo schisma d'Inghilterra e le altre operette di Bernardo Davanzati Bostichi* (Siena: F. Pigafetta, 1828), 29–30. The work first appeared posthumously in 1638. For Davanzati's wholehearted endorsement of Counter-Reformation ideals, see Leandro Perini, "Un patrizio fiorentino e il suo mondo: Bernardo Davanzati," *Studi storici*, 17 (1976): 161–70.

52. Cochrane *(Historians and Historiography,* 361) emphasizes Davanzati's dependence on Sleidan, but his further judgment that Davanzati had nothing new to add because he knew no English is neither fair nor accurate. Davanzati adduced a good deal of evidence from continental writers that Sleidan had not. Johannes Sleidan, *De statu religionis et reipublicae Carolo V Caesare commentarii* (n.p.: Eustace Vignon, 1573), treated Pole at sigs. 137^{r-v} and 169^{r-v}. Sleidan had read Pole's *De unitate* and criticized him as a controversialist whose writings did not serve to advance historical understanding (sig. Oiiii^r).

53. Fragnito, "Censura ecclesiastica," 10–11.

54. B. Varchi, *Opere,* 2 vols. (Triest: Lloyd Austriaco, 1859), 2:347. For him, see Ugo Pirotti, *Benedetto Varchi e la cultura del suo tempo* (Florence: Olschki, 1971); and Leatrice Mendelsohn, *Paragoni: Benedetto Varchi's Due Lezzioni and Cinquecento Art Theory* (Ann Arbor, MI: UMI Research Press, 1982).

55. Perini, "Davanzati," 163.

56. For some of this development, see the recent sketchy treatments in Rosemary O'Day, *The Debate on the English Reformation* (London: Methuen, 1986), 38–55; and A. G. Dickens, J. M. Tonkin, and Kenneth Powell, *The Reformation in Historical Thought* (Cambridge, MA: Harvard University Press, 1985), 105ff.

57. *Histoire du schisme d'Angleterre des Sanderus,* 1 (Lyon: Guillimin, 1685), sig. aiiii^v.

58. F. Maucroix, *Suite du schisme d'Angleterre, ou les vies des cardinaux Polus et Campege* (Lyon: Guillimin, 1685; added to vol. 2 of his translation of Sander), sig. Aii^{r-v}.

59. Renée Kohn sketched Maucroix's career in *Lettres de Maucroix* (Paris: Presses Universitaires de France, 1962), 17–35 (assessment at 27).

60. For a reading of *De unitate* as no more enamored of papal absolutism than of Henry VIII's, see T. F. Mayer, "Nursery of Resistance: Reginald Pole and his Friends," in P. A. Fideler and T. F. Mayer, eds., *Political Thought and the Tudor Commonwealth: Deep Structure, Discourse, and Disguise* (London: Routledge, 1992), 50–74.

61. Thomas Phillips, *The History of the Life of Reginald Pole* (Oxford: William Jackson, 1764), 66 followed Dudic very closely.

62. Gloucester Ridley, *A Review of Mr. Phillips's History of the Life of Reginald Pole* (London: J. Whiston, et al., 1766), 24 and 20.

63. *The Life of Cardinal Reginald Pole, Written originally in Italian by Lodovico Beccatelli,* translated by Benjamin Pye (London: Bathurst, 1766), ix, 27–28. Pye claimed in the preface (iv–v) that he had chosen to translate Beccadelli in order to correct Phillips's inaccuracies, but why Pye worked from Beccadelli's Italian instead of Dudic's Latin—as Phillips had—is unclear.

64. Gilbert Burnet, *The History of the Reformation of the Church of England,* ed. Nicholas Pocock, 6 vols. (Oxford: Clarendon Press, 1865), 4, 557–58. Burnet (545) cited the 1628 edition of Sander.

XIII

Reginald Pole in Paolo Giovio's *Descriptio*: A Strategy for Reconversion

Reginald Pole's partisans in the sixteenth century portrayed him as a saintly man who had been victimized by his schismatic cousin and prominent antagonist, Henry VIII; the present image of Pole is very similar to this sixteenth-century depiction. A more balanced view of Pole will require an attempt to get behind the tradition bearing this portrait. Recently, part of this "mito di santità" has been analyzed by Paolo Simoncelli, who argues that the image of Pole as a saint and victim was used to protect his allies, the *spirituali*, from heresy proceedings immediately after his death. The first of two contemporary lives of Pole, that by Lodovico Beccadelli, played a major role in this campaign.[1] Gigliola Fragnito has challenged this interpretation, but her approach to Beccadelli's life of Gasparo Contarini demonstrates the problem with lives of Pole. The literary construction of Renaissance biographies, although unnoticed by later historians, conditioned the approach taken by an author to the protagonist—"altering, if not deforming his physiognomy, and deviating from the elements for evaluating his political, diplomatic and religious action."[2] This happened to Pole in places other than Beccadelli's biography. He became a stock figure of Counter-Reformation historiography after Nicholas Sander's editor incorporated several especially choice stories about him into the second edition of his immensely successful *De origine ac progressu schismatis anglicani*.[3] Another important appearance of Pole has thus far escaped attention. Paolo Giovio introduced the figure of Pole into his *Descriptio Britanniae, Scotiae, Hyberniae, et Orchadum* in much the same way as Pole's more overt allies did. In this article Giovio's intentions and motives will be pursued

---

[1] Paolo Simoncelli, *Il caso Reginald Pole. Eresia e santità nelle polemiche religiose del cinquecento* (Rome: Edizioni di Storia e Letteratura, 1977), 15-17, and 33, 191-92 for Beccadelli. An earlier version of this article was given at the Central Renaissance conference in 1984, and I am especially grateful to James V. Mehl and Dennis Gilkey for their comments on it. Professor T. C. Price Zimmermann read a revised draft carefully and helped to strengthen it a good deal.

[2] Gigliola Fragnito, *Memoria individuale e costruzione biografica* (Urbino: Argolia, 1978), 12, 17-18.

[3] The first edition appeared in 1585 and was edited by Edward Rishton. The second came out the following year in Rome and was possibly the work of either Robert Persons or William Allen or of both in collaboration.

by literary and historical means. He may have had a very complex set of motives, some governing the work's conception, others Pole's place in it, and yet another two or three being fulfilled by its publication.[4]

Giovio was a native of Como, best known now for his enormous *Historiarum sui temporis libri*. He was trained in the arts and medicine, and he studied philosophy for a time with Pomponazzi at Padua. Near the beginning of Leo X's pontificate, he was summoned to Rome to teach philosophy and became a member of the Roman academy and unofficial papal historiographer. He was also Cardinal Giulio de' Medici's physician. After this "golden age," both metaphorical and real, Giovio spent the rest of his life as a client of the Farnese, primarily concentrating on his writing and assembling the magnificent portrait gallery of famous men. The *Descriptio* is dedicated to his old friend and the chief of the papal government, the cardinal nephew Alessandro Farnese.[5]

Pole appeared near the end of this work.

> And so he [Paul III] made Reginald Pole a cardinal, in the place of the dead Rochester [John Fisher], a man distinguished above the nobility of his origins by the learning of the best letters, and the praise of Christian virtue. . . . Not long after, because Pole was joined to the royal blood, and it seemed he would therefore command greater authority, he was sent into Britain as a legate, in order that he might remind it, by his familiar and pious words, what seemed to pertain to healing the King's mind.

A half-page retelling of Pole's 1537 legation follows, replete with details about English attempts by one "Brianius" (Sir Francis Bryan) to bring Francis I to honor his treaty obligations and have Pole trussed up and turned over to Henry as a traitor; these attempts were thwarted, however, by Pole's escape to refuge provided by the Cardinal of Liège. Giovio concluded this passage by making Henry's actions against Pole's family and other high ranking aristocrats in 1538 a product of his desire to be revenged on Pole.[6] He did not fail to emphasize that the Marquess of Exeter, the leader of the failed conspiracy,

---

[4]Quentin Skinner has sketched the distinction between motive and intention in "'Social Meaning' and the Explanation of Social Action," in *Philosophy, Politics and Society*, 4th ser., ed. P. Laslett, W. G. Runciman and Q. Skinner (Oxford: Blackwell, 1972), 136-57, esp. 114-17. I differ from him in arguing that both need to be taken into account, rather than according priority to a linguistically founded intention.

[5]For brief sketches of Giovio's life see Federico Chabod, "Paolo Giovio," in *Scritti sul rinascimento* (Turin: Einaudi, 1967), 241-70, 244, and T. C. Price Zimmermann, "A Note on Clement VII and the Divorce of Henry VIII," *English Historical Review* 82 (1967):549-52, 549. Zimmermann is completing a biography.

[6]This motive apparently came from Pole. It crops up in Beccadelli's life in G. B. Morandi, ed., *Monumenti di varia letteratura . . . di Monsignor Lodovico Beccadelli* I (Bologna, 1797): 292.

was the head of the White Rose faction, very popular with "the people," vocally opposed to the "throwing down" of the church, and hated by the upstart Thomas Cromwell.[7] At the very end of the book Pole was presented even more prominently, when Giovio suggested that had Henry only paid attention to "the most salubrious volume" which Pole had addressed to him, meaning *Pro ecclesiasticae unitatis defensione* (*De unitate*), he would have been led to model his behavior on Henry II's and, presumably, to do penance for his sins.[8]

There are a number of problems in determining what Giovio may have been up to in according such an important place to Pole, among them the relation between the *Descriptio* and the *Libri historiarum*, the source of his information, the date of the *Descriptio*, the genre to which it should be assigned, and the models Giovio followed in composing it.

The first two of these are closely connected. The title page of the *Descriptio* claimed it was drawn "from the book of Paolo Giovio . . . on the empires and people of the known world." This was a rather loose claim; as Ernesto Travi shows in the introduction to his forthcoming edition, the material in the *Descriptio* was collected incidentally as Giovio piled up information for his histories.[9] Books thirty-one and thirty-five, covering Henry's marriages, were written between 1535 and 1538, at about the same time Giovio began work on the *Descriptio*.[10] There are strong parallels between the two accounts, but Pole does not appear in the *Libri historiarum*. The information about him could thus have been collected in passing while working on the histories or, as Eric Cochrane states flatly, Pole himself may have been Giovio's

---

[7]Paolo Giovio, *Descriptio Britanniae, Scotiae, Hyberniae et Orchadum* (Venice, 1548), ff. 22v-23r. "Itaque in Roffensis interfecti Cardinalis locum, Reginaldum Polum Brittanum supra generis nobilitatem optimarum literarum eruditione, & christianae virtutis laude clarissimum, evocatum Patavio in Urbem, senatorem facit, . . . nec multo post, quod Polus sanguine Regi esset coniunctus, maioremque inde secum authoritatem allaturus esse videretur, legatus in Britanniam mittitur, ut familiaribus, piisque sermonibus ea commemoraret, quae ad sanandi Regis mentem pertinere viderentur, sed quum Polus in galliam pervenisset, venit ex Anglia Brianius [sic] ad Franciscum Regem, qui ipsum uti Henrici hostem ex foedere sibi vinctum tradi deposcebat, ita gallis Henrico studentibus in Belgium retrusus, ibique aliquamdiu luculentissimo usus hospitio Herardi Marchii Cardinalis Leodiensis, . . . exinde Rex adaucta tot claris funeribus animi feritate, Henricum Montacutum, Poli Cardinalis fratrem, & Corteneium Exoniae Marchionem . . . qui dudum tumultu Northlandico summa fide, virtuteque Regiis copiis praefuerant, insignique Regis amicitia erant conspicui, securi percuti iubet, eo nomine damnatos, quod in tanta templorum strage a consiliis Regiis libera voce discessissent, sed proculdubio gratia popularis, regiique sanguinis praeclara nobilitas, quod ad Albae Rosae principem domum genus referrent, invisos occulto metu, suspectosque reddiderant, premente praesertim Cromvele, qui degeneri odio nobilitati infestus, maximorum heroum ruina laetabatur."

[8]Ibid., f. 25r-v.

[9]Ernesto Travi, "Introduzione," Paolo Giovio, *De Imperiis et Gentibus Cogniti Orbis, Pauli Iovii Opera*, to appear as vol. X, 67-72, 70.

[10]T. C. Price Zimmermann, "Nota storico" to vol. III of *Historiarum sui temporis libri, Iovii Opera* V, 239-48, forthcoming.

principal source for recent English history.¹¹ There is much to support such a view, even if there is no explicit statement to that effect in the work. Giovio's account of the divorce crisis in the *Descriptio*, with its heavy emphasis on the University of Paris's opinion, could well have drawn on Pole's recollections since he played a leading role in procuring the theologians' judgment. It would seem that an Italian and an admirer of the republic of Venice, as was Giovio, would more probably have highlighted the equally successful negotiations with the Paduan theologians, had he been drawing on a source not intimately concerned with Paris.¹² Pole may also have stimulated Giovio's strong interest in the White Rose. Becadelli began his life of Pole with a detailed account of English factional struggles and gave a prominent place to his White Rose allegiance.¹³ Pole made much of his Plantagenet ancestry in the original draft of *De unitate*.¹⁴ Beccadelli and Giovio may have reflected Pole's own ambitions. There is also a close fit between Giovio's discussion and dating of Henry's claim to *imperium* over the church and Pole's early discovery of the drift of royal policy, at least in the version of events which he had worked out by the time of the *Descriptio*.¹⁵ Who better than Pole to furnish the detail about his 1537 legation?

Just here the first doubts arise, and the lack of textual warrant for Pole as Giovio's source quickly magnifies them. Giovio presented no evidence about

---

¹¹Eric Cochrane, *Historians and Historiography in the Italian Renaissance* (Chicago: University of Chicago Press, 1981), 366.

¹²Carlo Volpati, "Paolo Giovio e Venezia," *Archivio veneto* 5th ser., 15 (1934):132-56, and for Padua Edward Surtz, *Henry VIII's Great Matter in Italy: An Introduction to Representative Italians in the King's Divorce, mainly 1527-1535* (Ann Arbor, Mich.: University Microfilms, 1978). Pole's prominent role in the divorce is analyzed in T. F. Mayer, "A Mission Worse than Death: Reginald Pole and the Paris Theologians," *Journal of Ecclesiastical History*, forthcoming.

¹³Beccadelli, 277-80. The White Rose was the heraldic badge of Richard, duke of York, and hence the symbol of the Yorkist party during the fifteenth-century dynastic struggles in England. Despite his own claims and those of later apologists, Henry VII did not quite succeed in unifying his party, the Lancastrians, and the Yorkists after he overthrew Richard III. Pole was born into what should have been one of the most prominent Yorkist families. His mother was the daughter of Edward IV's brother the duke of Clarence, who wound up drowned in a butt of malmsey wine. In the early part of Henry VIII's reign, Richard de la Pole was the leader of the White Rose faction, but he spent his entire career on the continent in exile until his death in 1525. Pole's standing in that group could only have been enhanced by his sister's marriage to Henry, Lord Stafford, son of the third duke of Buckingham, whose father had been a Yorkist and one of Richard III's chief supporters before his treason. The White Rose retained some vitality into the 1530s, and Pole remained in relatively close touch with it, especially that section centered around Exeter.

¹⁴Thomas F. Dunn, "The Development of the Text of Pole's *De Unitate Ecclesiae*," *Papers of the Bibliographical Society of America* 70 (1976): 455-68, esp. 463.

¹⁵Much must be done to sort out how Pole contributed to his own myth, for example in the story of the interview with Henry in late 1530 or in Paris (see above). For his chronology of Henry's attack on the church, see T. F. Mayer, "Faction and Ideology: Thomas Starkey's *Dialogue*," *Historical Journal*, forthcoming.

the legation that he might not have drawn as easily from his close friend and steady informant, Rodolfo Pio, papal nuncio in Paris at the time of Pole's mission.[16] He had held that post for two years and was very eager for Pole's success by whatever means.[17] Pio passed on full reports about the legation, including Bryan's boast that he would kill Pole with his bare hands.[18] He received a long letter from Pole just after the latter was forced to leave Paris, complaining of Francis's breach of all human and divine law by his efforts to have Pole surrendered to Henry.[19] Very early in his nunciature, Pio discovered the importance of the White Rose, when he suggested to Cardinal Palmieri that Pole, a member of that faction, might be appointed to replace Fisher.[20] He would have been quite proud of the success of his recommendation. Thus, Pio could have supplied the essentials of Giovio's legation story: Pole's succession to Fisher, his White Rose loyalty, the threats against him. The suggestion that Pio was Giovio's source is strengthened by their close epistolary ties.[21] Some of the detail about the French role in the divorce, recounted in the histories (such as the especially juicy bit that Francis was willing to help Henry in hopes of breaking the Anglo-Imperial alliance and the emphasis on the Parisian theologians) could have come from either of two other highly placed correspondents—the du Bellay brothers: Guillaume, the principal French agent in the dickering over the theologians' decision, and Jean, then French

---

[16] Carlo Capasso summarizes his nunciature and relations with Pole. *Paolo III (1534-1549)* I (Messina-Rome: G. Principato, 1924): 387-92. His correspondence during his tenure in Paris was edited by J. Lestocquoy, but unfortunately often in highly expurgated form. *Correspondance des nonces en France Carpi et Ferrerio 1535-1540, Acta nuntiaturae Gallicae* I (Rome: Gregorian University Press, 1961). The summaries in J. S. Brewer, ed., *Letters and Papers Foreign and Domestic of the Reign of Henry VIII* (London: H. M. Stationery Office, 1862-1932) are much more thorough, especially for matters touching England. They are based on a transcription of Vatican MSS. (This collection will be cited as *LP*.)

[17] *LP* 11, no. 1173, 11 November 1536, to the principal papal secretary; Pole could be very useful in egging on the northern rebels.

[18] Lestocquoy, no. 217 (21 April 1537), 253 (*LP* 12:1, no. 996). Brian had said that "se lo [Pole] trovasse in mezza Francia lo amazzarebbe di sua mano."

[19] Reginald Pole, *Epistolarum Reginaldi Poli*, ed. A. M. Quirini (Brescia, 1744-1757) II, no. 17, p. 35, conjecturally dated and placed by Quirini as Paris, 20 February 1537, but actually Cambrai, 19 February. Both supplied from Biblioteca apostolica vaticana, Vat. lat. 12909, f. 139r.

[20] *LP* 8, no. 986, 4 July 1535. Whether or not the White Rose was a live option in England, many foreign observers thought it was and never failed to mention Pole's place in it. Martin de Çornoça, Spanish consul at Venice, singled out Pole's distinguished ancestry in a report on his value to the emperor in 1534. So had Eustace Chapuys, imperial ambassador in London, a year earlier. Pascual de Gazangos, ed., *Calendar of State Papers, Spanish*, 5:1 (London, 1886), nos. 80 and 109.

[21] Giovio wrote to Pio in Paris a week before the latter announced his arrival to the French. Paolo Giovio, *Lettere (Opere* I and II), ed. G. G. Ferrero (Rome: Istituto Typographico dello Stato, 1956, 1958) I, no. 47, 12 February 1535. His arrival announcement is in *LP* 8, no. 246.

ambassador to Henry and later a cardinal much resident in Rome.²² They could well have contributed to the *Descriptio* as well. Perhaps it does not matter a great deal who Giovio's source was. Even if Pole fed him the story, Giovio nevertheless used it for his own purposes.²³

Pio knew about Giovio's project right from the start, reinforcing the probability that Giovio persuaded him to contribute to it. Giovio began to write the *Descriptio* in early 1535 and promised Pio in the summer that he would have it finished that winter.²⁴ He reneged, but no explanation survives. Travi thinks he hoped for French support for the whole proposal to describe the "empires" of the known world, and when Francis refused, the scheme went on the back burner. Other than the date of its inception, next to nothing can be discovered about when the *Descriptio* was written. It was printed sometime in the first half of 1548.²⁵ Possibly the work took on book form between December 1546 and April 1548, judging from its set of privileges, including a delayed one from Francis I. In the earlier ones the printer, Michele Tramezzino, was granted only the generic copyright for Giovio's historical works, while in the last (from the Doge of Venice) he was given specific protection for the "descrittione della Anglia," among other titles.²⁶ Then again, this may simply indicate the time Tramezzino learned of the work. E. F.

---

²²Paolo Giovio, *Historiarum sui temporis [libri]*, ed. Dante Visconti (*Opere* IV and V) (Rome: Istituto Typographico dello Stato, 1964-1965) II, bk. 31, p. 346. V.-L. Bourrilly's is the best treatment of the du Bellays in his *Guillaume du Bellay, sieur de Langey* (Paris: Bellais, 1905). For Giovio's contacts with them, see *Lettere* I, no. 47, to Pio, complaining of de Langey's silence and also asking to be recommended to "Giovanni Giachino" de Passano, then Francis's resident ambassador in London. He did the same in another letter of December 1536 (ibid., 190). In August 1535 he noted that he had written to Cardinal du Bellay. Franca Bevilacqua Caldari presents other evidence of Giovio's borrowing from the cardinal; see her "Un brano delle Historiae in una lettera inedita del cardinale Jean du Bellay," *Studi romani* 19 (1971), cited in Cochrane, *Historians*, 573.

²³This *is* a point of great significance in Pole's biography, especially for its revelation of his attitude to the rest of the English nobility (who were his expected allies in opposition to Henry) and particularly to the duke of Buckingham, as well as for what it appears to say about Pole's ambitions. If Giovio's chronology of Henry's divorce maneuvers came from Pole, that would be of some value in unravelling Pole's notorious reworking of *cruces* in his career. It might also help to clear up the vexed problem of the prominence Thomas Starkey assigned to the constable in his elaborate system of checks on royal policy. Buckingham had claimed the office by hereditary right, but Henry's judges had refused his arguments. See Mayer, "Starkey's *Dialogue*." In other words, by the time the story came out in the *Descriptio*, it could have been fictional at two removes, both Pole and Giovio having had a crack at it.

²⁴Travi, 67.

²⁵Giovio sent a copy to Cosimo de'Medici on 16 June. *Lettere* II, no. 293.

²⁶There are six pages of privileges at the front of the volume. That from Venice occurs on the fourth and is dated 21 April. Tramezzino was a major Venetian publisher and printer who who would later be in the forefront of the struggle against the introduction of an Index. Paul F. Grendler, *The Roman Inquisition and the Venetian Press, 1540-1605* (Princeton: Princeton University Press, 1977), 5, 99-100, 118.

Hirsch long ago noted that the book could have been written well before this; it does, after all, stop with Henry's marriage to Catherine Parr in 1543.[27]

The question of the *Descriptio's* genre, like that of models for particular set-pieces, is of the essence since whatever genre a writer chose exercised powerful constraints on what could be written. As Peter Burke emphasizes, Renaissance literature was much concerned with genre, but also allowed the imitation of only one classical form at a time. Further, "what mattered to the Renaissance historian was not to convey any precise indication of the individuality of *this* man, or to describe precisely what was said on *this* occasion, but to give a general impression of *a* leader, *a* battle, *an* oration." In short, stereotypes abounded.[28] Any chance of distinguishing "reality" from "fiction" depends on knowledge of the forms into which raw perceptions were poured.

It is not yet possible to say what ancient format Giovio may have been following, as his readers would have expected, according to his claim in the work's preface. The printer took it to be some sort of history, as the privileges attest, and so does Cochrane.[29] Assuming for the moment that Tramezzino and Cochrane are correct, this raises as many problems as it solves. Giovio has not had a good press for his historical work until recently, when a more sympathetic appreciation of humanist historiography and its rhetorical grounding has cleared the way for a new understanding.[30] Fortunately, Giovio described

---

[27]E. F. Hirsh, "The Life and Works of George Lily," (Ph.D. dissertation, Yale University, 1935), pp. lv-lvi. Cochrane is in error when he claims it went no further than the marriage with Catherine Howard in 1540, *Historians*, 366.

[28]Peter Burke, *The Renaissance Sense of the Past* (New York: St. Martin's, 1970), 105-6.

[29]Cochrane, *Historians*, 366.

[30]A long tradition of polemic over his accuracy began almost immediately after the *Historiarum libri* was published. See Cochrane, *Historians*, 364-75. In the first part of this century, in what was long the standard survey, the Swiss journalist Edouard Fueter noted that Giovio's advance in mendacity over the rest of the humanists lay in trying to sell his product to more than one buyer. *Geschichte der neueren Historiographie* (Munich and Berlin: Oldenbourg, 1911) I:51-55. His assessment of Giovio as a mere journalist passed into W. K. Ferguson's *The Renaissance in Historical Thought* (Boston: Houghton Mifflin, 1948), 66. Even as late as 1977, Denys Hay still reproduced Fueter's judgment in all its essentials, adding a few details of his own about the "comical" side of Giovio's work, even though he elevates his status slightly by labeling him a "biographer " (should that be "mere biographer"?). *Annalists and Historians: Western Historiography from the VIIIth to the XVIIIth Century* (London: Methuen, 1977), 100-101. When Benedetto Croce took up the cudgels for Giovio, he initially set out to defend him against such charges. "Intorno a Paolo Giovio," originally in *La critica* 27 (1929):177-85, reprinted in his *Conversazioni critiche*, 3d ser. (Bari: Laterza, 1951), 296-308. Both Croce's later "La grandiosa aneddotica storica di Paolo Giovio," in *Poeti e scrittori del pieno e del tardo rinascimento* II (Bari: Laterza, 1958):27-55 and Chabod, "Giovio," still devote most of their attention to defending his exactitude. This is largely true of Cochrane's treatment as well, despite his structures on Fueter's approach; *Historians*, xi, 375. Donald Wilcox delivered one of the strongest attacks on Fueter for criticizing humanist historians for failing to ask questions considered relevant only later and consequently for an abject failure to take humanist history on its own terms. Donald J. Wilcox, *The Development of Florentine Humanist Historiography in the Fifteenth Century* (Cambridge: Harvard University Press, 1969), 27-28.

his work as a "corografia," which Travi explains was not history, but rather a complete description of an unknown country which was meant to contribute to the understanding of contemporary problems.[31] Whether it was history or *corografia*, the *Descriptio's* goal is markedly humanistic: in the preface Giovio hoped that his writings "should be judged to be able to educate gravely and delight with dignity . . . by famous examples."[32] After admitting that he took most of his materials for Britain's early history from Polydore Vergil, Giovio pointed out more directly that "our burden will be to add the most famous kings and to put the face of the present age under readers' eyes." Topographical description of the whole island would be followed by the major thing Giovio wished to express, "the fame of the King [Henry], who although early on he should have been carried along by famous piety and virtue of spirit into a supreme effort for true glory, he would at length act, moved strongly by an unaccustomed disturbance of mind."[33] The *Descriptio* was designed to present an unfavorable portrait of Henry, whom Giovio hoped to reform through Pole's agency.

The problem of which classical set-pieces Giovio might have chosen as models is similar to that of genre. Before trying to discern what Giovio may have been up to, it is necessary to lay out what he *could* have been doing. Giovio described his biographies as framed on Plutarch, but it seems likely that he fashioned his portrait of Pole on Polybius's story of Philip V's corruption by bad advice.[34] Philip began as the "darling of the whole of Greece," but he ended by seducing not only widows and married women, but finally any woman at all, succumbing to the lure of arbitrary power. The parallel to Henry is obvious. The good adviser/bad adviser *topos* helps to explain Philip's degeneration and supports the case for Giovio's borrowing. Just as the evil Demetrius urged Philip to break faith with the Messenians, triggering Philip's descent, while the good Aratus was just a step too slow, so did the wicked Thomas Wolsey hatch the divorce project, and Pole, like Aratus, was too late. If only Henry had read *De unitate*! The mere presence of a *topos*, though, as F.

---

[31]Travi, 72, 69. He also suggests that it was primarily English religious problems which concerned Giovio, 71.

[32]*Descriptio*, f. av. "[E]am minime defuturam arbitrabar, si scriptis nostris commendatione hominum tanta authoritas accederet, ut ea posteros illustribus exemplis copiose, & graviter erudire, ac oblectare cum dignitate posse censerentur."

[33]Ibid., f. 3r. "Nostri autem muneris erit attigisse clarissimos reges & praesentis seculi faciem legentium oculis subiecisse, universa scilicet insula in ampliores, nobilioresque provincias divisa representataque obiter fama regis, qui, cum antea ab illustri pietate virtuteque animi in summum verae gloriae fastigium esset provectus, ab inusitata demum mentis perturbatione commotus inde deciderit."

[34]*Virorum illustrium vitae*, preface. I am grateful to Professor Zimmermann for this reference.

W. Walbank argues for Polybius's original, need not mean that the story did not also reflect reality as Polybius saw it.³⁶

If Giovio were acting out of a similar positivist intention, trying to write the truth albeit within a classical framework, he was much less exacting than his defenders have claimed and the charges of mendacity leveled by critics would be fully justified. Hirsch's characterization of the *Descriptio's* last six folios as a "violently partisan account of the divorce and condemnation of Anne Boleyn" might seem fair enough.³⁶ The character of the bad adviser Wolsey is left a stick-figure, but Pole's is fully fleshed out; in fact, it may be the only well-developed character in the book. Even Henry is not so thoroughly limned Giovio could not have been striving for objectivity in his portrait of Pole. His story is simply too one-sided. Giovio made Henry the out-and-out aggressor and excluded altogether any mention of Pole's and his supporters' fire-breathing calls for popular revolt. Much as did Pole, Giovio carefully skirted exactly what Pole did on his 1537 mission. He mentioned the Pilgrimage of Grace only to illustrate Exeter's loyalty and did not tie it to Pole at all. Given his contacts in the papal court, with Pio (one of the ring-leaders), and with others in the French capital, at the very least, he must have known that the true purpose of Pole's legation was to stir up the rebels.³⁷

---

³⁵Polybius, *The Histories*, trans. W. R. Paton (London: Heinemann, 1922-1927) IV.77 (II:483), VII.11 (III:429), VII:12-14 (429-31, the climactic scene), and X.26 (IV:163). It is well within the realm of possibility that Giovio modeled the whole of his historical work on Polybius. True, he explicitly claimed to be leaving an unfinished monument like Livy's, but Livy did not write universal history and, as Arnaldo Momigliano observes, when Leonardo Bruni paraphrased Polybius in the early fifteenth century, he had tried to make him appear as much like Livy as possible. "Polybius' Reappearance in Western Europe," in *Polybe* (Geneva: Fondation Hardt, 1974), reprinted in his *Essays in Ancient and Modern Historiography* (Oxford: Blackwell, 1977), 79-98, esp. 84. Cochrane does everything in his power to avoid making a similar claim for Polybius's importance to Giovio, even noting that Giovio's was the most universal history since Polybius's; *Historians*, 373. The difficulty may be that Polybius has been made the patron saint of the "pragmatic" historians who supposedly arose as a reaction against the humanists. This distinction may be too neat. It should not be forgotten that Lodovico Domenichi, Giovio's literary executor, translated Polybius into Italian (even if he made a bad job of it), praising him in the preface as "a great historian, *a very great orator*, and best of all . . . a philosopher." Quoted in Peter Burke, "A Survey of the Popularity of Ancient Historians," *History and Theory* 5 (1966):135-52, esp. 144 (emphasis added). There were some twelve editions of Polybius between 1450 and 1549 (ibid., 137), and manuscripts of the *excerpta antiqua* (books V or VI to XVIII) abound. See J. M. Moore, *The Manuscript Tradition of Polybius* (Cambridge: Cambridge University Press, 1965), pt. II, and Momigliano, "Reappearance," 87-88. The connection between Giovio and Polybius would bear further study. It would hardly be surprising if a few new varieties of flora were to be discovered in what Perez Zagorin has called the "vast Amazonian forest" of humanist historiography. Review of Cochrane, *Historians, Renaissance Quarterly* 35 (1982): 590-92, esp. 590.

³⁶Hirsh, "Lily," p. lviii.

Giovio highlighted Pole's *De unitate* in much the same way. On one level, this is explained by Nancy Struever's observation that the humanists' concentration on fame led to an awareness of the power of ideas and consequently of the written word.[38] This meant much more than a mere intellectual gambit, though, again as Giovio must have known. Even without its inflammatory direct appeal to the emperor, *De unitate* was a potent anti-Henrician polemic, which the English greatly feared and numerous papal and imperial agents very much wanted printed.[39] Pole retained hopes that it would have an effect on Henry for some time after its composition in 1535-1536. He wrote a series of prefaces for it, addressed to various European monarchs and designed to bring them to act against Henry, including a very long *apologia* to Charles V, probably written as late as 1539.[40] Giovio betrayed little knowledge of the work's content, but he did know its chief thrust, the call to penance, and used it for the conclusion of his own work.[41]

Thus did Giovio magnify Pole. By the canons of humanist scholarship this was perfectly justified. Giovio may indeed have concerned himself with such positivist trappings as precise chronology, but he was doing much more.[42] As he wrote in the preface, he was after examples. By idealizing the character of Pole he was engaged in a political act, as well as a rhetorical effort to create reality.[43] His hopes for Henry need not have dictated any particular role for

[37]This was in Pole's mind from the beginning. In his memo for Paul III written before he left Rome, he ended with the quite practical matter of providing money for the rebels. Pole, *Epistolarum* II:cclxxvii. He wrote even more explicitly to the pope from Cambrai on 27 May 1537 that his presence there was the best way to put "terror" into the hearts of the English leaders and that he wished to remain in the Low Countries because, although the revolt had died down for the moment, its causes were still there and it was certain to break out again. Ibid., 52, 54. He wrote in more Biblical language to Cardinal Contarini in June, but the message–I hope I can stir up a popular revolt–was the same. Ibid., 67.

[38]Nancy S. Struever, *The Language of History in the Renaissance: Rhetoric and Historical Consciousness in Florentine Humanism* (Princeton: Princeton University Press, 1970), 72.

[39]Among them Pio, writing to Rome in November 1536. *LP* 11, no. 1173.

[40]Dunn, "*De Unitate*," 461.

[41]If we accept Pole's claim to have tried to suppress *De unitate*, then Giovio's knowledge of it is another sign of how close he was to Pole's circle. If, on the other hand, we credit an increasing body of evidence for a 1539 edition, Giovio's knowledge is not all that important. The case for this date seems to be clinched by a previously unnoticed marginal note in the Blado edition, *Reginaldi Poli ad Henricum Octavum Britanniae Regem, pro ecclesiasticae unitatis defensione*, f. Niiidr, "Cromuuellum nunc habet." He was executed in May 1540. Dunn argues that Contarini had the work printed without Pole's knowledge, and that may have been the case.

[42]Just to add my mite to the ongoing debate. A neat instance of Giovio's passion for correct chronology turns up in the *Descriptio* where he utterly confused the sequence of events in 1520 and 1521, chiefly because he had the date of the Field of Cloth of Gold wrong. *Descriptio*, f. 20r-v. Someone must have pointed out the problem, because in a letter to Antonio Buonagrazia four years later (*Lettere* II, no. 414, 4 July 1552), Giovio asked "quando fu l'abboccamento fra esso [Francis I] e 'l Re d'Inghilterra."

[43]Harvey C. Mansfield, Jr., review of Peter E. Bondanella, *Machiavelli and the Art of Renaissance History, Renaissance Quarterly* 28 (1975):68-70, esp. 69.

Pole, and he must be credited with the same sort of independence of mind when handling Pole as he showed in the histories.[44] He would have been unlikely to have simply swallowed Pole's self-presentation. The decision to cast him as hero must have sprung from precise motives.

Most of the evidence for Giovio's motives comes from his correspondence. Fortunately, all of the important letters are in Italian, and it is probable that Giovio was one of the few sixteenth-century writers who did not concern himself with literary form and future publication when writing in the *volgare*. For him, Italian was the vehicle of day-to-day business, as opposed to the highly polished Latin of his formal letters.[45] Equally fortunately, these letters come from a wide variety of sources, and many were left in manuscript. Therefore concerns about tampering are at a minimum. This is especially fortunate, for the editor of Giovio's published letters, Lodovico Domenichi, was highly suspect religiously and might well have used his collection to create a heterodox Giovio, much as Beccadelli, following common form, expurgated his *epistolario* to mold the *persona* he wished to leave behind.[46]

The search for Giovio's motives immediately strikes the snag of explaining why he went ahead with publication after the person against whom the *Descriptio* was most directly aimed had died. Henry breathed his last in January 1547. Hirsh suggested and Travi seconded a fairly neutral motive: a desire to provide information about England precisely because of the crisis following Henry's death.[47] This suggestion might be supported by his choice of Latin in order to reach a European audience, but that selection would have been automatic for a man who had labored for years on the Latin histories.[48] It also says nothing about how Giovio chose to present that information.

Three motives may be put forward. These may have been operative from the beginning, parallel to the more overt purpose of stimulating Henry's reconversion, or they may have taken over after Giovio's hopes for the king were necessarily crushed by his death. First, and perhaps most likely, Giovio may have meant to build Pole up as his candidate to bear the imperial standard

---

[44]He refused to bow to imperial pressure to change some of his stories about Charles V, for example. T. C. Price Zimmermann, "The Publication of Paolo Giovio's Histories: Charles V and the Revision of Book XXXIV," *La Bibliofilia* 74 (1972):49-90.

[45]Gigliola Fragnito, "Per lo studio dell'epistografia volgare del cinquecento: Le lettere di Ludovico Beccadelli," *Bibliothèque d'humanisme et renaissance* 53:1 (1981): 61-87, 69-70.

[46]Ibid., 80.

[47]Hirsh, "Lily," pp. liv-lv. Beatrice Corrigan noted the fascination of Italian historians with the strange form of the English government. She cited Girolamo Pollini and Bernardo Davanzati, both, interestingly enough, of great importance in the transmission of Pole's image. "Sir Thomas More: Personage and Symbol on the Italian Stage," in *Studies in the Continental Background of Renaissance English Literature*, ed. Dale B. J. Randall and G. W. Williams (Durham: Duke University Press, 1977), 91-108, esp. 92.

[48]Croce, "Grandiosa aneddotica," 37, citing a letter to Domenichi of 1549.

(or at least walk next to it) when Charles should invade England.[49] Giovio hoped for an invasion at the latest by the time of Henry's death, when his attitude toward the king became distinctly more hostile. Almost from the outset of the important letter to Pier Luigi Farnese reflecting on the state of England in early 1547, he called Henry the "cruente e impio tiranno d'Inghilterra." After remarks about the reign of force (and chance: Giovio described the new king's council playing at cards to decide whether to throw Mary into the Thames), Giovio presented his solution. The pope should send Pole with French and particularly German aid to wed Princess Mary, as part of a general plan for Charles's take-over.[50] This was perfectly feasible and fairly widely bruited. Pole remained in minor orders until 1553, and imperial agents several times reported rumors of a marriage, which could only have interested them. Count Cifuentes, imperial agent in Rome, for instance, wrote to Charles in May 1537, at the beginning of a dispatch about Pole's legation, that he might end up marrying Mary.[51] Giovio returned to this theme in August 1547, again suggesting that Charles should turn his arms against England in order to avenge the wrongs done to his cousin Mary.[52] This time, though, he wrote only that Charles should find Mary a suitable husband, rather than proposing Pole.[53] Charles was always reluctant to engage in what would later be called the enterprise of England, but he had long been aware of Pole's potential and would willingly acquiesce in his run for the papacy in 1549.[54] This remedy for English affairs dated back even further. In one of his many plans for imperial intervention, Giovio, in December 1539, thought the emperor could send an army to England to aid the White Rose, if only he did not have to worry about the corsair Barbarossa.[55] This could be highly significant. Then Pole was nearly the last representative of that faction—its former head, Exeter, and Pole's own older brother having been executed the year before.

It is also conceivable that Giovio meant to appeal to the English nobility to assist the emperor. In his life of the king (included in his *Vite d'huomini illustri di guerra*), he singled out Henry's attacks on the aristocracy along with those on the church arising form his "avaritia," and in his discussion of the 1538 "martyrs" in the *Descriptio*, he made much of Exeter's opposition to the

---

[49]Pole as part of an invasion force would not seem to square very well with Giovio's supposed belief that politics were best conducted when they had least to do with religion. Cochrane, *Historians*, 371. Perhaps this is one of many points at which Giovio's public and private views differed.

[50]Giovio, *Lettere* II, no. 249, pp. 69-70.

[51]British Library, Additional MS. 28,589, f. 216r (*LP* 12:1, no. 1141).

[52]To Pier Luigi Farnese, *Lettere* II, no. 270.

[53]To Cardinal Nicola de' Gaddi, 7 October [1548], ibid., no. 299, p. 128.

[54]See note 20 above and Simoncelli, *Caso Pole*, 60. Imperial agents supported Pole's creation as cardinal in 1536. Beccadelli, 292.

[55]To Nicola Renzi, secretary to the French ambassador in Rome, *Lettere* I, no. 101.

despoiling of the churches, constructing an inspirational *exemplum*.⁵⁶ Against this possibility it may be noted that when Giovio singled out the duke of Buckingham as a victim of Wolsey's tyranny, he wrote nothing about his piety. Two of the three military leaders whom he praised—the duke of Norfolk and Lord Dacre—were religious conservatives, but Norfolk put down the Pilgrimage, and the third, Charles Brandon, was one of Henry's closest companions.⁵⁷

Giovio's plan for imperial intervention probably would have won Pole's support, or, to say the same thing more emphatically, could almost have come from him. In *De unitate* Pole had addressed Charles directly, asking him to intervene in England.⁵⁸ This was a long-standing wish. As early as 1531 Pole had sketched out a scenario in which the emperor could bring England to its knees merely by cutting off trade with the Low Countries and then leaving Henry to the tender mercies of his enraged merchants.⁵⁹ Much the same scheme was probably canvassed during his 1537 legation.⁶⁰ More to the point, Pole harbored similar hopes about the time the *Descriptio* came out. In a long letter to Protector Somerset, perhaps written sometime in 1549, Pole described in great detail how the emperor could rightfully interfere in England and, amongst other things, restore Pole's family.⁶¹ This letter, together with one to Edward VI which was apparently intended as a preface to *De unitate*, reflects Pole's optimism that England could yet be returned to the fold.⁶² Perhaps Giovio shared that faith, despite his rather cynical description of Edward's government. The highly unflattering portrait of Henry may have been meant as an *exemplum* to Edward, while the favorable portrayal of Pole may have been a not so subtle hint to take him on as principal adviser.

Giovio's second and third motives might have sprung from an attempt to drum up support in Pole's circle for some sort of action against England, either directly in the imperial wake or more discreetly, by capturing the papal office for Pole. The *Descriptio* may have been in part a contribution to the *encomia* of Pole which cropped up during his *papabile* years.⁶³ In his prognostication near

⁵⁶Paolo Giovio, *Vite brevemente scritte d'huomini illustri di guerra, antichi et moderni*, trans. Lodovico Domenichi (Venice, 1559), 504-06.

⁵⁷*Descriptio*, ff. 21v, 17v.

⁵⁸This passage was cut out of the manuscript Pole sent to England. Dunn, "De Unitate," 463. The offending passage would have fallen at Public Record Office, London, State Papers Henry VIII (SP 1)/104, f. 160r.

⁵⁹Thomas Cranmer wrote a summary of Pole's opinion on 13 June 1531. B. L. Lansdowne 115, f. 2v.

⁶⁰Pole, *Epistolarum* II:37-38, to Pio.

⁶¹Biblioteca nazionale "Marciana," Venice, MS. Ital. X. 24 (6527), ff. 16v, 184 (*Calendar of State Papers, Venetian*, ed. Rawdon Brown [London, 1873], 5, no. 575).

⁶²Pole, *Epistolarum*, IV:306-54.

⁶³George B. Parks, "Italian Tributes to Cardinal Pole," in Randall and Williams, eds., *Continental Background* (above note 47), 43-66, esp. 58.

the beginning of the 1549 conclave, though Giovio tabbed his old friend Pio first and Cardinal del Monte, finally the winner, next. Pole was among "li abstratti," any of whom were suitable, but Giovio made nothing special out of him.[64] Carlo Dionisotti cites this passage as part of the evidence in his powerful case for Giovio's religious cynicism. According to him, Giovio was laughing at Pole, Morone, Cervini, and Carafa.[65] It is true that Giovio was not particularly taken with Carafa, sarcastically calling him the "cardinale riformatissimo in Christo," and he did introduce these four by writing "it is said" that any were worthy.[66] On the other hand, Cervini was at one time among Giovio's patrons, and Dionisotti overlooked the fact that this letter was written to one of Pole's Tridentine allies, Ottaviano Roverta.[67] Furthermore, if Giovio were so well informed, how on earth did he miss the tremendous support Pole would generate, coming within one vote of the papal throne? Either he claimed more inside knowledge than he had, or he may have trod a bit lightly around a dangerous spot in the ice.

A final possibility is worth attention. Giovio was closely tied to Pole and some of Pole's religious allies, whether or not they formed a party with a common core of beliefs.[68] Giovio's relative lack of concern about theological questions would seem to make it unlikely that he was attracted to them for religious reasons, but he may nevertheless have meant his work to rally Pole's friends behind his plans for England.[69] Giovio may simply have overlooked the theological subtleties involved in a quest for allies in defense of orthodoxy against an external enemy. Pole's crew was opposed to religious developments in England, *ergo* they were suitable material to help undo those changes. Delimiting the extent of Giovio's contacts with Pole's circle is complicated by his Farnese patronage. Carlo Gualteruzzi, for instance, was both an important *spirituale* and Alessandro Farnese's secretary.[70] Nor have any circumstances

[64]*Lettere* II, no. 342.

[65]Carlo Dionisotti, "Machiavellerie (IV)," *Rivista storica italiana* 87 (1975): 242-67, esp. 252.

[66]Chabod, "Giovio," 249.

[67]*Lettere* II, no. 218, 10 October 1545, informing Cervini of the completion of his lives of literary figures. For Roverta, see Dermot Fenlon, *Heresy and Obedience in Tridentine Italy: Cardinal Pole and the Counter Reformation* (Cambridge: Cambridge University Press, 1972), 144.

[68]Fenlon is one of the strongest defenders of the *spirituali* as a coherent party, with A. J. Schutte not far behind. "The *Lettere Volgari* and the Crisis of Evangelism in Italy," *Renaissance Quarterly* 28 (1975):639-88. Massimo Firpo has levelled some of the most devastating criticism at this claim. See especially his review of Alessandro Pastore, ed., Marcantonio Flaminio, *Lettere, Rivista storica italiana* 91 (1979): 653-62.

[69]Chabod called his outlook "secular and laic," in his "Giovio," 250, and Professor Zimmermann agrees, "Paolo Giovio: A Humanist Prelate, Unreformed and Unreforming," unpublished paper, which he very kindly let me read.

[70]Fragnito, "Epistografia volgare," 62.

which might have triggered this motive been isolated. No one knows what Pole was doing in 1547 and 1548.⁷¹ Nevertheless, quite apart from his hopes for Pole in early 1547, Giovio had long expressed regard for the cardinal, though it is always difficult to tell to what extent Renaissance expressions of respect should be taken at face value. In early 1537 he just missed paying homage to Pole when he set off on his legation to Flanders.⁷² In a letter to Cardinal Cervini, one of the three legates to the first session of Trent, Giovio asked to be recommended to Cardinal del Monte, one of the other two, and "al divin Reginaldo," probably Pole, who was the third.⁷³ In a letter of 1539 he called Pole and his long-time friend Jacopo Sadoleto "mirabili."⁷⁴ He had probably come to know Sadoleto when both were in the Roman academy in the late 1510s.⁷⁵ There he would also have come into contact with Pietro Bembo, one of Pole's earliest Italian admirers, later described by Giovio as "mio patrone."⁷⁶ Carlo Volpati detailed the "assidue e confidenziali" relations between Giovio and Bembo from 1530.⁷⁷ Giorgio Vasari, a close friend and client of Giovio's, took his recommendation to paint the trinity of Bembo, Sadoleto, and Pole, instead of three eunuchs, behind Paul III in the courtroom of the Cancelleria Palace.⁷⁸ This might have been a heavily ironic suggestion, on a par with Giovio's description of Pole as one of "li abstratti." All three cardinals, though, have been tabbed as at least heterodox, including Bembo. Simoncelli makes a solid case for labeling him a moderate *spirituale*.⁷⁹

Another mutual friend, whom Giovio also met in Rome, was Gianmatteo Giberti, then papal datary and later reforming bishop of Verona. In 1522 he sent Giovio some information for book ten of his histories.⁸⁰ A bit later Giberti patronized him.⁸¹ Giovio claimed to be impressed with the new discipline

---

⁷¹Fenlon skips over these two years and Marie Hallé [Martin Haile], otherwise the most thorough biographer, cited only the letter for Gualteruzzi's *Privilegio*. *Life of Reginald Pole* (London: Pitman, 1911), 343.

⁷²*Lettere* I, no. 73, 10 March 1537.

⁷³*Lettere* II, no. 218, 10 October 1545.

⁷⁴Ibid. I, no. 96, 7 August 1539 to Alessandro Farnese. This letter could be tremendously important since it laid out Giovio's opinion of two men whom Farnese would later regard less than favorably.

⁷⁵Ibid., no. 60 and Richard M. Douglas, *Jacopo Sadoleto: 1473-1547: Humanist and Reformer* (Cambridge: Harvard University Press, 1959), 9.

⁷⁶Ibid., 14-15; *Lettere* I, no. 115, to Carlo Gualteruzzi, 24 June 1540.

⁷⁷Volpati, "Giovio e Venezia," 138. He assigned Giovio to the same circle of Venetian humanists in which Pole moved.

⁷⁸*Lettere* I, no. 226, to Alessandro Farnese, 5 August 1546. Douglas, *Sadoleto*, xv reproduces the painting and discusses it on 208.

⁷⁹Paolo Simoncelli, "Pietro Bembo e l'evangelismo italiano," *Critica storica* 15 (1978):1-63.

⁸⁰*Lettere* I, no. 9.

⁸¹*Opere* X:256.

XIII

Giberti introduced in his diocese.[82] In 1540 Giovio twice mentioned Giberti, once in company with Bembo and Pole and the other time with "Battista Egnzio," long-time teacher of rhetoric in Venice and an intimate of Bembo and Pole.[83] In the same year he asked to have his *Libri historiarum* recommended to another of Pole's closest associates, Frederico Fregoso, the only man in the papal curia to defend the compromise formula on justification which Contarini had hammered out at Regensburg.[84] Giovio was also much taken with Vittoria Colonna, the woman whom Pole called his second mother, but this was before her fervently religious period.[85] According to Hirsh, George Lily, long a member of Pole's household and his chaplain when he returned to England in Mary's reign, was a "more than casual" friend of Giovio's, dedicating his *Elogia* to him, and Giovio in turn praised Lily's erudition in his *Descriptio*.[86]

This list amounts almost to a roll call of Pole's inner circle.[87] There is evidence to tie Giovio even more closely to this group. One of Giovio's most regular correspondents, Gualteruzzi, was a close friend of Pole's biographer Beccadelli, who is sometimes claimed as a leading *spirituale*, and Beccadelli wrote to him several times in a way that suggests Gualteruzzi was not only very interested in the *spirituali*, but well informed.[88] One of these letters is dated the day before Pole died, when the sky threatened to fall in on them. Beccadelli wrote that "voi sapete come hoggi si vive, et che osservatori si trovano de fatti d'altri, et non basta non far male, anzi il bene piglia sinistro senso spese volte."[89] Even later in July 1566 when things were becoming very difficult for this party, Gualteruzzi imprudently wrote to Beccadelli lamenting the arrest and imprisonment of Pietro Carnesecchi and revealing a high degree of familiarity with his household.[90] Gualteruzzi would have done well

---

[82]*Lettere* II, no. 19.

[83]Ibid. I, nos. 116, 239. It might be noted that Francesco Sarri thought Egnazio may have been forced to resign in 1549 because he had sheltered the fugitive Pierpaolo Vergerio on his way north. "Giovanni Fabrini da Figlione (1516-1580?)," *La rinascita* 2 (1939):617-40, 627-31.

[84]*Lettere* I, no. 109, to Gualteruzzi, 6 February 1540. Fenlon, *Heresy*, 59.

[85]Chabod, "Giovio," 247; Fenlon, *Heresy*, 71; Suzanne Therault, *Un cénacle humaniste de la renaissance: Autour de Vittoria Colonna châtelaine d'Ischia* (Florence: Sansoni, 1968), 229-32 in particular.

[86]Hirsh, "Lily," p. lv. There is little more to connect them. The *Descriptio* is quite independent of Lily's *Chronicon* of English history published in the same volume.

[87]Fenlon, *Heresy, passim*.

[88]Fragnito, *Memoria individuale*, esp. 158-64, strongly disputes Simoncelli's *spirituale* Beccadelli. Firpo, review of Flamino, *Lettere*, 659, agrees.

[89]Simoncelli, *Caso Pole*, 152. This letter is not quite so incriminating as Simoncelli argues.

[90]Fragnito, "Epistografia," 86.

to pay more attention to Beccadelli's advice to "mutar vela per accomodarsi a i venti," with specific reference to the Inquisition.⁹¹ How much this link should be discounted because of Gualteruzzi's official position is difficult to say. It should not be forgotten, though, that Paul III singled Pole out in his *ricordi* left for his son's guidance as "superiore agli altri di nobilita, bonta e dottrina."⁹² Simoncelli sees Gualteruzzi as a sort of *capo d'affari* for the *spirituali*, if not theologically very acute.⁹³ He once asked Marcantonio Flaminio for religious advice and received an exhortation to rely on *sola fides* in return.⁹⁴ Simoncelli and Fenlon regard Flaminio as a central theological influence on the *spirituali*, but in light of Massimo Firpo's heavy emphasis on the private character of Flaminio's religion, it may be wise to exercise caution in finding a party grouped around him.⁹⁵ Religious politics aside, Gualteruzzi apparently knew Pole well enough to induce him to intercede for a *privilegio* for him to print Bembo's works in 1548.⁹⁶ He was also the man Giovio asked to recommend his writings to Fregoso.

Whatever one makes of the Gualteruzzi connection and the rest of this circumstantial evidence of an alliance between Giovio and Pole's circle, there are other indications that his religious attitudes were not quite as *politique* as has often been thought. More than politics could have lain behind his plans for Pole. Giovio's close friend and literary executor, Domenichi, is one indicator. In the same year as the *Descriptio* was published and Pole intervened in behalf of Gualteruzzi, he issued John Calvin's broadside against Nicodemism—concealing one's Protestantism—and fell afoul of the Inquisition. Giovio helped to rescue his translator from prison, but the principal effort was probably made by Renata d'Este, sister of Marguerite de Navarre and notorious patron of reformed religion.⁹⁷ In this instance, little of Domenichi's action rubbed off on Giovio. It is more difficult to deny some role to Giovio in Domenichi's decision to undertake another translation at nearly the same time. As Cochrane notes, Domenichi rendered Heinrich Cornelius Agrippa's *De incertitudine et vanitate scientiarum* into Italian "for reasons unexplained."⁹⁸

⁹¹Ibid., 87.

⁹²Simoncelli, *Caso Pole*, 63.

⁹³Simoncelli, "Bembo," 8.

⁹⁴Fenlon, *Heresy*, 91-92. Farnese patronage may have connected Gualteruzzi and Flaminio. Although both Flaminio and Pole's closest friend Alvise Priuli turned down the post of secretary to the Council of Trent in 1545, they were in sufficiently good standing with the cardinal nephew to avoid falling into disfavor. Ibid., 209.

⁹⁵Firpo, review of Flaminio's *Lettere, passim*, esp. 656.

⁹⁶Hallé, *Pole*, 343.

⁹⁷G. K. Brown, *Italy and the Reformation to 1550* (Oxford: Blackwell, 1933), 173 and F. Bonaini, "Dell'imprigionamento per opinioni religiose di Renata d'Este e di Ludovico Domenichi e degli uffici da essa fatti per la liberazione," *Giornale storico degli Archivi Toscani* 3 (1859):268-81, esp. 271 and 276.

⁹⁸Cochrane, *Historians*, 481.

Giovio might well have helped to inspire the work. In his *Elogia clarorum virorum* Giovio had nothing but praise for Agrippa, noting that he had captured "the reasons of all sciences and arts . . . and called all religions into doubt," but in the end he had "confirmed all his novelties by the authority of sacred scripture." Both *De vanitate* and Agrippa's work on occult philosophy were "serious and grave" and "perhaps might seem eternal."[99] A specimen of Giovio's lack of theological acuity, this recommendation of Agrippa's fideistic scepticism?[100] Perhaps, but this position had strong affinities to Pole's, who roundly denigrated the possibility of merely human knowledge.[101] It may also be that this lack of confidence in human intellect was a common trait of the *spirituali*.[102]

Giovio danced another theologically dangerous turn with an ally of Pole. Although critical of Albert Pighe's behavior, Giovio declared himself highly impressed by his theology, once again in the *Elogia clarorum virorum*.[103] Giovio singled out his portrait of Pighe in a letter announcing the work's completion.[104] This could be quite important. Pole seems to have tried to help Pighe whenever he could, but Pighe was otherwise something of a pariah, even among Pole's friends, partly because of the violence of his polemics (Sadoleto's objection).[105] Giovio had probably known Pighe when both were in papal service in Rome in the 1520s. His good opinion is doubly worthy of notice since Pighe was a protégé of Adrian VI, whom Giovio, of course, thoroughly detested.[106] Giovio could well have been attracted to Pighe's sharp criticism of English religion, but he was also most unsound on justification.

One final possible point of contact between Giovio and many in Pole's acquaintance concerns one of the most burning issues of the mid-sixteenth century, a general council. Federico Chabod argued that Giovio looked forward to a council as a means to deal with the Lutherans, which is very much the attitude Fenlon suggests many *spirituali* held.[107] Dionisotti found no hostile refer-

[99]*Elogia veris clarorum virorum imaginibus apposita* (Venice, 1546), f. 63v.

[100]Charles G. Nauert, *Agrippa and the Crisis of Renaissance Thought* (Urbana: University of Illinois Press, 1965), 44-49, 98, 209. Nauert emphasizes the impact of Agrippa's Italian period on *De vanitate's* fideism.

[101]This was his position at the end of his two year debate with Sadoleto over the merits of philosophy and theology. The former's purpose was only to liberate the senses through its most important lesson: the impossibility of human knowledge. Pole, *Epistolarum* I, no. 16, 414-15.

[102]Fenlon, *Heresy*, 18.

[103]*Elogia clarorum virorum*, f. 66v.

[104]*Lettere* II, no. 218.

[105]Sadoleto to Johann Cochlaeus, 30 November 1538. Franz Dittrich, ed., *Regesten und Briefe des Cardinals Gasparo Contarini (1483-1542)* (Braunsberg: Huye, 1881), no. 374, p. 108.

[106]Hubert Jedin, *Studien über die Schriftstellerartigkeit Albert Pigges* (Münster: Aschendorff, 1931), 51-52.

[107]Fenlon, *Heresy*, 18.

ences to a council in Giovio's letters.[108] Contrariwise, Croce thought Giovio feared a council for the broils with the Lutherans it would probably cause.[109] He may also have thought a meeting would prove an embarrassment to the pope, and he showed little enthusiasm for Trent.[110] When Giovio did write favorably about a council, his end may well have been political—peace within Christendom would allow a crusade against the Turks—, but, to coin a phrase, politics makes strange religious bedfellows. Fenlon, however, probably painted with too broad a brush, as did Delio Cantimori in a different way, when he made the hope for restoration of the faith through a council a central belief of his diverse party which included what are now called the *spirituali*.[111] This is much too complex a problem to be sorted out here. The best approach is no doubt to consider each case individually. For example, Contarini's aspirations, if adequately reflected in the *Consilium de emendanda ecclesia* (1537), added up to administrative reform.[112] Pole's attitude was very complex: K. W. Beckmann simplifies a great deal when he makes Thomas Starkey's *Dialogue between Reginald Pole and Thomas Lupset*, the work of an undoubted conciliarist, a reflection of Pole's beliefs.[113] If there was a widespread desire for a council, it may have sprung more from a desire to heal the schism, than from any hope for doctrinal reform. This was the attitude of a good many influential conciliarists, Marco Mantova and Ortwin Gratius among them.[114]

I have outlined a rather complex set of motives and intentions behind the portrait of Reginald Pole in Paolo Giovio's *Descriptio*. At the formal level the figure of Pole was modeled on Polybius's treatment of Philip V, a variant of the good adviser/bad adviser *topos*, and his ideas were played up out of a humanist trust in the power of ideas. The original intention of the work, to effect Henry's reconversion, required the means, and Giovio was sanguine enough to expect that a reading of *De unitate* would do the trick. When Henry died before the work could be published, the motives behind it perforce changed. The

[108]Dionisotti, "Machiavellerie," 252.

[109]Croce, "Intorno a Giovio," 305.

[110]Zimmermann, "Humanist Prelate."

[111]Delio Cantimori, "Submission and Conformity: 'Nicodemism' and the Expectations of a Conciliar Solution to the Religious Question," trans. E. Cochrane, in E. Cochrane, ed., *The Late Italian Renaissance 1525-1630* (London: Macmillan, 1970), 244-65, 257-58.

[112]*Consilium delectorum cardinalium et aliorum prelatorum de emendanda ecclesia*, in *Documents Illustrative of the Continental Reformation*, ed. B. J. Kidd, (Oxford: Clarendon Press, 1911), now available in English translation with notes and commentary in Elizabeth G. Gleason, *Reform Thought in Sixteenth Century Italy* (Chico, Calif.: Scholars Press, 1981), 81-102. I am indebted to Professor Gleason for advice on this point.

[113]Kurt Wilhelm Beckmann, "Staatstheorie und Kirchenpolitik im Werke des englischen Humanisten Thomas Starkey," (Hamburg University Thesis, 1972), 38-39.

[114]T. F. Mayer, "Marco Mantova, a Bronze Age Conciliarist," *Annuarium Historiae Conciliorum* 14 (1984):171-94 and James V. Mehl, "Ortwin Gratius, Conciliarism and the Call for Church Reform," *Archiv für Reformationsgeschichte*, forthcoming. I am grateful to Professor Mehl for a copy of his paper.

most probable new one is that Giovio hoped for the emperor's intervention and proposed a leading role for Pole. Giovio may also have meant to make some sort of statement to Pole's religious party, to which he may have been sympathetic. Final resolution of the problem of Giovio's intentions and motives depends on three things: finding more direct evidence for the alternatives; uncovering the model behind the whole of the *Descriptio*; determining what Lily's part in its composition was, if any.[115] The first and last of these may be impossible, and we will never have more than plausible conjecture. Whether or not pessimism should be the order of the day, only when this sort of analysis has been done will it be possible to excavate the tradition by which the image of the saintly Pole has been handed down. If the *Descriptio* even approached the popularity of the *Libri historiarum*, it could have an important place.[116] Simoncelli worries that the myth is so pervasive that the "real" Pole cannot be unraveled from it, but only by decoding as many of that myth's constituent episodes as possible will there be any chance of establishing a more complete picture of Pole.

---

[115] Cochrane, *Historians*, 367, maintains that Lily edited the *Descriptio*, but presents no evidence. Hirsh had a similar suspicion, but no more luck in supporting it.

[116] Cochrane, *Historians*, 374 for the histories' popularity.

XIV

When Maecenas Was Broke: Cardinal Pole's "Spiritual" Patronage

Cardinal Pole's patronage makes an important test case as the study of patronage becomes an increasingly important part of the study of the Renaissance. Pole's patronage was "abnormal" in that it was conducted much more in terms of ideology than of material expectations and rewards. The explanation of the peculiar shape of Pole's patronage is twofold: (1) he was always short of cash, and (2) from very early on his clients regarded him as an icon, to whose burnishing they willingly contributed without making many further demands. Although a failure by the usual standards of patronage, Pole enjoyed much greater success both then and subsequently as an emblem/patron of a particular set of religious beliefs.

THE GIVING AND GETTING OF PATRONAGE is a subject of increasing importance in Renaissance studies.[1] Thus far the emphasis has fallen on successful patronage, even if results did not always fully satisfy patrons and clients. Before such an emphasis has a chance to establish the nature of "normal" patronage, it might be a good idea to examine a case which was neither normal nor successful, and whose effects were more potential than real: the patronage of Reginald Pole (1500–1558). Opponent of Henry VIII, cardinal, nearly successful candidate for pope, papal legate and archbishop of Canterbury under Mary I—in short, one of the most important political and religious figures of the mid-sixteenth century—Pole, by most definitions of a Renaissance patron, was a failure.

Pole passed none of the basic tests of a patron, beginning with the least stringent standard, protection extended. As papal legate, he resolved a dispute in Viterbo between shepherds and landowners (and between the commune and interlopers) to the benefit of the commune and the shepherds, but the winners had to pay their own freight.[2] He took care of his household, as any patron had to, but I have found but three cases of his intervention on behalf of his clients; only one of those is likely

---

[1] Diana Robin, *Filelfo in Milan* (Princeton: Princeton University Press, 1991), 13–17, provides a succinct analysis of forms of Renaissance patronage.
[2] Giuseppe Signorelli, *I Diritti d'uso civico nel Viterbese* (Viterbo: Monachi, 1907), 36ff., although Signorelli there mistakenly assigns responsibility to Pole's predecessor as legate, Nicolò Ridolfi.

Generous material support came from the National Endowment for the Humanities, I Tatti: The Harvard University Center for the Study of the Italian Renaissance, and the Gladys Krieble Delmas Foundation. Versions of various sections of this article were read as papers at the North American Conference on British Studies, Montreal, October 1993; the Sixteenth Century Studies Conference, St. Louis, December 1993; and the American Historical Association, San Francisco, January 1994.

although by no means certain to have succeeded.³ He did little better by the measure of successfully forwarding the careers of former clients. His recommendation in late 1553 of the physician and longtime lecturer at the University of Rome, Girolamo da Ponte or Pontano, to Cardinal Cicada (or Cicala) typifies the state of Pole's patronage: not only did he apparently have nothing of his own to give da Ponte, but the cardinal he chose to recommend him to, although well placed in the curial bureaucracy, found himself in need of a recommendation from Pole to Philip II four years later, at which time Pole described Cicada as being in dire financial straits.⁴ A few years later, in 1556, Pole recommended his secretary Mariano Vittori to Pierfrancesco Gagliano as coadjutor in Pistoia, but that good word is not known to have worked.⁵ Then again, Vittori may have gotten his canonry in Santa Maria in Cosmedin, Pole's titular church in Rome, through Pole's appointment, and Pole's enthusiastic letter on Vittori's behalf to Giovanni Morone may have helped Vittori eventually to find a place in Morone's household.⁶

Again, Pole falls down by the yardstick of tangible rewards dispensed, simply because he had little spare substance to disburse in that fashion. The paper evidence that he became quite wealthy once he made it to England proves to be largely an illusion. Someone submitted a huge bill for the maintenance of his household before he came back.⁷ Thereafter he turned over better than £20,000 per annum, according to his receiver Henry Pyning's records.⁸ Andras Dudic, Pole's second biographer and a member of his household in England, claimed that Pole had distributed no less than 10,000 crowns to it, besides providing horses to any member who wished to return to Italy.⁹ Dudic's claim came in a passage about Pole's aristo-

---

³Pole vigorously intervened on behalf of his major domo Bartolomeo Stella in a financial dispute with one of Cardinal Filonardi's clients in 1539; A. M. Querini, ed. *Epistolarum Reginaldi Poli*, 5 vols. (Brescia: Rizzardi, 1744–1757), 2, no. 76 (MSS Vaticani Latini, Biblioteca Apostolica Vaticana [hereafter VL] 5826, fols. 61r/62r–65r). In 1545/6 Pole backed up in a similar fashion the claim of his servant Richard Hilliard to a pension on the Major Penitentiary; Archivio di Stato, Florence, Carte Strozziane, ser. 1, 339, fols. 163r, 248r.

⁴Pole to Cardinal San Clemente, ca. August 11, or November 18, 1553. VL 6754, fol. 88v; Venice, Biblioteca Nazionale Marciana (hereafter BNM) MS Ital. X.24 [6527], fol. 67v); Rawdon Brown, G. Cavendish Bentinck, and Horatio F. Brown, eds., *Calendar of State Papers and Manuscripts, relating to English Affairs in the Archives and Collections of Venice* (hereafter CSPV), 9 vols. (London: Routledge and Kegan Paul, 1864–1898), 5, no. 826. Da Ponte earlier taught one of Pole's most important secretaries, Gianbattista Binardi. Ludovico Castelvetro-Binardi, Venice, April 10, 1543; see *Delle lettere facete et piacevoli de diversi huomini ... raccolte per M. Francesco Turchi* (Venice: Altobello Salicato, 1601), 2:127–129. If one can trust the weird testimony of Lorenzo Davidico, da Ponte—whom he described as one of Alvise Priuli's familiars—had his doubts about Priuli, Pole, and their circle, something Davidico claimed to know as da Ponte's confessor; see Dario Marcatto, *Il processo inquisitoriale di Lorenzo Davidico (1555–1560), Edizione critica* (Florence: Olschki, 1992), 110–111. For Pole's efforts to help Cicada, see his letter to Bartolomé Carranza of October 7, 1557: VL 6754, fol. 234r-v; BNM, MS Ital. X. 24 (6527), fol. 188r; CSPV, 6:3, no. 1099, falsely dated December 7; British Library (hereafter BL), Add. MS 41577, fol. 253r-v.

⁵VL 6754, fol. 217r.

⁶Angelo Sacchetti Sassetti, *La vita e gli scritti di M. Vittori* (Rieti: Trinchi, 1917), 30, 38 ff.

⁷The projected budget demanded not less than 1,000 crowns (probably meaning scudi) per month for the maintenance of Pole's household; see Cambridge, Corpus Christi College, MS 105, no. 43; printed in John Strype, *Ecclesiastical Memorials*, 3 vols. (Oxford: Clarendon Press, 1812), 3:2, 241–242.

⁸Public Record Office (PRO), State Papers (SP) 11/10, fols. 13–16v; other sets of accounts, with slightly different figures, are on fols. 126–135. The figure of £22,500 as Pole's annual turnover comes from SP 11/11/57.

⁹*Epistolarum Reginaldi Poli*, 1:52.

cratic magnificence, which was heavily reworked from Ludovico Beccadelli's version. That may make his assertion especially suspicious. The Venetian ambassador in London provided some confirmation of Dudic's figure in his report that the Queen's grants had underwritten "the liberality which [Pole] used towards some Italians, his servants, returned to Italy" to whom he gave 6,000 scudi.[10] Pyning's records for May 1556 include about £370 for gifts to Italians returning home, the only such reference.[11] More in line with Pyning than Dudic or the Venetian ambassador, Pole's executor, Alvise Priuli, averred that Pole had made nothing out of his legation, had never had much from Mary, and at best ran an annual deficit.[12] As Priuli also reported, rumors that Pole had acquired a huge treasure continued to circulate after his death; some were later recorded in a fantastic account of Pole's assets.[13] Yet the fact that Elizabeth I settled Pole's estate reasonably quickly with Priuli suggests that Priuli was probably telling something like the truth about Pole's finances.[14] By my best and most generous calculation, Pole probably cleared no more than £1,200 per annum after his return to England.[15]

[10] Paul Friedmann, *Les Dépeches de Giovanni Michiel, Ambassadeur de Venise en Angleterre pendant les années de 1554 à 1557,* (Venice: Commerce, 1869), 217, no. 77, May 12, 1556 (CSPV, 6:1, no. 482): "la liberalità che [Pole] ha usato verso alcuni italiani, servitori suoi, ritornati in Italia."

[11] PRO, SP 11/10, fol. 14r. It is nearly impossible to convert these various currencies into one another, but Pyning's figure is probably larger than either Dudic's or Michiel's. As for horses, it is impossible to attribute any cost specifically to those for Italians, although Pyning did record the total of £476 for horses and stables for the whole of the year from October 1, 1556; PRO SP 11/11/54, fol. 126r.

[12] VL 6754, fol. 255, Priuli? to [Antonio] Giberti, London, n.d.; BNM, MS Ital. X.24 (6527), fols. 202r–206r; BL, Add. MS 41577, fols. 274r–280r; Biblioteca Apostolica Vaticana (hereafter BAV), Ottob. 3166, fols., 398v–405v; English translation in Thomas Duffus Hardy, *Report ... upon the Documents in the Archives and Public Libraries of Venice* (London: Longmans, et al., 1866), 63–67, probably made from the transcript by Joseph Stevenson taken from BAV, Ottob. 3166, in PRO, 31/9, 5:255–264. Mary probably gave Pole more than Priuli admitted, but I have not yet been able to work out the precise value of her grants. See, e.g., *Calendar of Patent Rolls, Philip and Mary,* 4 vols. (London: HMSO, 1936–1939), 3:69–72, dated March 13, 1556, a huge gift of lands and annuities, or ibid., 4:450, November 5, 1558, a grant of various impropriations in exchange for Pole's offer of £7,000 in cash collected from his province.

[13] A memorandum in PRO, SP 12/1, fols. 140–143v, drawn up according to the endorsement in 1608, gave Pole an annual income of more than £25,000; see Robert Lemon and Mary A. E. Green, eds., *Calendar of State Papers Domestic, 1547–1580,* 12 vols. (London: Longman, Brown and Green, 1856–1872), 1, no. 64. Cf. Norman L. Jones, *Faith by Statute: Parliament and the Settlement of Religion 1559* (London: Royal Historical Society, 1982), 160.

[14] The final resolution of Pole's charges, which came to perhaps £1,800, took until November 1559; Bergamo, *Biblioteca Civica Angelo Mai: Carte Stella in Archivio Silvestri* (hereafter BCM:CS), 40/152; Giuseppe Bonelli, "Un archivio privato del Cinquecento: Le Carte Stella," *Archivio storico Lombardo,* 34 (1907): 332–386, no. 175.

[15] This figure differs substantially from that given for Pole's "disposable" income in David Loades, *The Reign of Mary Tudor: Politics, Government and Religion in England 1553–1558,* 2d ed. (London: Longman, 1991), 375, and my conclusion about Pole's revenues diverges widely from his. Loades begins from Pole's receiver Henry Pyning's tally of an annual income of £22,500, which is accurate but misleading (Loades here correctly cites SP 11/11/57, but identifies it as if it were no. 54). Despite that huge sum Pole was left with a profit of only about £450. Loades also claims that Pyning recorded grants from both Mary and Philip (the second of £1,055) which he took to represent the lion's share of a "disposable" income of £3,000. There are several problems in this reckoning. First, as far as I can see, Pole had no pension from Philip. Loades seems to have taken Pole's pension on the archbishopric of Burgos as in Philip's gift, but it was actually from Charles V; it is possible that Philip renewed it, but I have found no evidence for that; see VL 6754, fol. 34v (CSPV, 5, no. 681), to Charles V [n.d., but August 1550?], thank-

XIV

It is not surprising, therefore, that the only clear instances of Pole's generosity in England involve either very small sums or no financial considerations at all. He is known to have paid only two sets of pensions. One went to an old and faithful retainer, who got twenty-four scudi a year and continued room and board.[16] Pole granted the other pension, of 300 scudi, to the nephews of his long-time right-hand man, Vincenzo Parpaglia, when he and they left Pole's service in early 1556.[17] (These figures must be in two different kinds of scudi.) Pole, by contrast, drew at least one pension worth 2,000 scudi in theory. Otherwise, Pole chose to reward even other members of his household with largely meaningless titles (especially count of the Lateran), which he as a legate *a latere* was empowered to grant.[18] He also had some patronage of no particular import to dispense once he became archbishop of Canterbury. The only request that I have found for any of that is from Hugh Turnbull, a notorious pluralist, who nonetheless thought it worth sending Pole a particularly unctuous letter from Padua in 1555. Turnbull's reward may have been admission as an advocate to practice in the Consistory Court of Canterbury.[19] Pole's finances remained tight largely because he spent nearly all his surplus on "magnificence," especially in the form of a new wing of Lambeth Palace, built in 1556–1557. When he did have money, he is said to have distributed it both prodi-

---

[15](continued)
ing the emperor for the grant. The amount of this pension (£1,054) was already included in Pyning's records and thus must be backed out of any "disposable" assets. Second, the grant from Mary appears only in a set of Pyning's records (SP 11/11/60) other than the one Loades worked from, as worth £1,437; it is found again in the valuation of Pole's property made shortly before his death in September 1558, when it was said to be worth approximately £1,287 (PRO, SP 11/13/67. Together with the appearance for the first time of a pension on Winchester of £1,000, probably arranged by the queen, Pole still cleared less than £700 from the sources enumerated in September 1558. Thus Pole's gift from Mary turns out to have done him much less good than Loades thought. Even if Pyning's accounts and the September inventory are treated as recording essentially independent sources of income, Pole's net cash flow from both came to only about £1,200. I am grateful to Dr. C. S. Knighton for help on some of these points.

[16]Battista de Gervasis received a pension of twenty-four gold scudi in July 1555; Douai, Bibliothèque Publique (hereafter DBP) MS 922, vol. 3, fols. 58v–59. He was probably the "old master Battista," who had an exceptionally well-furnished room in Lambeth Palace, according to PRO, SP 12/1, fols. 20–29.

[17]Friedmann, *Dépêches de Michiel*, 217, no. 77, May 12, 1556 (CSPV, 6:1, no. 482).

[18]London, Westminster Diocesan Archives, MS 1, 319–351, Pole's bull of faculties common to all legates *a latere*. For his use of the power of conferring the title of Count of the Lateran and other honorifics, see e.g., DBP, MS 922, vol. 2, fols. 16–18v, 85v–87v. That was all that even one of Pole's own chaplains, John Oudenhagen, got directly from him; ibid., 3, fols. 21v–3v, April 29, 1555.

[19]Turnbull to Pole, Padua, March 7, 1555 (Oxford, Bodleian Library MS Rawlinson D 400, fols. 171v–172, an eighteenth-century copy). Unfortunately, the only evidence that Turnbull's suit to Pole succeeded comes from R. H. Pogson, "Cardinal Pole: Papal Legate to England in Mary Tudor's Reign" (Ph.D. thesis, University of Cambridge, 1972), 185. I found no support for this claim in Pole's archiepiscopal register in Lambeth Palace Library. When Turnbull was made a commissioner against heresy in 1558 he was identified merely as *sacrae theologiae professor;* Lambeth Palace Library, Pole's register, fols. 29v–30; printed in David Wilkins, *Concilia magnae Britanniae et Hiberniae*, 4 vols. (London: Gosling, et al., 1737), 4:173–174. It is also possible that Turnbull's putative reward had very little to do with Pole; his real patron may have been Anthony Hussey, Pole's registrar, two of whose sons Turnbull had tutored in Padua, and whom Turnbull cited as one of his two backers in his letter to Pole. For Hussey's sons in Padua see J. A. Giles, ed., *The Whole Works of Roger Ascham*, 2 vols. (London: J. R. Smith, 1864–1865), 1:410–411.

gally and in strict hierarchical order to his familiars.[20](I omit from consideration the huge number of benefices to which Pole presented, either in his own right as archbishop or during episcopal vacancies in his province. So far as is known, none of these presentations followed on a direct request for patronage. Many of them were couched as rewards, but only rarely does the language seem to say that Pole knew the grantee, and in very many cases it is clear that he was presenting on someone else's nomination.)

Thus the explanation of Pole's failure as a patron or dedicatee is crudely simple: he was a "poor cardinal" until the last three years of his life, and even then things did not improve much. According to his first biographer, he always insisted on living within his limited means.[21] Yet in proportion to his straitened resources, Pole did attract a fair number of potential clients, and had his patronage worked only a little better, it could have affected seriously the culture of the mid-sixteenth century.

Grasping the full extent of Pole's patronage requires putting aside the usual emphasis on outcomes and thinking in terms of process and potential. That must be so in part because Pole's patronage lay in a tricornered field mapped by straitened resources, religious and political ideology, and recurring disaster. During most of his career nonmaterial rewards had to compensate both for the limits imposed by thin substance and for political and religious fiascoes. Any study of Pole's patronage is further complicated by the fact that, like his works, Pole himself resulted from collaborative effort.[22] We need not accept Ludovico Castelvetro's canard that Gianbattista Binardi really authored some of Pole's works and translated most of the rest, nor the accusation that Binardi played the consummate courtier, a charge significantly cast in an imitation of Ariosto's great comic epic, *Orlando Furioso*.[23] Yet these two bunches of sour grapes make a vital point about the role of Pole's household, and especially Binardi, who had charge of all Pole's writings and whose hand is everywhere on Pole's surviving works in the Vatican: everything Pole did depended on interaction between himself and the extraordinary group of true believers that surrounded him. About the only normal aspect of Pole's patronage was this centrality of his household.

Lack of material rewards and collective, cooperative effort add up to a style of patronage driven by ideology. I shall refer to it as "spiritual" patronage. That label

---

[20]Ludovico Beccadelli, "Vita di Reginaldo Pole," BPP, MS Palatino 973/3, fol. 32r, recording an instance at Trent, probably in 1546.

[21]Ibid., fol. 31.

[22]Melissa Meriam Bullard, "Heroes and Their Workshops: Medici Patronage and the Problem of Shared Agency," *Journal of Medieval and Renaissance Studies* 24 (1994): 179–198. I differ from her in being reluctant to posit a directing presence, a position dictated in part by the nature of the sources.

[23]Ludovico Castelvetro, "Racconto delle vite d'alcuni letterati del suo tempo di M. L. C. Modenese scritte per suo piacere," printed in Giuseppe Cavazzuti, *Ludovico Castelvetro* (Modena: Società Tipografica Modenese, 1903), appendix, 7–8, and Alemanio Fino to Luca Michelonio, Crema, November 29, probably 1565 (BCM:CS, 41/197; Bonelli no. 346). Beccadelli also credited Binardi with having translated "other writings" of Pole's into Latin; Gigliola Fragnito, "Aspetti della censura ecclesiastica nell'Europa della Controriforma: L'edizione parigina delle opere di G. Contarini," *Rivista di storia e letteratura religiosa* 21 (1985): 3–48, at 23n.

covers a wide range of patron-client relationships. It includes Pole's link with Marcantonio Flaminio, which he defended as what might be called "patronage for reasons of conversion," claiming that he had taken Flaminio into his household to save him from the heretics. It included a major effort to preserve and redirect the course of English humanism. Sometimes it even included the disbursement of money, but always to causes and persons consistent with the antimaterialist bias built into Pole's patronage. It included a tightly overlapping circle of authors of works dedicated to Pole, the major "material" result of his patronage, all of them taking a similar religious line. And perhaps most important, it included the creation of Pole's own image as a spiritual figure of enormous power. What all these modes of patronage have in common is a complete lack of concern with material outcomes, the usual fuel of clientage, together with a stress on disseminating a particular message.

The precise nature of that message has proved frustratingly difficult to pin down, despite deep-seated suspicions about the orthodoxy of Pole and his friends as well as the mountains of evidence thrown up by investigations of those suspicions.[24] One of the views which got Pole and his circles into trouble seems to have resembled the profoundly contentious medieval doctrine of the apostolic poverty of the Church, a belief Pole almost certainly held.[25] Playing by that fundamental rule, and with the aims outlined above, Pole and his clients invented their own kind of patronage, one which produced its own satisfying rewards. In any event, Pole attracted and kept many clients over a long period of years, despite his usual inability to repay them in a tangible way for their loyalty. In this, Pole was ahead of his time. Poverty and humility—not to mention a small household—together with patronage of religious art and acts of charity became virtues in cardinals by the end of the century.[26] Pole's patronage ran through three phases. The second two are virtually unknown and will attract most of my attention. The first covers the years of Pole's education in Italy, from about 1519 to 1536. It was marked by his dependence on Henry VIII and largely successful performance of most of what Henry demanded of him. It ended in the upheavals of the mid-1530s, the first years of the English reformations. The second phase grew directly out of the first and lasted for another fifteen years. During it, Pole became an Italian and a patron for almost exclusively ideological reasons. His support came mainly from a papal pension. The final phase should have been the most obvious.[27] It began with Pole's triumphant

---

[24]Massimo Firpo and Dario Marcatto, eds., *Il processo inquisitoriale del Cardinal Giovanni Morone*, 5 vols. (Rome: Istituto italiano per la storia dell'età moderna e contemporanea, 1981–1989), passim, and Giacomo Manzoni, ed., "Il Processo Carnesecchi," *Miscellanea di storia italiana* 10 (1870): 189–573, passim. Cf. Sergio Pagano, ed., *Il processo di Endimio Calandra e l'Inquisizione a Mantova nel 1567–1568* (Vatican City: Biblioteca Apostolica Vaticana, 1991), Studi e Testi, no. 339, ad indices.

[25]The clearest statement of Pole's alleged plans to dismantle the church's financial machinery is in one of Girolamo Muzio's reports to Ferrante Gonzaga; see Amadio Ronchini, *Lettere di Girolamo Muzio giustinopolitano conservate nell'Archivio governativo di Parma* (Parma: F. Carmignani, 1864), 109.

[26]Gigliola Fragnito, "Cardinals' Courts in Sixteenth-Century Rome," *Journal of Modern History* 65 (1993): 26–56, 45; cf. Jean Delumeau, *Vita economica e sociale di Roma nel Cinquecento* (Florence: Sansoni, 1979), 112–113.

[27]Heinrich Lutz, *Nuntiaturberichte aus Deutschland: Erste Abteilung 1533–1559*, 15, *Friedenslegation des Reginald Pole zu Kaiser Karl V. und König Heinrich II. (1553–1556)* (Tübingen: Niemeyer, 1981), 63n, suggests the importance of Pole's cultural patronage.

return to England under Mary I in 1554 as legate, archbishop, and leading councillor. Thanks to royal generosity, Pole could finally live and act magnificently, and become a major cultural force. Pole brought with him a large household, full of skilled men, mainly writers, but also other kinds of artists, enough to start an Italian Renaissance cell in England. During it Pole and his household left perhaps their most enduring mark both on English humanism and on the historiography of the reformation.

* * *

The first moment of Pole's patronage witnessed his household in Padua consolidating Nicolò Leonico's earlier impact on English humanism.[28] Leonico had taught many of the first generation of English students in Padua, but his efforts with his pupil Pole and others of Pole's household produced deeper results. Pole learned to use literature as a tool to establish friendships, and then to memorialize them in life writing, as in the case of Christophe Longueil. Incidentally, Longueil offers a good example of Pole's failed patronage even during this relatively successful phase: he got very little out of Pole and died alone in Pole's house in Padua.[29] The second half of this phase turned on the disintegration of the household of the 1520s under the manifold pressures of the 1530s.[30] Throughout both these moments, Pole's patronage was Henry's. Thanks to the disgrace and murder of Pole's grandfather, the duke of Clarence, Pole's family had been stripped of its estates and reduced to nearly total dependence on royal favor. Henry entirely underwrote Pole's stay in Padua before 1536, and Pole duly acted his expected role by studying the political skills which would fit him for high office at home; dispensing a little patronage to Italians who might eventually prove useful in England (to Leonico, to Lazzaro Bonamico, another of his tutors, perhaps to Romolo Amaseo); and encouraging members of his household to train themselves for service to the commonwealth. Among them were Thomas Starkey, Richard Morison, John Friar, George Lily, and Henry Cole, all of whom took advantage especially of the Paduan legal faculty.[31]

By the early 1530s, most of Henry's plans had misfired in the crisis of divorce and incipient reformation. Not only did the king let slip the biggest prize when

---

[28]See the confused work of Adrian Gasquet, *Cardinal Pole and His Early Friends* (London: George Bell and Sons, 1927).

[29]Théophile Simar, *Christophe de Longueil, humaniste (1488–1522)*, Recueil de Travaux ... d'histoire et de philologie, no. 31 (Louvain: Université de Louvain, 1911), chap. 8.

[30]W. Gordon Zeeveld, *Foundations of Tudor Policy* (Cambridge: Harvard University Press, 1948), and an update in Kenneth R. Bartlett, *The English in Italy 1525–1558: A Study in Culture and Politics* (Geneva: Slatkine, 1991).

[31]See Pole's letter to Wolsey, BL, Cotton MS Vespasian F XIII, fols. 283–284; it is not in J. S. Brewer et al., eds., *Letters and Papers, Foreign and Domestic, of the Reign of Henry VIII*, 23 vols. (London: HMSO, 1862–1932). The letter was dated Oxford, October 6, and addressed to Wolsey as legate; the year must therefore be 1518 or 1519. In a letter sent directly to Henry, Pole again came cap in hand and again promised that his studies would glorify the king: he was born only to honor Henry; see BL, Nero B VI, fol. 122r, Padua, April 27, either 1519 or 1521. For Pole's relations with his clients, see Gasquet, *Early Friends* (mainly based on Pole's correspondence with Leonico); Zeeveld, *Foundations;* and, for their political expectations of Pole, Thomas F. Mayer, *Thomas Starkey and the Commonweal: Humanist Politics and Religion in the Reign of Henry VIII* (Cambridge: Cambridge University Press, 1989), passim and 49 ff.

Pole more or less openly refused to countenance Henry's divorce from Katharine of Aragon and, more obviously, the king's claim to supremacy over the English church, but most of the members of Pole's household followed his lead. Two who did not, Starkey and Morison, returned to England. Starkey wasted the advantage of earlier arrival by maintaining his allegiance to Pole; Morison ensured his fortune by repudiating his former patron. While Morison's propagandistic pamphlets advanced Henry's new policies, Starkey's design for an English commonwealth centered on Pole languished. Instead of successfully applying Italian categories of social and political analysis to the reform of England, Starkey had to content himself with preaching in pretty standard fashion the virtues of the royal supremacy.[32] Probably the only sign of patronage-seeking from outside Pole's household in the 1530s is a pair of dialogues by Antonio Brucioli in which Pole appears as speaker.[33] By the mid–1530s Pole's patronage had suffered its first major failure.

When Pole launched a new career in papal service, once more his patronage was not his own. When Paul III made him a cardinal in 1536, his pension was set at a modest 200 scudi per month. This would increase to 500 scudi for some of the time he was legate to the council of Trent in the mid–1540s, and he probably did somewhat better than that as legate to Viterbo (1541–1547) and then governor of Bagnoregio.[34] Pole's resources were now perhaps five or six times greater than they had been when he was drawing £100 a year from Henry, but they had to stretch much further.[35] By the time Pole moved to Viterbo, he had collected a new household, and shortly after he arrived it was reinforced by a contingent led by Marcantonio Flaminio. Flaminio's arrival confirmed Pole's religious and ideological movement since the beginning of his breach with Henry. Although there is some room for reservations on the specifics of this point, Massimo Firpo's contention that Flaminio meant to convert Pole's household into the foremost Valdesian cell in

---

[32] The best treatment of Morison is Zeeveld, *Foundations*, 157–189; see also David S. Berkowitz, ed., *Humanist Scholarship and Public Order: Two Tracts against the Pilgrimage of Grace by Sir Richard Morison* (Washington: Folger Shakespeare Library, 1984).

[33] Antonio Brucioli, *Dialogi*, ed. Aldo Landi (Naples: Prismi, 1982; Chicago: Newberry Library, 1982), "Della providentia divina" and "Della virtù"; see also George B. Parks, "Italian Tributes to Cardinal Pole" in Dale B. J. Randall and G. W. Williams, eds., *Studies in the Continental Background of Renaissance English Literature: Essays Presented to John L. Lievsay* (Durham: Duke University Press, 1977), 43–66, 63. For what little is known of Brucioli's possible ties to Pole and his circle, see Mayer, *Starkey*, 56–57.

[34] CSPV, xiii, and Beccadelli, "Vita," fol. 31, for Pole's basic stipend. Elisabeth Gleason has kindly confirmed that figure from the records of the datary; see Elisabeth G. Gleason, *Concilium Tridentinum Diariorum*, 3:2, ed. Umberto Mazzone (Freiburg: Herder, 1985), 119, 126, for his stipend at Trent. Between January 1548 and November 1549, Pole's pension was only 100 scudi per month; VL 10604, fols. 136v–175v. According to Eletto Ramacci's typescript history of the cardinals governor of Bagnoregio, Pole's salary was 75 scudi per annum (Ramacci, 119, from Bagnoregio, Archivio storico comunale, Consigli del Comune, 2, now destroyed).

[35] His pension was worth either about £55 per month (assuming it was paid in gold scudi da camera) or about £43 (if paid in scudi di moneta). I calculate the scudo as worth five shillings. For these values see Barbara M. Hallman, *Italian Cardinals, Reform and the Church as Property, 1492–1563* (Berkeley: University of California Press, 1985), 169, and M. J. Rodriquez-Salgado, *The Changing Face of Empire: Charles V, Philip II and Habsburg Authority, 1551–1559* (Cambridge: Cambridge University Press, 1988), xv.

Italy underscores the attraction it exercised.³⁶

Pole sank deep religious roots in Italy as one of the most important members of "the reform tendency." Nevertheless, not much grew from them throughout the 1540s. I have found only three or four oblique requests for patronage directed to Pole. In the first, from October 1542, Zanobio Ceffino sent from Montefiascone a pair of versified Psalms to Pole's major domo Bartolomeo Stella in nearby Viterbo. Given the centrality of the Psalms in reformed and heterodox circles, it is not surprising that Pole should have received these translations. Flaminio engaged in the 1540s in a similar project at the same time as he continued to write his slightly off-center poetry, and Pole had earlier joined in reading the Psalms with Jan van Kampen, who also produced paraphrases of some of them.³⁷ At an unknown time but probably later, Pole himself scrawled notes on various Psalms, and Priuli had a "librillo" of them in England.³⁸ If this Zanobio is the same as the "frate Zenobio" who appears in the *Processo Morone*, it would appear that his reward was "seduction" by Pole on the score of justification, making this case a classic instance of spiritual patronage.³⁹

The second instance is more complicated and involves perhaps the first use of Pole's image for religious and political purposes by someone other than Pole. Paolo Giovio's *Descriptio Britanniae*, published in 1548 but perhaps finished as early as 1543, casts Pole in the role he himself had chosen in 1536, the principled opponent of the corrupt tyrant Henry. Giovio made Pole try in his legation of 1537 "to remind it [England], by his familiar and pious words, [of] what seemed to pertain to healing the king's mind," and closed his work with Pole asking Henry to do penance, just as Pole had done in his own *Pro ecclesiasticae unitatis defensione (De unitate)*.⁴⁰ That Giovio should take an exalted view of Pole is perhaps not surprising; Pole's reputation as an unworldly reformer had grown steadily throughout the 1540s. It is more curious that Giovio, one of the all-time great patronage-mongers, does not seem to have looked for any reward from Pole. If he expected repayment, it would have had to come indirectly from Giovio's own patron Cardinal Alessandro Farnese, who would eventually make Pole his principal horse in the

---

³⁶Massimo Firpo, *Tra alumbrados e "spirituali": Studi su Juan de Valdés e il Valdesianesimo nella crisi religiosa del '500 italiano* (Florence: Olschki, 1990), 132–138.

³⁷Alessandro Pastore, ed., *Marcantonio Flaminio, Lettere*, Università degli studi di Trieste, Facoltà di lettere e filosofia, Isituto di storia medievale e moderna, n. s. 1 (Rome: Ateneo and Bizzari, 1978), no. 62. For van Kampen's Paraphrasis of the Psalms, see Henry de Vocht, *History of the Foundation and Rise of the Collegium Trilingue Lovaniense*, 3 vols. (Louvain: Bibliothèque de l'Université, 1951–1955), 3:191, 193.

³⁸Firpo, *Alumbrados*, 174–175; unfortunately the great majority of Pole's notes in VL 5969 are illegible, or nearly so.

³⁹*Processo Morone*, 1:198, "Compendium." The editors suggest (325) that Zanobio may have been the theologian of Ercole Gonzaga to whom Pier Paolo Vergerio wrote, but in the general index he became Zanobio Aiolla, without explanation or identification. Zanobio came into the *processo* through Bernardo de' Bartoli's first deposition, which named him, in company with Vittoria Colonna, as one of Pole's victims. That pairing may reinforce the notion that this Zanobio, like Stella's correspondent, was a poet; see *Processo Morone*, 2:264.

⁴⁰Paolo Giovio, *Descriptio Britanniae, Scotiae, Hyberniae et Orchadum* (Venice: Michele Tramezin, 1548), fols. 22v–23.

conclave of Julius III.[41] As I have shown elsewhere, one of the most likely explanations of Giovio's highly uncharacteristic behavior is a good measure of sympathy with Pole's reforming views.[42] In a peculiar twist, their execution would have hurt the pensioner (and one-time pluralist) Giovio severely, as well as spelling the final destruction of Leonine Rome, Giovio's natural habitat. Giovio's work therefore provides one of the strongest testimonials to Pole's spiritual (and anti–material) appeal.

The third possibility probably sprang from motives not unlike Giovio's, at more or less the same time. But when Gianbattista Folengo dedicated to Pole his *Commentaria in primam epistolam D. Ioanni*, published at the Aldine Press in Venice in 1546, he had in mind a different kind of conquest than Giovio had. The work was aimed at the Cassinese congregation of Benedictines, of which Pole was protector, although possibly not yet at that time.[43] Folengo touched on many themes of interest to Pole, especially the limitations of human erudition (a point aimed at the scholastic theologians assembled at Trent under Pole's legation), the gratuitous nature of divine grace, the "benefit and gift" of salvation through Christ's blood without any human merit, and above all, the necessity both of charity and love and of true penance in the actions of Christians.[44] Quite apart from its fairly obvious polemical purpose as a contribution to the debate over justification just then under way at Trent (and in which both the Cassinese and Pole would be defeated), Folengo's work once again testified to Pole's religious standing.

The plan for the final dedication to Pole was floated just a little later, but it was not executed until much later. The Portuguese writer Girolamo Osorio proposed to Priuli in early 1547 to dedicate a book of his, *De iustitia caelesti*, to Pole, significantly the book refuting heretical notions of grace. Pole's reputation as an expert on questions of justification spread as far as Portugal, where news of his ignominious flight from Trent when the issue was about to be decided might not yet have arrived. If Osorio sent the work to Priuli, there is no evidence that he received it (although Priuli was famously lazy and distracted, so the lack of evidence may not prove much).[45] About a decade later Roger Ascham revived Osorio's plan in roundabout fashion, and at least according to Mario Cosenza, the Cologne 1586 edition bore a dedication to Pole.[46]

---

[41]Thomas F. Mayer, "Il fallimento di una candidatura: Reginald Pole, la 'reform tendency' e il conclave di Giulio III," *Annali dell'Istituto storico italo-germanico in Trento* (forthcoming).

[42]Thomas F. Mayer, "Reginald Pole in Paolo Giovio's *Descriptio:* A Strategy for Reconversion," *Sixteenth Century Journal* 16 (1985): 431–450.

[43]Cf. the letter of dedication.

[44]Fols. 1r, 3r, 13v, 14r, 15r, 34, 91v ff. (for both penance and the necessity of humble learning at Trent). For another summary of the work and helpful discussion of its place in Cassinese theology, see Barry Collett, *Italian Benedictine Scholars and the Reformation: The Congregation of Santa Giustina of Padua* (Oxford: Clarendon Press, 1985), 191–194.

[45]Pio Paschini, *Un Amico del Card. Polo: Alvise Priuli*, Lateranum no. 2 (Rome: Pontificio Seminario Romano Maggiore, 1921), 98.

[46]I have not been able to see a copy of the work; for Ascham's presentation in 1555 of Girolamo Osorio, *De nobilitate* (Florence, 1552), to Pole along with fulsome praise of Pole's own nobility, see Lawrence Ryan, *Roger Ascham* (Stanford: Stanford University Press, 1963), 208. See also Mario Cosenza, *Biographical and Bibliographical Dictionary of the Italian Humanists* (Boston, G. K. Hall, 1962), 4:2900.

Cardinal Pole's "Spiritual" Patronage   429

Giovio's, Folengo's, and Osorio's books appeared during one of the blackest moments of Pole's career, the time of the Council of Trent's decision on justification. Yet Pole did not suffer many consequences from his defeat (and flight from the Council). Much the same was true after perhaps the lowest point in Pole's career, the aftermath of the conclave of 1549–1550. Shortly thereafter the death of Edward VI thrust him back into the midst of European politics. In August 1553 he became almost simultaneously legate for the reconciliation of England and for peace between Charles V and Henry II. Among the arrangements he made for his departure was the disposition of the proceeds from the abbey of Canalnuovo in the diocese of Adria, which he had received as commendatory abbot a few years earlier.[47] This transaction probably ranks as one of Pole's most significant pieces of spiritual patronage.[48] He instructed the income to be divided between his agent in Venice, who was to give his half to the poor priests of San Nicolò, and Pole's agent in Rome, who was to disburse his portion to similar effect. If the San Nicolò referred to is San Nicolò da Tolentino, then Pole was supporting the Theatines, whose church in Venice was San Nicolò. The strict order had been founded by Gian Pietro Carafa—often painted as Pole's bête noire—and Pole appears to have been very close to its Venetian *praepositus,* Bernardino Scotti, who would become Carafa's right-hand man when Carafa became Paul IV.[49] The amount of money in question was not terribly large. Beccadelli said Canalnuovo brought in 1,000 scudi per year, which nearly agrees with a nineteenth-century local historian's claim that the house had been worth 1,200 scudi in the fifteenth century.[50] According to an eighteenth-century survey of the property of the diocese of Adria, Canalnuovo was worth only eighty gold ducats per year.[51] However much money was involved and whichever house in Venice was meant, the arrangement seems to have been temporary. By 1557 the income was again being paid to Pole's receiver in

---

[47]Pole to Ercole, Duke of Ferrara, February 21, 1551. Archivio di Stato, Modena, Cancelleria ducale, Carteggio di principi esteri, Roma, 1408A. Cf. Giurisdizione sovrana, b. 298, fasc. Santa Maria di Gavello, the only surviving documents from the abbey.

[48]Venice, Archivio di Stato, Archivio Proprio Roma, 7, unfoliated (CSPV, 5, no. 586). Pole instructed his agent in Venice, Pietro Contarini, to dispose of his income in a letter of October 22, 1553, in VL 6754, fol. 274v.

[49]There are other religious institutions dedicated to San Nicolò in Venice, but the best candidate, the Benedictine abbey of that name on the Lido, seems excluded by the specification that the money was to go to "poor priests." That phrase instead fits the Theatines perfectly. Then again, Pole was at that time protector of the Benedictine order, and Contarini's nephew Placido, to whom Pole wrote a strongly worded letter about obedience, became prior there by 1557; DBP, MS 922, 4:115–121, Pole to Placido Contarini, September 16, 1553 (VL 5967, fols. 330r–337r; *Epistolarum Reginaldi Poli,* 4, no. 12); BPP, MS Palatino 1010, fol. 174r, Ludovico Beccadelli to Placido Contarini, Priore di San Nicolò a Vinetia, April 7, 1557. For Pole and Scotti, see e.g. the three letters in Giuseppe Silos, *Historiarum clericorum regularium,* 2 vols. (Rome: Mascardi, 1650), 2:333, 334–335, and those in VL 6754, fols. 187v, 195r–196r (CSPV, 6:1, no. 371); and fols. 215v–216v (CSPV, 6:1, no. 530). Thomas Goldwell, one of Pole's closest collaborators, was also a Theatine.

[50]"Vita," fol. 31v. Francesco Antonio Bocchi, *Della sede episcopale di Adria veneta* (Adria: Vianello, 1858), 192.

[51]Giovanni Pietro Ferretti, "Hadriensis Episcopatus Memorabilia," Rovigo, Accademia dei Concordi, MS Silvestrina 759, fol. 48v.

London.⁵² This uncharacteristically successful and indubitably spiritually motivated piece of patronage (whatever its further political utility) coincided with a substantial percentage increase in the number of dedications or encomia Pole attracted, although their raw number remained low. This increase could have been tied to Pole's twin legations, but something similar had not happened when he had almost secured the papacy four years earlier. George Parks listed ten "tributes" between 1554 and 1556, and I have added about a half dozen more. These include Lorenzo Davidico's *Gioiello del vero Christiano* (1552); Tommaso Campeggi's *De coelibatu* (1553); one book of Giovita Rapicio's *De numero oratorio*, to which he added another set of paraphrases of the Psalms (both published by Paolo Manuzio in 1554); Pier Francesco Zini's *Boni pastoris exemplum, ac specimen singulare* (written in 1554), dedicated to Pole's servant Gianfrancesco Stella, but calling Pole patron; Bernardino Tomitano's *Clonicus,* an encomiastic poem on Pole, dedicated to Carnesecchi (1556, also published by Manuzio); an emblem in Achille Bocchi's *Symbolicarum Quaestiones* (1555); a book of Pierio Valeriano's *Hieroglyphica* (1556); Marco Girolamo Vida's *De republica* (1556); Ellis Heywood's *Il Moro*, printed by Torrentino in Florence in 1556 and the only one of these written in Italian; and one chapter of Flavio Alessi Ugoni, *De maximis Italiae atque Graeciae calamitatibus* (published in 1559, but probably written earlier, perhaps in 1553 or shortly thereafter). Only one or perhaps two gained any worthwhile patronage for their authors. The probable successful case was Zini, whom Pole helped to acquire the archpresbytery of Lonato on Lago di Garda.⁵³ But to judge from the strongly worded letter Pole had to write Zini about taking up residence, Zini was less than pleased with the appointment, which came in any case before the publication of his book.⁵⁴ The doubtful instance is Heywood, who is supposed to have been one of Pole's secretaries in England, but his place in Pole's household remains undocumented. He was certainly not part of it at Pole's death.⁵⁵

The circle of those who dedicated works to Pole interlocks to a suspicious degree. Rapicio taught the humanities in Venice, and moved in the group of Paolo Ramusio (whom he tutored and to whom he dedicated the fifth book of *De numero*) and his father, both among Pole's Venetian admirers.⁵⁶ Like Ramusio, these authors had strong links to Manuzio, who would publish nearly all of Pole's works which appeared in the sixteenth century, and was undoubtedly an exponent of

---

⁵²PRO SP 11/11, fol. 134v. The total from a pension on Granada, the abbey, and a *luogho* on the Zecca of Venice was approximately £3,500, but there is no indication of the period covered.

⁵³VL 6754, fols. 279v–280, Pole to Julius III, perhaps in September 1553, and fol. 93v, Pole to the doge of Venice.

⁵⁴VL 6754, fol. 274, October 22, 1553.

⁵⁵Henry Foley, ed., *Records of the English Province of the Society of Jesus,* 7 vols. (London: Burns and Oates, 1877–1883), 7:1, 350, and Dennis E. Rhodes, "*Il Moro*: An Italian View of Sir Thomas More," in Edward Chaney and Peter Mack, eds., *England and the Continental Renaissance: Essays in Honour of J. B. Trapp* (Woodbridge: Boydell and Brewer, 1990), 67–72. Heywood had no room in Lambeth Palace, according to the detailed survey carried out by Elizabeth's commissioners in November 1558, recorded in PRO, SP 12/1, fols. 20r–29r. Since Heywood probably became a Jesuit at Dillingen, where Pole spent a good deal of time on his way back to England, it is possible that he was there already in 1553 and acted as Pole's secretary only during his stay.

what used to be called "evangelismo italiano."[57] Tomitano was in the extension of the same circle in Padua, and he had two close encounters with the Inquisition.[58] Zini belonged to much the same Venetian group owing to his post as tutor to the son of Bernardo Navagero, and of course, as a member of Pole's household. (As Venetian ambassador to Rome, Nagavero pursued a very favorable line on Pole's troubles with Paul IV and took in at least two key members of Pole's household after his death.)[59] Valeriano, too, had close ties to both Pole's Venetian and Paduan friends, perhaps especially Priuli, but also Gasparo Contarini (who ordained him in 1537), and Ludovico Beccadelli, Pole's first biographer.[60] Davidico is no doubt the oddest of these writers, but claimed to be close to Pole and, again, particularly to Priuli.[61] Bocchi had less direct ties to Pole, but had been Guido Ascanio Sforza's secretary in Rome, and Sforza probably had a better opinion of Pole than Paul III's other grandson, Cardinal Farnese. Further, Bocchi had been very close to Flaminio, whom he called his "maestro." Bocchi also had more than a few brushes with the Inquisition.[62] To judge from the inclusion of several of Vida's poems in Biblioteca Antoniana, Padua, MS XXIII 671, Vida belongs near, if not in, these same groups.[63] Vida had been close to Pole's model Gianmatteo Giberti in Rome between 1510 and 1520, and that seems to have set him on the path to a more spir-

[56]Luigi Boldrini, *Della vita e degli scritti di messer Giovita Rapicio* (Verona: Annichini, 1904). For Rapicio's earlier links to "evangelical" circles in Vicenza, see Achille Olivieri, *Riforma ed eresia a Vicenza nel Cinquecento* (Rome: Herder, 1992), 251–253. Pole acknowledged Ramusio's letter that accompanied Rapicio's dedication; see *Epistolarum Reginaldi Poli*, 4, no. 63 (May 1554); from this it appears that Ramusio was a friend of Donato Rullo, who accompanied Pole to England. The best life of Ramusio is in Emanuele Cicogna, *Delle Iscrizioni veneziane*, 8 vols. (Venice: Giuseppe Orlandelli, 1827), 2:330–336. George B. Parks, "Ramusio's Literary History," *Studies in Philology* 52 (1955): 127–148, must be used with extreme care.

[57]Fragnito, "Censura ecclesiastica," 26–28, and A. J. Schutte, "The *Lettere Volgari* and the Crisis of Evangelism in Italy," *Renaissance Quarterly* 28 (1975): 639–688.

[58]Silvana Seidel Menchi, "Sulla fortuna di Erasmo in Italia: Ortensio Lando e altri eterodossi della prima metà del Cinquecento," *Rivista storica svizzera* 24 (1974): 537–634, esp. 616–625, and Antonio Daniele, "Sperone Speroni, Bernardino Tomitano e l'Accademia degli Infiammati di Padova," *Sperone Speroni, Filologia Veneta* 2 (1989): 1–54.

[59]Agostino Valier, *Bernardi Navgerii [sic] S. R. E. Cardinalis. ... Vita*, in Agostino Valier, *De cautione adhibenda in edendis libris* (Padua: Giuseppe Comino, 1719), 90, 96.

[60]Giuliano Lucchetta, "Contributi per una biografia di Pierio Valeriano," *Italia medioevale e umanistica* 9 (1966): 461–476.

[61]Dario Marcatto, *Il processo inquisitoriale di Lorenzo Davidico (1555–1560): Edizione critica* (Florence: Olschki, 1992), 105–106, 111, 117–118, 122–125, 130–131. See also Massimo Firpo, *Nel labirinto del mondo: Lorenzo Davidico tra santi, eretici, inquisitori* (Florence: Olschki, 1992), 106, 240.

[62]See Antonio Rotondò in *Dizionario biografico degli Italiani* (Rome: Istituto dell'enciclopedia italiana, 1962–); "Per la storia dell'eresia a Bologna nel sec. XVI," *Rinascimento*, ser. 2, no. 2 (1961): 107–190, esp. 160–163, 165–167; Karen E. Pinkus, "The 'Symbolicae Quaestiones' of Achille Bocchi: Humanist Emblems and Counter-Reformation Communication (Ph.D. thesis, City University of New York, 1990); and Elizabeth See Watson, *Achille Bocchi and the Emblem Book as Symbolic Form* (Cambridge: Cambridge University Press, 1993), which tries to clear Bocchi of any association with heresy.

[63]According to Paul Oskar Kristeller, *Iter italicum*, 5 vols. (Leiden: E.J. Brill, 1964–1992), 2:4, the codex was assembled by Benedetto Ramberto, another of Pole's Venetian admirers; it includes nearly all the usual suspects. Vida's text, *Dialogi de rei publicae dignitate* (Cremona: Vincenzo Conte, 1556), together with an Italian translation is to be found in a truncated form in an appendix to Giuseppe Toffanin, *L'Umanesimo al concilio di Trento* (Bologna: Zanichelli, 1955). The best study of Vida is M. A. Di Cesare, *Vida's Christiad and Vergilian Epic* (New York: Columbia University Press, 1964), amplified by M. A. Di Cesare, *Bibliotheca Vidiana* (Florence: Sansoni, 1974).

itual religion, which he would pursue after leaving for his bishopric of Alba in 1533. Vida continued to correspond with Pole almost until the end.[64] Ugoni, like Folengo a Cassinese Benedictine, had spent time with Pole during his stop at Maguzzano in 1553, if not before, and wrote him a fulsome, if undated, letter saying how much he missed him.[65] Campeggi's dedication is superficially the hardest to explain. As one of the leading curialists, he should have wanted very little to do with Pole. But they had similar religious ideas, to judge from Campeggi's ties to the Theatines; had cooperated on the commission which produced the *Consilium de emendanda ecclesiae* in 1537; and in the drafting of the pope's reply to Charles V's protest against the transfer of the Council of Trent to Bologna in 1547. His career, like Pole's, had taken a turn for the worse in the aftermath of the conclave of Julius III, which may have reinforced their bond. Campeggi's work may also be a sign of the degree to which Pole had recovered by 1553.[66]

These writers failed in their quest for Pole's material patronage in part because he still had very little disposable cash. And yet the auspices for Pole's making a large impression had looked so good when he returned to England in November 1554. To speak metaphorically, he brought baggage full of the resources of Italian pictorial, plastic, and poetic art, and of humanism. In actuality, in addition to the members of his own household, the Habsburg court painter Antonis Mor likely joined his suite, a decision to which Pole may have had some input.[67] On arrival, Pole immediately opened lines of communication between his traveling household and a number of Englishmen whom he added to his inner administrative circle. They included his archdeacon of Canterbury, Nicholas Harpsfield; his relative David Pole (a man especially likely to have had a humanist bent, to judge from his library); Cole; John White; John Clerk; Anthony Hussey; and perhaps especially Seth Holland, who became president of All Souls'.[68] As the mixture of their hands with those of Pole's Italian secretaries throughout his administrative records, correspondence, and sometimes even more formal works indicates, the members of his household, both Italian and English, and his new English administrators dealt with each other on a daily basis. Language would have posed no problems. In addition to the always available Latin, many of Pole's English servants were fluent in Italian, and at least Binardi among the Italians knew English (he was widely thought a

---

[64] See his letter of January 1558 in BL, Add. MS 35830, fol. 20 r–v.

[65] Angelo Maria Querini to Cypriano Benaglia, June 23, 1744 (Biblioteca Civica Queriniana, Brescia, 3.a A. f. 1. 21). The letter is printed—probably from Ugoni's *Opera* (Venice, 1559)—in *Epistolarum Reginaldi Poli*, 5:286–287, immediately after the chapter dedicated to Pole.

[66] Hubert Jedin, "Campeggi, Tommaso," *Dizionario biografico degli Italiani*. Carnesecchi kept him informed of Pole's doings in 1555; see BAV, Chigiano R. 2.54 (no. 3122), fols. 267 r–274 r, and among the Carte Stella (42/5), there is a copy of his opinion on the King of England's powers over benefices.

[67] Joanna Woodall, "An Exemplary Consort: Antonis Mor's Portrait of Mary Tudor," *Art History* 14 (1991): 192–224, at 203, thinks that Mor "may" have traveled with Pole, but the coincidence of dates between their arrivals and the conditions of travel in the sixteenth century make it almost certain that they journeyed together.

[68] A. B. Emden, *A Biographical Register of the University of Oxford A. D. 1501 to 1540* (Oxford: Clarendon Press, 1974), appendix B, 730–733, lists David Pole's books; cf. Sears Jayne, *Library Catalogues of the English Renaissance*, 2d ed. (Godalming: St. Paul's Bibliographies, 1983), 120.

prodigy at languages).⁶⁹ Major cultural consequences of whatever duration should have followed upon the interactions of Pole's English servants with his foreign secretariat of Marcantonio Faita, principal secretary; Michele Facchetto; Antonio Fiordibello, who would return to Rome as a major cog in the papal secretariat; Mariano Vittorio; and above all Binardi; as well as two key non-Italian actors of deep humanist culture, Dudic and Lampson. Many of these interchanges took place in the idioms of humanism.

If Roger Ascham can be believed, Pole early on meant to invest in collecting on the humanist model, proposing to lay out 2,000 crowns to buy a manuscript of Cicero's missing *De republica* which had allegedly surfaced in Poland.⁷⁰ Such a plan was of a piece with Pole's deep-seated commitment to humanism (and apparently to humanist politics). Rhetoric was always his favorite weapon, writing his favorite mode of communication. However "Asiatic" (apparently meaning "long-winded") his style may have been, he had a great reputation as a writer of humanist Latin.⁷¹ He was credited with inventing a new kind of humanist theology in a work written in the favorite humanist form of dialogue, as were nearly all the rest of his works.⁷² Pole put considerable effort himself into preaching, the favorite humanist tool of reform, and probably intended to deploy other preachers as a means of bringing the English back to Rome.⁷³ That remained a matter of potential, and no members of

---

⁶⁹Among others, Pyning, Goldwell, Seth Holland, and Lily. For Pyning's Italian, see e.g. *Archivio segreto Vaticano* [ASV], Armaria 64:28, fols. 111–112, a letter in Italian to him, with his translations in the margin, or his letter to Pole of December 23, 1556, in BL, Add. MS 12529, fols. 5–6v, together with his household accounts (SP 11/11), kept in Italian. Goldwell's Italian is attested well enough by his highly successful career in Italy both before and after his service with Pole. A series of letters in Italian to Holland from Pole's datary Nicolò Ormanetto prove his knowledge of the language; see ASV, Nunziature, Inghilterra 3, fols. 124–126 (copy in ASV, Nunziature diverse 145, fols. 99–104v), and ibid., fols. 127r–v (copy in ASV, Nunz. div. 145, fols. 104v–106v). For Binardi's likely English, see ASV, Armaria 64:28, fol. 95, Copia della lettera di M. Enrico di Londra di 2. di Giugno tradotta d'Inglese, which is in Binardi's hand.

⁷⁰Ascham to Johann Sturm, September 14, 1555, in Giles, ed., *Works of Ascham*, 1:445–446. Cf. Ryan, *Roger Ascham*, 210. The story is made more plausible by Pole's good contacts in Poland, among them Cardinal Hosius and Jan Dantiscus.

⁷¹Ludovico Beccadelli, "Vita del cardinale Reginaldo Polo," in G. B. Morandi, ed., *Monumenta di varia letteratura*, 2 vols. (Bologna: Istituto per le scienze, 1797–1804), 1:2, 331. Beccadelli wrote: "He was broad, and more Asiatic than Attic in writing, which arose from the abundance of expressions which his fruitful intelligence supplied him." Fecund invention was, of course, the basis of successful humanist oratory.

⁷²Egidio Foscarari judged Pole's *De concilio* to represent a new departure in theological method in his letter to Giovanni Morone from Trent, September 11, 1561, in *Concilii tridentini*, vol. 8, ed. Stephan Ehses (Freiburg: Herder, 1919), 247–248. Ercole Gonzaga endorsed Foscarari's judgment, and helped to arrange free distribution of the work through Carlo Borromeo; ibid.

⁷³That at least was Mary's plan, and given their close cooperation on matters of religion, it is likely that Pole would have endorsed it. A memorandum setting out what could have been Mary's own ideas survives in numerous copies. That in PRO, SP 14/190, fol. 133, bears the title "Directions of Queen Mary to Her Council Touching the Reforming of the Church to the Roman Religion Out of Her Own Original." Others are BL, Harleian 444, fols. 27–28v; BL, Cotton Titus 107, fol. 120v; VL 6754, fols. 263v–264v, mistitled "Mary's Opinion about the Synod" BNM, MS Ital. X.24 (6527), fols. 208v–209; BL, Add. MS 41577, fols. 283v–284v; and BAV, Ottob. 3166, fols. 409–410. A similar set of memoranda in BL, Lansdowne 96, fol. 25, endorsed "Anno 1554," stresses the necessity for the bishops to find good preachers. Loades, *Reign of Mary Tudor*, 272, and Pogson, "Pole," 59, 77, and passim, are probably wrong to argue that Pole placed little emphasis on preaching. Both Loades and Pogson also make

his household seem to have exercised their talents in preaching, although they apparently did in other kinds of oration, or at least tried to. Fiordibello, for example, wrote but was prevented from delivering a congratulatory address to Philip and Mary, and Pole interrupted Harpsfield's welcoming oration just when the archdeacon was hitting his stride in praise of Pole.[74] But there can be no doubt that—following Pole's lead—his familia successfully employed the methods of humanist historiography to hijack the history of the English reformation; this highly effective piece of patronage also reinforces its ideological roots. Two of the foreign members of Pole's household, Dudic and Binardi, adopted Pole's own self-image in their collaborative biography of him, which was shortly thereafter taken into Nicholas Sander's enormously influential *De origine ac progressu schismatis anglicani,* whence it metastasized to take over virtually all histories of the English reformation, no matter the confessional allegiance of their authors.[75] Pole's images of John Fisher and Thomas More, originally created in *De unitate* (written in 1536), immediately became staple pieces of English polemical historiography, almost certainly through Pole's mediation. This took the form first of Harpsfield's life of More and shortly thereafter of William Roper's, both written during Pole's tenure as archbishop. Roper was deeply involved in the running of the archdiocese of Canterbury, in tandem with several key members of Pole's central administration. He served on the commission to reinstate Edmund Bonner in December 1553, and his name joined David Pole's and Nicholas Harpsfield's on the *inspeximus* of the sentence in that case. He was also apparently closely connected to one of Pole's chief financial officers in Canterbury, Cyriac Petit.[76]

---

[73] *(continued)*
Pole's alleged attitude to preaching a factor in explaining why he refused to admit the Jesuits, but see Thomas M. McCoog, "Loyola, the Early Jesuits and Italian Humanism," *Journal of Ecclesiastical History* , forthcoming (which I am grateful to Dr. McCoog for letting me see), and Thomas F. Mayer, "A Test of Wills: Cardinal Pole, Ignatius Loyola, and the Jesuits in England," in J. A. Munitiz and T. M. McCoog, eds., *The Reckoned Expense: Edmund Campion and the Early English Jesuits: Essays in Celebration of the First Centenary of Campion Hall, Oxford (1896–1996)* (Woodbridge: Boydel and Brewer, 1996). Some of Pole's sermons can be found in: VL 5968, strewn in nearly complete disorder throughout the volume; PRO, SP 69/8, fols. 94–112; and Strype, *Ecclesiastical Memorials,* 3:2, 482–510 (the original of which should be in the British Library somewhere, but I have been unable to find it). Strype also reported a lost sermon of Pole's, given at the installation of Sir Thomas Tresham as part of the restoration of the Knights of Saint John of Jerusalem in November 1557 (ibid., 21); Strype's source called Pole "the illustrious preacher." Dudic, *Epistolarum Reginaldi Poli,* 1:63, listed three sermons translated into Latin in his catalogue of Pole's writings, but it is not known whether they included any of these other texts, all but one of which are in Italian or English.

[74] Fiordibello's oration is in Jacopo Sadoleto, *Opera omnia,* 4 vols. (Verona: G. A. Tumerman, 1783; reprinted Ridgewood, N.J.: Gregg Press, 1964), 2:426–437; cf. VL 6754, fol. 149r, for the circumstances surrounding its misfire. *Epistolarum Reginaldi Poli,* 5:307, reported that Pole interrupted Harpsfield's welcoming oration at the point when he had just begun to expatiate on "Tu es Polus."

[75] See Thomas F. Mayer, "A Sticking-plaster Saint? Autobiography and Hagiography in the Making of Reginald Pole," in Thomas F. Mayer and D. R. Woolf, eds., *Rhetorics of Life-Writing in the Later Renaissance: Forms of Biography from Casandra Fedele to Louis XIV* (Ann Arbor: University of Michigan Press, 1995), 205-222.

[76] *Calendar of Patent Rolls, Philip and Mary,* 1:73–75, 102, 121. For Petit's role see PRO, SP 11/11, fol. 130v.

XIV

Cardinal Pole's "Spiritual" Patronage

In addition to reinforcing humanist taste in prose style, many of the Italians in Pole's circle took a passionate interest in poetry and what we would now call literary criticism. In the forefront were Binardi and Gianfrancesco Stella. For example, they took up the cudgels for Castelvetro in his controversy with Annibale Caro (thereby joining a small minority), and Stella left notes on Petrarch and Dante.[77] Binardi dedicated a *carmen* to Giovanni della Casa, and Stella wrote a number of sonnets.[78] Given the great popularity in England well into the eighteenth century of the *carmine* and other small poetic forms of Pole's earlier intimate Flaminio, and the vogue already well begun for Petrarch in England, possible links between Pole's poets and Elizabethan sonneteers require investigation.[79] Pole died under a cloud of quasiofficial accusations of heresy emanating from Rome; Paul IV certainly did not think his soul had been accompanied to heaven by winged sprites.[80] By at least 1550 he had become deeply suspicious of Pole's "seducer" Flaminio, going so far as to visit Flaminio's deathbed to be sure he died a good Christian. Both Pole and his first biographer defended Pole's relation to Flaminio by claiming that Pole had taken Flaminio under his protection in an effort to save him.[81] If so, that act must count both as perhaps the clearest instance of Pole's spiritual patronage, and as one of its most egregious failures. This final instance neatly brings out the peculiarity of all of Pole's patronage. Prepared to shun material rewards, or at least put them a distant second, Pole's clients came to him as a religious, political, and cultural icon. Despite their failure to gain much recompense and the dangers manifest in much of his patronage, Pole did better out of these relationships than most patrons, and his clients seem to have been better satisfied than most, even a grasping one like Lampson. "Il gran cardinale" Farnese had to wait until very recently to be restored to something like his original eminence as a patron (although he himself still does not come off very well).[82] Pole, by contrast, never left the stage once his clients put his image on paper and canvas. His patronage came to act as an engine which more than compensated for his original "failure."

---

[77] BCM:CS, 40/155 (Bonelli no. 178), Binardi to Stella, Ferrara, November 25, 1559. Stella's notes are BCM:CS, 42/19 (Bonelli no. 358).

[78] Binardi's poem (dated September 21, 1549) is in BPP, MS pal. 555, 82–83, and Stella's sonnets are BCM:CS, 42/39–41 (Bonelli no. 380), including one to Pole.

[79] Should there be such links, they are likely to have been reasonably indirect. For one thing, except for Tottel's *Miscellany*, published in 1557, there was very little Petrarchism in the 1550s and 1560s in England. I am greatly indebted to Steven May for much help on this point.

[80] Pole attracted one last request for patronage, which was written from Padua just after his death. On December 1, 1558, George Acworth introduced himself with a summary of his career and his literary merits; PRO, SP 1/70, fols. 42r–45v; English translation in L. Graham H. Horton-Smith, *George Acworth . . . a Full Account of his Life Together with a Translation of His Letters Written in Latin* (privately printed, 1953), 15–22.

[81] Pole offered that explanation of his relations with Flaminio to Carafa in 1553; Morandi, *Monumenta*, 1:2, 350; Beccadelli, "Vita," fol. 33r.

[82] Clare Robertson, *"Il gran cardinale": Alessandro Farnese, Patron of the Arts* (New Haven: Yale University Press, 1992).

XV

CARDINAL POLE'S FINANCES: THE PROPERTY OF A REFORMER

Over the last twenty years Reginald Pole (1500–1558), the first *inglese italianato, diavolo incarnato* according to Matthew Parker, has become the hero of one wing of the Italian Reformation, usually if uncomfortably called the *spirituali*.[1] At least this is a label used by contemporaries who derived it from the Pauline distinction between carnal and spiritual men, with the spiritual, of course, those who would be saved. Despite Pole's identification with those worthies, the difference between the two was not clear-cut in the sixteenth century, especially not in the case of a cardinal and archbishop of Canterbury who was also the grandson of George, Duke of Clarence. The vicissitudes of Pole's career determined the degree to which he became carnal, not in a physical sense, but an economic one. As Barbara McClung Hallman put the point, the church was property to the Italians in its upper ranks, regardless of their status as reformers, and this holds true of Pole as well.[2] Brilliant early academic performance and equally brilliant success in the early days of Henry VIII's first divorce produced the rewards that one of such high rank expected.[3] As John Gleason correctly observed, the young Pole was an egregious pluralist.[4] His protracted breach with the king left him temporarily in difficult financial straits, and perhaps not by coincidence it was then that he became most closely identified with efforts to reform, perhaps even undo, the

---

[1] Matthew Parker, with the collaboration of John Josselin and George Acworth, *De antiquitate britannicae ecclesiae* (London: [John Daye], 1572), p. 408. Massimo Firpo in particular makes Pole the central figure among the *spirituali*. See *Tra alumbrados e 'spirituali'. Studi su Juan de Valdés e il valdesianesimo nella crisi religiosa del '500 italiano* (Florence: Olschki, 1990), *Inquisizione romana e Controriforma. Studi sul Cardinal Giovanni Morone e il suo processo d'eresia* (Bologna: Il Mulino, 1992) and his and Dario Marcatto's edition of *Il processo inquisitoriale del Cardinal Giovanni Morone* (Rome: Istituto storico italiano per l'età moderna e contemporanea, 1981–1995; 6 vols).

[2] Barbara M. Hallman, *Italian cardinals, reform and the church as property, 1492–1563* (Berkeley: University of California Press, 1985).

[3] Thomas F. Mayer, 'A fate worse than death: Reginald Pole and the Parisian theologians', *English historical review*, 103 (1988), pp. 870–91 [this volume no. XI] and *Reginald Pole, prince and prophet* (Cambridge University Press, in press), chapter one.

[4] John B. Gleason, *John Colet* (Berkeley: University of California Press, 1989), p. 44.

church as property. In the last several phases of his career, first as one of the most highly regarded cardinals in the wake of the conclave of Julius III in which he was nearly elected pope, and even more after his return to England in 1554, Pole became a wealthy man. While his allegiance to 'spiritual' values did not therefore weaken, this did not prevent him from living a life not entirely distinguishable from that of his grasping predecessor Cardinal Wolsey, including holding a commendatory abbacy and engaging in extensive building at Lambeth Palace. To Wolsey both would have been small potatoes, but Wolsey never claimed to be a reformer of either belief or practice. Pole's finances have not received much attention since Ludovico Beccadelli's biography, no doubt because of the aura of sanctity that it helped to foster around him.[5] Yet it is significant that Beccadelli devoted a good deal of time to Pole's income in the course of creating his constant saint.

Henry took good care of his protégé. In 1512 the king paid Pole a pension of £12 and added in the following year another of unknown size.[6] The deanery of Wimborne Minster, to which the king presented him on 12 February 1518, was Pole's first substantial benefice, worth either £18 9s. 8d. or £29 8s. 4d.[7] In March 1518 he acquired the prebend of Ruscombe Southbury, Salisbury, but it was worth only ten marks.[8] In April 1519 he exchanged it for the more lucrative stall of Yetminster secunda which cleared £14 13s. 4d.[9] In 1520 he disposed of the advowson of Hinton Martin, apparently part of the deanery's patronage, but it may not have brought him any income.[10] It is possible that Henry helped to arrange Pole's election in

---

[5] See Thomas F. Mayer, 'A sticking-plaster saint? Autobiography and hagiography in the making of Reginald Pole' in Mayer and D. R. Woolf, eds, *The rhetorics of life-writing in early modern Europe: forms of biography from Cassandra Fedele to Louis XIV* (Ann Arbor: University of Michigan Press, 1995), pp. 205-22 [this volume no. XII] and my edition of Beccadelli's and Andras Dudic's lives of Pole forthcoming from MRTS.

[6] J. S. Brewer, James Gairdner and R. H. Brodie, eds, *Letters and papers, foreign and domestic of the reign of Henry VIII* (London: HMSO, 1862-1932; 21 volumes) (hereafter *L&P*), 2:2, p. 1455 (the pension paid through Mr Cole), and 1:2, p. 932, no. 35 (dated 26 April 1513), a royal grant ordering the prior of St Frideswide, Oxford, to give Pole a pension until a 'competent benefice' could be found.

[7] Thomas F. Mayer, ed., *The correspondence of Reginald Pole* (forthcoming) (hereafter *CRP*), no. 1. *Valor ecclesiasticus temp. Henr. VIII. auctoriate regia institutus* (London: [Record Commission], 1810-1834; 6 vols), 1, p. 272 and John Hutchins, *The history and antiquities of the county of Dorset*, ed. W. Shipp and J. W. Hodson (Westminster: J. B. Nichols and Sons, 1861-1874; reprinted EP Publishing, 1973; first published 1774; 4 vols), 3, p. 187. All values of benefices are drawn from the *Valor* and are current for 1535. Hutchins apparently used the same source, making it difficult to account for his variant figures.

[8] John LeNeve, *Fasti ecclesiae anglicanae (to 1541)*, 3, ed. J. M. Horn (London: Athlone Press, 1962- ; 13 volumes), p. 84 and *Valor*, 2, p. 155.

[9] LeNeve (to 1541), 3, p. 103; *Valor*, 2, p. 76.

[10] Pole granted it to his brothers Henry and Arthur together with Bernard Oldham. Wiltshire Record Office, Register Audley, fo. 167r, a reference I owe to S. J. Gunn's kindness.

1523 as a *socius compar* of Corpus Christi College, Oxford. This allowed him to draw a stipend of unknown size while studying overseas for three years.[11] According to Beccadelli, when Pole went to Italy for the first time, in addition to his royal pension of 300 *lire* (or approximately 500 *scudi* by Beccadelli's estimation, the number which Pole's second biographer Andras Dudic also gave) Pole had a further 1000 *scudi*, mostly from Exeter and other benefices resigned to him by Richard Pace.[12] Were Beccadelli's total correct, 1500 *scudi* would have made about £500.[13] As often, Beccadelli was weak on the details. For one thing, Pole did not have all this income as early as 1521, the date of his first trip to Italy, nor did the deanery of Exeter officially come to him until 1527, although it is possible that he had the income before that. For another, Pole's royal stipend was only £100, the figure at which it was originally set, and the level at which it continued.[14]

In 1527, probably more or less coincident with his return to England, Pole was showered with a suspiciously large income. First came the prebend of Knaresborough, York, worth £42 18s. 9.[15] Then in July and August he received another small prebend in Exeter (£4) and its rich deanery (£148).[16] At about the same time Pole acquired the parish of South Harting, worth £26 13s. 4d.[17] The imperial ambassador Eustace Chapuys gave the value of his benefices as 400 ducats in early 1532, which was also the sum John Walker remitted to Pole in June. This was probably only a half-year's revenue, since Walker was said to be having trouble getting together £100 for the second half

---

[11] G. R. M. Ward, *Statutes of the colleges of Oxford* (Oxford and London: J. H. Parker and Longmans, Brown, Green and Longmans, 1853; 3 vols), 2, p. 71.

[12] Ludovico Beccadelli, 'Vita del cardinale Reginaldo Polo', in G. B. Morandi, ed., *Monumenti di varia letteratura* (Bologna: Istituto per le scienze, 1797-1804; two vols) (hereafter *MMB*), 1:2, pp. 277-333, p. 282.

[13] I take the pound sterling as worth roughly three gold *scudi* (properly *d'oro in oro*), each of which contained three grams of gold. Peter Partner, *Renaissance Rome 1500–1559: a portrait of a society* (Berkeley: University of California Press, 1976), p. 21n and Jean Delumeau, *Vita economica e sociale di Roma nel Cinquecento*, translated by Sarah Cantoni and Davide Bigalli (Florence: Sansoni, 1979), p. 174. In several instances that can be checked, the range was from about 2.85:1 (in May 1556) to just about 3 in November 1558.

[14] Public Record Office, London (hereafter PRO), E 36/216, fo. 248r (*L&P*, 3, p. 1544), the king's book of payments for 1521, giving Pole 'finding' of £100 for one year in Italy. My thanks to Jonathan Woolfson for the PRO reference. Its payment is partially documented in 1525-1526, when Pole received one quarter's wages of £25. British Library, London (hereafter BL), Egerton 2604, fo. 5r, dated at front 17 Henry VIII, and at top fo. 7v, but year date added in different hand. In October 1529 Pole once more got £100. *L&P*, 5, p. 315. The £70 he received in April 1530 probably represents payment for his costs in Paris, perhaps including bribes. *Ibid.*, p. 749 and Mayer, 'Fate worse than death'.

[15] LeNeve (to 1541), 6, p. 61; *Valor*, 5, p. 2.

[16] *CRP*, nos 47-8; cf. J. A. F. Thomson, 'Two Exeter decanal elections, 1509', *Southern history*, 8 (1986), pp. 36-45, p. 45; *Valor*, 2, pp. 295-6.

[17] *CRP*, no. 44; *Valor*, 1, p. 326.

of the year. This accords with a calculation of Pole's income based on his assessment in the clerical subsidy that bought the pardon of the clergy in early 1531. Edward Wotton said Pole would owe about £30 towards it and the rate has been calculated as 2s. 8d. in the pound, making Pole's income about £225, near enough the totals derived from the figures in the *Valor ecclesiasticus*.[18] In December 1532 he added his final benefice on the presentation of his brothers and Walker, the rectory of Piddletown, Dorset, yielding a little more than £31 2s.[19] At this point, Pole brought in about £250 p. a.

Pole lost all or nearly all his income in 1537, not in 1536 as Beccadelli implied, and received in return only 200 *scudi* per month, the standard papal pension for 'poor' cardinals' (at a time when it was possible for one to live in the papal curia for three to ten *scudi* per month).[20] It was during this interval that Pole became most closely identified with efforts to overhaul papal finances. The evidence of his interest is largely inferential, based on a letter from his patron Cardinal Gasparo Contarini, and the *Consilium de emendanda ecclesia* of 1538 which Pole helped to draft.[21] Both Contarini's letter and the *Consilium* itemized abuses in papal financial policy that were blamed for most of the church's problems. Pole, preoccupied with preparations for his second legation, did not reply to Contarini's letter so exactly what he thought of its strictures cannot be said.[22] He is next known to have had a steady income when he became legate of Viterbo on 13 August 1541.[23] He drew at least 150 *scudi* per month from the post, although this figure may refer only to his pension after he had ceased to act as legate.[24] Two years later, Pole's material circumstances changed dramatically with the death of another of his patrons, Gianmatteo Giberti, bishop of Verona and former papal datary. He left Pole a

---

[18] *L&P*, 5, no. 737 and *CRP*, no. 62. Rate calculated by Roger Schofield given in J. A. Guy, 'Henry VIII and the *praemunire* manouevres of 1530–1531', *English historical review*, 97 (1982), pp. 481–503, p. 503.

[19] Hutchins, *Dorset*, 2, pp. 624–5; *Valor*, 1, p. 261.

[20] *MMB*, p. 322 and Hallman, *Property*, p. 15. For the loss of Pole's benefices, see the references in LeNeve cited above (notes 9–10 and 25). His prebend of Yetminster Secunda in Salisbury Cathedral did not go to Henry Cole until sometime before September 1539. John LeNeve, *Fasti ecclesiae anglicanae (post 1541)*, ed. J. M. Horn, 6 (London: Institute of Historical Research, 1986), p. 92.

[21] *CRP*, no. 230; Walter Friedensburg, 'Zwei Aktenstücke zur Geschichte der kirchlichen Reformbestrebungen an der römischen Kurie (1536–1538)', *Quellen und Forschungen aus italienischen Archiven und Bibliotheken*, 7 (1904), pp. 251–67, pp. 263–7; and *Prince and prophet*, chapter two.

[22] *CRP*, nos 235–6.

[23] *CRP*, no. 335.

[24] Archivio di Stato, Venice, Archivio proprio Roma (hereafter ASVe:APR), 7, fo. 363v (Rawdon Brown, ed., *Calendar of state papers and manuscripts, relating to English affairs in the archives and collections of Venice*, nine volumes [London: Longman, et al., 1864–98] [hereafter *CSPV*], 5, no. 670).

pension on the archbishopric of Granada, a large sum of cash of uncertain size, and according to Beccadelli, 800 *scudi* from the *capiscolia* of Valencia.[25] Pietro Bembo called the legacy *veramente eroica* and suggested that Pole should add at least one more member to his household who could take advantage of his new riches.[26] Jacopo Sadoleto too advised Pole to spend some of his money on liberality.[27] According to Beccadelli, Pole disbursed some of this cash to his household at Trent, after difficulties in collecting it.[28] Pole wrote Charles V's chief minister two letters in October 1544 asking for assistance with the pension, and much of the next year was also taken up in efforts to secure the money.[29] Pole may not have been paid the first installment until 1547, and had constantly to seek ways to extract the rest.

Pole apparently also profited handsomely from Vittoria Colonna's death in 1547. She left him 9,000 *scudi*, but he later claimed always to have intended to pass that to her niece as part of her dowry.[30] The legacy may thus have been a device to avoid having her brother Ascanio lay hands on the money. It did eventually go for his daughter's dowry, but Pole stipulated that if she were childless it should be put to pious uses.[31] He also claimed that Colonna had given it to him to succor his poor countrymen. In any case, Pole kept the credits on the Zecca of Venice he had from Colonna and paid the dowry out of other funds, so he gained to at least some degree.[32] At the death of another of

---

[25] *MMB*, p. 322. What *capiscolia* meant is unclear. Neither of the two versions of Giberti's will in the Archivio di Stato, Verona, records a bequest to Pole. My thanks to Dr.ssa Angela Miciluzzo for sending me copies of them. *L&P*, 19:2, no. 467 put the inheritance at 11,000 *scudi*.

[26] Ernesto Travi, ed., Pietro Bembo, *Lettere* (Bologna: Commissione per i testi di lingua, 1987-93), no. 2410. The act transferring the pension on Granada of 2000 gold *scudi* is dated 4 December 1543. Biblioteca Civica, Bergamo, Archivio Stella in Archivio Silvestri, 40/23 (Guiseppe Bonelli, 'Un archivio privato del Cinquecento: le carte Stella', *Archivio storico lombardo*, 34 [1907], pp. 332-86, no. 85)

[27] *CRP*, no. 413.

[28] *MMB*, p. 323.

[29] *CRP*, nos 416-17.

[30] Gottfried Buschbell, ed., *Concilium tridentinum epistolarum pars prima*, 10 (Freiburg: Herder, 1916), p. 802n.

[31] The possibly original draft of Pole's grant is Archivio segreto vaticano, Misc. Arm. II 84, fo. 36r; there is a copy in Biblioteca apostolica vaticana, MS Ferrajoli 433, pp. 18-30. Pietro Carnesecchi confirmed that this bequest eventually went for Colonna's niece's marriage (Giacomo Manzoni, ed., 'Il processo Carnesecchi', *Miscellanea di storia italiana*, 10 [1870], pp. 189-573, pp. 259, 267-8, and 276). Cf. *CRP*, no. 585 and René Ancel, *Nonciatures de France. Nonciatures de Paul IV. Nonciatures de Sebastiano Gualterio et de Cesare Brancatio* (Paris: Librairie Victor LeCoffre, 1909, 1911; 2 vols), 1, pp. 587-8.

[32] PRO, SP 11/11, no. 60 (C. S. Knighton, ed., *Calendar of state papers domestic series of the reign of Mary I, 1553-1558*, revised [London: PRO, 1998] [hereafter *CSPDR*], no. 665).

Pole's closest friends, Marcantonio Flaminio in early 1550, Pole was made universal heir, although he seems merely to have acted as executor.[33]

When Pole became governor of Bagnoregio, we find the first solid evidence both of income and outgoings. He derived only a little financial profit from his tenure, and probably wound up with a net loss. He was paid fifty *scudi* in July 1547, which probably represented his annual stipend.[34] In 1551 his salary, paid in bi-monthly installments, was seventy-five *scudi*.[35] In that year and the next, he lent the commune a total of 200 *scudi* to build a woolen mill, and perhaps made another loan in 1554. He tried to get his money back without success, and in 1557 converted some of it into a gift.[36]

During the conclave of 1549–50, Pole not only continued to number among the poor cardinals, but was also thought to pose a threat to the rich ones and to the notion of the church as property. One observer reported that Pole endorsed the plan to surrender Parma to Ottavio Farnese because he thought the papacy should have no temporal possessions.[37] One of Pole's appeals and simultaneously largest drawbacks arose from his identification with those cardinals who wished an overhaul of the papal bureaucracy, and consequently a change in the direction in which the papal monarchy had developed since at least Innocent III.[38] In the wake of the conclave Pole lost the legation of Viterbo, but he was handsomely compensated, and partly in a fashion that should have violated his reforming principles. In June 1550 Julius made Cardinal Corner legate in Pole's place, while assigning Pole an annual pension of 1800 *scudi*, some of it drawn on Viterbo.[39] This was an increase on his previous pension of 1080 *scudi*. During the conclave in the customary distribution of positions in the papal states, Pole had become governor of Ascoli, but nothing is known of his tenure (which may only have been for one year) or its income.[40] In addition, Pole gained an imperial pension of 2000

---

[33] *Marci Antonii, Joannis Antonii et Gabrielis Flaminiorum Fornocorneliensium Carmina* (Padua: Giuseppe Comino, 1743), pp. 342–4.

[34] Eletto Ramacci, untitled typescript history of the cardinals governor of Bagnoregio, p. 101. I am very grateful to Ramacci for letting me read his work, based on records in the Archivio comunale, now destroyed.

[35] *Ibid.*, p. 119. Cf. Eletto Ramacci, *Bagnoregio e Civita. Guida storico-turistica* (Montefiascone: Graffietti, 1986), p. 47 which says the governor's salary was 500 *scudi*. The seventy-five *scudi* of 1551 suggests this is a misprint.

[36] Ramacci, 'Cardinals governor', pp. 117 and 125.

[37] Archivio di Stato, Siena, Archivio del Balìa, b. 720, no. 57.

[38] Amadio Ronchini, *Lettere di Girolamo Muzio giustinopolitano conservate nell'archivio governativo di Parma* (Parma: F. Carmignani, 1864), p. 109 vs. the reference in the last note.

[39] ASVe:APR, 7, fo. 363v (*CSPV*, 5, no. 670) and *CRP*, no. 570.

[40] Sebastian Merkle, ed., *Concilium tridentinum diariorum pars secunda* (Freiburg: Herder, 1911), 2, p. 39; Thomas F. Mayer and Peter E. Starenko, 'An unknown diary of Julius III's conclave by Bartolomeo Stella, a servant of Cardinal Pole', *Annuarium historiae conciliorum*, 24 (1992), pp. 345–75, p. 356 [this volume no. V] and Archivio di Stato, Mantua, Archivio Gonzaga, b. 888

scudi, although despite the immediate appearance it may not necessarily have been a reward for him as an imperial partisan.⁴¹ This combined with the abbey of Gavello or Canalnuovo that he had received from Paul just before his death changed Pole's economic circumstances decidedly for the better. Gavello was part of Cardinal Accolti's enormous spoils, and was worth enough to be much fought-over, with Giandomenico de Cupis, the dean of the college of cardinals in whose diocese of Adria it lay, coming right out and asking Paul for it, only to be told that Pole deserved it.⁴² At the time Pole's legation was revoked, Alessandro Farnese tried to secure the abbey.⁴³ The only estimates I have seen make it a nearly worthless property, but Pole derived at least 300 *scudi* (probably per annum) from it, and Beccadelli claimed it yielded 1000.⁴⁴ The Venetians, reveling in the unusual circumstance of having three cardinals, quickly gave Pole possession, but he had to fight off the duke of Ferrara's efforts to tax the proceeds. Even more important, the letter making that request identified Pole as commendatory abbot.⁴⁵ This was in direct contradiction not only to the spirit of the *Consilium* on commendams, but, worse, a violation of canon law in the form of Leo X's bull on the reform of the curia promulgated during the Fifth Lateran Council which when abolishing monastic commendams laid heavy emphasis on the damage they did to good discipline.⁴⁶

(Inviati Roma 1540-1550), fos 430-35, Gianfrancesco Arrivabene-Sabino Calandra, Rome, 13 January 1550. For the significance of these appointments, see Hallman, *Property*, pp. 139-41.

⁴¹ *Concilium tridentinum*, 2, p. 180 and Hallman, *Property*, p. 57 for the lack of a direct link between Spanish and imperial pensions and suppport for the Habsburgs. Pole may have thanked the emperor for his gift – paid on the archbishopric of Burgos – in August 1550, but the wording of *CRP*, no. 583 could refer to any time thereafter.

⁴² ASVe:APR, 7, fo. 107v (*CSPV*, 5, no. 587). For the squabbling, see, *e.g.*, Archivio di Stato, Florence, Archivio mediceo del principato, 3268, fos 427r, 452r-v, 462r-v, 464r-v, and ASVe:APR, 7, fo. 106r (*CSPV*, 5, no. 586). Massimo Firpo and Dario Marcatto, eds., *I processi inquisitoriali di Pietro Carnesecchi (1557-1567)*, 1, *I processi sotto Paolo IV e Pio IV (1557-1561)* (Vatican City: Archivio Segreto Vaticano, 1998), p. XV mistakenly say Carnesecchi held Gavello at the time he lost his benefices (18 June 1556).

⁴³ Biblioteca Apostolica Vaticana, Vat. lat. 6407, fo. 245r, Farnese-Morone, 8 April 1557.

⁴⁴ For the estimates, Giovanni Pietro Ferretti, 'Hadriensis Episcopatus Memorabilia', Rovigo, Accademia dei Concordi, MS Silvestrina 759, fo. 48v and Francesco Antonio Bocchi, *Della sede episcopale di Adria veneta* (Adria: Vianello, 1858), p. 192. They are contradicted by a pension Pole granted on the abbey in 1556 for 300 *scudi* (*CSPV*, 6:1, no. 482). Beccadelli in *MMB*, p. 323. There are very few records from Gavello in the Archivio di Stato, Modena, Giurisdizione sovrana, b. 298, and according to the archivist at the Abbey of Nonantola, Francesco Gavioli, all the rest have been destroyed. I am grateful both to him and to the staff of the Archivio di Stato, Modena, and of the Accademia dei Concordi, Rovigo, for much help on this point.

⁴⁵ *CSPV*, 5, no. 590 and *CRP*, no. 586.

⁴⁶ B. J. Kidd, ed., *Documents illustrative of the continental reformation* (Oxford: Clarendon Press, 1911), p. 312, translated in Elisabeth G. Gleason, *Reform thought in sixteenth-century Italy* (Chico, Calif.: Scholars Press, 1981), p. 92. For Leo's bull, see Norman P. Tanner, S.J., ed., *Decrees of the ecumenical councils* (London and Washington: Sheed & Ward and Georgetown University Press, 1990; 2 vols), 2, p. 616.

Of course, it also allowed that the pope could override the law, as Paul IV did in Pole's case when appointing him to Canterbury in 1555, allowing him to hold any other benefices including monasteries.[47] Together with Giberti's and Colonna's legacies, then, it looks as if Pole now enjoyed an annual income of at least 4800 *scudi*. In 1553 it was claimed that he brought in 1000 gold *scudi per month*.[48] If the lower figure, equivalent to about £1,600, is correct, he was already very wealthy. If the higher sum, amounting to £4,000, is the true one, he was almost obscenely so. The 1000 gold crowns he bestowed on Cardinal Truchsess during his temporary exile in Rome in 1552 suggest the second conclusion, as does the forty *scudi* pension Pole allegedly gave his brother Sir Geoffrey.[49]

Julius continued to provide generously for Pole. When he was made legate to England and for peace in 1553, Pole received a stipend of either 772 1/2 or 1000 *scudi d'oro in oro*, the second figure representing a sum twice the ordinary legatine subvention.[50] The arrangements for its payment were almost identical to those made in 1550. In March 1554 according to the datary's records, Pole was paid 60 *scudi d'oro* on Camerino, as well as 95 1/2 *scudi d'oro in oro* in addition to his standard legate's stipend of 500 *scudi*, while a mandate for payment in the same month gave his provision as 1000 *scudi*, the balance from an unknown source.[51] The pope's extraordinary financial support allowed Pole to dispose of some of his income, dividing the proceeds from Gavello between the Theatines of Venice and other poor priests, perhaps more Theatines, in Rome.[52] This may have been unwise, no matter how spiritually acceptable (or politically astute). Pole at least once had to borrow from a merchant friend against an emergency advance from Rome.[53]

---

[47] *CRP*, no. 1459.

[48] Corpus Christi College, Cambridge [hereafter CCCC], MS 105, fo. 411r-v (in Latin), fo. 413r-v (in Italian) and 425r-v (in English); partially printed in John Strype, *Ecclesiastical memorials relating chiefly to religion, and its reformation, under the reigns of King Henry VIII, King Edward VI, and Queen Mary* (Oxford: Clarendon Press, 1816; 6 volumes), 3:2, pp. 241-42.

[49] Bernard Duhr, 'Die Quellen zu einer Biographie des Kardinals Otto Truchsess von Waldburg. Zugleich ein Beitrag zu seiner Charakteristik', *Historisches Jahrbuch*, 7 (1886), pp. 177-209, p. 194 and W. B. Turnbull, ed., *Calendar of state papers, foreign*, 1 (London: Longman *et al.*, 1861), p. 52. Sir Geoffrey's claim to a subvention may be corroborated by Priuli's statement that Pole had helped his brother financially when he (apparently meaning Reginald) was in Italy. *CRP*, no. 2312, fo. 259v.

[50] *CRP*, nos 625 and 684 and see the next note.

[51] Hallman, *Property*, p. 60 and Ancel, 'Reconciliation', p. 522n.

[52] *CRP*, nos 684 and 736. Thomas F. Mayer, 'When Maecenas was broke: Cardinal Pole's "spiritual" patronage', *Sixteenth century journal*, 27 (1996), pp. 419-35, p. 429 [this volume no. XIV]. I have subsequently failed to discover any record of a bequest to the Venetian Theatines in Archivio di Stato, Venice, Corporazioni religiose soppresse, S. Nicolò dei Tolentini, but the confusion of the records suggests that they may well be incomplete. If the bequest never arrived, the fault may be Pierfrancesco Zini's, whom Pole asked to pass on his order (*CRP*, no. 736).

[53] *CRP*, no. 980.

Cardinal Pole's Finances

As legate in England, Pole seems to have made virtually nothing, although the evidence is thin. Part of the problem is that very few original dispensations have survived, and most that do fail to mention fees. I have found only two. One went to David Vaughan, a Welsh priest, who paid 6s. in gold for his dispensation, and the other for 10s. to Thomas Twysden, an ex-monk of Battle Abbey.[54] Alvise Priuli, Pole's companion of twenty years and universal heir, claimed that Pole made nothing out of his legation, and this could be true.[55] The records of Pole's general receiver Henry Pyning include a single entry that might be related to it.[56] The only financial transaction in the legatine register is a quittance to Pole's receiver Tommaso Maggio or Madius in 1555.[57]

The lack of evidence that Pole profited from his legation is corroborated by Pietro Carnesecchi's report that only 12,000 *scudi* (£4,000) had been found in Pole's house at his death. Priuli's further claim that Pole had never had much from Mary I, and at best ran an annual deficit is open to question.[58] It contradicts the appearance that Pole's economic situation continued to look very rosy in England. We know his circumstances in fair detail from a request drawn up about the time he returned in November 1554. His income from all sources of 1000 gold *scudi* (£334) per month was topped by a projected budget demanding such a sum every month simply for the maintenance of his household.[59] Never the less, the record of expenses set against Pole's income agrees with Priuli's reckoning in showing a notable deficit.[60] Provisions for the human inmates of Pole's household came to 750 *scudi*, his forty horses ate up 170, and salaries amounted to 130 (75 for his 'old' household), leaving a monthly shortfall of fifty *scudi*, or 600 by the year.[61] In addition, Pole annually spent 1000 *scudi* for clothes for himself and his servants, a sum split equally between them, another 2000 *scudi* to repair his table service, 300 more for metal instruments of all kinds, 600 for linen, 400 for bedclothes, for building and repairs 500, and yet 200 more for furniture. This would have made a loss each year of 5600 *scudi*, or more than £1,800. Had Pole's income not

---

[54] *CRP*, nos 2038 and 1864. Wolsey made £200 from fees in 1525–26. Peter Gwyn, *The king's cardinal. The rise and fall of Thomas Wolsey* (London: Pimlico, 1990), p. 285.
[55] *CRP*, no. 2312.
[56] It amounts to either £151 17s. 0d. (SP 11/11, no. 57 [*CSPDR*, no. 662], fo. 130v) or £67 9s. 4d. (no. 60 [*CSPDR*, no. 665], fo. 134v).
[57] Bibliothèque municipale de Douai, MS 922, 3, fo. 58v.
[58] *CRP*, no. 2312. *Processo Carnesecchi*, p. 259. I am grateful to Charles Knighton for much help with this section. David Loades also graciously (and charitably) read through it.
[59] See note 48.
[60] Of the three lists in note 48, only that in Italian (fo. 413r-v) is complete. This suggests that it may have been drawn up by Pyning, who kept his later accounts in that language.
[61] Cf. Felicity Heal, *Of prelates and princes. A study of the economic and social position of the Tudor episcopate* (Cambridge: Cambridge University Press, 1980), p. 195.

increased, his shortfalls would have become astronomical, since none of these projected expenses came anywhere near as much as he actually spent. The smallest item on this list, 15 *scudi* (£5) for alms, boats and other miscellaneous items became almost £62 in January 1556, a month in which Pole's expenditure amounted to £475.[62] Pyning's accounts for most of 1556 and 1557 yield monthly totals for *ordinaria* in the range of between about £200 and £400, with occasional figures of more than £500.[63]

Fortunately, Queen Mary made Pole a rich man, although not immediately. Priuli claimed that in Pole's first year in England the queen gave him £3,000, but he spent 20,000 *scudi* (£6,667), making a huge deficit of almost £3,700.[64] Unfortunately, Pole's then receiver's accounts, certified as cleared on 8 July 1555, do not survive, so there is no way to check Priuli's claim.[65] Not until January 1556 after Pole had been appointed archbishop did Mary issue a privy seal creating an annual income of £5,000 including the see's ordinary revenues of £2,600, which represented a continuing decline from the £3,100 that came in as recently as 1553.[66] Lord Treasurer Winchester was to find the remaining £2,400 partly in a pension of £1,000 on Winchester, to be paid twice yearly, and partly from former archiepiscopal lands in Kent, Sussex and Surrey.[67] If they proved insufficient, he was to make up the shortfall from Exchequer receipts.[68] Winchester executed the queen's orders on 13 March, duly coming up with the remainder of £290 18s. 4d from the Exchequer, and Pole regularly received this grant, although its half-year installment due Michaelmas 1558 was held back.[69] A good deal of his

---

[62] PRO, SP 11/10, no. 8 (*CSPDR*, no. 544), fo. 13r.
[63] *Ibid.*, fos 13r–16v; other sets of accounts, with slightly different figures, are in SP 11/11, nos 54 and 57 (*CSPDR*, nos 659 and 662).
[64] *CRP*, no. 2312.
[65] Douai, MS 922, 3, fo. 58v.
[66] Heal, *Prelates*, p. 182.
[67] CCCC, MS 127, no. 1. *CSPV*, 6:1, no. 482 reported these arrangements almost exactly. The pension on Winchester gave rise in *De antiquitate* (p. 418) to the oft-repeated story that Pole had made a simoniacal contract with the bishop-elect, John White. When the pope provided White, it was stipulated that the pension could not exceed one-third of the see's revenues. William Maziere Brady, *The episcopal succession in England, Scotland and Ireland A. D. 1400 to 1875*, with a new introduction by A. F. Allison ([No place]: Gregg Press, 1971; three vols), 1, p. 14.
[68] According to SP 11/11, no. 60 (*CSPDR*, no. 665) the lands yielded £1,437 and in 1557–58 they were worth approximately £1,287 (SP 11/13, no. 67 [*ibid.*, no. 822]).
[69] *Calendar of patent rolls, Philip and Mary* (London: HMSO, 1936-1939; 4 vols), 3, pp. 69–72 and SP 11/13, no. 67 (*CSPDR*, no. 822) for 1558. Cf. David Loades, *The reign of Mary Tudor: politics, government and religion in England 1553-1558*, 2d ed. (London and New York: Longman, 1991), p. 290. Loades (p. 54) also says that Pole got a pension of £1,252 on the reversal of his attainder, citing an Elizabethan reckoning in SP 12/1, no. 64 (Robert Lemon, ed., *Calendar of state papers, domestic series, 1547-1580* [London: Longman, Brown, Green, Longman and Roberts, 1856], p. 119). It may be that the heading of the first list in this document 'Names of certain persons attainted. . .restored to name and lands by parliament in the time of

archiepiscopal revenue also went unpaid, almost £1,350 in 1558, some of it in arrears since 1553.[70] Beccadelli reported the total of the royal grant more or less accurately as 12,000 *scudi*, although he mistakenly assigned that figure to Canterbury alone, plus another 3,000 in a pension on Winchester, £5,000 in all.[71] Priuli made Pole's income 40,000 *scudi* (about £13,000) in a two-and-one-half year period, plus another 10,000 from the queen, which would yield about £6,500 total p. a., although the annual income is close to the figure in the royal grant.[72] The last transaction between Pole and the crown came as part of the effort to finance the recovery of Calais in November 1558. Perhaps in exchange for £1,000, perhaps gratis, the crown granted Pole some number (the sources differ) of advowsons once part of the archbishopric's property.[73]

That ecclesiastical revenues went through Pole's hands immediately points out the largest difficulty in making sense of his finances: private and public were inextricably mixed up together, and while we have several incomplete accountings of Pole's own income and expenditure, there are none for the monies coming to him from the church.[74] Priuli gave two summary accounts of ecclesiastical revenues, which may or may not be reliable and differ between themselves. To Pole's Roman agent Antonio Giberti, he said that Mary's surrenders did not even suffice to cover the pensions to ex-religious, but came up 8,000 *scudi* short. To his brother, Priuli alleged that church revenues did not come to more than 30,000 *scudi* (£10,000), discounting a rumor that Pole had 'hundreds of thousands of *scudi*' from that source. Stories that Pole had acquired a huge treasure continued to circulate

---

Queen Mary' brought Loades to connect the pension to Pole's attainder, but it appears on another list headed 'Lands given to divers persons which formerly were abbey lands'. It was thus probably the same as the pension granted in this patent. Winchester apparently regarded the first two sources of income as insufficiently reliable (the first was granted in reversion, and the second had previously been in the hands of Sir John Mason and Lord Clinton), and did not factor them into his final sum. Taking the patent's third sum of £1,109 1s. 7 7/8d. and adding the Exchequer annuities misses the target of £1,400 by 1/8d. That third figure must also be the sum Priuli mistakenly called a life annuity from Mary of £1,100 (*CRP*, no. 2312) which became 4000 *scudi* in his accounting of November 1558.

[70] SP 11/13, no. 67 (*CSPDR*, no. 822).
[71] *MMB*, p. 323.
[72] *CRP*, no. 2312.
[73] *CRP*, no. 2304. This transaction is almost certainly the one referred to in *De antiquitate* (p. 419) as involving nineteen benefices, the proceeds of which allegedly paid for Pole's building at Lambeth.
[74] Pyning's accounting did not distinguish between private and official sources of income, but at least he did not mix together Pole's revenues and those of the rest of the English church, for some of which he also accounted, against Loades, *Reign*, p. 375. Pyning did keep the records for the clerical subsidy of 1555 (PRO, SP 11/11, no. 53 [*CSPDR*, no. 723], in his hand), and according to Carnesecchi (*Processo Carnesecchi*, p. 259) some of the proceeds from it were found in Pole's house at his death, but there is no sign of these funds in Pyning's accounts for Pole.

after his death. Priuli ridiculed the figure of £100,000.[75] Similarly, Pole supposedly left 22,000 *scudi* (£7, 034) in his will, but the evidence is much too thin even to begin to corroborate this figure.[76] Another of £25,000 was recorded in an account copied in 1608 of Pole's assets including from the crown's surrenders to the church.[77]

It has been calculated that Pole had a 'disposable income' of £3,000 per year, making him one of the richest men in England, as Archbishop Warham had once been, and he surely did not live hand to mouth.[78] Although his income and the size of his household do not compare terribly favorably to Cranmer's, his servants did not go begging, either.[79] For example, in 1556 almost as soon as the grant from Mary went through, the Venetian ambassador in London reported that the money had allowed 'the liberality that Pole used towards some Italians, his servants, returned to Italy' to whom he gave 6,000 *scudi* (£2,000).[80] Dudic, who was with Pole in England, asserted that he had distributed no less than 10,000 crowns to his household, besides providing horses to any member who wished to return to Italy.[81] In one specific instance, Pole granted one of his *parafrenari* a pension of 24 gold *scudi*, in that case as in 1556 spending money as soon as he knew he had it.[82]

It is possible to make some rough computations of Pole's balance sheet on the basis of Pyning's records.[83] There are three sets of these, covering somewhat different periods. They are all in SP 11/11: 1) no. 54, about Michaelmas-Michaelmas 1556-57, expenditure only (cf. SP 11/10, no. 8); 2) no. 57, which covers 25 December 1556 to 19 November 1557; and 3) no. 60, which stretches from 1 January 1556 to 30 November 1557. In addition, 4) another accounting of the value of the archbishop's property for the year to

---

[75] *CRP*, no. 2312.
[76] *Processo Carnesecchi*, p. 302. No list of Pole's bequests has been found.
[77] PRO, SP 12/1, no. 64, fo. 140 (Lemon, ed., *Calendar*, p. 119). Cf. Norman L. Jones, *Faith by statute: parliament and the settlement of religion 1559* (London: Royal Historical Society, 1982), p. 160. The writer mistakenly called Pole 'Thomas' and made him archbishop of York, as if Wolsey were meant. One hopes he was a better accountant than prosopographer.
[78] Loades, *Reign*, p. 375. By disposable income Loades meant money 'that. . .does not seem to have been subject to regular or fixed deductions'. It is almost impossible to derive such a figure; Loades's is probably the best we can get. Heal, *Prelates*, p. 72 for Warham.
[79] Diarmaid MacCulloch, *Thomas Cranmer. A life* (New Haven and London: Yale University Press, 1996), p. 522.
[80] *CSPV*, 6:1, no. 482.
[81] Andras Dudic, 'Vita Reginaldi Poli' in Angelo Maria Querini, ed., *Epistolarum Reginaldi Poli...[Collectio]* (Brescia: Rizzardi, 1744-57; 5 vols), 1, p. 52. Dudic's claim came in a passage about Pole's aristocratic magnificence that was heavily reworked from Beccadelli's version. This may make his assertion especially suspicious.
[82] Douai, MS 922, 3, fos 58v-9r.
[83] I here correct several errors in 'Maecenas', pp. 421-2n.

Michaelmas 1558 in SP 11/13, no. 68 is of some help.[84] The difficulty of understanding Pyning's principles of accounting, together with marked inconsistencies between the two accounts covering virtually the same period (nos 2 and 3) makes it almost impossible to derive a satisfactory picture; why should there have been two? Pyning's totals can almost never be trusted. Part of the problem may be that these records are abstracts of accounts that must have been kept by someone other than Pyning, probably three or four household officials. It appears that Pyning accounted only once every two years, which may reduce the significance of his absence for six months right at the beginning of nos 2 and 3.

Some figures can still be generated, even if they are hardly as clear as one would like. According to the accounting in no. 2, Pole brought in £22,500 and spent all but barely £435 cash on hand. The only non-recurring expense was £1,000 for building. The figures for expenditure in a monthly accounting for the same period give a total of only about £7,000.[85] No. 3 gives yet another set of sometimes wildly different figures. In it, Pole's total revenues were said to be only £16,826. Of expenditures, far the largest sum went to the paymaster of the household, nearly £14,300, plus another £1,300 for other household expenses. The drain on Pole's resources caused by his household, already grown by some forty members over its travelling size, and which now had to accommodate another thirty or so *extraneos*, was obviously large.[86] The only non-recurring expense listed is again for building, this time £800. Excluding this last leaves a net of around £2,200, but Pyning claimed to have paid out all but about £451. That, at least, agrees well enough with the cash on hand in no. 1. No. 4 includes the pension on Winchester, missing in all of Pyning's accounts, and with this notable increase, Pole cleared about £800 from the sources enumerated in it.

Pole's 'foreign earned income' always caused problems. Its principal sources were two Spanish pensions, on Burgos and on Granada, in theory both of 2,000 *scudi* per year; the *luogo* on the Venetian Zecca inherited from Vittoria Colonna; and the commendam of Gavello. Both these pensions (and that on Winchester) violated points in the *Consilium*, but after the holding of plural bishoprics was prohibited, monastic commendams provided the principal source of income for cardinals, together with pensions, and this holds for Pole.[87] Otherwise, it is clear only that Pole never got his Spanish pensions in

---

[84] *CSPDR*, nos 659, 662, 665, and 822.
[85] PRO, SP 11/10, no. 8 (*CSPDR*, no. 544).
[86] CCCC, MS 105, no. 43, fol. 411r. Heal (*Prelates*, pp. 82, 85–6) noted that the household was always the biggest charge at Canterbury, approaching perhaps a third of the archbishopric's outlay.
[87] Kidd, *Documents*, pp. 310–11 (Gleason, *Reform thought*, pp. 89–90) and Hallman, *Property*, p. 39.

full, save perhaps in 1557–58. From the moment he was granted the two, he had problems being paid.[88] These continued, especially in the case of Burgos. Although Pole called the bishop, Cardinal Mendoza y Bobadilla, his *grande amico* in recommending him in 1554 to Mary, in December 1555 he had to demand payment, the Spanish merchants who were to forward the money having claimed that they were entitled to hold back one year's proceeds.[89] If Pole really spent as much as Priuli said in his first year in England, his anxiety to have his money is readily comprehensible. Five months later Pole had gotten no more than various excuses from Mendoza.[90] Finally, Juan Ugalde, one of Pole's chamberlains, was sent for the money both in 1556 and again in April 1558.[91] This second time it seems to have been paid, although perhaps not before Pole's death, when Mendoza demanded both the payment and also the pension itself back, claiming that Pole did not have a license to will it (and he did not, at least not in the main body of his testament). Likewise for Granada. In 1559 Priuli was still waiting for the last payment, which apparently did not figure in the 7,000 *scudi* from Spain which he then had in Antwerp.[92] Exactly how much Pole ever got is impossible to say. No. 3 lumps Granada, Zecca and abbey together as worth £3,476 (rounded) and says they were paid by Giberti, but No. 2's line for proceeds from him, which does not define the sources of the funds, gives £4,423. The discrepancy probably arises because Pyning included other money from Rome in No. 2, perhaps a partial payment of what Pole had coming from the papal chamber. At his death, Pole was still owed more than 6,000 *scudi* for the extraordinary expenses of his legation.[93] Similarly, the figures for Burgos diverge between the two accounts, £1,055 and £797 respectively. In this case, since the source of the money must be the same, the difference is harder to explain. In either case, the total should have been £1,334 (two years at 2,000 *scudi* p. a.). The shortfall in the first case may be explained by the payment arrangements Pole was forced to accept, which once had cost him 25%, and would appear to have done again.[94] Pole's *luogo* on the Zecca cannot be fully accounted for, either. Originally worth 9,000 *scudi*, it may have risen to as much as 12,000 by about 1555.[95]

---

[88] This was not a situation peculiar to Pole. Cardinal Gonzaga had the same trouble both with his pension on Granada and another on Badajoz. Archivio di Stato, Mantua, Archivio Gonzaga, b. 1928 (1556 Roma Diversi), unfoliated, Ippolito Capilupo-Gonzaga, Rome, 6 and 18 March 1556.
[89] *CRP*, nos 906 and 1464.
[90] *CRP*, no. 1560.
[91] *CRP*, nos 1659 and 2219.
[92] Archivio Stella 40/135 (Bonelli, no. 157).
[93] J. G. Nichols and J. Bruce, eds, *Wills from Doctors' Commons. A selection from the wills of eminent persons proved in the prerogative court of Canterbury, 1496-1695* (Camden Society, o. s., 83, 1863), pp. 48-53, p. 49 and *CRP*, no. 2286.
[94] *CRP*, no. 1464.
[95] Ab. note 20.

Taking no. 3's lower figure for Granada, Zecca and abbey of £3,476 and subtracting £1,334 (for the 4000 *scudi* from Granada), £568 (for Gavello, worth 1000 *scudi* according to Beccadelli, minus a probably one-time charge of 300 *scudi* granted to some of Pole's clients in 1556) leaves a sum for the Zecca of £1,574 which makes 4,722 *scudi* or 2,361 *scudi* p. a.[96] That would mean a return of 26.2% on 9,000 *scudi* deposited, 23.6% on 10,000, and 18.7% on 12,000, all of which are probably impossible. The official figures for interest (during the war crisis of 1570) go no higher than 14%.[97] This may mean that a Venetian pension was concealed under this entry. It may also be that Pole derived some income from his protectorship of the Cassinese Benedictines.[98] The most important illiquid part of his assets also came from overseas, the silver he brought from Italy, but it cannot be valued.[99] It was added to by at least one piece from the queen at New Year's 1557.[100]

Pole made a lot of money, and he spent a lot of money. That he did not pile up riches seems clear, most compellingly from the fact that Elizabeth I settled Pole's estate reasonably quickly with Priuli, apparently for only 2,000 *scudi* plus another £300 to Parker.[101] When Priuli reported the state of Pole's finances at his death, he was no doubt engaging in the universal practice of crying poor for the tax man, but whatever the discrepancies in Priuli's figures, they too indicate that Pole did not come out much ahead. In addition to spending what little came in from English sources, Pole had gone through all his income from Venice and Spain.[102] Unlike many of his peers, he never overspent his means, as Beccadelli carefully noted, although as both he and Dudic also observed, Pole knew how to 'use magnificence'.[103]

Magnificence and princely behavior typified the college of cardinals in the sixteenth century, and Pole was no exception. Yet change was slowly coming, and Pole reflected the transition in his at least nominal allegiance to the new norms.[104] This is clearest in his last financial document, his will. Although he had a license to testate which often became a pretext for massive transfers of clerical wealth to lay hands, Pole observed one of the most

---

[96] *MMB*, p. 323.
[97] Frederic C. Lane, *Venice. A maritime republic* (Baltimore: Johns Hopkins University Press, 1973), pp. 325-26 and Luciano Pezzolo, *L'oro dello stato: società, finanza e fisco nella Repubblica veneta del secondo '500* (Venice: Il Cardo, 1990), p. 175 and table on p. 180 which shows rates between 5 and 14% during the war of 1570-74.
[98] *CRP*, no. 1936.
[99] *CRP*, nos 2311-12.
[100] David Loades, *Mary Tudor. A life* (Oxford: Blackwell, 1989), p. 358.
[101] Archivio Stella, 40/135 (Bonelli, no. 157) and 40/152 (Bonelli, no. 175).
[102] *CRP*, no. 2312.
[103] *MMB*, p. 323 and Querini, *Collectio*, 1, p. 52.
[104] Gigliola Fragnito, 'Cardinals' courts in sixteenth-century Rome', *Journal of modern history*, 65 (1993), pp. 26-56 discusses a related transition, which Pole also anticipated.

important new standards by refusing to alienate ecclesiastical revenues to his kinsmen, even though that meant that he left them nothing.[105] In this he refused Priuli's suggestion to give some of his property to his poor relatives.[106] Rejection of such alienations was one of the most acerbic points in the *Consilium*.[107] The church might have remained property to Pole, but at least in so far as this was up to him its property would remain to it.

---

[105] *CRP*, no. 2286 and Hallman, *Property*, pp. 80-94.
[106] *CRP*, no. 2312.
[107] Kidd, ed., *Documents*, p. 312 (Gleason, *Reform thought*, pp. 90-91) and Hallman, *Property*, p. 80.

ADDENDA ET CORRIGENDA

I

p. 113: For 'whom our age ... [of the church]' read 'which our age and our fathers' consider eminent'.

III

For a critique see C. S. L. Davies, 'Tournai and the English crown, 1513-1519', *Historical Journal*, 41 (1998), pp. 1-26.

V

The diary may not be by Bartolomeo Stella. See no. IV, note 12.
p. 346: For 40/76 read 40/78.

VII

p. 308: Throckmorton as Pole's messenger is insignificant.

VIII

p. 388: *De concilio* was reprinted in the Venice 1728 edition of the conciliar collections of Philippe Labbé and Gabriel Cossart, app. 2, pp. 629-48 according to H. J. Sieben, 'Eine "ökumenische" Auslegung von Ap 15 in der Reformationszeit: Reginald Poles *De concilio*', *Theologie und Philosophie*, 60 (1985), pp. 16-42, p. 19n.
p. 389: Maggio could not have been legate to Venice. He may have been nuncio; the evidence is unclear.

XII

p. 210-11: For 'whom our age ... [of the church]' read 'which our age and our fathers' consider eminent'.

XIV

p. 422: Pole made much more use of Turnbull than I then knew. See my article in H. C. G. Matthew, ed., *New dictionary of national biography* (Oxford: Oxford University Press, forthcoming).

p. 425: Cole was probably never a member of Pole's household, although he traveled with him during Pole's legation of 1537. See my article in *New dictionary of national biography*.

p. 426: Pole was officially legate to Viterbo from 13 August 1541 until 13 June 1550 (Thomas F. Mayer, ed., *The correspondence of Reginald Pole*, forthcoming, nos 335 and 570).

p. 427: The speculation about Zanobio Ceffino is wrong. The Zanobio 'seduced' by Pole was de' Medici. See Massimo Firpo and Dario Marcatto, eds, *Il processo inquisitoriale del Cardinal Giovanni Morone*, 6 vols (Rome: Istituto storico italiano per l'età moderna e contemporanea, 1981-1995), 6, p. 164.

p. 430: The list of dedications to Pole should be dated from 1524, not 1554, and those by Rapicio, Bocchi, Tomitano and Valeriano were included in George Parks's list.

p. 434: The link between Roper's biography of More and Pole is not as direct as I implied. It was a private family effort in connection with John Rastell's edition of More's works (1557).

p. 435: Carafa's visit to Flaminio's deathbed is a myth. See my *Reginald Pole, prince and prophet* (Cambridge University Press, in press), chapter five.

See further my 'Cardinal Pole's finances: the property of a reformer', this volume no. XV.

INDEX

Accolti, Benedetto: XV 7
Adrian VI: XIII 448
Adria: XV 7
Agrippa, Heinrich Cornelius: XIII 447–8
Ailly, Pierre d': VIII 403–4
Alanus: III 265
Alciato, Andrea: VIII 389; IX 43
Allen, William: XII 212–13
Almain, Jacques: VIII 388, 404
Alvarez de Toledo, Juan: IV 3, 9, 11, 12, 14;
 V 349, 351, 352, 353, 357, 358, 361,
 364, 369, 371
Amboise, Georges d': V 361
Angulo, Agostino d': V 351
Anticlericalism: VIII 390; IX 49–50, 54;
 X 1, 10, 14
apostolic poverty of the church: XIV 424
Aragon, Katherine of: II 55, 63; VI 288;
 VII 305; XI 881; XII 205, 209; XIV 426
Ariosto, Ludovico: X *passim*
 Orlando Furioso: X *passim*
Armagnac, Georges d': IV 6, 12; V 367
Arrivabene, Gianfrancesco: IV 17, 20
Ascham, Roger: XIV 428, 433
Ascoli: XV 7
Aske, Robert: VII 330
Averroist Aristotelianism: IX 51
Ayala, Juan de: IV 13, 15, 18; V 349, 350
Azor, Juan: XII 213

Bagnoregio: XIV 426; XV 6
Bainham, James: VI 292
Bale, John: VI 304
Barignano, Pietro: IX 53
Barnes, Robert: VI 290–91
Bartolo da Sassoferrato: III 265; IX 42
Basel, Council of: VIII 393
Battle Abbey: XV 9
Baudouin, François: I 108
Baynton, Sir Edward: VII 328–9
Beccadelli, Ludovico: I 113, 115; II 52;
 IV 10, 21; V 347, 348; VI 311; IX 58;
 XI 874, 875; XII 205, 206, 207, 209,
 211, 214; XIII 431, 434, 441, 446;
 XIV 423, 431; XV 2–5, 7, 15–16
Beda, Noël: XI 881, 882, 887
Bellay, Guillaume du, Sieur de Langey: XI
 878, 880, 883, 884, 885, 887; XIII 435
Bellay, Jean du: IV 14, 15, 18; V 358, 374,
 VI 307; X 880, 881, 882; XIII 435
Bellay, Martin du: XI 887
Bembo, Pietro: II 55; IX 45, 56, 58; X 13;
 XIII 445; XV 5
Benci, Trifone: II:52
Beneficio di Cristo, Il: I 116; II 67; X 13
Berni, Francesco: II 52, 66
Bertano, Pietro: XII 210
Bible: I 109,111,114
Binardi, Gianbattista: I 107, 113; XII 209,
 211; XIV 423, 432–5
Bini, Gianfrancesco: II 66; V 355, 368
biography, in the Renaissance: XII *passim*;
 XIII *passim*
bishops: II 57; IV 2
Bobadilla, Nicolás: V 351
Boccaccio, Giovanni: IX 44; X:284
Bocchi, Achille: XIV 430–31
Bogaert, Cornelis: V 291
Boleyn, Anne: VI 294 304;VII 305
Boleyn, George, Lord Rochford: XI 880,
 882
Boleyn, Sir Thomas, Earl of Wiltshire:
 VI 294; XI 877, 878, 879, 882, 886,
 889
Bologna: VIII 407
Bonamico, Lazzaro: II 66; VIII 388; X 44;
 XIV 425
Bonner, Edmund: II16, 118; XIV 434
Borromeo, Carlo: IX 61
Bourbon de Vendôme, Charles: V 366
Bourbon de Vendôme, François Louis:
 V 358
Bèze, Theodore de: I 111–12
Brandon, Charles, Duke of Suffolk: I 304;
 VII 326; XIII 443
Brerewood, Thomas: VI 289

Brétigny, treaty of: III 260
Brie, Germaine: III 278
Browne, George: VI 292
Brucioli, Antonio: II 52, XIV 426
Bryan, Sir Francis: VI 300, 301, 309;
    VII 319–22, 324, 326–7; XI 883, 885,
    886, 887; XIII 432
Buonanni, Benedetto: IV 4, 12, 18; V 347,
    349, 350
Burnet, Gilbert: XII 213–14

Calais: XV 11
Calandro, Endimio: IV 17
Calvin, John: I 108, 118; II 67; XIII 447
Camaiano, Nofri: V 349, 351
Camaldoli: II 66; X 10, 13
Cambrai, War of the League of: IX 41
Camerino: XV 8
Campeggi, Tommaso: XIV 430, 432
Canalnuovo (*see* Gavello)
Canterbury: XV 8
Capodiferro, Girolamo: IV 6, 14; V 349
Cardinals: VIII 395; IX 54
Carnesecchi, Pietro: I 115; II 52; IV 19;
    XIII 446; XIV 430; XV 9
Caro, Annibale: I 113; XIV 435
Carranza, Bartolomé: I 117; II 52
Casa, Giovanni della: XIV 435
Cassinese Benedictines: XIV 428; XV 15
Castellesi, Adriano: IV 16
Castellio, Sebastian: I 107
Castelvetro, Ludovico: I 113, 116; XII
    209; XIV 423, 435
Castillon, Louis de Perreau, sieur de:
    VI 305, 307, 308, 309; VII 328
Caston, Stephen: VII 324
Ceffino, Zanobio: XIV 427
Cesi, Federico: IV 8
Chambre, Philippe de la: V 361, 362, 371
Chancery, Court of: III 262
Chapuys, Eustace: VI 299, 303, 305;
    XI 880, 881, 884, 886; XV 4
Charles II, king of France: III 261
Charles V, emperor: II 58, 63; IV 3, 5, 16;
    V 346, 350, 352; VI 290, 299, 300;
    VII 306, 312, 317, 318; X 9;
    XI 873, 875, 877, 886; XIII 440, 442–3; XIV 429, 432
Charles VII, king of France: III 260, 270
Châtillon, Odet de: V 358, 367
Cheke, Sir John: I 116
Chiesa degli Eremitani, Padua: IX 60
Chorography: XIII 438
church, definitions of: I 110, 111; II 56,
    57, 58, 59; IX 55
Cibo, Caterina: II 67

Cibo, Innocenzo: IV 11; V 348, 351, 352,
    363, 366, 371
Cicada (or Cicala), Giovanni Battista:
    XIV 420
Cifuentes, Fernando de Silva, count of:
    VII 317; XIII 442
Clement VII (Giulio de' Medici): III 268;
    XIII 432
Clement VIII (Ippolito Aldobrandini):
    XII 213
clergy, secular: X 8
Clerk, John: XIV 432
Cole, Henry: I 118; VIII: 406; XIV 425, 432
Colet, John: II 55; XI 888
Collins, George: VI 290
Collins, John: VII 316
Colonna, Ascanio: XV 5
Colonna, Vittoria: II 52; XIII 446; XV 5, 8,
    14
commonweal/commonwealth: II 50; III 261,
    270, 276
Como: XIII 432
Conciliarism: VIII *passim*; IX 55
conscience: I 111; III 269; X 6
Consilium de emendanda ecclesia: IV 2;
    XIII 449; XIV 432; XV 4, 8, 16
Constance, Council of: VIII 392
Constantine, emperor: II 57
    Donation of, VIII 399
Contarini, Gasparo: I 116; II 55, 65;
    VI 296, 299–300; VII 307, 311, 313;
    IX 58–60; XI 876; XII 206, 213;
    XIII 431, 440, 446, 449; XIV 431; XV
    4
Corner, Andrea: V 359, 361; XV 6
corporate metaphor: VIII 394
Corpus Christi College, Oxford: XV 3
Counsel: III 272–3
Courtenay, Gertrude, Marchioness of
    Exeter: VII 323
Courtenay, Henry, Marquess of Exeter:
    VI 305, 307; VII 325; XIII 432, 442
Cranmer, Thomas: I 113, 115–17; VI 290,
    294, 309; VII 310, 329; XI 889; XV 12
Cravetta, Aimone: III 265
Crescenzi, Marcello: V 356
Crispi, Tiberio: IV 14; V 349, 357
Crofts, George: VII 316, 327
Croke, Richard: XI 885
Cromwell, Thomas: III 270; VI 286, 289,
    292, 294, 296, 300, 301, 308, 309,
    311; VII 305, 306, 313–14, 320, 323,
    327–30; XI 875; XIII 433
Cueva, Bartolomeo della: V 357, 369
Cupis, Giandomenico de: IV 7–10, 12–13,
    16–19; V 354–57, 360, 362, 363, 365,

366, 368, 369, 371, 374; XV 7
Curzio (or di Corte), Francesco, the
   Younger: III 265
Cyprian of Carthage, St: I 110; II 57

Dacre of the North, Thomas, Lord: XIII 443
Dandolo, Matteo: IV 2, 14, 21; V 347, 374
Dante Alighieri: X 2
Darcy, Thomas, Lord Darcy: VI 305
Darrell, Elizabeth: VI 303, VII 323
Datary, papal: IV 2; V 350
Davanzati, Bernardo: XII 213
David, king: II 58
Davidico, Lorenzo: XIV 430–31
'De summo pontifice' IV 17
De unitate (Pro ecclesiasticae unitatis
   defensione): II 52, 56; VI 308, VII 305,
   307, 312, 327; XI 871, 874, 876;
   XII 205; XIII 440, 443; XIV 427,
   434
Decio, Filippo: VIII 388
Delgado, Francisco: XII 210
dialogue, humanist: VIII 390
Domenichi, Ludovico: XIII 439, 441, 447
Dominicans, Observant: X 13
dominium regale et politicum: III 270
Doria, Girolamo: V 351, 361, 365, 366
Dorigny, Nicholas: XI 884
Dudic, Andras: I 107, 111–13; II:53; IV 21;
   V 347; VI 311, 313; XI 874–5; XII
   206–10, 214; XIV 420, 433, 434; XV 3, 12
Duranti, Durante de: IV 20; V 354, 369

Edward III: III 260
Edward IV: III 273
Edward VI: III 274; XI 875; XII 206;
   XIV 429
Egnazio, Gianbattista: II 65; IX 45; III 446
Elizabeth I: XIV 421; XV 15
Enzinas (Dryander), Francisco de: VI 290
Erasmus, Desiderius: I 110–11; II 53, 64;
   III 258, 275, 278; VIII 389; X 14
      Adagia: III 276
      Querela pacis: III 275
Este, Alfonso d': X 8
Este, Ercole d': XV 7
Este family: X 1
Este, Ippolito d': IV 2, 7
Este, Renata d' (Renée de France): XIII 447
Eugenius IV (Gabriele Condulmer):VIII 393
Exeter: XV 3
Ezechiel: II 62, 64

Facchetto, Michele: XIV 433
Faction: III 258, 273, 279; VI 305, VII 322
Faita, Marcantonio: XIV 433

Farnese, Alessandro: IV 3, 4, 10, 13–16,
   18–20; V 346, 349, 352, 357, 359–60,
   364, 366–69, 371; XIII 427, 431–2,
   435, 444; XV 7
Farnese, Ottavio: XV 6
Farnese, Pier Luigi: XIII 442
Farnese, Ranuccio: V 357, 367
Farrington, Robert: VI 294
Ferdinand I of Habsburg, emperor: XII 211
Ferrara: X 12
Fief, Pierre du: VI 289–90
Fiennes, Sir Thomas, Lord Dacre of the
   South: VII 327
Filelfo, Francesco: II 53
Filonardi, Ennio: V 348, 354, 357, 374
Fiordibello, Antonio: XIV 433–4
Firmani, Luigi: IV 20; V 346, 356, 366,
   369, 370
Fisher, John: I 114; II 60–61, 63; VI 293;
   VII 307; XII 209; XIII 432; XIV 434
Fitzwilliam, Sir William: VI 305; VII 325
Flaminio, Marcantonio: I 113, 115–16;
   II 50–52, 66; IV 16, 18; V 347–8,
   366; IX 58; X 13; XIII 447;
   XIV 424, 426–7, 431, 435; XV 6
Flegge, Robert: VI 290, 294
Florence: IX 60
   Council of: II 57; VIII 392
Folengo, Gianbattista: XIV 428
Fortescue, Sir John: III 270
Foxe, Edward: XI 875, 877, 879, 884
Foxe, John: I 116; VI 288
Francis I: II 63; III 264, 278; VI 300, 303;
   VII 309, 317; X 9; XI 878, 883,
   887; XIII 436
Fregoso, Federico: XIII 446
Friar, John: XIV 425

Gabbrielle, Scipione: V 351
Gabriele, Trifone: IX 45, 52
Gaddi, Nicolò: IV 9, 11; V 356
Gagliano, Pierfrancesco: XIV 420
Garay, Pedro de: XI 881–2, 886–8
Gardiner, Stephen: VI 294, 300–301, 309;
   VII 313, 318–22, 324, 327, 330
Gavello (Canalnuovo): XIV 429; XV 7–8,
   14, 15
Gerson, Jean: VIII 388
Gheri, Cosmo: II 65
Gheri, Vincenzo: II 67
Giannotti, Donato: II 52, 54–5; IX 52
Giberti, Antonio: XV 12, 14
Giberti, Gian Matteo: II 66; V 354;
   VII 307, 309, 310–11, 318; IX 58;
   XIII 445–6; XIV 43; XV 5, 8
Gigli, Silvestro de: III 268

Giovenale, Latino: V 348, 357
Giovio, Paolo: IV 4; VI 311; VII 310; XI 891; XIII *passim*; XIV 427, 428
Giustinian, Paolo: II 65; IX 59
Glymes, Antonius van, Marquess of Bergen: VI 294
Goldwell, Thomas: IV 7
Gonzaga, Ercole: IV 2, 4, 17–8; V 351, 367–8, 370
Gonzaga, Ferrante: IV 6, 10, 18
Gonzaga, Guglielmo, duke of Mantua: IV 3
Gozzadini, Giovanni: VIII 404
Granada: XV 5
Gratius, Ortwin: XIII 449
Gritti, Andrea: II 55
Gualteri, Pier Paolo: V 346, 347, 348, 349, 354
Gualteri, Sebastiano: V 346
Gualteruzzi, Carlo: XIII 444, 446–7
Guillard, Louis: III 263–4, 266
Guise, Charles de: IV 14, 18–20; V 358, 359, 361, 364, 368, 370

Hackett, John: VI 293
Hall, Edward: VI 291
Harpsfield, Nicholas: II 52; VIII 389; XII 206–9, 211; XIV 432, 434
Harvel, Edmund: VII 326
Hastings, Francis, Baron Hastings: VII 327
Helyar, John: II 52; VI 309; VII 315, 324, 329
Henry VIII: I 107, 114; II 54, 56, 59, 62; III 257, 259, 266, 276; VI 287, 293, 297, 305, 307, 309, 313; VII 309, 311, 323, 327, 330; X 9; XI 872, 876, 880, 883, 884; XII 205, 206, XIII 438, 440–42, 449; XIV 424; XV 1, 2
Henry II, king of England: XIII 433
Henry II, king of France: IV 2, 16; XIV 429
Henry VI: III 263
Henry VII: II 59; III 274; VI 289
Herera, Alphonso de: XI 888
Heywood, Ellis: II 52; XIV 430
Historiography, of Pole: V 353; XII 205
Holland, Hugh: VI 309; VII 314, 315–16, 323, 329
Holland, Seth: XIV 432
Honor: III 259
Hosius, Stanislaus: XI 876; XII 211
Howard, Thomas, Duke of Norfolk: VI 305; VII 324, 326; XI 877, 881, 886; XII 206; XIII 443
humanism: IX 42

Hungary, Mary of: VI 288, 299; VII 318
Hussey, Anthony: XIV 432
Hutton, John: VI 293, 299–301, 309; VII 318, 320–21, 329–30

Imperium: III 277
Index of Prohibited Books: I 116
Innocent III (Lothar da Segni): IV 2; XV 6
Inquisition, Roman: IV: 3, 21; XIII 447;XIV 431
Isaiah: II 62, 63

Jerningham, Sir Richard: III 263
Johannes Monachus: VIII 398
Joye, George: VI 290
Julius II (Giuliano della Rovere): X 8
Julius III (Giovanni Maria Ciocchi del Monte): I 116; II 50; IV 1, 8–9, 11–12; V 345, 348, 350, 354, 358, 362, 368–70; XIII 444–5; XV 2, 8
justification: I 114; IV 15; VIII 390; IX 48, 54; XIII 446

Kampen, Jan van: XIV 427
kingship, conceptions of: II 59; III 259, 278

Lambeth Palace: XIV 422; XV 2
Lampridio, Benedetto: II 66; IX 45
Lampson (Lampsonius), Dominic: II 53; XIV 433
Lateran, fifth council of: XV 8
Latimer, Hugh: VI 292, 309; VII 324
Lee, Edward: XI 882
Legg, George: VII 327
Le Grand, Joachim: XII 213
Leo X (Giovanni de' Medici): III 257, 264, 268; X 8–10; XV 8
Leonico, Nicolò: II 54; IX 51–2; XIV 425
Lily, George: II 52; XI 872, 884, XIII 446, 449; XIV 425
Liège: VI 299
Lizet, Pierre: XI 887
Lok, William: VI 293
Longueil, Christophe (Christophoris Longolius): II 53–4; XIV 425
Lorraine, Charles de: V 364, 366, 371
Louis XI: III 268, 270
Louis XII: X 8
Lovati, Lovato: IX 43
Loyola, Ignatius: VII 316
Lupset, Thomas: I 108; II 52, 55; VII 316, XI 872, 884
Luther, Martin: I 109, 114

Machiavelli, Nicolò: II 65; X 9

Madius or Maggio, Tommaso: IV 7; XV 9
Madruzzo, Cristoforo: IV:3–4; V:362, 363, 365, 367, 369, 374; VIII 406; IX 57–8
Maffei, Bernardino: IV 8, 12; V 346; XII 209
Maggio, Roberto: VIII 389, 407; IX 46
Maino, Giason del: III 265; VIII 388, IX 42
Major, John: VIII 388
Mancini, Domenico: III 273–4
Mantova Benavides, Marco: II 58, 65; VIII *passim*; IX *passim*; X 13; XI:891; XIII 449
   Consiliorum sive responsorum: III 265
   Della eloquenza: IX 44, 53
   Dialogus de concilio: VIII *passim*; IX 45, 50, 54–7
   Discorsi sopra i dialoghi di M. Speron Sperone: IX 44
   L'heremita: IX 46–9
   Novelle: VIII 388
Mantova Benavides, Giovanni: IX 50, 58
Mantua: X 13
Manuzio, Paolo: I 112; XII 210; XIV 430
Marcellus II (Marcello Cervini): II 50; IV 2, 5, 9–13; V 346, 349, 352, 356, 360, 362, 366, 368, 374; VIII 407; XII 211; XIII 444
Marck, Erard de la: VI 297, 299; VII 310, 318; XIII 432
Marino, Pascale: IX 53
Marsilio of Padua: VIII 387; IX 56
Martyrology: II 53, 56, 62
Mary I: XIII 442; XIV 421, 425; XV 9, 10, 12, 15
Massarelli, Angelo: IV 6, 13; V 346, 348, 349, 350, 352
Maucroix, François: XII 213–14
Maximilian I, emperor: X 9
Medici, Cosimo I, de', duke of Florence: II 67; IV 3, 11; V 349, 351, 352; XII 213
Mendoza, Diego Hurtado de: IV 3, 7, 9, 10, 14, 16; V 347, 348, 350, 352
Mendoza, Francisco de, cardinal Coria, V 350, 361, 369; XV 14
Merum et mixtum imperium: III 263
Meudon, Antoine de Sanguine: V 374
Mewtas, Peter: VI 300–301, 303, 309; VII 315, 319, 323, 329–30
Michelangelo Buonarotti: II 52, 66; V 354
Michiel, Giovanni: XIV 421; XV 12
Mignanelli, Fabio: VIII 407
monks and monasticism: X 8 and *passim*
Montefiascone: XIV 427

Montmorency, Anne de: IV 18; VI 305, 307; XI 880, 882, 886, 887
More, Sir Thomas: I 114; II 56, 60, 61, 63; III 257, 258, 271, 273, 278,–9; VI 291–2; XI 872, 881; XII 209; XIV 434
Mor, Antonis: XIV 432
Morison, Sir Richard: VI 300; VII 314, 330; VIII 406; XIV 425–6
Morone, Giovanni: I 115; II 52; IV 12; V 353, 364, 367, 374; XII 211; XIII 444; XIV 420
Morton, John: III 258, 274
Moses: II 57
Mountjoy, William, Lord: III 263
Mussato, Albertino: IX 43
Musso, Cornelio: IX 61
Muzio, Girolamo: IV 10

Navagero, Bernardo: XII 210; XIV 431
Navarra, Francisco de: II 52; IV 8
Navarre, Marguerite de: V 364; XIII 447
Negri, Francesco: I 108
Negri, Girolamo: IX 58
neo–platonism: IX 51
Neville, Sir Edward: VI 304; VII 323
Neville, Sir George, Lord Abergavenny: VII 327
Nicaea, Council of: II 57
Nicodemism: XIII 447
Niconitio, Francesco: IX 46, 54
Nobility: II 59, 61

Ochino, Bernardino: I 111
Oldoino, Agostino: IV 8
Orphinstrange, John: VIII 406
Ortiz, Pedro: XI 888
Osório, Jeronimo: XIV 428
Oxford: I 108

Pace, Richard: XV 3
Pacheco, Pedro: IV 9, 13; V 356, 366, 370
Padua: II 54; IX 43; IX *passim*; XII 206; XIII 432; XIV 425, 431
   university of: VIII 385, 405; IX 42, 59–60
Paleario, Aonio: II 52
Palladio, Blosio: II 66
Palmer, Sir Thomas: VI 300, 304; VII 319, 321, 325
Palmieri, Andrea Matteo: VII 307; XIII 435
Panormitanus (Nicolò da Tudeschis): VIII 387, 392, 398, 405; IX 55
Panziroli, Guido: VIII 389
papacy, conceptions of: II 57–8; III 259
Paris: II:55
   parlement of: III 262, 264

university of: II 60; XI 870, 879, XIII 434
Parisio, Pietro Paolo: III 265; VIII 407
Parker, Matthew: XV 1, 16
Parma: IV 5; V 365; XV 6
Parpaglia, Vincenzo: V 354; XIV 422
Parr, Catherine: XIII 437
Pate, Richard VI 303
Patronage: XIV 419
Paul, St: I 110; II 64; X 6, 14
Paul III (Alessandro Farnese): II 66; IV 1, 8; V 372; VI 297; VII 305–6, 311; VIII 392, 407; IX 57; XIII 445, 447; XIV 426; XV 7
Paul IV (Gianpietro Carafa): I 115; II 65; IV 2, 5, 7, 9–10, 13–14, 16–18, 21; V 346, 348–50, 352–54, 356–59, 361, 363, 365–6, 369, 374; XIII 444; XIV 429, 435; XV 8
Paulet, Sir William: VI 305; VII 324; XV 10
Paulus de Castro: III 265
Penitentiary, papal: IV 2; V 350, 357
Perrenot de Granvelle, Nicholas: XV 5
Personae: II 61; VI 296, 311; XI 871, 873; XII 205, 209, 215
Persons, Robert: XII 212
Peter, St: II 57
Petit, Cyriac: XIV 434
Petit, Guillaume: XI 887
Peto, William: VI 288
Petrarch, Francesco: IX 44
 and Petrarchism: IX 46; XIV 435
Philip II: XIV 420
Phillips, Harry: VI 289, 291, 294, 301, 310; VII 320–21, 330
Phillips, Thomas: XII 214
Piddletown, Dors.: XV 4
Pighe, Albert: I 108; VIII 393; XIII 448
Pilgrimage of Grace: II 64; VI 287, 303; VII 305, 307, 322, 326; XIII 439
Pinelle, Charles: XI 888
Pio da Carpi, Rodolfo: IV 10; V 355, 357, 362, 369, 374; VI 297, 303, 307–9; VII 307, 322; IX 61; XI 877; XIII 435–6, 439, 444
Pisani, Francesco: V 359
Pitigliano, Giovambattista da: IX 52
Pius IV (Gianangelo de' Medici): V 351, 361, 367; VIII 406
Plantagenet, Arthur, Lord Lisle: VI 304–5; VII 321, 324, 327
Plantagenet, George, Duke of Clarence: II 54; XV 1
Plutarch: XIII 438
Poland: I 111
Pole, David: XIV 432, 434

Pole, Sir Geoffrey: IV 14; VI 308; VII 314–16, 323, 329; XV 8
Pole, Sir Henry, Lord Montagu: II 54; VI 307; VII 315, 323; XIII 442
Pole, Margaret, Countess of Salisbury: II 54; VII 315, 323
Pole, Richard de la: VI 288
Pollini, Girolamo: XII 212
Polybius: XIII 438–9, 449
Pomponazzi, Pietro: XIII 432
Ponte, Girolamo da: XIV 420
Poyntz, Thomas: VI 289, 291
Preaching: I 110, 111
Predestination: IX 48
Priuli, Alvise: II 50, 65; IV 6, 8, 11; XII 210; XIV 421, 431; XV 9–12, 14, 16
Privy Chamber: III 279
Pro ecclesiasticae unitatis defensione see De unitate
Prophecy: II 53, 56, 58; X, 10; XI 871
Prudence: II 53, 56, 58–9, 61, 65; XI 875
Pye, Benjamin: XII 214
Pyning, Henry: XV 9, 10, 13, 15

Querini, Vincenzo: II 65
Quirini, Luigi: IX 58

Ragland, Jerome: VII 315
Ramusio, Paolo: XIV 430
Rapicio, Giovita: XIV 430
Regalia, 'regalie', regality: III 263–4, 266, 268
Renard, Simon: IV 12
representation, concept of: VIII 398, 403–4
republic: II 59; III 258, 271; IX 42, 55
rex imperator: II 59; III 257, 265, 270
Ribadeneira, Pedro de: XII 212
Ricalcato, Ambrogio: VII 307
Ricasoli, Gianbattista: IV 19
Richard II: II 67
Ricoboni, Antonio: VIII 389
Ridley, Gloucester: XII 214
Ridolfi, Nicolò: IV 7; V 362, 365, 368, 371
Ripa, Gianbattista della: IV 7
Rishton, Edward: XII 212
Roper, William: XIV 434
Rovere, Giulio della: IV 5, 17; V 351, 365
Roverta, Ottaviano: XIII 444
Ruino, Carlo: III 265; VIII 388
Rullo, Donato: II 52
Russell, Sir John: VI 305; VII 326; XI 889

Sadler, Ralph: VII 330
Sadoleto, Jacopo: XIII 445, 448; XV 5

Salviati, Giovanni: IV 3, 6, 7, 9; V 362, 367, 368, 371
Sampson, Richard: II 60–61; III 257, 259, 263–4, 268–9, 270; VI 288, 305; VII 325
Sander, Nicholas: II 52; XII 211, 213; XIII 431; XIV 434
Sandro, Bernardino: VII 314
Sandys, William Lord: VI 305
San Nicolò da Tolentino, Venice: XIV 429
Savonarola, Girolamo: IX 59; X 13
Savoy, Margaret of: III 264
Schard, Simon: VIII 406
Scotti, Bernardino: XIV 429
Segni, Bernardo, *Istorie fiorentine*: IV 11; V 349
Selve, Jean de: XI 887
Seripando, Girolamo: II 52
Serristori, Averardo: IV 13, 18; V 347, 351
Servetus, Miguel: I 111
Seymour, Edward, Duke of Somerset: XII 206–7; XIII 443
Sfondrati, Francesco: IV 5, 7
Sforza, Guido Ascanio: V 355–7, 362, 367, 370; XIV 431
Sforza, Ludovico, 'Il Moro': X 8
Silva, Miguel de: IV 5; V 363, 366
Silvestri, Francesco: X 13
Sleidan, Johannes: XII 213
Socini, Mariano, the elder: III 265
Socini, Mariano, the younger: III 265
Soto, Pedro de: I 117
South Harting, Sussex: XV 4
Sovereignty: III *passim*; VIII 401–2
Sovereignty, divided: III 271; VIII 394; IX 55
Spadafora, Bartolomeo: II 52
Speroni, Sperone: VIII 388; IX 44
spirituali: IX 57–8; X 13–14; XIII 446–7; XV 1
Starkey, Thomas: I 107, 108; II 52, 55, 58; VI 303, 308–9; VII 314, 323, 325–6, 330; VIII 406; XI 876, 884, XIII 449, XIV 425–6
Stella, Bartolomeo: II 66; IV 7; V 346, 354; XIV 427
Stella, Gianfrancesco: V 354; XII 210, XIV 430, 435
Stokesley, John: VI 291–2, 294, 303, 311; XI 880–82, 887–88
Stridonio, Phillipo: IX 58

Talbot, George, Earl of Shrewsbury: VI 305; VII 326
Tartagni, Alessandro: III 265
Theatines: XIV 432

Theobald, Thomas: VI 290, 291, 294; VII 310
Throckmorton, Michael: VI 300; VII 308, 310, 312–14, 329
Tisen, John: VI 292
Toledo, Pedro de: IV 12, 14, 18; V 349, 351, 352
Tomitano, Bernardino: XIV 430–31
Torelli, Lelio: II 67
Torquemada, Juan de: VIII 393
Tournon, François de: V 358, 367
Tramezzino, Michele: XIII 436
Transylvania: I 112
Tregonwell, John: VII 329
Trent, Council of: I 113, 116; II 50; IV 2, 9; XII 210; XIII 449; XIV 432
Truchsess, Otto: IV 13–14; V 351, 361, 366, 368, 369; XV 8
Tunstall, Cuthbert: VI 291, 305; VII 325
Turnbull, Hugh: XIV 422
Tyberino, Alessandro: IX 52
Tyndale, William: VI 287, 291, 292
Tyranny: II 51; III 258, 271, 273, 275, 279

Underhill, John: VI 289
Urfé, Claude d': IV 9; V 353, 374

Valdés, Juan de: I 115; II 67
Valencia: XV 5
Valeriano, Pierio: XIV 430
Vallombrosa: X 5, 10
Vannes, Peter: VI 303
Varchi, Benedetto: XII 213
Vasari, Giorgio: XIII 445
Vaughan, David: XV 9
Vaughan, Stephen: VI 288, 291, 293
Vaughan, William: VII 320
Venice: II 55; XIII 434; XV 16
Verallo, Girolamo: IV 5, 11, 14; V 348–9, 350, 352, 356, 357
Vergerio, Pierpaolo: I 108; VIII 406
Vergil, Polydore: III 273–4; XIII 438
Verona: XIII 445
Vicenza: VIII 390
Vida, Marco Gerolamo: II 50–51; XIV 430–31
Villagarcia, Juan de: I 117
Viterbo: I 115; V 354; XIV 419, 426; XV 5
Vittori, Mariano: XIV 420, 433
Vives, Juan Luis: VII 316

Walker, John: VII 314–15; XV 4
Wallop, Sir John: VI 303, 309; VII 308, 323
Walsingham, Sir Francis: VIII 406
Wellisbourne, John: XI 883

Wells, Morgan: VII 315, 327
West, Sir Thomas, Lord Delawarr: VII 317, 327
White, John: XIV 432
'White Rose', English faction: VII 328; XIII 433–4, 442
Wimborne Minster, Dors.: XV 2
Winchester, bishopric of: XV 10, 14
Windsor, Sir Andrew: VII 324
Windsor, Sir Antony: VII 324–5
Wingfield, Sir Robert: VI 304, 305; VII 321
Wolsey, Thomas: II 54; III 257, 259, 263, 264, 268, 270, 278–9; VI 288, 290; XI 880, 884; XIII 438; XV 2
Wotton, Sir Edward: XV 4
Wriothesley, Sir Thomas: VI 293; VII 327
Wyatt, Sir Thomas: VI 303; VII 323; XI 872

Zabarella, Francesco: VIII 387, 392, 395, 398–9, 402, 404–5; IX 55–6
Zanetti, Guido, da Fano: II 52
Zecca of Venice: XV 6, 14, 15
Zini, Pier Francesco: XIV 430-31
Zwichem van Aytta, Viglius: XIII 389; IX 43